Study Guide

Cornelius Rea Douglas College

Study Guide

to accompany

Psychology
second edition

Don H. Hockenbury
Sandra E. Hockenbury

WORTH PUBLISHERS

Study Guide by Rea
to accompany
Hockenbury & Hockenbury **Psychology**, second edition

Printed in the United States of America

ISBN 1-57259-825-5

Printing: 5 4 3 2 1
Year: 04 03 02 01 00

Cover: *First Time / Second Line* by Phoebe Beasley (collage, 28" × 16", 1997)

Worth Publishers
41 Madison Avenue
New York, NY 10010
www.worthpublishers.com
Faculty Services: 1-800-446-8923

Contents

To the Student

This study guide is designed to help you to study effectively and to learn the important concepts in *Psychology*, 2nd edition, by Don and Sandy Hockenbury. Use this study guide in an active manner and as a complement to the textbook, not as a substitute for it. By actively interacting with the text material and this study guide, you will be able to master the chapter concepts in a straightforward and enjoyable manner. Our goal is to create independent, motivated students who enjoy learning for its own sake, who can think critically, and who have a deep conceptual understanding of the information presented in the text.

Your first course in psychology is very exciting but it is also challenging. Besides the volume of new information you will be asked to learn, you are faced with learning new terminology, novel concepts, unfamiliar theories, and, most important, the scientific way of thinking. "How to Use This Guide," which outlines this Study Guide, explains how best to use the study guide to learn all the new material. "Study Tips" (p. ix) provides some practical suggestions for improving your ability to learn, understand, and remember.

HOW TO USE THIS GUIDE

Scanning

Scanning is a useful strategy that can facilitate learning. When you scan a chapter, you get a better idea of what lies ahead. So survey the text chapter first. Spend some time looking at the graphics, and examine the special features, boxed inserts, and concept reviews; note the parts that look interesting to you. Pay attention to the diagrams, graphs, photographs, cartoons, and tables. This preview will give you a clearer impression of what is going to be covered in the chapter. Don't worry about the details at this point; just try to get the big picture.

Next read the chapter overview (Chapter . . . At A Glance) in the study guide. This will give you a general, but more detailed, summary of what you are about to encounter in the chapter. This type of previewing activity will help you to develop a conceptual framework (or cognitive map) that will allow you to more readily understand the details of what you are about to read and will make learning the material easier. For example, imagine trying to put together a large jigsaw puzzle without knowing what the finished picture looked like. Do you think it would be easier if you could see the finished picture? Of course it would! Likewise, when you scan the chapter and read the preview, you will have some idea of the big picture and of how the various pieces of the chapter fit together.

Advance Organizers and Learning Objectives

The text authors have provided advance organizers at the beginning of each major section of a chapter. These will help you to start thinking about the material and will give you an overview of what lies ahead. The preview questions at the beginning of each main section in the study guide are derived from these advance organizers. So, read these preview questions before you read each section of the text chapter and before you start the exercises in the study guide. Both the advance organizers and the preview questions are directly linked to the true/false tests, matching exercises, progress tests, and graphic organizers in the study guide. Successful completion of these activities will prepare you for tests, quizzes, exams, and other evaluation procedures.

Structured Note Taking

Good note taking is very important to learning. So we encourage you to take notes. The study guide structures your note taking by prompting you to write definitions, to paraphrase information, and to complete sentences. Simply highlighting sentences in the textbook is not sufficient. Highlighting does not involve active cognitive processing of the information, whereas writing, especially using your own words, does.

Graphic Organizers

An important aid to better understanding text material is the use of visualization. Completing the graphs, charts, and flow diagrams will provide a visual synopsis that will help you understand and remember the material. So be sure to complete all these exercises, and practice making up your own graphic organizers.

Learning Checks: Matching Exercises, True/False Tests, and Progress Tests

At the end of each major section in the study guide are learning checks in the form of conceptual questions, matching exercises, and true/false tests. These exercises provide you with feedback as you progress through the chapter. Be sure to complete each of these before going on to the next section. Three progress tests containing multiple-choice questions conclude each chapter. These are designed to help you assess your mastery of the material. If you don't know the answers to these questions, go back and study the parts of the text that you didn't understand.

If your instructor gives a quiz or test after each chapter, complete all three progress tests before the exam. Testing, and the corrective feedback it provides, will give you a more realistic idea of how well prepared you actually are and thus reduces the tendency for "overconfidence."

If your exam covers a number of chapters, it is a good idea to complete progress tests 1 and 2 after you have studied each chapter, then create a "comprehensive pretest" from progress test 3 in all the relevant chapters. Taking this larger test will give you a better idea of what the exam is going to be like.

One additional point: It is important not to confuse your recognition ability with your ability to recall and write about a topic. Multiple-choice questions tap your ability to recognize the correct answer, but do not assess your ability to express your ideas logically and coherently. You need to develop both types of skills.

Something To Think About

Each study guide chapter concludes with a special feature called Something to Think About, which contains thought-provoking questions about the material. We encourage you to think actively about what you have read in the chapter. Discuss these topics with friends and family members. This will help you remember the concepts and make learning more enjoyable.

You can also use the ideas from these sections as a guide for writing short essays or papers or for preparing for a presentation.

Answers

The answers to all the questions are included at the end of each chapter. Check your answers as you work your way through the material: Getting immediate corrective feedback facilitates the learning process.

STUDY TIPS

What are the five or ten most effective ways to improve your ability to learn, comprehend, and remember the material in this course? The truth is that there is probably no single list of techniques, no matter who develops it, that will work for all learners all the time. Everyone has a different way or style of learning; becoming familiar with your own unique learning style is the first step in becoming a successful student. However, we can all improve our ability to learn and to remember what we have learned. On that optimistic note, here are some general strategies that can be of value and can benefit almost anyone who makes the effort to use them. So, when faced with the challenge of mastering a large amount of new material try some, or all, of the following:

Use Distributed Practice

You know that you should not cram. Cramming, or what psychologists called massed practice, is not good for long-term retention of material. Spacing out your studying, or distributed practice, on the other hand, enhances your ability to remember. This is one of the most well-established principles in psychology—the spacing effect. Instead of studying for five straight hours at one time, you would be much better off studying one hour a day over five days. This technique also works at shorter intervals. For example, if you have to memorize a formula, your tendency is to repeat it over and over (say, ten times) until you feel confident you have it memorized. This, of course is massed practice, and the sense of confidence that typically accompanies it is often misleading. A better way to maximize the benefits of those ten rehearsals is to space them over time, allowing a longer interval after each rehearsal than the one before.

Reduce Interference

One reason we tend to forget new information is that other information (either previously learned or learned later) can interfere with the material we are trying to master. So, if you are studying for a number of courses at the same time, try to study subjects that are different from each other. The more similar they are, the greater the interference. Another source of interference comes from social activities, such as watching TV or interacting with friends. When you engage in these activities after studying, you increase the risk of interference. In addition, playing loud music, having the TV on, or listening to other people's conversations while you are studying can cause distraction and interfere with learning. The best advice? Go to sleep after studying. A good sleep is the best way to cut down on interference and it helps consolidate memories. The worst thing to do? Stay up all night cramming for an exam that is being given the next day.

Try Overlearning

Overlearning is another very effective, and relatively simple, technique for preventing forgetting. When you feel you have mastered the material in a chapter, and you have just answered all the progress test questions correctly, you usually feel relieved and put away the books. It is at this point, however, that overlearning is useful. If you had spent, say, an hour and a half getting to this level, what you need to do now is spend another 10 to 15 minutes reviewing the material one more time. These few extra minutes of studying are the most beneficial minutes you can spend in terms of consolidating your memory and preventing the forgetting of material you have just learned. Hermann Ebbinghaus showed, over a hundred years ago, that most of the information is lost very soon after it is learned. He was the first to demonstrate the powerful effect of overlearning as a way of dealing with this problem.

Get Corrective Feedback

If you studied hard and felt you really knew the material, it is a bit of a shock to find that you did poorly on the test. What could have happened? One possibility is that you only thought you knew the material and you were suffering from "the overconfidence effect." A simple way of prevent this is to get corrective feedback on what you know before taking the exam. For example, using the True/False tests and the Matching Tests, completing the Graphic Organizers, and, of course, taking the Progress Tests will give you the feedback you need.

Be aware, however, that this is not necessarily a perfect gauge of how you will do on the real exam. When you are testing yourself, you tend to be in a much more relaxed state: You have just studied the material and you are in no particular rush. If you make a mistake, it is no big deal; you can simply look up the answers at the end of the chapter (this is not something that you can do in the exam!). These factors often lead students to the false conclusion that the questions on the real exam were much harder than the ones in the progress tests, sample exams, and so forth. Try to make your self-testing as real as possible (get a little anxious); that way you will benefit most from corrective feedback.

Use Mnemonics

Use of memory aids, called mnemonics, can help in memorizing new material and in preventing forgetting. Visual imagery, in particular, is very effective with some material. Try to vividly imagine what it is you are attempting to memorize. A picture is worth a thousand words and is much more memorable. For other material, try making up a story that links elements together. Create acronyms for lists of terms or complex concept names, for example (it is easier to remember SCUBA than self-contained underwater breathing apparatus). Look ahead in your textbook to Chapter 6 and read about how memory works, why we forget, and how we can make memories last; specifically, read the Application for more study tips.

Develop Good Study Habits

Most top students get good grades because of effective study habits (not sheer brilliance). Evaluate your current study habits. Manage your time effectively. Remember, we are usually poor judges about how long things take to do (late papers are a typical example that is the result of our poor judgment). So, after you have made your plans, allow yourself some extra time.

Make studying a priority and firmly commit to doing well in school. Don't let other people interfere with your goal of getting good grades. Study by yourself (too much socializing takes place in study groups). Reward yourself with social activities, if that's what is important to you, AFTER you have successfully completed your study and have achieved an A+ on the progress tests. If you like music, play soft instrumental music (the suggestion has been made that some classical music, such as Mozart, has a relaxing and beneficial effect). Take a short break after an hour or so of studying—walk around for a few minutes. Do some exercise. Don't study when you are sleep deprived, very tired, or stressed out. If you are getting nowhere and can't concentrate on the material. do something else for a while (a breath of fresh air, a brief nap, a little walk, a chat with a friend, a little meditation or exercise, can all be helpful).

Try Exercise
Exercising before you study will help relieve stress and will induce a more relaxed state. This is because exercise causes the brain to release pain-killing chemicals called endorphins (you have your own little drug-producing factory). It is also a good idea to exercise before a major exam for the same reasons. If aerobic exercise is not your thing (if it makes you tired and unable to concentrate), try meditation, or some other relaxation technique. Anxiety interferes with performance, so anything you can do to effectively control and reduce your anxiety will help. Have fun, good luck, and enjoy your introductory psychology course.

Study Guide

Introduction and Research Methods

PREVIEW

Reading the section below first will give you a general sense of the chapter's contents and an initial introduction to some of the major concepts and terms. This will prime you for what you are about to read and help you to develop a "cognitive map" that will guide your study of the material in this chapter. Likewise, reading the **preview questions** at the beginning of each major section will improve your ability to understand, learn, and retain the information.

CHAPTER 1. . . AT A GLANCE

Chapter 1 first defines psychology, then gives a brief history of the people and events that influenced its development. Beginning with the contributions of philosophy and physiology, the chapter discusses the two early schools, structuralism and functionalism; the emergence of the major perspectives in twentieth-century psychology; and the major specialty areas.

The four goals of psychology are used to introduce the scientific method. The descriptive and experimental research methods are outlined, and the advantages and disadvantages of each are discussed.

Important issues such as the need for representative sampling and random selection are raised. The section concludes with a discussion of the uses and limitations of correlational studies. The concepts of correlation, the correlation coefficient, and negative and positive correlations are described and explained.

The experimental method is explained in detail, using a specific study to illustrate important concepts such as dependent and independent variables, experimental and control groups, and random assignment. Also presented are variations in experimental design.

The chapter concludes with an important discussion of the ethical guidelines that regulate psychological research and the role played by the American Psychological Association.

Introduction: The Origins of Psychology

Preview Questions

Consider the following questions as you study this section of the chapter.

- How is psychology defined today?
- Which two disciplines influenced the emergence of psychology as a science?
- Who founded the first two schools of psychology, and what were these schools called?
- Who founded psychoanalysis, and what contributions did he make to psychology?
- What are the goals of behaviorism, and who were the three main proponents of this perspective?
- What is the emphasis of humanistic psychology, how does it differ from behaviorism and psychoanalysis, and what are the names of its two major advocates?

Read the section "Introduction: The Origins of Psychology?" and **write** *your answers to the following:*

1. (a) Psychology is now defined as
   _____ .

   (b) The definition of psychology has changed and _____ over time.

   (c) The early psychologists struggled over such fundamental issues as how psychology should be defined, what its proper _____ should be, which areas of human experience should be studied, what _____ should be used to investigate psychological issues, whether psychology should include the study of _____ , and whether its findings should be _____ to enhance human behavior.

2. (a) Early philosophers such as Aristotle were interested in psychological topics such as _____ , _____ , _____ , _____ , and _____ .

   (b) French philosopher and mathematician

_____ promoted interactive dualism, which refers to the idea that
_____ .

   (c) Another issue raised by philosophers was the _____ issue, in which _____ refers to the inborn characteristics of the individual and _____ refers to the environmental influences that shape the individual.

   (d) Today, this issue is often framed in terms of _____ versus _____ .

   (e) Unlike philosophers who rely on logic and intuition, modern psychologists base their conclusions on the
   _____ .

3. (a) The branch of biology that studies the functions and parts of living organisms, including humans, is _____ .

   (b) Scientists such as Hermann von Helmholtz established the foundation for an idea crucial to the development of psychology, that _____ could be applied to understanding
   _____ .

4. (a) In his text, *Principles of Physiological Psychology*, _____ outlined the connections between _____ and psychology and promoted the idea that psychology should be established as a separate scientific discipline.

   (b) He is credited with opening the first _____ at the University of Leipzig in 1879.

   (c) He defined psychology as the study of _____ and emphasized the use of _____ to study and measure consciousness.

5. (a) Wundt's student _____ established structuralism, the first major school in psychology.

(b) This school held that even our most complex experiences could be broken down into elemental _____ and could be studied through a procedure called _____ .

6. Structuralism had several significant limitations:

   (a) Different subjects often provided very different _____ about the same stimulus, and the same subjects _____ in their responses to the same stimulus from trial to trial.

   (b) _____ could not be used to study children or animals.

   (c) Complex topics such as _____ , _____ , _____ , and _____ did not lend themselves to scientific investigation using introspection.

7. (a) The functionalist school of psychology was based on the ideas of _____ .

   (b) Functionalism stressed the importance of how behavior _____ to allow organisms to _____ to their environment.

   (c) Functionalism expanded psychology to include applications to _____ , _____ , and _____ .

8. (a) The common goal of functionalism and structuralism is an emphasis on the study of _____ .

   (b) In contrast to the structuralists, William James saw _____ as an ongoing stream of mental activity.

   (c) Functionalism's twin themes, the importance of the _____ role of behavior and _____ psychology to enhance human behavior, continue to be evident in modern psychology.

9. (a) One of James's students, _____ , established the first _____ in

the United States and founded the American Psychological Association.

   (b) Another student, who founded a psychological laboratory at Wellesley College in 1891 and became the first woman president of the American Psychological Association, was _____ , who conducted research in many areas, including _____ , _____ , and _____ .

   (c) The first American woman to officially earn a Ph.D. in psychology was _____ . She strongly advocated the scientific study of the _____ of different animal species and, in 1921, became the second woman president of the American Psychological Association.

10. (a) The Austrian physician who developed a theory of personality based on uncovering causes of behavior that were hidden from the person's conscious awareness was _____ .

   (b) His school of psychology, which focuses on the role of unconscious conflicts in determining behavior and personality, was called _____ . These unconscious conflicts are almost always _____ or _____ in nature.

   (c) He further believed that past experiences, especially childhood experiences, were critical in the formation of adult personality and behavior and that glimpses of unconscious impulses are revealed in _____ , _____ , _____ , and _____ .

11. (a) Behaviorism rejected the emphasis on _____ promoted by structuralim and functionalim and rejected Freudian notions about _____ influences.

   (b) Instead, behaviorism focused on the scientific study of _____ that could be objectively measured and verified.

(c) Behaviorism grew out of the pioneering work of Russian physiologist _____ , whose work on salivation in dogs led him to believe that he had discovered the mechanism by which all behaviors are _____ .

(d) The American psychologist who championed behaviorism as a new school in psychology was _____ ; he rejected both _____ as a scientific methodology and _____ as the subject matter of psychology.

(e) The goal of the behaviorists was to discover the fundamental principles of _____ , and for the most part they studied _____ behavior under carefully controlled laboratory conditions.

(f) Behaviorism was later championed by _____ who also believed that psychology should restrict itself to studying _____ that could be measured and verified.

(g) Behaviorism dominated American psychology for almost 50 years; during that time, the study of _____ was largely ignored as a topic in psychology.

12. (a) Humanistic psychology is sometimes referred to as the "third force" because it is distinctly different from both _____ and _____ .

(b) The person credited with founding humanistic psychology is _____ . Unlike the psychoanalysts, he stressed the role of _____ experiences in people's lives; unlike the behaviorists, he emphasized _____ , _____ , and the importance of choice in human behavior.

(c) The humanistic psychologist who developed a theory of motivation that emphasizes psy-chological growth and self-direction was _____ .

13. Read the following and write the correct term in the space provided.

(a) A psychologist who stresses the importance of how behavior enables organisms to adapt to their environment would be classified as belonging to the _____ school of psychology.

(b) Dr. Levine adheres to the theory that emphasizes the role of unconscious conflicts in determining behavior and personality. This viewpoint is most consistent with the _____ school of psychology.

(c) Environmental influences and overt measurable behavior are to _____ as conscious experience, psychological growth, and self-determination are to _____ .

(d) While researching a paper on the history of psychology, John discovered that René Descartes, a seventeenth-century philosopher and mathematician, promoted the idea that the mind and body are separate entities that interact to produce sensations, emotions, and other conscious experiences. Descartes' view is called _____ .

(e) Dr. Brunac's research focuses on the question of the degree to which heredity and environment influence the development of human abilities such as intelligence and personality characteristics. Dr. Brunac is interested in the _____ issue.

(f) Alvira believes that our most complex conscious experiences can be broken down into elemental structures or basic components of sensations and feelings through the research method of introspection. Alvira's view is most consistent with the school of thought in psychology called _____ .

Review of Terms, Concepts, and Names 1

Use the terms in this list to complete the Matching Test, then to help you answer the True/False items correctly.

psychology
interactive dualism
nature-nurture issue
   (heredity versus
   environment)
physiology
Wilhelm Wundt
Edward B. Titchener
structuralism
introspection
William James
functionalism
G. Stanley Hall

Mary Whiton Calkins
Margaret Floy
   Washburn
behaviorism
Ivan Pavlov
John B. Watson
B. F. Skinner
Sigmund Freud
psychoanalysis
humanistic psychology
Carl Rogers
Abraham Maslow

Matching Exercise

Match the appropriate term/name with its definition or description.

1. _____ American psychologist who conducted research on memory, personality, and dreams; established one of the first U.S. psychology research laboratories; first woman president of the American Psychological Association.

2. _____ Looking inward in an attempt to reconstruct feelings and sensations experienced immediately after viewing a stimulus object.

3. _____ School of psychology and theoretical viewpoint that emphasizes each person's unique potential for psychological growth and self-direction.

4. _____ American psychologist who founded behaviorism, emphasizing the study of observable behavior and rejecting the study of mental processes.

5. _____ Early school of psychology that emphasized studying the purpose, or function, of behavior and mental experiences.

6. _____ The scientific study of behavior and mental processes.

7. _____ The idea that the mind and body are separate entities that interact to produce sensations, emotions, and other conscious experiences.

8. _____ German physiologist who founded psychology as a formal science; he opened the first psychology research laboratory in 1879.

9. _____ British-born American psychologist who founded structuralism, the first school of psychology.

10. _____ School of psychology and theoretical viewpoint that emphasizes the study of observable behaviors, especially as they pertain to the process of learning.

11. _____ American psychologist who founded the school of humanistic psychology.

True/False Test

Indicate whether each statement is true or false by placing T or F in the blank space next to each item.

1. ___ G. Stanley Hall was an American psychologist who established the first psychology research laboratory in the United States and founded the American Psychological Association.

2. ___ Structuralism stresses the importance of how behavior functions to allow people and animals to adapt to their environment.

3. ___ Physiology is a branch of biology that studies the functions and parts of living organisms, including human beings.

4. ___ William James was an American philosopher and psychologist who founded psychology in the United States and established the psychological school called functionalism.

5. ___ The issue of heredity versus environment is the same as the nature-nurture issue and refers to the debate over which is more important, the inborn charactristics of the individual or the impact of the environment.

6. ___ Margaret Floy Washburn was an American psychologist who published research on mental processes in animals and was the first woman in the United States to earn a doctorate in psychology.

7. ___ Ivan Pavlov was an Austrian physician whose work focused on the unconscious causes of behavior and personality formation and who founded psychoanalysis.

8. ___ B. F. Skinner was a famous American psychologist who championed behaviorism.

9. ___ Abraham Maslow was a humanistic psychologist who developed a theory of motivation that emphasized psychological growth.

10. ___ Psychoanalysis studies environmental influences on behavior and personality without

reference to mental processes and is concerned with understanding how we learn to become who we are.

11. ___ Sigmund Freud was a Russian psychologist whose pioneering research on learning contributed to the development of behaviorism and who discovered the basic learning process that is now called classical conditioning.

Check your answers and review any areas of weakness before going on to the next section.

Contemporary Psychology

Preview Questions

Consider the following questions as you study this section of the chapter.

- What are the seven major perspectives in contemporary psychology, and how do they differ?
- What is the difference between a *perspective* and a *specialty* area?
- What is the focus of each of the main specialty areas in contemporary psychology?
- How do clinical psychologists and psychiatrists differ, and what role do psychoanalysts play in the mental health profession?

*Read the section "Contemporary Psychology" and **write** your answers to the following:*

1. (a) Today's psychologists tend to characterize themselves according to (1) the _____ they emphasize in investigating psychological topics and (2) the _____ in which they have been trained and practice.

2. (a) The biological perspective emphasizes studying the _____ bases of human and animal behavior, including the _____ system, _____ system, _____ system, and _____ .

    (b) In recent decades, the influence of biological psychology has been increased by advances in _____ and _____ .

(c) The relative success of _____ that help control symptoms of psychological disorders such as schizophrenia and depression have raised questions about the interaction between _____ factors and human behavior, emotions and thought processes.

(d) Technological advances that allow scientists to study the structure and activity of the intact brain include _____ , _____ , and _____ ; these and other advances have produced new insights into the _____ bases of memory, learning, mental disorders, and other behaviors.

3. (a) The perspective that emphasizes the importance of unconscious influences, early life experiences, and interpersonal relationships in explaining the underlying dynamics of behavior or treating people with psychological problems is called the _____ perspective.

    (b) While the key ideas and themes of Freud and his theory of _____ are still important among many psychologists, they have been expanded and modified by his followers; today, psychologists who adopt this perspective are called _____ psychologists.

4. (a) The view that psychology should focus on observable behaviors and fundamental laws of learning is evident today in the behavioral perspective, advocated by _____ and _____ .

    (b) Contemporary psychologists who take this perspective continue to study how behavior is acquired or modified by _____ consequences. Many who work in the field of mental health use this viewpoint in explaining and treating psychological disorders.

5. (a) Psychologists who take the humanistic perspective continue to be influenced by _____ and _____ .

   (b) The humanistic perspective focuses on the motivation of people to _____ , the influence of interpersonal relationships on a person's self-concept, and the importance of _____ and _____ in striving to reach one's potential.

6. (a) The cognitive perspective focuses on the important role of _____ in how people process _____ , develop _____ , solve _____ , and think.

   (b) An important factor in the cognitive revolution was the development of the first _____ , which gave psychologists a model for human mental processes.

7. (a) Psychologists who study the diversity of human behavior in different cultural settings and countries are called _____ psychologists.

   (b) The phenomenon of social loafing in some countries and its opposite effect in others points to the enormous influence of _____ and _____ factors on behavior.

8. (a) Growing out of renewed interest in the work of British naturalist _____ , the _____ perspective focuses on the application of his principles to explain psychological processes and phenomena.

   (b) This theory proposes that _____ for survival between individual members of a species and the heritability of characteristics that increase their chances of survival are part of the process that reflects the principle of _____ .

   (c) Psychologists who take this perspective assume that psychological processes that

helped individuals _____ to their environment also helped them survive, reproduce, and pass those abilities on to their offspring.

   (d) The _____ perspective has been applied to such psychological problems as _____ , which are extreme fears of particular objects or situations, as well as human relationships, mate selection, and sex differences.

9. Which specialty area is represented by each of the following?

   (a) Dr. Matthews studies the relationship between behavior and the nervous system. She would most likely be classified as a(n) _____ psychologist.

   (b) Michele wants to study physical, social, and psychological changes that occur over the lifespan when she attends graduate school. Michele is planning to be a(n) _____ psychologist.

   (c) Dr. Bowman studies the causes, treatment, and prevention of different types of psychological disorders. Dr. Bowman is most likely a(n) _____ psychologist.

   (d) Dr. Ying explores how individuals are affected by people and situations and the factors that influence conformity and obedience. Dr. Ying is a(n) _____ psychologist.

   (e) Dr. Steinberg examines individual differences and the characteristics that make each person unique. He is most likely a(n) _____ psychologist.

   (f) Ingrid is interested in investigating mental processes such as reasoning, thinking, and problem solving. Ingrid is probably planning a career as a(n) _____ psychologist.

   (g) Dr. Whinney develops instructional methods and materials used to train people in both educational and work settings; she also studies how people of all ages learn. She is a(n) _____ psychologist. Her colleague, Dr. Marx focuses on designing programs that promote the intellectual, social, and emotional development of children, including those with special needs. He is a(n) _____ psychologist.

(h) Dr. Barton is concerned with stress and coping, the relationship between psychological factors and well-being, and ways of promoting health-enhancing behaviors. Dr. Barton is probably a(n) _____ psychologist.

(i) Pitor, who just completed his Ph.D., applied for a job concerned with the relationship between people and work, including the study of job satisfaction, worker productivity, personnel selection, and the interaction between people and equipment. Pitor has applied for a job as a(n) _____ psychologist.

10. (a) A practitioner with a medical degree plus years of specialized training in the treatment of psychological disorders is a(n)

_____ .

(b) A practitioner with a doctorate in psychology and intensive training in treating people with psychological disorders is a(n)

_____ .

(c) A practitioner who has extensive training in Freud's psychoanalytic method of psychotherapy is a(n) _____ and could be a(n) _____ ,
a(n) _____ , or some other mental health professional.

Graphic Organizer 1

The statements in the table below represent some of the major perspectives and specialty areas in contemporary psychology. Which perspective is reflected by each statement and which specialty area is being described? Write your answers in the spaces provided.

Statement	Perspective	Specialty
1. I'm interested in how different parenting styles and techniques influence each child's individual potential for growth and self-determination.		
2. I study the relationship between people and work and, more specifically, how to increase productivity. I believe that by changing environmental factors, increasing the use of rewards and praise for correct behavior, and providing corrective feedback, workers' overt behavior can be changed.		
3. I study how people of all ages learn, and I develop instructional methods and materials to help the learning process. In particular, I stress the role played by thinking, problem solving, memory, and mental imagery.		
4. I work mostly with people who suffer from mental disorders, and I believe that the main causes of mental illness are either genetic or due to some malfunction in the central nervous system or endocrine system. I often prescribe medications and order medical procedures such as electroshock treatment.		
5. I often travel to different countries to research people's attitudes and group relations. My research tends to show that many behavioral patterns—for instance, the amount of personal space people require to feel comfortable—vary from one country to another.		
6. I believe that unconscious conflicts, early childhood experiences, and repressed sexual and aggressive feelings make us who we are, and I use this point of view in my work on individual differences and in trying to determine which characteristics make each of us unique.		
7. I focus on the relationship between psychological factors and health, in particular on how people cope with stress in their lives. It is not what happens to us that is important; rather, how we perceive and think about potentially stressful events determines our well-being.		
8. My research keeps me in the lab most of the time, and I focus on the principles and conditions of learning and motivation. Recently, I have been investigating how quickly rats learn the layout of a maze as a function of either large or small amounts of reinforcement.		
9. Psychological processes that have helped individuals adapt to their environment also helped them to survive, reproduce, and pass those abilities to their offspring. I adopt this point of view in my investigations of interpersonal attraction, prejudice, and aggression.		

Graphic Organizer 2

Origins of Psychology, First Schools, Key Figures, and Major Perspectives in Contemporary Psychology

Flow diagram exercise: To help you develop the technique of creating your own graphic organizers, we encourage you to try making a flow diagram/ timeline, using boxes, lines, and arrows, that contains the following information. Use a separate sheet of paper and generate your own graphic organizer, then compare it to the sample provided in the answer section. To help you in this early stage of your study, we've filled in portions of the first two boxes.

Philosophy (list key figures)	Physiology (list key figure)

1. Two areas that influenced the beginnings of psychology and the key figures in each.

2. The founder of psychology and the year the first psychology research lab was established.

3. First school in psychology and key figure.

4. First American school in psychology and key figures.

5. Two new approaches (and key figures in each) that challenged the first two schools in psychology.

6. New school that emerged in the 1950s and key figures.

7. The seven major perspectives in contemporary psychology and the key figures (if any) and emphasis of each.

Review of Terms and Names 2

Use the terms in this list to complete the Matching Test, then to help you answer the True/False items correctly.

perspective
specialty area
biological perspective
psychodynamic
    perspective
behavioral perspective
humanistic perspective
cognitive perspective
cross-cultural
    perspective

culture
ethnocentrism
individualistic cultures
collectivistic cultures
evolutionary perspective
Charles Darwin
biological psychology
cognitive psychology
experimental psychology

developmental
    psychology
social psychology
personality psychology
health psychology
educational psychology
school psychology

industrial/organizational
    psychology
clinical psychologist
counseling psychology
psychiatrist
psychoanalyst

Matching Exercise

Match the appropriate term/name with its definition or description.

1. _____ Psychologist who has a doctorate in psychology and intensive training in diagnosing and treating people with psychological disorders.

2. _____ The study of physical, social, and psychological changes over the lifespan, from conception to death.

3. _____ Mental health professional who has a medical degree plus years of specialized training in the diagnosis and treatment of psychological disorders.

4. _____ Specialists who help develop the instructional methods and materials used to train people in both educational and work settings and who study how people of all ages learn.

5. _____ General term that describes research focused on such basic topics as sensory processes, principles of learning, emotion, and motivation.

6. _____ Point of view or general framework that reflects a psychologist's emphasis in investigating psychological topics.

7. _____ Specific area in psychology in which psychologists are trained and in which they work or practice.

8. _____ Broad term that refers to the attitudes, values, beliefs, and behaviors shared by a group of people and communicated from one generation to another.

9. _____ Specialty area that investigates mental processes, information processing, reasoning, thinking, problem solving, memory, perception, mental imagery, and language.

10. _____ Professional who could be a psychologist, a psychiatrist, or other mental health specialist and has extensive training in Freud's method of psychotherapy.

11. _____ Area of psychology that examines individual differences and the characteristics and traits that make each person unique.

12. _____ Perspective in psychology that studies how behavior is acquired or modified by environmental consequences and whose focus is on observable behavior and the fundamental laws of learning.

13. _____ The tendency to use your own culture as the standard for judging other cultures.

14. _____ Perspective in psychology that emphasizes studying the physical bases of human and animal behavior, including the nervous system, endocrine system, immune system, and genetics.

True/False Test

Indicate whether each statement is true or false by placing T or F in the blank space next to each item.

1. ____ Biological psychology studies the physical bases of human and animal behavior.

2. ____ The evolutionary perspective uses Darwin's theory of evolution by natural selection to explain psychological processes and phenomena.

3. ____ Counseling psychology is concerned with the relationship between people and work, and it includes the study of job satisfaction, worker productivity, personnel selection, and the interaction between people and equipment.

4. ____ The cross-cultural perspective stresses the importance of cultural and ethnic influences on behavior.

5. ____ School psychology focuses on designing programs that promote the intellectual, social, and emotional development of children, including those with special needs.

6. ____ Charles Darwin was a British naturalist and scientist whose theory of evolution through natural selection was first published in *On the Origin of the Species* in 1859.

7. ____ Psychologists who explore how individuals are affected by people and situations and what factors influence conformity, obedience, persuasion, interpersonal attraction, and other related phenomena are called social psychologists.

8. ____ Individualistic cultures emphasize the needs and goals of the group over the needs and goals of the individual.

9. ____ Health psychology is concerned with stress and coping, the relationship between psychological factors and well-being, and ways of promoting health-enhancing behaviors.

10. ____ Industrial/organizational psychology aims to improve everyday functioning by helping people solve problems in daily living and cope more effectively with challenging situations in their lives either through one-to-one sessions or group therapy.

11. ____ Psychologists who take the humanistic perspective emphasize the importance of unconscious influences, early life experiences, and interpersonal relationships in explaining the underlying dynamics of behavior or treating people with psychological problems.

12. ____ Collectivistic cultures emphasize the needs and goals of the individual over the needs and goals of the group.

13. ____ The psychodynamic perspective focuses on the motivation of people to grow psychologically, the influence of interpersonal relationships on a person's self-concept, the importance of choice and self-direction in striving to reach one's potential.

14. ____ The cognitive perspective stresses the important role of mental processes in how people process information, develop language, solve problems, and think.

Check your answers and review any areas of weakness before going on to the next section.

The Scientific Method

Preview Questions

Consider the following questions as you study this section of the chapter.

- What are the four goals of psychology?

- What is the scientific method?

- What assumptions and attitudes guide psychologists?

- What is meant by empirical evidence, and what are the four basic steps of the scientific method?

- How does the scientific method generate new knowledge and challenge established ways of thinking?

*Read the section "The Scientific Method" and **write** your answers to the following:*

1. The four basic goals of psychology are to
   (a) _____ , (b) _____ ,
   (c) _____ , and
   (d) _____
   behavior and mental processes.

2. (a) The scientific method refers to a set of
   _____ , _____ , and
   _____ that guide researchers in
   creating questions to investigate, in generating evidence, and in drawing conclusions.

   (b) Psychologists are guided by the basic scientific assumption that all events are lawful,
   which means that psychologists assume that
   _____ .

   (c) They are also guided by the scientific
   assumption that events are explainable, and
   this means that psychologists assume that
   _____

   _____ .

   (d) Psychologists share a set of attitudes in trying to achieve the goals of psychology, these
   including a willingness to consider new or
   alternative explanations, or being
   _____ ; critically evaluating the
   evidence, or having a healthy sense of
   _____ ; and being
   _____ in the claims they make.

3. (a) Evidence that is the result of observation,
   measurement, and experimentation is called
   _____ evidence.

   (b) As part of the overall process of producing
   scientific evidence psychologists follow the
   four steps of the scientific method:
   (1) _____
   (2) _____
   (3) _____
   (4) _____

4. (a) When a researcher has identified a question
   or issue to be investigated, it must be posed
   in the form of a tentative statement that
   describes the relationship between two or
   more variables, or a _____ ,
   that can be tested empirically.

   (b) Factors that can change or vary and are
   capable of being observed, measured, and
   verified are called _____ .

   (c) A precise description of how a variable in a
   study will be manipulated or measured is an
   _____ . It is critical
   because many concepts that psychologists
   investigate can be measured in more than
   one way.

5. (a) In designing a study, investigators must
   decide between two categories of research
   methods: _____ and
   _____ .

   (b) Naturalistic observation, surveys, case studies, and correlational studies are commonly
   used _____ methods, which
   involve strategies for observing and describing behavior.

   (c) Cause-and-effect relationships are measured
   by the _____ method.

6. (a) To summarize, analyze, and draw conclusions about data, researchers use a branch
   of math known as _____ .

   (b) If the results of research are not likely to
   have occurred by chance, they are called
   _____

   (c) Meta-analysis is a statistical technique that
   involves the analysis of _____
   on a specific topic in order to identify overall
   trends.

7. (a) Along with reporting their results, psychologists provide a detailed description of the
   study itself, including who
   _____ in the study, how
   _____ were selected, how
   _____ were operationally
   defined, what _____ or _____

were used, how the _____ were analyzed, and what the _____ seem to suggest.

(b) Psychologists describe their methods and explain their procedures in detail so that other investigators may _____ , or repeat, the study.

8. (a) A tentative explanation that tries to account for the diverse findings on the same topic is called a _____ , or a model.

(b) Whereas a _____ is a specific question or prediction to be tested, a _____ is a tentative explanation that tries to integrate, summarize, and account for the relationship among a large number of findings and observations; a good _____ often generates new _____ that can be tested by further research.

(c) When new results challenge the established way of thinking about a phenomenon, a _____ is expanded, modified, and even replaced; thus, the _____ base of psychology is constantly evolving and changing.

9. Read the following and write the correct term in the space provided.

(a) Dr. Marlow is interested in drinking and driving behavior and wants to know the frequency with which people will drive after receiving feedback from a breathalyzer test. In one condition she sets up her equipment in a bar and administers the test to patrons who are leaving and planning to drive and then observes whether or not feedback on their level of intoxication influenced their decision to drive. Dr. Marlow is using _____ research.

(b) In the above example, Dr. Marlow makes this prediction: the majority of people who are told that they are over the legal limit

will still drive; the higher the level on the breathalyzer test, the more likely it is that they will drive. Dr. Marlow has formulated a _____ .

(c) After collecting data over many weeks, Dr. Marlow performs calculations and mathematical tests to see if her prediction was correct. Dr. Marlow is using _____ to analyze her data.

(d) Dr. Marlow next writes a report describing the background of this research and details her research design, data collection methods, results, analyses, and conclusions. She submits her report to a respected psychology journal for peer review and publication. She is following step _____ of producing scientific evidence by _____ .

Review of Terms and Concepts 3

Use the terms in this list to complete the Matching Test, then to help you answer the True/False items correctly.

scientific method
critical thinking
empirical evidence
hypothesis
variable
operational definition
descriptive method
experimental method

cause-and-effect
  relationship
statistics
statistical significance
meta-analysis
replicate
theory

Matching Exercise

Match the appropriate term/name with its definition or description.

1. _____ Statistical technique that involves combining and analyzing the results of many research studies on a specific topic in order to identify overall trends.

2. _____ To repeat or duplicate a scientific study in order to increase confidence in the validity of the original findings.

3. _____ A set of assumptions, attitudes, and procedures that guide researchers in creating questions to investigate, in generating evidence, and in drawing conclusions.

4. _____ Tentative statement that describes the relationship between two or more variables.

5. _____ Precise description of how the variables in a study will be manipulated or measured.

6. _____ Method of investigation used to demonstrate cause-and-effect relationships by purposely manipulating a factor thought to produce change in a second factor.

7. _____ Mathematical methods used to summarize data and draw conclusions based on the data.

True/False Test

Indicate whether each statement is true or false by placing T or F in the blank space next to each item.

1. ____ A statistically significant finding is one that is not likely to have occurred by chance.

2. ____ Empirical evidence is evidence that is the result of observation, measurement, and experimentation.

3. ____ A variable is a tentative statement that describes the relationship between two or more factors.

4. ____ Descriptive methods are research strategies for observing and describing behavior and include naturalistic observation, survey, case studies, and correlational studies.

5. ____ The cause-and-effect relationship demonstrated by the experimental method is one in which a change in one variable causes a change in a second variable.

6. ____ A theory is a statistical technique that involves the analysis of many research studies on a specific topic in order to identify overall trends.

7. ____ Critical thinking is the active process of trying to minimize the influence of preconceptions and biases while rationally evaluating evidence, determining what conclusions can be drawn from the evidence, and considering alternative explanations.

> Check your answers and review any areas of weakness before going on to the next section.

Descriptive Methods

Preview Questions

Consider the following questions as you study this section of the chapter.

- What are descriptive methods, and what are the four types discussed in the text?
- How is naturalistic observation typically conducted?
- What are case studies, and when are they normally used?
- How do researchers ensure that their sample closely parallels the larger group on relevant characteristics, and why is this important for obtaining accurate results?
- What does a correlational study involve, and what are its limitations?
- What is the correlation coefficient, and how does a negative correlation differ from a positive correlation?

*Read the section "Descriptive Methods" and **write** your answers to the following:*

1. (a) Descriptive methods are research strategies for _____ and _____ behavior.

   (b) Using descriptive methods, researchers can answer important questions such as when certain behaviors take place, how often they occur, and whether they are _____ such as a person's age, ethnic group, or educational level.

   (c) Descriptive methods can provide a wealth of information about behavior that would be difficult or impossible to study _____ .

2. (a) The systematic observation and recording of behaviors as they occur in their natural setting is called _____ .

   (b) One advantage of this method is that it allows researchers to study human behaviors that could not ethically be _____ in an experimental situation. Another advantage is that results often can be _____ more confidently to real-life situations than can artificially or staged situations.

3. (a) An intensive, in-depth investigation of an individual, involving the compilation of data from a wide variety of different sources, is called a _____ .

   (b) When a small group of individuals are intensively studied, it is called _____ . If information from several case studies that focus on the same type of behavior are combined, it is called _____ . In both methods, psychologists look for characteristics or patterns of behavior that are _____ across individual cases.

4. (a) Subjects asked to respond to a structured set of questions about their experiences, beliefs, behaviors, or attitudes are taking part in a _____ .

   (b) A key advantage of this type of research is that investigators are able to gather information from a _____ of people than could be obtained through other research methods.

   (c) Typically, this research method involves a carefully designed _____ in a paper-and-pencil format that is mailed or otherwise distributed to a selected group of people.

   (d) This research can also be conducted over the telephone or in person, using an _____ format in which a structured set of questions are asked and the person's responses are recorded.

   (e) Interview-based surveys are typically more _____ and _____ than questionnaire-based surveys.

5. (a) Surveys are administered to a segment of a larger group or population, or a _____ . The key to meaninful results is a _____

that very closely parallels or matches the larger group on relevant characteristics such as age, sex, race, marital status, and educational level.

   (b) Random selection means that _____ of the larger group has an _____ chance of being selected for inclusion in the sample.

6. (a) A correlational study examines how strongly two _____ are related to, or associated with, each other.

   (b) The numerical indicator of how strongly related two factors seem to be is the _____ ; it always falls in the range from _____ to _____ .

   (c) The number indicates the _____ of the relationship, and the sign shows the _____ of the relationship between the two variables.

   (d) The closer the number is to _____ , whether positive or negative, the stronger the association between the two factors.

7. (a) A positive correlation indicates that two variables vary systematically in the _____ direction, either _____ or _____ together.

   (b) A negative correlation indicates that two variables vary systematically in the _____ direction; as one _____ , the other _____ .

   (c) That two variables may be strongly correlated (either positively or negatively) is not evidence of a _____ relationship.

   (d) Correlational research has two advantages: first, it can be used to _____ some factors and _____ others that merit more intensive study, and second, the results of correlational research can allow researchers to make meaninful _____ .

Graphic Organizer 3
POSITIVE AND NEGATIVE CORRELATIONS

The following box shows both positive and negative correlations between variables. In cells A through D the arrows indicate a relationship between the amount students study (variable X) and their grade point average (GPA) (variable Y). Fill in the appropriate term in each space provided.

Amount of Study (X)

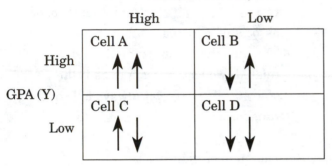

1. Cell A indicates a _____ correlation, and cell D indicates a _____ correlation.

2. Cell C indicates a _____ correlation, and cell B indicates a _____ correlation.

3. Cell A: _____ amounts of X are associated with _____ levels of Y.

   Cell D: _____ amounts of X are associated with _____ levels of Y.

4. Cell C: _____ amounts of X are associated with _____ levels of Y.

   Cell B: _____ amounts of X are associated with _____ levels of Y.

8. Read the following and decide which term applies in each case.

   (a) If a researcher found a correlation coefficient of −0.85, between the amount of exercise people do and their weight, this would indicate that the _____ people exercise, the _____ they weigh.

(b) If an organization wants to find out about the spending habits of high-income people, they would be advised to conduct a _____ , using a representative _____ that would be _____ selected from this population.

(c) Dr. Klatz is interested in whether there is a difference in the way males and females carry objects such as textbooks, bags, and other large objects, so she sets up a hidden camera on the main concourse of a large university and videotapes people at various times throughout the day. Dr. Klatz is using _____ .

(d) A psychologist discovers that the more control people feel they have over what happens in their work environments, the more productive they are. The psychologist has discovered a _____ correlation between perceived control and productivity.

(e) A psychologist who wants to find out about the lives and experiences of people who claim to have been abducted by aliens and to know how these people are viewed by their families, friends, and coworkers would be advised to use the _____ method of research.

Review of Terms and Concepts 4

Use the terms in this list to complete the Matching Test, then to help you answer the True/False items correctly.

descriptive methods
naturalistic observation
case study
survey
sample
representative sample

random selection
correlational study
correlation coefficient
positive correlation
negative correlation

Matching Exercise

Match the appropriate term with its definition or description.

1. _____ A questionnaire or interview designed to investigate the opinions, behaviors, or characteristics of a particular group.

2. _____ General term for scientific procedures that involve systematically observing behavior in order to describe the relationships among behaviors and events.

3. _____ Selected segment of the population under study.

4. _____ Selected segment of a population that very closely parallels the larger group being studied on relevant characteristics.

5. _____ Research strategy that allows the precise calculation of how strongly related two factors are to each other.

6. _____ Type of research in which psychologists combine information from several case studies that focus on the same type of behavior.

True/False Test

Indicate whether each statement is true or false by placing T or F in the blank space next to each item.

1. ____ A case study is an intensive, in-depth investigation of an individual.

2. ____ A negative correlation between two variables means that the two factors are totally unrelated.

3. ____ Naturalistic observation is the systematic observation and recording of behaviors as they occur in their natural setting.

4. ____ A correlation coefficient is a numerical indicator of how strongly related two factors seem to be.

5. ____ Random selection means that every member of the larger group or population has an equal chance of being selected for inclusion in the sample.

6. ____ In a multiple case study, a small group of individuals are intensively studied.

7. ____ A positive correlation is one in which the two variables move in opposite directions; as one factor increases, the other decreases.

Check your answers and review any areas of weakness before going on to the next section.

The Experimental Method

Preview Questions

Consider the following questions as you study this section of the chapter.

- What is the experimental method, and what is its main purpose?

- What are independent and dependent variables, and why do researchers use random assignment?

- What is a placebo control group, and when is it likely to be used?

- Why do researchers use the double-blind technique, and what is meant by expectancy effects?

- What are some of the limitations of the experimental method?

Read the section "The Experimental Method" and ***write*** *your answers to the following:*

1. (a) The _____ method is used to demonstrate a cause-and-effect relationship between _____ in one variable and the _____ on another variable.

   (b) Conducting an experiment involves deliberately varying one factor, called the _____ variable, and measuring the changes it produces in a second factor, called the _____ variable.

   (c) If all other factors are held constant, then any changes in the _____ variable can be attributed to the changes in the _____ variable, and that's why an experiment can demonstrate a _____ relationship between the two variables.

2. (a) Random assignment means that _____

_____ .

(b) Random assignment is important because it ensures _____

_____ .

and that _____

_____ .

3. (a) In the Sam Stone study, the _____ that was deliberately manipulated was exposing one group of children to suggestive questioning after Sam Stone's visit; the children assigned to the suggestive questioning condition represented the _____ group.

(b) Children randomly assigned to the control group experienced all the experimental conditions except the _____ variable; these children were asked neutral rather than suggestive questions.

(c) The control group serves two important functions. First, it serves as a _____ to which changes in the experimental group can be compared; second, it can be used to check for changes that occur _____ or _____ over time.

(d) Because the control group is not exposed to the _____ variable, whatever changes occur in the _____ variable (their memory) in the control group cannot have been caused by the _____ variable.

4. (a) In the Sam Stone study, the number of factual errors the children made in the fifth interview was the _____ .

(b) To ensure objectivity in rating the video-taped behavior, the rater was _____ , or unaware of the experimental condition to which each child had been assigned.

5. (a) Leichtman and Ceci (1995) concluded that repeated exposure to suggestive questioning can produce a _____ (high/low) rate of factual errors in the recollections of young children.

(b) The Sam Stone study repeated, or _____ , the findings of earlier studies, and the _____ (low/high) rate of factual errors made by children in the control group demonstrates that even young children _____ (can/cannot) accurately report an event if the situation remains free of suggestive or leading questions.

6. (a) A group exposed to a fake treatment or a substance with no known effects is called the _____ group and is used in experiments to help check for changes that may occur simply because subjects think changes are going to occur, or _____ effects. These are also referred to as _____ effects.

(b) A double-blind study is one in which neither the _____ nor the _____ are aware of the experimental condition to which participants have been assigned.

(c) A single-blind study is one in which the _____ but not the _____ is aware of the critical information about the experiment.

(d) The purpose of the double-blind technique is to guard against the possibility that the researcher will inadvertently display _____ , which are subtle cues or signals that communicate what is expected of particular subjects.

7. (a) In a natural experiment, researchers carefully observe and measure the impact of a _____ event on their study participants.

(b) A natural experiment that measured the effects of prolonged exposure to a noisy urban environment found that children exposed to chronic noise (the _____ variable) showed increased psychological and physical stress (the _____ variable).

8. The experimental method has several limitations:

(a) The artificial conditions of some experiments may produce results that do not _____ well and thus cannot be _____ to real situations or to a more general population beyond the study participants.

(b) Even experiments conducted in natural settings have disadvantages, such as a _____ in experimental control.

(c) Sometimes it is not be feasible to create experimentally the kinds of conditions that researchers want to study for _____ reasons.

9. Dr. Denton studies the effects of marijuana on memory. He designs an ethically approved experiment that consists of two groups: group A gets the active ingredient in cannabis, THC, and group B gets a harmless inert substance, and neither the researcher nor the participants know who is getting the drug and who is not. Subjects are assigned to each group by chance, and all subjects are given a long list of word pairs to learn and are later given a memory test.

(a) The independent variable in this study is

_____ .

(b) The dependent variable is the

_____ .

(c) Group A is the _____ group, and group B is the

_____ group.

(d) Dr. Denton has used a

_____ technique in designing the experiment; along with the control pro-

cedure used, this should help guard against

_____ .

(e) Subjects ended up in group A or group B on the basis of _____ .

10. Five of the key provisions of the APA ethical guidelines regulating research with human participants are

(a) _____

(b) _____

(c) _____

(d) _____

(e) _____

Review of Terms and Concepts 5

Use the terms in this list to complete the Matching Test, then to help you answer the True/False items correctly.

experimental method	double-blind study
independent variable	single-blind study
dependent variable	demand characteristics
random assignment	natural experiment
control group	pseudoscience
experimental group	paranormal phenomena
placebo control group	rule of falsifiability
placebo	illusory correlation
expectancy (placebo) effect	

Matching Exercise

Match the appropriate term with its definition or description.

1. _____ Experimental technique in which the researchers, but not the subjects, are aware of the critical information about the experiment.

2. _____ Method of investigation used to demonstrate cause-and-effect relationships by purposely manipulating a factor thought to produce change in a second factor.

3. _____ The factor that is observed and measured for change in an experiment.

4. _____ Alleged abilities that fall outside the range of normal experience and established scientific explanations.

5. _____ Change in a subject's behavior produced by the subject's belief that change should happen.

6. _____ Group of subjects who are exposed to all experimental conditions except the independent variable.

7. _____ In order for a claim to be proved true, there must be identifiable evidence that could prove the claim false.

8. _____ Subtle cues or signals that communicate what is expected of particular subjects in an experiment.

9. _____ A fake treatment or a substance with no known effects.

True/False Test

Indicate whether each item is true or false by placing T or F in the blank space next to each item.

1. ____ Random assignment means that all subjects have an equal chance of being assigned to any of the conditions or groups in the study.

2. ____ Subjects in the placebo control group receive a fake treatment or substance with no known effects.

3. ____ Subjects in the experimental group receive all the experimental conditions including the independent variable.

4. ____ The independent variable in an experiment is purposely manipulated in order to effect a change in another variable.

5. ____ The experimental technique in which neither the participants nor the researcher is aware of the experimental conditions to which each subject has been assigned is called the double-blind technique.

6. ____ A pseudoscience is a fake or a false science.

7. ____ In a natural experiment researchers carefully observe and measure the impact of naturally occurring events on their study participants.

> Check your answers and review any areas of weakness before going on to the next section.

Something to Think About

1. When family and friends find out you are taking a psychology course, someone typically makes some comment about "headshrinking" and "psychoanalyzing," or notes that "psychology is just plain old common sense." To prepare yourself for these remarks, think about how you would explain what psychology really is and how you might "educate" your family and friends about the difference among psychiatry, clinical psychology, and psychoanalysis.

2. If you are like most introductory psychology students, you were probably motivated to take this course, at least in part, because of a number of questions you have about human behavior and mental processes. For example, students often wonder if hypnosis can really help recover repressed memories and memories of past lives; if a lie detector really can detect lies; if "satanic messages" embedded in the lyrics of rock music can cause people to commit suicide; if ESP really exists; or whether subliminal tapes can really improve memory, clear up acne, or improve self-esteem. Now that you know more about the science of psychology, take one of your questions and think about how a psychologist tries to answer it.

> Check your answers and review any areas of weakness before doing the following progress tests.

Progress Test 1

Review the complete chapter (including Concept Reviews and the boxed inserts), review all your study notes, and then test yourself on the following progress test. Check your answers. If you make a mistake, review your notes, the relevant section in the study guide, and, if necessary, go back and read the appropriate part of your textbook.

1. Two disciplines influenced the founding of psychology. The discipline that concerns itself with questions such as mind-body dualism and the nature-nurture issue is _____ ; the discipline that is a branch of biology and studies functions and structures of living organisms is _____ .
   (a) chemistry; physics
   (b) neurology; sociology
   (c) physics; neurology
   (d) philosophy; physiology

2. A Japanese psychologist investigating the relationship between worker satisfaction and productivity was surprised to find that North American workers were less productive when working as part of a group than when working alone. In some Asian countries he had found the opposite to be true. This researcher probably has a _____ perspective and his specialty area is _____ psychology.
   (a) cross-cultural; developmental
   (b) behavioral; health
   (c) behavioral; developmental
   (d) cross-cultural; industrial/organizational

3. Dr. Hammersly focuses on the role of unconscious factors in his patients' behaviors and spends time analyzing their dreams and delving into their early childhood experiences. Dr. Finkleman is more concerned with the way her patients think and reason, and her psychotherapy involves teaching her patients how to recognize irrational thinking and to find different ways of thinking about their situation. Dr. Hammersly's perspective is _____ , and Dr. Finkleman's perspective is _____ .
   (a) cognitive; behavioral
   (b) psychoanalytic; cognitive
   (c) humanistic; biological
   (d) cognitive; psychoanalytic

4. In the above example, Dr. Hammersly would most likely be classified as a _____ , and Dr. Finkleman is most probably a _____ .
   (a) psychoanalyst; social psychologist
   (b) biological psychologist; developmental psychologist
   (c) clinical psychologist; educational psychologist
   (d) psychoanalyst; clinical psychologist

5. A researcher who investigates how people differ on such characteristics as shyness, assertiveness, and self-esteem is most likely a _____ psychologist.
   (a) clinical
   (b) biological
   (c) developmental
   (d) personality

6. To ensure that differences among subjects are evenly distributed across all experimental conditions and that there is no bias in how subjects are assigned to their respective groups, a researcher studying the effects of violence on TV and its effect on children should
   (a) operationally define the role each subject is expected to play and assign subjects on the basis of how closely they fit the definition.
   (b) make sure that the smartest people are assigned to the experimental condition.
   (c) make sure that there is an equal number of males and females, young and old, smart and stupid, short and tall, and so on, in each group.
   (d) randomly assign the subjects to each condition in the experiment.

7. A researcher is interested in how sleep deprivation affects performance and cognitive abilities. She proposes that there is a relationship between the amount of sleep deprivation and the ability to solve complex mental tasks; the more sleep-deprived people are, the more mistakes they are likely to make. She has
   (a) developed a theory.
   (b) formulated a hypothesis.
   (c) produced empirical evidence.
   (d) merely stated the obvious.

8. In a study investigating the effects of sleep deprivation and cognitive performance, a researcher discovers a statistically significant difference between the cognitive scores of subjects who were sleep-deprived for one hour each night and those who were sleep-deprived for four hours per night. This finding indicates that
   (a) the group members were not randomly assigned.
   (b) sleep deprivation improves mental health.
   (c) smarter people need less sleep than less intelligent people.
   (d) the differences between the groups are not likely to have occurred by chance.

9. An experimenter who decides to repeat the essence of an earlier study using different subjects is
   (a) replicating the previous study.
   (b) wasting his time.
   (c) doing a meta-analysis.
   (d) conducting a correlational study.

10. In an experiment designed to test the effects of alcohol on motor coordination group 1 subjects are given a precise amount of alcohol in a mixed drink and group 2 participants are given a drink that smells and tastes exactly like the alcoholic drink but contains no alcohol. Which of the following is true?
    (a) Group 1 is the control group.
    (b) Group 2 is the experimental group.
    (c) Group 2 is the placebo control group.
    (d) Group 1 will have much more fun than group 2.

11. A researcher is interested in whether people talk when they are riding in elevators, so she and her research assistants spend many hours riding in elevators and unobtrusively noting when they hear a conversation. This researcher is using
    (a) naturalistic observation.
    (b) experimental research.
    (c) correlational research.
    (d) case study research.

12. In an attempt to understand how traumatic brain injuries affect behavior, Dr. Nicolai extensively and carefully observes and questions three accident victims who had suffered brain injuries. Which research method is Dr. Nicolai utilizing?
    (a) naturalistic observation
    (b) experimental research
    (c) correlational research
    (d) case study research

13. In her research, Dr. Cranshaw focuses on the application of principles of natural selection to explain psychological processes and phenomena. Dr. Cranshaw is most likely a(n) _____ psychologist.
    (a) evolutionary   (c) behavioral
    (b) biological   (d) psychodynamic

14. According to Culture and Human Behavior 1.1, individualistic cultures emphasize the needs and goals of the _____ over the needs and goals of the _____ .
    (a) individual; group
    (b) country; company
    (c) group; individual
    (d) collective; group

15. According to the Application, which of the following is true of pseudoscience?
    (a) It is a legitimate science that uses both established and unorthodox methods in the search for the truth.
    (b) It is a fake or false science.
    (c) It is not accepted by most of the scientific establishment because pseudoscientists have discovered truths that threaten all the fundamental laws and principles of science.
    (d) It does not use sophisticated jargon, impressive looking statistical graphs, or elaborate theories, and virtually no pseudoscientist has impressive-sounding credentials.

Progress Test 2

After you have checked your understanding of the material in Progress Test 1 and have done a complete chapter review with special focus on any areas of weakness, you are ready to assess your knowledge on Progress Test 2. Check your answers. If you make a mistake, review your notes, and the relevant section of the study guide, and if necessary, review the appropriate part of your textbook.

1. In an experiment, children were randomly assigned to a group that watched a violent video or to a group that watched a nonviolent video; later, the level of aggression in both groups was measured under controlled laboratory conditions. In this example, the measure of the children's aggression was the
   (a) dependent variable.
   (b) independent variable.
   (c) control variable.
   (d) naturalistic variable.

2. Dr. Ames researches changes in people's intellectual abilities as they grow older. Dr. Ames's specialty area is _____ psychology.
   (a) social   (c) developmental
   (b) educational   (d) clinical

3. Which of the major perspectives in psychology today would Wilhelm Wundt say most resembled his point of view?
   - (a) behavioral
   - (b) psychoanalytic
   - (c) cognitive
   - (d) humanistic

4. Dr. Sandman investigates the relationship between sleep deprivation and cognitive abilities. He decides to test subjects in his sleep research lab under varying conditions. First, he allows all his subjects to get a number of uninterrupted nights' sleep and records how long each subject sleeps on average. Next, he decides that sleep deprivation would be either two, three, or four hours less than the average for each subject. Dr. Sandman
   - (a) has operationally defined one of his variables.
   - (b) is using cruel and unusual punishment.
   - (c) has empirically demonstrated a cause-and-effect relationship.
   - (d) has proposed a theory.

5. An educational psychologist is interested in whether student evaluations of instructors' performance is actually a good measure of teaching ability. A review of the literature showed some inconsistent findings across hundreds of different studies. To get a sense of the overall trends in this body of research, the investigator would be advised to use a technique called
   - (a) the correlation coefficient.
   - (b) meta-analysis.
   - (c) case study research.
   - (d) replication.

6. Compared to clinical psychologists, psychiatrists are more likely to
   - (a) prescribe drugs and other medical procedures for their clients.
   - (b) assume that psychological disorders result from unconscious conflicts.
   - (c) use a cognitively based therapy rather than a biologically based therapy.
   - (d) favor a humanistic perspective rather than a psychoanalytic perspective.

7. In an experiment testing the effects of subliminal persuasion on memory and self-esteem, while asleep group A participants listened to a memory tape and were told it would improve their memory, group B heard the same tape but were told it would improve their self-esteem, group C participants listened to a self-esteem tape and were told it would improve their self-

esteem, and group D heard the same tape but were told it would enhance memory. All subjects were given a pretest and posttest measure of self-esteem and memory. The dependent variable in the experiment was
   - (a) the random assignment to the four groups.
   - (b) the scores on the pretest and the posttest.
   - (c) listening to either the self-esteem tapes or the memory tapes.
   - (d) the level of deception used.

8. In the above experiment, subjects were randomly assigned to one of four conditions. The purpose of random assignment is to
   - (a) increase the probability that the same number of subjects end up in each condition.
   - (b) increase the likelihood that the subjects are representative of people in general.
   - (c) decrease the probability of expectancy effects.
   - (d) reduce the possibility of bias and ensure that differences among participants are spread out across all experimental conditions.

9. Researchers and participants in a study examining the effects of marijuana on memory are both unaware of which subjects actually received the active ingredient and which were given a placebo. This study involves the use of
   - (a) replication.
   - (b) the single-blind procedure.
   - (c) the double-blind procedure.
   - (d) correlational techniques.

10. Researchers using a form of descriptive research have found that the bigger a person's line of credit, the more money he or she is likely to owe. The researchers have found a _____ between the size of a credit line and the amount of debt.
   - (a) positive correlation
   - (b) negative correlation
   - (c) cause-and-effect relationship
   - (d) zero correlation

11. Mary is interviewed in depth, and her friends, family, and coworkers are contacted for further information. She also takes a number of psychological tests, and her behavior in various situations is observed. This is an example of _____ research.
   - (a) survey
   - (b) correlational
   - (c) case study
   - (d) experimental

12. In an attempt to predict the winner in the next election, The Kneed to Know Kompany contacts a randomly selected representative sample of the voting population and questions them about their voting plans. This is an example of _____ research.
    (a) correlational
    (b) survey
    (c) case study
    (d) experimental

13. Behaviorism and psychoanalysis dominated psychology for many decades early in the century, but in the 1950s a new school of thought emerged, _____ , which emphasized conscious experience, each person's unique potential for psychological growth, self-determination, and free will.
    (a) structuralism
    (b) functionalism
    (c) humanistic psychology
    (d) cross-cultural psychology

14. According to Culture and Human Behavior 1.1, ethnocentrism is
    (a) the tendency to use one's own culture as the standard for judging other cultures.
    (b) introspective self-centered analysis.
    (c) much more common in individualistic cultures than in collectivistic cultures.
    (d) much more common in collectivistic cultures than in individualistic cultures.

15. When evaluating claims made in the media about psychology-related topics, the Application makes the point that
    (a) skepticism is the rule, not the exception, in science.
    (b) there is no way to sort out true claims from false claims.
    (c) testimonials are the most reliable source of information.
    (d) pseudoscientific claims are legitimate scientific claims.

Progress Test 3

After you have checked your understanding of the material in Progress Tests 1 and 2 and have done a complete chapter review with special focus on any areas of weakness, you are ready to assess your knowledge on Progress Test 3. Check your answers. If you make a mistake, review your notes, and the relevant section of the study guide, and if necessary, review the appropriate part of your textbook.

1. An emphasis on the physical bases of behavior is to the _____ perspective as an emphasis on the influence of culture on behavior is to the _____ perspective.
   (a) biological; evolutionary
   (b) behavioral; humanistic
   (c) biological; cross-cultural
   (d) behavioral; cognitive

2. The evolutionary perspective focuses on _____ , whereas the cognitive perspective emphasizes _____ .
   (a) the physical bases of behavior; environmental influences on behavior
   (b) unconscious influences on behavior and personality; psychological growth and personal potential
   (c) mental processes, information processing, problem solving, and thinking; the influence of culture on behavior
   (d) the application of principles of natural selection to explain psychological processes and phenomena; information processing, problem solving, and thinking

3. Psychologists went to Slogaria after the fall of the dictatorship. There they discovered that many children in orphanages had suffered extreme physical and psychological deprivation. Children from these orphanages, who were later adopted, were matched with a control group of children of the same ages, gender, and so on, who had not experienced deprived conditions. The psychological, emotional, cognitive, and physical development of each group was then measured and monitored over a number of years. This example best illustrates which kind of research?
   (a) correlational research
   (b) naturalistic observation
   (c) a natural experiment
   (d) a double-blind study

4. In the above example, the measurements of psychological and physical health taken over the years constitute the
   (a) independent variable.
   (b) expectancy effects.
   (c) dependent variable.
   (d) demand characteristics.

5. In conducting research on the effects of a new memory enhancing drug, Dr. Simpleton used the double-blind technique. The purpose of doing so was to guard against the possibility that the researcher will inadvertently display
   (a) expectancy effects.
   (b) demand characteristics.
   (c) placebo effects.
   (d) ethnocentrism.

6. In order to find out students' opinions about the recent cut-backs at her university, Gira sent a questionnaire to every twentieth person on the list of currently enrolled students. Gira used the technique of
   (a) replication.   (c) random sampling.
   (b) meta-analysis.   (d) interviewing.

7. Research showing that students with the highest GPAs study approximately twice as many hours per week as those with the lowest GPAs would indicate that
   (a) there is a positive correlation between study behavior and GPA.
   (b) there is a negative correlation between study behavior and GPA.
   (c) high GPA causes good study behavior.
   (d) that the correlation coefficient would probably exceed +1.50.

8. Ethical principles developed by the American Psychological Association require psychologists to
   (a) always tell the participants the exact nature of the experiment and inform them of the hypothesis that will be tested.
   (b) never, under any circumstances, use deception with potential participants.
   (c) withhold all information about the nature, results, and conclusions of the study because of the confidentiality principle.
   (d) obtain informed consent and voluntary participation of potential participants.

9. Dr. Joyce supports the view that the goal of psychology should be to discover the fundamental principles of learning and psychologists should focus exclusively on overt behavior rather than on mental processes. Dr. Joyce would be classified as a _____ psychologist.
   (a) behavioral   (c) psychoanalytic
   (b) cognitive   (d) humanistic

10. An experimenter found that variable A and variable B had a correlation coefficient of +.55, and variable C and variable D had a correlation coefficient of −.75. She can conclude that
    (a) variables A and B have a stronger correlation than variables C and D.
    (b) variable A causes variable B, but C and D are unrelated.
    (c) variables A and B have a weaker correlation than variables C and D.
    (d) variables A and B are strongly correlated, but C and D have no relationship.

11. If researchers wanted to discover the extent to which education level can be used to predict political preferences, they would most likely use
    (a) correlational research.
    (b) naturalistic observation.
    (c) experimental research.
    (d) a natural experiment.

12. "Psychology should study the purpose of behavior and mental processes and how they function to allow organisms to adapt to their environment." This is what a _____ might say.
    (a) functionalist   (c) behaviorist
    (b) structuralist   (d) psychoanalyst

13. According to In Focus 1.3, animal research is condoned by the American Psychological Association as long as the research
    (a) has an acceptable scientific purpose.
    (b) will likely increase knowledge about behavior.
    (c) will likely increase understanding of the species under study.
    (d) produces results that benefit the health and welfare of humans or other animals.
    (e) will do all of the above.

14. According to Culture and Human Behavior 1.1, collectivistic cultures emphasize the needs and goals of the _____ over the needs and goals of the _____ .
    (a) individual; group
    (b) country; company
    (c) group; individual
    (d) collective; group

15. According to Critical Thinking 1.2, critical thinking involves
    (a) minimizing the influence of preconceptions and biases while rationally evaluating evidence.
    (b) determining the conclusions that can be drawn from the evidence.
    (c) considering alternative explanations.
    (d) all of the above.

Answers

Introduction: The Origins of Psychology

1. (a) science of behavior and mental processes
   (b) evolved
   (c) subject matter; methods; animal behavior; applied

2. (a) sleep, dreaming, the senses, memory; learning
   (b) René Descartes; mind and body are separate entities that interact to produce sensations, emotions, and other conscious experiences
   (c) nature-nurture; nature; nurture
   (d) heredity; environment
   (e) systematic gathering of evidence to test and support ideas

3. (a) physiology
   (b) scientific methods; human behavior and mental processes

4. (a) Wilhelm Wundt; physiology
   (b) psychology research laboratory
   (c) consciousness; experimental methods

5. (a) Edward B. Titchener
   (b) structures; introspection

6. (a) introspective reports; varied
   (b) Introspection
   (c) learning, development, mental disorders, personality

7. (a) William James
   (b) functions; adapt
   (c) education, child-rearing; the work environment

8. (a) conscious experiences
   (b) consciousness
   (c) adaptive; applying

9. (a) G. Stanley Hall; psychology research laboratory
   (b) Mary Whiton Calkins; dreams, memory, personality
   (c) Margaret Floy Washburn; mental processes

10. (a) Sigmund Freud
    (b) psychoanalysis; sexual or aggressive
    (c) dreams, memory blocks, slips of the tongue; spontaneous humor

11. (a) consciousness; unconscious
    (b) overt behaviors
    (c) Ivan Pavlov; learned
    (d) John B. Watson; introspection; conscious mental processes
    (e) learning; animal
    (f) B. F. Skinner; outwardly observable behaviors (overt behaviors)
    (g) conscious experiences

12. (a) behaviorism; psychoanalysis
    (b) Carl Rogers; conscious; self-determination, free will
    (c) Abraham Maslow

13. (a) functionalist
    (b) psychoanalytic
    (c) behaviorism; humanistic psychology
    (d) interactive dualism
    (e) nature-nurture
    (f) structuralism

Matching Exercise 1

1. Mary Whiton Calkins
2. introspection
3. humanistic psychology
4. John B. Watson
5. functionalism
6. psychology
7. interactive dualism
8. Wilhelm Wundt
9. Edward B. Titchener
10. behaviorism
11. Carl Rogers

True/False Test 1

1. T	7. F
2. F	8. T
3. T	9. T
4. T	10. F
5. T	11. F
6. T	

Contemporary Psychology

1. (a) perspective; specialty area
2. (a) physical; nervous; endocrine; immune; genetics
   (b) technology; medicine
   (c) drugs; biological
   (d) CAT scan; PET scan; MRI; biological
3. (a) psychodynamic
   (b) psychoanalysis; psychodynamic
4. (a) Watson; Skinner
   (b) environmental
5. (a) Carl Rogers; Abraham Maslow
   (b) grow psychologically; choice; self-direction
6. (a) mental processes; information; language; problems
   (b) computers
7. (a) cross-cultural
   (b) cultural; ethnic
8. (a) Charles Darwin; evolutionary
   (b) competition; natural selection
   (c) adapt
   (d) evolutionary; phobias
9. (a) biological
   (b) developmental
   (c) clinical
   (d) social
   (e) personality
   (f) cognitive
   (g) educational; school
   (h) health
   (i) industrial/organizational
10. (a) psychiatrist
    (b) clinical psychologist
    (c) psychoanalyst; clinical psychologist; psychiatrist

Graphic Organizer 1

PERSPECTIVE	SPECIALTY
1. humanistic	developmental
2. behavioral	industrial/organizational
3. cognitive	educational
4. biological	psychiatrist
5. cross-cultural	social
6. psychoanalytic	personality
7. cognitive	health
8. behavioral	experimental
9. evolutionary	social

Graphic Organizer 2

Origins of Psychology, First Schools, Key Figures, and Major Perspectives in Psychology

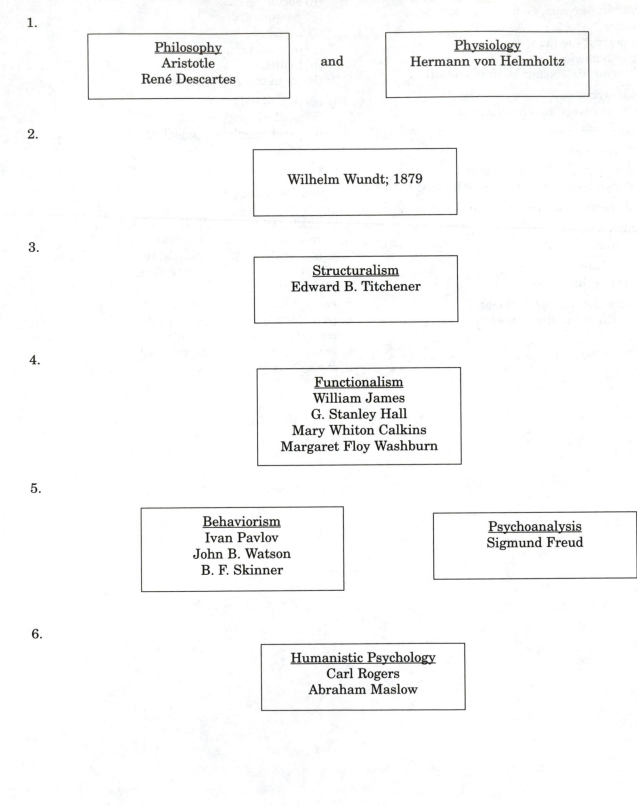

1.

Philosophy		Physiology
Aristotle	and	Hermann von Helmholtz
René Descartes		

2.

Wilhelm Wundt; 1879

3.

Structuralism
Edward B. Titchener

4.

Functionalism
William James
G. Stanley Hall
Mary Whiton Calkins
Margaret Floy Washburn

5.

Behaviorism
Ivan Pavlov
John B. Watson
B. F. Skinner

Psychoanalysis
Sigmund Freud

6.

Humanistic Psychology
Carl Rogers
Abraham Maslow

7.

Perspective	Major emphasis	Key figure
Biological	Physical bases of behavior	
Psychodynamic	Unconscious influences, early childhood experiences	Freud
Behavioral	Environmental influences	Watson, Pavlov, Skinner
Humanistic	Psychological growth, choice, self-direction	Rogers, Maslow
Cognitive	Mental processes such as information processing, language, thinking	
Cross-cultural	Diversity of human behavior in different countries and culture	
Evolutionary	Application of evolutionary principles to explain psychological processes and phenomena	Darwin

Seven Major Perspectives in Contemporary Psychology

Matching Exercise 2

1. clinical psychologist
2. developmental psychology
3. psychiatrist
4. educational psychologists
5. experimental psychology
6. perspective
7. specialty area
8. culture
9. cognitive psychology
10. psychoanalyst
11. personality psychology
12. behavioral perspective
13. ethnocentrism
14. biological perspective

True/False Test 2

1. T
2. T
3. F
4. T
5. T
6. T
7. T
8. F
9. T
10. F
11. F
12. F
13. F
14. T

The Scientific Method

1. (a) describe
   (b) explain
   (c) predict
   (d) control or influence
2. (a) assumptions, attitudes; procedures
   (b) behavior and mental processes follow consistent patterns
   (c) behavior and mental processes have a cause or causes
   (d) open-minded; scientific skepticism; cautious
3. (a) empirical
   (b) (1) formulate a question that can be tested
       (2) design a study to collect relevant data
       (3) analyze the data to arrive at conclusions
       (4) report the results
4. (a) hypothesis
   (b) variables
   (c) operational definition
5. (a) descriptive; experimental
   (b) descriptive
   (c) experimental
6. (a) statistics
   (b) statistically significant
   (c) many research studies
7. (a) participated; participants; variables; procedures; methods; data; results
   (b) replicate
8. (a) theory
   (b) hypothesis; theory; theory; hypotheses
   (c) theory; knowledge

9. (a) experimental (in a natural setting)
    (b) hypothesis
    (c) statistics
    (d) 4; reporting her findings

Matching Exercise 3

1. meta-analysis
2. replicate
3. scientific method
4. hypothesis
5. operational definition
6. experimental method
7. statistics

True/False Test 3

1. T   4. T   7. T
2. T   5. T
3. F   6. F

Descriptive Methods

1. (a) observing; describing
    (b) related to other factors
    (c) experimentally

2. (a) naturalistic observation
    (b) manipulated; generalized

3. (a) case study
    (b) multiple case study; case study research; consistent

4. (a) survey
    (b) larger group
    (c) questionnaire
    (d) interview
    (e) expensive; time-consuming

5. (a) sample; representative sample
    (b) every member; equal

6. (a) variables
    (b) correlation coefficient; −1.00 to +1.00
    (c) strength; direction
    (d) 1.00

7. (a) same; increasing; decreasing
    (b) opposite; increases; decreases
    (c) cause-and-effect
    (d) rule out; identify; predictions

Graphic Organizer 3

1. positive; positive
2. negative; negative

3. high; high; low; low
4. high; low; low; high

8. (a) more; less
    (b) survey; sample; randomly
    (c) naturalistic observation
    (d) positive
    (e) case study

Matching Exercise 4

1. survey
2. descriptive methods
3. sample
4. representative sample
5. correlational study
6. case study research

True/False Test 4

1. T   5. T
2. F   6. T
3. T   7. F
4. T

The Experimental Method

1. (a) experimental; changes; effects
    (b) independent; dependent
    (c) dependent; independent; cause-and-effect

2. (a) all subjects have an equal chance of being assigned to any of the experimental conditions
    (b) that the differences among subjects are spread out across all experimental conditions; the assignment of subjects is done in an unbiased manner

3. (a) independent variable; experimental
    (b) independent variable
    (c) baseline; naturally; spontaneously
    (d) independent; dependent; independent

4. (a) dependent variable
    (b) blind

5. (a) high
    (b) replicated; low; can

6. (a) placebo control; expectancy effects; placebo
    (b) participants (subjects); researchers
    (c) researcher; participants (subjects)
    (d) demand characteristics

7. (a) naturally occurring
    (b) independent; dependent

8. (a) generalize; applied
   (b) decrease
   (c) ethical

9. (a) the drug and placebo conditions
   (b) participants' scores on the memory tests
   (c) experimental; placebo control
   (d) double-blind; expectancy effects
   (e) random assignment

10. (a) Informed consent and voluntary participation of subjects is required.
    (b) Students must be given the option of not participating in research involving credits without being penalized in any way.
    (c) Psychologists are restricted in their use of deception.
    (d) All records must be kept confidential.
    (e) Participants must be allowed the opportunity to obtain information about the study once it is completed and must be debriefed about the nature of their involvement in the study.

Matching Exercise 5

1. single-blind study
2. experimental method
3. dependent variable
4. paranormal phenomena
5. expectancy effect (placebo effect)
6. control group
7. rule of falsifiability
8. demand characteristics
9. placebo

True/False Test 5

1. T	4. T	6. T
2. T	5. T	7. T
3. T		

Something to Think About

1. (a) Psychology tackles questions that people have grappled with for thousands of years. Instead of using anecdotal evidence, intuition, philosophical discussion, and speculation, psychology uses the scientific method to answer questions that are amenable to empirical testing. It uses four steps in generating empirical evidence. First, questions are formulated into testable hypotheses; next, the study is designed and the data are collected, then statistical analyses are prepared and conclusions are drawn, and finally, the results are reported. Psychologists operationally define all variables and precisely specify the method of measurement or manipulation. Following this process, they can be confident in the reliability and validity of their results.

   (b) The difference between clinical psychologists, psychiatrists, and psychoanalysts is training. Clinical psychologists have a doctorate in psychology and extensive training in the assessment, diagnosis, and treatment of people with psychological disorders. Psychiatrists, on the other hand, have an M.D. plus years of training in dealing with people with psychological disorders; because of their medical qualifications, they can prescribe drugs and order medical procedures such as electroshock therapy. A psychoanalyst can be a psychologist, psychiatrist, or other mental health professional who has extensive training in Freudian psychotherapeutic methods.

2. Many of the questions that students have coming into psychology can be tested empirically and quite a few have, in fact, been answered. For example, how would you test the claim that subliminal messages can influence our behavior? It turns out that psychologists have done just that.

   The essence of their experimental design was the use of two subliminal tapes, one claiming to improve self-esteem and the other claiming to improve memory. They randomly assigned subjects to one of four groups and gave them all pretests on measures of self-esteem and memory. Members of group 1 were given the memory tape to listen to for a set period of time and told it would help improve their memory; those in group 2 were given the same memory tape but were told it would improve their self-esteem. (Remember, on subliminal tapes you can't, by definition, hear the messages, only the surface music.) Group 3 was given the self-esteem tape and told it would improve self-esteem, and group 4 was given the same self-esteem tape but were told that it would improve memory. All subjects listened to their respective tapes for exactly the same length of time, at the same times of the day, etc. Later they were given another test of self-esteem and memory. The pretest and posttest scores for all conditions were compared.

   What do you think the results showed? If

you believe the claims of those who promote the power of subliminal tapes, then groups 1 and 3 should have shown significant improvement in memory and self-esteem scores, respectively. And, one would assume, if the results were not due to some placebo effect, then groups 2 and 4 should have shown some memory improvement for group 2 and self-esteem improvement for group 4—because that is what they were actually exposed to.

The results were clear and unequivocal: there was no improvement in any of the groups between their pretest and posttest scores. In contrast to the claims of their promoters, subliminal tapes were shown to be of no value in improving memory or self-esteem.

This is a good example of how useful the scientific method is in answering questions of a psychological nature. Can you apply what you know about scientific psychology to answer other questions you may have?

Progress Test 1

1. d	6. d	11. a
2. d	7. b	12. d
3. b	8. d	13. a
4. d	9. a	14. a
5. d	10. c	15. b

Progress Test 2

1. a	6. a	11. c
2. c	7. b	12. b
3. c	8. d	13. c
4. a	9. c	14. a
5. b	10. a	15. a

Progress Test 3

1. c	6. c	11. a
2. d	7. a	12. a
3. c	8. d	13. e
4. c	9. a	14. c
5. b	10. c	15. d

CHAPTER
2

The Biological Foundations of Behavior

Reading the section below first will give you a general sense of the chapter's contents and an initial introduction to some of the major concepts and terms. This will prime you for what you are about to read and help you to develop a "cognitive map" that will guide your study of the material in this chapter. Likewise, reading the **preview questions** at the beginning of each major section will improve your ability to understand, learn, and retain the information.

CHAPTER 2. . . AT A GLANCE

Chapter 2 first outlines the scope and diversity of biological psychology, then reminds you that biological psychologists investigate the physical processes underlying psychological experiences and behavior.

The first section describes the structure and functions of the neuron. Neural activation, synaptic transmission, and the role of neurotransmitters are outlined. The functions and effects of five neurotransmitters (acetylcholine, dopamine, serotonin, norepinephrine, and endorphins) are discussed.

The next section discusses the structures and functions of the divisions of the nervous system: the central nervous system, which consists of the brain and spinal cord; and the peripheral nervous system, with its two main subdivisions, the somatic and autonomic nervous systems. The sympathetic and parasympathetic systems, which make up the autonomic nervous system, are described. This section ends by focusing on the endocrine system, its glands, and its chemical messengers, called hormones.

The core section, on the brain, begins with a description of how the brain's complex operations are studied—through case studies, EEG, MRI, CAT scans, PET scans, and fMRI. A guided tour of the brain takes you through the regions of the hindbrain, midbrain, and forebrai, including their structures and functions. The different roles of the four lobes of the brain (temporal, occipital, parietal, and frontal) are explained, and the functions of forebrain structures in the limbic system, the thalamus, hypothalamus, hippocampus, and amygdala are described.

The chapter ends with a discussion of hemispheric specialization and the part played by split-brain patients in discovering the specialized functions of the brain's hemispheres.

Introduction: The Scope of Biological Psychology

Preview Questions

Consider the following questions as you study this section of the chapter.

- What is biological psychology?
- What systems and structures are of interest to biopsychologists?

*Read the section "Introduction: The Scope of Biological Psychology" and **write** your answers to the following.*

1. (a) Biological psychology is the study of the

   _____

   _____ that correspond with our

   _____ and _____ .

   (b) Also called biopsychology, this area of research reflects the contributions of psychologists as well as other kinds of scientists, including _____ ,

   _____ , _____ ,

   _____ , and _____ .

2. Biological psychology is concerned with

   (a) the _____ system, the body's primary communication network, and its most essential cells called

   _____ ;

   (b) a closely linked communication network called the _____ system;

   (c) the _____ and how certain areas are specialized to handle different functions, like language, vision, and touch.

The Neuron: The Basic Unit of Communication

Preview Questions

Consider the following questions as you study this section of the chapter.

- How do neurons and glial cells function in the nervous system?
- What are the three types of neuron, and what does each do?

- How do neurons function, and how is information transmitted between them?
- What are some common neurotransmitters, and how do they function?
- How can drugs affect synaptic transmission?

*Read the section "The Neuron: The Basic Unit of Communication" and **write** your answers to the following:*

1. (a) The basic units of communication in the nervous system are the _____ .

   (b) These cells are highly specialized to _____ and _____ information from one part of the body to another.

   (c) The cells that help neurons by providing support and nutrition, removing waste products, and enhancing the speed of communication between neurons are the

   _____ .

2. Name the three different types of neurons, and describe their functions.

   (a) _____

   _____

   _____

   (b) _____

   _____

   _____

   (c) _____

   _____

   _____

3. The three basic components of the neuron are the (a) _____ ,

   (b) _____ , and (c) _____ .

4. (a) Information is received by the

   _____ , transmitted to the

   _____ , and then passed

   along the _____ to other cells in the body.

   (b) The myelin sheath is a _____

   _____

   that _____ the rate at which neural messages are sent.

5. (a) Within the neuron, information is communicated in the form of brief electrical impulses called _____ .

(b) The _____ is the minimum level of stimulation required to activate a particular neuron.

(c) The resting potential is the state in which a neuron _____ _____ .

(d) The _____ law states that either a neuron is sufficiently stimulated and an action potential occurs or a neuron is not sufficiently stimulated and an action potential does not occur.

6. (a) The _____ and _____ neurons are separated by a tiny fluid-filled space called the _____ .

(b) At the end of the axon are several small branches called _____ .

(c) On these branches are synaptic vesicles, which contain chemicals called _____ .

(d) Synaptic transmission refers to the process _____ _____ .

(e) The process by which neurotransmitter molecules detach from a postsynaptic neuron and are reabsorbed by the presynaptic neuron so they can be recycled and used again is called _____ .

(f) If a neuron's message increases the likelihood that the postsynaptic neuron will activate and generate an action potential, it is _____ ; if it decreases the likelihood that the postsynaptic neuron will activate and generate an action potential, it is _____ .

7. (a) Our ability to perceive, feel, think, move, act, and react depends on the delicate balance of chemicals, or _____ , in the nervous system.

(b) Although the connection between particular _____ and particular effects are far from simple, and many behaviors are the result of complex neurochemical interactions, researchers have linked abnormal levels of specific neurochemicals to various _____ and _____ problems.

8. Identify the neurotransmitters according to their functions.

(a) _____ stimulates muscles to contract and is important in memory, learning, and general intellectual functioning. Severe depletion of this and several other neurotransmitters in the brain is found in victims of _____ disease.

(b) _____ is involved in movement, attention, learning, and pleasurable or rewarding sensations. Diminished production of this neurotransmitter in one brain area may result in _____ disease; the hallucinations and perceptual distortions that characterize schizophrenia may involve excessive brain levels of this neurotransmitter.

(c) _____ is involved in sleep, moods, and emotional states, including depression; antidepressant drugs such as _____ increase the availability of _____ in certain brain regions.

(d) _____ is implicated in the activation of neurons throughout the brain and helps the body react to threats or danger. It is also involved in _____ and _____ , and, like some other neurotransmitters, may play a role in a number of mental disorders, especially depression.

(e) _____ usually communicates an inhibitory message to other neurons, helping to balance and offset excitatory messages; antianxiety medications such as _____ and _____ work by increasing the activity of this transmitter, which inhibits _____ and slows brain activity.

(f) _____ , which are chemically similar to the opiates, regulate the perception of pain and are involved in the pain reducing effects of _____ , an ancient Chinese medical treatment, as well as the positive moods associated with aerobic exercise.

9. (a) Much of what is known about different neurotransmitters has come from observing the effects of _____ and other substances.

(b) A _____ bite causes acetylcholine to be released continuously by motor neurons, causing severe muscle spasms.

(c) Both _____ and _____ inhibit or interfere with the reuptake of serotonin, increasing the availability of this neurotransmitter in the brain.

(d) Chemically similar to acetylcholine, _____ mimics its effects by occupying its receptor sites and stimulating skeletal muscles and causing the heart to beat more rapidly.

(e) The drug _____ works by blocking acetylcholine receptor sites, causing almost instantaneous paralysis.

(f) _____ eliminates the effects of both endorphins and opiates by blocking opiate receptor sites.

10. Read the following and decide which neurotransmitter is most likely involved:

(a) Mrs. Cartwright's memory functions have deteriorated, and she has been diagnosed as suffering from Alzheimer's disease. _____

(b) When Gerald was bitten by a black widow spider, he suffered severe, uncontrollable muscle spasms and had great difficulty breathing. _____

(c) When Melanie was suffering from severe depression, her doctor prescribed Prozac, which he said would help alleviate the symptoms of her mood disorder by increasing the availability of a particular neurotransmitter. _____

(d) Patients afflicted with Parkinson's disease suffer from rigidity, muscle tremors, and poor balance and have trouble initiating movements. These symptoms are believed to result from diminished production of the neurotransmitter _____ .

(e) George suffers from chronic anxiety. His doctor has prescribed the antianxiety drug Valium because it works by increasing _____ , which inhibits action potentials and slows brain activity.

(f) Mr. Lee had his back pain treated by an ancient Chinese medical technique called acupuncture. Inserting needles in various parts of his body may have reduced his perception of pain because of the involvement of _____ .

Graphic Organizer 1

Identify the parts of the neuron in the figure below:

a. _____   f. _____

b. _____   g. _____

c. _____   h. _____

d. _____   i. _____

e. _____

Review of Terms and Concepts 1

Use the terms in this list to complete the Matching Test, then to help you answer the True/False items correctly.

biological psychology
  (biopsychology)
neuron
glial cells
sensory neuron
motor neuron
interneuron
cell body
dendrites
axon
myelin sheath
action potential
stimulus threshold
resting potential
all-or-none law

synapse
synaptic gap
axon terminals
synaptic vesicles
neurotransmitter
synaptic transmission
reuptake
acetylcholine
dopamine
serotonin
norepinephrine
GABA (gamma-
  amniobutyric acid)
endorphins

Matching Exercise

Match the appropriate term from the list with its definition or description.

1. _____ Highly specialized cell that communicates information in electrical and chemical form.

2. _____ Neurotransmitter that usually communicates an inhibitory message.

3. _____ Neurotransmitters that regulate pain perception.

4. _____ Type of neuron that signals muscles to contract or relax.

5. _____ Neurotransmitter that is involved in sleep, pain perception, sexual behavior, and emotions such as aggression and depression; also involved in regulating sensations.

6. _____ The part of a neuron that contains the nucleus.

7. _____ A brief electrical impulse by which information is transmitted along the axon of a neuron.

8. _____ Chemical messenger manufactured in the synaptic vesicles of a neuron.

9. _____ The long, fluid-filled tube that carries a neuron's messages to other body areas.

10. _____ The point of communication between two neurons.

11. _____ Tiny pouches or sacs in the axon terminals that contain chemicals called neurotransmitters.

12. _____ The neurotransmitter that is involved in the regulation of bodily movements and thought processes.

13. _____ Minimum level of stimulation required to activate a particular neuron.

True/False Test

Indicate whether each statement is true or false by placing T or F in the blank space next to each item.

1. ___ Norepinephrine is involved in activation of neurons throughout the brain, is critical in the body's response to danger, and is implicated in learning and memory retrieval.

2. ___ Biological psychology is the specialized branch of psychology concerned with the diagnosis and treatment of mental disorders.

3. ____ Reuptake is the process in which neuro-transmitters are released by one neuron, cross the synaptic gap, and affect adjoining neurons.

4. ____ Glial cells assist neurons by providing structural support, nutrition, and removal of cell wastes; they manufacture myelin.

5. ____ Interneurons communicate information from one neuron to the next.

6. ____ Synaptic transmission is the process by which neurotransmitter molecules detach from a postsynaptic neuron and are reabsorbed by a presynaptic neuron so that they can be recycled and used again.

7. ____ Axon terminals are branches at the end of the axon that contain tiny pouches or sacs called synaptic vesicles.

8. ____ Sensory neurons communicate information to the muscles and glands of the body and signal muscles to contract or relax.

9. ____ Dendrites are the long, fluid-filled tubes that carry information *from* the neuron *to* other cells in the body, including other neurons, glands, and muscles.

10. ____ The myelin sheath is a white, fatty covering wrapped around the axons of some neurons that increases their speed of communication.

11. ____ The resting potential is a brief electrical impulse by which information is transmitted along the axon of a neuron.

12. ____ Acetylcholine is a neurotransmitter that produces muscle contractions and is involved in memory functions.

13. ____ The synaptic gap is a tiny space between the axon terminal of one neuron and the dendrite of an adjoining neuron.

14. ____ The all-or-none law states that either a neuron is sufficiently stimulated and an action potential occurs or a neuron is not sufficiently stimulated and an action potential does not occur.

Check your answers and review any areas of weakness before going on to the next section.

The Nervous System and the Endocrine System: Communication Throughout the Body

Preview Questions

Consider the following questions as you study this section of the chapter.

- What are the two main divisions of the nervous system, and what are their functions?
- How do spinal reflexes work?
- What are the key components of the peripheral nervous system, and what are their functions?
- What is the function of the endocrine system, and what role do hormones play?
- How does information transmission in the endocrine system differ from that in the nervous system?
- What are the specific functions of the pituitary gland, the hypothalamus, the gonads, and the adrenal glands?

*Read the section "The Nervous System and the Endocrine System: Communication Throughout the Body" and **write** your answers to the following:*

1. (a) The _____ system is a complex, organized communication network of neurons and nerves; it has two main divisions, the _____ and the _____ .

   (b) The _____ is the most important transmitter of messages in the _____ nervous system; in the peripheral nervous system, communication occurs along _____ .

   (c) Large bundles of neuron axons are called _____ .

2. (a) The central nervous system includes the _____ and the _____ .

   (b) Simple, automatic behaviors that are produced by the spinal cord and occur without involvement of the brain are referred to as _____ .

(c) In the simplest spinal reflex, sensation is communicated to the spinal cord via a(n) _____ , a(n) _____ relays information within the spinal cord, and a _____ leading from the spinal cord signals muscles to react.

3. (a) The peripheral nervous system has two subdivisions, the

_____

and the _____ .

(b) Sensory information received by sense organ receptors is carried by the _____ nervous system to the central nervous system, which then carries messages from the central nervous system along motor nerves to the muscles.

(c) Involuntary functions such as heartbeat, blood pressure, digestion, and breathing are regulated by the _____ nervous system.

4. (a) The autonomic nervous system has two branches, the

_____ and

the _____ .

(b) The _____ nervous system is the body's emergency system and produces rapid physical arousal in response to perceived threats or in response to emotions such as anger or anxiety.

(c) The fight-or-flight response refers to

_____

_____

_____ .

(d) The _____ nervous system maintains normal body functions and conserves the body's physical resources.

Graphic Organizer 2

Mapping the Divisions and Functions of the Nervous System

In the following organizational chart of the nervous system, write the name of each division and choose the appropriate function of each from the list below (e.g., A is the appropriate choice for the nervous system).

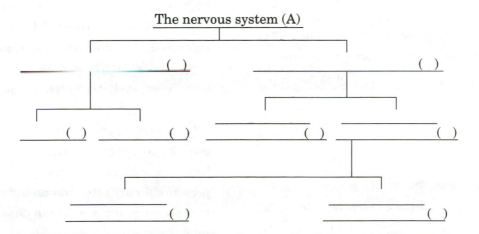

A. Complex organized communication system of nerves and neurons.
B. Maintains normal body functions and conserves physical resources.
C. Produces rapid physical changes to perceived threats and emergencies.
D. Includes all nerves lying outside the central nervous system.

E. Communicates sensory and motor information.
F. Consists of the brain and the spinal cord.
G. Regulates involuntary functions such as heartbeat and respiration.
H. Main organ of the nervous system; made up of billions of neurons.
I. System that handles both incoming and outgoing messages to and from the brain.

5. (a) The _____ system is made up of glands located throughout the body and uses chemical messengers called _____ , which are secreted into the _____ , to transmit information from one part of the body to another.

   (b) Metabolism, growth rate, digestion, blood pressure, and sexual development and reproduction are all processes regulated by _____ .

6. (a) The signals that trigger the secretion of hormones are regulated primarily by a brain structure called the _____ .

   (b) This structure serves as the main link between the _____ system and the _____ system, and directly regulates the release of hormones by the _____ gland.

   (c) Under the direction of the _____ , the _____ gland directly controls hormone production in other endocrine glands.

7. (a) The set of endocrine glands involved in the human stress response are the _____ .

   (b) The inner part of each gland, the medulla, produces two hormones that also act as neurotransmitters, _____ and _____ .

8. (a) The sex organs—the ovaries in women and testes in men—are called the _____ .

   (b) The testes secrete the hormone _____ and the ovaries secrete the hormones _____ and _____ .

   (c) The sex hormones affect _____ , _____ , and _____

9. Other important endocrine glands include (a) the thyroid gland, which controls _____ ; (b) the pancreas,

which regulates _____ levels and plays a key role in hunger and eating; and (c) the pineal gland, which produces the hormone _____ and regulates sleep and wakefulness.

10. Read the following and complete the sentence with the correct term:

   (a) Allison accidentally touched a hot stove top and immediately withdrew her hand before becoming consciously aware of the sensation or movement. She was able to do this because of her _____ .

   (b) Always a daredevil, Michael dove off the cliff into the river below. Unfortunately, he landed on his head and is now paralyzed from the shoulders down. Apart from his paralysis, all his mental functions are intact and he is attempting to complete his college degree. His present inability to move the lower part of his body is a result of permanent damage to his _____ .

   (c) At home alone late at night Jason had just finished watching the most frightening video he had ever seen when there was a sudden knock on the door. His heart rate suddenly increased, his breathing accelerated, and he began to sweat. These physiological changes were most likely triggered by his _____ .

   (d) When Jason answered the door, he discovered it was only the pizza delivery and before long he calmed down and his blood pressure, heart rate, and breathing returned to their normal state. These physical reactions were most likely regulated by his _____ .

   (e) Jason's initial reaction to the knock on the door (his fight-or-flight response) resulted in his adrenal glands (in particular the adrenal medulla) releasing the two hormones _____ and _____ .

Review of Terms and Concepts 2

Use the terms in this list to complete the Matching Test, then to help you answer the True/False items correctly.

nervous system
central nervous system
nerve
spinal reflexes
peripheral nervous
    system
somatic nervous system
autonomic nervous
    system
sympathetic nervous
    system
parasympathetic
    nervous system
fight-or-flight response
endocrine system

hormones
hypothalamus
pituitary gland
adrenal glands
adrenal cortex
adrenal medulla
gonads
testosterone
estrogen
progesterone
thyroid
pancreas
pineal gland
melatonin

Matching Exercise

Match the appropriate term with its definition or description.

1. _____ The endocrine gland that controls metabolism.

2. _____ Bundle of neuron axons that carries information in the peripheral nervous system.

3. _____ Communication system composed of glands located throughout the body that secrete hormones into the bloodstream.

4. _____ Simple, automatic behaviors that are processed in the spinal cord without any brain involvement.

5. _____ Set of endocrine glands that are involved in the human stress response.

6. _____ Branch of the autonomic nervous system that maintains normal body functions and conserves the body's physical resources.

7. _____ Brain structure that regulates the release of hormones by the pituitary gland.

8. _____ Sex hormone secreted by the testes in males.

9. _____ Outer portion of the adrenal gland.

10. _____ Division of the nervous system that includes all the nerves lying outside the central nervous system.

11. _____ Subdivision of the peripheral nervous system that regulates involuntary functions.

12. _____ Hormone involved in the regulation of sleep and wakefulness.

13. _____ Endocrine gland that produces melatonin.

True/False Test

Indicate whether each statement is true or false by placing T or F in the blank space next to each item.

1. ___ The nervous system is the primary internal communication network of the body; it is divided into the central nervous system and the peripheral nervous systems.

2. ___ Progesterone is a sex hormone secreted only by the testes in males.

3. ___ The gonads are the sex organs—the testes in males and the ovaries in females.

4. ___ The central nervous system is a major division of the nervous system and consists of the brain and the spinal cord.

5. ___ Estrogen is one of the hormones secreted by the ovaries in females.

6. ___ The pituitary gland is the inner portion of the adrenal medulla and secretes epinephrine and norepinephrine.

7. ___ The fight-or-flight response refers to physiological changes such as increased heart rate, accelerated breathing, dry mouth, and perspiration that occur in response to perceived threats or danger.

8. ___ The sympathetic nervous system maintains normal bodily functions and conserves physical resources.

9. ___ Hormones are chemical messengers that are secreted into the bloodstream by endocrine glands.

10. ___ The somatic nervous system regulates involuntary functions such as heartbeat, digestion, breathing, and blood pressure.

11. ___ The adrenal medulla is the outer portion of the adrenal gland.

12. ___ The pancreas regulates blood-sugar levels and plays a key role in hunger and eating.

> Check your answers and review any areas of weakness before going on to the next section.

Studying the Brain: The Toughest Case to Crack

Preview Questions

Consider the following questions as you study this section of the chapter.

- Why have scientists used case studies of brain-damaged people to study the brain?
- How has the production of *lesions* been useful in advancing knowledge of the brain?
- What are the five main imaging techniques used to study the brain, and how does each attempt to accomplish the task?

*Read the section "Studying the Brain: The Toughest Case to Crack" and **write** your answers to the following:*

1. (a) The brain is made up of billions of _____ organized into a complex, integrated hierarchy of structures.

   (b) The brain has been difficult to study because _____ and because _____ .

2. (a) Using the case study, researchers systematically _____ and _____ the behavior of people whose brains have been _____ by illness or injury.

   (b) What are the limitations of the case study method?
   (1) _____
   (2) _____

3. (a) Lesions are produced by _____ .

   (b) After the brain of a human or an animal has been lesioned, experimenters observe _____ .

   (c) By electrically stimulating specific brain

areas with implanted bipolar electrodes, researchers can study the _____ ; electrical stimulation causes activation of the neurons in the area around the tip of the electrode, and usually produces the _____ (same/opposite) effect of a lesion in the same brain area.

4. Identify and describe the four methods used to study the living brain.

   (a) The _____ uses disk-shaped electrodes placed on the scalp to _____ .

   (b) _____ is an imaging technique that produces two-dimensional pictures of brain structures using multiple _____ that are reassembled by a computer.

   (c) _____ is an imaging technique that creates highly detailed images through computer analysis of electromagnetic signals generated by the brain in response to bombardment by _____ .

   (d) An imaging technique that provides color-coded images of the brain's activity while the subject reads, talks, plays chess, etc., by tracking the brain's use of _____ tagged compounds such as glucose, oxygen, or a particular drug is called _____ .

   (e) A new technique that tracks changes in the brain's blood flow as measured by fluctuations in blood oxygen levels, and provides a picture of brain activity averaged over seconds, is called _____

A Guided Tour of the Brain

Preview Questions

Consider the following questions as you study this section of the chapter.

- How does the brain develop, and what are its three main divisions?
- What are the key structures of the hindbrain and midbrain, and what functions are associated with each structure?
- What are the two main structures of the forebrain, and what functions have been identified with each of the four lobes of the cerebral cortex?
- What are the key limbic system structures, and what role do they play in behavior?

*Read the section "A Guided Tour of the Brain" and **write** your answers to the following:*

1. (a) Many brain functions involve the activation of _____ , which are formed by groups of neuron _____ . These communication circuits link different brain areas and structures; thus, damage to one area of the brain may disrupt many _____ and affect many different functions.

    (b) Although the brain centers and structures involved in different aspects of behavior are discussed separately, it is best to think of the brain as an _____ system.

2. (a) The human brain begins as a fluid-filled tube that gradually expands and develops into separate fluid-filled cavities called _____ , which are at the core of the fully developed brain; the fluid that is manufactured in these cavities by special glial cells is called _____ fluid.

    (b) Between conception and birth, the number of neurons _____ (increases/decreases) dramatically. Neurons compete to form synaptic connections; those that fail to do so are eliminated.

    (c) At birth, the infant's brain weighs _____ and is only about _____ the size of the adult brain; After birth, neurons grow in size, continue to develop new dendrites, and _____ forms on neuron axons in key areas of the brain. By adulthood, the fully mature human brain weighs about _____ .

    (d) Traditionally, it was believed that people and most animals _____ (have/do not have) the capacity to develop new neurons after birth. New evidence suggests that the hippocampus, at least, _____ (has/does not have) the capacity to generate new neurons during the lifespan.

3. (a) The three major divisions of the brain are the _____ , the _____ , and the _____ .

    (b) Located at the base of the brain, the brainstem includes the _____ and the _____ .

4. (a) The region that connects the spinal cord with the rest of the brain is the _____ .

    (b) The three structures that make up the hindbrain are the _____ , the _____ , and the _____ .

    (c) The medulla controls vital life functions such as _____ _____ .

    (d) The _____ connects other regions of the brain to the _____ , which helps coordinate and integrate movements on each side of the body.

    (e) The _____ is a large, two-sided structure at the back of the brain responsible for muscle coordination, fine motor movements, and maintaining posture and equilibrium.

(f) At the core of the medulla and the pons is a network of neurons called the _____ , which plays an important role in regulating _____ , _____ , and _____ .

5. Decide which area of the brain is most likely involved in each of the following.
   (a) Marcel had a stroke on the *right* side of his brain in an area that controls motor movement; as a result, he has trouble moving the *left* side of his body. This is because incoming sensory messages and outgoing motor messages cross over at the _____ level of the brain.
   (b) If this area of your brain was electrically stimulated while you were fast asleep, you would wake up instantly. _____
   (c) After being hit in the head by a baseball, Larry now has jerky, uncoordinated movements and can no longer type or play his guitar. _____
   (d) In the third round of a boxing match Bruno caught a right hook that snapped his head back; when he hit the canvas, his breathing stopped. _____

6. (a) The _____ is an important relay station that helps coordinate auditory and visual information before sending it on to higher brain centers.
   (b) The substantia nigra is involved in _____ and contains a large concentration of neurons that produce _____ .

7. (a) The outer portion of the forebrain, which is called the _____ , is divided into two _____ .
   (b) A thick bundle of axons called the _____ connects the two hemispheres and serves as their primary communication link.

8. Name the four lobes of the cerebral cortex, and complete the descriptions of their functions.

(a) Located near the temples, the _____ lobe contains the _____ , which receives _____ information.
(b) The _____ lobe, located at the back of the brain, contains the _____ , which receives _____ information.
(c) The _____ lobe is involved in processing _____ information, such as temperature , _____ , _____ , and _____ .
(d) The _____ lobe processes _____ and is involved in thinking, planning, and emotional control.

9. (a) The areas involved in processing and integrating sensory and motor information, the formation of perceptions, and the integration of perceptions and memories is the _____ .
   (b) The prefrontal association cortex is involved in the _____

10. (a) The four forebrain structures located beneath the cerebral cortex are all components of the _____ and in various combinations form complex neural circuits that play critical roles in _____ , _____ , and _____ control.
    (b) The finding that rats and other animals would work hard to obtain electrical brain stimulation led researchers to speculate that there might be _____ in certain regions of the limbic system.

11. (a) The structure that processes and integrates sensory information for all the senses except smell and relays it to higher brain centers is the _____ .

(b) The peanut-sized structure that is involved in diverse functions, including eating, drinking, frequency of sexual activity, fear, aggression, and exerting control over the secretion of endocrine hormones, is called the

_____ ;

the area of this structure that plays a key role in regulating daily sleep-wake cycles and other rhythms of the body is the

_____ .

(c) The curved structure that is involved in learning and forming new memories is the

_____ .

(d) The almond-shaped structure that is involved in controlling a variety of emotional response patterns, including fear, anger, and disgust, and that play a role in learning and forming memories, especially those with a strong emotional component, is the

_____ .

Graphic Organizer 3

Chart Diagram Exercise: The Key Structures of the Limbic System

To help you develop the technique of creating your own graphic organizers, we encourage you to try to locate the structures listed below in the following outline of a brain. Then, on a separate piece of paper, write a description of each structure.

Locate and describe the following:
   (a)   Hypothalamus
   (b)   Thalamus
   (c)   Amygdala
   (d)   Hippocampus

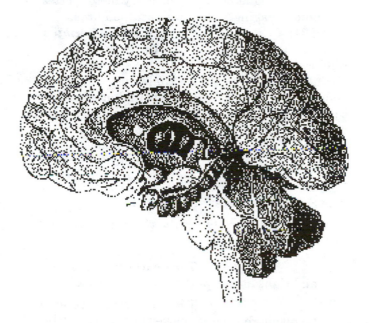

Review of Terms and Concepts 3

Use the terms in this list to complete the Matching Test, then to help you answer the True/False items correctly.

electroencephalograph (EEG)

computerized axial tomography (CAT or CT scan)

magnetic resonance imaging scanner (MRI)

positron emission tomography (PET scan)

functional magnetic resonance imaging (fMRI)

brainstem

hindbrain

medulla

pons

cerebellum

reticular formation

midbrain

substantia nigra

forebrain

cerebral cortex

cerebral hemispheres

temporal lobe

primary auditory cortex

occipital lobe

primary visual cortex

parietal lobe

somatosensory cortex

frontal lobe

primary motor cortex

association areas

prefrontal association cortex

limbic system

thalamus

hypothalamus

suprachiasmatic nucleus (SCN)

hippocampus

amygdala

Matching Exercise

Match the appropriate term with its definition or description.

1. _____ The nearly symmetrical left and right halves of the cerebral cortex.

2. _____ The area on each cerebral hemisphere located above the temporal lobe that processes somatic sensations.

3. _____ Midbrain area involved in motor control and containing a large concentration of dopamine-producing neurons.

4. _____ The part of the temporal lobe that enables hearing.

5. _____ Hindbrain structure that connects the medulla to the two sides of the cerebellum; helps coordinate and integrate movement on each side of the body.

6. _____ Forebrain structure that processes sensory information from all the senses except smell and relays it to higher brain centers.

7. _____ The part of the occipital lobe that receives information from the eyes.

8. _____ The curved forebrain struc-

ture that is part of the limbic system and is involved in learning and forming new memories.

9. _____ Region of the brain made up of the hindbrain and the midbrain.

10. _____ Band of tissue in the frontal lobe on which the movements of different parts of the body are represented.

11. _____ Large association area of the brain, situated in front of the primary motor cortex, that is involved in the planning of voluntary movements.

12. _____ Hindbrain structure that controls vital life functions such as breathing, circulation, heart rate, and digestion.

13. _____ Instrument that produces a graphic record of the brain's electrical activity by using large electrodes placed on the scalp.

14. _____ Network of nerve fibers located in the center of the medulla that helps regulate attention, arousal, and sleep.

15. _____ Imaging technique that provides three-dimensional, highly detailed images of the brain using electrical signals generated by the brain in response to magnetic fields.

16. _____ Area of the hypothalamus that plays a key role in regulating daily sleep-wake cycles and other rhythms of the body.

True/False Test

Indicate whether each statement is true or false by placing T or F in the blank space next to each item.

1. ____ The frontal lobe is the largest lobe of the cerebral cortex; processes voluntary muscle movement and is involved in thinking, planning, and emotional expression and control.

2. ____ The somatosensory cortex is a band of tissue on the parietal lobe that receives information from touch receptors in different parts of the body.

3. ____ The midbrain is a region at the base of the brain that controls several structures that regulate basic life functions.

4. ____ The cerebellum is an almond-shaped forebrain structure that is part of the limbic system and involved in emotion and memory.

5. ___ The forebrain, the largest and most complex brain region, contains centers for complex behaviors and mental processes.

6. ___ The cerebral cortex is the wrinkled outer portion of the forebrain that contains the most sophisticated brain centers.

7. ___ The amygdala is the large, two-sided hindbrain structure at the back of the brain that is responsible for muscle coordination and maintaining posture and equilibrium.

8. ___ The occipital lobe is a region at the back of each cerebral cortex hemisphere that is the primary receiving area for visual information.

9. ___ The association areas, which make up the bulk of the cerebral cortex and are the regions in which sensory and motor information is combined, produce complex, sophisticated human behaviors.

10. ___ The temporal lobe is an area on each hemisphere that is the primary receiving area for auditory information.

11. ___ The hindbrain is the middle and smallest brain region that is involved in processing auditory and visual sensory information.

12. ___ Computerized axial tomography (CAT scan or CT scan) is an imaging technique that provides color-coded images of brain activity by measuring the amount of a radioactive compound glucose, or oxygen, used in different brain regions.

13. ___ The limbic system consists of three forebrain structures—the hypothalamus, amygdala, and hippocampus—and is involved in emotions, motivation, learning, and memory.

14. ___ The hypothalamus is a peanut-sized forebrain structure that is part of the limbic system and is involved in diverse functions such as eating, drinking, sexual activity, and fear and aggression and exerts control over the secretion of endocrine hormones by directly influencing the pituitary gland.

15. ___ Positron emission tomography (PET scan) is an imaging technique that produces two-dimensional pictures of brain structures or other body parts using multiple X-rays that are reassembled by a computer; also called computed tomography.

16. ___ Functional magnetic resonance imaging (fMRI) is an imaging technique that uses magnetic fields to map brain activity by measuring changes in the brain's blood supply during different mental activities.

> Check your answers and review any areas of weakness before going on to the next section.

Specialization in the Cerebral Hemispheres

Preview Questions

Consider the following questions as you study this section of the chapter.

- What did Broca and Wernicke contribute to our knowledge of the brain?

- What is aphasia, and how did clinical findings on aphasia contribute to understanding the brain?

- How were split-brain patients tested to reveal differences in the abilities of the two hemispheres?

- What are the most important functions of each cerebral hemisphere?

*Read the section "Specialization in the Cerebral Hemispheres" and **write** your answers to the following:*

1. (a) Cortical localization refers to

   _____

   _____ .

   (b) Clinical evidence for cortical localization came from the work of _____ , who treated patients who had great difficulty speaking but could comprehend written or spoken language.

   (c) An area in the lower left frontal lobe, known to play a crucial role in speech production, is called _____ area.

2. (a) The area on the left temporal lobe that is involved in the ability to understand spoken and written communication was discovered by _____ .

   (b) Patients who have difficulty comprehending language and whose speech often makes little sense are most likely to have damage on the left _____ lobe in _____ area.

3. (a) The notion that one hemisphere exerts more control over or is more involved in the processing of a particular psychological function is termed _____ _____ .

   (b) Speech and language functions are controlled by the _____ hemisphere.

4. (a) Someone who is either partially or completely unable to articulate ideas or understand spoken or written language due to brain injury or brain damage is likely to be diagnosed with some form of _____ .

   (b) People who find it difficult to produce speech but their comprehension of verbal or written words is unaffected are victims of _____ aphasia.

   (c) People who can produce speech but often have difficulty finding the right words and have great difficulty understanding written or spoken communication are victims of _____ aphasia.

5. (a) Patients who suffered epilepsy underwent an operation in which the _____was cut.

   (b) This operation is called a _____ .

   (c) These patients are called _____ patients.

6. (a) The American psychologist who pioneered research on brain specialization in split-brain patients was _____ .

   (b) Sensations and movements on the left side of the body are processed by the _____ hemisphere, so a blindfolded split-brain patient who has an object placed in her left hand will _____ (be able/not be able) to state what the object is.

   (c) Explain your answer to (b): _____ _____ _____ .

(d) A procedure for presenting stimuli to each hemisphere separately involves split-brain patients focusing on a midpoint and words or pictures are flashed to the _____ or _____ of the midpoint.

(e) Visual information presented to the right of the midpoint is projected to the person's _____ hemisphere, and visual information to the left of the midpoint is projected to the person's _____ hemisphere.

(f) A split-brain patient who is presented with a picture or a word to the left of the midpoint will _____ (be able/not be able) to state what was seen, and if the stimulus is to the right of the midpoint, the patient will _____ (be able/not be able) to state what was seen.

7. (a) List the main areas of specialization of the left hemisphere: _____ _____ _____

   (b) List the main areas of specialization of the right hemisphere: _____ _____ _____

8. Complete the following examples by placing the term *right* or *left* in each blank:

   (a) A blindfolded split-brain patient would be able to verbally identify an object placed in her _____ hand but not in her _____ hand.

   (b) When the picture of an apple was flashed to the _____ of the midpoint during an experiment with a split-brain patient, the patient was not able to say what he saw. However, he could draw a picture of the object with his _____ hand.

   (c) When a swear word was flashed to her _____ hemisphere, a split-brain patient could not say what she saw but showed some nonverbal signs of embarrassment.

(d) The fact that a split-brain patient had trouble assembling colored blocks to match a design with his left hand but not his right hand suggests that the _____ hemisphere is superior to the _____ hemisphere at perceptual tasks that involve deciphering visual cues, reading maps, copying designs, and so on.

Review of Terms, Concepts, and Names 4

Use the terms in this list to complete the Matching Test, then to help you answer the True/False items correctly.

cortical localization
Pierre Paul Broca
Broca's area
Karl Wernicke
Wernicke's area
aphasia
Broca's aphasia
Wernicke's aphasia
lateralization of function

corpus callosum
split-brain operation
Roger Sperry
split-brain patient
functional plasticity
structural plasticity

Matching Exercise

Match the appropriate term/name with its definition or description.

1. _____ The American psychologist who received the Nobel Prize in 1981 for his pioneering research on brain specialization in split-brain patients.

2. _____ The partial or complete inability to articulate ideas or understand spoken or written language due to brain damage or injury.

3. _____ A person who has had his or her corpus callosum surgically cut.

4. _____ The language area on the left temporal lobe concerned with speech comprehension.

5. _____ A thick band of nerve fibers that connects the two cerebral hemispheres and acts as a communication link between them.

6. _____ The notion that different functions are located or localized in different areas of the brain; also referred to as localization of function.

7. _____ The phenomenon in which brain structures physically change in response to environmental influences.

8. _____ The notion that specific psychological or cognitive functions are processed primarily on one side of the brain; also referred to as lateralization.

True/False Test

Indicate whether each statement is true or false by placing T or F in the blank space next to each item.

1. ___ Karl Wernicke was a German neurologist who discovered an area on the left temporal lobe that, when damaged, produces meaningless or nonsensical speech and difficulties in verbal or written comprehension.

2. ___ The split-brain operation was performed on patients specifically to enable psychologists to scientifically study hemispheric specialization in the cerebral cortex of humans.

3. ___ Broca's aphasia is a speech disorder that results from the surgical severing of the corpus callosum.

4. ___ Patients with Wernicke's aphasia can speak but may have problems finding the right words and typically have great difficulty understanding written or spoken communication.

5. ___ Broca's area is a language area on the lower left frontal lobe of the cerebral cortex.

6. ___ Pierre Paul Broca was a French surgeon and neuroanatomist who discovered an area on the lower left frontal lobe that, when damaged, produces speech disturbances but no loss of comprehension.

7. ___ Functional plasticity refers to the brain's ability to shift functions from damaged to undamaged areas.

Check your answers and review any areas of weakness before going on to the next section.

Something to Think About

1. A biological psychologist who specializes in the assessment and diagnosis of people with brain-related problems is faced with the following cases. Based on what you now know about biological psychology, the brain, and nervous system functioning, give some thought to what the specialist's assessment might be.
   (a) Fraser slipped on ice and hit the back of his head on the sidewalk, and now his vision is seriously affected. Which brain area is most likely affected?
   (b) Following an operation to remove a brain tumor, Yoko is able to read and understand written and spoken language but has difficulty speaking and expressing herself clearly. It is likely that she has damage in which part of the brain?
   (c) Ever since a brain lesion destroyed part of her limbic system, Vanessa has had trouble controlling her appetite and has had a constant urge to eat and drink. Which structure was most likely damaged?
   (d) Raphael is now 12 years old but is only four feet tall. What is the probable reason for his growth problem?

2. Family members and friends who know you are taking a psychology course may ask you some interesting and curious questions. One often-asked question is, "I know that regular exercise helps keep me in shape physically, but is there anything I can do to prevent mental deterioration?" What advice would you give in response to that question?

Check your answers and review any areas of weakness before doing the following progress tests.

Progress Test 1

Review the complete chapter (including Concept Reviews and all boxed inserts), review all your study notes, and then test yourself on the following progress test. Check your answers. If you make a mistake, review your notes, the appropriate section in the study guide, and, if necessary, the relevant part of the chapter in your textbook.

1. A hunter in a South American jungle uses the poison curare on the tip of his arrow; when the arrow strikes an animal, the animal becomes almost instantly limp and quickly suffocates because its respiratory system has become paralyzed. The curare has _____ the neurotransmitter_____
   (a) blocked the release of; acetylcholine
   (b) blocked the receptors for; acetylcholine
   (c) increased the release of; acetylcholine
   (d) increased the reuptake of; acetylcholine

2. Miguel has been diagnosed with schizophrenia. His psychologist believes that Miguel's hallucinations and perceptual distortions may, in part, be caused by _____ amounts of the neurotransmitter _____ .
   (a) diminished; dopamine
   (b) excessive; dopamine
   (c) diminished; serotonin
   (d) excessive; serotonin

3. Jenny has just finished running a very tough marathon (26.22 miles) but seems to be very happy and elated. One cause of her "runner's high" may be due to abnormally high levels of chemical substances in her brain called
   (a) acetylcholines.   (c) endorphins.
   (b) serotonins.   (d) dopamines.

4. Mrs. Danvers has multiple sclerosis. She experiences muscle weakness, loss of coordination and speech, and visual disturbances that result from the slowdown or interruption of neural transmission. The cause of these symptoms probably involves the degeneration of the
   (a) dendrites.   (c) myelin sheath.
   (b) corpus callosum.   (d) synaptic vesicles.

5. When Dr. Maxwell electrically stimulated a specific area of a patient's right cerebral hemisphere, the patient's left hand twitched. The part of the cortex that was stimulated was
   (a) Broca's area.
   (b) the primary motor cortex.
   (c) Wernicke's area.
   (d) the somatosensory cortex.

6. While Rupert was reading a poem, researchers studied his brain activity by tracking changes in his brain's blood supply as a function of fluctuations in blood oxygen levels. They were most likely using an imaging technique called
   (a) functional magnetic resonance imaging (fMRI).
   (b) electroencephalography (EEG).
   (c) positron emission tomography (PET scan).
   (d) computerized axial tomography (CAT or CT scan).

7. Neurotransmitters are to hormones as _____ is to _____ .
   (a) nervous system; endocrine system
   (b) nerves; neurons
   (c) hypothalamus; pituitary gland
   (d) brain; spinal cord

8. When Mike was faced with a final exam worth 80 percent of his grade in his graduate statistics class he was totally stressed out. The particular gland(s) in his endocrine system that is (are) likely to be stimulated is (are) the
   (a) gonads.
   (c) adrenal glands.
   (b) pituitary gland.
   (d) nervous glands.

9. If researchers electrically stimulate the reticular formation in a sleeping cat, it is most likely that the cat will
   (a) aggressively attack the researchers.
   (b) stop breathing.
   (c) become paralyzed on both sides of the body.
   (d) instantly wake up, fully alert.

10. If researchers destroy or lesion the amygdala of a timid cat, it is likely that the cat will
    (a) become even more fearful.
    (b) lose its timidity and fearfulness.
    (c) become a vicious predator and start attacking large dogs.
    (d) stop breathing and die.

11. If a normal right-handed individual sustained severe damage to the right cerebral hemisphere, this would most likely reduce a number of abilities. Damage to the right hemisphere is *not* likely to affect his ability to
    (a) manipulate blocks to match a particular design.
    (b) recognize people's faces.
    (c) appreciate art and music.
    (d) decipher visual cues related to emotional expression.
    (e) produce and understand written and spoken language.

12. The occipital lobe is to _____ as the temporal lobe is to _____ .
    (a) anticipatory thinking; seeing
    (b) seeing; anticipatory thinking
    (c) seeing; hearing
    (d) hearing; seeing

13. If someone taps you on the back, you sense the touch because the _____ cortex in the _____ lobe receives this tactile information.
    (a) primary motor; frontal
    (b) primary visual; occipital
    (c) primary somatosensory; parietal
    (d) primary auditory; temporal

14. According to In Focus 2.3, most left-handed people
    (a) process language in the left hemisphere.
    (b) process language in the right hemisphere.
    (c) are intellectually challenged.
    (d) are female.

15. After a tamping iron accidentally went through his skull, Phineas Gage recovered physically, but his personality was profoundly changed; he could no longer make rational decisions, he became emotionally unstable, and he could no longer do his job. According to In Focus 2.2, the part of his brain that was damaged was the
    (a) frontal lobe.
    (c) temporal lobe.
    (b) occipital lobe.
    (d) parietal lobe.

Progress Test 2

After you have checked your understanding of the material in Progress Test 1 and have done a complete chapter review with special focus on any areas of weakness, you are ready to further assess your knowledge on Progress Test 2. Check your answers. If you make a mistake, review your notes, the appropriate parts of the study guide, and, if necessary, the relevant sections of your textbook.

1. A patient is suffering from a number of symptoms, including depression, sleep disturbances, and mood fluctuations, and has problems in learning and memory retrieval. Her doctor prescribes Prozac and some other drugs because the patient's problems are probably due to abnormal levels of the neurotransmitters
   (a) dopamine and acetylcholine.
   (b) serotonin and endorphins.
   (c) acetylcholine and norepinephrine.
   (d) serotonin and norepinephrine.

2. Signal reception is to _____ as signal transmission is to _____ .
   (a) myelin sheath; cell body
   (b) dendrite; axon
   (c) action potential; resting potential
   (d) axon; dendrite

3. As a result of a stroke, 75-year-old Mrs. Yee suffered brain damage. While she is no longer able to speak, she can understand what is being said to her. Mrs. Yee suffers from
   (a) damage to her occipital lobe.
   (b) Wernicke's aphasia.
   (c) damage to her left temporal lobe.
   (d) Broca's aphasia.

4. Your brain is involved in every perception, thought, and emotion, as are its neurons and their neurotransmitters. These neurotransmitters are chemical messengers that
   (a) carry information primarily in the endocrine system.
   (b) travel from the cell body along the axon and create an action potential.
   (c) assist neurons by providing physical support, nutrition, and waste removal.
   (d) travel across the synaptic gap and affect adjoining neurons.

5. If a patient suffers damage to the hippocampus, she is likely to have problems
   (a) learning and forming new memories.
   (b) remembering events and things that happened before her brain injury.
   (c) comprehending spoken and written language.
   (d) controlling emotions such as aggression, fear, anger, and disgust.

6. After Eduardo's serious skiing accident, doctors detected damage to his cerebellum. Eduardo is most likely to have trouble
   (a) swallowing, coughing, and breathing.
   (b) sleeping.
   (c) staying awake.
   (d) playing tennis, typing, and walking with a smooth gait.

7. In a typical test situation with a split-brain patient, a picture of an apple is briefly presented to the right of the center point. If the patient is asked to name the object, she will
   (a) be unable to say what she saw.
   (b) be able to draw a picture of the object with her left hand.
   (c) report that she saw nothing.
   (d) say she saw an apple.

8. If a researcher anesthetizes the entire right hemisphere of a right-handed patient who is asked to recite the alphabet aloud while reclining on the operating table with both arms extended upward, it is most probable that the patient's
   (a) left arm will fall limp but she will continue saying the alphabet.
   (b) right arm will fall limp but she will continue saying the alphabet.
   (c) left arm will fall limp and she will become speechless.
   (d) right arm will fall limp and she will become speechless.

9. A champion athlete loses his medal after officials discover that he has taken anabolic steroids, a synthetic version of the male sex hormone testosterone. Anabolic steroids, like other hormones, circulate through the _____ and primarily affect _____ functioning.
   (a) cerebrospinal fluid; central nervous system
   (b) bloodstream; endocrine system
   (c) cerebrospinal fluid; peripheral nervous system
   (d) bloodstream; limbic system

10. Doctors found a cancerous tumor in 50-year-old Milton's gonads, and so surgically removed the gonads. This operation will most likely affect his ability to
    (a) learn and form new memories.
    (b) produce epinephrine and norepinephrine.
    (c) produce dopamine and serotonin.
    (d) produce testosterone.
    (e) get a job as a baritone singer.

11. Dr. Jones systematically observes and records the behavior of people whose brains have been damaged by illness or injury. He is using an investigative technique called
    (a) MRI.   (c) PET scan.
    (b) CAT scan.   (d) case study.

12. The parietal lobe is to _____ as the frontal lobe is to _____ .
    (a) anticipatory thinking; hearing
    (b) sensing touch; anticipatory thinking
    (c) seeing; hearing
    (d) tasting; smelling

13. The chapter prologue tells the story of Asha, who suffered a stroke. This story illustrates that the brain has a remarkable ability to gradually shift functions from damaged to undamaged areas, a phenomenon called
    (a) lateralization of function.
    (b) structural plasticity.
    (c) synaptic transmission.
    (d) functional plasticity.

14. Structural plasticity refers to the capacity of some brain structures to
    (a) change in response to environmental stimulation.
    (b) remain rigid or "hard-wired" for life.
    (c) deteriorate with age and cause forgetfulness.
    (d) wear out if they are used too much.

15. Despite the fact that phrenology was eventually dismissed as a pseudoscience, it was pointed out in Box 2.1 that phrenology played a significant role in advancing the scientific study of the brain by triggering interest in
    (a) split-brain operations for epilepsy.
    (b) the role neurotransmitters play in regulating behavior.
    (c) cortical localization or localization of function.
    (d) how drugs affect synaptic transmission.

Progress Test 3

After you have checked your understanding of the material in Progress Tests 1 and 2, and have done a complete chapter review with special focus on any areas of weakness, you are ready to further assess your knowledge on Progress Test 3. Check your answers. If you make a mistake, review your notes, the appropriate parts of the study guide, and, if necessary, the relevant sections of your textbook.

1. When doctors removed a tumor from Andrew's occipital lobe, they also had to remove healthy brain tissue from the same area. When he recovers, Andrew is most likely to suffer some loss of
   (a) language comprehension.
   (b) muscular coordination.
   (c) visual perception.
   (d) taste perception.

2. Nancy suffers from severe epilepsy that so far has not responded to any treatment. As a final resort, her doctor operates on her brain and surgically cuts the
   (b) amygdala.
   (b) hippocampus.
   (c) corpus callosum.
   (d) adrenal cortex.

3. After a police car with flashing lights and blaring siren passes him and pulls over another driver for speeding, Jerry's heartbeat soon slows down, his blood pressure decreases, and he stops sweating so much. These calming physical reactions are most directly regulated by his
   (a) sympathetic nervous system.
   (b) parasympathetic nervous system.
   (c) somatic nervous system.
   (d) central nervous system.

4. While cooking dinner for a large family gathering, Mindy was so distracted by the conversations around her that she forgot to use an oven mitt when she grabbed a very hot roaster pan. She instantly withdrew her hand before becoming consciously aware of the sensation or her own hand movement. Mindy was able to do this because of her
   (a) spinal reflexes.
   (b) parasympathetic nervous system.
   (c) high levels of endorphins.
   (d) limbic system.

5. As a result of a stroke, Mr. Nelson can no longer understand what he reads or what is being said to him, and he often has trouble finding the right words when he tries to speak. Mr. Nelson suffers from
   (a) Wernicke's aphasia.
   (b) Broca's aphasia.
   (c) Parkinson's disease.
   (d) Alzheimer's disease.

6. If a picture of a hammer is flashed to the left of the midpoint during an experiment with a split-brain patient and she is asked to indicate what she saw, the patient will
   (a) verbally report what she saw.
   (b) be able to draw a picture of the hammer with her right hand.
   (c) be unable to verbally report what she saw.
   (d) most likely draw a picture of a nail with her right hand.

7. In order to determine which area of Drucilla's brain was most active when she read a passage from a book, neuroscientists radioactively tagged glucose and used a technique involving a(n)
   (a) PET scan.
   (b) CAT scan.
   (c) MRI.
   (d) EEG.

8. Sonny suffered brain damage when he was knocked down in a boxing match; he can no longer hear in one ear. It is most probable that one of his _____ lobes was injured.
   (a) ear
   (b) occipital
   (c) temporal
   (d) frontal
   (e) parietal

9. In an effort to relax after a stress-filled week, Joanne had a couple of glasses of wine and her coworker Jim took a Valium. Both alcohol and Valium work by increasing the activity of the neurotransmitter _____ , which inhibits action potentials and slows brain activity.
   (a) GABA
   (b) dopamine
   (c) norepinephrine
   (d) serotonin

10. If Dr. Doonan's research showed that the left hemisphere is dominant for speech and language in virtually all right-handed people and the majority of left-handers, this would argue strongly for the notion of
    (a) lateralization of function.
    (b) the all-or-none law.
    (c) structural plasticity.
    (d) functional plasticity.

11. In his medical practice Dr. Setiadi uses acupuncture, an ancient Chinese procedure that involves inserting needles at various points in the body. This pain-killing technique is assumed to involve the production of _____ by the brain.
    (a) endorphins
    (b) dopamine
    (c) GABA
    (d) acetylcholine

12. The production of the hormone melatonin is to the _____ as the regulation of blood sugar levels is to the _____ .
    (a) gonads; pineal gland
    (b) pineal gland; pancreas
    (c) pituitary gland; gonads
    (d) thyroid gland; adrenal glands

13. A researcher plans to survey 1,000 randomly selected individuals about hand preference. According to In Focus 2.3, the results are likely to indicate that
    (a) about 50 percent will be left-handed.
    (b) about 25 percent will be left-handed.
    (c) about 8 percent will be left-handed.
    (d) about one-third will be left-handed, one-third right-handed, and one-third ambidextrous.

14. During the early 1800s, Franz Gall developed a theory that the shape of the skull reflects abilities and personality characteristics. According to Box 2.1, this idea was called
    (a) philosophy.
    (b) bumpology.
    (c) phrenology.
    (d) physiology.

15. According to the Application, research has shown that compared with high school dropouts, university graduates had 40 percent more
    (a) synaptic connections.
    (b) brain mass.
    (c) neurons in their brains.
    (d) axons in the corpus callosum.

Answers

Introduction: The Scope of Biological Psychology

1. (a) the internal physical events and processes; experiences; behavior
   (b) biologists, physiologists, chemists, neurologists; psychiatrists

2. (a) nervous; neurons
   (b) endocrine
   (c) brain

The Neuron: The Basic Unit of Communication

1. (a) neurons
   (b) receive; transmit
   (c) glial cells

2. (a) Sensory neurons convey information to the brain from specialized receptor cells in the sense organs, the skin, and the internal organs.
   (b) Motor neurons send information to the muscles and glands.
   (c) Interneurons communicate information from one cell to the next and are the most common type of cell in the body.

3. (a) cell body
   (b) dendrites
   (c) axon

4. (a) dendrites; cell body; axon
   (b) white, fatty covering manufactured by special glial cells; increases

5. (a) action potentials
   (b) stimulus threshold
   (c) is prepared to activate and is polarized so that it is negative on the inside and positive on the outside
   (d) all-or-none

6. (a) presynaptic (sending); postsynaptic (receiving); synaptic gap
   (b) axon terminals
   (c) neurotransmitters
   (d) in which neurotransmitters are released by one neuron, cross the synaptic gap, and affect adjoining neurons
   (e) reuptake
   (f) excitatory; inhibitory

7. (a) neurotransmitters
   (b) neurotransmitters; physical; behavioral

8. (a) Acetylcholine; Alzheimer's
   (b) Dopamine; Parkinson's
   (c) Serotonin; Prozac; serotonin
   (d) Norepinephrine; learning; memory retrieval
   (e) GABA (gamma-amniobutyric acid); Valium; Xanax; action potentials
   (f) Endorphins; acupuncture

9. (a) drugs
   (b) black widow spider's
   (c) Prozac; cocaine
   (d) nicotine
   (e) curare
   (f) Naloxone

10. (a) acetylcholine
    (b) acetylcholine
    (c) serotonin
    (d) dopamine
    (e) GABA
    (f) endorphins

Graphic Organizer 1

a. dentrites
b. cell body
c. axon
d. myelin sheath
e. synaptic gap
f. neurotransmitter
g. synaptic vesicles
h. postsynaptic neuron
i. presynaptic neuron

Matching Exercise 1

1. neuron
2. GABA (gamma-amniobutyric acid)
3. endorphins
4. motor neuron
5. serotonin
6. cell body
7. action potential
8. neurotransmitter
9. axon
10. synapse
11. synaptic vesicles
12. dopamine
13. stimulus threshold

True/False Test 1

1. T	6. F	11. F
2. F	7. T	12. T
3. F	8. F	13. T
4. T	9. F	14. T
5. T	10. T	

The Nervous System and the Endocrine System: Communication Throughout the Body

1. (a) nervous; central nervous system; peripheral nervous system
   (b) neuron; central; nerves
   (c) nerves

2. (a) brain; spinal cord
   (b) spinal reflexes
   (c) sensory neuron; interneuron; motor neuron

3. (a) somatic nervous system; autonomic nervous system

(b) somatic
(c) autonomic

4. (a) sympathetic nervous system; parasympathetic nervous system
   (b) sympathetic
   (c) physiological changes, such as increased heart rate, accelerated breathing, dry mouth, and perspiration, in response to perceived threat or danger
   (d) parasympathetic

Graphic Organizer 2

Mapping the Divisions and Functions of the Nervous System

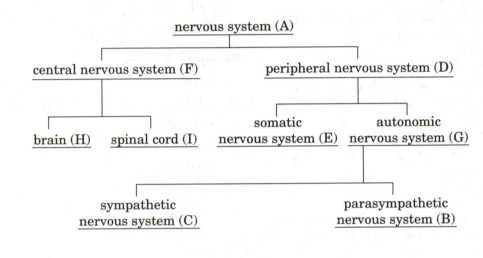

5. (a) endocrine; hormones; bloodstream
   (b) endocrine hormones

6. (a) hypothalamus
   (b) endocrine; nervous; pituitary
   (c) hypothalamus; pituitary

7. (a) adrenal glands
   (b) epinephrine; norepinephrine

8. (a) gonads
   (b) testosterone; estrogen; progesterone
   (c) sexual development, reproduction; sexual behavior

9. (a) metabolism
   (b) blood-sugar
   (c) melatonin

10. (a) spinal reflexes
    (b) spinal cord
    (c) sympathetic nervous system
    (d) parasympathetic nervous system
    (e) norepinephrine; epinephrine

Matching Exercise 2

1. thyroid gland
2. nerve
3. endocrine system
4. spinal reflexes
5. adrenal glands
6. parasympathetic nervous system
7. hypothalamus
8. testosterone
9. adrenal cortex
10. peripheral nervous system
11. autonomic nervous system
12. melatonin
13. pineal gland

True/False Test 2

1. T	5. T	9. T
2. F	6. F	10. F
3. T	7. T	11. F
4. T	8. F	12. T

Studying the Brain: The Toughest Case to Crack

1. (a) neurons
   (b) it is entirely encased by bone; it is extremely complex
2. (a) observe; record; damaged
   (b) (1) Because they focus on unusual situations, generalizing results from a case study must be done cautiously.
   (2) Injuries to the brain are rarely limited to specific, localized areas. Also, because brain areas are linked, damage in one area may also disrupt functioning in otherwise normal areas.
3. (a) surgically altering, removing, or destroying specific portions of the brain
   (b) the subsequent effects on behavior
   (c) behavioral effects; opposite
4. (a) electroencephalograph (EEG); record the brain's electrical activity
   (b) Computerized axial tomography (CAT or CT scan); X-rays
   (c) Magnetic resonance imaging (MRI); magnetic fields
   (d) radioactively; positron emission tomography (PET scan)
   (e) functional magnetic resonance imaging (fMRI)

A Guided Tour of the Brain

1. (a) neural pathways; cell bodies; neural pathways
   (b) integrated

2. (a) ventricles; cerebrospinal
   (b) increases
   (c) less than a pound; one-quarter; myelin; 3 pounds
   (d) do not have; has
3. (a) hindbrain; midbrain; forebrain
   (b) hindbrain; midbrain
4. (a) hindbrain
   (b) medulla; pons; cerebellum
   (c) breathing, circulation, heart rate, and digestion
   (d) pons; cerebellum
   (e) cerebellum
   (f) reticular formation; attention; arousal; sleep
5. (a) hindbrain (more specifically, the medulla is the point at which neural messages cross over)
   (b) reticular formation
   (c) cerebellum
   (d) medulla
6. (a) midbrain
   (b) motor control; dopamine
7. (a) cerebral cortex; cerebral hemispheres
   (b) corpus callosum
8. (a) temporal; primary auditory cortex; auditory
   (b) occipital; primary visual cortex; visual
   (c) parietal; somatosensory; touch; pressure; body position
   (d) frontal; voluntary muscle movements
9. (a) association areas
   (b) planning of voluntary movements
10. (a) limbic system; learning; memory; emotional
    (b) pleasure centers
11. (a) thalamus
    (b) hypothalamus; suprachiasmatic nucleus (SCN)
    (c) hippocampus
    (d) amygdala

Graphic Organizer 3
Chart Diagram Exercise: The Key Structures
of the Limbic System

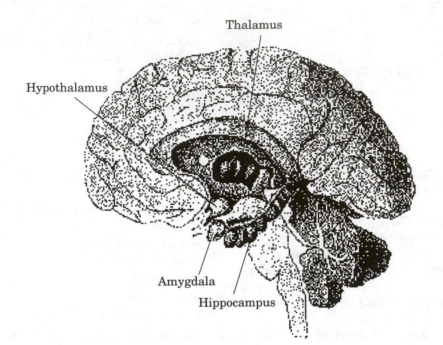

Thalamus

Hypothalamus

Amygdala

Hippocampus

(a) Hypothalamus; a peanut-sized forebrain struc-
    ture that regulates behaviors related to sur-
    vival, such as eating, drinking, and sexual
    activity
(b) Thalamus; a forebrain structure that processes
    sensory information for all the senses except
    smell and relays it to the cerebral cortex
(c) Amygdala; an almond-shaped forebrain struc-
    ture that is involved in emotion and memory
(d) Hippocampus; a curved forebrain structure that
    is involved in learning and forming new memo-
    ries

Matching Exercise 3

1. cerebral hemispheres

2. parietal lobe

3. substantia nigra

4. primary auditory cortex

5. pons

6. thalamus

7. primary visual cortex

8. hippocampus

9. brainstem

10. primary motor cortex

11. prefrontal association area

12. medulla

13. electroencephalograph (EEG)

14. reticular formation

15. magnetic resonance imaging (MRI)

16. suprachiasmatic nucleus (SCN)

True/False Test 3

1. T	7. F	13. T
2. T	8. T	14. T
3. F	9. T	15. F
4. F	10. T	16. T
5. T	11. F	
6. T	12. F	

Specialization in the Cerebral Hemispheres

1. (a) the idea that particular areas of the human
       brain are associated with particular func-
       tions (also referred to as localization of func-
       tion)
   (a) Pierre Paul Broca
   (b) Broca's

2. (a) Karl Wernicke
   (b) temporal; Wernicke's

3. (a) lateralization of function
   (b) left
4. (a) aphasia
   (b) Broca's
   (c) Wernicke's
5. (a) corpus callosum
   (b) split-brain operation
   (c) split-brain
6. (a) Roger Sperry
   (b) right; not be able
   (c) The information about the object went to her right hemisphere, which cannot communicate verbally. The left hemisphere, which can "talk," did not receive the information because in split-brain people the corpus callosum is severed.
   (d) left; right (right; left)
   (e) left; right
   (f) not be able; be able
7. (a) language abilities, speech, reading, and writing; musical ability (but not necessarily appreciation or responsiveness) involves both right and left hemispheres
   (b) nonverbal emotional expression, visual-spatial tasks such as completing a puzzle, face recognition, reading maps, copying designs, drawing, and musical appreciation or responsiveness (but not necessarily ability)
8. (a) right; left
   (b) left; left
   (c) right
   (d) right; left

Matching Exercise 4

1. Roger Sperry
2. aphasia
3. split-brain patient
4. Wernicke's area
5. corpus callosum
6. cortical localization
7. structural plasticity
8. lateralization of function

True/False Test 4

1. T   3. F   5. T   7. T
2. F   4. T   6. T

Something to Think About

1. (a) The occipital lobe is most likely affected because it includes the primary visual cortex where visual information is received, so damage to this area could affect vision.
   (b) Yoko probably has damage to the left frontal lobe, Broca's area. Damage here would not affect comprehension but would influence speech production.
   (c) Vanessa's hypothalamus was most likely damaged. The hypothalamus is part of the limbic system and regulates appetite, among its many functions.
   (d) The hypothalamus exerts considerable control over the secretion of endocrine hormones by directly influencing the pituitary gland. The pituitary gland produces *growth hormone*, which, not surprisingly, stimulates growth. So we can guess that Raphael's short stature is the result of a malfunction in this system.

2. In answer to this question, the news is good. Because of the brain's structural plasticity, some brain structures can change in response to environmental stimulation. Research with rats has demonstrated that, in addition to other changes, an enriched environment increases the number and length of dendrites, enlarges the size of neurons, and increases the number of neural connections. More important, there is an impressive amount of correlational research showing that the human brain also seems to benefit from enriched environments. Getting a good education, as long as the process is challenging, is one way to "exercise" the brain. Another piece of advice is to remain mentally active throughout the lifespan and to get involved in complex and stimulating activities.

   It is important to point out that intellectual decline is not the inevitable result of aging. To increase the number of synaptic connections and dendritic growth, the best advice is to get involved in novel, challenging, and unfamiliar pursuits. Keep pumping those neurons and remember, "If you don't use it, you lose it!"

Progress Test 1

1. b	6. a	11. e
2. c	7. a	12. c
3. c	8. c	13. c
4. c	9. d	14. a
5. b	10. b	15. a

Progress Test 3

1. c	6. c	11. a
2. c	7. a	12. b
3. b	8. c	13. c
4. a	9. a	14. c
5. a	10. a	15. a

Progress Test 2

1. d	6. d	11. d
2. b	7. d	12. b
3. d	8. a	13. d
4. d	9. b	14. a
5. a	10. d	15. c

Sensation and Perception

<table>
<tr><td>

PREVIEW

</td><td>

Reading the section below first will give you a general sense of the chapter's contents and an initial introduction to some of the major concepts and terms. This will prime you for what you are about to read and help you to develop a "cognitive map" that will guide your study of the material in this chapter. Likewise, reading the **preview questions** at the beginning of each major section will improve your ability to understand, learn, and retain the information.

</td></tr>
</table>

CHAPTER 3. . . AT A GLANCE

Chapter 3 describes both sensation and perception. Beginning with the basic principles of sensation—sensory threshold, Weber's law, and sensory adaptation—the chapter then explains the senses of vision, hearing, smell, taste, and touch. This is followed by a discussion of pain, pain perception, and the gate-control theory of pain. The section concludes with the kinesthetic and vestibular senses.

The discussion of perception first distinguishes between bottom-up and top-down processing. How we perceive shape and depth are explained, including a description of monocular and binocular cues. The perception of motion is explained, followed by the phenomenon of perceptual constancy. How we misperceive objects and events in our world is illustrated through various illusions and impossible figures. That perception is a psychological process is made clear through a discussion of how perceptual sets—expectations, learning experiences, and cultural factors—influence our interpretations.

The Application at the end of the chapter is devoted to how we can use various perceptual strategies and techniques in the control of pain.

Introduction: What Is Sensation and Perception?

Preview Questions

Consider the following questions as you study this section of the chapter.

- What are the definitions of sensation and perception?
- How do sensation and perception differ?

*Read the section "Introduction: What Is Sensation and Perception?" and **write** your answers to the following:*

1. (a) The primary function of the nervous system is _____ of information from one part of the body to another.

   (b) Being able to detect patches of color and edges of objects reflects _____ , and integrating and organizing them so that we interpret (identify) them reflects

   _____ .

Some Basic Principles of Sensation

Preview Questions

Consider the following questions as you study this section of the chapter.

- What are sensory receptors; how do they help us hear, taste, smell, feel, and see; and what is transduction?
- What are the two types of sensory thresholds?
- How does Weber's law relate to the just noticeable difference (jnd)?
- Why does sensory adaptation occur, and why is it important?

*Read the section "Some Basic Principles of Sensation" and **write** the answers to the following:*

1. (a) The vibrations of physical energy in the air are called _____ waves; the response to dissolvable chemicals in the mouth is _____ ; the detection of airborne chemical molecules inhaled through the nose is

   _____ ; the response to pressure on the skin is called _____ ; and

vision is the result of physical energy called _____ waves.

   (b) These different forms of physical energy are converted by the _____ into electrical impulses that are transmitted via neurons to the brain.

   (c) The process by which a form of physical energy is converted into a coded neural signal that can be processed by the nervous system is called _____ .

2. (a) The point at which a stimulus is strong enough to be detected by activating sensory receptors is the _____ .

   (b) The smallest possible strength of a stimulus that can be detected half the time is the

   _____ , and the smallest possible difference between two stimuli that can be detected half the time is the

   _____ .

   (c) The just noticeable difference (jnd) is another term for the _____ .

   (d) The principle that the jnd will vary depending on its relation to the strength of the original stimulus is called

   _____ . It states that for each sense the size of the jnd is a

   _____ proportion of the size of the initial stimulus. In other words, our psychological experience of sensation is

   _____ .

3. (a) The gradual decline in sensitivity to a constant stimulus is called

   _____ .

   (b) Our experience of sensation is

   _____ to the duration of exposure.

4. Read the following and write the correct term in the space provided.

   (a) When Anton went to have his hearing tested, he was presented with many different tones; in fact, some were at such a low level of intensity he could hardly detect them. These sounds were below Anton's

   _____ threshold.

(b) Detecting a sequence of sounds as a series of different tones involves the process of _____ ; recognizing the sequence of sounds as a melody is _____ .

(c) Jan was exposed to a 100-watt light. When its brightness was increased by 5 watts, she was not aware of the increase. However, when a 20-watt light was increased by 5 watts, she detected the increase immediately. Jan's experience illustrates a principle of sensation called

_____ .

(d) The school bell rings at lunch time. The process by which our ears convert the sound waves from the bell into a coded neural signal that can be processed by the nervous system is called _____ .

(e) Not realizing how cold it is after you have been on the ski slope for a while is an example of _____ .

(f) Not being able to detect a sound because its level is too low is to the _____ threshold as being able to just barely notice that two sounds are not the same is to the _____ threshold.

Review of Terms and Concepts 1

Use the terms in this list to complete the Matching Test, then to help you answer the True/False items correctly.

sensation	difference threshold
perception	just noticeable difference
sensory receptors	(jnd)
transduction	Weber's law
threshold	sensory adaptation
absolute threshold	subliminal perception

Matching Exercise

Match the appropriate term with its definition or description.

1. _____ The level at which a stimulus is strong enough to be detected by activating sensory receptors.

2. _____ The process by which a form of physical energy is converted into a coded neural signal that can be processed by the nervous system.

3. _____ The smallest possible strength of a stimulus that can be detected half the time.

4. _____ Specialized cells unique to each sense organ that respond to a particular form of sensory stimulation.

5. _____ The smallest possible difference between two stimuli that can be detected half the time; also called the just noticeable difference.

6. _____ The perception of stimuli that are below the threshold of conscious awareness.

True/False Test

Indicate whether each statement is true or false by placing T or F in the blank space next to each item.

1. ____ Perception refers to the process of detecting a physical stimulus, such as sound, light, heat, or pressure.

2. ____ Sensory adaptation refers to the decline in sensitivity to a constant stimulus.

3. ____ Weber's law is a principle of sensation that holds that the size of the just noticeable difference will vary depending on its relation to the strength of the original stimulus.

4. ____ The process of integrating, organizing, and interpreting sensations is called sensation.

5. ____ The smallest possible difference between two stimuli that can be detected half the time is called the difference threshold.

> Check your answers and review any areas of weakness before going on to the next section.

Vision: From Light to Sight

Preview Questions

Consider the following questions as you study this section of the chapter.

- How do we see, and what is the electromagnetic energy spectrum?
- What are the key structures of the eye and what causes nearsightedness, farsightedness, and astigmatism?

- What are the functions of the rods and cones, and how do the bipolar and ganglion cells process visual information for transmission to the brain?
- What properties of light determine our experience of color, and how do the two theories of color vision explain the process?

Read the section "Vision: From Light to Sight" and **write** *your answers to the following.*

1. (a) The sense organ for vision is the _____ , which contains receptor cells that are sensitive to the physical energy of _____ .

    (b) X-rays, microwaves, and ultraviolet rays are forms of _____ energy; they differ in terms of their _____ .

    (c) The difference from one wave peak to another is called a _____ .

    (d) Humans are capable of visually detecting only a minuscule portion of the _____ spectrum.

2. (a) The clear membrane covering the visible part of the eye that helps gather and direct incoming light is the _____ .

    (b) The black opening in the middle of your eye is called the _____ ; it is surrounded by the colored part of the eye called the _____ , which is actually a ring of muscles that expand or contract to precisely control the size of the _____ .

    (c) In dim light, the iris _____ the pupil; in bright light, it _____ the pupil.

    (d) The transparent structure located behind the pupil that actively focuses, or bends, light as it enters the eye is the _____ ; this bending process is called _____ .

    (e) If the eyeball is abnormally shaped, the _____ may not properly focus the incoming light on the _____ , resulting in visual disorders.

    (f) When light from a distant object is focused in front of the retina, it is called myopia, or _____ . When light from a nearby object or image is focused behind the retina, it called hyperopia, or _____ . An abnormally curved eyeball resulting in blurry vision for lines in a particular direction produces _____ .

    (g) During middle age, another form of _____ , called presbyopia, often occurs and is caused by the lens becoming brittle and inflexible. Corrective glasses remedy these visual disorders by intercepting and bending light so that the image falls properly on the _____ .

3. (a) The thin, light-sensitive membrane located at the back of the eye that contains the sensory receptors for light is the _____ .

    (b) The two kinds of sensory receptors on this membrane are the _____ and the _____ ; when exposed to light, they undergo a chemical reaction that results in a _____ signal.

    (c) The eye contains far _____ (less/more) rods than cones. Although both are light receptors, the _____ are much more sensitive to light than are the _____ .

    (d) We rely on the _____ for our vision in dim light and at night, and we rely on our _____ for vision in bright light, for sensing fine details, and for color vision.

    (e) Rods reach their maximum sensitivity to the available light in about _____ minutes whereas cones take about _____ minutes.

    (f) The small area in the center of the retina that is composed entirely of cones, where visual information is most sharply focused, is the _____ .

(g) Rods are more prevalent in the outlying area of the retina; as a result, in dim light or at night, we are better off using our _____ vision.

4. (a) The part of the retina that lacks rods and cones—the point where the fibers that make up the optic nerve leave the back of the eye—is the _____ .

(b) Because there are no photoreceptors in this part of the retina, there is a tiny hole, or _____ , in our field of vision.

5. (a) Most visual information is processed in the _____ , but it undergoes some preliminary processing in the _____ .

(b) Information from the sensory receptors, the rods and cones, is collected by specialized neurons called _____ cells, which in turn funnel information to other specialized neurons called _____ cells.

(c) These cells receive information from photoreceptors in their _____ field. In this early stage of visual processing, each _____ cell combines, analyzes, and encodes this information before transmitting it to the brain.

(d) For the most part, a single ganglion cell receives information from one or two _____ , but might receive information from hundreds of _____ ; consequently, the _____ can send messages of much greater visual detail to the brain, whereas the visual information transmitted by the _____ is far less specific.

(e) Cones are especially important in visual acuity, which refers to the _____ .

(f) Visual acuity is strongest when images are focused on the _____ because of the strong concentration of cones there.

6. (a) The thick bundle of ganglion cell axons that exits from the back of the eye and carries visual information to the brain is the _____ .

(b) After leaving the back of each eye, the left and right _____ meet and converge at the the point in the brain where they partly cross over to the opposite of the brain, called the _____ .

(c) From the _____ , most of the optic-nerve axons project to the thalamus; from there signals are sent to the _____ cortex, where they are decoded and interpreted.

(d) Specialized neurons that respond to particular aspects of visual stimulation such as edges, lines, and other forms are called _____ .

7. Our experience of color involves three properties of light waves.

(a) What we know as color, referred to as _____ , varies with the different wavelengths of light, which in turn correspond to our subjective experience of different colors; wavelengths of about 400 nanometers (nm) are perceived as _____ , those of 700 nm are perceived as _____ , and those in between are perceived as _____ , _____ , _____ , and blue.

(b) The property of color that corresponds to the purity of the light waves is its _____ ; a highly _____ color is vivid and rich, whereas a less _____ color is faded and washed out.

(c) The property of color that corresponds to the intensity or amplitude of the light wave is its _____ ; the higher the amplitude, the greater the degree of _____ .

8. (a) White light (such as sunlight) contains all _____ and thus all colors of the visible part of the electromagnetic spectrum; on the other hand, an object appears black because it _____ all wavelengths and _____ none.

(b) The color of any object is determined by the _____ of light that the object _____ .

9. There are two theories of color vision.

(a) According to the _____ theory, cones in the retina are especially sensitive to red, green, or blue light, and colors other than these result from the stimulation of a combination of these cones.

(b) According to the _____ theory, there are four basic colors that are divided into two pairs of color-sensitive neurons, red-green and blue-yellow, that oppose each other; when one member of a color pair is stimulated, the other is inhibited. In addition, _____ and _____ act as an opposing pair.

10. (a) An inherited form of color deficiency or weakness in which an individual cannot distinguish between certain colors is called _____ .

(b) A visual experience that occurs after the original stimulus is no longer present is called a(n) _____

(c) Trichromatic theory provides the best explanation for _____ , and opponent-process theory best accounts for _____

(d) Both theories of color vision are accurate because each theory correctly describes color vision at a _____ of visual processing.

11. Decide which term applies to the following.

(a) According to the trichromatic theory, if Mr.

Colorado's red- , green- , and blue-sensitive cones are stimulated simultaneously, he should see _____ .

(b) If a person with normal vision stares at a red circle for a couple of minutes, then shifts his or her eyes to a white surface, the afterimage of the circle will be _____ .

(c) Following an accident the fovea in Harbinder's right eye was destroyed. Although he can still see with this eye, it is likely that he will have trouble seeing _____ and _____ when his left eye is closed.

(d) Frederico's dog Fido lacks receptor cells for long wavelengths of about 700 nanometers. Most likely, Fido cannot see the color _____ .

(e) According to the opponent-process theory, if certain cells in Dale's retina are stimulated by exposure to green light, they are likely to be inhibited by exposure to _____ light.

Graphic Organizer 1

Identify each part of the eye by writing the name on the appropriate line; then match its function by placing the corresponding number next to the name. [For example, "1. retina" is the first answer.]

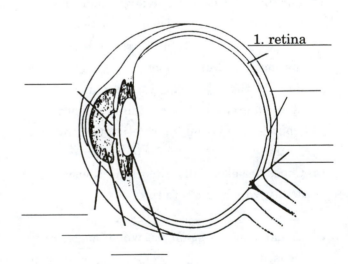

1. retina

1. A light-sensitive membrane located at the back of the eye that contains sensory receptors for vision.

2. The black opening in the middle of the eye that changes size to let in different amounts of light.

3. A clear membrane covering the visible part of the eye that helps gather and direct incoming light.

4. The colored part of the eye that is the muscle that controls the size of the pupil.

5. A transparent structure located behind the pupil that actively focuses, or bends, light as it enters the eye.

6. A small area in the center of the retina that contains cones but not rods.

7. The area of the retina without rods or cones where the optic nerve leaves the eye.

Review of Terms and Concepts 2

Use the terms in this list to complete the Matching Test, then to help you answer the True/False items correctly.

wavelength	fovea
cornea	optic disk
pupil	blind spot
iris	bipolar cells
iridology	ganglion cells
lens	visual acuity
accommodation	optic nerve
nearsightedness	optic chiasm
(myopia)	color
farsightedness	hue
(hyperopia)	saturation
presbyopia	brightness
astigmatism	trichromatic theory
retina	color blindness
rods	afterimage
cones	opponent-process theory

Matching Exercise

Match the appropriate term with its definition or description:

1. _____ The visual ability to see fine details.

2. _____ Common visual deficiency in which distant objects are seen clearly but close objects appear blurry because the focus of close objects falls behind the retina.

3. _____ Visual experience that occurs after the original source of stimulation is no longer present.

4. _____ Distance from one wave peak to another.

5. _____ Process by which the lens changes shape to focus incoming light so that it falls on the retina.

6. _____ Perceived intensity of color that corresponds to the amplitude of the light wave.

7. _____ Thick nerve that exits from the back of the eye and carries visual information to the visual cortex in the brain.

8. _____ Theory that the sensation of color is due to cones in the retina that are especially sensitive to red, green, or blue light.

9. _____ Short, thick, pointed sensory receptors of the eye that detect color and are responsible for color vision and visual acuity.

10. _____ Property of wavelengths of light, what we know as color, in which different wavelengths correspond to our subjective experience of different colors.

11. _____ Long, thin, blunt sensory receptors that are highly sensitive to light but not color and are primarily responsible for peripheral vision and night vision.

12. _____ Specialized neurons in the retina that collect sensory information from the rods and cones and then funnel it to other specialized neurons before it is transmitted to the brain.

13. _____ Perceptual experience of different wavelengths of light, involving hue, saturation (purity), and brightness (intensity).

14. _____ Area of the retina without rods or cones, where the optic nerve exits the back of the eye.

15. _____ Point in the brain where the optic fibers from each eye meet and partly cross over to the opposite side of the brain.

True/False Test

Indicate whether each statement is true or false by placing T or F in the blank space next to each item.

1. ____ The cornea is the transparent structure located behind the pupil that actively focuses, or bends, light as it enters the eye.

2. ____ The opponent-process theory states that color vision is the product of opposing pairs of color receptors, red-green, black-white, and

blue-yellow; when one member of a color pair is stimulated, the other is inhibited.

3. ___ The lens is the clear membrane covering the visible part of the eye that helps gather and direct incoming light.

4. ___ A single ganglion cell might receive information from only one or two cones or it might receive information from a hundred or more rods.

5. ___ The retina is a small area in the center of the back of the eye that is composed entirely of cones, where visual information is most sharply focused.

6. ___ The colored part of the eye, which is actually a ring of muscles that controls the size of the pupil, is called the iris.

7. ___ The pupil is the opening in the middle of the iris that changes size to let in different amounts of light.

8. ___ The fovea is a thin, light-sensitive membrane located at the back of the eye that contains two kinds of sensory receptors for light and vision.

9. ___ Nearsightedness occurs when close objects are seen clearly but distant objects appear blurry because the focus of light from distant objects falls a little short of the retina.

10. ___ Saturation is the property of color that corresponds to the purity of the light wave.

11. ___ Color blindness occurs because there are no receptor cells in the area where the optic nerve exits the eye.

12. ___ Iridology is based on the unproven notion that physical and psychological functioning are reflected in the iris, the colored part of the eye.

13. ___ During middle age, another form of farsightedness, called presbyopia, often occurs due to the lens becoming brittle and inflexible.

14. ___ In astigmatism, an abnormally curved eyeball results in blurry vision for lines of a particular direction.

15. ___ The blind spot is the point where the optic nerve leaves the eye, producing a small gap in the field of vision.

> Check your answers and review any areas of weakness before going on to the next section.

Hearing: From Vibration to Sound

Preview Questions

Consider the following questions as you study this section of the chapter.

- What is audition, and how do we hear?
- What properties of a sound wave correspond to our perception of sound?
- What are the key structures of the ear, and what are their functions?
- How do place theory and frequency theory explain pitch?

Read the section "Hearing: From Vibration to Sound" and **write** *your answers to the following:*

1. (a) The technical term for the sense of hearing is _____ .

   (b) The ability to sense and perceive very subtle differences in sound is important to _____ survival, _____ interactions, and _____ development.

2. (a) The physical stimuli that produce our sensory experience of sound are the

   _____ .

   (b) Loudness is determined by the intensity, or _____ , of a sound wave and is measured in units called _____ .

   (c) Zero decibels represents the softest sound a human can hear, or the _____ . As decibels increase, perceived _____ increases.

   (d) Pitch refers to the relative _____ or _____ of a sound and is determined by the _____ of a sound wave.

   (e) _____ refers to the rate of vibration, or number of waves per second, and is measured in units called _____ .

(f) The distinctive quality of a sound produced by the combination of several sound-wave frequencies is called _____

3. (a) The human ear is made up of the _____ ear, where sound waves are collected; the _____ ear, where they are amplified; and the _____ ear, where they are transduced into neural messages.

(b) The three structures of the outer ear are the _____

(c) The outer ear is separated from the middle ear by the _____ ; the _____ separates the middle ear from the inner ear.

(d) The middle ear contains three tiny bones called the _____

(e) Hearing loss that occurs if the tiny bones of the middle ear are damaged or become brittle, as happens in old age, is called _____ deafness. This type of deafness _____ (can/cannot) be helped with a hearing aid, which amplifies sound.

(f) A coiled, fluid-filled tube that is the main structure of the inner ear is the _____ ; it contains the _____ and tiny projecting fibers called _____ , which are responsible for transducing, or transforming, the vibrations of sound waves into neural impulses.

(g) Damage to the hair cells or auditory nerve causes _____ deafness. This type of deafness _____ (can/cannot) be helped by a hearing aid.

4. (a) The membrane within the cochlea, the _____ , is a key structure involved in the discrimination of pitch.

(b) According to the _____ theory, the basilar membrane vibrates at a frequency that is _____ (lower than/the same as/higher than) the sound wave. This theory can explain sounds up to about 1,000 hertz.

(c) The _____ theory suggests that different frequencies cause larger vibrations at different locations along the basilar membrane.

(d) Higher-frequency sounds cause maximum vibration near the _____ end of the basilar membrane, and lower-frequency sounds cause maximum vibration at the _____ end.

(e) Different pitches excite different _____ along the basilar membrane; higher-pitched sounds are interpreted according to the _____ where the hair cells are most active.

(f) _____ theory helps explain our discrimination of lower-frequency sounds, and _____ theory helps explain our discrimination of higher-pitched sounds; for midrange pitches, both _____ and _____ are involved.

5. Read the following and write the correct term in the space provided.

(a) The retina in the eye performs a function that parallels the function of the _____ in the ear.

(b) Rita, who has suffered damage to the bones in her middle ear, has been told by the experts that a hearing aid that artificially amplifies sounds will help restore her hearing. Rita probably has _____ deafness.

(c) After a small area of his basilar membrane was damaged, Hamish could no longer hear high-pitched sounds. This loss of hearing can best be explained by the _____ theory.

(d) Mrs. Newbold is 75 years old and has had some hearing loss due to stiffness of the tiny bones in her middle ear. It is possible that her deafness can be helped by a

_____ .

(e) Dr. Emison's research, which found that high-frequency sounds trigger activity near the stirrup end of the basilar membrane, supports the _____ theory of pitch.

Graphic Organizer 2

Identify each part of the ear by writing the name on the appropriate line and then match its function by placing the corresponding number next to the name. [For example, "1. pinna" is the first answer.]

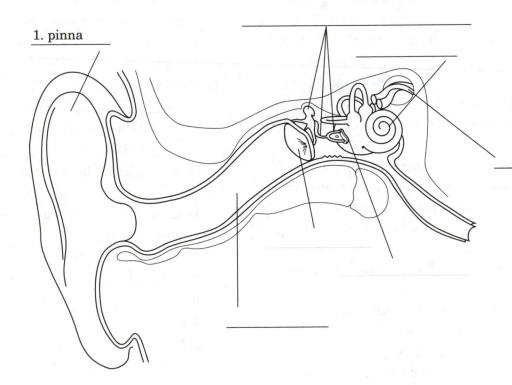

1. pinna

1. The oddly shaped flap of skin and cartilage that is attached to each side of the head.

2. A tightly stretched membrane at the end of the ear canal that vibrates when sound waves hit it.

3. A fluid-filled coiled structure that contains the sensory receptors for sound.

4. The tunnel through which sound waves travel to reach the eardrum.

5. The tightly stretched membrane that separates the middle ear from the inner ear.

6. The small structures of the middle ear whose joint action almost doubles the amplification of the sound.

7. The nerve that carries the neural information to the thalamus and the auditory cortex in the brain.

Review of Terms and Concepts 3

Use the terms in this list to complete the Matching Test, then to help you answer the True/False items correctly.

audition
sound waves
amplitude
decibels
pitch
frequency
hertz
timbre
outer ear
pinna
ear canal
eardrum

oval window
middle ear
hammer, anvil,
    and stirrup
conduction deafness
inner ear
cochlea
basilar membrane
hair cells
nerve deafness
frequency theory
place theory

Matching Exercise

Match the appropriate term with its definition or description.

1. _____ Type of deafness due to damage to the hair cells or auditory nerve.

2. _____ Technical term for the sense of hearing.

3. _____ Rate of vibration, or number of waves per second.

4. _____ Hairlike sensory receptors for sound embedded in the basilar membrane.

5. _____ Physical stimuli that produce our sensory experience of sound.

6. _____ The distinctive quality of a sound, determined by the complexity of the sound waves.

7. _____ Part of the ear that collects sound waves and consists of the pinna, the ear canal, and the eardrum.

8. _____ Relative highness or lowness of a sound, determined by the frequency of the sound wave.

9. _____ The view that different frequencies cause larger vibrations at different locations along the basilar membrane.

10. _____ Unit of measurement for loudness.

11. _____ Intensity or amount of energy of a wave, reflected in the height of the wave; determines a sound's loudness.

12. _____ The part of the ear that amplifies sound waves; consists of three small bones—the hammer, the anvil, and the stirrup.

True/False Test

Indicate whether each statement is true or false by placing T or F in the blank space next to each item.

1. ____ According to frequency theory, the basilar membrane vibrates at the same frequency as the sound wave, thereby enabling low-frequency sound to be transmitted to the brain.

2. ____ The oval window is a tightly stretched membrane that separates the middle ear from the inner ear.

3. ____ Conduction deafness results from mechanical problems that prevent parts of the ear from conducting vibrations to the hair cells in the inner ear.

4. ____ The hammer, anvil, and stirrup are important transduction structures in the inner ear.

5. ____ The cochlea is a coiled, fluid-filled structure that contains the sensory receptors for sound.

6. ____ Hertz refers to the number of wave peaks per second.

7. ____ The ear canal is the fluid-filled section of the ear that contains the cochlea.

8. ____ The structure within the cochlea that contains the hair cells is called the basilar membrane.

9. ____ The eardrum is a tightly stretched membrane at the end of the ear canal that vibrates when sound waves hit it.

10. ____ The pinna is the oddly shaped flap of skin and cartilage that is attached to each side of your head.

11. ____ The inner ear is the part of the ear where sound is transduced into neural impulses; it consists of the cochlea and semicircular canals.

> Check your answers and review any areas of weakness before going on to the next section.

The Chemical and Body Senses: Smell and Taste (Part 1)

Preview Questions

Consider the following questions as you study this section of the chapter.

• How are olfaction and gustation defined, and what is meant by the chemical senses?

- How do airborne molecules result in the sensation of odor?
- What are the primary tastes, and how do we perceive different tastes?

*Read the section "The Chemical and Body Senses" (through taste) and **write** your answers to the following:*

1. (a) The technical term for the sense of smell is _____ ; for taste, the term is _____ .

   (b) Sensory receptors for taste and smell respond to different types of _____ substances, and which is why they are sometimes called the _____ senses.

2. (a) The sensory stimuli that produce our sensation of odor are _____ , which encounter millions of _____ cells high in the nasal cavity.

   (b) Stimulation is converted by these cells into neural messages that travel along the axons that make up the _____ .

   (c) Hundreds of different odor receptors have been identified, but we can identify many more different odors. It appears that a given smell activates a _____ of different receptors and that specific odors are identified by the brain when it interprets the _____ of receptors that are stimulated.

   (d) The olfactory _____ connect to the olfactory _____ in the brain, which is actually the enlarged ending of the _____ at the front of the brain.

   (e) Axons from the olfactory bulb form the _____ , which projects to different areas of the brain, including the _____ lobe and the _____ system.

3. (a) Several studies have shown that _____ (males/females) tend to be more sensitive to odors than _____ (males/females) and that many animals display greater sensitivity than humans.

   (b) Humans have a remarkable ability to recognize _____ smells.

   (c) As with other senses, we experience sensory _____ to odors when exposed to them for a period of time, with maximum _____ occurring in less than a minute.

4. (a) Our sense of taste, or _____ , results from stimulation of special receptors in the mouth.

   (b) The stimuli that produce the sensation of taste are _____ substances in whatever you eat or drink. These substances are dissolved by saliva, which allows them to activate the _____ .

   (c) The specialized receptors for taste, or _____ , when activated, send neural messages to the _____ , which then directs the information to several regions in the cortex.

   (d) The four primary taste qualities are _____ , _____ , _____ , and _____ ; all other tastes are a combination of these.

5. Read the following and write the correct term in the space provided.

   (a) After eating his salad with vinegar dressing, Mario thinks that his very expensive vintage wine tastes strange. This change in perceived taste is probably due to the vine-

(f) The olfactory sense is the only sense with a direct connection to the brain (and to the outside world), and unlike the other senses, it does not pass through the _____ before being relayed to the higher centers of the cortex.

gar causing some disruption to his

_____ .

(b) As a result of damage to her olfactory bulb, Danielle has lost the ability to detect the _____ of whatever she eats or drinks.

(c) If a person experiences damage to the thalamus, his or her sense of _____ will be least affected.

(d) In a study investigating olfaction, women are asked to smell a number of T-shirts and decide which one has been worn for a number of days by their spouse. Based on the research presented in the text, the women are very _____ (likely/unlikely) to be able to accurately identify the correct T-shirt.

The Chemical and Body Senses: Touch and Position (Part 2)

Preview Questions

Consider the following questions as you study this section of the chapter.

- What are the skin and body senses, and what sensory receptors are involved in touch and temperature?
- How is the sensation of pain produced, and what causes pain?
- What is the gate-control theory of pain?
- What are the kinesthetic and vestibular senses, and where are their receptors located?

Read the section "The Chemical and Body Senses" ("Movement, Position, and Balance") and **write** *your answers to the following:*

1. (a) Essential information about your physical status and your physical interaction with objects in your environment is provided by the _____ senses.

(b) The largest and heaviest organ in the body, which weighs about 6 pounds, is the

_____ .

(c) This organ has many different kinds of receptors; some are specialized to respond to

just one kind of stimulus, such as

_____ , _____ , or

_____ .

(d) One important receptor involved in the sense of touch is called the _____ , which is located beneath the skin; if pressure stimulation is constant, this receptor either reduces the number of signals sent or stops responding altogether; in other words, _____ takes place.

(e) When a cold spot is stimulated by either a cold or a hot stimulus, it produces a sensation of _____ , but warm spots respond only to warm stimuli.

(f) The sensation of hot is produced when warm and cold spots are stimulated

_____ .

2. (a) Because pain provides us with information about our body and what is happening to it, it is important to our _____ .

(b) Pain is the sensation of _____ or _____ , and virtually any stimulus, external or internal, that can produce tissue damage can cause pain.

(c) The most influential theory for understanding how pain is processed is called the _____ theory; this model suggests that the sensation of pain is controlled by a series of _____ that open and close in the spinal cord.

(d) Pain begins when an intense stimulus activates small-diameter sensory fibers, called _____ endings, in the skin, muscles, or internal organs. These fibers carry messages to the spinal cord, releasing a neurotransmitter called _____ , which causes other neurons to become activated; these neurons send the pain message through open signal gates to the _____ in the brain.

(e) Psychological and emotional factors that can
_____ the experience of pain
include anxiety, fear, and a sense of helplessness, and factors that can _____
the experience of pain include positive emotions, a sense of control, distraction, and
laughter.

(f) The pain experience is also influenced by
_____ and
_____ learning
experiences about the meaning of pain and
how one should react to pain.

(g) Psychological factors also influence the
release of _____ , the body's
natural painkillers, which are produced in
many parts of the brain and the body.

(h) In the brain, _____ can inhibit
the transmission of pain signals, and in the
spinal cord they inhibit the release of
_____ .

(i) A person's _____ and
_____ state can influence other
bodily processes, such as muscle tension,
psychological arousal, and rapid heart rate,
that affect the experience of pain.

3. (a) Information about the location of body parts
in relation to one another, called the
_____ sense, involves specialized sensory neurons called
_____ , which are located in the
muscles and joints.

(b) Our sense of balance or equilibrium is provided by the _____ sense, which
responds to changes in gravity, motion, and
body position.

(c) The two sources of vestibular sensory information, both located in the ear are the
_____ canals and the
_____ sacs. These structures
are filled with fluid and lined with hairlike
receptor cells that shift in response to

_____ , changes in body
_____ , or changes in
_____ .

(d) Maintaining our equilibrium also involves
information from other senses, particularly
_____ .

(e) When information from the
_____ conflicts with
information from the vestibular system, the
result can be _____ ,
_____ , and _____ .

4. Read the following and write the correct term
in the space provided.

(a) On the day of her final statistics exam,
Nadia has a sore ankle. According to the
gate-control theory, it is likely that Nadia's
anxiety about the exam will
_____ her perception
of the pain in her ankle.

(b) While fishing in a small boat, Mortimer
becomes nauseous from the motion of the
waves. Mortimer's _____ and
_____ are most likely responsible for making him feel ill.

(c) During a psychology lab demonstration,
Gary is blindfolded and asked to grasp with
his hand two intertwined pipes, one containing warm water and the other containing
cold water. Gary is likely to experience the
sensation of _____ .

(d) If you are blindfolded and asked to touch
your chin, nose, and forehead with your
index finger, you probably will have no trouble doing so. This ability is due to your
_____ sense.

(e) Arleigh accidentally scrapes the skin off his
knuckles while working on his car. The pain
he feels following the injury is caused in
part by the release of the neurotransmitter
_____ .

Review of Terms and Concepts 4

Use the terms in this list to complete the Matching Test, then to help you answer the True/False items correctly.

olfaction
gustation
chemical senses
airborne molecules
olfactory receptor cells
olfactory nerves
olfactory bulb
olfactory cortex
olfactory tract
pheromones
taste buds
skin senses

body senses
Pacinian corpuscle
pain
gate-control theory
free nerve endings
substance P
endorphins
kinesthetic sense
proprioceptors
vestibular sense
semicircular canals
vestibular sacs

Matching Exercise

Match the appropriate term with its definition or description.

1. _____ Technical term for our sense of taste.

2. _____ Fluid-filled sacs that are lined with hairlike receptor cells that shift in response to motion, changes in body position, and gravity.

3. _____ Touch receptor located beneath the skin; when stimulated by pressure, it converts the stimulation into neural messages that are relayed to the brain.

4. _____ The name sometimes given to our senses of taste and smell because they both involve sensory receptors for chemical substances.

5. _____ Small-diameter sensory fibers in the skin, muscles, or internal organs that, when activated by an intense stimulus, begin the process of pain perception.

6. _____ Cells located high in the nasal cavity that are stimulated by inhaled molecules in the air.

7. _____ Enlarged ending of the olfactory cortex at the front of the brain where the sensation of smell is registered.

8. _____ Specialized sensory receptors for taste that are located on the tongue and inside the mouth and throat.

9. _____ Tract formed by bundles of axons from the olfactory bulb that projects to different brain area, including the temporal lobe and structures in the limbic system.

10. _____ The sense of balance or equilibrium.

11. _____ The body's natural painkillers that are produced in many parts of the brain and the body.

12. _____ The sense of location and position of body parts in relation to one another.

True/False Test

Indicate whether each item is true or false by placing T or F in the space next to each item.

1. ____ Pain is the unpleasant sensation of physical discomfort or suffering that can occur in varying degrees of intensity.

2. ____ Gate-control theory suggests that pain is the product of both physiological and psychological factors that cause spinal "gates" to open and relay patterns of intense stimulation to the brain, which perceives them as pain.

3. ____ Airborne chemical molecules are emitted by the substances we are smelling; we inhale them through the nose and through the opening in the palate at the back of the throat.

4. ____ The olfactory nerves connect directly to the olfactory bulb, where smells are perceived by the brain.

5. ____ Proprioceptors are sensory neurons in the spinal cord that regulate the release of endorphins.

6. ____ Olfaction is the technical term for our sense of smell.

7. ____ The semicircular canals are fluid-filled structures lined with hairlike receptors that shift in response to motion, changes in bodily position, and gravity and are a source of information for our vestibular sense.

8. ____ The olfactory cortex is at the front of the brain and is directly linked to the outside world via neural pathways.

9. ____ The body senses provide essential information about our physical status and our physical interaction with objects in our environment.

10. ___ Substance P is one of the body's natural painkillers and is produced in many parts of the brain and body in response to intense stimulation.

11. ___ The skin senses keep us informed as to our position and orientation in space.

12. ___ Chemical signals used by animals to communicate boundaries and sexual receptiveness are called pheromones.

> Check your answers and review any areas of weakness before going on to the next section.

Perception (Part 1)

Preview Questions

Consider the following questions as you study this section of the chapter.

- What is perception?
- How does bottom-up processing differ from top-down processing?
- What three questions does perception answer about the stimuli we sense?
- Who founded Gestalt psychology, and what is the main focus of this perspective?

Read the section "Perception" (the introduction only) and ***write*** *your answers to the following:*

1. (a) Perception is the process of

   _____ , _____ , and

   _____ sensory information

   in a meaningful way.

   (b) Psychologists sometimes refer to the flow of

   sensory data from the sensory receptors to

   the brain as _____ pro-

   cessing, or data-driven processing.

   (c) As we interact with our environment, many

   of our perceptions are shaped by

   _____ processing, or con-

   ceptually driven processing; this occurs

   when we draw on our _____ ,

   _____ , _____ ,

   and other cognitive processes to arrive at

   meaningful perceptions.

(d) _____ and _____

   processing are involved in our everyday per-

   ceptions and both are necessary to explain

   how we arrive at perceptual conclusions.

2. Perceptual processes help us organize our sensations to answer three basic questions:

   (a) _____

   (b) _____

   (c) _____

3. (a) The German psychologists who investigated

   and established many perceptual principles

   were called _____ psy-

   chologists; this school was founded by

   German psychologist _____

   in the early 1900s.

   (b) The German word _____

   means a unified whole, which makes sense

   because this perspective maintains that we

   perceive whole objects or figures rather than

   isolated bits and pieces of information.

Perception: The Perception of Shape (Part 2)

Preview Questions

Consider the following questions as you study this section of the chapter.

- How important is shape in identifying objects and other elements of our environment?
- What is the figure-ground relationship, and how significant is it to perception?
- What perceptual principles do we follow in determining figure-ground relationships?
- What perceptual principles do we follow when we group visual elements?
- What is the law of Pragnanz, and what does it explain?

Read the section "Perception: The Perception of Shape" (up to depth perception) and ***write*** *your answers to the following:*

1. (a) Although we rely to some degree on size,

   color, and texture to determine what an

   object might be, we rely primarily on an

   object's _____ to identify it.

(b) When we view a scene, we automatically separate the elements of that scene into the feature that clearly stands out and its less distinct background; this is called the

_____ .

(c) Our ability to separate a scene into

_____ and _____ is a psychological accomplishment, not a function of the actual elements of the scene we are viewing.

(d) The perception of an image in two different ways (as with the vase example in text Figure 3.14) is called

_____ ; this ability underscores the notion that our perception of figure is a _____ phenomenon.

(e) The markings and colorations of some animals help them avoid predation by allowing them to blend with the background; the predator cannot distinguish the animal (the

_____) from the natural background (the _____).

2. (a) We actively organize elements to try to produce the stable perception of well-defined, whole objects, according to a number of Gestalt _____ or laws. These laws include _____ ,

_____ , _____ ,

and _____ .

(b) The law of Prägnanz states that when several perceptual organizations are possible, the perceptual interpretation that will occur will be the one that produces the

" _____ , _____ ,

and most stable shape." For this reason, it is also called the

_____ .

(c) The law of Prägnanz encompasses all the other _____ , including

the figure-ground relationship.

(d) Our perceptual system works in an economical and efficient way to reveal "the essence of something," which is roughly what the German word _____ means.

Perception: Depth Perception (Part 3)

Preview Questions

Consider the following questions as you study this section of the chapter.

- Why is depth perception important, and how is it defined?
- What are monocular cues, and how do they contribute to depth perception?
- What are binocular cues, and how do they differ from monocular cues?
- How is binocular disparity involved in our ability to see three-dimensional images in stereograms?

Read the section "Perception: Depth Perception" (up to motion perception) and **write** *your answers to the following:*

1. (a) The ability to perceive distance or the location of three-dimensional objects is called

_____ .

   (b) The cues used to judge the distance of objects that require the use of only one eye are called _____ cues.

2. Identify the following monocular cues.

   (a) When two similar-sized objects are observed, the object that appears larger is perceived as being closer: _____

   (b) When one object partially blocks or obscures the view of another object, the partially blocked object is perceived as being farther away: _____

   (c) Faraway objects appear hazy or slightly blurred by the atmosphere:

   _____

   (d) The details of a distinct surface texture gradually become less clearly defined as distance increases: _____

(e) Parallel lines seem to meet in the distance:
_____

(f) A moving person observes that nearby objects seem to move faster as they pass by than objects that are far away:

_____

3. (a) Artists using monocular cues to create the perception of distance or depth in paintings are using _____ cues.

(b) A monocular cue that utilizes information about changes in the shape of the lens of the eye to help us estimate distance is called

_____ .

4. (a) In contrast to monocular cues, _____ cues for distance or depth perception require information from both eyes.

(b) A binocular cue based on the degree to which muscles rotate the eyes to focus on an object is called _____ .

(c) Focusing on an object held about six inches from the eyes will require a greater degree of _____ than will focusing on it at arm's length; the information provided by these signals from the eyes is used to judge distance.

(d) The distance cue that relies on information provided by the two slightly different images that result from having our eyes a number of inches apart is called

_____ .

(e) When the two retinal images of an object are very different, we perceptually interpret the object as being _____ ; when they are almost identical, the object is perceived as being _____ .

(f) Stereograms use the binocular depth cue of _____ to create the perception of a three-dimensional image.

Perception: The Perception of Motion (Part 4)

Preview Questions

Consider the following questions as you study this section of the chapter.

- Which sources of information contribute to our perception of motion?
- Who first studied induced motion, and how did he go about demonstrating this phenomenon?
- How does stroboscopic motion work, and how does it relate to the perception of motion?
- How do we use auditory cues to perceive distance and location?

*Read the section "Perception: The Perception of Motion" (up to perceptual constancies) and **write** your answers to the following:*

1. (a) When a moving object moves across the retina, our eye muscles make microfine _____ to keep the object in focus.

(b) We also compare the moving object to the _____ , which is usually stationary.

(c) We perceive movement when complex neural pathways combine information from _____ activity, the changing _____ image, and the contrast of the moving object with its stationary _____ .

(d) Some neurons are highly specialized to detect the _____ of motion, whereas other neurons are specialized to detect motion at one particular

_____ .

2. (a) We typically assume that the _____ we are observing moves while the background or frame remains stationary; this sometimes leads to the illusion of motion called _____ motion.

(b) In Gestalt psychologist Karl Dunker's experiment on _____ motion, when the _____ slowly moved to the right, the subjects perceived the dot as moving to the left despite the fact that the dot never moved.

3. (a) The phenomenon in which two spaced-apart lights that flash on and off in succession create the perception of one light moving back and forth in space is referred to as _____ motion.

(b) Although no actual movement takes place and the two flashing lights are detected at two different points on the retina, the brain's _____ somehow combines this rapid sequence of visual information to arrive at the perceptual conclusion of motion.

(c) The perception of smooth motion in a movie is due to _____ motion.

4. (a) We also use _____ information to judge distance and direction.

(b) Using only one ear, the _____ a sound is, the closer it is perceived to be, but using two ears allows more accurate location of the _____ as well as the distance of a sound.

(c) The direction and distance of a sound are calculated by the brain on the basis of differences in _____ and _____ detected by each ear.

5. Read the following and write the correct term in the space provided.

(a) Dr. Schwartz, whose research focus is perceptual organization, believes that we perceive whole objects or figures rather than isolated bits and pieces of sensory information. Dr. Schwartz is most likely a _____ psychologist.

(b) At a noisy party, Ben focuses on his girlfriend's conversation, while tuning out the other conversations. Using a Gestalt perceptual principle to analyze this example, the noisy environment is the _____ and his girlfriend's voice is the

_____ .

(c) While viewing a stereogram, Nina experiences the perceptual illusion of three-dimensional depth from the two-dimensional scene. The binocular cue responsible for this phenomenon is _____ .

(d) Chan knows that the red bicycle in the parking lot is closer to him than the green bicycle because the red one casts a larger retinal image. This illustrates the distance cue known as _____ .

(e) Emily paints a long garden pathway bordered with flowers. She shows the flowers as decreasing in size as they approach the horizon, where they seem to meet; Emily is using _____ to convey depth on the canvas.

(f) Ricardo uses sequentially flashing Christmas lights in front of his house to make it look as though Santa and his sleigh are moving from the garden to the roof. Ricardo is using the perceptual illusion of

_____ .

(g) To make the task of completing the jigsaw puzzle more challenging, Zahra attempted to assemble it without the finished picture in front of her. Zahra is most likely to use _____ , or data-driven processing, to accomplish the task.

Review of Terms, Concepts, and Names 5

Use the terms in this list to complete the Matching Test, then to help you answer the True/False items correctly.

perception
bottom-up processing
  (data-driven
  processing)
top-down processing
  (conceptually driven
  processing)
extrasensory perception
  (ESP)
parapsychology
Gestalt psychology
Max Wertheimer
figure-ground
  relationship
figure-ground reversal
law of Prägnanz
  (law of simplicity)
depth perception

monocular cues
relative size
overlap
aerial perspective
texture gradient
linear perspective
motion parallax
pictorial cues
accommodation
binocular cues
convergence
binocular disparity
stereogram
induced motion
Karl Dunker
stroboscopic motion
auditory cues

Matching Exercise

Match the appropriate term with its definition or description.

1. _____ School of psychology founded in Germany in the early 1900s that maintained that our sensations are actively processed according to consistent perceptual rules that result in meaningful whole perceptions.

2. _____ Law that states that when several perceptual organizations are possible, the perceptual interpretation that will occur will be the one that produces the best, simplest, and most stable shape.

3. _____ Monocular cue that suggests that faraway objects often appear hazy or slightly blurred by the atmosphere.

4. _____ Binocular cue that relies on the fact that our eyes are set a couple of inches apart and thus cast slightly different images on the retina of each eye.

5. _____ Gestalt principle of perceptual organization that states that we automatically separate the elements of a perception into the feature that clearly stands out from its less distinct background.

6. _____ Monocular cue in which an object partially blocked or obscured by another object is perceived as being farther away.

7. _____ Distance or depth cues that require the use of both eyes.

8. _____ Monocular cue that utilizes information about changes in the shape of the lens of the eye to help us gauge depth and distance.

9. _____ German Gestalt psychologist who is best known for his studies on the perception of motion; also studied the perception of pain and the effects of past experience on perception; emigrated to the United States in 1938.

10. _____ An illusion of movement that results when two separate, carefully timed flashing lights are perceived as one light moving back and forth.

11. _____ The use of visual cues (either monocular or binocular) to perceive the distance or three-dimensional characteristics of objects.

12. _____ The perception of an image in which the ground can be perceived as the figure and the figure as the ground; underscores that our perception of figure and ground is a psychological phenomenon.

13. _____ German psychologist who founded Gestalt psychology in the early 1900s; emigrated to the United States in 1933; studied the optical illusions of apparent movement and described principles of perception.

14. _____ The scientific investigation of claims of various paranormal phenomena.

True/False Test

Indicate whether each item is true or false by placing T or F in the space next to each item.

1. ___ Perception is defined as the process of integrating, organizing, and interpreting sensory information in a meaningful way.

2. ___ Induced motion occurs when a sound reaches one ear slightly before reaching the other and results in the perception of movement.

3. ___ Relative size is the monocular cue in which an object partially blocked or obscured by another object appears farther away.

4. ___ Monocular cues for distance or depth require information from both eyes.

5. ____ The depth cue that occurs when parallel lines seem to meet in the distance (and the closer together the lines appear to be, the greater the perception of depth) is called linear perspective.

6. ____ Convergence is a binocular cue that relies on the degree to which muscles rotate the eyes to focus on an object; the less convergence, the farther away the object appears to be.

7. ____ When we are in motion, we can use the speed of passing objects to estimate their distance; nearby objects will appear to move much faster relative to distant objects. This monocular cue is called motion parallax.

8. ____ In addition to monocular and binocular visual cues, auditory cues can also be used to judge distance and direction.

9. ____ Texture gradient is a binocular cue for distance in which parallel lines seem to meet in the distance and their surface or texture become less clearly defined the farther away they are.

10. ____ Monocular cues used by artists to create the perception of distance or depth in paintings are called pictorial cues.

11. ____ Top-down processing is information processing that emphasizes the importance of sensory receptors in detecting the basic features of a stimulus in the process of recognizing a whole pattern; it involves analysis from the parts to the whole.

12. ____ A stereogram is a picture that uses the principle of binocular disparity to create the perception of a three-dimensional image.

13. ____ Bottom-up processing is information processing that emphasizes the importance of the observer's knowledge, expectations, and other cognitive processes in arriving at meaningful perceptions and involves analysis from the whole to the parts.

14. ____ Extrasensory perception (ESP) is based on the idea that sensory information can be detected by some means other than through the normal processes of sensation.

> Check your answers and review any areas of weakness before going on to the next section.

Perception: Perceptual Constancies (Part 5)

Preview Questions

Consider the following questions as you study this section of the chapter.

- What is perceptual constancy?
- What principles guide our perception of size constancy?
- What are shape constancy and brightness constancy?

*Read the section "Perception: Perceptual Constancies" and **write** your answers to the following:*

1. (a) The tendency to perceive objects, especially familiar objects, as unchanging despite changes in sensory input is called

   _____ .

   (b) Without this perceptual ability our perception of reality _____
   instead of the stable view of the world we normally perceive.

2. (a) Size constancy is the perception that an object remains the same size despite its changing image on the _____ .

   (b) An important aspect of size constancy is that if the retinal image of an object does not change but the perception of its distance increases, we will perceive the object as

   _____ ; this principle is easily demonstrated with the phenomenon of the _____ .

3. (a) The tendency to perceive familiar objects as having a fixed shape regardless of the image they cast on our retinas is called

   _____ .

   (b) If we observe a door opening toward us, the retinal image of its rectangular shape changes but our _____ of its shape remains constant.

4. (a) With brightness constancy, the brightness of an object stays the _____ though the lighting conditions

   _____ .

(b) The perception of brightness constancy occurs because objects always reflect the same _____ of available light, even if the lighting conditions change dramatically.

Perceptual Illusions and the Effects of Experience on Perceptual Interpretations

Preview Questions

Consider the following questions as you study this section of the chapter.

- What are perceptual illusions, and why are psychologists interested in them?
- How are the Müller-Lyer and moon illusions explained?
- What do illusions and impossible figures reveal about normal perceptual processes?
- How do perceptual sets influence the perceptual conclusions we reach?

Read the sections "Perceptual Illusions" and "The Effects of Experience on Perceptual Interpretations" and **write** *your answers to the following:*

1. (a) When we misperceive the true characteristics of an object or an image, we experience a(n) _____ .

    (b) The perceptual contradictions of _____ not only are fascinating but also can shed light on how the _____ processes of perception guide us to perceptual conclusions.

2. (a) The Müller-Lyer illusion involves the misperception of the _____ .

    (b) Visual depth cues that promote the perception that a line with outward-pointing arrows is _____ from us and a line with inward-pointing arrows is _____ to us contribute to the Müller-Lyer illusion.

    (c) _____ constancy plays an important role in the Müller-Lyer illusion.

    (d) Although two identical lines produce _____ retinal images, one line is embedded in visual depth cues that make

us perceive it as farther away; thus, our brain interprets it as being

_____ .

3. (a) The moon illusion is the misperception that a full moon is _____ when viewed on the horizon than in the overhead sky.

    (b) The retinal image of a full moon on the horizon is _____ (the same as/larger than/smaller than) that of a full moon in the overhead sky.

    (c) A partial explanation of the moon illusion is that people perceive objects on the horizon as _____ than objects that are directly overhead in the sky. This perception is enhanced by the monocular depth cue of _____ .

    (d) The moon illusion also involves the misapplication of _____ constancy, and even though the retinal image of the moon remains constant, we perceive the moon as _____ because it seems farther away on the horizon.

    (e) If all distance cues are removed, the size of the moon on the horizon will look _____ as it does when directly overhead.

4. (a) Although impossible figures are not _____ in the true sense, they baffle our natural tendency to perceptually organize a scene.

    (b) Perceptual illusions underscore the fact that what we see is not merely a simple reflection of the world, but rather our subjective perceptual _____ of it.

    (c) Perception, in the final analysis, is clearly a _____ process and may be influenced by many factors such as our expectations and our prior experiences.

5. (a) What we perceive is shaped by our _____ , _____ , and _____ experiences.

(b) The influence of prior assumptions and expectations on perceptual interpretations is referred to as our _____ .

(c) People who have reported sightings of UFOs, the Loch Ness monster, mermaids, and so on have interpreted ambiguous stimuli in terms of the _____ they held in the situation, seeing what their expectations led them to see.

6. Read the following and write the correct term in the space provided.

(a) Stereotypes are mental conceptions that we have about individuals belonging to specific racial or ethnic groups and can influence how we interpret their behaviors. Stereotypes are most similar to the perceptual phenomenon of _____ .

(b) William noticed that the full moon seemed to be much larger on the horizon than when it was overhead. His friend Jane, a psychology major, explained that the illusion results from distance cues that make the horizon moon seem _____ (farther away/closer) than an overhead moon.

(c) Your unopened introductory psychology textbook produces a trapezoidal retinal image, but you typically perceive the book as a rectangular object. This is due to _____ constancy.

(d) When asked to judge the length of two equal lines, people consistently report the one with outward-pointing arrows as being longer than the one with inward-pointing arrows. These people are experiencing the _____ illusion.

Review of Terms and Concepts 6

Use the terms in this list to complete the Matching Test, then to help you answer the True/False items correctly.

perceptual constancy
size constancy
shape constancy
brightness constancy
perceptual illusion

Müller-Lyer illusion
moon illusion
impossible figures
perceptual set

Matching Exercise

Match the appropriate term with its definition or description.

1. _____ The influence of prior assumptions and expectations on perceptual interpretations.

2. _____ The tendency to perceive objects, especially familiar objects, as constant and unchanging despite changes in sensory input.

3. _____ Famous visual illusion involving the misperception of the identical length of two lines, one with arrows pointed inward and one with arrows pointed outward.

4. _____ The perception of an object as maintaining the same size despite changing images on the retina.

5. _____ Visual riddles, though not true illusions, that capitalize on our urge to perceptually organize visual elements into a meaningful whole.

True/False Test

Indicate whether each item is true or false by placing T or F in the space next to each item.

1. ____ A perceptual illusion is the tendency to perceive objects as constant and unchanging despite changes in sensory input.

2. ____ The moon illusion involves the misperception that the moon is larger when it is on the horizon than when it is directly overhead.

3. ____ The perception of a familiar object as maintaining the same shape regardless of the image produced on the retina is called shape constancy.

4. ____ Brightness constancy is the perception that the brightness of an object remains the same even though the lighting conditions change.

Check your answers and review any areas of weakness before going on to the next section.

Something to Think About

1. Many people have reported strange experiences that they interpret as extrasensory perception, or ESP. Suppose that a friend or family member told you about such an experience. This person might be convinced that something extraordinary has occurred. Based on what you have learned in this chapter, how would you go about explaining to them what has most likely taken place?

2. Imagine that you have decided to become an artist. You want to paint a picture that includes a variety of elements such as buildings, fields, a river, a mountain, and some people and animals. Using what you know about sensation and perception, think of all the monocular cues that you could use to give your masterpiece a sense of depth. In addition, can you think of any perceptual components that might add interest to your canvas?

> Check your answers and review any areas of weakness before doing the progress tests.

Progress Test 1

Review the complete chapter (including Concept Reviews and all boxed inserts), review all your study notes, and then test yourself on the following progress test. Check your answers. If you make a mistake, review your notes, the appropriate section in the study guide, and if necessary, the relevant part of the chapter in your textbook.

1. Dr. Kandola's research showed that the vibrations of hair cells in the basilar membrane were at the same frequency as the low-frequency sound waves that stimulated them. This research supports the _____ theory of pitch.
   (a) place
   (b) frequency
   (c) timbre
   (d) amplitude

2. Dr. Frankenstein's younger brother built a monster but omitted a very important part of his anatomy. As a result, the monster cannot transform sounds into neural messages. The missing part is the
   (a) eardrum.
   (b) middle ear with its tiny bones.
   (c) vestibular sacs.
   (d) basilar membrane.

3. A red pen is displayed in Roger's peripheral vision while he stares straight ahead. He correctly identifies the object but is unable to name the color. The reason for this is that
   (a) there are many rods but very few cones in the periphery of the retina.
   (b) there are many cones but very few rods in the periphery of the retina.
   (c) there are no receptor cells for vision in the periphery of the retina.
   (d) the stimulus was below Roger's difference threshold.

4. After staring at a blue light for a few minutes, Yoko shifts her gaze to a white wall and experiences an afterimage in the color _____; Yoko's experience provides support for the _____ theory of color vision.
   (a) red; opponent-process
   (b) yellow; opponent-process
   (c) red; trichromatic
   (d) yellow; trichromatic

5. Neville is color-blind and cannot see red or green, yet he can see blue with no problem. Which theory of color vision can most easily explain this?
   (a) trichromatic theory
   (b) place theory
   (c) opponent-process theory
   (d) frequency theory

6. Ever since her operation, Madame Burgundi can no longer experience the flavors of the gourmet foods and wines she serves in her restaurant. It is most likely that she has suffered damage to her
   (a) kinesthetic sense.   (c) sense of humor.
   (b) sense of smell.   (d) vestibular sense.

7. The dizziness and disorientation Shelly felt after she rolled down the hill are a function of her
   (a) basilar membrane.
   (b) Pacinian corpuscles.
   (c) semicircular canals and vestibular sacs.
   (d) proprioceptors.

8. As Pancho gazed down the railway tracks it seemed to him that the two parallel rails actually met in the distance. Pancho is experiencing the monocular depth cue
   (a) linear perspective.   (c) motion parallax.
   (b) aerial perspective.   (d) texture gradient.

9. Many people have mistaken a floating log for Ogopogo, the alleged Okanagan Lake monster. The most likely reason for this misperception is
   (a) a perceptual set.
   (b) monocular vision.
   (c) rye whisky.
   (d) extrasensory perception.

10. If Fred holds a letter very close to his nose as he reads it and Charlie holds it at arm's length when he reads it, Fred will experience _____ Charlie.
    (a) more convergence than
    (b) the identical level of convergence as
    (c) less convergence than
    (d) more motion parallax than

11. In an experiment, you are seated in a darkened room and shown a large lighted frame with a single dot of light inside it. The frame slowly moves to the left, and the dot remains stationary. It is very probable that you will perceive
    (a) induced motion.
    (b) the dot moving to the right.
    (c) the frame as remaining stationary.
    (d) all of the above.

12. As Demi moves away from the camera, her image on the screen grows smaller and smaller, yet viewers do not perceive Demi as the incredible shrinking woman. This illustrates
    (a) convergence.   (c) size constancy.
    (b) binocular disparity. (d) motion parallax.

13. Nedzad claims that by examining the color and markings of your iris he can tell a lot about you, including level of mental stress, presence of any mental disorders, personality characteristics, past history of disease and injuries, and much more. According to Science versus Pseudoscience 3.2, Nedzad is probably
    (a) a psychic palm reader.
    (b) an iridologist.
    (c) mentally ill.
    (d) a biological psychologist.

14. Whether perceptual principles are universal and inborn (nativist position) or vary from culture to culture and are influenced by experience and learning (empiricist position) has been the subject of a longstanding debate. According to

Culture and Human Behavior 3.5, research using the Müller-Lyer illusion tends to support
   (a) the nativist position.
   (b) the empiricist position.
   (c) neither the nativist nor the empiricist position.
   (d) the nativist position slightly more than the empiricist position.

15. If advertisers were to expose moviegoers to the subliminally flashing words EAT POPCORN and DRINK COKE during a movie
    (a) sales of popcorn and coke would increase dramatically.
    (b) the moviegoers would feel hungry and thirsty for days after seeing the movie.
    (c) the subliminal messages are not likely to have any discernible effect on the sale of popcorn and coke.
    (d) the moviegoers will have recurring nightmare involving popcorn and coke.

Progress Test 2

After you have checked your understanding of the material in Progress Test 1 and have done a complete chapter review with special focus on any areas of weakness, you are ready to further assess your knowledge on Progress Test 2. Check your answers. If you make a mistake, review your notes, the relevant sections of the study guide, and if necessary, review the appropriate parts of your textbook.

1. Detection of stimulus energy is to the interpretation of the information as _____ is to _____ .
   (a) transduction; accommodation
   (b) hue; saturation
   (c) hearing; vision
   (d) sensation; perception

2. When Julius returns from getting a drink of water, he resumes weightlifting a 150-pound free weight and doesn't notice that someone has added a five-pound ring to each end. For Julius the additional ten pounds
   (a) is not a just noticeable difference (jnd).
   (b) is below his absolute threshold.
   (c) is not sensed because of sensory adaptation.
   (d) is easy to lift because water releases endorphins.

3. When Vincent arrived home, the first thing he noticed was the smell of freshly baked bread. The process by which the odor of baking bread was converted into neural signals that Vincent's brain could interpret is called

(a) sensory adaptation.
(b) transduction.
(c) accommodation.
(d) conduction.

4. Mario was born with a genetically inherited visual deficiency. It is most probable that Mario suffers from

(a) red-green color blindness.
(b) blue-yellow color blindness.
(c) stroboscopic vision.
(d) binocular disparity.

5. When Tony was painting a landscape, he used many different colors. The technical term for each of the different wavelengths of light that produce the subjective sensation of different colors in Tony's painting is

(a) saturation.   (c) brightness.
(b) hue.   (d) timbre.

6. As Rodney was setting up the equipment for the concert, he adjusted the amplitude of the speaker system. This is most likely to affect the _____ of the music.

(a) pitch   (c) timbre
(b) frequency   (d) loudness

7. Eight-year-old Sean can hear sounds close to 20,000 hertz. This sensory capacity is best explained by

(a) extrasensory perception (ESP) theory.
(b) opponent-process theory.
(c) frequency theory.
(d) place theory.

8. When Derrick removed all visual distance cues, he noticed that the moon on the horizon looked to be the same size as it was when directly overhead. Derrick concluded correctly that the distance cues make the horizon moon seem _____ the overhead moon.

(a) farther away than   (c) smaller than
(b) closer than   (d) the same size as

9. Using a small ice cube tray, Jason replaces every other ice cube with warm water. He blindfolds Richard and then simultaneously stimulates both cold and warm receptors on Richard's skin by placing his arm in direct con-

tact with the tray. When Jason asks Richard what he is experiencing, he woud probably say he feels

(a) cold.   (c) hot.
(b) warm.   (d) like an idiot.

10. On the day of an important job interview, Madeline wakes up with a slight toothache. As the time for the stressful interview approaches, her anxiety increases and so does her perception of the pain from her tooth. When the interview is over, Madeline is elated because she feels it has gone well and, to her surprise, she feels hardly any pain from her tooth. Madeline's experience is best explained by the _____ theory and the contribution of her psychological and emotional state.

(a) opponent-process   (c) place
(b) gate-control   (d) frequency

11. Astrid holds a pencil quite close to her nose and opens and closes her left and right eyes a couple of times in succession. She notices that the images are quite different. When she views the same pencil in a similar manner from across the room, she sees almost identical images. Astrid has demonstrated the _____ cue of_____ .

(a) binocular; binocular disparity
(b) monocular; motion parallax
(c) binocular; overlap
(d) monocular; convergence

12. When blindfolded, most people are not able to accurately and consistently identify the location of an object that makes a sound directly above the precise midpoint of their heads. The reason for this is that

(a) they cannot judge distance and direction from auditory cues.
(b) when deprived of one sense, all the other senses are adversely affected.
(c) the sound waves reach each ear at the same time, and people need to detect a difference in time lag and loudness to pinpoint the location of a sound.
(d) the blindfold obscures all visual cues; without these cues, they cannot judge location or distance.

13. As dusk descends Carmen thinks that the yellow tulips are just as yellow as they had been earlier when there was more daylight. Despite the changing lighting conditions, Carmen's perception of the color of the flowers did not

change. This is best explained by _____ constancy and the fact that objects always reflect the same _____ of available light.

(a) brightness; amount
(b) brightness; proportion
(c) size; degree
(d) shape; amount

14. According to the Application, the process of learning voluntary control over largely autonomic body functions such as heartbeat, blood pressure, and muscle tension by using specialized sensitive equipment is called

(a) iridology.   (c) acupuncture.
(b) psychokinesis.   (d) biofeedback.

15. Willard believes he can influence the mechanical systems within slot machines with the power of his mind alone. Willard is claiming to possess the power of

(a) telepathy.   (c) psychokinesis.
(b) clairvoyance.   (d) precognition.

Progress Test 3

After you have checked your understanding of the material in Progress Tests 1 and 2, and have done a complete chapter review with special focus on any areas of weakness, you are ready to further assess your knowledge on Progress Test 3. Check your answers. If you make a mistake, review your notes, the appropriate parts of the study guide, and if necessary, the relevant sections of your textbook.

1. During a psychology lab demonstration the instructor set up two flashing lights about three feet apart in a darkened room. About one-tenth of a second after the first light flashed, the second light flashed, and then the first light flashed again, and so on. Most of the students experienced the illusion of apparent motion, perceiving just one light traveling back and forth. The instructor is most likely to explain this phenomenon in terms of

(a) the principles of stroboscopic motion.
(b) the kinesthetic sense.
(c) motion parallax.
(d) binocular disparity.

2. You have just arrived at the beach and the texture of the sand toward the water appears smooth, even, and perfectly flat, yet the sand beneath your feet is rough and uneven and you can see individual small stones, seashells, and

other debris. You are experiencing the monocular distance cue of

(a) motion parallax.
(b) aerial perspective.
(c) linear perspective.
(d) texture gradient.

3. José notices that near the horizon the moon appears larger than when it is overhead in the sky. The effect is mainly the result of

(a) distance cues that make the horizon moon seem farther away.
(b) the retinal image of the horizon moon being larger than the retinal image of the overhead moon.
(c) distance cues that make the horizon moon seem nearer.
(d) having to tilt your head upward when looking at the overhead moon.

4. While carrying out a sensory demonstration in which a small object is positioned so that its retinal image would be cast on the exact spot where her optic nerve exits the eye, Deidre should expect the image of the object to

(a) change to its opposite color.
(b) look twice as large as it had before.
(c) produce an afterimage if she shifts her gaze to a white surface.
(d) disappear from sight.

5. Analysis that moves from the parts to the whole is to _____ as analysis that moves from the whole to the parts is to

_____ .

(a) figure-ground relationship; figure-ground reversal
(b) bottom-up processing; top-down processing
(c) size constancy; shape constancy
(d) the moon illusion; the Muller-Lyer illusion

6. While strolling through the garden, Jamal suddenly noticed the beautiful odor of roses. Jamal is using her _____ sense, and the process by which the odor is converted into neural signals that her brain can understand is called _____ .

(a) gustatory; saturation
(b) olfactory: transduction
(c) gustatory; adaptation
(d) olfactory; accommodation

7. Whenever Robyn looks at her boyfriend, her pupils dilate. The eye structure responsible for this response is called the
   (a) retina.   (c) iris.
   (b) fovea.   (d) optic disk.

8. When looking carefully at a picture of a country scene we are able to detect fine visual details, especially those that are focused on the fovea. One reason for this visual acuity is that
   (a) the fovea contains rods, which have many individual neural connections to the cortex.
   (b) the fovea contains cones, which have many individual neural connections to the cortex.
   (c) the fovea is the spot where the optic nerve leaves the eye.
   (d) there are only bipolar cells in the fovea and these are specialized for feature detection.

9. After Jackson has been in the hot tub for a few minutes he no longer notices how hot the water is. This is because of
   (a) sensory adaptation.
   (b) the just noticeable difference.
   (c) Jackson's thick skin.
   (d) sensory saturation.

10. After playing in a heavy metal rock band for most of his young adult life, Edwin has suffered a significant hearing loss. Unfortunately for Edwin, his hearing problem cannot be helped by a hearing aid. It is most likely that he is suffering from
    (a) damage to the auditory cortex in his left temporal lobe.
    (b) nerve deafness.
    (c) damage to his proprioceptors.
    (d) conduction deafness.

11. Graham suffers from a visual disorder called nearsightedness, and Grace is farsighted. Both disorders are caused by
    (a) the lack of rods and cones in the visual disk.
    (b) clouding of the cornea.
    (c) ganglion and bipolar cells malfunctioning.
    (d) the fact that images are not properly focused on the retina.

12. In a replication of a famous experiment, 3-year-old children were shown an object and told it was a "dax." Later, the children were shown a variety of objects, some shaped like the original dax, but different in color, size, and texture, and other objects identical to the dax but

shaped differently. The results showed that the main characteristic that the children used to determine whether the object was a dax or not a dax, was the object's
(a) shape.   (c) color.
(b) size.   (d) texture.

13. To reduce the experience of pain, Dexter looks away and focuses on a picture on the wall as a nurse sticks a hypodermic needle into his arm. Dexter is using the pain control technique of
(a) counter-irritation.   (c) biofeedback.
(b) relaxation.   (d) distraction.

14. Dr. Frederick believes that people living in urban, industrialized environments have a great deal of perceptual experience in judging lines, corners, edges, and other rectangular, manufactured objects, and thus should be more susceptible to the Müller-Lyer illusion than people in cultures whose experience has been primarily with more natural objects. This idea is called
(a) Weber's law.
(b) gate-control theory.
(c) the carpentered-world hypothesis.
(d) the opponent-process theory.

15. Maxwell is a male pig and, like most male pigs, he releases a chemical substance in the sweat glands to communicate territorial boundaries and sexual receptiveness. Female pigs use their _____ sense to detect these airborne chemical scents called _____ .
(a) gustatory; vestibulars
(b) olfactory; pheromones
(c) gustatory; pheromones
(d) olfactory; vestibulars

Answers
Introduction: What Is Sensation and Perception?
1. (a) communication
   (b) sensation; perception

Some Basic Principles of Sensation
1. (a) sound; taste; smell; touch; light
   (b) sensory receptors
   (c) transduction
2. (a) threshold
   (b) absolute threshold; difference threshold
   (c) difference threshold

(d) Weber's law
(e) constant; relative

3. (a) sensory adaptation
   (b) relative

4. (a) absolute
   (b) sensation; perception
   (c) Weber's law
   (d) transduction
   (e) sensory adaptation
   (f) absolute; difference

Matching Exercise 1

1. threshold

2. transduction

3. absolute threshold

4. sensory receptors

5. difference threshold

6. subliminal perception

True/False Test 1

1. F   3. T   5. T
2. T   4. F

Vision: From Light to Sight

1. (a) eye; light
   (b) electromagnetic; wavelengths
   (c) wavelength
   (d) electromagnetic

2. (a) cornea
   (b) pupil; iris; pupil
   (c) widens (expands); narrows (contracts)
   (d) lens; accommodation
   (e) lens; retina
   (f) nearsightedness; farsightedness; astigmatism
   (g) farsightedness; retina

3. (a) retina
   (b) rods; cones; neural
   (c) more; rods; cones
   (d) rods; cones
   (e) 30; 5
   (f) fovea
   (g) peripheral

4. (a) optic disk
   (b) blind spot

5. (a) brain; retina
   (b) bipolar; ganglion
   (c) receptive; ganglion
   (d) cones; rods; cones; rods

(e) ability to see fine detail
(f) fovea

6. (a) optic nerve
   (b) optic nerves; optic chiasm
   (c) optic chiasm; visual
   (d) feature detectors

7. (a) hue; violet; red; orange, yellow, green
   (b) saturation; saturated; saturated
   (c) brightness; brightness

8. (a) wavelengths; absorbs; reflects
   (b) wavelength; reflects

9. (a) trichromatic
   (b) opponent-process; black; white

10. (a) color blindness
    (b) afterimage
    (c) color blindness; afterimages
    (d) different level

11. (a) white
    (b) green
    (c) color; fine detail
    (d) red
    (e) red

Graphic Organizer 1

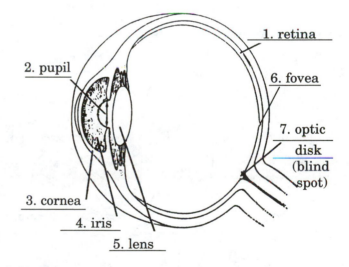

1. retina
2. pupil
6. fovea
7. optic disk (blind spot)
3. cornea
4. iris
5. lens

Matching Exercise 2

1. visual acuity

2. farsightedness

3. afterimage

4. wavelength

5. accommodation

6. brightness

7. optic nerve

8. trichromatic theory

9. cones

10. hue

11. rods

12. bipolar cells

13. color

14. optic disk

15. optic chiasm

True/False Test 2

1. F	5. F	9. T	13. T
2. T	6. T	10. T	14. T
3. F	7. T	11. F	15. T
4. T	8. F	12. T	

Hearing: From Vibration to Sound

1. (a) audition
   (b) physical; social; language

2. (a) sound waves
   (b) amplitude; decibels
   (c) absolute threshold; loudness
   (d) highness; lowness; frequency

   (e) Frequency; hertz
   (f) timbre

3. (a) outer; middle; inner
   (b) pinna, ear canal, and eardrum
   (c) eardrum; oval window
   (d) hammer, anvil, and stirrup
   (e) conduction; can
   (f) cochlea; basilar membrane; hair cells
   (g) nerve; cannot

4. (a) basilar membrane
   (b) frequency; the same as
   (c) place
   (d) stirrup; opposite
   (e) hair cells; place
   (f) Frequency; place; frequency; place

5. (a) cochlea
   (b) conduction
   (c) place
   (d) hearing aid
   (e) place

Graphic Organizer 2

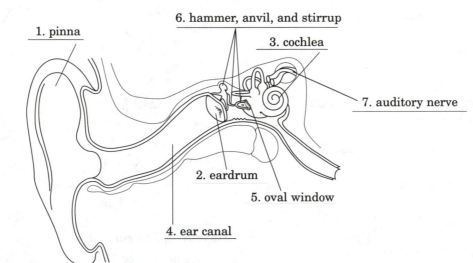

6. hammer, anvil, and stirrup

1. pinna

3. cochlea

7. auditory nerve

2. eardrum

5. oval window

4. ear canal

Matching Exercise 3

1. nerve deafness

2. audition

3. frequency

4. hair cells

5. sound waves

6. timbre

7. outer ear

8. pitch

9. place theory

10. decibels

11. amplitude
12. middle ear

True/False Test 3

1. T   5. T   9. T
2. T   6. T   10. T
3. T   7. F   11. T
4. F   8. T

The Chemical and Body Senses: Smell and Taste (Part 1)

1. (a) olfaction; gustation
   (b) chemical; chemical
2. (a) molecules in the air; specialized olfactory receptor
   (b) olfactory nerves
   (c) group; pattern
   (d) nerves; bulb; olfactory cortex
   (e) olfactory tract; temporal; limbic
   (f) thalamus
3. (a) females; males
   (b) familiar
   (c) adaptation; adaptation
4. (a) gustation
   (b) chemical; taste buds
   (c) taste buds; thalamus
   (d) sweet, salty, sour; bitter
5. (a) taste buds
   (b) smell (olfaction)
   (c) smell (olfaction)
   (d) likely

The Chemical and Body Senses: Touch and Position (Part 2)

1. (a) skin
   (b) skin
   (c) pressure; warmth; cold
   (d) Pacinian corpuscle; sensory adaptation
   (e) cold
   (f) simultaneously
2. (a) survival
   (b) discomfort; suffering
   (c) gate-control; gates
   (d) free nerve; substance P; thalamus
   (e) intensify; reduce
   (f) social; cultural
   (g) endorphins
   (h) endorphins; substance P
   (i) mental (psychological); emotional
3. (a) kinesthetic; proprioceptors

(b) vestibular
(c) semicircular; vestibular; motion; position; gravity
(d) vision
(e) eye; dizziness, disorientation; nausea
4. (a) intensify
   (b) semicircular canals; vestibular sacs
   (c) hot
   (d) kinesthetic
   (e) substance P

Matching Exercise 4

1. gustation
2. vestibular sacs
3. Pacinian corpuscle
4. chemical senses
5. free nerve endings
6. olfactory receptor cells
7. olfactory bulb
8. taste buds
9. olfactory tract
10. vestibular sense
11. endorphins
12. kinesthetic sense

True/False Test 4

1. T   5. F   9. F
2. T   6. T   10. F
3. T   7. T   11. F
4. T   8. T   12. T

Perception (Part 1)

1. (a) integrating, organizing; interpreting
   (b) bottom-up
   (c) top-down; knowledge, experiences, expectations
   (d) Bottom-up; top-down
2. (a) What is it?
   (b) How far away is it?
   (c) Where is it going?
3. (a) Gestalt; Max Wertheimer
   (b) *gestalt*

Perception: The Perception of Shape (Part 2)

1. (a) shape
   (b) figure-ground relationship
   (c) figure; ground

(d) figure-ground reversal; psychological
(e) figure; ground

2. (a) principles; similarity, closure, good continuation, proximity
(b) best, simplest; *law of simplicity*
(c) Gestalt principles
(d) *Prägnanz*

Perception: Depth Perception (Part 3)

1. (a) depth perception
(b) monocular

2. (a) relative size
(b) overlap
(c) aerial perspective
(d) texture gradient
(e) linear perspective
(f) motion parallax

3. (a) pictorial
(b) accommodation

4. (a) binocular
(b) convergence
(c) convergence
(d) binocular disparity
(e) close by; farther away
(f) binocular disparity

Perception: The Perception of Motion (Part 4)

1. (a) movements
(b) background
(c) eye muscle; retinal; background
(d) direction; speed

2. (a) object; induced
(b) induced; frame

3. (a) stroboscopic
(b) visual system
(c) stroboscopic

4. (a) auditory
(b) louder; direction
(c) time lag; loudness

5. (a) Gestalt
(b) ground; figure
(c) retinal disparity
(d) relative size
(e) linear perspective
(f) stroboscopic motion
(g) bottom-up processing

Matching Exercise 5

1. Gestalt psychology
2. law of Prägnanz

3. aerial perspective
4. binocular disparity
5. figure-ground relationship
6. overlap
7. binocular cues
8. accommodation
9. Karl Dunker
10. stroboscopic motion
11. depth perception
12. figure-ground reversal
13. Max Wertheimer
14. parapsychology

True/False Test 5

1. T	6. T	11. F
2. F	7. T	12. T
3. F	8. T	13. F
4. F	9. F	14. T
5. T	10. T	

Perception: Perceptual Constancies (Part 5)

1. (a) perceptual constancy
(b) would be in a constant state of flux

2. (a) retina
(b) larger; afterimage

3. (a) shape constancy
(b) perception

4. (a) same; change
(b) proportion

Perceptual Illusions and the Effects of Experience on Perceptual Interpretations

1. (a) perceptual illusion
(b) illusions; normal

2. (a) lengths of lines
(b) farther away; closer
(c) Size
(d) identical; longer

3. (a) bigger (larger)
(b) the same as
(c) more distant (farther away); overlap
(d) size; larger
(e) the same size

4. (a) illusions
(b) interpretation
(c) psychological

5. (a) educational, cultural; life
   (b) perceptual set
   (c) perceptual sets
6. (a) perceptual sets
   (b) farther away
   (c) shape
   (d) Müller-Lyer

Matching Exercise 6

1. perceptual set
2. perceptual constancy
3. Müller-Lyer illusion
4. size constancy
5. impossible figures

True/False Test 6

1. F   3. T
2. T   4. T

Something to Think About

1. First, you would note that these strange experiences happen to many people, that there is nothing particularly unique about them. The problem arises in the way people interpret these experiences. These experiences, of course, do not constitute proof of ESP, no matter how strongly someone believes they do. Two less extraordinary concepts can explain these occurrences: coincidence and the fallacy of positive instances. Coincidence, which refers to an event occuring simply by chance, can account for many of the experiences reported by people. Combine coincidence with our tendency to remember coincidental events that seem to confirm our belief about unusual phenomena—the fallacy of positive instances—and the feeling that something unusual has happened can be very strong, even though there are no rational grounds for it. Finally, there is no strong scientific evidence for the existence of ESP, despite years of intensive study by psychologists interested in this topic. To date, no parapsychology experiment that has claimed to show evidence of ESP has been successfully replicated. This, of course, does not prove conclusively that ESP does not exist; however, although one should keep an open mind, there is not a shred of evidence or any rational reason to believe in its existence.

2. Some of the most common monocular or pictorial cues that are useful in conveying a sense of depth on the canvas are overlap, in which "nearer" objects are depicted as blocking or obscuring more "distant" objects; linear perspective, in which parallel lines are depicted as converging toward the top of the painting, for instance; and texture gradient, in which surfaces that are supposed to be close to the observer have distinct, clearly defined textures and those that are gradually less and less clearly defined depict distance. Relative size and aerial perspective are also useful devices to convey depth.

   To make your picture more interesting you might want to attempt to incorporate some of the elements from impossible figures (such as the Escher drawings) or perceptual illusions.

Progresst Test 1

1. b	6. b	11. d
2. d	7. c	12. c
3. a	8. a	13. b
4. b	9. a	14. b
5. a	10. a	15. c

Progress Test 2

1. d	6. d	11. a
2. a	7. d	12. c
3. b	8. a	13. b
4. a	9. c	14. d
5. b	10. b	15. c

Progress Test 3

1. a	6. b	11. d
2. d	7. c	12. a
3. a	8. b	13. d
4. d	9. a	14. c
5. b	10. b	15. b

Consciousness and Its Variations

PREVIEW

Reading the section below first will give you a general sense of the chapter's contents and an initial introduction to some of the major concepts and terms. This will prime you for what you are about to read and help you to develop a "cognitive map" that will guide your study of the material in this chapter. Likewise, reading the **preview questions** at the beginning of each major section will improve your ability to understand, learn, and retain the information.

CHAPTER 4 . . . AT A GLANCE

Chapter 4 examines the different forms of human consciousness, beginning with how biological and environmental "clocks" regulate our circadian rhythms and sleep-wake cycles. The discovery of REM sleep and how the EEG is used to measure brain-wave activity are discussed. This is followed by an examination of the different stages of sleep and their associated brain-wave activity and behavioral patterns, including the various sleep disorders. The section concludes with an exploration of dreams and mental activity during sleep. Two major theories of the meaning of dreams and their relevance to psychological and physiological functioning are presented.

Altered states of consciousness are introduced next, and both hypnosis and meditation are discussed in this context. Under hypnosis, profound sensory and perceptual changes may be experienced. This section focuses on phenomena such as posthypnotic suggestion, posthypnotic amnesia, and hypermnesia. Hilgard's notions of dissociation and the hidden observer are examined, and the controversy surrounding how to explain hypnosis is discussed. Finally, meditation is defined, and techniques for inducing a meditative state are presented along with research findings on transcendental meditation, or TM.

The final section of the chapter is concerned with using drugs to alter consciousness. The psychoactive drugs are classified and listed along with their various effects on brain activity and physiological and psychological functioning. Drug dependence, drug tolerance, withdrawal symptoms, and drug abuse are discussed.

Introduction: Consciousness: Experiencing the "Private I"

Preview Questions

Consider the following questions as you study this section of the chapter.

- How is consciousness defined, and what did William James mean by "stream of consciousness"?
- Why was research on consciousness abandoned for a time, and why did it regain legitimacy?

Read the section "Introduction: Consciousness: Experiencing the 'Private I'" and **write** *your answers to the following:*

1. (a) Your immediate awareness of

   _____ , _____ ,

   _____ , and the world around

   you represents the experience of consciousness.

   (b) Even though your conscious experience is

   constantly _____ , you don't

   experience your personal consciousness as

   _____ .

2. (a) The psychologist who described consciousness as a stream or river—always changing but unified and unbroken—was

   _____ .

   (b) The subjective experience of consciousness

   has a feeling of _____ , which

   helps provide us with a sense of personal

   identity.

3. (a) In the late 1800s, the first psychologists tried to capture the structure of conscious experience through the technique of

   _____ ; this approach was aban-

   doned because such subjective

   _____ were not objectively

   verifiable.

   (b) As a result of the problem of verification, psychologists at the turn of the century emphasized the scientific study of

   _____ , which could be directly

   observed, measured, and verified.

4. In the late 1950s, psychologists returned to the study of consciousness because

   (a) It was becoming abundantly clear that a complete understanding of behavior was not possible until the role of

   _____ in behavior

   was considered.

   (b) Psychologists had developed

   _____ of

   study. Technological advances in studying

   _____ activity were producing

   intriguing results.

The Biological and Environmental "Clocks" Regulating Consciousness

Preview Questions

Consider the following questions as you study this section of the chapter.

- What are circadian rhythms?
- What roles do the suprachiasmatic nucleus (SCN), sunlight, and melatonin play in regulating circadian rhythms?
- How do "free-running" conditions affect circadian rhythms?
- Why do people suffer jet-lag symptoms, and what role does melatonin play in producing these symptoms?

Read the section "The Biological and Environmental 'Clocks' Regulating Consciousness" and **write** *the answers to the following:*

1. (a) The most obvious variation in consciousness that we experience is the daily

   _____ cycle.

   (b) The psychological and biological fluctuations that systematically vary over a period of about 24 hours refers to our

   _____ . Examples of

   things that undergo daily highs and lows

   include _____ alertness and

   the _____ cycle.

   (c) Researchers have identified over 100

   _____ that ebb and flow over any

given 24-hour period, such as blood pressure, the secretion of different hormones, and pain sensitivity.

2. (a) All your many circadian rhythms are controlled by a master biological clock in a tiny cluster of neurons in the brain's _____—called the _____ .

(b) The _____ is the internal pacemaker that governs the timing of circadian rhythms, including the sleep-wake and mental alertness cycles.

(c) One of the most important environmental time cues that helps keep the circadian rhythms synchronized to one another on a 24-hour schedule is _____ , especially _____ .

(d) As the sun sets each day, the decrease in available light is detected by the _____ through its connections to the visual system; this triggers an increase in the pineal gland's production of a hormone called _____ .

(e) Increased blood levels of the hormone _____ make you sleepy; at night the level of this hormone peaks between 1:00 and 3:00 A.M.; shortly before sunrise, or if exposed to bright lights, the _____ gland all but stops producing the hormone, and you soon wake up.

(f) Sunlight sets, or _____ , the SCN so that it keeps circadian cycles _____ and operating on a 24-hour schedule.

3. (a) Researchers have had volunteers live in underground bunkers or caves for various periods of time in order to deprive them of all _____ and create "free-running" conditions.

(b) Under free-running conditions two effects occur: first, people tend to drift to the SCN's natural rhythm of roughly a _____

day and, second, their _____ lose their normal synchronization with one another.

(c) When people leave the free-running condition and are once again exposed to normal daylight, sunlight _____ the biological clock within days, and circadian rhythms become _____ with one another once again and resume operating on a 24-hour cycle.

4. (a) When environmental time cues are out of sync with our internal biological clock, we may experience _____ effects, such as fatigue and disrupted sleep, and _____ effects, such as unclear thinking, loss of concentration, memory problems, depression, irritability, and mental fatigue, which collectively are called _____ .

(b) The circadian cycle of the hormone _____ seems to play a key role in making you feel very sleepy, sluggish, and groggy after a long flight over many time zones.

(c) Night-shift workers such as nurses, doctors, and people who work in law enforcement, the military, broadcasting, and weather services can all experience the symptoms of _____ because their circadian rhythms are out of sync with daylight/darkness time cues.

(d) After working a night shift, people returning home are often exposed to bright morning light, which is a potent stimulus and can reset the person's _____ to a day schedule.

5. Read the following and write the correct term in the space provided.
(a) Sheena works night shifts and has found that she can sleep quite well during the day now that she has hung heavy curtains in her bedroom that effectively block out any

daylight. She is able to get restful sleep in the daytime because her _____ are staying in sync with her night work schedule, and she has prevented sunlight from resetting her _____ .

(b) Although Marvin was very tired after pulling an "all-nighter" to finish a paper, he began to feel much less drowsy as the morning proceeded. His reaction is probably due to decreased levels of the hormone _____ .

(c) David typically experiences a slump in his mental alertness around midafternoon but feels very energetic in the early evening. These daily highs and lows are examples of _____ .

(d) During a history lecture, Alfie is listening and taking notes but at times he is also thinking about his girlfriend and the argument they had last night. He wonders what he will say to her when he phones her that afternoon, which gets him thinking about how often his parents fight and whether arguing is genetic, which reminds him about his biology exam next week. This description reflects Alfie's _____ .

(e) Dr. Parizeau arranges for volunteers to spend several weeks in underground bunkers without exposure to sunlight, clocks, or other environmental time cues, and during this time he monitors their sleep-wake cycles and other biological changes. Dr. Parizeau is attempting to create _____ in his research on circadian rhythms.

Review of Terms, Concepts, and Names 1

Use the terms in this list to complete the Matching Test, then to help you answer the True/False items correctly.

consciousness
William James
introspection
circadian rhythm
biological clock
suprachiasmatic nucleus (SCN)
melatonin
pineal gland
free-running condition
jet lag
biorhythms

Matching Exercise

Match the appropriate term/name with its definition or description:

1. _____ Personal awareness of mental activities, internal sensations, and the external environment.

2. _____ Subjective verbal reports that try to capture the structure of conscious experience through examining one's present mental state.

3. _____ Cluster of neurons in the brain's hypothalamus that governs the timing of circadian rhythms.

4. _____ Symptoms such as physical and mental fatigue, depression, irritability, disrupted sleep, and fuzziness in concentration, thinking, and memory that result from circadian rhythms being out of sync with daylight/darkness cues.

5. _____ Hormone manufactured by the pineal gland that produces sleepiness.

6. _____ A pseudoscience based on the unproven notion that from birth onward, three rigidly fixed natural rhythms reflect high, low, and critical periods of a person's physical, emotional, and intellectual functioning.

True/False Test

Indicate whether each statement is true or false by placing T or F in the blank space next to each item.

1. ___ The "biological clock" is another name for the tiny cluster of neurons in the hypothalamus called the suprachiasmatic nucleus, or SCN.

2. ___ William James was the American psychologist who proposed that psychology should not study consciousness because it could not be objectively investigated; instead, psychology should emphasize the scientific study of overt, observable behavior.

3. ___ The pineal gland is an endocrine gland located in the brain that regulates the production of the hormone melatonin.

4. ___ Researchers have had volunteers live in underground bunkers, depriving them of all environmental time cues for various periods of time, in order to create free-running conditions.

5. ___ Circadian rhythm refers to a cycle or rhythm that is roughly 24 hours long and involves cyclical daily fluctuations in biological and psychological processes.

> Check your answers and review any areas of weakness before going on to the next section.

Sleep

Preview Questions

Consider the following questions as you study this section of the chapter.

- How did the invention of the electroencephalograph and the discovery of REM sleep contribute to modern sleep research?
- What are the characteristics of the sleep stages?
- How do sleep patterns change over the life-span?
- Why do we need to sleep?
- How do the restorative and adaptive theories of sleep explain the function of sleep?

*Read the section "Sleep" and **write** your answers to the following:*

1. (a) The electroencephalograph measures the rhythmic electrical activity of the brain called _____ .

   (b) The electroencephalograph produces a graphic record called a(n) _____ , or _____ .

   (c) Along with brain activity, sleep researchers monitor a variety of other _____ functions during sleep, such as eye movements, muscle movements, body temperature, blood pressure, and breathing rate.

2. (a) Researchers found that particular brain-wave activity, as measured by the EEG, was often associated with rapid movements of the sleeper's eyes; this heralded the discovery of _____ sleep,

abbreviated as _____ .

   (b) Today, researchers distinguish between _____ sleep, often called active sleep or paradoxical sleep, and _____ sleep, or _____ . sleep, often called quiet sleep.

   (c) Active sleep is associated with heightened bodily and brain activity during which _____ consistently occurs; in quiet sleep, the body's physiological functions and brain activity _____ .

3. (a) When you are awake and reasonably alert, your brain generates small, fast brain waves, called _____ brain waves; when you relax and close your eyes, your brain's electrical activity slows down, generating _____ brain waves.

   (b) During the drowsy transition from wakefulness to light sleep, you may experience odd but vividly realistic sensations called _____ .

   (c) The vivid sensation of falling is probably the most common _____ . It is often accompanied by an involuntary muscle spasm of the whole body that can jolt the person awake, called a _____ , or sleep start.

4. (a) As people drift off to sleep, they initially enter NREM sleep and begin a progression through _____ stages of NREM sleep; each stage is characterized by corresponding _____ (increases/decreases) in brain and body activity, and progression through these NREM stages occupies the first 50 to 70 minutes of sleep.

   (b) When you enter the first stage of sleep, the _____ brain waves associated with drowsiness are replaced by even slower _____ brain waves.

(c) Stage 1 NREM sleep lasts only a few minutes; during this stage, a person is _____ (easily awakened/difficult to awaken).

(d) Stage 2 represents the onset of true sleep and is marked by the appearance of bursts of brain activity called _____ .

(e) Theta brain waves are predominant in stage 2, but large, slow brain waves called _____ brain waves also begin to emerge and gradually increase in frequency over the 15 to 20 minutes spent in stage 2.

5. (a) Stages 3 and 4 of NREM sleep are physiologically very _____ (similar/different); both stages are defined by the amount of delta brain wave activity, and combined they are referred to as _____ sleep.

(b) When delta brain waves represent more than 20 percent of total brain activity, the sleeper is said to be in stage _____ NREM sleep; when they exceed 50 percent, the sleeper is said to be in stage _____ NREM sleep.

(c) During the 20 to 40 minutes spent in the night's first episode of stage 4 NREM sleep, delta waves eventually come to represent 100 percent of brain activity; during this stage, the person is _____ (easily awakened/difficult to awaken).

(d) During stage 4 NREM sleep, blood pressure and other physiological functions are at their_____ (highest levels/lowest levels) and the muscles are still capable of movement; _____ can occur during this stage.

(e) When researchers briefly awaken people during stage _____ and ask

them to perform some simple task, they can do so but generally don't remember it the next morning.

(f) After approximately 70 minutes into a typical night's sleep, the sequence of stages reverses itself; within minutes, the sleeper cycles back from stage _____ to stage_____ to stage _____ , and then enters a dramatic new phase, the night's first episode of _____ sleep.

6. (a) During _____ sleep, the brain becomes more active, generating smaller and faster brain waves, and visual and motor neurons fire repeatedly, just as they do during wakefulness.

(b) _____ usually occur during REM sleep. Although the brain is very active, voluntary _____ activity is suppressed.

(c) REM sleep is accompanied by considerable _____ arousal; heart rate, blood pressure, and respiration can fluctuate up and down, muscles twitch, and in both sexes, sexual arousal may occur.

(d) Throughout the night, the sleeping person cycles between NREM and REM sleep, with each cycle lasting about _____ minutes on average, but the duration of cycles may vary from _____ to _____ minutes.

(e) As the night progresses, episodes of _____ sleep become increasingly longer and less time is spent in _____ sleep.

(f) Stage _____ and stage _____ slow-wave sleep usually occur only during the first two ninety-minute cycles; during the last two 90-minute cycles before awakening, periods of REM sleep can last as long as 40 minutes; NREM sleep is composed primarily of stage _____ sleep.

7. (a) Over the course of our lives, the
_____ and _____
of sleep change considerably.

(b) Four months before birth, virtually all of
fetal life is spent in _____
sleep; one month before birth, the fetus
demonstrates distinct _____
cycles, spending 12 hours each day in REM
sleep; at birth, the newborn sleeps about 16
hours a day, up to _____ per-
cent of which is in REM sleep.

(c) From birth onward, the average amount of
time spent sleeping gradually
_____ ; the amount of time
devoted to REM sleep and slow-wave NREM
sleep also gradually _____ over
the lifespan, with more time being spent in
lighter stage _____ NREM sleep.

8. (a) That we have a biological need for sleep has
been demonstrated by _____
studies, and with as little as one day's sleep
deprivation research subjects will develop
_____ , episodes of sleep last-
ing only a few seconds that occur during
wakefulness.

(b) People who do not sleep for a day or more
also experience disruptions in mood, mental
abilities, _____ ,
_____ , and complex
motor skills.

(c) If subjects in one group are selectively
deprived of REM sleep and those in another
group are selectively deprived of slow-wave
NREM sleep, subjects in the first group will
experience _____ whereas those in the
second group will experience
_____ when allowed to sleep
uninterrupted.

9. (a) Sleep and dreaming promote physiological
processes that renew, repair, and rejuvenate
the body and mind, according to the
_____ theory of sleep.

(b) Research suggests that NREM sleep is
important for restoring the
_____ ; the secretion of growth
hormone, testosterone, prolactin, and other
hormones _____ (increases/
decreases) during NREM sleep. REM sleep
is important for restoring the
_____ .

(c) The sleep patterns exhibited by different
animals, including humans, reflect the survival value of being prevented from interacting with the environment when doing so is
most hazardous, according to the
_____ theory of
sleep.

(d) Animals with few natural predators, such as
gorillas and lions, sleep _____ (more/less)
than grazing animals such as cattle and
horses.

(e) Although researchers still aren't sure exactly what functions are served by sleep, there
is evidence to support the
_____ theory of
sleep _____ (and/but not) the
_____ theory of
sleep.

Sleep Disorders: Troubled Sleep

Preview Questions

*Consider the following questions as you study this
section of the chapter.*

- What are sleep disorders, who suffers from
  them, and how common are they?
- How is insomnia defined?
- What are the characteristics of sleep apnea,
  sleepwalking, night terrors, REM sleep behavior disorder, and narcolepsy?

*Read the section "Sleep Disorders: Troubled Sleep"
and **write** your answers to the following:*

1. Sleep disorders are _____
_____ .

2. (a) The most common sleep complaint among adults is _____ , which occurs when people repeatedly complain about the quality or duration of their sleep, when they experience difficulty going to sleep or staying asleep, or when they wake before it is time to get up.

   (b) A treatment strategy in which the person is conditioned to associate the bed only with sleepiness and sleep, called _____ , has been used to help people develop better sleep habits.

   (c) Alcohol, over-the-counter medications, and even sleep-inducing medications that physicians sometimes prescribe are generally not recommended for dealing with _____ .

3. (a) The second most common sleep disorder is _____ , which affects some 20 million Americans. It is more common in older men, especially those with a weight problem.

   (b) In this disorder, the sleeper repeatedly _____ during the night and carbon dioxide builds up in the blood, causing a momentary awakening during which the sleeper snorts or gulps in air.

4. (a) Unlike insomnia, sleepwalking and night terrors are much more common in _____ than in adults.

   (b) Sleepwalking and night terrors usually occur during stages _____ and _____ of NREM sleep.

   (c) As compared with adolescents or adults, children spend considerably more time each night in _____ sleep; thus, most episodes of bedwetting, or _____ , occur then.

   (d) About 25 percent of all children have at least one episode of somnambulism, or

   _____ , which typically occurs during the first three hours of sleep.

   (e) Like sleepwalking, sleep terrors, or _____ , typically occur during stage 3 or 4 of NREM sleep; nightmares and dreams, on the other hand, usually occur during _____ sleep.

   (f) The first sign of a sleep terror in a child is sharply increased _____—restlessness, sweating, and racing heart. The child abruptly sits up in bed and lets out a panic-stricken cry or scream as he or she thrashes about in bed or even sleepwalks.

   (g) Surprisingly, the child quickly goes back to sleep and wakes in the morning _____ (with a clear/with no) memory of the incident.

   (h) A sleep disorder in which people grind their teeth during sleep is called _____ . Along with night terrors and sleepwalking, it is categorized as a _____ , a general category of sleep disorders that involve arousal or activation during sleep or sleep transitions.

5. (a) The behavior of a person (typically a male over 60) with _____ may involve leaping out of bed, running around the room, lashing out at imagined intruders, or tackling furniture.

   (b) It is believed that a person with this disorder is acting out his dreams because of the brain's failure to suppress _____ during _____ sleep.

   (c) Excessive daytime sleepiness and brief lapses into sleep throughout the day, usually lasting an hour or less, is the most common symptom of _____ ; some people with the disorder experience dramatic sudden daytime _____ that last up to several minutes.

(d) Laughter, anger, surprise, sexual arousal, and other forms of arousal can trigger _____ , in which sufferers instantly enter REM sleep and experience _____ ; that is, their muscle go limp and they collapse.

(e) Vivid and sometimes terrifying _____ are common during sleep attacks.

6. Read the following and write the correct term in the space provided.

(a) James went to bed a short while ago; although his eyes are closed and he is very relaxed, he has not yet fallen asleep. If James's brain is relatively normal, it is probably generating _____ brain waves.

(b) Shortly after falling asleep, James experiences a muscle spasm that jolts him awake. James has most likely experienced the most common hypnagogic hallucination of _____ accompanied by a _____ .

(c) Bjorn, who has been under a lot of stress ever since he started college, is having trouble sleeping. He repeatedly complains about the quality and duration of his sleep, and worry about not sleeping well often keeps him awake at night. Bjorn is most likely to be diagnosed as suffering from _____ .

(d) In an attempt to deal with his sleep disturbance, Bjorn decides to try an over-the-counter sleep medication combined with alcohol. Bjorn's approach is most likely to make his problem _____ (better/worse) in the long run.

(e) After being asleep for about 2 hours, eight-year-old Soo Mee suddenly sits up in bed screaming incoherently. Her mother has trouble waking her and calming her down. Soo Mee is experiencing a(n) _____ and is probably in stage _____ or _____ of NREM sleep.

(f) Salim is enjoying a night out with a bunch of his college friends at Yuk Yuks comedy club. While laughing heartily at a very funny act, he suddenly goes limp and falls asleep for a few minutes. It is likely that Salim is suffering an attack of _____ and has instantly entered REM sleep and experienced _____ .

(g) Mrs. Eastman has just turned 65 and is worried because she is waking up more easily nowadays, sleeps less than 7 hours most nights, and feels less rested and less satisfied after sleeping. A sleep specialist is most likely to say that she _____ _____ .

(h) Azra has been asleep for about ten minutes and is now in stage 2 sleep. Her brain-wave activity is likely to be predominantly _____ waves and to be marked by _____ .

Graphic Organizer 1

The diagram below shows the brain waves typical of each stage in a 90-minute (approximately) sleep cycle. Match the term or description with the correct brain-wave pattern.

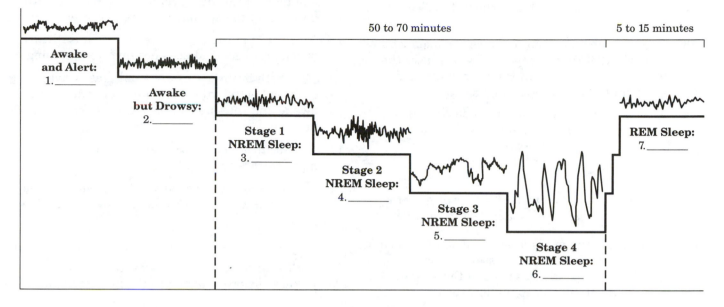

A. Brain waves associated with dreaming

B. Sleep spindles

C. Beta brain waves

D. Mixture of theta and delta brain waves

E. Alpha brain waves

F. Delta brain waves

G. Mixture of alpha and theta brain waves

Review of Terms and Concepts 2

Use the terms in this list to complete the Matching Test, then to help you answer the True/False items correctly.

electroencephalograph
electroencephalogram (EEG)
REM sleep (active or paradoxical sleep)
NREM sleep (quiet sleep)
beta brain waves
alpha brain waves
hypnagogic hallucinations
myoclonic jerk (sleep starts)
theta brain waves
sleep spindles
slow-wave sleep
delta brain waves
microsleeps
REM rebound

NREM rebound
restorative theory of sleep
adaptive (evolutionary) theory of sleep
sleep disorders
insomnia
sleepwalking (somnambulism)
nocturnal enuresis
night terrors (sleep terrors)
sleep bruxism
parasomnias
REM sleep behavior disorder
sleep apnea
narcolepsy
sleep paralysis

Matching Exercise

Match the appropriate term with its definition or description.

1. _____ Condition in which a person regularly is unable to fall asleep, stay asleep, or feel adequately rested by sleep.

2. _____ Type of sleep during which rapid eye movements and dreaming occur, and voluntary muscle activity is suppressed; also called active sleep or paradoxical sleep.

3. _____ The view that sleep and dreaming are essential to normal physical and mental functioning.

4. _____ Brain-wave pattern associated with relaxed wakefulness and drowsiness.

5. _____ Sleep disorder in which the person repeatedly stops breathing during sleep.

6. _____ Graphic record of brain activity produced by an electroencephalograph.

7. _____ Short bursts of brain activity that characterize stage 2 NREM sleep.

8. _____ Vivid sensory phenomena that can occur during the onset of sleep.

9. _____ Term applied to the combination of stage 3 and stage 4 sleep.

10. _____ Involuntary muscle spasm of the whole body that jolts the person completely awake and often accompanies the hypnagogic hallucination of falling.

11. _____ Bodily state of narcoleptics when, during a sleep attack, their muscles go limp and they collapse.

12. _____ Sleep disorder in which the sleeper acts out his or her dreams.

13. _____ Phenomenon in which a person who is deprived of REM sleep greatly increases the amount of time spent in REM sleep at the first opportunity for uninterrupted sleep.

14. _____ Instrument that uses electrodes placed on the scalp to measure and record the brain's electrical activity.

True/False Test

Indicate whether each statement is true or false by placing T or F in the blank space next to each item.

1. ___ NREM rebound is a phenomenon in which a person who is deprived of stage 3 and 4 NREM sleep spends less time in these stages when permitted to sleep undisturbed.

2. ___ The adaptive (evolutionary) theory of sleep suggests that unique sleep patterns of different animals evolved over time to help promote survival and environmental adaptation.

3. ___ Sleep disorders are serious disturbances in the normal sleep pattern that interfere with daytime functioning and cause subjective distress.

4. ___ Narcolepsy is a sleep disorder in which the person repeatedly stops breathing during sleep and awakens momentarily.

5. ___ Sleep bruxism is a sleep disorder in which people grind their teeth loudly during sleep.

6. ___ Sleepwalking (somnambulism) is a sleep disturbance characterized by an episode of walking or performing other actions during stage 3 or stage 4 NREM sleep.

7. ___ Parasomnias are sleep disorders characterized by arousal or activation during sleep or sleep transitions; they include sleepwalking, night terrors, sleep bruxism, and REM sleep behavior disorder.

8. ___ Beta brain waves are patterns of electrical activity that begin in stage 1 NREM sleep and predominate in stage 2 NREM sleep.

9. ___ Episodes of sleep lasting only a few seconds that occur during wakefulness are called microsleeps; they can occur after as little as one day's sleep deprivation.

10. ___ Night terrors typically occur during stage 3 or stage 4 NREM sleep and are characterized by increased physiological arousal, intense fear and panic, frightening hallucinations, and with no recall of the episode the next morning.

11. ___ NREM sleep is quiet sleep, which is divided into four stages and does not involve dreaming.

12. ___ Theta brain waves are small, fast waves of electrical activity in the brain that reflect an awake and reasonably alert state of consciousness.

13. ___ *Nocturnal enuresis* is another name for night terrors or sleep terrors.

14. ___ Delta brain waves are the long, slow waves associated with stage 3 and stage 4 of NREM sleep.

Check your answers and review any areas of weakness before going on to the next section.

Dreams and Mental Activity During Sleep

Preview Questions

Consider the following questions as you study this section of the chapter.

- What is the difference between sleep thinking and dreaming?
- What are the main characteristics of dreams, and what are the most common themes in dreams?
- Why do we remember some dreams and forget others?
- How do nightmares and lucid dreams differ?
- How does Freud's theory of the meaning of dreams differ from the activation-synthesis model?
- What conclusions can we draw about the meaning of dreams?

Read the section "Dreams and Mental Activity During Sleep" and **write** *your answers to the following:*

1. (a) More prevalent than dreams is _____ , which occurs during

NREM sleep and consists of vague, uncreative, bland, and thoughtlike ruminations about real-life events.

(b) In contrast, a dream is an unfolding episode of mental images that is _____ , involving characters and events.

2. The five basic characteristics of a dream are
   (a) _____ can be intense;
   (b) _____ and _____ are usually illogical;
   (c) _____ are sometimes bizarre;
   (d) even bizarre details are
   _____ ;
   (e) the dream _____ are difficult to remember.

3. (a) Although dreams usually occur during _____ sleep, they can also occur during _____ sleep.
   (b) When people are awakened during _____ sleep, up to 90 percent of the time they will report a dream.

4. (a) Research has shown that the brain's activity during REM sleep is very _____ (similar to/different from) its activity during wakefulness and very _____ (similar to/different from) its activity during slow-wave NREM sleep.
   (b) During REM sleep, both the _____ and the _____ are essentially shut down, and thus the sleeper is cut off from both information about the external world and from the brain centers involved in rational thought.
   (c) Areas of the brain that are highly active during REM sleep include the _____ and the _____ (structures in the limbic system that are involved in emotion and memory); other parts of the brain's visual system are involved in generating _____ .

(d) REM sleep seems to be necessary to consolidate _____ for certain types of new information; REM sleep _____ (increases/decreases) after learning a novel task, and deprivation of REM following training _____ (disrupts/enhances) learning.

5. (a) The _____ of our dreams usually reflects our daily concerns, including worry about exams, money, health, or troubled relationships.
   (b) Certain themes such as _____ , being _____ , or being attacked are common across cultures; negative events are _____ (more/less) frequently reported than positive events.
   (c) In sleep labs, researchers have successfully influenced dream _____ while the subjects were asleep and dreaming.

6. (a) On average, we forget approximately 95 percent of our dreams. One theory suggests that this happens because fundamental changes in brain _____ and brain _____ during sleep fail to support our ability to process information and store it.
   (b) You are much more likely to recall a dream if you _____ during it.
   (c) The more vivid, bizarre, or emotionally intense a dream is, the more likely it is to be _____ the following morning.
   (d) Also, our ability to recall dreams is affected by the interference of _____ upon awakening.
   (e) It is difficult to remember _____ during sleep, not just dreams; during sleep, it seems that the brain is largely _____ to forget most experiences.

7. (a) An unpleasant anxiety dream that occurs during REM sleep and has a frightening or unpleasant theme is called a _____ ; these dreams are especially common in young children.

(b) In adults, an occasional _____ is a natural and relatively common experience and is not indicative of a psychological disorder or sleep disorder unless it frequently causes personal distress.

8. (a) A lucid dream is one in which a person becomes _____ that he or she is _____ .

(b) Lucid dreamers can often _____ the course of the dream.

9. (a) Freud believed that _____ and _____ instincts are the motivating forces that dictate human behavior, but because they are consciously unacceptable, they are pushed into the unconscious, or _____ .

(b) Freud proposed that fulfillments of repressed wishes and urges are found in disguised form in _____ , which function as a sort of psychological safety valve for the release of these unconscious and unacceptable desires.

(c) The actual images of a dream is the _____ ; the disguised psychological meaning is its _____ .

(d) According to Freud, dreams can be analyzed and the _____ content revealed by looking for symbolic expressions of repressed urges and wishes in the images of the _____ content; this belief _____ (has/has not) been substantiated by psychological research.

10. (a) Dreaming is our subjective awareness of the brain's internally generated signals during sleep, according to the _____ model.

(b) Specifically, this model maintains that the experience of dreaming is due to the automatic _____ of brain-stem circuits at the base of the brain that arouse more sophisticated brain areas, including the visual and auditory pathways and the amygdala and hippocampus, that we normally use to assess the external world.

(c) The activated brain combines, or _____ , internally generated sensory signals and imposes meaning on them; the dream story itself is derived from a hodgepodge of memories, emotions, and sensations that are internally triggered.

(d) The _____ model suggests that dreams make sense to the extent that they reflect how dreamers impose _____ on the images generated by their brain.

(e) Our dreams appear to mirror our real-life concerns. When we are awake, we monitor and try to make sense of the _____ environment; during sleep, we try to make sense of the less orderly _____ stimuli produced by the brain.

(f) The _____ of dreams occurs when you're awake, so it may be that conscious speculations about dreams reveal more about the characteristics of the interpreter than about the dream itself.

11. Read the following and write the correct term in the space provided.

(a) Meredith recalls having a dream about dancing in a ballet with a very big, strong, muscled male dancer when suddenly the music switches to loud rock music and the man disappears. According to Freud, Meredith's account represents the _____ of the dream.

(b) Dr. Dormo believes that Meredith's dream could be the result of a burst of neural activity that spread upward from the brain stem and activated more sophisticated brain areas. This interpretation is most consistent with the _____ model of dreaming.

(c) After falling asleep, Ricardo finds that his mind keeps returning to the material he has been studying all day in preparation for his exam the next morning. Ricardo is experiencing the most common form of mental activity during sleep, called

_____ .

(d) Dr. Roach is a cross-cultural psychologist interested in investigating sleep and dreams. His cross-cultural data are likely to show that the dreams of people in various parts of the world have _____ (common/no common) themes.

(e) Maxwell claims that he has no recollection of any dream when he wakes up in the morning, and he is convinced that he never dreams. One way to demonstrate to Maxwell that he does dream is to wake him up after he has been asleep for about

_____ minutes, when he is clearly in _____ sleep.

(f) Kerry is sometimes aware that she is dreaming, even though she is asleep, and can often determine the course and outcome of the dream. Kerry often says she feels like a movie director in these nighttime productions: Kerry is most probably a

_____ .

Review of Terms, Concepts, and Names 3

Use the terms in this list to complete the Matching Test, then to help you answer the True/False items correctly.

sleep thinking
dream
nightmare
lucid dream
Sigmund Freud
manifest content

latent content
J. Allan Hobson
Robert McCarley
activation-synthesis model

Matching Exercise

Match the appropriate term/name with its definition or description:

1. _____ Contemporary American psychiatrist and neurobiologist who extensively researched sleep and dreaming; proposed the activation-synthesis model of dreaming with coresearcher Robert McCarley.

2. _____ The founder of psychoanalysis who proposed that dream images are disguised and symbolic expressions of unconscious wishes and urges.

3. _____ Repetitive, bland, and uncreative ruminations about real-life events during sleep.

4. _____ Contemporary American psychiatrist and neuroscientist who extensively researched sleep and dreaming; proposed the activation-synthesis model of dreaming with coresearcher J. Allan Hobson.

5. _____ Dream in which the sleeper is aware that he or she is dreaming.

True/False Test

Indicate whether each item is true or false by placing T or F in the space next to each item

1. ___ A nightmare is a frightening or unpleasant anxiety dream that occurs during REM sleep.

2. ___ In Freud's psychoanalytic theory, the latent content of a dream refers to the elements that are consciously experienced and remembered by the dreamer.

3. ___ A dream is a storylike episode of unfolding mental imagery during sleep.

4. ___ The activation-synthesis model of dreaming states that brain activity during sleep produces dream images (*activation*), which are combined by the brain into a dream story (*synthesis*).

5. ___ In Freud's psychoanalytic theory, the manifest content of a dream refers to the unconscious wishes, thoughts, and urges that are concealed in the latent content of a dream.

Check your answers and review any areas of weakness before going on to the next section.

Hypnosis

Preview Questions

Consider the following questions as you study this section of the chapter.

- What is hypnosis, and what are the characteristics of the hypnotic state?
- What are the main characteristics of people who are susceptible to hypnosis?
- What are the effects of hypnosis, and what are its limits?
- How has hypnosis been explained?

*Read the section "Hypnosis" and **write** your answers to the following:*

1. (a) _____ is a cooperative social interaction in which one person, the subject, responds to suggestions by another person, which produces changes in perception, memory, and behavior.

   (b) It is characterized by highly focused _____ , increased responsiveness to _____ , vivid images and fantasies, and a willingness to accept _____ of logic or reality.

   (c) Children tend to be _____ (less/more) responsive to hypnosis than adults, and there is some evidence that the degree of hypnotic susceptibility may run in families.

   (d) The best candidates for hypnosis are individuals who approach the hypnotic experience with positive, receptive _____ and _____ and who have the ability to become deeply absorbed in _____ and _____ .

2. (a) Deeply hypnotized subjects sometimes experience feelings of _____ from their bodies, profound _____ , and sensations of _____ , but more often they can converse normally and remain fully aware of their surroundings.

   (b) Sensory changes that can be induced through hypnosis include temporary _____ , temporary _____ , or a complete loss of _____ in some part of the body.

   (c) Painful _____ and _____ procedures, including surgery, have been performed successfully with hypnosis as the only anesthesia.

   (d) People can also experience _____ while under hypnosis.

3. (a) When a _____ suggestion is made during hypnosis, the subject will carry out that specific suggestion after the hypnotic session is over; usually, these effects last only a few hours or days before they wear off.

   (b) Research on the effectiveness of hypnosis in modifying habitual behaviors such as smoking has provided _____ (little/lots of) evidence in support of this technique. Coupled with _____ , however, it enhances the effectiveness of weight-loss programs.

4. (a) In posthypnotic amnesia, a subject is unable to recall information or events that occurred _____ or _____ hypnosis, whereas in hypermnesia a subject's memory is supposedly enhanced for _____ .

   (b) Many studies have shown that efforts to enhance memories hypnotically can lead to _____ and _____ ; false memories, or _____ , can be inadvertently created when hypnosis is used to aid recall.

   (c) The problem of inaccurate, distorted, or contrived memories also frequently occurs in _____ , which refers to the use of hypnosis to recall or reexperience an earlier developmental period.

(d) As a general rule, hypnosis is much more effective in enhancing _____ in memories than in enhancing the accuracy of memories.

5. (a) A person _____ (can/cannot) be hypnotized against his or her will.

(b) Hypnosis _____ (can/cannot) make you stronger than your physical capabilities or induce talents that are not already present.

(c) Hypnosis _____ (can/cannot) enhance physical skills and athletic ability by increasing motivation and concentration or by reducing anxiety.

(d) Hypnosis _____ (can/cannot) make you perform behaviors that are contrary to your morals or values.

6. (a) Dissociation refers to the splitting of _____ into two or more simultaneous streams of mental activity.

(b) According to Hilgard's _____ , one stream responds to the hypnotist's suggestions, whereas the other, dissociated stream processes information that is unavailable to the consciousness of the hypnotized subject.

(c) The second, dissociated stream of mental activity is referred to as the _____ , but this does not mean that the hypnotized person has multiple personalities.

(d) Not all psychologists agree that hypnotic phenomena are due to dissociation, divided _____ , or a _____ , but rather it can be understood in terms of _____ and _____ factors.

(e) Hypnosis has been used in _____ , _____ , and _____ as well as in sports and business in attempts to improve performance and enhance motivation.

Meditation

Preview Questions

Consider the following questions as you study this section of the chapter.

- What is meditation, and what is it intended to accomplish?
- What are the two general categories of meditation?
- How does meditation work, and what are its effects?

*Read the section "Meditation" and **write** your answers to the following:*

1. (a) Meditation refers to a group of techniques that induce an altered state of focused _____ and heightened _____ .

(b) Meditation takes many forms, religious and nonreligious. Common to all forms of meditation are the goals of controlling or retraining _____ .

(c) Although meditation techniques vary a great deal, they can be divided into two general categories. In one technique, you focus awareness on a visual image, your breathing, a word, or a phrase; these are called _____ techniques. When a sound is used, it is typically a short word or a religious phrase, called a _____ , that is mentally repeated.

(d) Techniques involving a present-centered awareness of the passing moment without mental judgment, and a quiet awareness of the here and now without distracting thoughts are referred to as _____ techniques.

2. (a) A meditation technique widely used in research is _____ , in which the subjects sit quietly with eyes closed, mentally repeat their mantra, and use a strategy for getting rid of distracting thoughts.

(b) Numerous studies have shown that even beginning meditators practicing _____ experience a state of lowered physiological arousal, including lowered blood pressure, a decrease in heart rate, and changes in brain waves.

(c) Meditators show EEG patterns that are dominated by _____ brain-wave activity, which is similar to the state of drowsiness that precedes stage 1 sleep.

(d) Meditation appears to be _____ (more/no more) effective than mental relaxation. However, many experienced meditators describe the meditative experience as simultaneously producing _____ and a state of _____ , whereas people who practice mental relaxation with their eyes closed often describe the experience as relaxing but boring.

(e) Many studies have shown that transcendental meditation, or TM, _____ (does not enhance/enhances) physical and psychological functioning.

(f) Hypnosis and meditation are similar in that both involve the deliberate use of mental techniques to change the experience of _____ .

3. Read the following and write the correct term in the space provided.

(a) Janna quickly becomes deeply absorbed while reading novels or watching movies. It is very likely that Janna is among the 15 percent of adults who are _____ to hypnosis.

(b) While under hypnosis, Karl describes a very frightening experience of being lost at the fairground when he was 6 years old. When his therapist makes the suggestion that Karl will soon forget this traumatic event, he is attempting to induce _____ .

(c) During every final exam period, Declan gets very uptight and anxious. At the suggestion of a friend, he has tried using a meditation technique in which he focuses his awareness and attention by repeating a simple phrase over and over to himself. Declan is using a _____ technique of meditation.

(d) A researcher suggests to a hypnotized subject that the letter D does not exist. After being brought out of the trance, the subject is asked to recite the alphabet; when she does, she skips the letter D. This example illustrates the use of

_____ .

(e) An eyewitness to a robbery (who couldn't remember much of the incident) was hypnotized. When the hypnotherapist suggested that there had been three white men and one black woman involved in the robbery, the subject agreed and described them in some detail. All the other five witnesses reported that only one white male robber was involved. The hypnotherapist has created a _____ .

(f) Lynda has an irrational fear and dislike of cats. Her therapist hypnotizes her and asks her to remember her earliest childhood experience with a cat. The therapist is attempting to use _____ to uncover hidden memories.

Review of Terms, Concepts, and Names 4

Use the terms in this list to complete the Matching Test, then to help you answer the True/False items correctly.

hypnosis	neodissociation theory of
posthypnotic suggestion	hypnosis
posthypnotic amnesia	hidden observer
hypermnesia	meditation
pseudomemory	concentration technique
age regression	opening-up techniques
Ernest R. Hilgard	transcendental
dissociation	meditation (TM)

Matching Exercise

Match the appropriate term/name with its definition or description.

1. _____ Ernest Hilgard's theory that attributes hypnotic effects to the splitting of consciousness into two simultaneous streams of mental activity, only one of which is unavailable to the consciousness of the hypnotized subject.

2. _____ Meditative technique that has been widely used in research in which practitioners sit quietly with eyes closed, mentally repeat the mantra they have been given, and practice a strategy for getting rid of distracting thoughts.

3. _____ A cooperative social interaction in which the hypnotized person responds to the hypnotist's suggestions with changes in perception, memory, and behavior.

4. _____ The splitting of consciousness into two or more simultaneous streams of mental activity.

5. _____ Suggestion made during hypnosis that the person carry out a specific instruction following the hypnotic session.

6. _____ Hypnotic suggestion that supposedly enhances the person's memory for past events.

7. _____ Hilgard's term for the hidden, or dissociated, stream of mental activity during hypnosis.

True/False Test

Indicate whether each item is true or false by placing T or F in the space next to each item.

1. ___ Ernest Hilgard was an Austrian physician who discovered "animal magnetism" and whose pioneering work is associated with the origins of hypnotism.

2. ___ A concentration meditative technique involves a present-centered awareness of the passing moment without mental judgment and does not involve concentrating on a mantra or object or activity.

3. ___ In posthypnotic amnesia, the result of a posthypnotic suggestion, the subject is unable to recall specific information or events that occurred before or during hypnosis.

4. ___ The use of hypnosis to recall or reexperience an earlier developmental period is called age regression.

5. ___ Pseudomemories are false memories (even though the person may be very confident that the memories are real) that result when suggestions are made during hypnosis that create distortions and inaccuracies in recall.

6. ___ The opening-up meditative techniques involve focusing awareness on a visual image or your breathing, or mentally repeating a sound called a mantra.

7. ___ Meditation is any of a number of sustained concentration techniques that focus attention and heighten awareness.

Check your answers and review any areas of weakness before going on to the next section.

Psychoactive Drugs

Preview Questions

Consider the following questions as you study this section of the chapter.

- What are psychoactive drugs, and what properties do they have in common?
- What factors influence the effects, use, and abuse of drugs?
- How do depressants work, and what effects do alcohol, barbiturates, tranquilizers, and inhalants have?
- How do opiates affect the brain and relieve pain?
- How do stimulants affect the brain and psychological functioning?
- How do the most common psychedelic drugs influence perception, mood, and thinking?

*Read the section "Psychoactive Drugs" and **write** your answers to the following:*

1. (a) Two of the most widely used psychoactive drugs are _____ and _____ .

(b) Psychoactive drugs are _____ substances that can alter arousal, mood, thinking, sensation, and perception.

2. There are four broad categories of psychoactive drugs.

   (a) Drugs that depress, or inhibit, brain activity are called _____ .

   (b) Drugs that are chemically similar to morphine and that relieve pain and produce euphoria are the _____ .

   (c) Drugs that excite brain activity are called _____ .

   (d) Drugs that distort sensory perception are called _____ .

3. (a) The broad term that refers to a condition in which a person feels psychologically and physically compelled to take a specific drug is _____ .

   (b) When an individual experiences _____ , his body and brain chemistries have physically adapted to the drug.

   (c) Many physically addictive drugs gradually produce _____ , which means that increasing amounts of the drug are needed to gain the original, desired effect.

   (d) When a person is physically dependent on a drug, abstaining from the drug produces _____ , which are unpleasant physical reactions to the lack of the drug, plus an intense craving for it.

   (e) Withdrawal from stimulating drugs may produce _____ and fatigue, whereas withdrawal from depressant drugs may produce _____ ; the withdrawal symptoms are opposite to the drug's action, a phenomenon called the _____ .

4. (a) Biologically, psychoactive drugs disrupt brain activity by interfering with _____ transmission among neurons.

   (b) Drug effects can be influenced by the person's _____ , _____ , _____ , or _____ as well as whether the drug is taken on a full or empty stomach and whether the drug is taken alone or in combination with other drugs. How a drug is metabolized is affected by _____ and _____ differences.

   (c) Personality characteristics, mood, expectations, experience with the drug, and the _____ in which the drug is taken can also affect the drug response.

   (d) Recurrent drug use that results in disruptions in academic, social, or occupational functioning or in legal or psychological problems is referred to as _____ .

5. List six situations in which drug use is most likely to occur.

   (a) _____

   (b) _____

   (c) _____

   (d) _____

   (e) _____

   (f) _____

6. (a) The depressants are a class of drugs that depress or _____ central nervous system activity and result in drowsiness, sedation, or sleep and are potentially physically addictive. In addition, when taken in combination, their effects are _____ .

   (b) Used in _____ (large/small) amounts, alcohol reduces tension, anxiety, and possibly the risk of heart disease; it is also a dangerous drug with a high potential for misuse, or _____ .

   (c) Besides the amount of alcohol consumed,

factors such as body weight, gender, food consumption, and the rate of alcohol consumption also affect _____ levels.

(d) Alcohol depresses the activity of neurons throughout the brain and impairs cognitive abilities such as _____ , _____, and _____ and physical abilities such as muscle coordination and balance; in excessive amounts, alcohol can cause _____ .

(e) A particularly risky practice that involves having quite a few drinks in a row (five or more for men, and four or more for women) is called _____ .

(f) Because alcohol is physically addictive, _____ can include disrupted sleep, anxiety, and mild tremors for a low level of dependence, and confusion, hallucinations, severe tremors, and seizures for a high level of dependence; the severest symptoms are collectively called _____ .

(g) Psychological effects of alcohol depend on the person's environment and expectations, but the variety of experiences produced are due to the fact that alcohol _____ by depressing the brain centers responsible for judgment and self-control.

7. (a) "Downers," or _____ , are powerful drugs that reduce anxiety and promote sleep by depressing activity in the brain centers that control arousal, wakefulness, and alertness; they produce physical and psychological dependence.

(b) _____are depressants that are prescribed to relieve anxiety and, although chemically different, produce similar, although less powerful, effects as those produced by barbiturates.

(c) Inhalants refer to a number of chemical substances that are inhaled to produce an alteration in _____ ; they include

paint solvents, model airplane glue, gasoline, nitrous oxide, and certain aerosol sprays, all of which act as _____ depressants.

8. (a) A group of addictive drugs that relieve pain and produce feelings of euphoria are called _____ , or _____ .

(b) Natural opiates include _____ , which is derived from the opium poppy; _____ , the active ingredient in opium; and codeine, which can be derived from either _____ or _____ .

(c) Synthetic and semisynthetic opiates include _____ , methadone, and the prescription painkillers Percodan and Demerol.

(d) Opiates produce their powerful effects by mimicking the brain's own natural painkillers, called _____ .

(e) When used medically, opiates alter an individual's reaction to _____ by reducing the brain's perception of _____ ; people who take opiates for relief after surgery _____ (rarely/frequently) develop drug tolerance or dependence.

(f) The most frequently abused opiate is _____ , which produces an intense "rush" of euphoria followed by feelings of contentment, peacefulness, and warmth; ceasing to take the drug produces unpleasant _____ symptoms.

9. (a) All _____ drugs are at least mildly addicting, and all tend to increase brain activity.

(b) _____ is the drug found in coffee, tea, cola drinks, and many over-the-counter medications and is the most widely used _____ drug in the world; it stimulates the cerebral cortex, resulting in increased mental alertness and wakefulness, and is physically addictive.

(c) Regular coffee, tea, or cola drinkers will experience _____ _____ symptoms (headache, irritability, drowsiness, and fatigue) if they abruptly stop caffeine intake; in high doses, caffeine can produce anxiety, restlessness, insomnia, and increased heart rate.

(d) Another widely used, legal, and extremely addictive stimulant is _____ ; it is found in all tobacco products and can increase mental alertness and reduce fatigue and drowsiness.

(e) Functional MRI scans show that _____ increases neural activity in many areas of the brain, including the frontal lobes, thalamus, hippocampus, and amygdala.

(f) Smokers report that tobacco _____ (enhances/depresses) mood, attention, arousal, and vigilance; _____ symptoms include jumpiness, irritability, tremors, craving, headaches, drowsiness, brain fog, and light-headedness.

10. (a) Sometimes called "speed" or "uppers," _____ suppress appetite and can elevate mood and produce a sense of euphoria, but when abused, they can produce severe psychological and physical problems.

(b) Using any type of _____ for an extended period of time is followed by _____ , a term used to describe withdrawal symptoms of fatigue, deep sleep, intense mental depression, and increased appetite.

(c) Cocaine is an illegal _____ derived from the leaves of the coca tree, which is found in South America; when "snorted" in purified form, it reaches the brain in minutes and provides intense euphoria, mental alertness, and self-confidence, which last for several minutes.

(d) A more concentrated form of cocaine called _____ is smoked rather than inhaled.

(e) Prolonged use of either amphetamines or cocaine can result in _____ , which is characterized by schizophrenia-like symptoms, including auditory hallucinations of "voices" and bizarrely paranoid ideas; some people itch and tingle, claiming that insects or small animals are crawling on or under their skin.

11. (a) The term _____ was coined in the 1950s to describe a group of drugs that create profound perceptual distortions, alter mood, and affect thinking.

(b) Two such drugs, _____ , which is derived from the mushroom of the same name, and _____ , which is derived from the peyote cactus, have both been used for hundreds of years in religious rites in Mexico and Central America.

(c) In contrast to naturally occurring psychedelics, _____ is a much more potent and powerful synthetic psychedelic that can produce psychological effects with relatively few physiological changes.

(d) _____ and _____ are very similar chemically to the neurotransmitter serotonin, which is involved in regulating moods and sensations.

(e) Depending on an individual's personality, current emotional state, surroundings, and the other people present, the effects of a _____ experience vary greatly; adverse reactions to _____ include flashbacks, depression, long-term psychological instability, and prolonged psychotic reactions.

12. (a) One of the world's most widely used illegal drugs, _____ , is made from the dried and crushed leaves, stems, flowers, and seeds of the common plant *Cannabis sativa*; its active ingredient is the chemical _____ .

(b) Low to moderate doses of THC produce a sense of _____ , mild _____ , and a dreamy state of _____ , with enhanced taste, touch, and smell; higher doses can sometimes produce sensory distortions that resemble a mild _____ experience.

(c) This drug has been shown to be helpful in the treatment of _____ , epilepsy, _____ , asthma, and _____ ; in cancer patients it can prevent the nausea and vomiting caused by chemotherapy. Its medical use, however, is very limited and politically controversial.

(d) Most marijuana users _____ (do/do not) develop tolerance or physical dependence; some of the negative effects include interference with muscle coordination, perception, learning, memory, cognitive functions, and reproductive processes.

13. Read the following and write the correct term in the space provided.

(a) Sian regularly drinks five or six cups of strong coffee a day. If she is like most people, she would probably be surprised to find out that caffeine is a _____ drug and is _____ addictive.

(b) Zachary has been using a mood-altering, euphoria-enhancing psychoactive drug; with continued use, he needs to take larger and larger doses in order to experience its original effects. Zachary is developing _____ for the drug.

(c) At a party where he has had too much to drink, the normally shy Darryl keeps people entertained for quite a while with his silly antics. Darryl's unusual behavior is probably caused by the fact that alcohol lessens inhibitions by depressing the brain centers responsible for _____ and _____ .

(d) If he continues drinking at the party, Darryl will probably lose his coordination and balance; the next day, he might _____ (remember/not remember) very clearly the events of the evening before.

(e) While undergoing chemotherapy for cancer, Brendan is given marijuana to help prevent nausea and vomiting. It is very likely that Brendan _____ (will/will not) develop tolerance and physical dependence.

(f) Dora has been suffering from severe anxiety, so her doctor prescribes a depressant drug called Valium, which is a commonly prescribed _____ .

(g) Shortly after "snorting" an illegal psychoactive drug, Samuel experiences intense euphoria, mental alertness, and self-confidence that lasts for several minutes. It is most likely that Samuel has inhaled the stimulant drug _____ .

Graphic Organizer 2

Read the following examples, identify the drug involved, and indicate the type of drug it is.

Example	Drug Name	Drug Class
1. During a party Jordy becomes less and less inhibited as the night wears on, and by the time the party is nearly over, he is very unco-ordinated and unbalanced and has trouble walking.		
2. After taking her prescription drug for a number of weeks, Janet no longer feels the intense anxiety she used to suffer.		
3. Mrs. Smothers, who suffers from glaucoma, and Mr. Hartley, who has asthma, have both been given an ordinarily illegal drug at the university hospital.		
4. Harold has used a powerful synthetic drug for a number of years to create sensory and perceptual distortions and to alter his mood, but now he is experiencing flashbacks, depression, and occasional psychotic reactions.		
5. Henrietta was a very heavy coffee drinker until she quit cold turkey. She is now experiencing headaches, irritability, drowsiness, and fatigue.		
6. Following surgery, Gregory was given a common prescription drug under medical supervision in order to alleviate his pain.		
7. Just before his exam, Juan smokes a couple of cigarettes and finds he is less tired, more mentally alert, and yet fairly relaxed.		

Review of Terms and Concepts 5

Use the terms in this list to complete the Matching Test, then to help you answer the True/False items correctly.

psychoactive drug
physical dependence
tolerance
withdrawal symptoms
drug-rebound effect
drug abuse
depressants
binge-drinking
delirium tremens (DTs)
barbiturates
tranquilizers
inhalants
opiates (narcotics)
opium
morphine
stimulants

caffeine
nicotine
amphetamines
cocaine
stimulant-induced
    psychosis
psychedelic drugs
mescaline
LSD
psilocybin
marijuana
THC
hashish
sleep inertia
    (morning brain fog)

Matching Exercise

Match the appropriate term with its definition or description.

1. _____ The active ingredient of marijuana and other preparations derived from the hemp plant.

2. _____ Category of psychoactive drugs that depress or inhibit brain activity.

3. _____ Stimulant drug found in tobacco products.

4. _____ Recurrent drug use that results in dis-ruptions in academic, social, or occupational functioning or in legal or psychological prob-lems.

5. _____ Drug that alters normal conscious-ness, perception, mood, and behavior.

6. _____ Schizophrenia-like symptoms that can occur as the result of prolonged amphetamine or cocaine use.

7. _____ Psychedelic drug derived from the peyote cactus.

8. _____ Condition in which increasing amounts of a physically addictive drug are needed to produce the original, desired effect.

9. _____ Potent form of marijuana made from the resin of the hemp plant.

10. _____ Unpleasant physical reactions, combined with intense drug cravings, that occur when a person abstains from a drug on which he or she is physically dependent.

11. _____ Stimulant drug derived from the coca tree.

12. _____ Chemical substances that are inhaled to produce an alteration in consciousness.

13. _____ Class of stimulant drugs that arouse the central nervous system and suppress appetite.

14. _____ The collective term for withdrawal symptoms associated with high levels of alcohol dependence; may involve confusion, hallucinations, severe tremors, or seizures.

15. _____ Feelings of grogginess upon waking from sleep that interfere with the ability to perform mental or physical tasks.

True/False Test

Indicate whether each item is true or false by placing T or F in the space next to each item.

1. ___ Marijuana is a psychoactive drug derived from the hemp plant.

2. ___ Barbiturates are a category of depressant drugs that reduce anxiety and produce sleepiness.

3. ___ When withdrawal symptoms occur that are the opposite of a physically addictive drug's action, this is referred to as the drug-rebound effect.

4. ___ Caffeine is the stimulant drug found in tobacco products.

5. ___ Opium is a natural opiate derived from the opium poppy.

6. ___ Binge-drinking is defined as five or more drinks in a row for men, or four or more drinks in a row for women.

7. ___ Psilocybin is a psychedelic drug derived from the psilocybe mushroom, which is sometimes called "magic mushroom."

8. ___ LSD is the active ingredient of marijuana and other preparations derived from the hemp plant.

9. ___ Morphine is the active ingredient of the natural opiate called opium.

10. ___ Tranquilizers such as Valium and Librium are depressants that are prescribed to relieve anxiety.

11. ___ Psychedelic drugs are a category of psychoactive drugs that increase brain activity, as reflected in aroused behavior and increased mental alertness.

12. ___ Physical dependence is a condition in which a person has physically adapted to a drug so that the person must take the drug regularly in order to avoid withdrawal symptoms.

13. ___ Opiates are a category of psychoactive drugs that are chemically similar to morphine and have strong pain-relieving properties.

14. ___ Stimulants are a category of psychoactive drugs that create sensory and perceptual distortions, alter mood, and affect judgment by altering brain chemistry or activity.

> Check your answers and review any areas of weakness before going on to the next section.

Something To Think About

1. We've all heard the complaint, "there's so much to do, and so little time!" When people are busy and feel pressured, they often end up sleep-deprived, making them less efficient or productive than well-rested people. More important, they are more likely to make potentially dangerous mistakes. Those most at risk are shift workers or people who suffer jet-lag symptoms for other reasons.

    Imagine you are a consultant and have been asked to prepare a report for an organization concerned with these problems among its employees. Based on what you have learned about the sleep-wake cycle, circadian rhythms, biological and environmental clocks, and so on, what would you recommend in your report?

2. Almost everybody has some fascination with dreams and what they mean. Some people believe that dreams can foretell the future or are important in other mysterious ways. Suppose a friend tells you that she has dreamed that she could not understand a single question on a very important math exam. She just stared at the exam until the professor announced the exam was over and removed the

paper from in front of her. At this point, she awoke in a very anxious state. Now she is worried that when she takes the real exam next week, her dream will come true. What would you say to her about dreams and their meaning, lucid dreaming, theories of dreams, and such?

Check your answers and review any areas of weakness before doing the progress tests.

Progress Test 1

Review the complete chapter (including Concept Reviews and the boxed inserts), review all your study notes, and then test yourself on the following progress test. Check your answers. If you make a mistake, review your notes, the relevant section of the study guide, and, if necessary, go back and read the appropriate part of your textbook.

1. Nightmares are to _____ as night terrors are to _____ .
   (a) sleep spindles; beta waves
   (b) alpha waves; beta waves
   (c) REM sleep; slow-wave NREM sleep
   (d) slow-wave NREM sleep; REM sleep

2. The best predictor(s) of whether someone is likely to abuse drugs is (are)
   (a) being rebellious and feeling alienated.
   (b) having friends who use drugs.
   (c) social and cultural norms that are favorable to drug taking.
   (d) the availability and cost of the drug.
   (e) all of the above.

3. After ingesting a small dose of a psychoactive drug, Graham experiences vivid visual hallucinations and other perceptual distortions; he feels as if he is floating above his body. Graham is most likely experiencing the effects of
   (a) cocaine.   (d) LSD.
   (b) barbiturates.   (e) cappuccino.
   (c) tranquilizers.

4. "Consciousness is like a stream or river; it is continuous and cannot be divided or broken down into component parts." The person most likely to have made that statement is
   (a) Sigmund Freud.   (c) Ernest Hilgard.
   (b) William James.   (d) J. Allan Hobson.

5. After flying from San Diego to New York, Jasmine experiences a restless, sleepless night; the next day, she is irritable and cannot concentrate on her work. Jasmine's problems are likely due to
   (a) disruption in her circadian rhythms.
   (b) high blood levels of melatonin.
   (c) jet lag.
   (d) all of the above.

6. Justine believes that dreaming is simply our subjective awareness of the brain's internally generated signals during sleep, which start with automatic activation of brain-stem circuits that then arouse more sophisticated brain areas. Justine's views are most consistent with which theory of dreams?
   (a) adaptive theory
   (b) restorative theory
   (c) activation-synthesis theory
   (d) wish-fulfillment theory

7. In order to find out what goes on in people's brains during a typical night's sleep, researchers are most likely to
   (a) ask people to try to remember as much as possible when they awake in the morning
   (b) closely watch the actions of subjects sleeping in the sleep research lab.
   (c) wake people up every fifteen minutes and ask them what is going on in their mind.
   (d) use an electroencephalograph to measure their brain-wave activity throughout the night.

8. Just as you are about to fall asleep, you have the sudden feeling of falling and your body gives an involuntary spasm. You have experienced
   (a) a sleep spindle.
   (b) a myoclonic jerk.
   (c) sleep apnea.
   (d) a microsleep.

9. Harry has been asleep for about an hour or so, and his heart begins to beat faster, his breathing becomes irregular, his voluntary-muscle activity is suppressed, and his closed eyes move rapidly back and forth. It is most probable that Harry is in _____ and is therefore experiencing _____ .
   (a) REM sleep; a myoclonic jerk
   (b) NREM: sleep spindles
   (c) REM; paradoxical sleep
   (d) NREM; quiet sleep

10. Eight-year-old Billy gets out of bed at 1 A.M. and starts to sleepwalk. He is most likely
    (a) in slow-wave stage 3 or 4 NREM sleep.
    (b) suffering from narcolepsy.
    (c) in REM sleep.
    (d) suffering from sleep apnea.

11. After Zufina has been asleep for a period of time in the sleep lab, the EEG monitor indicates the presence of theta waves and sleep spindles. Zufina is in _____ sleep.
    (a) Stage 3 NREM   (c) Stage 2 NREM
    (b) REM   (d) Stage 4 NREM

12. Mr. Jensen repeatedly complains about the quality and duration of his sleep; he claims that he can't fall asleep and stay asleep and usually wakes up before it is time to get up. Mr. Jensen apparently suffers from
    (a) sleep apnea.   (c) nocturnal enuresis.
    (b) narcolepsy.   (d) insomnia.

13. People have no problem staying up a little later each night on the weekend. The most likely explanation for this is that
    (a) the SCN naturally tends toward a 25-hour day.
    (b) the SCN naturally tends toward a 23-hour day.
    (c) there are no obvious environmental time cues during the weekend.
    (d) there are much better late-night movies on TV during the weekend.

14. According to the Application, Improving Sleep and Mental Alertness, sleep inertia refers to
    (a) feelings of grogginess upon awakening from sleep that interfere with the ability to perform mental or physical tasks.
    (b) a sleep disorder in which the person stops breathing during sleep and awakens momentarily, only to return immediately to sleep.
    (c) the paralysis that accompanies stage 3 and 4 deep sleep.
    (d) the sudden involuntary spasm of the whole body during stage 1 sleep.

15. According to Critical Thinking 4.6, _____ theory suggests that hypnotic subjects are responding to social demands by acting the way they think good hypnotic subjects should act and by conforming to expectations and situational cues.
    (a) neodissociation   (c) activation-synthesis
    (b) social-cognitive   (d) adaptive

Progress Test 2

After you have checked your understanding of the material in Progress Test 1 and have done a complete chapter review with special focus on any areas of weakness, you are now ready to assess your knowledge in Progress Test 2. Check your answers. If you make a mistake, review your notes, the relevant section of the study guide, and, if necessary, the appropriate part of your textbook.

1. Dr. Benjamin hypnotizes a client and suggests that she will no longer feel a craving for chocolates. Dr. Benjamin is making use of
   (a) posthypnotic suggestion.
   (b) hypermnesia.
   (c) posthypnotic amnesia.
   (d) meditation.

2. Amber sits in a relaxed position, closes her eyes, and begins to recite her mantra. Amber is practicing
   (a) hypnosis.
   (b) meditation.
   (c) sleep inertia.
   (d) dissociation.
   (e) laziness.

3. Researchers who have found evidence that subjects appear to have a "hidden observer" are likely to suggest that hypnosis involves
   (a) dissociation.
   (b) social factors.
   (c) stages 3 and 4 NREM sleep.
   (d) experimenter bias.

4. John drinks five or six cups of coffee every day; if he doesn't, he feels irritable, drowsy, and fatigued. John is _____ a(n) _____ drug.
   (a) addicted to; psychedelic
   (b) physically dependent on; opiate
   (c) addicted to; depressant
   (d) physically dependent on; stimulant

5. Richard has just finished his fourth night shift and is driving home from work in the bright morning light. The most likely effect of this exposure is that
   (a) the bright light will reset his body clock to a day schedule.
   (b) he will become very drowsy and sleepy.
   (c) he will experience an increase in the production of melatonin.
   (d) all of the above will occur.

6. Nancy's parents took her to the doctor because she grinds her teeth loudly in her sleep. The doctor is likely to diagnose her with _____called _____ .
   (a) a parasomnia; nocturnal enuresis
   (b) a hypermnesia; somnambulism
   (c) a parasomnia; sleep bruxism
   (d) a hypermnesia; sleep inertia

7. Phelan has just had a very painful operation. His doctors are most likely to prescribe _____for pain relief.
   (a) a tranquilizer   (c) morphine
   (b) marijuana   (d) alcohol

8. Mr. Godfrey has cancer and was given marijuana to counter the nausea and vomiting following chemotherapy. The active ingredient that makes this a useful drug in such cases is
   (a) psilocybin.   (c) LSD.
   (b) cannabis.   (d) THC.

9. Sleep researchers deprive subjects of REM sleep for a number of nights but allow them an otherwise normal sleep; the subjects are likely to experience_____ when next allowed to sleep uninterrupted.
   (a) narcolepsy   (c) sleep inertia
   (b) REM rebound   (d) NREM rebound

10. Harold dreams that he is on a train traveling through mountains in what he thinks is Switzerland. He can see the train very clearly going in and out of tunnels over and over again. Harold's therapist suggests that the dream is not about travel in a foreign country but about Harold's concern with his sexual performance. The therapist adheres to the _____ theory of dreams and is attempting to reveal the _____ of Harold's dream.
    (a) evolutionary; adaptive aspects
    (b) Freud's wish fulfillment; manifest content
    (c) Freud's wish fulfillment; latent content
    (d) activation-synthesis; restorative aspects

11. During a very intense game of pool Gary attempts a very difficult shot that will win him the game when he suddenly collapses and falls fast asleep on the pool table. Gary probably suffers from _____ and is experiencing _____ .
    (a) sleep apnea; sleep paralysis
    (b) narcolepsy; a sleep attack
    (c) insomnia; sleep inertia
    (d) REM sleep behavior disorder; sleep paralysis

12. Nicotine is to alcohol as a _____ drug is to a _____
    (a) stimulant; depressant
    (b) psychedelic; stimulant
    (c) depressant; stimulant
    (d) depressant; psychedelic

13. According to In Focus 4.3, which of the following is true?
    (a) Some people never sleep.
    (b) It is extremely dangerous to awaken a sleepwalker.
    (c) If you dream you are falling and you hit the ground, you will wake up dead.
    (d) In a relatively common phenomenon called sleep paralysis, the paralysis of REM sleep carries over to the waking state for up to 10 minutes.

14. According to Culture and Human Behavior 4.4, having siestas, or afternoon naps, is
    (a) the leading cause of insomnia.
    (b) a normal, even beneficial, aspect of our daily sleep-wake circadian rhythm.
    (c) the reason most Third World countries are poverty-stricken.
    (d) directly correlated with high birth rates.

15. According to In Focus 4.5, What You Really Want to Know About Dreams, which of the following is true?
    (a) People who have been blind all their lives don't dream.
    (b) Up until the widespread use of color TV, most people's dreams were in black and white.
    (c) Virtually all mammals experience sleep cycles in which REM sleep alternates with slow-wave NREM sleep, and it is reasonable to conclude that they all experience dreams.
    (d) Eating cheese before going to sleep is a good way to ensure you have interesting, juicy dreams.

Progress Test 3

After you have checked your understanding of the material in Progress Tests 1 and 2, and have done a complete chapter review with special focus on any areas of weakness, you are ready to further assess your knowledge on Progress Test 3. Check your answers. If you make a mistake, review your notes, the appropriate parts of the study guide, and if necessary, the relevant sections of your textbook.

1. Mrs. Cadogan complains that her overweight 65-year-old husband snores and snorts throughout the night and appears to be gasping for breath. She notes that this happens most often when he is sleeping on his back. Mr. Cadogan suffers from
   (a) sleep apnea.   (c) sleep inertia.
   (b) sleep terrors.   (d) sleep bruxism.

2. Dr. Gerhardt believes that sleep promotes physiological processes that repair and rejuvenate the body and mind. Dr. Gerhardt's view is consistent with the _____ theory of sleep.
   (a) evolutionary
   (b) activation-synthesis
   (c) wish-fulfillment
   (d) restorative

3. Liam uses airplane glue to induce an altered state of consciousness, relaxation, giddiness, and reduced inhibitions. Liam is using
   (a) THC.   (c) an opiate.
   (b) LSD.   (d) an inhalant.

4. Stage 2 sleep is to _____ as stage 4 is to _____ .
   (a) beta waves; alpha waves
   (b) alpha waves; beta waves
   (c) sleep spindles; delta waves
   (d) dreams; nightmares

5. Dr. Hayward uses hypnosis on a patient during a root canal procedure. When he asks her to raise her hand if some part of her can feel pain, she raises her hand. This illustrates
   (a) the hidden observer.
   (b) paradoxical sleep.
   (c) posthypnotic amnesia.
   (d) tolerance.

6. While asleep, Kerry is sometimes aware that she is dreaming and, is able to influence the course and outcome of her dream. She feels like a movie director in these nighttime productions. Kerry is most probably a(n)
   (a) heavy drug user.   (c) insomniac.
   (b) lucid dreamer.   (d) myoclonic jerk.

7. Due to prolonged and heavy use of cocaine, Andrew suffered schizophrenia-like symptoms, including auditory hallucinations of "voices, bizarre paranoid ideas, and the "cocaine bugs" hallucination in which he felt like insects were crawling under his skin. Andrew's symptoms suggest that he has

   (a) stimulant-induced psychosis (cocaine psychosis).
   (b) delirium tremens (DTs).
   (c) hypermnesia.
   (d) a parasomnia.

8. Research indicates that the percentage of total sleep spent in REM sleep is higher in _____ than in _____ .
   (a) infants; adults   (c) old people; children
   (b) females; males   (d) cats; dogs

9. After he abruptly stops taking a depressant psychoactive drug, Ernie suffers from sleep problems, excitability, and restlessness. Ernie is suffering from
   (a) drug-rebound effect. (c) inertia.
   (b) parasomnia.   (d) apnea.

10. Maya uses the zazen, or the "just sitting" technique of Zen Buddhism, in which she engages in quiet awareness of the "here and now" without any distracting thoughts. Maya is using a type of _____ meditation.
    (a) opening-up
    (b) inertia
    (c) concentration
    (d) parasomnia

11. According to his wife, 70-year-old Hugo sometimes jumps out of bed during the night and appears to be acting out his dreams. It is very likely that Hugo suffers from a sleep disorder called
    (a) narcolepsy.
    (b) REM sleep behavior disorder.
    (c) sleep apnea.
    (d) nocturnal enuresis.

12. Jason frequently experiences morning brain fog. One way to deal with his sleep inertia, according to the Application, is to
    (a) stay in bed, in a deep sleep, until the last possible minute after the alarm has gone off.
    (b) get up very gradually and spend the first 30 minutes or so in very low-level light conditions.
    (c) set his alarm clock 15 minutes earlier than usual, get up as soon as it goes off, sip some coffee, and expose himself to bright light.
    (d) Stay up about 15 minutes later than usual each night for a week, but get up at the same time each morning.

13. According to In Focus 4.1, research suggests that
    (a) the skin, as well as the retina in the eye, contains specialized circadian photoreceptors.
    (b) jet lag is due mainly to a change in diet and has little or nothing to do with the disruption of circadian rhythms.
    (c) staying in complete darkness for 8 to 12 hours after you arrive at your destination will alleviate all the symptoms of jet lag and reset your biological clock.
    (d) staying in complete darkness for 8 to 12 hours before you depart will alleviate all the symptoms of jet lag and reset your biological clock.

14. Biorhythms are discussed in Science Versus Pseudoscience 4.2. Which of the following point(s) is (are) made?
    (a) Biorhythms is a popular pseudoscience.
    (b) The notion that there are three "natural biorhythms" rigidly fixed from birth on is unproved.
    (c) Although "biorhythms" and "biological rhythms" sound very similar, they have virtually nothing in common.
    (d) The legitimate scientific study of biological rhythms examines the consistent but potentially varying cycles of living organisms over time.
    (e) All of the above points were made.

15. In Focus 4.3 presents information about sleep. Which of the following is (are) true according to this section?
    (a) Deaf people who use sign language sometimes "sleep sign" during sleep.
    (b) Some people are "morning larks" and others are "night owls"; they differ in terms of the timing of their circadian rhythms.
    (c) It is not possible to learn foreign languages, chemistry, etc., by listening to tape recordings while fast asleep.
    (d) All of the above are true.

Answers

Introduction: Consciousness: Experiencing the "Private I"

1. (a) thoughts, sensations, memories
   (b) changing; disjointed (discontinuous)
2. (a) William James

(b) continuity
3. (a) introspection; self-reports
   (b) overt behavior
4. (a) conscious mental processes
   (b) new and more objective methods; brain

The Biological and Environmental "Clocks" Regulating Consciousness

1. (a) sleep-wake
   (b) circadian rhythms; mental; sleep-wake
   (c) bodily processes
2. (a) hypothalamus; SCN, or suprachiasmatic nucleus
   (b) SCN, or suprachiasmatic nucleus
   (c) bright light; sunlight
   (d) SCN; melatonin
   (e) melatonin; pineal
   (f) entrains; synchronized
3. (a) environmental time cues
   (b) 25-hour; circadian rhythms
   (c) resets; synchronized
4. (a) physiological; psychological; jet lag
   (b) melatonin
   (c) jet lag
   (d) body clock (the SCN)
5. (a) biological clock/circadian rhythms; SCN (body clock)
   (b) melatonin
   (c) circadian rhythms
   (d) consciousness
   (e) free-running conditions

Matching Exercise 1

1. consciousness
2. introspection
3. suprachiasmatic nucleus (SCN)
4. jet lag
5. melatonin
6. biorhythms

True/False Test 1

1. T   3. T   5. T
2. F   4. T

Sleep

1. (a) brain waves
   (b) electroencephalogram; EEG
   (c) physical

2. (a) rapid-eye-movement; REM
   (b) REM; NREM; non-rapid-eye-movement
   (c) dreaming; slow down

3. (a) beta; alpha
   (b) hypnagogic hallucinations
   (c) hypnagogic hallucination; myoclonic jerk

4. (a) four; decreases
   (b) alpha; theta
   (c) easily awakened
   (d) sleep spindles
   (e) delta

5. (a) similar; slow-wave
   (b) 3; 4
   (c) difficult to awaken
   (d) lowest levels; sleepwalking
   (e) 4 NREM
   (f) 4; 3; 2; REM

6. (a) REM
   (b) Dreams; muscle
   (c) physiological
   (d) 90; 70; 120
   (e) REM; slow-wave (NREM)
   (f) 3; 4; 2

7. (a) quantity; quality
   (b) REM; sleep-wake cycles; 50
   (c) decreases; decrease; 2

8. (a) sleep-deprivation; microsleeps
   (b) reaction time; perceptual skills
   (c) REM rebound; slow-wave NREM rebound

9. (a) restorative
   (b) body; increases; mental and brain functions
   (c) adaptive (evolutionary)
   (d) more
   (e) restorative; and; adaptive

Sleep Disorders: Troubled Sleep

1. serious disturbances in the normal sleep pattern that interfere with daytime functioning and cause subjective distress.

2. (a) insomnia
   (b) stimulus control
   (c) insomnia

3. (a) sleep apnea
   (b) stops breathing

4. (a) children
   (b) 3; 4
   (c) deep (slow-wave); nocturnal enuresis
   (d) sleepwalking
   (e) night terrors; REM
   (f) physiological arousal
   (g) with no
   (h) sleep bruxism; parasomnia

5. (a) REM sleep behavior disorder
   (b) muscle movements; REM
   (c) narcolepsy; sleep attacks
   (d) sleep attacks; sleep paralysis
   (e) hypnagogic hallucinations

6. (a) alpha
   (b) falling; myoclonic jerk
   (c) insomnia
   (d) worse
   (e) night terror; 3; 4
   (f) narcolepsy; sleep paralysis
   (g) is experiencing sleep disturbances that are normal for her age
   (h) theta; sleep spindles

Graphic Organizer 1

1. C   4. B   6. F
2. E   5. D   7. A
3. G

Matching Exercise 2

1. insomnia
2. REM sleep
3. restorative theory of sleep
4. alpha brain waves
5. sleep apnea
6. electroencephalogram (EEG)
7. sleep spindles
8. hypnagogic hallucinations
9. slow-wave sleep
10. myoclonic jerk (sleep start)
11. sleep paralysis
12. REM sleep behavior disorder
13. REM rebound
14. electroencephalograph

True/False Test 2

1. F   6. T   11. T
2. T   7. T   12. F
3. T   8. F   13. F
4. F   9. T   14. T
5. T   10. T

Dreams and Mental Activity During Sleep

1. (a) sleep thinking
   (b) storylike

2. (a) emotions

(b) content; organization
(c) sensations
(d) uncritically accepted
(e) images

3. (a) REM; NREM
   (b) REM

4. (a) different from; different from
   (b) primary visual cortex; frontal lobes
   (c) amygdala; hippocampus; visual images
   (d) memories; increases; disrupts

5. (a) content
   (b) falling; chased; more
   (c) content

6. (a) chemistry; functioning
   (b) wake up
   (c) remembered
   (d) distractions
   (e) any experience; programmed

7. (a) nightmare
   (b) nightmare

8. (a) aware; dreaming
   (b) guide

9. (a) sexual; aggressive; repressed
   (b) dreams
   (c) manifest content; latent content
   (d) latent; manifest; has not

10. (a) activation-synthesis
    (b) activation
    (c) synthesizes
    (d) activation-synthesis; personal meaning
    (e) external; internal
    (f) interpretation

11. (a) manifest content
    (b) activation-synthesis
    (c) sleep thinking
    (d) common
    (e) 70; REM
    (f) lucid dreamer

Matching Exercise 3

1. J. Allan Hobson
2. Sigmund Freud
3. sleep thinking
4. Robert McCarley
5. lucid dream

True/False Test 3

1. T   3. T   5. F
2. F   4. T

Hypnosis

1. (a) hypnosis
   (b) attention; suggestions; distortions
   (c) more
   (d) attitudes; expectations; fantasy; imaginary experience

2. (a) detachment; relaxation; timelessness
   (b) blindness; deafness; sensations
   (c) medical; dental
   (d) hallucinations

3. (a) posthypnotic
   (b) little; cognitive-behavior therapy

4. (a) before; during; past events
   (b) distortions; inaccuracies; pseudomemories
   (c) age regression
   (d) confidence

5. (a) cannot
   (b) cannot
   (c) can
   (d) cannot

6. (a) consciousness
   (b) neodissociation theory of hypnosis
   (c) hidden observer
   (d) consciousness; hidden observer; social; cognitive
   (e) medicine, dentistry; psychotherapy

Meditation

1. (a) attention; awareness
   (b) attention
   (c) concentration; mantra
   (d) opening-up

2. (a) transcendental meditation, or TM
   (b) TM
   (c) alpha
   (d) no more; relaxation; alertness
   (e) enhances
   (f) consciousness

3. (a) highly susceptible
   (b) posthypnotic amnesia
   (c) concentration
   (d) posthypnotic suggestion
   (e) pseudomemory
   (f) age regression

Matching Exercise 4

1. neodissociation theory of hypnosis
2. transcendental meditation (TM)
3. hypnosis

4. dissociation

5. posthypnotic suggestion

6. hypermnesia

7. hidden observer

True/False Test 4

1. T   4. T   6. F
2. F   5. T   7. T
3. T

Psychoactive Drugs

1. (a) caffeine; alcohol
   (b) chemical

2. (a) depressants
   (b) opiates
   (c) stimulants
   (d) psychedelic drugs

3. (a) addiction
   (b) physical dependence
   (c) tolerance
   (d) withdrawal symptoms
   (e) depression; excitability; drug rebound effect

4. (a) synaptic
   (b) weight, gender, age; racial; ethnic
   (c) setting (context)
   (d) drug abuse

5. (a) when social and cultural norms are favorable toward drug taking;
   (b) when the drug is fairly readily available at a reasonable cost;
   (c) when role models and family members engage in drug taking;
   (d) when the person has occupational, social, or academic problems;
   (e) if the person associates with drug-using peers; and
   (f) if there is a history of rebelliousness or alienation from society as a whole.

6. (a) inhibit; additive
   (b) small; abuse
   (c) blood alcohol
   (d) concentration, memory; speech; death
   (e) binge-drinking
   (f) withdrawal symptoms; delirium tremens, or DTs
   (g) lessens inhibitions

7. (a) barbiturates
   (b) Tranquilizers
   (c) consciousness; central nervous system

8. (a) opiates; narcotics
   (b) opium; morphine; opium; morphine
   (c) heroin
   (d) endorphins
   (e) pain; pain; rarely
   (f) heroin; drug rebound (withdrawal)

9. (a) stimulant
   (b) Caffeine; psychoactive
   (c) withdrawal
   (d) nicotine
   (e) nicotine
   (f) enhances; withdrawal

10. (a) amphetamines
    (b) amphetamines; "crashing"
    (c) stimulant drug
    (d) crack
    (e) stimulant-induced psychosis

11. (a) psychedelic drug
    (b) psilocybin; mescaline
    (c) LSD (lysergic acid diethylamide)
    (d) LSD; mescaline
    (e) psychedelic; LSD

12. (a) marijuana; THC
    (b) well-being; euphoria; relaxation; psychedelic
    (c) pain; hypertension; glaucoma
    (d) do not

13. (a) psychoactive; physically
    (b) tolerance
    (c) judgment; self-control
    (d) not remember
    (e) will not
    (f) tranquilizer
    (g) cocaine

Graphic Organizer 2

1. alcohol; depressant

2. tranquilizer; depressant

3. marijuana; psychedelic

4. LSD; psychedelic

5. caffeine; stimulant

6. morphine; opiate

7. nicotine; stimulant

Matching Exercise 5

1. THC

2. depressants

3. nicotine

4. drug abuse

5. psychoactive drug

6. stimulant-induced psychosis

7. mescaline

8. tolerance

9. hashish

10. withdrawal symptoms

11. cocaine

12. inhalants

13. amphetamines

14. delirium tremens (DTs)

15. sleep inertia

True/False Test 5

1. T	6. T	11. F
2. T	7. T	12. T
3. T	8. F	13. T
4. F	9. T	14. F
5. T	10. T	

Something to Think About

1. Generally speaking, humans are very adapt-able; in fact, most people can easily adapt to shift work. If shifts are scheduled to take into account our natural tendencies and use knowledge about sleep-wake cycles, circadian rhythms, and the role of the SCN, they need not produce the usual jet-lag symptoms.

   Begin your report with a discussion of how to rotate a person's shifts. Because we tend to drift to longer days (the 25-hour day rather than the 24-hour day), as we often do on weekends, it would seem best to rotate shifts forward: first shift, 8 A.M. to 4 P.M., second shift 4 P.M. to 12 midnight, and then midnight to 8 A.M. for the third shift.

   The length of the shift rotation is the next issue to address. Every shift change is going to take some time to get used to and will be accompanied by some jet-lag symptoms, so the less someone has to change the better. It would probably be best to have people do the same shift for at least a month before changing to the next shift forward.

   Shift workers should be given as much information as possible about circadian rhythms, sleep-wake cycles, and the role of the SCN in the production of melatonin. People finishing a night shift, for example, could be told the value

of black-out curtains to avoid having their biological clock reset by bright light; those suffering from sleep inertia could be given the information presented in the Application section (Improving Sleep and Mental Alertness). For instance, for the midnight to 8 A.M. shift, having bright lights, especially in the early part of the shift, can help people adjust to the night shift.

   Finally, present the organization with a somewhat radical idea. Introduce the idea of the siesta or nap and explain how the low points in our circadian rhythms produce fatigue, especially in sleep-deprived people. Taking a nap is a normal, even beneficial, aspect of our daily sleep-wake cycle. In fact, research has shown that naps reduce fatigue and sleepiness, improve mood and mental alertness, and can improve overall productivity.

2. This dream sounds like a real nightmare. The first thing to tell your friend is that dreams cannot predict the future. She is not likely to fail the exam because of her dream. Her dream reflects the fact that she is concerned and worried about the course. The best way to do well on the exam, and to deal with exam anxiety, is to study the material completely. The text presents two theories of dreams. Freud's view is that the manifest content is relatively unimportant; he would suggest looking for disguised symbolic meaning that reflects the latent content. The activation-synthesis theory suggests that if someone is worried and anxious, these concerns are likely to show up in a dream if these well-worn neural pathways are activated. In other words, the brain produces dream images that are synthesized into a meaningful story using memories about daily events, past experiences, concerns, and worries.

   The person's interpretation of the dream may tell us more about the dreamer than anything else. If that is the case, it would be fairly safe to assume that this dreamer is experiencing some perceived difficulty with the course (or some aspect of it) and/or the course material itself.

   Finally, you could suggest that she try lucid dreaming. If she is not already a lucid dreamer, you could present the suggestions outlined in the text for increasing this ability. It is quite possible that she could go to sleep and have the same dream again, but this time, with her lucid dreaming ability, have a completely different and much more positive outcome.

Progresst Test 1

1. c	6. c	11. c
2. e	7. d	12. d
3. d	8. b	13. a
4. b	9. c	14. a
5. d	10. a	15. b

Progress Test 2

1. a	6. c	11. b
2. b	7. c	12. a
3. a	8. d	13. d
4. d	9. b	14. b
5. a	10. c	15. c

Progress Test 3

1. a	6. b	11. b
2. d	7. a	12. c
3. d	8. a	13. a
4. c	9. a	14. e
5. a	10. a	15. d

Learning

CHAPTER 5. . . AT A GLANCE

Chapter 5 answers the question "What is learning?" in its discussions of classical conditioning, operant conditioning, and observational learning. Conditioning focuses on how we form associations between environmental events and behavioral responses. Classical conditioning (discovered by Ivan Pavlov) involves repeatedly pairing a neutral stimulus with a stimulus that naturally elicits a response until the neutral stimulus elicits the same response. Behaviorism was founded by John B. Watson and was concerned with the scientific study of observable behaviors, especially as they pertain to learning. Classical conditioning is used to explain conditioned emotional reactions and conditioned physiological responses. Contemporary psychology has modified the basics of classical conditioning to account for cognitive functioning and biological predispositions.

Operant conditioning (developed by B. F. Skinner) demonstrates how voluntary, active behaviors are acquired through shaping, reinforcement (positive and negative), and punishment (by application and by removal). Once acquired, behaviors are maintained through different schedules of reinforcement. Behaviors that are partially reinforced are more resistant to extinction than are behaviors that are continuously reinforced. Behavior modification is the application of principles of operant conditioning to help people develop more adaptive behaviors. Operant conditioning theory has also been modified by contemporary cognitive and biological views.

Observational learning (studied by Albert Bandura) shows how new behaviors can be acquired through watching the actions of others; it involves the processes of attention, memory, motor skills, and motivation. This type of learning is not limited to humans but has been demonstrated in many nonhuman animals as well. Applications involve education, work performance, psychotherapy, and counseling.

Introduction: What Is Learning?

Preview Questions

Consider the following questions as you study this section of the chapter.

- How is learning defined?
- What is conditioning?
- What are three basic types of learning?

Read the section "Introduction: What Is Learning?" and **write** *your answers to the following:*

1. (a) Psychologists formally define learning as a process that produces a relatively

   _____ .

   (b) Learning new behaviors often reflects _____ to the environment; it occurs in every type of setting; and it is an important aspect of the behavior of virtually all animals, not just human beings.

   (c) Psychologists have often studied learning by observing and recording the learning experiences of _____ in carefully controlled laboratory situations. The goal of much of this research has been to identify the _____ that apply across a wide range of species, including humans.

2. (a) Conditioning is the process of learning _____ between _____ events and _____ responses.

   (b) The two types of conditioning are _____ and _____ .

   (c) The process by which we acquire new behaviors by seeing the actions of others is called _____ learning.

Classical Conditioning: Associating Stimuli

Preview Questions

Consider the following questions as you study this section of the chapter.

- Who discovered classical conditioning, and how did he investigate it?
- What is the basic process of classical conditioning?
- How does classical conditioning occur, and what factors can affect the strength of a classically conditioned response?
- What phenomena did Pavlov discover when he varied the stimuli during conditioning?
- Who founded behaviorism, and what were its basic assumptions?
- How can classical conditioning be used to explain emotional responses, and how does it affect physiological reactions?

Read the section "Classical Conditioning: Associating Stimuli" and **write** *your answers to the following:*

1. (a) Ivan Pavlov was a _____ whose involvement with psychology began as a result of an observation he made while investigating the role of saliva in digestion in dogs.

   (b) The learning process that Pavlov discovered was the first to be extensively studied in psychology; thus, it is called

   _____ .

2. (a) Classical conditioning deals with behaviors that are _____ automatically by some stimulus; thus, in classical conditioning the stimulus doesn't produce a "new" behavior, but rather it

   _____ .

   (b) A relatively simple unlearned behavior, governed by the nervous system, is a _____ . It occurs _____ when the appropriate stimulus is presented. In Pavlov's studies of digestion, the dogs salivated _____ when food was placed on their tongues .

   (c) When the dogs began salivating in response to the sight of Pavlov or to the sound of an experimenter's footsteps, a new

_____ stimulus elicited the salivary response; thus, a new

_____ sequence was learned.

3. (a) Classical conditioning is the process of learning an _____ between two stimuli and involves pairing a(n) _____ (e.g., the sight of Pavlov) stimulus with a(n)_____ stimulus (food in the mouth) that automatically elicits a(n) _____ response (the dog salivates).

(b) If the two stimuli, (Pavlov + food), are repeatedly paired, eventually the _____ stimulus (Pavlov), elicits the same basic _____ response as the natural stimulus (food), even in the absence of the natural stimulus.

4. (a) The natural stimulus (such as food in the dog's mouth) that reflexively produces a response without any prior learning is called the

_____

(abbreviated _____).

(b) The unlearned reflexive response (such as the dog's salivation to food in its mouth) is called the

_____

(abbreviated _____).

(c) The stimulus that is originally neutral (such as the sound of a bell or the sight of Pavlov) but comes to elicit a reflexive response is called the _____

_____ (abbreviated _____)

(d) The learned reflexive response to a previously neutral stimulus (such as the dog's salivation to the sound of the bell or the sight of Pavlov) is called the

_____

(abbreviated _____).

(e) Think of the word "conditioned" as meaning the same as "learned"; thus, the

_____ stimulus would be the learned stimulus, the _____ response the learned response, the _____ stimulus the unlearned stimulus, and the _____ response the unlearned response.

(f) When a dog salivates in response to a natural stimulus that is not acquired through learning, it is a(n) _____ response; when the dog learns to salivate to a neutral stimulus that doesn't normally produce the automatic response, it is a(n) _____ response. In both cases, the response is virtually the same but the label given (CR or UCR) depends on which stimulus elicits the response.

5. (a) Pavlov discovered that the more _____ the conditioned stimulus and the unconditioned stimulus are paired, the stronger the association between the two.

(b) Pavlov also discovered that the timing of stimulus presentations affected the strength of the conditioned response; the conditioned stimulus should be presented _____ (shortly before/at the same time as/shortly after) the unconditioned stimulus.

(c) When stimuli similar to the original conditioned stimulus also elicit the conditioned response, the phenomenon _____ is said to have occurred. When a particular conditioned response is made to one stimulus but not to the other stimuli, _____ has occurred.

(d) If the conditioned stimulus (CS) is repeatedly presented without being paired with the unconditioned stimulus (UCS), the conditioned response (CR) seems to gradually _____ ; Pavlov called the phenomenon _____ .

(e) If an animal is allowed a rest period after a response has been extinguished, the conditioned response (CR) will _____ when the conditioned stimulus (CS) is presented again; Pavlov called this phenomenon _____ .

6. (a) The person who changed the definition of psychology from the *scientific study of the mind* to the *scientific study of behavior* was the American psychologist

_____ .

(b) The school of psychology and theoretical viewpoint that emphasizes the scientific study of observable behaviors, especially as they pertain to the process of learning, is

_____ .

(c) The belief that virtually all human behavior is a result of conditioning and learning (i.e., due to past experience and environmental influences) and that neither talent, personality, or intelligence is inherited, was a basic assumption of _____ . He identified three emotions that he believed represented inborn, natural reflexes: _____ , _____ , and _____ .

7. (a) Your text describes the classical conditioning of Little Albert by Watson and Rayner. What were the CS, the UCS, and the UCR in their experiment?

CS	UCS	UCR

(b) What was the CR? _____

(c) This classical conditioning experiment demonstrated how _____ form.

(d) Little Albert reacted with fear to other animals such as a rabbit, a dog, and a sealskin coat. What is this process called?

_____

(e) This study would not be allowed today for _____ reasons.

8. (a) Caffeine-dependent people often feel alert after just a few sips of coffee in the morning even though it can take up to 45 minutes for the caffeine to reach significant levels in the bloodstream. This illustrates the fact that

_____

responses can be classically conditioned.

(b) The sight, taste, and smell of the coffee in the above example act as _____ stimuli to elicit the sense of increased alertness, which is the _____ response.

(c) Originally, when the caffeine entered the bloodstream, it automatically elicited a natural reaction of increased alertness; in this case, the caffeine is the _____ stimulus, and the increased alertness to caffeine in the bloodstream is the

_____ response.

9. Research with cancer patients who had undergone a series of chemotherapy treatments indicates that the human immune system can be classically conditioned. Initially, only the chemotherapy treatments affected the patients' immune systems, but after many treatments, cues related to the hospital environment produced reduced immune functioning. Using this example, identify the components that constitute the CS, UCS, UCR, and CR.

(a) The UCS in this research was the

_____ and the

_____

was the UCR.

(b) After repeated treatments, the

_____ related to the hospital environment (called the CS) became associated with the chemotherapy treatments.

(c) Now, the CS produced a response of

_____ , which is the CR.

10. Read the following and write the correct term in the space provided.

(a) About five hours after extinguishing the classically conditioned response (CR) in an experimental animal, Dr. Taylor presented the conditioned stimulus (CS) and obtained a CR. Dr. Taylor has demonstrated

_____ .

(b) Fido drools whenever he hears the sound of the electric can opener but does not drool when he hears the sound of the blender, which makes a similar noise. It appears that Fido has learned to

_____ between the

two sounds.

(c) Ahmood, who is a regular coffee drinker,

notices that he now feels alert at just the sight and smell of the coffee. In classical conditioning terms, Ahmood's physiological response to these cues is called a

_____ .

(d) Ahmood also observed that he has a similar physiological response to the smell of other beverages such as herbal tea and hot chocolate. In this situation, he is experiencing a phenomenon called

_____ .

Graphic Organizer 1

In his classic experiment Pavlov repeatedly presented a neutral stimulus, such as a tone, just before putting food in the dog's mouth, which automatically elicited salivation. After several repetitions the tone alone triggered the salivation. Label the following graph using the correct terms (UCS, UCR, CS, CR):

Before Conditioning

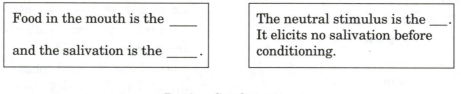

Food in the mouth is the ____ and the salivation is the ____ .

The neutral stimulus is the ___ . It elicits no salivation before conditioning.

During Conditioning

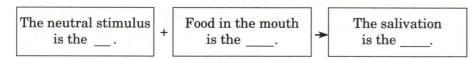

The neutral stimulus is the ___ . + Food in the mouth is the ____ . → The salivation is the ____ .

After Conditioning

The tone alone is the ___ . → The salivation is now the ___ .

Contemporary Views of Classical Conditioning

Preview Questions

Consider the following questions as you study this section of the chapter.

- How does the cognitive explanation of learning differ from the behavioral explanation?
- What kinds of cognitive processes are involved in classical conditioning, and how have they been demonstrated experimentally?
- How does the evolutionary perspective account for the conditioning process?
- How do taste aversions challenge the principles of classical conditioning, and how can they be explained?
- What is biological preparedness?

*Read the section "Contemporary Views of Classical Conditioning" and **write** your answers to the following:*

1. (a) According to the traditional behavioral perspective, mental processes such as thinking, anticipating, or deciding were _____ (needed/not needed) to explain the conditioning process.

   (b) According to the cognitive perspective, learning new behaviors involves _____ as well as external events.

2. (a) Rescorla suggested that classical conditioning depends on the _____ the conditioned stimulus provides about the unconditioned stimulus.

   (b) For learning to occur, the conditioned stimulus must be a(n) _____ that predicts the presentation of the unconditioned stimulus.

   (c) Animals actively process _____ about the reliability of the signals they encounter; in other words, they assess the _____ of stimuli.

   (d) According to Rescorla, animals use _____ processes to

draw inferences about signals they encounter in their environment; thus, from this perspective classical conditioning involves learning about the _____ between events.

3. (a) According to Darwin's theory of evolution by _____ , both the physical characteristics and the natural behavior patterns of any species have been shaped by evolution to maximize _____ to the environment. According to some psychologists, this might affect how an animal learned new behavior patterns, especially those important to survival.

   (b) The traditional behaviorist view was that the general principles of learning applied to virtually all_____ and all _____ situations; thus, they argued that the general learning principles of classical conditioning would be the same regardless of the species or the response being conditioned; the study of _____ argued against this position

4. (a) Don got sick several hours after eating Sandy's spaghetti. Stomach flu was the actual cause of his illness, yet he now dislikes the taste, smell, or sight of spaghetti. Don has developed a_____ .

   (b) In _____ , a single pairing can result in classical conditioning, and the timespan between the two stimuli (CS and UCS) can be _____ , not just a matter of seconds; these findings violate two basic principles of classical conditioning.

   (c) This type of conditioning was demonstrated experimentally in laboratory rats by _____ .

5. (a) Contrary to Pavlov's claim, this research showed that associations _____ (can/cannot) be formed between just any stimulus and any response; rats were much more likely to associate a painful stimulus such as shock with _____ (lights and noise), and were much more likely to associate taste with _____ (the physical discomfort of illness).

(b) One factor that helps explain Garcia's results is _____ , the idea that an organism is innately predisposed to form some associations and not others; organisms seem to be _____ to associate illness with a taste rather than a location, a person, or an object.

(c) Associations that are easily learned may reflect the _____ history and _____ mechanisms of particular animal species.

(d) Research on taste aversion and similar findings emphasized that the study of learning must consider the unique _____ and capabilities of different species; as a result of _____ , animals have developed unique forms of behavior to adapt to their natural environment, which ultimately influence what an animal is capable of learning and how easily it can be conditioned.

6. Read the following and write the correct term in the space provided.

(a) Dr. Munchausen believes that the general principles of learning apply to virtually all species and all learning situations, whereas his colleague Dr. Milstein believes that an animal's natural behavioral patterns and unique characteristics can influence what it is capable of learning. Dr. Munchausen supports the _____ perspective, and Dr. Milstein views are consistent with an _____ perspective.

(b) Dr. Wells decided to classically condition some rats. He used a tone (CS) followed by a shock (UCS) for group 1; for group 2, he used a taste (CS) followed by a shock. It is very _____ (likely/unlikely) that the rats in group 1 will be classically conditioned; it is very _____ (likely/unlikely) that the rats in group 2 will be classically conditioned.

(c) It appears that Dr. Wells in the above example is investigating how _____ affects learning through classical conditioning.

(d) Dr. Manly believes that classical conditioning depends on the information the CS provides about the UCS and that for learning to occur, the CS must be a reliable signal that predicts the presentation of the UCS. Dr. Manly's views are most consistent with the _____ perceptive.

Review of Terms, Concepts, and Names 1

Use the terms in this list to complete the Matching Test, then to help you answer the True/False items correctly.

learning
conditioning
Ivan Pavlov
classical conditioning
elicit
unconditioned stimulus
unconditioned response
conditioned stimulus
conditioned response
extinction
spontaneous recovery

stimulus generalization
stimulus discrimination
John B. Watson
behaviorism
cognitive perspective
Robert A. Rescorla
taste aversion
John Garcia
biological preparedness
phobia

Matching Exercise

Match the appropriate term/name with its definition or description.

1. _____ The gradual weakening and disappearance of conditioned behavior; in classical conditioning, it occurs when the conditioned stimulus is repeatedly presented without the unconditioned stimulus.

2. _____ The process of learning associations between environmental events and behavioral responses.

3. _____ A relatively enduring change in behavior or knowledge as a result of past experience.

4. _____ Classically conditioned dislike for and avoidance of a particular food that develops when an organism becomes ill after eating the food.

5. _____ American psychologist who founded behaviorism in the early 1900s, an approach that emphasized the scientific study of outwardly observable behavior rather than subjective mental states.

6. _____ School of psychology and theoretical viewpoint that emphasizes the scientific study of observable behaviors, especially as they pertain to the process of learning.

7. _____ Natural stimulus that reflexively elicits a response without the necessity of prior learning.

8. _____ Russian physiologist who first described the basic learning process of associating stimuli that is now called classical conditioning.

9. _____ Extreme, irrational fear of a specific object, animal, or situation.

10. _____ Unlearned, reflexive response that is elicited by an unconditioned stimulus.

11. _____ In learning theory, the idea that an organism is innately predisposed to form associations between certain stimuli and not others.

True/False Test

Indicate whether each statement is true or false by placing T or F in the blank space next to each item.

1. ____ Classical conditioning is the basic learning process that involves repeatedly pairing a neutral stimulus with a response-producing stimulus until the neutral stimulus elicits the same response.

2. ____ "Elicit" means to draw out or bring forth and causes an existing behavior to occur.

3. ____ The American psychologist who experimentally demonstrated the involvement of cognitive processes in classical conditioning is John Garcia.

4. ____ The occurrence of a learned response not only to the original stimulus but to other, similar stimuli as well, is called stimulus discrimination.

5. ____ The conditioned stimulus is a formerly neutral stimulus that acquires the capacity to elicit a reflexive response.

6. ____ The reappearance of a previously extinguished conditioned response after a period of time without exposure to the conditioned stimulus is called spontaneous recovery.

7. ____ Stimulus generalization occurs when a learned response is made to a specific stimulus but not to other, similar stimuli.

8. ____ Robert A. Rescorla is the American psychologist who experimentally demonstrated the learning of taste aversions in animals, a finding that challenged several of the basic assumptions of classical conditioning.

9. ____ The conditioned response is the learned, reflexive response to a conditioned stimulus.

10. ____ The cognitive perspective holds that mental processes as well as external events are an important component in the learning of new behaviors.

> Check your answers and review any areas of weakness before going on to the next section.

Operant Conditioning: Associating Behaviors and Consequences (Part 1)

Preview Questions

Consider the following questions as you study the first three parts of this section of the chapter (up to and including Punishment):

- What types of behavior are subject to operant conditioning?

- What were B. F. Skinner's key assumptions, and what is the fundamental premise of operant conditioning?

- How are positive and negative reinforcement similar, and how are they different?
- What is punishment, and what factors influence its effectiveness?
- What negative effects are associated with the use of punishment?

Read the section "Operant Conditioning: Associating Behaviors and Consequences (Part 1)" and **write** *your answers to the following:*

1. (a) The law of effect was formulated by
   _____ .

   (b) Cats learned to escape from his "puzzle box" through a process of _____ and _____ learning.

   (c) The law of effect states that responses followed by a(n) "_____"
   are strengthened and more likely to occur again in the same situation, and responses followed by a(n) "_____"
   are weakened and less likely to occur again.

2. (a) Like Watson, Skinner believed that psychology _____ (should/should not) restrict itself to studying only phenomena that could be objectively measured and verified (that is, outwardly observable behavior); he believed that internal thoughts, beliefs, emotions, or motives _____ (could/could not) be used to scientifically explain behavior.

   (b) To Skinner, the most important form of learning was demonstrated by new behaviors that were actively
   _____ by the organism; he coined the term *operant* to describe active behaviors that _____ upon the environment to generate or produce

   _____ .

   (c) Skinner's operant conditioning model explains learning as a process in which behavior is _____ and maintained by its _____ . In this

model, the active response that is emitted is called a(n) _____ ; if it is followed by a _____ , it is strengthened and is more likely to occur again in the future.

   (d) Reinforcement is said to occur when a(n) _____ or a(n) _____
   follows an operant and increases the likelihood of the operant being repeated.

3. (a) Reinforcement can take two forms, positive and negative. Positive reinforcement involves following an operant with

   _____ ;
   negative reinforcement involves the

   _____
   from a situation.

   (b) Reinforcement (positive or negative) always _____ the probability of behavior occurring in the future.

   (c) Aversive stimuli typically involve physical or psychological discomfort that an organism seeks to _____ or

   _____ .

   (d) A behavior is negatively reinforced when it lets you terminate aversive stimuli that are already present (this is called
   _____ behavior); a behavior that precludes the presentation of aversive stimuli is also negatively reinforced because it prevents the occurrence of some unpleasant or undesirable consequence (this is called
   _____ behavior).

4. (a) A reinforcer that is naturally reinforcing for a given species is a _____ reinforcer; one that has acquired reinforcing value by being associated with a primary reinforcer is called a _____ reinforcer, or secondary reinforcer.

   (b) Food, water, adequate warmth, and sexual contact are examples of _____ reinforcers; money, frequent-flyer points, respect of your peers, and the approval of significant others are examples of _____ reinforcers.

5. The following are examples of negative reinforcement. Decide which illustrates *escape* and which illustrates *avoidance*.

   (a) You go to the dentist on a regular basis; as a result, you don't experience problems such as toothaches. This an example of _____ .

   (b) Your partner is complaining about your messy habits, so you put on your running gear and go for a five-mile jog. This is an example of _____ .

   (c) You study hard all semester because you don't want to end up with a low grade-point average. This is an example of _____ .

   (d) You turn the air conditioner on when the temperature in your room gets too hot and uncomfortable. This is an example of _____ .

6. (a) Punishment refers to the presentation of an event or stimulus following a behavior that acts to _____ the likelihood of the behavior being repeated.

   (b) The difference between negative reinforcement and punishment is that negative reinforcement always _____ the likelihood that an operant will be repeated in the future, and punishment always _____ the future performance of an operant.

   (c) Punishment by application involves the _____ of a punishing stimulus following a response, and punishment by removal involves the _____ or _____ of a reinforcing stimulus following a response.

(d) Both reinforcement and punishment are defined by the _____ they produce.

7. (a) Punishment is not always effective because it is often _____ ; to be effective, punishment should _____ follow the response and must be consistently applied.

   (b) Punishment has several drawbacks: even though it may suppress a response, it does not _____ the appropriate behavior; when it is intense, it may produce undesirable results, such as complete passivity, _____ , _____ , or hostility; and its effects are likely to be _____ , with the behavior reappearing after the punitive consequences are withdrawn.

   (c) Skinner strongly opposed the use of punishment; instead, he advocated the greater use of _____ to strengthen desirable behaviors.

8. For each of the following, decide whether the example illustrates negative reinforcement (N) or punishment (P).

   (a) _____ Marco always wears his seatbelt whenever he drives his car because he doesn't want to be thrown against the windshield if his car is hit from behind.

   (b) _____ Darryl has tried some new aftershave lotion. "It smells like diesel oil!" comments his girlfriend. Darryl never uses that aftershave lotion again.

   (c) _____ Maria does not misbehave at the dinner table because she knows that misbehavior will result in her forfeiting dessert.

   (d) _____ Greta's cigarette lighter ignites the hair spray she has just put on her hair and burns her bangs and eyebrows. Greta no longer smokes when she is doing her hair.

(e) _____ Jim no longer picks up hitchhikers after the last one robbed him at gun point.

(f) _____ Before pouring milk on her cereal, Carmelitta smells the carton to make sure the milk has not gone sour.

(g) _____ Astrid brushes her teeth after every meal because she wants to cut down on the number of visits she needs to make to the dentist.

Graphic Organizer 2

The following is a very useful way to organize the procedures used in operant conditioning. The arrow ↑ or ↓ indicates whether the behavior increases or decreases. Fill in the blanks in cells 1, 2, 3, and 4.

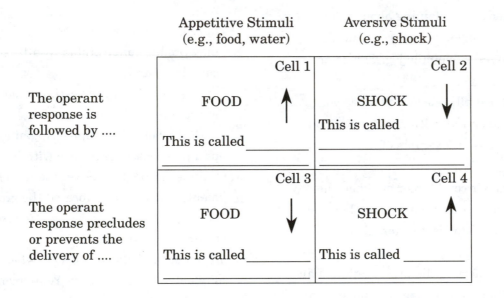

	Appetitive Stimuli (e.g., food, water)	Aversive Stimuli (e.g., shock)
The operant response is followed by ….	**Cell 1** FOOD ↑ This is called _____	**Cell 2** SHOCK ↓ This is called _____
The operant response precludes or prevents the delivery of ….	**Cell 3** FOOD ↓ This is called _____	**Cell 4** SHOCK ↑ This is called _____

9. Read the following and write the correct term or word in the space provided.

   (a) Ashley holds the view that responses followed by a satisfying state of affairs are strengthened and are more likely to occur again in the same situation and that responses followed by an unpleasant or annoying state of affairs are less likely to recur. This view is most consistent with a fundamental principle of learning called the _____.

   (b) April burned her fingers when she picked up a hot saucepan with her bare hands. She now always dons her oven mitts before touching any hot pan or pot. The aversive stimulus of getting burned reduced her tendency to pick up pots with her bare hands and is therefore is an example of _____ ; her increased tendency to use oven mitts because it reduces the possibility of getting burned is an example of

   _____ .

   (c) Whenever young Simon wants something, such as a new toy or candy, he cries and screams until his parents give in and give him what he wants. Simon's whining behavior is _____ reinforced by his parents giving in, and the parents behavior is _____ reinforced because it stops the annoying crying and screaming.

   (d) While researching a term paper for his history of psychology class, Rupert discovered the name of the first psychologist to investigate how voluntary behaviors are influenced by their consequences. That psychologist was _____ .

Revew of Terms, Concepts, and Names 2

Use the terms in this list to complete the Matching Test, then to help you answer the True/False items correctly.

Edward L. Thorndike
law of effect
B. F. Skinner
operant
operant conditioning
reinforcement
positive reinforcement
negative reinforcement

primary reinforcer
conditioned reinforcer
punishment
punishment by
   application
punishment by removal
Premack's principle

Matching Exercise

Match the appropriate term/name with its definition or description.

1. _____ American psychologist who developed the operant conditioning model of learning and emphasized studying the relationship between environmental factors and observable actions, not mental processes, in trying to achieve a scientific explanation of behavior.

2. _____ Situation in which a response results in the removal, avoidance, or escape of a punishing stimulus, increasing the likelihood of the response being repeated in similar situations.

3. _____ American psychologist who was the first to experimentally study animal behavior and document how active behaviors are influenced by their consequences; postulated the law of effect.

4. _____ Presentation of a stimulus or event following a behavior that acts to decrease the likelihood of the behavior being repeated.

5. _____ Stimulus or event that has acquired reinforcing value by being associated with a primary reinforcer; also called a secondary reinforcer.

6. _____ Occurrence of a stimulus or event following a response that increases the likelihood of the response being repeated.

7. _____ Skinner's term for an actively emitted behavior that operates on the environment to produce consequences.

True/False Test

Indicate whether each statement is true or false by placing T or F in the blank space next to each item.

1. ___ A primary reinforcer is a stimulus or event that is naturally or inherently reinforcing for a given species, such as food, water, or other biological necessities.

2. ___ Punishment by application involves the loss or withdrawal of a reinforcing stimulus following a response.

3. ___ Positive reinforcement refers to a situation in which a response is followed by the addition of a reinforcing stimulus, increasing the likelihood of the response being repeated in a similar situation.

4. ___ Punishment by removal involves the presentation of an unpleasant or aversive event or stimulus following a response.

5. ___ The law of effect states that responses followed by a satisfying effect become strengthened and are more likely to recur in a particular situation, whereas responses followed by a dissatisfying effect are weakened and less likely to recur in a particular situation.

6. ___ Operant conditioning is the basic learning process that involves changing the probability of a response being repeated by manipulating the consequences of that response.

7. ___ Premack's principle refers to the finding that a more preferred activity or behavior can be used to reinforce a less preferred activity or behavior.

Check your answers and review any areas of weakness before going on to the next section.

Operant Conditioning: Associating Behaviors and Consequences (Part 2)

Preview Questions

Consider the following questions as you study the last parts of this section of the chapter (up to and including Applications of Operant Conditioning):

- What are discriminative stimuli, and what important role do they play in operant conditioning?

- What is shaping, and how does it work?
- How does partial reinforcement affect behavior?
- What are the four basic schedules of reinforcement?
- What are some practical applications of operant conditioning principles?
- How has behavior modification been used to change human behavior?

Read the section "Operant Conditioning: Associating Behaviors and Consequences (Part 2)" and **write** *your answers to the following:*

1. (a) A discriminative stimulus is a specific stimulus in the presence of which a particular _____ is more likely to be

     _____ .

   (b) A ringing telephone is a

       _____ for picking up

       the receiver.

2. (a) According to Skinner, behavior is

       _____ and _____ by

       the stimuli that are present in a given situation and not by a personal choice or a conscious decision.

   (b) In the presence of a particular environmental stimulus (the _____ stimulus), we emit a particular behavior (the _____), which is followed by a consequence (_____ or _____).

   (c) If the consequence is either positive or negative reinforcement we are _____ (more/less) likely to repeat the operant when we encounter the same or similar discriminative stimuli in the future. If the consequence is some form of punishment, we are _____ (more/less) likely to repeat the operant when we encounter the same or similar discriminative stimuli in the future.

   (d) To scientifically study the relationship between behavior and its consequences, Skinner invented the _____ , more popularly known as a Skinner box.

3. (a) Reinforcing successively closer approximations to a behavior until the correct behavior is displayed is the process called

     _____ .

   (b) If parents use praise and encouragement to gradually teach a child how to dress herself, they are using a _____ procedure.

4. (a) Once a rat had acquired a lever-pressing behavior, Skinner found that the most efficient way to strengthen the response was to immediately reinforce every occurrence of bar pressing; this pattern of reinforcement is called _____ .

   (b) When behaviors are reinforced only on some occasions, the pattern of reinforcement is called

     _____ .

   (c) In operant conditioning, when a learned response no longer results in reinforcement, the likelihood of the behavior being repeated gradually declines; this is called

     _____ .

   (d) The partial reinforcement effect states that partially reinforced behaviors tend to be much _____ (more/less) resistant to extinction than behaviors conditioned using _____ reinforcement.

5. (a) Skinner found that specific, preset arrangements of partial reinforcement produce different patterns and rates of responding; these different reinforcement arrangements are called

     _____ .

   (b) When reinforcement occurs after a preset number of responses, it is a _____ schedule. This schedules produce a _____ (high/low) rate of responding that follows a burst-pause-burst pattern.

   (c) When reinforcement occurs after an average

number of responses, which changes from trial to trial, it is a _____ schedule. This schedule produces a _____ (high/low), steady rate of responding because the number of responses required on any particular trial is _____ .

(d) When reinforcement is delivered for the first response emitted after a preset amount of time has elapsed, it is a _____ schedule. With this schedule, the number of responses typically tends to _____ (increase/decrease) as the time for the next reinforcer draws near, producing a scallop-shaped pattern.

(e) When reinforcement occurs for the first response emitted after an average amount of time has elapsed, but the length of time changes from trial to trial, it is a _____ schedule. This schedule tends to produce a _____ (high/moderate), steady rate of responding because reinforcement depends on the passage of time rather than on the number of responses.

6. (a) The application of learning principles to help people develop more effective or adaptive behaviors is called

_____ .

(b) _____ has been used in such diverse situations as improving worker performance, increasing social skills in schoolchildren, promoting sleep at night, increasing automobile seatbelt use, helping athletic performance, and in the specialized training of animals to help people who are physically challenged in some way.

7. What type of schedule do each of these examples illustrate?

(a) Your instructor, Dr. Jones, decides to give surprise quizzes throughout the semester. Your studying will be reinforced on a _____ schedule.

(b) Your instructor, Dr. Wong, schedules a quiz every two weeks throughout the semester. Your studying will be reinforced on a _____ schedule.

(c) A rat gets a food pellet for every 20 responses. It is reinforced on a _____ schedule.

(d) Maria sells magazine subscriptions by phone. She makes many calls but only gets paid for making a sale. She is reinforced on a _____ schedule.

(e) Juanita and her colleagues assemble TV sets in a factory. They get paid a bonus for every ten TVs they produce. They are being rewarded on a(n) _____ schedule.

Graphic Organizer 3

Fill in each cell with the name of the appropriate partial reinforcement schedule.

	Based on the number of responses made	Based on the elapsed time
Fixed	Cell 1 _____	Cell 2 _____
Variable	Cell 3 _____	Cell 4 _____

Review of Terms, Concepts, and Names 3

Use the terms in this list to complete the Matching Test, then to help you answer the True/False items correctly.

Skinner box
discriminative stimulus
shaping
continuous
   reinforcement
partial reinforcement
partial reinforcement
   effect

schedule of
   reinforcement
fixed ratio
variable ratio
extinction
fixed interval
variable interval
behavior modification

Matching Exercise

Match the appropriate term/name with its definition or description:

1. _____ The application of learning principles to help people develop more effective or adaptive behaviors.

2. _____ Schedule of reinforcement in which every occurrence of a particular response is reinforced.

3. _____ The popular name for an operant chamber, the experimental apparatus invented by B. F. Skinner to study the relationship between environmental events and active behaviors.

4. _____ Reinforcement schedule in which a reinforcer is delivered after a fixed number of responses has occurred.

5. _____ Operant conditioning procedure in which successively closer approximations of a goal behavior are selectively reinforced until the goal behavior is displayed.

6. _____ Reinforcement schedule in which a reinforcer is delivered for the first response that occurs after a fixed time interval has elapsed.

7. _____ The delivery of a reinforcer according to a preset pattern based on the number of responses or the time interval between responses.

True/False Test

Indicate whether each statement is true or false by placing T or F in the blank space next to each item.

1. ___ Partial reinforcement refers to a situation in which the occurrence of a particular response is only sometimes followed by a reinforcer.

2. ___ A variable-ratio schedule is one in which a reinforcer is delivered for the first response that occurs after an average time interval has elapsed but the time varies unpredictably from trial to trial.

3. ___ A discriminative stimulus is a specific stimulus in the presence of which a particular response is more likely to be reinforced.

4. ___ A variable-interval schedule is one in which a reinforcer is delivered after an average number of responses but the number varies unpredictably from trial to trial.

5. ___ The partial reinforcement effect refers to the fact that continuously reinforced behaviors are more resistant to extinction than behaviors that are only sometimes reinforced.

6. ___ The gradual weakening and disappearance of conditioned behavior in operant conditioning is called extinction; it occurs when an emitted behavior is no longer followed by a reinforcer.

> Check your answers and review any areas of weakness before going on to the next section.

Contemporary Views of Operant Conditioning

Preview Questions

Consider the following questions as you study this section of the chapter.

- What factors do contemporary learning researchers suggest are involved in operant conditioning?

- How did Tolman's research demonstrate the involvement of cognitive processes in learning?

- What are cognitive maps and latent learning?

- How is operant conditioning influenced by an animal's natural behavior pattern?

- What is instinctive drift, and how does it challenge the traditional behavioral view of operant conditioning?

*Read the section "Contemporary Views of Operant Conditioning" and **write** your answers to the following:*

1. (a) In Skinner's view, operant conditioning did not need to invoke _____ factors to explain the acquisition of operant behaviors.

(b) Similarly, Thorndike and other early behaviorists believed that complex, active behaviors were no more than a chain of _____ connections that had been "stamped in" by their effects.

2. (a) Tolman firmly believed that _____ processes played an important role in the learning of complex behavior; although these processes could not be observed directly, they could still be experimentally _____ and _____ by careful observation of outward behavior.

(b) Traditional behaviorists believed that rats in a maze learned a _____ , whereas Tolman believed that rats learned a mental representation of the layout of the maze, which he called a _____ .

(c) As a result of his research, Tolman concluded that _____ or _____ is not necessary for learning to take place. He also made the distinction between _____ (behavior that is observed) and _____ (which is inferred from performance).

(d) Learning that is not reflected in actual performance or overt behavior is called _____ learning.

(e) Many contemporary cognitive learning theorists follow Tolman in their belief that operant conditioning involves the _____ of the relationship between a behavior and its consequences; that is, operant conditioning is seen as involving the cognitive _____ that a given consequence will follow a given behavior.

3. (a) Like those studying classical conditioning, psychologists studying operant conditioning found that an animal's _____ behavior patterns could influence the learning of new behaviors.

(b) The Brelands noted that certain nonreinforced behaviors, which seemed to reflect innate, _____ tendencies, prevented the animal from getting reinforced for the correct behaviors.

(c) The biological predisposition to perform natural behaviors that interfere with the performance of operant behaviors is called _____ .

Observational Learning: Imitating the Actions of Others

Preview Questions

Consider the following questions as you study this section of the chapter.

- What type of learning is indirect?
- What four mental processes are involved in observational learning?
- How has observational learning been applied?

Read the section "Observational Learning: Imitating the Actions of Others" and **write** *your answers to the following:*

1. (a) Classical and operant conditioning emphasize the role of _____ experiences in learning, but much of human learning occurs _____ , by watching what other people do, then imitating their behaviors.

(b) The type of learning in which changes in behavior take place through watching the actions of others is called _____ . The psychologist most strongly identified with this type of learning is _____ , who believes that such learning is the result of _____ processes that are actively judgmental and constructive, not merely mechanical copying.

(c) In one famous experiment, three separate groups of four-year-old children watched a short film, which had a different ending for each group. Some children saw an adult who behaved aggressively being _____ with soft drinks and candy; other children saw the adult being _____ , and some watched a version in which there were _____ for the aggressive behavior. As expected, when the children were allowed to play alone, the consequences they observed _____ (did/did not) affect their behavior.

(d) When asked to show the experimenter what the adult did in the film, almost all the children, who were promised reinforcement, _____ (did not imitate/imitated) the aggressive model despite the fact that this learning _____ (was/was not) evident in their earlier behavior.

(e) Bandura explained his results in much the same way Tolman explained latent learning; reinforcement _____ (is/is not) essential for learning; rather, the _____ of reinforcement affects the performance of what had been learned.

2. Bandura suggests that four cognitive processes interact to determine whether imitation will occur:

(a) You must pay _____ to the model's behavior.

(b) You must _____ the model's behavior.

(c) You must be able to transform the mental representations into _____ .

(d) There must be some _____ to imitate the model's behavior.

3. (a) Nonhuman animals _____ (are/are not) capable of learning new behaviors through observation and imitation.

(b) _____ factors seem to play a role in observational learning by primates; high status rather than low status models were _____ (more/less) likely to be imitated, and

those with whom the animals had a close relationship were _____ (more/less) likely to be imitated than were strangers.

(c) Like classical and operant conditioning, _____ has been applied in a variety of settings, including education, vocational and job training, psychotherapy, and counseling.

5. Read the following and write the correct term or word in the space provided.

(a) Maria watches the cooking show Cucina Amore on public TV on Saturday afternoon and often cooks one of the dishes she sees the chef prepare. Maria's culinary ability is the result of _____ learning.

(b) Dr. Bristow believes that reinforcement is not necessary for learning to occur but that the *expectation* of reinforcement can affect the performance of what has been learned. Dr. Bristow is emphasizing the importance of _____ factors in learning.

(c) If a rat has been allowed to explore a maze for a number of trials without ever getting a reinforcer, it is very _____ (likely/unlikely) that when food is made available in the goal box, the rat will find it very quickly with few errors.

(d) An animal trainer has a hard time operantly conditioning a pig to pick up a large wooden penny and put it in a big "piggy bank" because the pig seems to prefer to push the coin with its snout even though it is not reinforced for this behavior. The Brelands called this phenomenon _____ .

(e) Mr. and Mrs. Delbrook both stopped smoking when they started a family because they wanted to model healthy behavior patterns for their children. They are apparently aware of the importance of _____ learning in children's development.

Review of Terms, Concepts, and Names 4

Use the terms in this list to complete the Matching Test, then to help you answer the True/False items correctly.

Edward C. Tolman
cognitive map
latent learning
learned helplessness

instinctive drift
Albert Bandura
observational learning

Matching Exercise

Match the appropriate term/name with its definition or description:

1. _____ Learning that occurs through observing the actions of others.

2. _____ Tolman's term for learning that occurs in the absence of reinforcement but is not behaviorally demonstrated until a reinforcer becomes available.

3. _____ American psychologist who used the terms *cognitive map* and *latent learning* to describe experimental findings that strongly suggested that cognitive factors play a role in animal learning.

4. _____ Tolman's term for the mental representation of the layout of a familiar environment.

5. _____ American psychologist who experimentally investigated observational learning, emphasizing the role of cognitive factors.

6. _____ The tendency of an animal to revert to instinctive behaviors, which can interfere with the performance of an operantly conditioned response.

7. _____ A phenomenon in which exposure to inescapable and uncontrollable aversive events produces passive behavior.

Check your answers and review any areas of weakness before going on to the next section.

Something to Think About

1. Imagine that you are a behavioral therapist whose client has a real fear of going to the dentist. Despite the need for some important dental work, he can't bring himself to make an appointment. Using what you know about classical conditioning, explain how his phobia might have come about and describe how to extinguish the fear.

2. Mrs. Denton can't understand why scolding her ten-year-old son for misbehaving only seems to make the problem worse. Using what you know about operant conditioning techniques, what advice would you give Mrs. Denton about how she might (a) reduce the disruptive behavior and (b) increase more appropriate behavior.

3. Imagine your family has decided to get a new puppy dog. Using what you know about operant conditioning techniques, what advice would you give them about how they should train the dog to be obedient and do some neat pet tricks.

Check your answers and review any areas of weakness before doing the progress tests.

Progress Test 1

Review the complete chapter (including Concept Reviews and all the boxed inserts), review all your study notes, and then test yourself on the following progress test. Check your answers. If you make a mistake, review your notes, review the relevant section of the study guide, and, if necessary, go back and read the appropriate part of your textbook.

1. Dr. Ramos is a behavioral psychologist who conducts basic research using animals in carefully controlled laboratory studies. The goal of his research is most probably to
   (a) train animals to do tricks.
   (b) collect and sell saliva from dogs and other animals.
   (c) identify the general learning principles of learning that apply across a wide range of species, including humans.
   (d) observe changes in animal behavior that result from biological maturation.

2. Dr. Frolov classically conditioned a dog to flex his hind leg at the sound of a bell by pairing the ringing of a bell with a mild electric shock to the leg. In this example, the ringing bell is the
   (a) unconditioned stimulus (UCS)
   (b) conditioned response (CR)
   (c) unconditioned response (UCR)
   (d) conditioned stimulus (CS)

3. Some forms of chemotherapy make patients sick. A patient who has eaten vegetarian pizza just before the therapy (and is then sick) later feels ill when she sees or smells pizza. In this example of taste aversion learning, the conditioned response is the

(a) vegetarian pizza.
(b) chemotherapy.
(c) illness induced by the therapy.
(d) nausea felt at the sight or smell of pizza.

4. Zoran has a classically conditioned fear of rivers and lakes after he was attacked by an alligator while swimming in a river near his home. A behavioral psychologist is likely to suggest that his conditioned response (CR) can be weakened and may eventually disappear through a process called

(a) spontaneous recovery.
(b) extinction.
(c) instinctive drift.
(d) stimulus generalization.

5. Dr. Redner believes that classical conditioning depends on the information the conditioned stimulus provides about the unconditioned stimulus, and that for learning to occur, the conditioned stimulus must be a reliable signal that predicts the presentation of the unconditioned stimulus. Dr. Redner's views are most consistent with those of the learning theorist

(a) Robert A. Rescorla.
(b) Edward L. Thorndike.
(c) Ivan Pavlov.
(d) B. F. Skinner.

6. Ricardo always gets nervous and apprehensive whenever his professor uses the word "exam" but he seldom feels the same anxiety when the word "quiz" is mentioned. Assuming that classical conditioning is involved in these two different reactions at the mention of tests, it appears that Ricardo is exhibiting

(a) stimulus discrimination.
(b) spontaneous recovery.
(c) latent learning.
(d) stimulus generalization.

7. About five hours after she had successfully extinguished a dog's classically conditioned response of salivating to the sound of a bell, Dr. Sheckenov discovered that the dog once again salivated in the presence of the bell. This example illustrate the phenomenon of

(a) stimulus generalization.
(b) spontaneous recovery.
(c) latent learning.
(d) instinctive drift.

8. Dr. Radersched conducts research on the phenomenon of biological preparedness. She is most likely to discover that

(a) organisms are innately predisposed to form associations between some stimuli and responses and not others.
(b) that the general principles of learning apply to virtually all animal species and all learning situations.
(c) classical conditioning occurs because two stimuli are associated closely in time and that frequency and contiguity are the only variables that affect learning.
(d) mental processes, but not innate predispositions, are the crucial variables involved in classical conditioning.

9. After studying very hard last semester Sasha got very good grades in all her courses. This semester Sasha is once again studying very hard. It appears that good grades are _____ for Sasha's studying behavior.

(a) conditioned stimuli
(b) discriminative stimuli
(c) positively reinforcing
(d) negatively reinforcing

10. Rachel studies very hard to avoid getting bad grades because for her a bad grade is a devastating experience. Rachel's studying behavior is maintained by

(a) negative reinforcement.
(b) primary reinforcement.
(c) positive reinforcement.
(d) punishment by removal.

11. Helmut is employed by his university as a telephone solicitor for a fundraising drive. He is paid a set amount of money for every ten calls he makes regardless of whether he is successful in raising funds. Helmut's telephoning is reinforced on a _____ schedule of reinforcement.

(a) fixed-interval (FI)
(b) variable-interval (VI)
(c) fixed-ratio (FR)
(d) variable-ratio (VR)

12. Ever since Thelma got her new fax machine and hooked up her computer to the Internet, her phone line is often busy. It is difficult for her parents to know when to call her so they try at random times. It appears that phoning Thelma is reinforced on a _____ schedule.
    (a) fixed-interval (FI)
    (b) variable-interval (VI)
    (c) fixed-ratio (FR)
    (d) variable-ratio (VR)

13. After they had been watching Superman cartoons all morning, five-year-old Jim and six-year-old John, each using a beach towel as a cape, climbed on top of the garage roof and got ready to fly. Their startled mother stopped them in time and realized the powerful influence of _____ on behavior.
    (a) observational learning
    (b) classical conditioning
    (c) operant conditioning
    (d) stimulus generalization

14. According to the Critical Thinking 5.4, B. F. Skinner maintained that
    (a) human freedom is an illusion.
    (b) all behavior arises from causes that are within the individual, and environmental factors have little or no influence.
    (c) cognitive factors are the crucial elements in all learning.
    (d) the evolutionary perspective best explains animal behavior but can't be applied to human beings.

15. According to In Focus 5.5, the phenomenon of learned helplessness demonstrated that
    (a) cognitive factors, such as expectations, are involved in learning.
    (b) fixed-ratio schedules produce greater responding than fixed-interval schedules.
    (c) biological predispositions are involved in classical conditioning.
    (d) continuously reinforced behaviors are more resistant to extinction than are partially reinforced behaviors.

Progress Test 2

After you have checked your understanding of the material in Progress Test 1 and have done a com-plete chapter review with special focus on any areas of weakness, you are now ready to assess your knowledge on Progress Test 2. Check your answers. If you make a mistake, review your notes, the relevant section of the study guide, and, if necessary, the appropriate part of your textbook.

1. Which of the following best illustrates classical conditioning?
    (a) Henry feels ill at the sight or smell of peanut butter because it once made him sick.
    (b) Annalee studies hard because she wants to get good grades.
    (c) Virginia goes shopping for new clothes fairly frequently because it makes her feel good.
    (d) Lyndle drives at the posted speed limit after getting a number of speeding tickets.

2. Erv developed a fear of attics after he was accidentally locked in his own attic by his wife. Erv's present fear and apprehension of the attic is a(n)
    (a) example of instinctive drift.
    (b) conditioned emotional response.
    (c) form of learned helplessness.
    (d) conditioned physiological response.

3. Little Richard receives attention from his teacher in the form of a scolding every time he misbehaves. As a result, Richard misbehaves quite frequently. In this instance, it would appear that the teacher's scolding is a
    (a) form of punishment by application.
    (b) positively reinforcing stimulus.
    (c) form of punishment by removal.
    (d) negatively reinforcing stimulus.

4. A group of four-year-old children watch a video showing an adult hitting, kicking, and punching a large Bobo doll. These children are later asked to imitate the model and are promised a reward for every behavior they can imitate. It is very probable that the children will
    (a) not imitate the adult model.
    (b) verbally describe what they saw but will refuse to imitate the adult model.
    (c) quite readily imitate the adult's aggressive behavior.
    (d) become very upset as a result of watching the aggressive behavior.

5. Lauren spent the first week of the semester exploring the campus. Later, she had no trouble locating the library, although she had never been there before. According to Tolman, Lauren

(a) has developed biological preparedness.
(b) has formed a cognitive map.
(c) is suffering from instinctive drift.
(d) has developed a sense of direction.

6. Gerry puts up her umbrella soon after it starts to rain in order prevent her clothes from getting any wetter. This example illustrates _____ behavior and _____ reinforcement.

(a) avoidance; positive
(b) escape; negative
(c) avoidance; negative
(d) escape; positive

7. When Juanita gets paid she uses her money to buy food to feed her family. For Juanita, money is a _____ reinforcer and food is a _____ reinforcer

(a) conditioned; primary
(b) primary; negative
(c) conditioned; secondary
(d) primary; positive

8. At dinner one night, Amanda created quite a disturbance using her spoon as a drumstick. Her mother told her that she would get no dessert if she persisted with her unruly behavior. Amanda soon stopped the banging. This example most clearly illustrates

(a) negative reinforcement.
(b) punishment by removal.
(c) positive reinforcement.
(d) punishment by application.

9. Dr. Penrose uses a fixed-interval schedule of tests throughout the term. It is likely her student's studying behavior will

(a) be slow, steady, and moderate.
(b) demonstrate a burst-pause-burst pattern.
(c) follow a scallop-shaped pattern.
(d) be extinguished because of lack of consistent reinforcement.

10. Zeno tried to train his potbellied pig to pick up the newspaper on the doorstep and bring it into the house. However, the pig pushed the paper with his snout into the garden, even though this behavior would not be rewarded. It appears that Zeno's attempt to operantly condition his pig has been subject to

(a) instinctive drift.
(b) stimulus discrimination.
(c) spontaneous recovery.
(d) extinction.

11. Greta loves playing the slot machines even though she wins money only once in a while. Greta's gambling behavior is likely to be very resistant to extinction because of

(a) the partial reinforcement effect.
(b) Premack's principle.
(c) the law of effect.
(d) instinctive drift.

12. Dalbir believes that reinforcement is not necessary for learning to occur but it does affect the performance of what has been learned. Dalbir's view is most consistent with the phenomenon of

(a) instinctive drift.
(b) biological preparedness.
(c) learned helplessness.
(d) latent learning.

13. Sebastian has often had stir-fried yak with his girlfriend at their favorite Mongolian restaurant. On one occasion, he got very sick a few hours later. In the future, he will most likely avoid which of the following?

(a) his girlfriend
(b) Mongolians
(c) stir-fried yak
(d) all restaurants

14. According to the Application, we often choose a short-term reinforcer over a more valuable long-term goal. Your text suggests that we do this because

(a) the relative value of a reinforcer can shift over time.
(b) as the availability of a reinforcer gets closer, the subjective value of the reinforcer increases.
(c) when we make our decision, we'll choose whichever reinforcer has the greatest subjective value.
(d) of all of the above reasons.

15. According to Seligman (In Focus 5.2), people are more likely to develop phobias of spiders, snakes, or heights—as compared to doorknobs, knives, washing machines, and ladders—because
    (a) of instinctive drift.
    (b) we are biologically prepared to do so.
    (c) doorknobs, knives, and ladders are inherently safer than spiders, snakes, and heights.
    (d) of latent learning.

Progress Test 3

After you have checked your understanding of the material in Progress Tests 1 and 2, and have done a complete chapter review with special focus on any areas of weakness, you are ready to further assess your knowledge on Progress Test 3. Check your answers. If you make a mistake, review your notes, the appropriate parts of the study guide, and if necessary, the relevant sections of your textbook.

1. Arturo, a psychology major, was asked by his roommate to explain conditioning. He is most likely to point out
   (a) that conditioning is the process of learning associations between environmental events and behavioral responses.
   (b) that there are two basic types of conditioning, operant conditioning and classical conditioning.
   (c) that contemporary learning theorists also consider the process of observational learning.
   (d) all of the above.

2. When Harjit jumped into the swimming pool, she was surprised by the coldness of the water and reflexively started shivering. Her automatic shivering response to the cold temperature is a(n)
   (a) conditioned response (CR).
   (b) unconditioned stimulus (UCS).
   (c) unconditioned response (UCR).
   (d) conditioned stimulus (CS).

3. Justine got sick after eating a chicken burger. Now she not only has an intense dislike of chicken burgers but feels nauseated at the sight of beef burgers, fish burgers, soybean burgers, or anything that even resembles a burger. It would appear that Justine has experienced the phenomenon Pavlov called
   (a) stimulus discrimination.
   (b) spontaneous recovery.
   (c) extinction.
   (d) stimulus generalization.

4. By presenting the CS over and over again without the UCS, Dr. Laslove discovered that the subject's conditioned response (CR) gradually weakened and disappeared. Dr. Laslove has carried out a procedure called
   (a) latent learning.
   (b) spontaneous recovery.
   (c) extinction.
   (d) stimulus discrimination.

5. Rolando got very sick after eating a big dish of oysters. Ever since that experience Rolando feels ill whenever he sees or smells oysters. It appears that Rolando
   (a) has developed a taste aversion.
   (b) has experienced latent learning.
   (c) is suffering from instinctive drift.
   (d) is experiencing spontaneous recovery.

6. Dr. Alonzo takes a cognitive perspective in his research on learning. He is most likely to suggest that classical conditioning
   (a) involves learning the relations between events and that the CS must be a reliable predictor of the UCS.
   (b) results from simply pairing the CS with the UCS for a number of trials.
   (c) is constrained by biological predispositions.
   (d) follows general principles of learning that apply to virtually all animals species and all learning situations.

7. Positive reinforcement is to _____ as negative reinforcement is to _____ .
   (a) increased responding; decreased responding
   (b) decreased responding decreased responding
   (c) increased responding; decreased responding
   (d) increased responding; increased responding

8. When Bella used his knife to release a piece of toast that was jammed in the toaster he got a severe electric shock. Bella has never used his knife to get toast out of the toaster again. It appears that Bella's behavior has been changed by
   (a) punishment by application.
   (b) negative reinforcement.
   (c) punishment by removal.
   (d) extinction.

9. Whenever the doorbell rings, Rex runs to the door and barks and growls. For Rex the ringing doorbell is a(n) _____ for his growling and barking behavior.
   (a) discriminative stimulus
   (b) unconditioned stimulus
   (c) reinforcing stimulus
   (d) primary reinforcer

10. Tammy wants to train her dog to "shake hands" with people so she reinforcers closer and closer approximations to the desired behavior. First she rewards him for sitting on command, then for slightly raising his front paw, then for fully raising his paw, then for moving his paw up and down until it is grasped, and so on. Tammy has used a process called
    (a) latent learning.
    (b) extinction.
    (c) partial reinforcement.
    (d) shaping.

11. Arnie always drives at the posted speed limit and obeys all the rules of the road because he can't afford to pay fines for driving offenses. Arnie's good driving habits are maintained by
    (a) positive reinforcement.
    (b) partial reinforcement.
    (c) secondary reinforcement.
    (d) negative reinforcement.

12. Harry works on an assembly line as part of a team of eight workers. They get paid a bonus for every one hundred products they assemble. Harry and his coworkers are being rewarded on a _____ schedule of reinforcement.
    (a) fixed-interval (FI)
    (b) variable-interval (VI)
    (c) fixed-ratio (FR)
    (d) variable-ratio (VR)

13. Wilma's psychology instructor schedules tests every two weeks throughout the semester but her sociology instructor has surprise quizzes throughout the semester. The psychology instructor is using a _____ schedule and the sociology instructor is using a _____ schedule.
    (a) fixed-interval (FI); variable-interval (VI)
    (b) variable-interval (VI); variable-ratio (VR)
    (c) fixed-ratio (FR); variable-ratio (VR)
    (d) variable-ratio (VR); fixed-interval (FI)

14. According to In Focus 5.1, John B. Watson
    (a) believed that punishment was the best and most desirable way to change behavior.
    (b) vehemently opposed Skinner's idea that freedom is just an illusion.
    (c) was a pioneer in the application of classical conditioning principles to advertising.
    (d) discovered the phenomenon of learned helplessness.

15. According to In Focus 5.3, which of the following is true?
    (a) Punishment is the most effective way to change undesirable behavior.
    (b) Punishment works better than any other behavioral strategy in changing undesirable behavior.
    (c) There are no effective strategies for reducing undesirable behaviors.
    (d) A number of strategies other than punishment can be used to change undesirable behavior.

Answers

Introduction: What Is Learning?

1. (a) enduring change in behavior or knowledge as a result of an individual's experience
   (b) adapting
   (c) animals; general principles of learning

2. (a) associations; environmental; behavioral
   (b) classical; operant
   (c) observational

Classical Conditioning: Associating Stimuli

1. (a) physiologist
   (b) classical conditioning

2. (a) elicited; causes an existing behavior to occur
   (b) reflex; automatically or reflexively; automatically or reflexively
   (c) learned; stimulus-response

3. (a) association; neutral (later to be a conditioned stimulus); unconditioned; unconditioned
   (b) conditioned; reflexive

4. (a) unconditioned stimulus; UCS
   (b) unconditioned response; UCR
   (c) conditioned stimulus; CS
   (d) conditioned response; CR
   (e) conditioned; conditioned; unconditioned; unconditioned
   (f) unconditioned; conditioned

5. (a) frequently
   (b) shortly before
   (c) stimulus generalization; stimulus discrimination
   (d) disappear; extinction
   (e) reappear; spontaneous recovery

6. (a) John B. Watson
   (b) behaviorism
   (c) Watson; love, rage; fear

7. (a)

(b) fear

CS	UCS	UCR
white rat	loud noise	fear

8. (a) physiological
   (b) conditioned; conditioned
   (c) unconditioned; unconditioned

9. (a) chemotherapy treatment; drop in immune response
   (b) cues
   (c) reduced immune functioning

10. (a) spontaneous recovery
    (b) discriminate
    (c) conditioned response (CR)
    (d) generalization

(c) emotional responses
(d) generalization
(e) ethical

Graphic Organizer 1

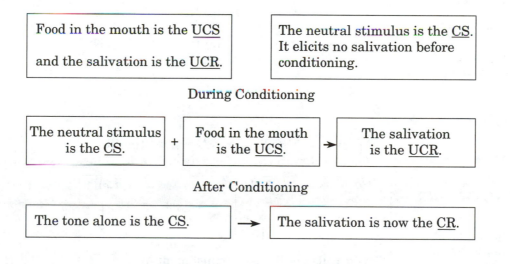

Before Conditioning

Food in the mouth is the UCS and the salivation is the UCR.

The neutral stimulus is the CS. It elicits no salivation before conditioning.

During Conditioning

The neutral stimulus is the CS. + Food in the mouth is the UCS. → The salivation is the UCR.

After Conditioning

The tone alone is the CS. → The salivation is now the CR.

Contemporary Views of Classical Conditioning

1. (a) not needed
   (b) mental processes

2. (a) information
   (b) reliable signal
   (c) information; predictive value
   (d) cognitive; relationships

3. (a) natural selection; adaptation
   (b) animal species; learning; taste aversion

4. (a) taste aversion
   (b) taste aversion learning; several hours

(c) John Garcia

5. (a) cannot; external stimuli; internal stimuli
   (b) biological preparedness; biologically prepared
   (c) evolutionary; survival
   (d) behavior patterns; evolution

6. (a) behavioral; evolutionary
   (b) likely; unlikely
   (c) biological preparedness
   (d) cognitive

Matching Exercise 1

1. extinction
2. conditioning
3. learning
4. taste aversion
5. John B. Watson
6. behaviorism
7. unconditioned stimulus (UCS)
8. Ivan Pavlov
9. phobia
10. unconditioned response (UCR)
11. biological preparedness

True/False Test 1

1. T	5. T	9. T
2. T	6. T	10. T
3. F	7. F	
4. F	8. F	

Operant Conditioning: Associating Behaviors and Consequences (Part 1)

1. (a) Edward L. Thorndike
   (b) trial; error
   (c) satisfying state of affairs; unpleasant, annoying state of affairs

2. (a) should; could not
   (b) emitted; operate; consequences
   (c) shaped; consequences; operant; reinforcing stimulus (reinforcer)
   (d) stimulus; event

3. (a) addition of a reinforcing stimulus; removal of an aversive or unpleasant stimulus
   (b) strengthens (increases)
   (c) escape; avoid
   (d) escape; avoidance

4. (a) primary; conditioned
   (b) primary; conditioned

5. (a) avoidance
   (b) escape
   (c) avoidance
   (d) escape

6. (a) decrease
   (b) increases; decreases
   (c) presentation; loss; withdrawal
   (d) effects

7. (a) delayed; immediately
   (b) teach or promote; fear; anxiety; temporary
   (c) positive reinforcement

8. (a) N   (e) P
   (b) P   (f) N
   (c) P   (g) N
   (d) P

Graphic Organizer 2

	Appetitive Stimuli (e.g., food, water)	Aversive Stimuli (e.g., shock)
The operant response is followed by	Cell 1 — FOOD ↑ This is called <u>positive reinforcement</u>	Cell 2 — SHOCK ↓ This is called <u>punishment by application</u>
The operant response precludes or prevents the delivery of	Cell 3 — FOOD ↓ This is called <u>punishment by removal</u>	Cell 4 — SHOCK ↑ This is called <u>negative reinforcement</u>

9. (a) law of effect
   (b) punishment by application; negative reinforcement
   (c) positively; negatively
   (d) Edward L. Thorndike

Matching Exercise 2

1. B. F. Skinner
2. negative reinforcement
3. Edward L. Thorndike

4. punishment

5. conditioned reinforcer

6. reinforcement

7. operant

True/False Test 2

1. T	3. T	5. T	7. T
2. F	4. F	6. T	

Operant Conditioning: Associating Behaviors and Consequences (Part 2)

1. (a) operant; reinforced
   (b) discriminative stimulus

2. (a) determined; controlled
   (b) discriminative; operant; reinforcement; punishment
   (c) more; less
   (d) operant chamber

3. (a) shaping
   (b) shaping

4. (a) continuous reinforcement
   (b) partial reinforcement
   (c) extinction
   (d) more; continuous

5. (a) schedules of reinforcement
   (b) fixed-ratio (FR); high
   (c) variable-ratio (VR) high; unpredictable
   (d) fixed-interval (FI); increase
   (e) variable-interval (VI); moderate

6. (a) behavior modification
   (b) Behavior modification

7. (a) variable-interval (VI)
   (b) fixed-interval (FI)
   (c) fixed-ratio (FR)
   (d) variable-ratio (VR)
   (e) fixed-ratio (FR)

Graphic Organizer 3

	Based on the number of responses made	Based on the elapsed time
Fixed	Cell 1 Fixed ratio	Cell 2 Fixed interval
Variable	Cell 3 Variable ratio	Cell 4 Variable interval

Matching Exercise 3

1. behavior modification
2. continuous reinforcement
3. Skinner box
4. fixed ratio (FR)
5. shaping
6. fixed interval (FI)
7. schedules of reinforcement

True/False Test 3

1. T	3. T	5. F
2. F	4. F	6. T

Contemporary Views of Operant Conditioning

1. (a) cognitive
   (b) stimulus-response

2. (a) cognitive; verified; inferred
   (b) sequence of responses; cognitive map
   (c) reward; reinforcement; performance; learning
   (d) latent
   (e) cognitive representations; expectancy

3. (a) natural
   (b) instinctive
   (c) instinctive drift

Observational Learning: Imitating the Actions of Others

1. (a) direct; indirectly
   (b) observational learning; Albert Bandura; cognitive
   (c) reinforced; punished; no consequences; did
   (d) imitated; was not
   (e) is not; expectation

2. (a) attention
   (b) remember
   (c) actions capable of being reproduced
   (d) motivation

3. (a) are
   (b) Motivational; more; more
   (c) observational learning

5. (a) observational
   (b) cognitive
   (c) likely
   (d) instinctive drift
   (e) observational

Matching Exercise 4

1. observational learning
2. latent learning
3. Edward C. Tolman

4. cognitive map
5. Albert Bandura
6. instinctive drift

Something to Think About

1. The first assumption that someone who adheres to the behavioral perspective would make is that the irrational fear, or phobia, was the result of a classical conditioning process. In the past, the client had a very unpleasant experience at a dentist's office. One could speculate that as a child he was taken to the dentist and experienced pain and fear when a hypodermic needle was inserted into his gum or a drill struck a nerve. If this were the case, the dentist (CS) has become associated with the needle or drill (UCS), which elicited pain and fear (UCR). The dentist (CS) now evokes a fear response (CR), which may have generalized to all dentists.

   One way to get rid of the irrational fear would be to use an extinction procedure in which the CS (the dentist) is presented over and over without the UCS until the fear subsides. This might mean that the client will have to find a very understanding dentist who will allow him to make many visits to the office without having any work done. The behavioral perspective predicts that this would eventually result in a reduction of the irrational fear and therefore allow the client to get some much-needed dental work done. It would also be important to point out that following a prolonged absence from the dentist, spontaneous recovery may occur.

2. It is possible that Mrs. Denton's "scolding" may in fact be reinforcing the undesirable behavior. Attention, in almost any form, from an adult can be a powerful positive reinforcer for a child. If this is the case, then withholding reinforcement (scolding) will tend to extinguish the target behavior, but only if it is consistent. Inconsistent or intermittent reinforcement will make the behavior very resistant to extinction.

   In addition, she should encourage desirable behavior. She should pay attention to any instance of good behavior, or any close approximation of the goal behavior, by praising her son or providing some other positive reinforcer. In other words, she should use a shaping procedure initially, then use partial reinforcement to ensure that the desirable behavior becomes resistant to extinction. It is also important that she model the appropriate behavior and avoid punishing the child, especially using punishment by application.

3. Operant conditioning techniques can be used to train animals. Decide on the target behavior(s) and start by using a shaping procedure and continuous positive reinforcement. Pick one of the behaviors you want to train—for example having the dog sit at the command "sit"—and use a reinforcer such as "good dog!" while patting the dog on the head or chest. The command "sit" should be followed with gentle pressure on the dog's rear end to make him sit; he should be reinforced immediately. After just a few trials, the dog will sit on command without the application of pressure to his back; he should always be immediately reinforced. It is important to let the dog know who is in command at all times without using punishment. After the dog is obeying the commands regularly, then switch to a partial reinforcement schedule, only occasionally reinforcing the dog for obeying. This will ensure greater resistance to extinction. Dogs can be trained to do many tricks in this manner, but remember to work with the animal's natural repertoire of behaviors (biological predispositions). Dogs can learn some behaviors more easily than others.

Progresst Test 1

1. c	6. a	11. c
2. d	7. b	12. b
3. d	8. a	13. a
4. b	9. c	14. a
5. a	10. a	15. a

Progress Test 2

1. a	6. b	11. a
2. b	7. a	12. d
3. b	8. b	13. c
4. c	9. c	14. d
5. b	10. a	15. b

Progress Test 3

1. d	6. a	11. d
2. c	7. d	12. c
3. d	8. a	13. a
4. c	9. a	14. c
5. a	10. d	15. d

Memory

Reading the section below first will give you a general sense of the chapter's contents and an initial introduction to some of the major concepts and terms. This will prime you for what you are about to read and help you to develop a "cognitive map" that will guide your study of the material in this chapter. Likewise, reading the **preview questions** at the beginning of each major section will improve your ability to understand, learn, and retain the information.

CHAPTER 6 . . . AT A GLANCE

Chapter 6 examines memory and the mechanisms involved in remembering and forgetting. The first section begins with the fundamental processes of encoding, storage, and retrieval, followed by a discussion of the capacity, duration, and function of each of the three stages of memory: sensory memory, short-term memory, and long-term memory. The levels-of-processing framework is presented, as are the types of information stored in long-term memory and the ways in which that information is organized.

How retrieval works and the problems associated with retrieval failure, as in the tip-of-the-tongue phenomenon, are examined. How the serial position effect, encoding specificity principle, and flashbulb memories contribute to our ability to remember—or not remember—information is explored. An explanation of the fact that memories are constructed and reconstructed lays the groundwork for a discussion of the sources of potential memory problems resulting from schema distortion, source confusion, and the misinformation effect. The influence of such problems on eyewitness testimony and false memories are also considered in this section.

Forgetting, theories of forgetting, and relevant research findings are explored next. Finally, the biological basis of memory is explained and the contributions of empirical research and case studies of people with amnesia are presented. The chapter ends with an examination of the role played by brain structures such as the hippocampus and the amygdala.

Introduction: What Is Memory?

Preview Questions

Consider the following questions as you study this section of the chapter.

- How is memory defined?
- What are encoding, storage, and retrieval?
- What is the three-stage model of memory?

*Read the section "Introduction: What is Memory?" and **write** your answers to the following:*

1. (a) Memory refers to the mental processes that enable us to _____ , _____ , and _____ information.

    (b) Rather than being a single process, memory involves three fundamental processes: _____ is the process of transforming information into a form that can be entered and retained by the memory system; _____ is the process of retaining information in memory so that it can be used at a later time; and _____ involves recovering the stored information so that we can be consciously aware of it.

2. (a) The stage model of memory divides memory into three distinct stages, _____ memory, _____ memory, and _____ memory; information is transferred from one stage to another.

    (b) Each memory stage is thought to differ in terms of _____ (how much information can be stored), _____ (how long the information can be stored), and _____ (what is done with the stored information).

3. (a) A great deal of information from the environment is first registered in _____ memory, where it is held for a very brief period of time; after a few seconds or less, the information fades.

    (b) During this very brief period of time, if you select or pay _____ to some aspect of the environmental information that's being registered, it will be transferred to the second stage of memory, _____ memory.

    (c) Also known as working memory, _____ memory refers to the active, working memory system that can temporarily hold all current information that you are consciously aware of for up to about _____ seconds.

    (d) Working memory is where cognitive activities such as _____ , _____ , and _____ take place. Information that is actively processed in working memory may be encoded for storage in _____ memory.

    (e) The third stage of memory, _____ memory, represents the storage of memories that may last for a lifetime.

    (f) The transfer of information between these stages involves an interaction; not only does information flow from _____ to _____ , but much information also flows in the opposite direction, from _____ to _____ .

Sensory Memory: Fleeting Impressions of Reality

Preview Questions

Consider the following questions as you study this section of the chapter.

- How long is information from the environment held in sensory memory?
- How did Sperling's experiment establish the duration of visual sensory memory?
- What are the functions of sensory memory?

Read the section "Sensory Memory: Fleeting Impressions of Reality" and **write** *your answers to the following:*

1. (a) The characteristics of visual sensory memory were first identified in 1960 in large part through the research of

   _____ .

   (b) Visual sensory memory holds a great deal of information very briefly, for about

   _____ , just long enough for us to pay attention to specific elements that are significant to us. This meaningful information is transferred to

   _____ memory.

2. (a) Visual sensory memory is sometimes referred to as _____ memory because it is the brief memory of an image, or _____ ; auditory sensory memory is sometimes referred to as _____ memory, meaning a brief memory that is like a(n)

   _____ .

   (b) The duration of visual sensory memory is about _____ to

   _____ a second, whereas auditory sensory memory holds information for up to _____ seconds.

   (c) An important function of sensory memory is to very briefly store our sensory impressions so that they _____ slightly with one another; this gives rise to our perception of the world around us as

   _____ rather than a series of disconnected images or disjointed sounds.

Short-Term, Working Memory: The Workshop of Consciousness

Preview Questions

Consider the following questions as you study this section of the chapter.

- What is the main function of short-term, or working, memory?

- What is the duration and capacity of short-term memory?

- How do we overcome the limitations of short-term memory?

Read the section "Short-term, Working Memory: The Workshop of Consciousness" and **write** *your answers to the following:*

1. (a) Short-term, or working, memory is the stage of memory in which information transferred from _____ memory and information retrieved from

   _____

   memory become conscious.

   (b) An important function of working memory is that it provides temporary _____ for information that is currently being used in some _____ cognitive activity.

   (c) If information in short-term memory is repeated over and over again, or

   _____ , it can be maintained in short-term memory much longer than 30 seconds; this is called

   _____ .

2. (a) The capacity of short-term memory is limited to about _____

   items, or bits of information, at one time; when short-term memory is filled to capacity, new information will bump out, or

   _____ , currently held information unless it is consciously and constantly repeated.

   (b) The amount of information that can be held in short-term memory can be increased through a process called

   _____ , the grouping of related items into a single unit; it often involves the retrieval of meaningful information from _____ .

Long-Term Memory

Preview Questions

Consider the following questions as you study this section of the chapter.

- How much information can be stored in long-term memory?
- What factors increase the efficiency of encoding?
- What is the levels-of-processing framework?
- What three major categories of information are stored in long-term memory, and how are they divided into subsystems?
- How is information organized in long-term memory?

Read the section "Long-Term Memory" and **write** *your answers to the following:*

1. (a) Long-term memory refers to the _____ of information over extended periods of time; it can involve recalling what you were doing just minutes ago or ten years ago.

    (b) The amount of information that can be held in long-term memory is _____ .

    (c) One common method of getting information into long-term memory is to repeat the to-be-remembered information over and over again; this strategy, called _____ rehearsal, is less effective than _____ rehearsal, which involves focusing on the meaning of information to help encode and transfer it to long-term memory.

    (d) Two additional factors enhance encoding and improve memory: applying information to yourself is the _____ effect; trying to picture the information in a vivid manner is the use of _____ .

2. (a) According to the levels-of-processing framework, information is more likely to be remembered if it is processed at a "_____" level than if it is processed at a "_____" level because elaborative _____ involves processing the meaning of new information, rather than its more superficial characteristics.

    (b) The levels-of-processing framework suggests that maintenance rehearsal, or simple repetition, would represent _____ processing, and elaborative rehearsal would represent _____ processing.

3. Three major categories of information are stored in long-term memory:

    (a) _____ information refers to the long-term memory of how to perform different skills, operations, and actions.

    (b) _____ information refers to long-term memory of events or episodes in your life; it is also called autobiographical memory.

    (c) _____ information is a general store of knowledge of facts, names, definitions, concepts, and ideas.

4. (a) Long-term memory is not a simple, unitary system; it appears to be composed of separate but interacting _____ and abilities.

    (b) A basic distinction has been made between explicit (or declarative) memory, which is described as _____ , and implicit (or nondeclarative) memory, which is described as _____ (procedural memories, including skills and habits, typically reflect implicit memory processes).

5. (a) Information in long-term memory is not just a random jumble of information—it is _____ —but the processes involved are not very well understood.

    (b) The process whereby information is actively

organized into related groups during recall from long-term memory is called

_____ ; usually, there is some logical _____ between bits of information stored in long-term memory.

(c) The _____ model accounts for the way information is organized in long-term memory by noting that concepts are logically linked, or associated, among different clusters of information.

(d) When one concept is activated in the

_____ , it can spread in any number of directions, activating other _____ , especially those with strong connections.

6. Read the following and write in the correct term in the space provided:

(a) During a math exam Trevor is desperately trying to think of the correct formula for the area of a triangle. Although he knew the formula when he was studying last week, it just won't come to mind, despite all his efforts. Trevor is experiencing trouble with one of the three fundamental processes of memory, called

_____ .

(b) To help learn the number of days in each month, eight-year-old Gloria has been reciting a short rhyme over and over:"Thirty days hath September, April, June, and November; all the rest have thirty-one except February, which has twenty-eight." She is using the fundamental process of _____ to transform the information into a form that can be entered and retained by the memory system.

(c) In the above example, Gloria is using a type of rehearsal that is giving some meaning to

an otherwise hard-to-remember string of numbers; this is called

_____ rehearsal.

(d) After looking up a phone number, Alysha is able to remember it only long enough to press all the correct numbers on the keypad. The phone number is in her

_____ memory and is briefly stored there by the use of

_____ rehearsal.

(e) Vito is an excellent chess player and can easily recall the exact positions of most of the chess pieces after a brief glance at the board. He explains his ability by pointing out that he does not try to memorize the locations of all the individual pieces but instead focuses on their relatively few attack patterns. Vito is using

_____ to improve the capacity of his short-term memory.

(f) Fifty-five-year-old Mr. Adams put on roller skates for the first time in over forty years; much to his surprise, he had no trouble remembering how to skate. In this instance, Mr. Adams is using one of the three categories of information stored in long-term memory, called _____ information.

(g) When Stephan was consciously reviewing the information he had researched for a term paper, he was using a dimension of long-term memory called

_____ (or declarative memory); later, when he was typing his paper without conscious awareness of the exact layout of the letters on the keyboard, he was using _____ (or nondeclarative memory).

Review of Terms, Concepts, and Names 1

Use the terms in this list to complete the Matching Test, then to help you answer the True/False items correctly.

memory
encoding
storage
retrieval
stage model of memory
sensory memory
short-term memory
  (working memory)
long-term memory
George Sperling
visual sensory memory
  (iconic memory)
auditory sensory
  memory
  (echoic memory)

maintenance rehearsal
chunking
elaborative rehearsal
self-reference effect
visual imagery
levels-of-processing
  framework
procedural information
episodic information
semantic information
explicit memory
implicit memory
clustering
association
semantic network model

Matching Exercise

Match the appropriate term/name with its definition or description.

1. _____ Rehearsal that involves focusing on the meaning of information to help encode and transfer it to long-term memory.

2. _____ Model that describes units of information in long-term memory as being organized in a complex network of associations.

3. _____ The process of recovering information stored in memory so that we are consciously aware of it.

4. _____ Organizing items into related groups during recall from long-term memory.

5. _____ Mental representations, or pictures, especially vivid ones, used to enhance encoding.

6. _____ Active stage of memory in which information is stored for about thirty seconds.

7. _____ Long-term memory of events in your life; also called autobiographical memory.

8. _____ The process of transforming information into a form that can be entered and retained by the memory system.

9. _____ Model that describes memory as consisting of three distinct stages: sensory memory, short-term memory, and long-term memory.

10. _____ The mental processes that enable us to retain and use information over time.

11. _____ Long-term memory of how to perform different skills, operations, and actions.

12. _____ American psychologist who identified the duration of visual sensory memory in a series of classic experiments in 1960.

13. _____ The stage of memory that represents the long-term storage of information.

True/False Test

Indicate whether each statement is true or false by placing T or F in the blank space next to each item.

1. ____ Information or knowledge that can be consciously recollected is called implicit, or nondeclarative, memory.

2. ____ Auditory sensory memory is sometimes referred to as iconic memory because it is a brief memory of an image, or icon.

3. ____ Applying information to oneself to help you remember that information is called the self-reference effect.

4. ____ Semantic information is the general knowledge of facts, names, concepts, and ideas stored in long-term memory.

5. ____ When people are presented with the stimulus word *salt*, they frequently respond with the word *pepper*, and this suggests that there is some logical association between bits of information in long-term memory.

6. ____ Storage is the process of transforming information into a form that can be entered and retained by the memory system.

7. ____ Sensory memory is the stage of memory that registers information from the environment and holds it for a very brief period of time.

8. ____ The levels-of-processing framework describes units of information in long-term memory as being organized in a complex network of associations.

9. ____ Maintenance rehearsal involves focusing on the meaning of information to help people encode and transfer it to long-term memory.

10. ____ Increasing the amount of information that can be held in short-term memory by grouping related items together as a single unit is called chunking.

11. ____ Auditory sensory memory is sometimes

referred to as echoic memory, meaning a brief memory that is like an echo.

12. ___ Information or knowledge that affects behavior or task performance but cannot be consciously recollected is called explicit, or declarative, memory.

> Check your answers and review any areas of weakness before going on to the next section.

Retrieval: Getting Information from Long-Term Memory

Preview Questions

Consider the following questions as you study this section of the chapter.

- How is retrieval defined, and what is a retrieval cue?
- What does the TOT experience tell us about the nature of memory?
- How is retrieval tested, and what is the serial position effect?
- What is the encoding specificity principle, and how is it reflected in context effects, state-dependent retrieval, and mood congruence?
- What role does distinctiveness play in retrieval, and how accurate are flashbulb memories?

Read the section "Retrieval: Getting Information from Long-Term Memory" and **write** *your answers to the following:*

1. (a) Retrieval refers to the process of accessing, or retrieving, stored information; in many instances, the ability to retrieve stored memories hinges on having an appropriate _____ .

   (b) The inability to recall long-term memories because of inadequate or missing retrieval cues is referred to as

   _____ .

2. The TOT experience refers to the inability to get at a bit of information that you're absolutely certain is stored in your memory and illustrates the following points:

   (a) Retrieving information is not an

   _____ process.

   (b) In many instances, information is stored in memory but not accessible without the right

   _____ .

   (c) Information stored in memory is

   _____ and connected in relatively logical ways.

3. (a) Producing information using no retrieval cues is called _____ ; it is the memory measure used on essay tests.

   (b) Remembering an item of information in response to a retrieval cue is called

   _____ ; it is the memory measure used on matching questions and fill-in-the-blank tests.

   (c) Identifying the correct information out of several possible choices is the memory measure called _____ ; multiple-choice tests are an example of this type of retrieval .

   (d) From a student's point of view,

   _____ and

   _____ tests are probably easiest, because they provide retrieval cues that help access stored information.

4. (a) The serial position effect refers to the tendency to retrieve information more easily from the _____ and the

   _____ of a list rather than the _____ .

   (b) The tendency to recall the first items in a list is called the _____ effect; the tendency to recall the final items in a list is called the

   _____ effect.

   (c) The _____ effect is especially prominent when you have to engage in serial recall, that is, when you have to remember a list of items in their original order.

5. The encoding specificity principle, which states that recreating the original conditions improves retrieval effectiveness, can take several forms.

    (a) The tendency to remember information more easily when the retrieval occurs in the same setting in which the information was originally learned is the

    _____ .

    (b) When the pharmacological state of learning and retrieval match, recall of information is better because of

    _____ .

    (c) The idea that a given mood tends to evoke memories that are consistent with that mood is referred to as

    _____ ; when in a

    _____ mood, you're more likely to recall positive memories; when in a

    _____ mood, you're more likely to recall negative or unpleasant memories.

6. (a) Encoded information representing a unique, different, or unusual event is easier to recall than routine events because such memories are said to be characterized by a high degree of _____ .

    (b) The recall of very specific images or details surrounding a significant, rare, or vivid event is called a _____ memory. Although there is usually a high level of

    _____ in the accuracy of these memories, research suggests that they are no better recalled than everyday memories.

Reconstructing Memories: Sources of Potential Errors

Preview Questions

Consider the following questions as you study this section of the chapter.

- Why do errors and distortions in memory occur during the process of retrieval?
- What are schemas, and how can they contribute to memory distortion?

- What is source confusion, and how can it produce false memories?
- What factors can reduce the accuracy of eyewitness testimony?

Read the section "Reconstructing Memories: Sources of Potential Errors" and **write** *your answers to the following:*

1. (a) Every new memory formed is not simply recorded, but actively

    _____ .

    (b) To form a new memory, you actively organize and encode information; later, when retrieval is attempted, details from memory are actively _____ , or rebuilt.

    (c) In the process of constructing and reconstructing a memory, two general factors can contribute to errors and distortions: the information stored _____ the memory occurs and the information acquired _____ the memory occurs.

2. (a) Organized clusters of knowledge and information about particular topics are called _____ ; these can be useful in forming new memories but can also contribute to memory distortions.

    (b) Research shows how _____ we already hold can influence what we remember, that once a memory is formed it has the potential to be _____ by new information, and that it is very easy for memories to become _____ .

3. (a) A memory distortion that arises when the true source of a memory is forgotten is called _____ .

    (b) The result can be a distorted or inaccurate memory that feels completely real and is often accompanied by all the emotional impact of a real memory, called a

    _____ .

(c) Research clearly shows that eyewitness testimony _____ (is/is not) subject to memory distortion, which can have serious implications in real life.

(d) A phenomenon in which people's existing memories can be altered by exposing them to misleading information is called the _____ . People _____ (are/are not) as confident of their fabricated memories as they are about their genuine memories.

4. (a) Despite the ways in which memory can be distorted, people's memories _____ (are/are not) accurate for overall details.

(b) When memory distortions occur, they usually involve _____ bits of information; nevertheless, the surprising ease with which bits of memory can be distorted is unnerving and suggests that rather than being set in stone, human memories are malleable.

5. Read the following and write the correct term in the space provided.

(a) When Cathy feels depressed, she remembers certain sad childhood events that she never thinks about otherwise. Cathy is experiencing the effects of _____ .

(b) Hendrik has a vivid memory of exactly what he was doing when President Bush declared war on Iraq. This example illustrates a _____ memory.

(c) Although elderly Mrs. Haggerty always answers her family's questions completely, she appears to be filling in blanks with logical, though often incorrect, information. This example illustrates the _____ nature of memory.

(d) Jessie cannot remember the newer name of the small Central American country that was formerly called British Honduras until she is told it starts with the letter B. The letter B acts as a _____ for the name *Belize*.

(e) The progress tests in this study guide use which measure of memory? _____

(f) When Mr. Melvin questioned a witness, he deliberately kept referring to the murder weapon as large scissors instead of garden shears. When the witness was later asked to identify the garden shears as the murder weapon, he appeared slightly confused and said he believed the weapon was a large pair of scissors. Mr. Melvin has successfully used the _____ .

(g) Research subjects memorized long lists of words while in a room full of fresh flowers. Later, half the subjects were tested in the same room and half were tested in a room with no flowers. Those tested in the same room recalled significantly more than those in the different room. This is one form of the _____ principle called the _____ .

Graphic Organizer 1

Read the definitions and fill in the correct term next to the appropriate number in the puzzle below (items 1–6). When you have finished, the letters in the boxes will spell a significant memory term. Write out the definition of this term (item 7).

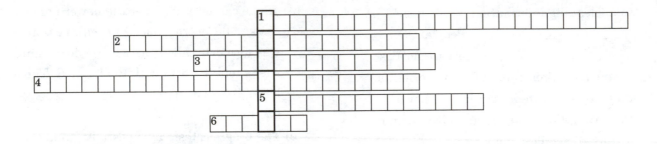

1. An encoding specificity phenomenon in which information learned in a particular mental state is more likely to be recalled while the person is in the same state.

2. The inability to recall long-term memories because of inadequate or missing retrieval cues.

3. The recall of very specific images or details surrounding a vivid, rare, or significant personal event.

4. A memory phenomenon that involves the sensation of knowing that specific information is stored in long-term memory but being temporarily unable to retrieve it.

5. An encoding specificity phenomenon in which a given mood tends to evoke memories that are consistent with that mood.

6. A test of long-term memory that involves retrieving information without the aid of retrieval cues.

7. Write the definition of the memory term:

_____

_____

_____

Review of Terms, Concepts, and Names 2

Use the terms in this list to complete the Matching Test, then to help you answer the True/False items correctly.

retrieval	context effect
retrieval cue	state-dependent
retrieval cue failure	retrieval
tip-of-the-tongue (TOT)	mood congruence
experience	distinctiveness
recall	flashbulb memory
cued recall	schema
recognition	false memory
serial position effect	source confusion
serial recall	eyewitness testimony
primacy effect	Elizabeth Loftus
recency effect	misinformation effect
encoding specificity	cryptomnesia
principle	

Matching Exercise

Match the appropriate term with its definition or description.

1. _____ Tendency to recover information more easily when the retrieval occurs in the same setting as the original learning of the information.

2. _____ The process of accessing stored information.

3. _____ Organized cluster of information about a particular topic.

4. _____ The tendency to remember items at the beginning and end of a list better than items in the middle.

5. _____ A memory distortion that occurs when the true source of the memory is forgotten.

6. _____ American psychologist who has conducted extensive research on the memory distortions that can occur in eyewitness testimony.

7. _____ Test of long-term memory that involves remembering an item of information in response to a retrieval cue.

8. _____ Memory distortion in which people's existing memories can be altered by exposing them to misleading information.

9. _____ Clue, prompt, or hint that helps trigger recall of a given piece of information stored in long-term memory.

10. _____ Encoding specificity phenomenon in which a given mood tends to evoke memories that are consistent with that mood.

11. _____ Principle that when the conditions of information retrieval are similar to the conditions of information encoding, retrieval is more likely to be successful.

12. _____ Memory distortion in which "hidden," or unremembered, memory becomes the basis for a seemingly "new" memory.

True/False Test

Indicate whether each statement is true or false by placing T or F in the blank space next to each item.

1. ____ The primacy effect refers to the tendency to recall the final items in a list during serial recall.

2. ____ Eyewitness testimony is the most reliable and accurate source of information about events that people have observed and almost always results in the conviction of only the guilty people.

3. ____ State-dependent retrieval is an encoding specificity phenomenon in which information learned in a particular mental state is more likely to be recalled while the person is in the same mental state.

4. ____ A test of long-term memory that involves retrieving information without the aid of retrieval cues is called recall, or free recall.

5. ____ The tip-of-the-tongue (TOT) experience involves the sensation of knowing that specific information is stored in long-term memory but being temporarily unable to retrieve it.

6. ____ Serial recall refers to remembering a list of items in their original order.

7. ____ When the encoded information represents a unique, different, or unusual memory, it is said to be characterized by a high degree of distinctiveness.

8. ____ A distorted or inaccurate memory that feels completely real and is often accompanied by all the emotional impact of a real memory is called a false memory.

9. ____ The inability to recall long-term memories because of inadequate or missing retrieval cues is called retrieval cue failure.

10. ____ The recency effect refers to the tendency to recall the first items in a list during serial recall.

11. ____ Recognition refers to a test of long-term memory that involves identifying correct information from several possible choices.

12. ____ Flashbulb memory refers to recall of very specific images or details surrounding a vivid, rare, or significant personal event.

> Check your answers and review any areas of weakness before going on to the next section.

Forgetting: You *Forgot* the Plane Tickets?!

Preview Questions

Consider the following questions as you study this section of the chapter.

- How is forgetting defined, and why does it occur?

- What did Ebbinghaus contribute to the study of forgetting?

- How do encoding failure, interference, motivated forgetting, and decay contribute to forgetting?

*Read the section "Forgetting: You Forgot the Plane Tickets?!" and **write** your answers to the following:*

1. Forgetting is _____ _____ .

2. (a) The scientific study of forgetting was begun over a century ago by _____ .

   (b) To be sure that he was studying memory and the forgetting of completely new material, rather than information that had preexisting associations in his memory, he used _____ in his research.

   (c) Ebbinghaus plotted the results of his recall test on a line graph, which he called the _____ ; this graph revealed two distinct patterns in the relationship between _____ and the passage of time.

   (d) First, much of what we learn is lost _____ (immediatley/relatively soon/sometime later) after we learn it. If we learn something in a matter of minutes on one occasion, forgetting will occur in a _____ ; if we spend many sessions over many weeks or months, most forgetting will be during the first _____ after learning the information.

   (e) The amount of forgetting eventually _____ , and information that is not quickly forgotten seems to be remarkably stable in memory over long periods of time.

3. Researchers have identified four potential causes of forgetting:

   (a) The inability to recall specific information because of insufficient encoding for storage in long-term memory is referred to as _____ . It explains why, for example, you forget a person's name five minutes after being introduced.

   (b) Forgetting can also be caused by one memory competing with or replacing another memory, with similarity between the two memories being the critical factor. This is the _____ theory of forgetting.

   (c) When a new memory competes with remembering an old memory, it is called _____ ; the misinformation effect may be a function of this type of forgetting.

   (d) _____ occurs when an old memory interferes with a new memory, for example, when you refer to your current partner by a previous partner's name.

   (e) Motivated forgetting (a Freudian idea) refers to the idea that we forget because we are motivated to forget, usually because a memory is _____ or _____ .

   (f) There are two forms of motivated forgetting: _____ , in which a person makes a deliberate, conscious effort to forget information, and _____ , which is forgetting that occurs unconsciously, with all awareness of an event or experience is blocked from conscious awareness.

   (g) According to _____ theory, we forget memories because we don't use them, and they fade away over time as a matter of normal brain processes; when a new memory is formed, it creates a _____ , which is a change in brain structure or chemistry that, if not used, gets eroded by normal metabolic brain processes.

Graphic Organizer 2

Use the following to review forgetting due to interference in the test phase. Write in the type of *interference that is responsible for forgetting in the test phase.*

Memorizing Phase	Test Phase	Type of Interference
1. Learn A first; later learn B	Test A	
2. Learn A first; later learn B	Test B	

The Search for the Biological Basis of Memory

Preview Questions

Consider the following questions as you study this section of the chapter.

- How did research by Lashley and Thompson contribute to our understanding of the physical basis of memory?

- How do neurons change when a memory is formed?

- How have case studies of people with retrograde and anterograde amnesia provided important insights into the brain structures involved in memory?

- What brain structures are involved in normal memory, and what roles do they play?

*Read the section "The Search for the Biological Basis of Memory" and **write** your answers to the following:*

1. (a) _____ speculated that the memory involved in learning a classically conditioned response would ultimately be explained as a matter of changes in the brain, but it was _____ who set out in the 1920s to find experimental evidence to support this idea.

(b) The brain changes associated with the formation of a long-term memory and whose theoretical existence suggests localization of a memory in a specific brain area are called _____ , or engrams.

(c) The search for the engram led to the conclusion that memories are not localized in specific locations but are _____ , or stored throughout the brain. Research by _____ has shown that some memories seem to be localized at specific spots in the brain.

(d) Research on memory and the brain suggests that memories have the potential to be both _____ and _____ , with very simple memories being the former and more complex memories the latter.

2. (a) The notion of a memory _____ suggests that some change must occur in the workings of the brain when a new long-term memory is stored.

(b) Research has shown that both the _____ and _____ of neurons in the brain change when a new memory is acquired and that these changes create a memory circuit.

(c) Each time a memory is recalled, the neurons in the circuit are activated, the communication links are strengthened, and the memory becomes established as a _____ memory.

3. (a) Amnesia is the technical term for severe _____ .

(b) Two types have been identified, retrograde and anterograde. People who suffer from retrograde amnesia are unable to remember some or all of their _____ , especially _____ memories for recent events.

(c) The process of setting a new memory permanently in the brain is called memory _____ ; if the process is disrupted before it is complete, a long-term memory is vulnerable and may be lost.

4. (a) Anterograde amnesia is the inability to _____ memories.

(b) Case studies of people with brain damage suggest that the _____ is not involved in most short-term memory tasks, nor in the storage or retrieval of long-term memories; rather, it seems to play a critical role in the encoding and transfer of new memories from short-term to long-term memory.

(c) Destruction of the hippocampus does not affect the formation of _____ memories (which reflect the implicit memory system) but has a critical effect on the formation of new _____ or _____ memories (which reflect the explicit memory system).

(d) Research with patients suffering from anterograde amnesia suggest that implicit and explicit memory processes involve _____ (the same/different) brain regions; these finding have led to a new understanding of the role played by various brain regions in different types of memory abilities.

(e) The inability to remember infant experiences (events from the first few years of life) during adulthood is called _____ ; explanations for this phenomenon rely on the encoding specificity principle and immature brain development in infancy.

(f) Along with the hippocampus, several other brain regions are involved in memory tasks. The _____ is involved in classically conditioning simple reflexes. The _____ seems to be responsible for the encoding of emotional qualities associated with particular memories, such as fear or anger, and for associating memories that involve different senses. The _____ is important to our ability to remember the order of information.

(g) The condition characterized by impairment of memory and intellectual functions—most commonly caused by Alzheimer's disease—is _____ .

5. Read the following and write the correct term in the space provided.

(a) When he first moved to his new apartment, Adam could not remember his new phone number; instead, he would give people his old phone number. Adam's inability to remember his new number is due to _____ interference.

(b) At a recent orientation meeting. Juan was introduced to five of the directors; much to his embarrassment, after a short while he could not remember their names. Juan's memory lapse is probably due to _____ .

(c) Later that night, while thinking about his embarrassment at the meeting, Juan decided that because it was normal to forget names under such circumstances, he was just not going to think about it any more. Juan is using a form of motivated forgetting called _____ .

(d) Bruno, who was knocked out in his last boxing match, cannot remember anything about the fight or events that happened before the bout. Bruno is most likely suffering from a form of amnesia called _____ amnesia.

(e) Mrs. O'Meara, whose hippocampus was removed during a recent brain operation, is most likely to have trouble forming _____ memories.

(f) Jackson has just finished a course in Spanish and is experiencing problems in remembering the Italian he learned last semester. Jackson's memory problem is a result of _____ .

Review of Terms, Concepts, and Names 3

Use the terms in this list to complete the Matching Test, then to help you answer the True/False items correctly.

forgetting	memory trace
Hermann Ebbinghaus	engram
nonsense syllable	Karl Lashley
forgetting curve	Richard F. Thompson
encoding failure	amnesia
interference theory	retrograde amnesia
retroactive interference	memory consolidation
proactive interference	anterograde amnesia
motivated forgetting	hippocampus
suppression	infantile amnesia
repression	amygdala
decay theory	senile dementia

Matching Exercise

Match the appropriate term/name with its definition or description.

1. _____ Motivated forgetting that occurs consciously.

2. _____ Loss of memory caused by the inability to store new memories; foward-acting amnesia.

3. _____ The brain changes associated with a particular stored memory.

4. _____ Severe memory loss.

5. _____ American psychologist and neuroscientist who conducted extensive research on the neurobiological foundations of learning and memory.

6. _____ The inability to recall previously available information.

7. _____ Theory that forgetting is due to normal metabolic processes that occur in the brain over time.

8. _____ Motivated forgetting that occurs unconsciously.

9. _____ The theory that forgetting is caused by one memory competing with or replacing another.

10. _____ German psychologist who originated the scientific study of forgetting; plotted the first "forgetting curve," which describes the basic pattern by which learned information is forgotten over time.

11. _____ Inability to recall specific information because of insufficient encoding for storage in long-term memory.

12. _____ The inability to remember infant experiences during adulthood.

True/False Test

Indicate whether each item is true or false by placing T or F in the space next to each item.

1. ____ Karl Lashley was the American physiological psychologist who attempted to find the specific brain location of particular memories.

2. ____ With retroactive interference, an old memory interferes with remembering a new memory; forward-acting memory interference.

3. ____ The idea that forgetting occurs because an undesired memory is held back from awareness is called motivated forgetting.

4. ____ Memory consolidation is the gradual, physical process of converting new long-term memories to stable, enduring long-term memory codes.

5. ____ Retrograde amnesia is the loss of memory caused by the inability to store new memories; forward-acting amnesia.

6. ____ Damage or destruction of the hippocampus can affect the ability to transfer short-term memories into long-term memories.

7. ____ Hermann Ebbinghaus used nonsense syllables to study memory and the forgetting of completely new material rather than information that had preexisting associations in memory.

8. ____ The engram is the name given to the memory trace in the brain associated with the formation of long-term memories.

9. ___ Proactive interference is forgetting in which a new memory interferes with remembering an old memory; backward-acting memory interference.

10. ___ Damage or destruction of the amygdala will make monkeys lose their normal fear of snakes and other natural predators.

11. ___ The forgetting curve reveals two distinct patterns in the relationship between forgetting and the passage of time; much of what is learned is forgotten relatively quickly and the amount of forgetting eventually levels off.

12. ___ Senile dementia is a condition characterized by impairment of memory and intellectual functions, and its most common cause is Alzheimer's disease.

> Check your answers and review any areas of weakness before going on to the next section.

Something to Think About

1. You may have met that rare person who seems to have a perfect memory and rarely forgets anything. Most of us, however, have to struggle to learn and retain at least some of the vast amount of material we are constantly exposed to in the "information age." If someone were to ask you what you have learned about memory and forgetting that could help them, what would you say?

2. Suppose a friend of yours is falsely identified as being the culprit in a grocery store hold-up and comes to you for help. Based on what you know about eyewitness testimony and related phenomena, what advice would you give him?

> Check your answers and review any areas of weakness before doing the progress tests.

Progress Test 1

Review the complete chapter (including Concept Reviews and the boxed inserts), review all your study notes, and then test yourself on the following progress test. Check your answers. If you make a mistake, review your notes and the relevant section of the study guide, and, if necessary, go back and read the appropriate part of your textbook.

1. In preparation for his biology exam, Lionel repeats the list of terms and their definitions over and over. Lionel's rehearsal strategy involves the fundamental memory process of
   (a) encoding.   (c) retrieval.
   (b) storage.   (d) wasting his time.

2. Michael, whose aggressive, arrogant behavior and indifferent attitude have resulted in the break-up of many relationships, is again contemplating getting married for the third time. Michael is confident that this time it will work and that his previous relationship problems were never his fault. Michael is either actively _____ or unconsciously _____ memory of his own behavior.
   (a) consolidating; schematizing
   (b) schematizing; consolidating
   (c) suppressing; repressing
   (d) repressing; suppressing

3. Five-year-old Betty can recite the alphabet perfectly every time she is asked to do so. Betty's ability to do this involves the fundamental memory process of
   (a) repression.   (c) retrograde amnesia.
   (b) retrieval.   (d) encoding.

4. Acquisition is to retention as _____ is to _____ .
   (a) retrograde; retroactive
   (b) procedural; episodic
   (c) encoding; storage
   (d) storage; retrieval

5. Dirk can remember in vivid detail where he was and what he was doing when he heard about Princess Diana's tragic death in a car crash in Paris. Dirk's flashbulb memory is stored in his
   (a) iconic memory.   (c) long-term memory.
   (b) short-term memory.   (d) echoic memory.

6. Whenever Killian is introduced to someone, he usually remembers the name by repeating it over and over to himself. Killian is using a memory strategy called
   (a) rehearsal.
   (b) retroactive interference.
   (c) clustering.
   (d) chunking.

7. One conclusion that can be drawn from Ebbinghaus's work on forgetting is that
   (a) we can remember only about seven non-sense syllables at one time.
   (b) when we memorize new information, most forgetting occurs relatively soon after we learn it.
   (c) the duration of visual sensory memory is less than half a second.
   (d) the capacity of long-term memory is large but fleeting.

8. Mrs. Carson was very busy when she phoned her husband and quickly listed the twelve items she wanted him to pick up at the store. After she hung up, Mr. Carson attempted to write down the items. It is likely that he will
   (a) forget the items in the middle.
   (b) remember only the middle and the last items.
   (c) remember only the first and middle items.
   (d) forget the first and last items and remember the items in the middle.

9. According to the levels-of-processing framework, shallow processing is to deep processing as _____ is to _____ .
   (a) visual sensory memory; echoic sensory memory
   (b) maintenance rehearsal; elaborative rehearsal
   (c) clustering; chunking
   (d) state-dependent memory; mood-dependent memory

10. Charlie finds it easier to remember a list of words that includes *automobile, cigarettes, encyclopedia, lampshade, geranium,* and *seashell,* as compared to a list of the same length that includes *philosophy, processes, justice, abstraction, fundamental,* and *inherent,* because with the first list it is easier to use
    (a) echoic processing.
    (b) maintenance rehearsal.
    (c) procedural memory.
    (d) visual imagery.

11. Karen can remember very clearly when and where she met Jim and how she felt when he first spoke to her. This information, which is stored in Karen's long-term memory, is called
    (a) procedural information.
    (b) episodic information.
    (c) semantic information.
    (d) retroactive information.

12. After his hippocampus was destroyed by a tumor, Mr. Locke is likely to experience problems
    (a) forming procedural memories.
    (b) recognizing common objects.
    (c) correctly repeating items over and over.
    (d) transferring short-term memories into long-term memory.

13. Mr. Locke (in the above example) is likely to be classified as suffering from
    (a) retrograde amnesia.
    (b) anterograde amnesia.
    (c) retrieval cue failure.
    (d) cryptomnesia.

14. According to the Application, one way to make memories last is to learn material over several sessions rather than cramming learning into one long session. This method of study is called
    (a) distributed practice.
    (b) massed practice.
    (c) maintenance rehearsal.
    (d) serial position learning.

15. According to Critical Thinking 6.2, which of the following regarding childhood sexual abuse is true?
    (a) Physical and sexual abuse of children does happen.
    (b) Memories of childhood abuse can become repressed and surface later in life.
    (c) Repressed memories recovered in therapy need to be regarded with caution.
    (d) A person's confidence in a memory is no guarantee that the memory is accurate.
    (e) All of the above are true.

Progress Test 2

After you have checked your understanding of the material in Progress Test 1 and have done a complete chapter review with special focus on any areas of weakness, you are ready to assess your knowledge in Progress Test 2. Check your answers. If you make a mistake, review your notes, the relevant section of the study guide, and if necessary, the appropriate part of your textbook.

1. When Gary was preparing for an exam, he tried a number of different strategies to make the material meaningful. According to the levels-of-processing framework, Gary is using _____ to help him remember the information.
   (a) elaborative rehearsal
   (b) maintenance rehearsal
   (c) retroactive interference
   (d) proactive interference

2. Shortly after he finished reading an exciting novel, Sean fell down the stairs and suffered a concussion; now, he has no recall of ever having read the novel. Sean's memory problem is probably the result of
   (a) retrieval cue failure.
   (b) source confusion.
   (c) disruption of memory consolidation.
   (d) mood incongruence.

3. Sean (in the above example) is most likely to be classified as suffering from
   (a) anterograde amnesia.
   (b) proactive forgetting.
   (c) retrograde amnesia.
   (d) retroactive forgetting.

4. Richard F. Thompson classically conditioned rabbits to eye-blink to a tone; he later found that there was change in brain activity in the rabbit's cerebellum. This result suggests that some long-term memories
   (a) are stored in a localized region of the brain.
   (b) are distributed and stored across multiple brain locations.
   (c) have no biological or physical basis in the brain.
   (d) are very vulnerable if they are not given enough time to consolidate.

5. Dr. Dement believes that forgetting is due to memory traces being eroded by normal metabolic processes in the brain. Dr. Dement supports the
   (a) interference theory.
   (b) motivated forgetting theory.
   (c) levels-of-processing framework.
   (d) decay theory.

6. When Manfred, who used to be a compulsive gambler, is asked how he did, he recalls losing much less money than was actually the case. Manfred's memory failure best illustrates
   (a) motivated forgetting.
   (b) retrieval cue failure.
   (c) retroactive interference.
   (d) proactive interference.

7. Natasha has memorized the new personal identity code she was given by security; now, she can't remember her old personal identity code. Natasha is experiencing the effects of
   (a) mood congruence.
   (b) source confusion.
   (c) proactive interference.
   (d) retroactive interference

8. Jeffery, who was an eyewitness to a robbery, initially thought the robber looked like a female. During questioning, a police detective suggested to him many times that the robber was probably a man with long hair. Later, when he was giving testimony on the witness stand, Jeffery was quite sure that it was a man who robbed the store. This example illustrates
   (a) state-dependent retrieval.
   (b) mood congruence.
   (c) a flashbulb memory.
   (d) the misinformation effect.

9. State-dependent retrieval is to _____ as mood-dependent memory is to

   _____ .
   (a) a pharmacological state; an emotional state
   (b) retroactive interference; proactive interference
   (c) an emotional state; a pharmacological state
   (d) proactive interference; retroactive interference

10. The smell of cherry blossoms awakened in Mrs. Yamomoto vivid memories of her childhood in Osaka. The aroma of the blossoms apparently acted as an effective
    (a) schema.   (c) flashbulb cue.
    (b) echoic cue.   (d) retrieval cue.

11. During a discussion about old movies, Grace could not bring to mind the name of the actor who played Sidney Greenstreet's sidekick in *The Maltese Falcon*, despite the fact that she felt she knew the name and had, in fact, talked about his role in the movie on other occasions. Grace is experiencing
    (a) the serial position effect.
    (b) encoding failure.
    (c) the tip-of-the-tongue (TOT) phenomenon.
    (d) anterograde amnesia.

12. Multiple-choice exam questions measure _____ ; short essay questions measure _____ .
    (a) recall; recognition
    (b) recognition; recall
    (c) short-term memory; long-term memory
    (d) long-term memory; short-term memory

13. Harold, who was in the kitchen, asked Jane, who was reading a book in the living room, whether she wanted a diet or a regular soft drink. Jane replied, "What did you say?" but before Harold could respond, Jane said, "Make it a regular Coke, please." This example illustrates

   (a) iconic memory.
   (b) repression.
   (c) echoic memory.
   (d) a flashbulb memory.

14. The Application lists a number of strategies that can be used to improve memory for important information. Which of the following is *not* one of those strategies?

   (a) Use visual imagery.
   (b) Organize the information.
   (c) Counteract the serial position effect.
   (d) Use contextual cues to jog memories during a test.
   (e) Always use massed practice, especially during all-night cramming sessions before a test.

15. According to Science Versus Pseudoscience 6.1, which of the following is true?

   (a) There is ample scientific evidence that people can remember actual past lives.
   (b) There is good reason to believe that many memories of past lives are examples of cryptomnesia.
   (c) Most reincarnation memories can only be recovered by a skilled hypnotherapist.
   (d) Most people cannot recall memories of past lives because of repression.

Progress Test 3

After you have checked your understanding of the material in Progress Tests 1 and 2, and have done a complete chapter review with special focus on any areas of weakness, you are ready to further assess your knowledge on Progress Test 3. Check your answers. If you make a mistake, review your notes, the appropriate parts of the study guide, and if necessary, the relevant sections of your textbook.

1. Memory with awareness is to _____ as memory without awareness is to _____ .

   (a) explicit memory; implicit memory
   (b) retroactive interference; proactive interference

   (c) implicit memory; explicit memory
   (d) proactive interference; retroactive interference

2. Dr. Rhodes believes that when the conditions of information retrieval are similar to the conditions of information encoding, retrieval is more likely to be successful. This view is most consistent with

   (a) the levels-of-processing framework.
   (b) the semantic network model.
   (c) the encoding specificity principle.
   (d) interference theory.

3. Elizabeth Loftus's story, presented in the Prologue, demonstrates how it is possible to form an extremely vivid, but inaccurate, memory. A common cause of such false memories is

   (a) retrograde amnesia.
   (b) source confusion.
   (c) anterograde amnesia.
   (d) retrieval cue failure.

4. The _____ is to encoding emotional aspects of memory as the _____ is to the encoding and transfer of new information from short-term to long-term memory.

   (a) amygdala; hippocampus
   (b) prefrontal cortex; amygdala
   (c) hippocampus; amygdala
   (d) cerebellum; hippocampus

5. When Danny "the Dynamo" was thrown out of the ring during a wrestling match he hit his head on the floor and was knocked unconscious. When he finally came to he had no recollection of the wrestling match or the events leading up to it. It is most probable that Danny is suffering from

   (a) anterograde amnesia.
   (b) cryptomnesia.
   (c) retrograde amnesia.
   (d) senile dementia.

6. Neddy cannot accurately remember the order of the numbers on the small calculator he has owned for ten years and uses quite frequently. Neddy's problem in recall is most likely a function of

   (a) retrieval cue failure.
   (b) proactive interference.
   (c) encoding failure.
   (d) retroactive interference.

7. Most subjects in an experiment responded with *sky* and *grass* to the stimulus words *blue* and *green*. Results such as these support
    (a) the semantic network model.
    (b) decay theory.
    (c) the levels-of-processing framework.
    (d) interference theory.

8. Emelia can quite easily list all fifty U.S. states and Canada's ten provinces and two territories. This type of information in long-term memory is called _____ information.
    (a) procedural
    (b) episodic
    (c) semantic
    (d) state-dependent

9. Marcus, like most adults, cannot recall events and experiences from the first few years of his life. His infantile amnesia most likely reflects
    (a) the fact that early childhood events were never effectively encoded and stored in the first place.
    (b) motivated repressed memories.
    (c) the fact that childhood memories are forgotten after they have been encoded and stored.
    (d) the fact that the brain does not contain brain structures, such as the hippocampus and amygdala, until after the age of three.

10. Lisa took a strong mood-altering prescription medication while studying for her exam; the following week, she took the same pills before the exam because she wanted to be in the same positive emotional state on both occasions. Lisa appears to believe in the effects of
    (a) maintenance rehearsal.
    (b) elaborative rehearsal.
    (c) mood congruence.
    (d) source confusion.

11. When Kirk was given a long list of items to memorize, he found it easier to remember them when he regrouped all the items according to whether they were vegetables, furniture, animals, and so on. Kirk is using a memory aid called
    (a) the serial position effect.
    (b) the self-referencing technique.
    (c) the context effect.
    (d) chunking.

12. When she first transferred from a college to a university, Kelly had trouble remembering her new student number; she would always recall her old college student number instead. Kelly's memory problem is an example of
    (a) retrograde amnesia.
    (b) proactive interference.
    (c) anterograde amnesia.
    (d) retroactive interference.

13. Mrs. Kahn experienced no trouble skiing despite the fact that she had not been on the slopes for almost fifteen years. Mrs. Kahn's current skiing ability is probably due to _____ information stored in her long-term memory.
    (a) procedural
    (b) episodic
    (c) semantic
    (d) repressed

14. According to Culture and Human Behavior 6.3, declines in memory ability
    (a) are due entirely to a natural, biological aging process.
    (b) may be influenced by cultural expectations about aging and memory abilities.
    (c) are predominantly the function of diseases such as Alzheimer's.
    (d) are most evident in members of the deaf culture who communicate with American Sign Language.

15. According to Science Versus Pseudoscience 6.1, cryptomnesia refers to
    (a) memories of being buried in a mausoleum or crypt.
    (b) a memory distortion in which a seemingly "new" or "original" memory is actually based on an unrecalled previous memory.
    (c) loss of memory caused by the inability to store new memories.
    (d) severe memory loss following a near-death experience.

Answers

Introduction: What Is Memory?

1. (a) acquire; retain; retrieve
   (b) encoding; storage; retrieval

2. (a) sensory; short-term; long-term
   (b) capacity; duration; function

3. (a) sensory
   (b) attention; short-term
   (c) short-term; 30
   (d) imagining; remembering; problem solving; long-term
   (e) long-term
   (f) short-term; long-term memory; long-term; short-term memory

Sensory Memory: Fleeting Impressions of Reality

1. (a) George Sperling
   (b) half a second; short-term

2. (a) iconic; icon; echoic; echo
   (b) one-quarter; one-half; a few
   (c) overlap; continuous

Short-Term, Working Memory: The Workshop of Consciousness

1. (a) sensory; long-term
   (b) storage; conscious
   (c) rehearsed; maintenance rehearsal

2. (a) seven; displace
   (b) chunking; long-term memory

Long-Term Memory

1. (a) storage
   (b) limitless
   (c) maintenance; elaborative
   (d) self-reference; visual imagery

2. (a) deeper; shallow; rehearsal
   (b) shallow; deep

3. (a) Procedural
   (b) Episodic
   (c) Semantic

4. (a) subsystems
   (b) memory with awareness; memory without awareness

5. (a) organized
   (b) clustering; association or connection
   (c) semantic network
   (d) semantic network; associations

6. (a) retrieval
   (b) encoding

(c) elaborative
(d) short-term; maintenance
(e) chunking
(f) procedural
(g) explicit memory; implicit memory

Matching Exercise 1

1. elaborative rehearsal
2. semantic network model
3. retrieval
4. clustering
5. visual imagery
6. short-term memory
7. episodic information
8. encoding
9. stage model of memory
10. memory
11. procedural information
12. George Sperling

True/False Test 1

1. F	6. F	11. T
2. T	7. T	12. F
3. T	8. F	
4. T	9. F	
5. T	10. T	

Retrieval: Getting Information from Long-Term Memory

1. (a) retrieval cue
   (b) retrieval cue failure

2. (a) all-or-nothing
   (b) retrieval cue
   (c) organized

3. (a) recall
   (b) cued recall
   (c) recognition
   (d) cued-recall; recognition

4. (a) beginning; end; middle
   (b) primacy; recency
   (c) primacy

5. (a) context effect
   (b) state-dependent retrieval
   (c) mood congruence; positive; blue (bad)

6. (a) distinctiveness
   (b) flashbulb; confidence

Reconstructing Memories: Sources of Potential Errors

1. (a) constructed
   (b) reconstructed
   (c) before; after

2. (a) schemas
   (b) schemas; changed; distorted

3. (a) source confusion
   (b) false memory
   (c) is
   (d) misinformation effect; are

4. (a) are
   (b) limited

5. (a) mood congruence
   (b) flashbulb
   (c) reconstructive
   (d) retrieval cue
   (e) recognition
   (f) misinformation effect
   (g) encoding specificity; context effect

Graphic Organizer 1

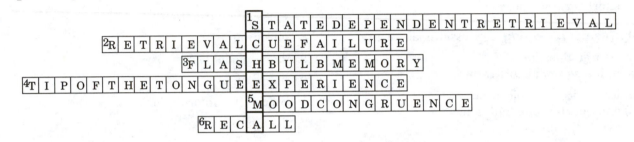

7. An organized cluster of information about a particular topic

Matching Exercise 2

1. context effect
2. retrieval
3. schema
4. serial position effect
5. source confusion
6. Elizabeth Loftus
7. cued recall
8. misinformation effect
9. retrieval cue
10. mood congruence
11. encoding specificity principle
12. cryptomnesia

True/False Test 2

1. F	5. T	9. T
2. F	6. T	10. F
3. T	7. T	11. T
4. T	8. T	12. T

Forgetting: You *Forgot* the Plane Tickets?!

1. the inability to recall information that was previously available

2. (a) Hermann Ebbinghaus
   (b) nonsense syllables
   (c) forgetting curve; forgetting
   (d) relatively soon; matter of minutes; few months
   (e) levels off (stabilizes)

3. (a) encoding failure
   (b) interference
   (c) retroactive interference
   (d) Proactive interference
   (e) unpleasant; disturbing
   (f) suppression; repression
   (g) decay; memory trace

Graphic Organizer 2

1. retroactive interference
2. proactive interference

The Search for the Biological Basis of Memory

1. (a) Ivan Pavlov; Karl Lashley
   (b) memory traces
   (c) distributed; Richard F. Thompson
   (d) localized; distributed

2. (a) trace
   (b) structure; function
   (c) long-term
3. (a) memory loss
   (b) past memories; episodic
   (c) consolidation
4. (a) form new
   (b) hippocampus
   (c) procedural; episodic; semantic
   (d) different
   (e) infantile amnesia
   (f) cerebellum; amygdala; frontal cortex
   (g) senile dementia
5. (a) proactive
   (b) encoding failure
   (c) suppression
   (d) retrograde
   (e) long-term
   (f) retroactive interference

Matching Exercise 3

1. suppression
2. anterograde amnesia
3. memory trace
4. amnesia
5. Richard F. Thompson
6. forgetting
7. decay theory
8. repression
9. interference theory
10. Hermann Ebbinghaus
11. encoding failure
12. infantile amnesia

True/False Test 3

1. T	5. F	9. F
2. F	6. T	10. T
3. T	7. T	11. T
4. T	8. T	12. T

Something to Think About

1. We are all vulnerable to forgetting, and sometimes the consequences can be serious. What can we do to improve memory? Fortunately, a number of strategies can help us to remember important information. You might begin your answer with a discussion of the fundamental processes of encoding, storage, and retrieval, then explain the function, capacity, and duration of each of the three stages of memory. Aspects of the levels-of-processing framework are also relevant to your discussion. Of course, no discussion of the topic of memory would be complete without mentioning Ebbinghaus's work on forgetting as well as the contributions of the various theories of forgetting to our understanding of memory. Finally, mention the ten most important strategies that could help improve memory, as described in the Application.

2. It is a real nightmare to contemplate the prospect of being falsely accused of a crime, and having an eyewitness pointing at you and saying very confidently, "Yes, that is the person. There's no doubt about it, he did it!" What can be done in such a situation? If you don't have an alibi, the jury is very likely to believe a confident eyewitness who, under oath, points a finger at the accused. First, you might consider hiring an expert witness, such as Elizabeth Loftus, to testify to the problems inherent in eyewitness testimony. Such testimony, based on scientific evidence, is difficult to refute. If your friend cannot afford the testimony of an expert witness, then we suggest he try to educate his defense lawyer about the relevant research findings in this important area of psychology. These include source confusion, the personal schema of the eyewitness, the power of the misinformation effect, evidence related to false memories, and relevant aspects of the encoding specificity principle.

Progress Test 1

1. a	6. a	11. b
2. c	7. b	12. d
3. b	8. a	13. b
4. c	9. b	14. a
5. c	10. d	15. e

Progress Test 2

1. a	6. a	11. c
2. c	7. d	12. b
3. c	8. d	13. c
4. a	9. a	14. e
5. d	10. d	15. b

Progress Test 3

1. a	6. c	11. d
2. c	7. a	12. b
3. b	8. c	13. a
4. a	9. a	14. b
5. c	10. c	15. b

CHAPTER 7

Thinking, Language, and Intelligence

PREVIEW Reading the section below first will give you a general sense of the chapter's contents and an initial introduction to some of the major concepts and terms. This will prime you for what you are about to read and help you to develop a "cognitive map" that will guide your study of the material in this chapter. Likewise, reading the **preview questions** at the beginning of each major section will improve your ability to understand, learn, and retain the information.

CHAPTER 7. . . AT A GLANCE Chapter 7 combines thinking, language, and intelligence, three closely related cognitive functions. The section on thinking begins with discussions of the use of mental imagery and concept formation. This leads to a description of problem-solving strategies, followed by an explanation of two common obstacles to effective problem solving, functional fixedness and mental sets. The section concludes with a discussion of different decision-making models.

The next section, on our remarkable cognitive capacity for language, first explains the character of language, then explores the various ways in which language influences thought. Animal communication and the controversial debate over whether or not animals are capable of language finishes up this section.

Our ability to think and use language are aspects of what we call intelligence. Because the measurement of intelligence has been a controversial issue, this section provides some background into the development of intelligence testing and the contributions of various psychologists. The difference between aptitude tests and achievement tests is explained, and the requirements of standardization, reliability, and validity are described as a way of understanding the problems of testing.

The debate over the nature of intelligence centers on whether intelligence is a single, general ability or a cluster of different abilities, and on whether intelligence should be narrowly or broadly defined. Four theories regarding this issue are presented. The heredity-environment debate regarding the origins of intelligence is examined in detail.

Introduction: Thinking, Language, and Intellegence

Preview Questions

Consider the following questions as you study this section of the chapter.

- What role do mental images and concepts play in thinking?
- What are some of the basic characteristics of mental images, and how do we manipulate them?
- What are concepts, and how are they formed?
- What is a prototype, and what role do prototypes play in concept formation?

*Read the section "Introduction: Thinking, Language, and Intelligence" and **write** your answers to the following:*

1. (a) Cognition is a general term that refers to the _____ activities involved in _____ , _____ , and _____ knowledge.

   (b) A key dimension of _____ is how we use our cognitive abilities and accumulated knowledge to think, solve problems, make decisions, and use language.

2. (a) In the most general sense, all conscious mental activity involves _____ . This includes acquiring new knowledge, remembering, planning ahead, or daydreaming.

   (b) More narrowly, thinking involves manipulating _____ of information in order to draw inferences and conclusions; it is often directed toward some goal, purpose, or conclusion.

3. (a) A mental representation of objects or events that are not physically present is called a(n) _____ .

   (b) Experiments on the cognitive ability to manipulate mental images by scanning them or rotating them seem to indicate that we treat them much like the _____ they represent, although they are not always exact duplicates of real images.

4. (a) A mental category formed to group objects, events, or situations that share similar features is a _____ .

   (b) A mental category formed by learning the rules or features that define it is called a(n) _____ .

   (c) If the defining features, or _____ , are missing, the object _____ (is/is not) included as a member or example of that category.

   (d) A _____ is formed as a result of everyday experience rather than by logically determining whether an object or event fits a specific set of rules; these have "fuzzy boundaries" because the rules or attributes _____ (are/are not) always sharply defined.

   (e) The best or most typical instance of a particular concept is called a _____ ; the more closely an item matches the _____ , the more quickly it is identified as being an example of that concept.

Problem Solving: Searching for the IDEAL Solution

Preview Questions

Consider the following questions as you study this section of the chapter.

- How is problem solving defined, and what are the basic steps in problem solving?
- What are four problem-solving strategies, and what are the advantages and disadvantages of each?
- How can functional fixedness and mental set interfere with problem solving?

*Read the section "Problem Solving: Searching for the IDEAL Solution" and **write** your answers to the following:*

1. Problem solving refers to thinking and behavior directed toward attaining a goal that is not readily available. The IDEAL problem solver involves five steps:

    (a) _____ the problem.

    (b) _____ and represent the problem.

    (c) _____ possible strategies or solutions.

    (d) _____ on a selected strategy or solution.

    (e) _____ and evaluate the solution.

2. (a) Before you can begin to solve any problem, you have to (1) _____ that a problem exists and (2) accurately _____ the problem; you must sort out the important and unimportant information and determine which aspects of the problem are relevant to its solution.

    (b) To help focus attention on critical details that can improve accuracy in interpreting a problem, you should _____ all the relevant information. When problems are complicated or involve weighing many different factors, creating a _____ or _____ can be useful for identifying the relationships between the important elements of the problem.

3. (a) Actually trying a variety of solutions and eliminating those that don't work is a strategy called _____ , which can be useful if there is a limited range of possible solutions.

    (b) A procedure or method that, when followed step by step, always produces the correct solution is a(n) _____ .

    Although guaranteed to eventually generate a solution, it is not always practical.

    (c) A general rule-of-thumb strategy that may or may not work is called a(n) _____ . Although not guaranteed to solve a given problem, _____ can reduce the number of possible solutions so that trial and error can be employed to eventually arrive at the correct one.

    (d) One common _____ for solving a problem, such as writing a term paper, is to break the problem down into a series of _____ ; a second is _____ from the end point and determining the steps necessary to reach the final goal.

    (e) The solution to a problem may arrive as a sudden realization, or flash of _____ , that happens after you mull over the problem. This can occur when you recognize how the problem is similar to a previously solved problem or that an object can be used in a novel way.

    (f) The final step in problem solving is to look back and _____ the solution.

4. (a) When we view objects as functioning only in the usual or customary way, we're engaging in a tendency called _____ ; this may prevent us from seeing the full range of ways in which an object can be used.

    (b) The tendency to persist in solving problems with solutions that have worked in the past are called _____ ; while these can sometimes suggest a useful heuristic, they can also prevent us from coming up with new, possibly simpler or more effective solutions.

Decisions, Decisions, Decisions: Should I or Shouldn't I?

Preview Questions

Consider the following questions as you study this section of the chapter.

- What cognitive strategies do we use to make decisions?
- What are the single-feature, additive, and elimination by aspects models of decision making?
- Under what conditions is each strategy appropriate?
- When are the availability and representative heuristics used, and what potential problems are associated with each?

Read the section "Decisions, Decisions, Decisions: Should I or Shouldn't I?" and **write** *your answers to the following:*

1. (a) The decision-making process becomes complicated when each option involves the consideration of several _____ , or aspects.

   (b) In order to simplify the choice among many alternatives, a decision-making strategy called the _____ model can be used; this is useful for minor decisions but can increase the riskiness of an important or complex decision.

   (c) A better strategy for complex decisions is to systematically evaluate the important features of each alternative; one such decision-making model is called the _____ model.

   (d) In the _____ model, you first generate a list of the important factors, then rate each factor using an arbitrary scale. This strategy can often reveal the best overall choice.

   (e) The _____ model proposes that we evaluate all alternatives on one characteristic at a time, starting with the most important feature and discarding

each alternative if it doesn't meet that criterion; as the range of possible choices is narrowed down, the remaining alternatives are compared, one feature at a time, until just one alternative is left.

   (f) Good decision makers adapt their strategy to the demands of the specific situation; if there are just a few choices and features to compare, the _____ model is most appropriate, but if the decision is complex, with multiple features, begin by using the _____ model, then use the _____ model to make the final decision.

2. Some decisions must be made under conditions of uncertainty in which we must estimate the probability of a particular event occurring; in such instances, we tend to rely on two rule-of-thumb heuristics.

   (a) To estimate the likelihood of an event based on how easily other instances of the event are available in memory, we use the _____ heuristic. When instances of an event are readily recalled, we tend to consider the event more likely to occur.

   (b) When a rare event makes a vivid impression on us, we may overestimate its likelihood; thus, the _____ heuristic can produce inaccurate estimates.

   (c) The key point is that the _____ (less/more) accurately our memory of an event reflects the actual frequency of the event, the _____ (less/more) accurate our estimate of the event's likelihood will be.

   (d) When we estimate an event's likelihood by comparing how similar its essential features are to our prototype of the event, we are using the _____ heuristic.

(e) If we fail to consider possible variations from the prototype or if we fail to consider the approximate number of prototypes that actually exist, the _____ heuristic can produce faulty estimates.

3. Read the following and write the correct term or word in the space provided.

   (a) After a chimpanzee tries unsuccessfully to get bananas that are out of reach, she sits for a long time staring at them. Suddenly, she looks around the cage, picks up a stick, and uses it to pull the bananas within her reach, something she has never done before. Her solution to the banana problem is probably the result of _____ .

   (b) You learn that one of the Russell children is taking ballet classes; you immediately conclude that it is their one daughter rather than any of their three sons. You reached a possibly erroneous conclusion by using the

   _____ .

   (c) Dr. Mendleson studies how people manipulate mental representations to draw inferences and conclusions. Dr. Mendleson is most likely a _____ psychologist interested in people's _____ ability.

   (d) You are asked to decide which city is farther north, Edinburgh, Scotland, or Stockholm, Sweden, so you try to picture a map of Europe in your mind. You are using a

   _____ .

   (e) Marisa has learned the rules and features that define a square, a rectangle, and a right-angle triangle. Marisa has learned a _____ concept.

   (f) Henry had trouble recognizing that a seahorse is a fish because it does not closely resemble his _____ concept of fish.

   (g) In order to convert liters into U.S. gallons Natalie multiplies the number of liters by 0.264178. She is using a(n) _____ to arrive at the correct answer.

   (h) Hilda is asked to complete the sequence "J, F, M, A, _, _, _, _, _, _, _, _." After trying a few different possibilities she comes up with the correct answer—M, J, J, A, S, O, N, D, (the first letter of the months of the year). It appears that Hilda is using a(n)

   _____ strategy to solve the problem.

   (i) Anatole is trying to decide which of two equally affordable and attractive cars to purchase, so he makes a list of the advantages and disadvantages of each using an arbitrary rating scale. Andy is using the _____ model to help him make a decision.

Graphic Organizer 1

James has to work to support himself while going to college; he is very concerned about his grade point average because he plans to go to graduate school. When he works long hours, he finds that his grades suffer; if he cuts back on work, he suffers from lack of funds. Decide what aspect of the IDEAL problem solver is illustrated by each of the following or, if appropriate, identify the problem-solving strategy being described.

1. James often feels stressed—like he is caught between a rock and a hard place. He comes to the realization that he has a problem.

   _____

2. James's friend Al has him make a list of all the relevant information, thinking that this would help James focus his attention on the critical details and improve his accuracy in interpreting the problem. _____

3. James explains his dilemma to Al. Graduate school is his ultimate goal, and he feels pressured to complete his undergraduate degree within four or five years at the most. He has to maintain a high GPA, yet he needs to work to support himself. _____

4. Before talking to his friend, James had tried to juggle all his commitments to work, school, and friends in a haphazard manner but nothing really worked. _____

5. Al, a computer programmer, thought that if James could feed all the information into a special problem-solving computer program, the answer could be found by evaluating every possible variable through multiple comparisons.

    _____

6. Given that, as far as James knew, no such program existed, he decided to start with his ultimate goal—going to graduate school—and, in an attempt to determine the steps necessary to get to his goal, work backward to his current situation. _____

7. While working out in the gym, it suddenly occurred to James that maybe his self-imposed five-year limit to complete his BA was unrealistic. After all, why should being a somewhat older graduate student be such a big deal?

    _____

8. Al suggested that the problem could be broken down into a series of subproblems and then James should tackle each problem one at a time. _____

9. James thought that the best solution was to take fewer courses, work enough to support himself in a reasonable manner, and plan on graduating in seven to eight years instead of four or five, but with a very good GPA. This strategy, in retrospect, would give him a better chance of getting into graduate school while avoiding getting into debt.

    _____

Review of Terms and Concepts 1

Use the terms in this list to complete the Matching Test, then to help you answer the True/False items correctly.

cognition	insight
thinking	functional fixedness
mental image	mental set
concepts	intuition
formal concept	single-feature model
natural concept	additive model
prototype	elimination by aspects
problem solving	model
trial and error	availability heuristic
algorithms	representativeness
heuristic	heuristic
subgoals	
working backward	

Matching Exercise

Match the appropriate term with its definition or description.

1. _____ Decision-making model in which all the alternatives are evaluated one characteristic at a time, starting with the most important feature and scratching each alternative off the list of possible choices if it fails to meet the criterion.

2. _____ The manipulation of mental representations of information in order to draw inferences or conclusions.

3. _____ Most typical instance of a particular concept.

4. _____ Sudden realization of how a problem can be solved.

5. _____ Decision-making strategy in which the choice among many alternatives is simplified by basing the decision on a single feature.

6. _____ Strategy in which the likelihood of an event is estimated by comparing how similar it is to the typical prototype of the event.

7. _____ Problem-solving strategy that involves attempting different solutions and eliminating those that do not work.

8. _____ Mental category that is formed by learning the rules or features that define it.

9. _____ The mental activities involved in acquiring, retaining, and using knowledge.

10. _____ Mental category of objects or ideas based on properties that they share.

11. _____ Problem-solving strategy that involves following a general rule of thumb to reduce the number of possible solutions.

True/False Test

Indicate whether each statement is true or false by placing T or F in the blank space next to each item.

1. ___ Working backward is a common heuristic used to break a problem down into a series of smaller problems; as each subproblem is solved, you get closer to solving the larger problem.

2. ___ A mental representation of objects or events that are not physically present is called a mental image.

3. ___ Problem solving is thinking and behavior directed toward attaining a goal that is not readily available.

4. ___ The tendency to persist in solving problems with solutions that have worked in the past is called functional fixedness.

5. ___ The additive model of decision making involves generating a list of the most important factors, then using an arbitrary rating scale to rate each alternative on each factor, and finally adding the ratings together for comparison purposes.

6. ___ The availability heuristic is a strategy in which the likelihood of an event is estimated on the basis of how easily other instances of the event are available in memory.

7. ___ A natural concept is a mental category that is formed as a result of everyday experience.

8. ___ A useful heuristic in which you start at the end point and determine the steps necessary to reach your goal uses the analysis of subgoals.

9. ___ A mental set is the tendency to view objects as functioning only in their usual or customary manner.

10. ___ Intuition refers to the process of coming to a conclusion or making a judgment without conscious awareness.

11. ___ A problem-solving strategy that involves following a specific rule, procedure, or method that inevitably produces the correct solution is referred to as an algorithm.

> Check your answers and review any areas of weakness before going on to the next section.

Language and Thought

Preview Questions

Consider the following questions as you study this section of the chapter.

- How is language defined?
- What are the five most important characteristics of language?
- In what ways does language influence thinking?
- Can animals use language?

Read the section "Language and Thought" and **write** *your answers to the following:*

1. (a) The primary function of language is to _____ .

   (b) Language is a system for combining arbitrary _____ to produce an infinite number of meaningful statements.

2. (a) To express meaningful information in a way that can be understood by others, language requires the use of _____ .

   (b) For the vast majority of words the connection between the symbol and the meaning is completely _____ ; as a result, language is tremendously flexible.

   (c) An important characteristic of language is that the _____ of the symbols is shared by others who speak the same language.

   (d) Language is a system; it is highly structured and follows specific rules for combining words called _____ .

   (e) Language is creative, or _____ ; an infinite number of new and different phrases and sentences can be created.

   (f) A characteristic of language, the ability to communicate meaningfully about ideas, objects, and activities that are not physically present, is called _____ .

3. (a) All your _____ abilities are involved in understanding and producing language.

   (b) Language can affect our thoughts by influencing what we _____ .

   (c) Another important way in which language can influence thought has to do with our _____ of others; for example, the nuances of words can reinforce or minimize negative _____ .

   (d) The tendency to use a male pronoun can lead to _____ .

4. (a) Animals communicate with each other and with other species, but psychologists question whether animals can learn to use language; this active area of psychological research is referred to as _____ cognition or _____ cognition.

   (b) The results of several ongoing studies have produced some compelling demonstrations of animal _____ learning, but many psychologists caution against jumping to the conclusion that animals can think or that they possess self-awareness because such conclusions are far from proven.

Measuring Intelligence

Preview Questions

Consider the following questions as you study this section of the chapter.

- How is intelligence defined?
- What roles did Binet, Terman, and Wechsler play in the development of intelligence tests?
- How do achievement tests differ from aptitude tests?
- What does it mean to standardize a test?
- What is the role of norms in standardization, and what is the normal curve?
- How are reliability and validity defined and how are they determined?

*Read the section "Measuring Intelligence" and **write** your answers to the following:*

1. (a) The use of mental images and concepts, problem solving and decision making, and language capabilities are cognitive abilities that are aspects of what is commonly called _____ .

   (b) Wechsler defined _____ as the global capacity to think rationally, act purposefully, and deal effectively with the environment.

   (c) Intelligence tests attempt to measure general _____ , rather than accumulated knowledge or aptitude for a specific subject or area.

2. (a) In the early 1900s, the French government commissioned psychologist _____ to develop procedures to identify students who might require special help.

   (b) Along with Théodore Simon, Binet devised a series of tests to measure different kinds of elementary _____ , such as memory, attention, and the ability to understand similarities and differences.

   (c) Binet noticed that brighter children performed like _____ children, whereas less capable children performed like _____ children; this observation led him to the idea of a mental level or mental age that was different from a child's _____ age.

   (d) Binet _____ (did/did not) believe that he was measuring an inborn or permanent level of intelligence. He also believed that intelligence was too complex a quality to describe with a _____ and that an individual's score could _____ (vary/not vary) over time.

3. (a) Binet's test was translated and adapted by American psychologist Lewis Terman and is called the _____ .

   (b) The _____ , or _____ , is a number derived by dividing the individual's mental age by the chronological age and multiplying the result by 100.

   (c) During World War I, army psychologists developed two group intelligence tests; the _____ test, which was administered in writing, and the _____ test, which was administered orally to those who could not read. They were later adapted for civilian use.

   (d) Despite concerns about the misuse of the so-called _____ tests, they quickly became popular and were used in a wide variety of settings, not just to identify children who might benefit from special educational help. It soon came to be believed that the _____ score was a fixed, inborn characteristic resistant to change.

4. (a) David Wechsler designed a new intelligence test called the

   _____ , or _____ for short.

   (b) Wechsler's test was specifically designed for adults rather than for children and provided scores on 11 _____ measuring different abilities grouped to provide an overall _____ score and _____ score.

   (c) The scores on subtests of vocabulary, comprehension, knowledge of general information, and other such tasks were included in the _____ score. The subtests in which test-takers had to identify missing parts in incomplete pictures, arrange pictures to tell a story, or arrange

blocks to match a given pattern were part of the _____ score.

   (d) Because the _____ provided an individualized profile of the subject's strengths and weakness on specific tasks, it marked a return to the attidudes and goals of _____ .

   (e) Wechsler calculated the _____ by comparing an individual's score to the scores of others in the same general age group whose average score was statistically fixed at 100. The range of scores is statistically defined so that _____ of all scores fall between 85 and 115, which is considered to indicate "normal" or "average" intelligence.

   (f) Wechsler also developed two tests for children: the

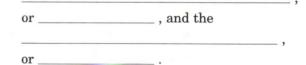

   or _____ , and the

   _____ , or _____ .

5. (a) Tests designed to measure a person's level of knowledge, skill, or accomplishment in a particular area, such as mathematics or a foreign language, are _____ tests; in contrast, tests designed to assess a person's capacity to benefit from education or training are _____ tests.

   (b) _____ means that the test is given to a large number of subjects who are representative of the group of people for whom the test is designed. The scores of this group establish the _____ , or standards, against which an individual's score is compared and interpreted.

   (c) For IQ tests, these standards closely follow a bell-shaped pattern of individual differences called the _____ , or _____ , with most scores clustering around the average.

(d) If a test consistently produces similar scores on different occasions, it is said to be

_____ .

(e) To determine a test's _____ , psychologists check whether test and retest scores using two different versions of the test or two different halves of the test are highly similar.

(f) If a test measures what it is supposed to measure, it is said to be _____ ; one test of this essential requirement is to demonstrate its predictive value.

6. Read the following and write the correct term in the space provided.

(a) A Norwegian visitor to England asks the hotel clerk, "Can you please my key to my room give me?" This visitor has apparently not yet mastered the _____ of the English language.

(b) When Elinore's husband refers to her psychiatrist as a "headshrinker" during discussions with friends or family, he may be influencing their _____ perceptions of Elinore and her therapist.

(c) Ten-year-old Jean performed at the same level as most 12-year-olds on Binet's test. Her _____ age is different from her _____ age.

(d) According to his score on the Standard-Binet test, Marcel's mental age is identical to his chronological age. Marcel's IQ score is likely to be _____ .

(e) When 25-year-old Dagmar applied for a position with the Department of Defense, she was given a test; she scored slightly above the norm on overall verbal ability but well above the norm in overall performance for her age group. The test Dagmar was given was a(n) _____ called the _____ .

(f) The test and retest scores on the new Zander jealousy scale were highly similar but lacked predictive value; furthermore, it was not clear exactly what human attribute it was measuring. The Zander test was high in _____ but low in _____ .

Review of Terms, Concepts, and Names 2

Use the terms in this list to complete the Matching Test, then to help you answer the True/False items correctly.

language
linguistic relativity hypothesis
syntax
generative
displacement
animal cognition (comparative cognition)
intelligence
Alfred Binet
mental age
Lewis Terman
Stanford-Binet Intelligence Scale
intelligence quotient (IQ)
David Wechsler
Wechsler Adult Intelligence Scale (WAIS)
verbal score
performance score
achievement test
aptitude test
standardization
normal curve (normal distribution)
reliability
validity

Matching Exercise

Match the appropriate term/name with its definition or description.

1. _____ Every language's unique rules for combining words.

2. _____ The French psychologist who, along with French psychiatrist Théodore Simon, developed the first widely used intelligence test.

3. _____ The ability to communicate meaningfully about ideas, objects, and activities that are not physically present.

4. _____ Measure of intelligence in which an individual's mental level is expressed in terms of the average abilities of a given age group.

5. _____ Name of Lewis Terman's translation and revision of the Binet-Simon intelligence test.

6. _____ The ability of a test to measure what it is intended to measure.

7. _____ Characteristic of language that allows one to create an infinite number of new and different phrases and sentences.

8. _____ Active area of psychology concerned with all aspects of animal language research.

9. _____ Bell-shaped distribution of individual differences in a normal population in which most scores cluster around the average score.

10. _____ The global capacity to think rationally, act purposefully, and deal effectively with the environment.

11. _____ System for combining arbitrary symbols to produce an infinite number of meaningful statements.

True/False Test

Indicate whether each item is true or false by placing T or F in the space next to each item.

1. ____ Lewis Terman was a French psychiatrist who, along with French psychologist Alfred Binet, developed the first widely used intelligence test, called the Binet-Terman IQ Test.

2. ____ David Wechsler was the American psychologist who developed the Wechsler Adult Intelligence Scale (WAIS), the most widely used intelligence scale.

3. ____ An aptitude test is designed to measure a person's level of knowledge, skill, or accomplishments in a particular area, such as mathematics or a foreign language.

4. ____ The intelligence quotient (IQ) is a global measure of intelligence derived by comparing an individual's score to that of others in the same age group.

5. ____ The *verbal score* on the WAIS reflects scores on subtests such as identifying missing parts in incomplete pictures, arranging pictures to tell a story, or arranging blocks to match a given pattern.

6. ____ Reliability refers to the ability of a test to produce consistent results when administered on repeated occasions under similar conditions.

7. ____ Standardization is the process of administering a test to a large, representative sample of people under uniform conditions for the purpose of establishing norms.

8. ____ An achievement test is designed to measure a person's capacity to benefit from education or training.

9. ____ The *performance score* on the WAIS represents scores on subtests of vocabulary, comprehension, knowledge of general information, and other similar tasks.

10. ____ The Wechsler Adult Intelligence Scale (WAIS) was designed as an achievement test but is now widely used as an aptitude test.

11. ____ The notion that differences among languages cause differences in the thoughts of their speakers is called the linguistic relativity hypothesis.

Check your answers and review any areas of weakness before going on to the next section.

The Nature of Intelligence

Preview Questions

Consider the following questions as you study this section of the chapter.

- What are the two key issues involved in the debate over the nature of intelligence?
- Is intelligence a single, general ability, or is it a cluster of different abilities?
- How narrowly should intelligence be defined?
- How do Spearman, Thurstone, Gardner, and Sternberg differ in their views of intelligence?

*Read the section "The Nature of Intelligence" and **write** your answers to the following:*

1. Much of the controversy over the definition and nature of intelligence centers on two key issues:

   (a) Is intelligence a _____ , _____ ability or a _____ of different abilities?

   (b) Should the _____ of intelligence be restricted to mental abilities measured by intelligence tests, or should intelligence be _____ more broadly?

2. (a) The belief that a common factor, or general mental capacity, is at the core of different mental abilities originated with British psychologist _____ .

   (b) Psychologists who follow the approach that _____ , or a _____ factor, is responsible for overall performance on mental ability tests think that intelligence can be accurately expressed by a single measure of general cognitive ability, such as the IQ score.

   (c) Lewis Terman's approach to measuring and defining intelligence as a single, overall IQ score was in the tradition of British psychologist _____ .

3. (a) Psychologist L. L. Thurstone disagreed that intelligence is a single mental capacity and proposed that there were seven different "_____," each a relatively independent element of intelligence.

   (b) To Thurstone, the _____ factor was simply an overall average score of such independent abilities and consequently was less important than an individual's specific _____ of mental abilities.

   (c) The approach of American psychologist _____ to measuring and defining intelligence as a pattern of different abilities was very similar to Thurstone's approach.

4. (a) More recently, Howard Gardner has expanded _____ basic notion of intelligence as different mental abilities that operate independently by postulating the notion of _____

   (b) To Gardner, "_____" is the ability to solve problems, or create products, that are valued within one or more cultural settings and therefore must be viewed in the context of a particular culture.

   (c) Some abilities emphasized by Gardner may be tapped by a standard intelligence test, such as _____ intelligence, but other abilities, such as _____ intelligence or _____ intelligence, may not be, despite being recognized and highly valued in many different cultures, including our own.

5. (a) Robert Sternberg agrees with _____ that intelligence is a much broader quality than the narrow range of mental abilities tested by a conventional IQ test, but he disagrees with the notion of multiple, independent _____ , which he regards as specialized "talents."

   (b) Sternberg's _____ theory of intelligence emphasizes both the universal aspects of intelligent behavior and the importance of adapting to a particular social and cultural environment; Sternberg's conception of intelligence is called _____ intelligence.

   (c) Sternberg contends that intelligence involves three distinct types of mental abilities:

      (1) _____ intelligence refers to the mental processes used in learning how to solve problems: picking a problem-solving strategy and applying it to solve problems.

      (2) _____ intelligence is the ability to deal with novel situations by drawing on previous experiences and transferring existing skills and knowledge to new information.

      (3) _____ intelligence involves the ability to adapt to the environment and is loosely equivalent to "street smarts"; behaviors that reflect _____ intelligence can vary depending on the particular situation, environment, or culture.

6. (a) Despite _____ (agreement/dis-agreement) on the specific nature and definition of intelligence, psychologists generally _____ (agree/disagree) that factors such as abstract thinking, problem solving, and the capacity to acquire knowledge (all typically assessed on standard IQ tests) are important elements of intelligence.

(b) Other important aspects of intelligence that exist and are not measured in conventional intelligence tests include _____

_____ , _____

behavior, and the ability to adapt to one's environment.

The Roles of Genetics and Environment in Determining Intelligence

Preview Questions

Consider the following questions as you study this section of the chapter.

- What is the heredity-environment issue?
- How are twin studies used to measure genetic and environmental influences?
- What is a heritability estimate, and why can't heritability estimates be used to explain differences between groups?
- How can social discriminatioin affect intelligence test scores?
- Are IQ tests culturally biased?

*Read the section "The Roles of Genetics and Environment in Determining Intelligence" and **write** your answers to the following:*

1. (a) The debate on the origins of intelligence involves two basic questions: (1) Do we essentially _____ our intellectual potential from our parents, grandparents, and great-grandparents? (2) Is our intellectual potential primarily determined by our _____ and upbringing?

(b) Virtually all psychologists agree that both _____ and _____

are important in determining intelligence levels; how much each contributes is the crucial issue.

(c) Eye color is completely _____ determined but height is a function of the interplay between _____ and _____ ; you inherit a potential range for height but where your actual height falls within that range is influenced by environmental factors.

(d) How people's intelligence and personalities are determined is extremely complex; the genetic range of intellectual potential is influenced by _____ (one/many) gene(s), and _____ factors are not stable but constantly changing.

2. (a) To deal with the complexities involved in the study of the role of heredity and environment, psychologists have used

_____ .

(b) Identical twins share exactly the same genes, because they developed from a single fertilized egg that split into two; consequently, any dissimilarities between them must be due to _____ factors rather than _____ differences.

(c) Fraternal twins develop from two different fertilized eggs and therefore _____ (are/are not) like any other pair of siblings, but because they are the same age, their _____ experiences are likely to be more similar than those of siblings of different ages.

(d) Both genetic and environmental influences are important:

(1) Genetic influence is shown by the fact that identical twins raised together have very _____ IQ scores.

(2) Environmental influences are shown when two identical twins who are raised in different homes have

_____ IQ scores, and two genetically unrelated people raised in the same home have IQs much more _____ than unrelated people from randomly selected homes.

3. (a) Using studies based on degree of genetic relatedness, researchers have scientifically estimated _____ , which is the percentage of variation within a given population that is due to heredity.

   (b) It is estimated that approximately 50 percent (or possibly 65 percent) of the difference in IQ scores within a specific group of people, or a given population, is due to _____ factors; this figure _____ (does/does not) apply to a single individual's IQ score.

4. (a) Much of the controversy over the role of _____ in intelligence is due to attempts to explain the differences in average IQ scores for different racial groups.

   (b) Although *group* differences in *average* IQ scores have been found, it is important to note that they do not predict _____ differences in IQ scores.

   (c) The most fundamental problem related to the controversy over genetics and IQ scores is the inappropriate comparison of _____ differences in IQ scores.

5. (a) Unless the environmental conditions of two racial groups are virtually identical, it is impossible to estimate the overall _____ differences between the two groups, and even if intelligence were primarily determined by heredity, IQ differences between groups could still be due entirely to the _____ .

   (b) Scarr and Weinberg, who explored the relationship between racial IQ differences and the environment, concluded that IQ differences are due not to race, but rather to the _____ conditions and

_____ values to which children are exposed.

   (c) Changes in average IQ scores in many countries in just one generation can be accounted for only by _____ changes, because the amount of time is far too short for _____ influenced changes to have occurred.

6. (a) The effect of social discrimination on intelligence test scores has been shown in numerous _____ studies; in many different societies, the average IQ is lower for members of a discriminated-against minority, even when that group is of the same race as the dominant group.

   (b) Children belonging to _____ groups score 10 to 15 IQ points lower, are often one or two years behind in basic reading and math skills, are overrepresented in remedial programs and the number of school dropouts, and are underrepresented among students in higher education, as compared with children belonging to _____ groups.

   (c) The impact of _____ on group differences in IQ remains even when the minority-group and dominant-group members are of similar socioeconomic backgrounds.

7. (a) Another approach to explaining group differences in IQ scores has been to look at _____ in the tests themselves; if standardized intelligence tests reflect white, middle-class cultural knowledge and values, minority-group members might do poorly not because of lower intelligence but because of unfamiliarity with the white, middle-class _____ .

   (b) It is now generally recognized that it is _____ (quite possible/virtually impossible) to design a test that is completely culture free. A test will tend to favor the people from the culture in which it was developed and within that culture the intelligence test may be _____ . (valid/invalid).

(c) Cultural differences may also be involved in _____ behavior. People from different cultural backgrounds may use different organizational and problem-solving _____ than those required on standardized intelligence test; in addition, factors such as _____ , _____ toward test taking, and previous experience with test taking can all influence performance and test scores.

(d) Being aware that you are not expected to do well on a particular test can create anxiety and apprehension about being evaluated and can lower both the _____ and _____ of responses on standardized test questions.

8. On the basis of the discussion about influences of heredity and environment in intelligence, three broad conclusions can be drawn about the debate surrounding intelligence and race:

(a) The IQ of any given individual, regardless of which racial group he or she may belong to, is the result of the complex interaction of _____ and _____ influences.

(b) The IQ differences between racial groups are influenced much more by _____ factors than by _____ factors.

(c) Within a given racial group, the differences among people are due at least as much to _____ influences as to _____ influences.

9. Read the following and write the correct term in the space provided.

(a) Although Dr. Bowman recognizes that particular individuals might excel in specific areas, she believes that a factor, called general intelligence, or the *g* factor, is responsible for overall performance on mental ability

tests. Her belief about the nature of intelligence is most consistent with the approach taken by psychologist _____ .

(b) Jamal is a highly valued maintenance worker because of his almost uncanny ability to be able to fix almost any piece of equipment that breaks down. Jamal is demonstrating what Robert Sternberg would call _____ intelligence.

(c) Selma is a very successful, highly motivated, goal-directed, creative graphic designer. These aspects of her intelligence are _____ (not likely/very likely) to be assessed and measured on a conventional intelligence test.

(d) Dicky and Ricky are identical twins and have almost identical IQ scores despite the fact that they were separated at birth and raised separately. Fraternal twins Joel and Joanna were raised together but their IQ scores are much less similar than Dicky's and Ricky's scores. This example provides the most support for the _____ side in the heredity-environment debate.

(e) As compared with the scores of two randomly selected unrelated people of the same age, Joel and Joanna's IQ scores are much more similar. This finding provides most support for the _____ side in the heredity-environment debate.

(f) Dr. Yokomoto, like the majority of experts on intelligence testing, is most likely to attribute the finding that Japanese and Chinese children outperform American children on mathematics achievement tests to _____ factors.

(g) When Dr. Parsei, an expert on intelligence testing, was asked if a completely culture-free intelligence test could be designed, he replied that it _____ (was/was not) because group ability tests reflect the values, knowledge, and communication strategies of their culture of origin.

Graphic Organizer 2

Read the following statements and decide which
psychologist is most associated with each:

Statement	Psychologist
1. I define intelligence as the global capacity to think rationally, act purposefully, and deal effectively with the environment; a good IQ test should have both verbal and performance scores representing subtests that measure a variety of abilities.	
2. My theory of intelligence emphasizes both universal aspects of intelligent behavior and the importance of adapting to the individual's particular social and cultural environment; there are essentially three forms of intelligence: analytical, creative, and practical intelligence.	
3. I'm not sure I have a fully developed theory of intelligence, but I do believe that we can help children do better in school if we devise tests that can identify those who need help and then provide that help. There is a great deal of variation in intelligence in any age group of children.	
4. I am convinced that a factor called general intelligence, or the *g* factor, is responsible for the overall performance on mental ability tests. Furthermore, I would go so far as to say that intelligence can be accurately expressed as a single number that reflects an individual's intellectual abilities.	
5. I disagree with those who say that intelligence is a single, general mental capacity. On the basis of my observations of what is valued in different cultures, I've concluded that there are multiple intelligences (at least seven), each independent of the other, and these must be viewed in the context of a particular culture.	
6. I tend to agree with statement 4 above. In addition, I believe that intelligence can best be expressed by a number I call the intelligence quotient, or IQ, which is derived by dividing the mental age by the chronological age and multiplying the result by 100.	

Review of Terms, Concepts, and Names 3

Use the terms in this list to complete the Matching Test, then to help you answer the True/False items correctly.

Charles Spearman
g factor (general
   intelligence)
L. L. Thurstone
primary mental abilities
Howard Gardner
Robert Sternberg
triarchic theory of
   intelligence

analytical intelligence
creative intelligence
practical intelligence
heredity
environment
heritability
identical twins
fraternal twins
creativity

Matching Exercise

Match the appropriate term/name with its definition or description.

1. _____ A contemporary American psychologist whose triarchic theory of intelligence includes three forms of intelligence (analytical, creative, and practical).

2. _____ The percentage of variation within a given population that is due to heredity.

3. _____ A factor of intelligence that is responsible for a person's overall performance on tests of mental ability.

4. _____ A group of cognitive processes used to generate useful, original, and novel ideas or solutions.

5. _____ American psychologist who advanced the theory that intelligence is composed of several primary mental abilities and cannot be accurately described by a general intelligence, or g, factor.

6. _____ Sternberg's type of intelligence that involves the ability to adapt to the environment and often reflects what is commonly described as street smarts.

7. _____ British psychologist who advanced the theory that a general intelligence factor, called the g factor, is responsible for overall intellectual functioning.

8. _____ A form of intelligence that involves the ability to deal with novel situations by drawing on existing skills and knowledge.

True/False Test

Indicate whether each item is true or false by placing T or F in the space next to each item.

1. ____ Howard Gardner is a contemporary American psychologist whose theory of intelligence states that there is not one intelligence but multiple intelligences, the importance of each being determined by cultural values.

2. ____ Identical twins develop from two different fertilized eggs and are 50 percent genetically similar to each other.

3. ____ Heredity refers to the traits, capacities, and intellectual potential that we inherit from our parents, grandparents, and great-grandparents.

4. ____ Analytical intelligence refers to the mental processes used in learning how to solve problems, that is, in picking a problem-solving strategy and applying it to solve problems.

5. ____ In the debate over what determines intelligence, environment refers to factors such as type of upbringing, nutritional and health standards, social and cultural factors, and other influences that may have an impact on intellectual development.

6. ____ Fraternal twins share exactly the same genes because they developed from a single fertilized egg that split into two.

7. ____ Sternberg's theory that there are three forms of intelligence—analytical, creative, and practical—is called the triarchic theory of intelligence.

8. ____ According to Thurstone, primary mental abilities are relatively independent elements of intelligence and include verbal comprehension, numerical ability, reasoning, and perceptual speed.

Check your answers and review any areas of weakness before going on to the next section.

Something to Think About

1. Many people mistakenly believe that creativity is restricted to a few gifted, genius-level, artistic people. What would you tell someone who wants to be creative but does not believe he or she possesses an artistic temperament?

2. People vary in their IQ test scores, but about 68 percent of scores on tests such as the WAIS-R are between 85 and 115, the range for normal intelligence. A friend comes up to you and says, "Wouldn't it be great if we all had above-average IQ scores? Just think how wonderful life would be and how happy and successful we'd be!" How might you enlighten your friend about IQ tests and IQ scores?

> Check your answers and review any areas of weakness before doing the progress tests.

Progress Test 1

Review the complete chapter (including Concept Reviews and all the boxed inserts), review all your study notes, and then test yourself on the following progress test. Check your answers. If you make a mistake, review your notes, review the relevant section of the study guide, and, if necessary, go back and read the appropriate part of your textbook.

1. In applying for a job at O'Hare Airport, Lynda is given a test to see if she is suited to be an air traffic controller. This is an example of _____ testing.
   - (a) intelligence
   - (b) achievement
   - (c) aptitude
   - (d) motivational

2. When Aaron is asked to define *weapon*, he responds that it is anything you could use to beat someone with. Aaron is using the word *weapon* as a
   - (a) natural concept.
   - (b) prototype.
   - (c) formal concept.
   - (d) heuristic.

3. When Michelle is asked the same question as Aaron, she replies that a weapon is one of a variety of instruments, or objects, that can be used to defend, attack, hurt, maim, or kill. Furthermore, the term *weapon* can even refer to words in a phrase, as in "the pen is mightier than the sword." Michelle is using the word *weapon* as a
   - (a) natural concept.
   - (b) prototype
   - (c) formal concept.
   - (d) heuristic

4. When three-year-old Claudia is asked which letter of the alphabet comes before *G*, she recites the alphabet from the beginning until she arrives at the solution. Claudia is using _____ to solve the problem.
   - (a) trial and error
   - (b) insight
   - (c) an algorithm
   - (d) a heuristic

5. Louis forgot to bring his pillow when he went camping for the weekend, so he spent a very uncomfortable night. It didn't occur to Louis that he could use his down-filled jacket as a pillow. This example best illustrates
   - (a) functional fixedness.
   - (b) mental set.
   - (c) the availability heuristic.
   - (d) use of an algorithm.

6. When Vasilis is faced with the decision of which of two equally attractive apartments to rent, he makes a list of what is most important and gives each factor a numerical rating. It appears that Vasilis is using the _____ model of decision making.
   - (a) elimination by aspects
   - (b) additive
   - (c) single-feature
   - (d) heuristic

7. Jerome *recently* saw a TV special in which most of the psychologists interviewed were middle-aged males. When he took his first psychology class, he was surprised to find that his professor was a young female rather than an older bearded male. Jerome's surprise is probably due to his use of the
   - (a) availability heuristic.
   - (b) representativeness heuristic.
   - (c) single-feature model.
   - (d) additive model.

8. When Heidi tells Hans that she is going to enter a foot race to raise funds to end the arms race, he has no trouble understanding that she is going to run in a race to generate support for an anti-weapons cause. Hans's correct interpretation best illustrates the importance of
   - (a) syntax.
   - (b) displacement.
   - (c) generativity.
   - (d) prototypes.

9. When asked what she does for a living, Krista always replies that she is a sanitary engineer rather than a garbage collector. Krista is probably aware of the effect of language on
   - (a) memory.
   - (b) gender bias.
   - (c) social perception.
   - (d) income level.

10. Six-year-old Bruce's performance on an intelligence test is at a level characteristic of an average four-year-old. Bruce's mental age is
    (a) eight.   (c) six.
    (b) four.   (d) five.

11. Scott is a very bright ten-year-old with a mental age of thirteen. If tested on the Stanford-Binet Intelligence Scale, his IQ score would most likely be
    (a) 100.   (c) 150.
    (b) 77.   (d) 130.

12. Twenty-year-old Val has just taken a test that includes vocabulary, comprehension, general knowledge, object assembly, and other subtests. Val has completed the
    (a) WAIS.   (c) WISC.
    (b) WPPSI.   (d) Stanford-Binet.

13. In his research on very young black children adopted into white middle-class families, Dr. Wilson found that their IQ scores were several points above the average of both blacks and whites. Dr. Wilson, like most experts in this area, is most likely to conclude that
    (a) intelligence is determined primarily by heredity.
    (b) IQ scores cannot be improved by environmental factors.
    (c) improved diet and health standards are the crucial factor in improving IQ scores.
    (d) socioeconomic conditions, cultural values, and other such environmental factors can affect IQ scores.

14. In Focus 7.1 suggests that intuition
    (a) involves two stages, the guiding stage and the integrative stage.
    (b) is the process of coming to a conclusion or making a judgment without conscious awareness of the thought processes involved.
    (c) may involve what are commonly called hunches.
    (d) involves all of the above.

15. Which of the following is *not* one of the obstacles to logical thinking that can account for much of the persistence of unwarranted beliefs in pseudosciences?
    (a) the belief bias effect
    (b) confirmation bias
    (c) the underestimation effect
    (d) the fallacy of positive instances
    (e) the overestimation effect

Progress Test 2

After you have checked your understanding of the material in Progress Test 1 and have done a complete chapter review with special focus on any areas of weakness, you are now ready to assess your knowledge of Progress Test 2. Check your answers. If you make a mistake, review your notes, the relevant section of the study guide, and, if necessary, the appropriate part of your textbook.

1. As part of his overall vocational assessment Steven took a test that measured his level of knowledge, skills, and accomplishments in particular areas such as mathematics and writing ability. Steven took a(n)
    (a) aptitude test.
    (b) achievement test.
    (c) intelligence test.
    (d) motivational test.

2. When Katrina is asked to identify the letters of the alphabet that do not have curved lines, she tries to mentally picture each letter as she completes the task. Katrina is using
    (a) mental imagery.   (c) a formal concept.
    (b) a natural concept. (d) a prototype.

3. Shawn is asked to memorize a map of an island that has a hut, a lake, a tree, a beach, and a grassy area, all clearly marked at distinct locations. Later, he is asked to imagine a specific location, such as the hut; when a second location, the tree, is named, he has to press a button when he reaches the tree on the visual image in his mind. The results of this experiment will most likely reveal that the _____ the distance between the two points, the _____ time it will take to scan the mental image of the map.
    (a) greater; more
    (b) greater; less
    (c) shorter; more
    (d) All of the above are false; there is no relationship between distance and time taken to mentally scan points on the map.

4. When Earl is asked what object or objects come to mind in response to the word *vegetable*, he answers "potatoes and carrots." For Earl, potatoes and carrots are
    (a) formal concepts.   (c) algorithms.
    (b) prototypes.   (d) heuristics.

5. Ian wants to improve his problem-solving ability so he adopts a strategy that involves identifying and defining the problem, exploring possible strategies and acting on one, and then looking back and evaluating the solution. Ian has adopted the _____ of problem solving.
    (a) single-feature model
    (b) additive model
    (c) elimination by aspects model
    (d) IDEAL model

6. When Elana got her new VCR, she spent hours trying different approaches to programming the machine rather than consulting the manual. Elana is using the _____ approach to problem solving.
    (a) algorithm   (c) heuristic
    (b) trial-and-error   (d) insight

7. After spending weeks studying a variety of sources and materials, Terry still couldn't decide on a topic for her seminar presentation. However, when she was out for her daily jog, she suddenly had a flash of inspiration about her topic. Terry solved her problem
    (a) through insight.
    (b) by using an algorithm.
    (c) through functional fixedness.
    (d) by using the representativeness heuristic.

8. When his TV picture became fuzzy, Lloyd would bang the top of the TV set and the picture would clear. Recently, when he was playing a video on his new VCR, tracking problems created a fuzzy picture; Lloyd banged the top of the TV over and over but to no avail. Lloyd appears to be experiencing an obstacle to solving the problem called
    (a) functional fixedness.
    (b) subgoal analysis.
    (c) a mental set.
    (d) confirmation bias.
    (e) prototypical male stupidity.

9. When writing term papers, assignments, and exams, Gary is very careful to use "he or she" in place of the masculine pronoun and "people" instead of "man." Gary is apparently aware of the relationship between language and
    (a) memory.   (c) social perception.
    (b) gender bias.   (d) functional fixedness.

10. Dr. Peerless has designed a test to measure the level of scientific knowledge in high school graduates. To establish a norm against which individual scores may be interpreted and compared, she is presently administering the test to a large representative sample of high school graduates. Dr. Peerless is in the process of
    (a) establishing the test's reliability.
    (b) establishing the test's validity.
    (c) standardizing the test.
    (d) determining the test's aptitude.

11. After completing the above process, Dr. Peerless needs to check whether her test measures what it was designed to measure. She does this by comparing scores on her test with the scores and grades obtained by students in high school science courses. In this instance, Dr. Peerless is in the process of
    (a) establishing the test's reliability.
    (b) establishing the test's validity.
    (c) standardizing the test.
    (d) determining the test's aptitude.

12. Arnie is very adept at dealing with novel situations by drawing on previous experience and can often find unusual ways to relate old information to solve new problems. Robert Sternberg would call this _____ intelligence.
    (a) analytical   (c) creative
    (b) practical   (d) motivational

13. As part of a bizarre experiment in a science fiction story, Dr. Igor places 100 genetically identical individual infants in different homes. Because they are all identical, the heritability of intelligence (that is, the percentage of variation within the group that is due to genetic factors) should be _____ percent.
    (a) 0   (c) 65
    (b) 50   (d) 100

14. According to In Focus 7.4, "Does a High IQ Score Predict Success in Life?," which of the following is true?
    (a) IQ scores reliably predict academic success.
    (b) Academic success is no guarantee of success beyond school.
    (c) Many different personality factors are involved in achieving success, such as motivation, emotional maturity, commitment to goals, creativity, and a willingness to work hard.
    (d) All of the above are true.

15. According to the Application, which of the following is *not* a way to increase your creative potential?
    (a) Focus almost exclusively on extrinsic motivation.
    (b) Choose the goal of creativity.
    (c) Try different approaches.
    (d) Acquire relevant knowledge.
    (e) Engage in problem finding.

Progress Test 3

After you have checked your understanding of the material in Progress Tests 1 and 2, and have done a complete chapter review with special focus on any areas of weakness, you are ready to further assess your knowledge on Progress Test 3. Check your answers. If you make a mistake, review your notes, the appropriate parts of the study guide, and if necessary, the relevant sections of your textbook.

1. Adrian took the WAIS test. One aspect of his general cognitive ability that is not likely to have been measured is his
    (a) linguistic ability.
    (b) problem-solving ability.
    (c) general knowledge.
    (d) creativity.

2. Dr. Larch is a renowned researcher and theorist in the area of intelligence testing. Like most experts in his field, Dr. Larch is most likely to agree that
    (a) genetic factors, rather than environmental influences, are the primary cause of any IQ differences found between racial groups.
    (b) within a given racial group, the differences among people are due at least as much to environmental influences as they are to genetic influences.
    (c) the IQ of any individual, regardless of his or her race, is determined almost exclusively by genetic factors and is relatively uninfluenced by environmental influences.
    (d) the IQ of any given individual, regardless of his or her race, is determined almost exclusively by environmental factors and is relatively uninfluenced by genetics.

3. With little or no hesitation, Matthew was able to state that cats and dogs are both examples of the concept of mammal; he was slower to respond when asked whether dolphins and whales were also examples of mammals. This example suggests that

    (a) formal concepts have fuzzy boundaries and that cats and dogs are prototypes of the category.
    (b) natural concepts have fuzzy boundaries and that cats and dogs are prototypes of the category.
    (c) formal concepts have fuzzy boundaries and that dolphins and whales are prototypes of the category.
    (d) natural concepts have fuzzy boundaries and that dolphins and whales are prototypes of the category.

4. Tom created the novel sentence, "The faceless bureaucrat was finally faced with making a face-saving decision but could not face up to the fact that he was in a fatal face-off with his favorite facetious faculty." Tom's ability to do this illustrates the _____ nature of language.
    (a) syntactic
    (b) inflexible
    (c) generative
    (d) practical

5. Dr. Adatia, a cross-cultural psychologist, discovered that children of immigrant Buraku families living in the United States had IQ scores no different from other Japanese-Americans, but that the Burakumin in Japan had IQ scores 10 to 15 points lower than those of other Japanese. Dr. Adatia is most likely to conclude that
    (a) IQ scores are genetically determined.
    (b) social discrimination can affect IQ scores.
    (c) better nutrition is the main factor that influences IQ scores.
    (d) the U.S. educational system is better than that of Japan.

6. Dr. Bishop assesses the correlation between scores obtained on two halves of his new abstract reasoning test in order to measure the _____ of her test.
    (a) reliability   (c) norms
    (b) validity   (d) aptitude

7. Miguel is extremely adept at learning how to solve problems, that is, in picking problem-solving strategies and applying them to problems. Robert Sternberg would call this ability a form of
    (a) analytical intelligence.
    (b) creative intelligence.
    (c) practical intelligence.
    (d) general intelligence, or the *g* factor.

8. Dr. Welch believes that there are multiple independent intelligences that cannot be reflected in a single measure of mental ability and that each intelligence must be viewed within a cultural context. Dr. Welch's position is most consistent with the views of
    (a) Charles Spearman.
    (b) L. L. Thurstone.
    (c) Howard Gardner.
    (d) Robert Sternberg.

9. When Allison goes to graduate school, she plans to investigate aspects of the heredity-environment debate as it relates to intelligence. She is most likely to
    (a) use animals, such as rats and pigeons, in her research.
    (b) get involved in twin studies.
    (c) study the language abilities of primates.
    (d) explore creativity and intuition.

10. Maja is writing a paper for her course in comparative cognition. After reviewing all the relevant research on animal language, Maja is likely to conclude that
    (a) only humans possess language capabilities.
    (b) animals can communicate with each other but are not capable of mastering any aspect of language.
    (c) some species have demonstrated an elementary understanding of syntax and certain other limited aspects of language.
    (d) many animal species can "think," use language and possess self-awareness.

11. Martin has had some difficulties in school and has fallen behind in academic achievement. His chronological age is ten and his IQ score on the Stanford-Binet is 70. Martin's mental age is therefore
    (a) seven.   (c) thirteen.
    (b) ten.   (d) five.

12. Cynthia always buys the brand of paper towels that is on sale whether or not it is the highest quality towel. Cynthia makes her decision about which paper towel to purchase based on the _____ model of decision making.
    (a) single-feature
    (b) additive
    (c) elimination by aspects
    (d) heuristic

13. Jan is orderly, neat, quiet, and shy. She enjoys reading in her spare time and is an avid chess player. Given this description, most people would guess that she is a librarian rather than a real estate agent. This tendency to classify Jan as a librarian illustrates the influence of
    (a) the availability heuristic.
    (b) belief perseverance.
    (c) the representativeness heuristic.
    (d) the elimination by aspects strategy.

14. According to Culture and Human Behavior 7.3, the linguistic relativity hypothesis (or Whorfian hypothesis)
    (a) proposes that the differences among languages cause differences in the thoughts of their speakers.
    (b) has been supported by the results of dozens of cross-cultural studies.
    (c) accounts for the fact that the English language has more than a dozen words for *snow* but Eskimos have only one or two.
    (d) holds that language does not determine cultural differences but instead language reflects cultural differences.

15. According to the Application, creativity
    (a) is something that only a few very gifted people possess.
    (b) refers to a group of cognitive processes used to generate useful, novel, and original ideas and solutions.
    (c) is only concerned with artistic expression, with little or no practical value.
    (d) refers to the ability to arrive at conclusions or make judgments without conscious awareness of the thought processes involved.

Answers

Introduction: Thinking, Language, and Intelligence

1. (a) mental; acquiring, retaining; using
   (b) intelligence

2. (a) thinking
   (b) mental representations

3. (a) mental image
   (b) actual objects

4. (a) concept
   (b) formal concept
   (c) attributes (rules); is not
   (d) natural concept; are not
   (e) prototype; prototype

Problem Solving: Searching for the IDEAL Solution

1. (a) Identify
   (b) Define
   (c) Explore
   (d) Act
   (e) Look back

2. (a) recognize; understand
   (b) list; graphic; table

3. (a) trial and error
   (b) algorithm
   (c) heuristic; heuristics
   (d) heuristic; subgoals; working backward
   (e) insight
   (f) evaluate

4. (a) functional fixedness
   (b) mental sets

Decisions, Decisions, Decisions: Should I or Shouldn't I?

1. (a) features
   (b) single-feature
   (c) additive
   (d) additive
   (e) elimination by aspects
   (f) additive; elimination by aspects; additive

2. (a) availability
   (b) availability
   (c) less; less
   (d) representativeness
   (e) representativeness

3. (a) insight
   (b) representativeness heuristic
   (c) cognitive; thinking
   (d) mental image
   (e) formal
   (f) natural
   (g) algorithm
   (h) trial-and-error
   (i) additive

Graphic Organizer 1

1. Identifying the problem
2. Defining the problem
3. Defining the problem
4. Trial and error
5. Using an algorithm
6. Using a heuristic (working backward)
7. Insight
8. Using a heuristic (subgoal analysis)
9. Looking back and evaluating the solution

Matching Exercise 1

1. elimination by aspects model
2. thinking
3. prototype
4. insight
5. single-feature model
6. representativeness heuristic
7. trial and error
8. formal concept
9. cognition
10. concept
11. heuristic

True/False Test 1

1. F	5. T	9. F
2. T	6. T	10. T
3. T	7. T	11. T
4. F	8. F	

Language and Thought

1. (a) communicate
   (b) symbols

2. (a) symbols
   (b) arbitrary
   (c) meaning
   (d) syntax
   (e) generative
   (f) displacement

3. (a) cognitive
   (b) remember
   (c) social perception; stereotypes
   (d) gender bias

4. (a) animal; comparative
   (b) language

Measuring Intelligence

1. (a) intelligence
   (b) intelligence
   (c) mental abilities

2. (a) Alfred Binet
   (b) mental abilities
   (c) older; younger; chronological
   (d) did not; single number; vary

3. (a) Stanford–Binet Intelligence Scale
   (b) intelligence quotient; IQ
   (c) Army Alpha; Army Beta
   (d) IQ; IQ

4. (a) Wechsler Adult Intelligence Scale; WAIS

(b) subtests; verbal; performance

(c) verbal; performance

(d) WAIS; Alfred Binet

(e) IQ; two-thirds

(f) Wechsler Intelligence Scale for Children; WISC; Wechsler Preschool and Primary Scale of Intelligence; WPPSI

5. (a) achievement; aptitude

(b) Standardization; norms

(c) normal curve; normal distribution

(d) reliable

(e) reliability

(f) valid

6. (a) syntax

(b) social

(c) mental; chronological

(d) 100

(e) IQ test; WAIS

(f) reliability; validity

Matching Exercise 2

1. syntax

2. Alfred Binet

3. displacement

4. mental age

5. Stanford-Binet Intelligence Scale

6. validity

7. generative

8. animal cognition (comparative cognition)

9. normal curve (normal distribution)

10. intelligence

11. language

True/False Test 2

1. F	5. F	9. F
2. T	6. T	10. F
3. F	7. T	11. T
4. T	8. F	

The Nature of Intelligence

1. (a) single, general; cluster

(b) definition; defined

2. (a) Charles Spearman

(b) general intelligence; g

(c) Charles Spearman

3. (a) primary mental abilities

(b) g; pattern

(c) David Wechsler

4. (a) Thurstone's; multiple intelligences

(b) intelligence

(c) logical-mathematical; bodily kinesthetic; musical

5. (a) Gardner; intelligences

(b) triarchic; successful

(c) analytical; creative; practical; practical

6. (a) disagreement; agree

(b) creativity; achievement motivation, goal-directed

The Roles of Genetics and Environment in Determining Intelligence

1. (a) inherit; environment

(b) heredity; environment

(c) genetically; heredity; environment

(d) many; environmental

2. (a) twin studies

(b) environmental; hereditary

(c) are; environmental

(d) similar; different; similar

3. (a) heritability

(b) genetic; does not

4. (a) heredity

(b) individual

(c) group

5. (a) genetic; environment

(b) socioeconomic; cultural

(c) environmental; genetically

6. (a) cross-cultural

(b) minority; majority (dominant)

(c) discrimination

7. (a) cultural bias; culture

(b) virtually impossible; valid

(c) test-taking; strategies; motivation, attitude

(d) speed; accuracy

8. (a) hereditary; environmental

(b) environmental; genetic

(c) environmental; genetic

9. (a) Charles Spearman

(b) practical

(c) not likely

(d) heredity

(e) environment

(f) environmental

(g) was not

Graphic Organizer 2

1. David Wechsler
2. Robert Sternberg
3. Alfred Binet
4. Charles Spearman
5. Howard Gardner
6. Lewis Terman

Matching Exercise 3

1. Robert Sternberg
2. heritability
3. *g* factor (general intelligence)
4. creativity
5. L. L. Thurstone
6. practical intelligence
7. Charles Spearman
8. creative intelligence

True/False Test 3

1. T	4. T	7. T
2. F	5. T	8. T
3. T	6. F	

Something to Think About

1. Many people would like to be more creative. Fortunately, much can be done to increase our creative potential. The first thing to tell someone is that creativity is hard to define precisely but that most cognitive psychologists agree that creativity is a group of cognitive processes used to generate useful, original, and novel ideas and solutions. Creativity is not confined to artistic expression; as indicated in the definition, creativity involves usefulness as well as originality. Based on information in the Application, you could then conduct your own mini-workshop on creativity. You can summarize the workshop by using the letters of the word **CREATE** as an acronym: **C**hoose the goal of creativity; **R**einforce creative behavior; **E**ngage in problem finding; **A**cquire relevant knowledge; **T**ry different approaches; **E**xert effort and expect setbacks.

2. First, you could tell your friend that we can't all be above average. The distribution for intelligence will follow a normal, or bell-shaped, curve, with about 50 percent above average and 50 percent below average. Next, you could talk a little about the problems involved in defining intelligence. Not even the experts agree. Some think that performance on mental ability tests reflects a general intelligence, or *g* factor; others think there are three forms of intelligence; and some postulate multiple intelligences. Despite these disagreements, psychologists do agree that intelligence involves such elements as abstract thinking, problem solving, and the capacity to acquire knowledge. They also tend to agree that aspects of intelligent behavior such as creativity, motivation, goal-directed behavior, and adaptation to one's environment are not measured by conventional intelligence tests. Thus, IQ scores reflect the limitations of existing intelligence tests. Finally, according to In Focus Box 7.4, whereas IQ scores may predict academic success, success in school is no guarantee of success and happiness in life in general. Many different personality factors are involved in achieving success, such as motivation, emotional maturity, commitment to goals, creativity, and, perhaps most important of all, a willingness to work hard. None of these attributes are measured by traditional IQ tests.

Progresst Test 1

1. c	6. b	11. d
2. a	7. a	12. a
3. c	8. a	13. d
4. c	9. c	14. d
5. a	10. b	15. c

Progress Test 2

1. b	6. b	11. b
2. a	7. a	12. c
3. a	8. c	13. a
4. b	9. b	14. d
5. d	10. c	15. a

Progress Test 3

1. d	6. a	11. a
2. b	7. a	12. a
3. b	8. c	13. c
4. c	9. b	14. a
5. b	10. c	15. b

CHAPTER

8

Motivation and Emotion

PREVIEW

Reading the section below first will give you a general sense of the chapter's contents and an initial introduction to some of the major concepts and terms. This will prime you for what you are about to read and help you to develop a "cognitive map" that will guide your study of the material in this chapter. Likewise, reading the **preview questions** at the beginning of each major section will improve your ability to understand, learn, and retain the information.

CHAPTER 8. . . AT A GLANCE

Chapter 8 is concerned with motivation and emotion. Motivation refers to the forces that act on or within an organism to initiate and direct behavior. Instinct theories, drive theories, incentive theories, and humanistic theories are introduced. The point is made that the motivation of any behavior is determined by the interaction of multiple factors, including biological, behavioral, cognitive, and social components.

The motivation to eat is influenced by psychological, biological, social, and cultural factors. Several internal and external signals are involved in hunger and satiation. The energy balance model, set-point theory, and the rate at which the body uses energy (basal metabolic rate, or BMR) are discussed in relation to the regulation of body weight. Factors influencing obesity, anorexia nervosa, and bulimia nervosa are examined, and the authors conclude that much is yet to be discovered about these disorders.

Curiosity, sensation seeking, and arousal motives are discussed next. Although there are individual differences, all people seek to maintain an optimal level of arousal, which sometimes involves seeking out stimulation. Competence motivation and achievement motivation are compared, and the Thematic Apperception Test (TAT) is introduced.

Emotions, which serve many different functions in human behavior and relationships, have three basic components: subjective experience, physical arousal, and a behavioral or expressive response. Facial expressions for some basic emotions seem to be universal and innate, but expression is also influenced by cultural display rules.

The key theories of emotion—the James-Lange theory, the Cannon-Bard theory, Schachter and Singer's two-factor theory of emotion, and Richard Lazarus's cognitive-mediational theory—are examined. A synthesis is suggested by an interactive approach that emphasizes the idea that cognitive appraisals, physiological arousal, and behavioral expression all contribute to subjective emotional experiences.

Introduction: Motivation and Emotion

Preview Questions

Consider the following questions as you study this section of the chapter.

- How is motivation defined?
- What three characteristics are associated with motivation?
- How is emotion related to motivation?

*Read the section "Introduction: Motivation and Emotion" and **write** your answers to the following:*

1. (a) Motivation refers to the forces that act on or within an organism to _____ and _____ behavior.

    (b) The fact that people use the word *motivation* to understand and explain other people's behavior reflects the three basic characteristics commonly associated with motivation: _____ is seen in the initiation or production of behavior; _____ is demonstrated by continued efforts or determination to achieve a particular goal, often in the face of obstacles; and _____ is seen in the greater vigor of responding that usually accompanies motivated behavior.

2. (a) Motivational processes are closely tied to _____ , and vice versa.

    (b) A psychological state involving three distinct components: subjective experience, physical arousal, and a behavioral or expressive response is the definition of _____ .

The Study of Motivation: From Then to Now

Preview Questions

Consider the following questions as you study this section of the chapter.

- What four theories have historically been included in the study of motivation?

- How does each theory explain motivation, and what are the limits of each?
- What characterizes the study of motivation today?

*Read the section "The Study of Motivation: From Then to Now" and **write** your answers to the following:*

1. (a) In the late 1800s, the newly founded science of psychology initially embraced the idea that people are motivated to engage in certain behaviors because of genetic programming, which is the basis of _____ theories.

    (b) Drawing from the work of Charles Darwin and his scientifically based theory of evolution, psychologists devised lengthy lists of _____ to account for every conceivable human behavior.

    (c) The problem with these early theories was that they merely _____ and _____ behaviors, rather than actually _____ them.

    (d) By the 1920s and 1930s, instinct theories fell out of favor, although the more general idea that some human behaviors are _____ and _____ programmed has remained an important element in the overall understanding of motivation.

2. (a) During the 1940s and 1950s, instinct theories were replaced by theories that behavior is motivated by the desire to reduce internal tension caused by unmet biological needs such as hunger and thirst; these are called _____ theories.

    (b) Leading theorists, including psychologists Clark Hull and Robert Woodworth, believed that _____ are triggered by the internal mechanism of _____ .

(c) The principle of _____ states that the body monitors and maintains relatively constant levels of internal states, such as body temperature, fluid levels, and energy supplies.

(d) If any of theses internal conditions deviates very far from the optimal level, the body initiates processes to bring the condition back to the normal or optimal range and tries to maintain a(n) _____ , or _____ .

(e) When an internal imbalance is detected by homeostatic mechanisms, a _____ is produced that activates behavior to reduce the _____ and to reestablish the balance of internal conditions.

(f) Today, the _____ concept remains useful in explaining some motivated behaviors that have biological components but may be inadequate for explaining other behaviors, such as those directed at _____ (increasing/ decreasing) tension and physiological arousal.

3. (a) Theories that behavior is motivated by the pull of external goals, such as rewards, are called _____ theories.

(b) These theories of motivation drew heavily from well-established _____ principles such as reinforcement and the work of influential learning theorists such as Pavlov, Watson, Skinner, and Tolman.

(c) Tolman also stressed the importance of cognitive factors in learning and motivation, especially the _____ that a particular behavior will lead to a particular goal.

(d) When combined, the _____ and _____ theories seem to account for a broad range of behaviors, but, even then, the most obvious shortcoming of _____ theory was its inability to explain behaviors that are not primarily motivated by any kind of external factors, such as playing, mastering a new task, or simply trying to satisfy curiosity.

4. (a) While not discounting biological and external motivators, humanistic theories emphasized the importance of _____ and _____ components in human motivation (for example, how we perceive the world, how we think about ourselves and others, and our beliefs about our abilities and skills).

(b) Although the motivation to strive for a positive self-concept and personal potential was thought to be _____ , this viewpoint also recognized the importance of the _____ ; without personal, social, and cultural support, the motivation to strive toward one's highest potential could be jeopardized.

(c) One of the most famous models of motivation, devised by Abraham Maslow, is called the _____ .

(d) Maslow believed that people are motivated to satisfy the needs at each level of the hierarchy before moving to the next level; people progressively move up the hierarchy, striving to eventually reach _____ .

(e) At the lowest levels of Maslow's hierarchy are fundamental _____ , _____ , and _____ needs; at the highest levels the needs become more individualized and _____ .

(f) The full use and exploitation of talents, capacities, potentialities, and so on is Maslow's definition of _____ .

(g) Limitations of Maslow's model are related to the vagueness of some concepts, studies with limited samples and questionable reliability, and the fact that most people do not experience _____ , despite the claim that it is an inborn goal toward which all people supposedly strive.

(h) The humanistic model of motivation is not as influential as it once was, but it did help establish the important role played by _____ and _____ factors in human motivation.

5. (a) Rather than continuing to search for a grand theory of motivation, researchers today study _____ .

(b) Today, motivation researchers assume that the motivation of any behavior is determined by multiple factors that include _____ , _____ , _____ , and social components. Exactly how these different factors interact to energize and motivate behavior is still the subject of much research.

6. Read the following and write the correct term in the space provided.

(a) Amber is a graduate student studying the various forces acting on or within organisms that initiate and direct behavior. Her area of research is _____ .

(b) When Trevor is hungry, he eats. The consumption of food serves to maintain _____ .

(c) Manuel is struggling to make enough money to feed and clothe himself and pay the rent. According to Maslow, it is _____ (likely/unlikely) that Manuel is close to reaching the goal of self-actualization.

(d) Mrs. Lewis gives a gold star to any child in her class who gets 100 percent on the weekly spelling test. This example illustrates _____ theory.

(e) Bruno the bear hibernates every winter. This behavior is an example of an _____ .

(f) When Bernice finished her first 10-mile race in less than 90 minutes, she felt totally exhilarated and overjoyed by having achieved her goal. Her intense feelings suggest that _____ are closely tied to motivation.

Review of Terms and Concepts 1

Use the terms in this list to complete the Matching Test, then to help you answer the True/False items correctly.

motivation	homeostasis
activation	drive
persistence	incentive theories
intensity	humanistic theories
emotion	hierarchy of needs
instinct theories	Abraham Maslow
drive theories	self-actualization

Matching Exercise

Match the appropriate term/name with its definition or description.

1. _____ The view that we are innately motivated to strive for a positive self-concept and the realization of our personal potential.

2. _____ The forces that act on or within an organism to initiate and direct behavior.

3. _____ Basic characteristic commonly associated with motivation that is seen in a person's continued efforts or determination to achieve a particular goal, often in the face of obstacles.

4. _____ American psychologist who developed a hierarchical model of human motivation in which basic needs must first be satisfied before people can strive for self-actualization.

5. _____ Impulse that activates behavior to reduce a need and restore homeostasis.

6. _____ View that some motives are innate and due to genetic programming.

7. _____ Maslow's levels of motivation that progress from basic physical needs to psychological needs to self-fulfillment needs.

True/False Test

Indicate whether each statement is true or false by placing T or F in the blank space next to each item.

1. ____ Incentive theories propose that behavior is motivated by the pull of external goals, such as rewards.

2. ____ *Self-actualization* is defined by Maslow as "the full use and exploitation of talents, capacities, and potentialities."

3. ____ Activation, one of the basic characteristics commonly associated with motivation, is seen in the greater vigor of responding that usually accompanies motivated behavior.

4. ____ Drive theories propose that behavior is motivated by the desire to reduce internal tension caused by unmet biological needs, such as hunger or thirst.

5. ____ Homeostasis refers to the notion that the body monitors and maintains internal states, such as body temperature and energy supplies, at relatively constant levels.

6. ____ Intensity, one of the basic characteristics commonly associated with motivation, is seen in the initiation or production of behavior.

7. ____ Emotion is a subjective and conscious psychological state that includes physiological arousal and an expressive response.

> Check your answers and review any areas of weakness before going on to the next section.

The Motivation to Eat: What Causes Us to Start and Stop Eating (Part 1)

Preview Questions

Consider the following questions as you study this section of the chapter.

- What four broad categories of factors influence the motivation to eat?

- How do oral signals, stomach signals, CCK, insulin, and the hypothalamus seem to influence hunger and eating behavior?

*Read the section "The Motivation to Eat: What Causes Us to Start and Stop Eating" (up to " The Regulation of Weight") and **write** your answers to the following:*

1. (a) What, when, and how much you eat are influenced by diverse _____ , _____ , _____ , and cultural factors.

   (b) Psychologically, eating can be related to _____ , such as depression, anxiety, or stress.

   (c) Interpersonally, eating is often used to foster _____ , as when you have friends over for dinner or take a potential customer to lunch.

2. (a) The oral sensations involved in tasting and chewing food contribute greatly to the subjective pleasure and satisfaction of eating and provide important sensory signals in eating behavior; they _____ (do/do not) seem to be what causes us to start or stop eating. They _____ (do/do not) help maintain or slow down eating behavior once it has begun.

   (b) The stomach has sensory _____ that detect the stretching of the stomach muscles; as the stomach stretches to accommodate food, these signals are relayed to the brain, helping to trigger feelings of _____ .

   (c) A _____ called cholecystokinin, or CCK, also seems to play a role in signaling satiation; as food moves from the stomach to the intestines, CKK is secreted into the bloodstream and conveyed to the brain, where it acts as a(n) _____ .

   (d) CCK seems to magnify the satiety-producing effects of food in the stomach by

_____ (slowing/speeding up) the rate at which the stomach empties and by heightening the sensitivity of _____ in the stomach.

3. (a) The hormone secreted by the pancreas that helps regulate the metabolism of carbohydrates, fats, and starches in the body is _____ . Higher levels lead us to experience _____ (less/more) hunger and eat _____ (less/more) food.

(b) Normally, _____ levels begin to rise shortly after we start eating, but Judith Rodin has shown that we can become _____ to produce increased levels *before* consuming food.

(c) People who are highly responsive to food cues are called _____ , whereas people who are less responsive to food cues are called _____ .

(d) When _____ are exposed to an environmental stimulus that they've learned to associate with food, they produce significantly more insulin in anticipation of eating than do _____ .

4. (a) In the 1940s, a small structure buried deep within the brain, the _____ , was first implicated in the regulation of eating behavior. An experimental animal would eat until it became obese if its _____ was damaged.

(b) A decade later, it was discovered that an animal would stop eating if the _____ was damaged; and if left to its own devices, the animal would starve to death.

(c) On the basis of these initial findings, it became widely believed that this structure and its surrounding regions contained the "_____" and

"_____" centers, but later research cast serious doubts on this simple model.

(d) It seems that whether damage to the VMH produced obesity depended on the _____ of the food.

5. Psychologists have reached a number of conclusions about the factors that regulate eating behavior:

(a) _____ signals from oral sensations, stretch receptors, and chemicals such as CCK and insulin appear to be involved, each providing some form of feedback to the brain.

(b) It appears that the _____ and its surrounding regions detect these varied signals and, in turn, initiate or suppress eating behavior.

(c) Our _____ response to external signals may trigger physiological changes in responsive individuals, such as increased insulin production, that lead to increased feelings of hunger.

(d) What motivates us to eat at a particular moment is governed by a complex system involving the _____ of physiological, behavioral, cognitive, and environmental factors.

The Motivation to Eat: The Regulation of Body Weight (Part 2)

Preview Questions

Consider the following questions as you study this section of the chapter.

- What model has been used to explain the regulation of body weight, and how does it work?
- What role does basal metabolic rate play in weight regulation?
- How does set-point theory account for the regulation of body weight?
- How is obesity defined, and how do obese individuals differ from nonobese individuals in their response to food?

- Why is it difficult to maintain weight loss?
- What are the characteristics of anorexia nervosa and bulimia nervosa?

*Read the section "The Motivation to Eat: The Regulation of Body Weight" and **write** your answers to the following:*

1. (a) Typically, we gain a few pounds during the winter and shed a few pounds during the summer, but for the most part our weight stays pretty much the same; traditionally, this has been explained in terms of the

    _____

    model.

   (b) If the _____ we consume equals the _____ we expend, our weight remains constant.

   (c) The main source of energy is the simple sugar _____ . If there is more of this sugar than your body needs for its requirements, the excess is converted to

    _____ .

   (c) About _____ (one-third/two-thirds) of your body's energy is used for routine physical activities; the remaining _____ (one-third/two-thirds) is used for continuous body functions that are essential for life.

   (d) The rate at which your body uses energy for vital body functions when at rest is referred to as your _____ , abbreviated _____ .

2. (a) The finding that matched pairs of individuals maintained the same weight despite the fact that one ate twice as much as the other demonstrates that a constant body weight depends on the critical balance between _____ and basal metabolic rate.

   (b) A variety of factors influences a person's basal metabolic rate; on average, women have a _____ (higher/lower)

metabolic rate than men, heavy people have a _____ (higher/lower) metabolic rate than slender people, and the BMR _____ (increases/decreases) with age.

   (c) Usually, one can reliably predict a child's approximate adult weight by considering the adult weight of his or her biological parents; this suggests that _____ can also play a role in determining a person's BMR.

3. (a) Set-point weight is the particular weight that the body is naturally set to maintain by increasing or decreasing _____ .

   (b) Set-point theory is based on the well-established principle of _____ ; increases or decreases in body weight are followed by corresponding changes in the body's _____ .

   (c) Research suggests that the _____ and _____ of fat cells are established very early in life (by about the age of two) and are at least partly determined by genetic factors.

   (d) Environmental factors, such as what and how much you eat, also play an important role in the amount of fat stored. At first, overeating produces an increase in the _____ of the fat cells; if overeating continues, the _____ of fat cells will increase.

   (e) Once acquired, fat cells are with you for life; your body essentially becomes programmed to maintain a higher _____ weight. If you reduce your weight, the _____ of fat cells does not decrease; fat cells simply decrease in _____ .

   (f) One criticism of set-point theory is that it merely _____ what occurs rather than _____ the underlying mechanisms. Set-point theory nevertheless remains a useful model in helping us understand many aspects of body weight regulation.

4. (a) People are said to be obese when their weight is _____ percent or more above their optimal weight for their age, sex, and body type. Although a brain tumor or a hereditary disease causes obesity in a small percentage of individuals, for most obese people a specific cause _____ (can/cannot) be identified.

(b) Several studies have demonstrated that many obese individuals tend to be highly responsive to _____ cues associated with food, such as time of day, how appetizing the food is, and easy availability of food.

(c) Individuals who are highly responsive to food-related stimuli tend to react physiologically by producing more _____ .

(d) Obese individuals generally operate with _____ (higher/lower) body levels of insulin.

(e) The more _____ that circulates throughout a person's body, the faster fat deposits build from glucose not used for energy and the more weight the person gains; the more weight gained, the easier it becomes to gain additional weight.

(f) When an obese person restricts food intake, the body vigorously defends against the loss by sharply reducing the rate of _____ ; far fewer calories are now needed to maintain the obese weight because the body's expenditure of energy is sharply reduced, and fat requires _____ (less/more) energy to maintain than to maintain lean body tissue.

(g) Another critical finding is that the _____ rate remains decreased for as long as the person's body weight remains below the obese set-point weight.

(h) To maintain their lower weight, people must modify their eating patterns and follow a regular _____ program.

5. (a) Anorexia nervosa is a potentially life-threatening psychological disorder that involves _____ and has three key symptoms: the individual (1) _____ to maintain a minimally normal body weight, (2) is extremely afraid of gaining _____ or becoming _____ , and (3) has a distorted perception about the size of his or her _____ .

(b) Approximately 90 percent of cases of anorexia nervosa occur in adolescent or young adult _____ (males/females).

(c) It is rare for people with anorexia to completely lose their _____ ; rather, they tend to place themselves on a very restricted _____ , exercise excessively, engage in fasting and self-induced vomiting, and misuse laxatives.

(d) Depression, social withdrawal, insomnia, and, in women, failure to menstruate, along with a distorted _____ , frequently accompany the disorder; despite emaciation, the person with anorexia views a mirror image as overweight.

6. (a) People who have bulimia nervosa _____ (are/are not) within their normal weight range and may even be slightly _____ .

(b) Bulimic people engage in _____ eating and then purge themselves of the excessive food consumption by self-induced vomiting and less often by the use of laxatives or enemas.

(c) People with bulimia usually _____ (do/do not) conceal their eating problems from others. Also, their binges usually include the consumption of _____ , sweet foods that can be swallowed quickly; as much as 50,000 calories may be consumed at one time.

(d) Diverse cultural, psychological, social, and _____ factors seem to be involved in both anorexia nervosa and bulimia nervosa; both female identical twins _____ (are/are not) more likely than nonidentical twins to develop anorexia.

7. Read the following and write the correct term in the space provided.

(a) Farah skipped lunch; later in the afternoon, while walking by the cafeteria, she smells french fries, and her mouth begins to water. At this time it is likely that her blood level of insulin is _____ (high/ low).

(b) Farah is very responsive to food-related environmental stimuli even when she hasn't skipped a meal. Judith Rodin would classify her as a(n) _____ (external/ nonexternal).

(c) While Dr. Fleming was investigating the relationship between the brain and eating behavior, he discovered that rats would stop eating if he destroyed an area of their brain called the _____ hypothalamus, or _____ .

(d) Although he leads a somewhat sedentary lifestyle, 35-year-old Joshua has been about the same weight, give or take a pound or two, since his late teens. His set-point weight is most likely maintained by his _____ , or _____ .

(e) Despite trying many different weight-loss approaches, Roger is still about 30 percent above his "ideal" weight. According to most definitions, Roger would be classified as _____ .

(f) Claire is a 15-year-old of average height who weighs only 85 pounds. She has lost 30 pounds over the past eight or nine months by eating very little and going to aerobics classes twice a day. Claire probably suffers from _____ .

Review of Terms and Concepts 2

Use the terms in this list to complete the Matching Test, then to help you answer the True/False items correctly.

satiation
oral signals
stomach signals
cholecystokinin (CCK)
insulin
externals/nonexternals
ventromedial hypothalamus (VMH)
lateral hypothalamus (LH)

energy balance model
basal metabolic rate (BMR)
set-point weight
set-point theory
obese
anorexia nervosa
bulimia nervosa

Matching Exercise

Match the appropriate term with its definition or description.

1. _____ Hormone that seems to play a role in signaling satiation, or fullness.

2. _____ The sensations involved in tasting and chewing food that contribute greatly to the subjective pleasure and satisfaction of eating.

3. _____ The rate at which the body uses energy for vital body functions when at rest.

4. _____ Judith Rodin's terms for people who are highly responsive to environmental food-related stimuli and for those who are less responsive to food cues.

5. _____ Area of the hypothalamus that, when damaged, causes an experimental animal to eat until it becomes obese.

6. _____ The particular weight that is set and maintained by increases or decreases in basal metabolic rate.

7. _____ Hormone secreted by the pancreas that helps regulate the metabolism of carbohydrates, fats, and starches in the body.

8. _____ Weighing 20 percent or more above one's optimal body weight.

True/False Test

Indicate whether each statement is true or false by placing T or F in the blank space next to each item.

1. ___ The energy balance model suggests that if the food (energy) we consume equals the energy we expend, our weight remains constant.

2. ___ Bulimia nervosa is an eating disorder characterized by the individual's refusal to maintain a minimally normal body weight, is extremely afraid of gaining weight or becoming fat, and a distorted perception of his or her body size.

3. ___ If the lateral hypothalamus (LH) is damaged, an experimental animal will stop eating.

4. ___ Satiation is the feeling of fullness and diminished desire to eat.

5. ___ The stomach has sensory receptors that detect the stretching of the stomach muscles as it accommodates food; these stomach signals are relayed to the brain, helping to trigger feelings of satiation.

6. ___ Anorexia nervosa is an eating disorder in which a person engages in binge eating and then purges the excessive food consumption by self-induced vomiting or, less often, by taking laxatives or enemas.

7. ___ Set-point theory is based on the well-established principle of homeostasis; increases or decreases in body weight are followed by corresponding changes in the body's basal metabolic rate.

Check your answers and review any areas of weakness before going on to the next section.

Arousal Motives: Curiosity and Sensation Seeking

Preview Questions

Consider the following questions as you study this section of the chapter.

- How does arousal theory account for people's motivation to maintain an optimal level of arousal?
- What factors influence curiosity and exploratory behavior?
- How does arousal theory help explain the pacing of curious behavior?
- What is sensation seeking?

*Read the section "Arousal Motives: Curiosity and Sensation Seeking" and **write** your answers to the following:*

1. (a) Motivation researchers have long noted that people can be highly motivated to seek out experiences that _____ tension rather than _____ tension.

   (b) Behaviors such as _____ , _____ , and seeking stimulation cannot be adequately explained by drive theories of motivation. _____ theories also fall short in explaining such behavior.

2. (a) Arousal theory is based on the observation that people find both very high and very low levels of arousal quite _____ .

   (b) When arousal is too _____ , we experience boredom and try to _____ arousal by seeking out stimulating experiences; when arousal is too _____ , we seek to _____ arousal in a less stimulating environment.

   (c) According to arousal theory, people are motivated to maintain a(n) _____ level of arousal, one that is neither too high nor too low; this level can vary from person to person, from time to time, and from one situation to another.

3. (a) One purpose of curiosity and exploratory behavior is to become familiar with and to understand our world; in pursuit of this goal, we "_____" the rate at which we gradually expose ourselves to increasing complexity and novelty.

   (b) As we become familiar with a stimulus, we move toward stimuli that are slightly more complex, and this _____ produces the optimal level of physical and cognitive arousal that helps motivate curiosity.

   (c) If a stimulus is more complex than we can process at the _____ that we can tolerate, uncomfortable levels of physical or cognitive arousal can occur; if this happens, the curiosity drive becomes _____ , and we withdraw from the stimulus and may even experience intense anxiety and fear.

4. (a) What is considered novel or complex is relative to each individual's _____ ; as an individual becomes more familiar with his or her environment through exploratory behavior, the complexity or novelty of the objects or situations that inspire that person's curiosity also progressively _____ .

(b) Some children respond positively to novel stimuli and easily adjust to changes in their environment, whereas other children do not. These _____ differences seem to be based on a genetic predisposition and are often remarkably consistent throughout a person's life.

5. (a) People who are highly motivated to experience the high levels of arousal associated with varied and novel activities that often involve some degree of physical or social risk are called _____ .

(b) _____ are not attracted to danger per se but view themselves as independent, open-minded, and unconventional people who like feeling uninhibited, especially in relaxed social situations; they are _____ (flexible/ inflexible) in their style of thinking, are _____ (tolerant/intolerant) of uncertainty, and enjoy the discovery of new knowledge.

Competence and Achievement Motivation

Preview Questions

Consider the following questions as you study this section of the chapter.

- How do competence motivation and achievement motivation differ?
- How is each type of motivation measured?
- What is self-efficacy?

*Read the section "Competence and Achievement Motivation" and **write** your answers to the following:*

1. (a) When you strive to use your cognitive, social, and behavioral skills to be capable and exercise control in a situation, you are displaying _____ motivation.

(b) If you have a drive to excel, succeed, or outperform others at some task, you are exhibiting _____ motivation.

(c) Henry Murray first defined the _____ as the tendency to overcome obstacles, exercise power, and strive to do something difficult as well as as quickly as possible.

(d) Achievement motivation has been most commonly measured by a test called the _____ , abbreviated as _____ .

(e) In this test, the person being tested is asked to make up a story about each of a series of ambiguous pictures; the story is then coded in terms of its _____ themes and imagery. The TAT _____ (does/does not) generally correlate with various measures of success.

2. When it is broadly defined as the desire for excellence, achievement motivation is found in many, if not all, cultures; in _____ cultures the need to achieve emphasizes personal, individual success rather than the success of the group; in _____ cultures, achievement motivation tends to be more socially, family, or group oriented.

3. (a) The degree to which we are convinced of our ability to effectively meet the demands of a situation is our sense of _____ .

(b) At virtually any age, we tend to

_____ (seek out/avoid) challenging situations or tasks that we believe exceed our capabilities; increasing motivation, particularly achievement motivation, often involves convincing ourselves that we can rise to the challenge.

4. Read the following and write the correct term in the space provided.

(a) Young Alec practices at the golf range for one or two hours most days because he plans to become a professional golfer. His goal and behavior suggest that Alec has a high level of _____ motivation.

(b) Jasmine was very excited by her first trip to the zoo. She was particularly curious and a little nervous about what she would find in the reptile house. As Jasmine and her parents entered the reptile facility, she became more and more anxious, and when she saw the lizards and snakes, she burst into tears. It appears that the situation was moving faster than Jasmine's curiosity and exploratory _____ .

(c) Roland loves the quiet routine of his life. He goes to work at the same time every day, meets his friends for bridge every Tuesday and Thursday evening, and works out at the gym on Monday, Wednesday, and Friday. Every year, he vacations at the same hotel in Aruba. Roland is likely to score very

_____ (high/low) on Marvin Zuckerman's Sensation Seeking Scale.

(d) Yen Shih and her fellow students believe that it is unacceptable to express pride for personal achievements, but it is acceptable to feel pride in achievements that benefit others. Yen Shih most likely lives in a

_____ culture.

(e) Allison wants to prove to herself that she is capable of mastering basic mathematical concepts, so she enrolls in an algebra course and an introductory statistics course. Allison is demonstrating _____ motivation.

Graphic Organizer 1

Identify the theory associated with each of the following statements:

Statement	Theory
1. I believe that behavior is motivated by the desire to reduce internal tension caused by unmet biological needs that push us to behave in certain ways.	
2. I emphasize the importance of psychological and cognitive components in human motivation and believe that we are innately driven to strive for a positive self-concept and the realization of our personal potential.	
3. I take my lead from Charles Darwin, and although my ideas may not be popular today, I strongly believe that we are motivated to engage in certain behaviors because of genetic programming.	
4. We do what we do because of the pull of external goals, such as rewards. I think that learning theorists have it right when they say reinforcement is a key factor in motivation.	
5. How do we explain curiosity and exploratory behavior? I believe that we are motivated to maintain an optimal level of arousal. When arousal is too low, we try to increase it by seeking out stimulating experiences; when it is too high, we seek to reduce arousal in a less stimulating environment.	

Review of Terms and Concepts 3

Use the terms in this list to complete the Matching Test, then to help you answer the True/False items correctly.

arousal theory
sensation seeking
competence motivation
achievement motivation
Thematic Apperception
    Test (TAT)

individualistic cultures
collectivistic cultures
self-efficacy

Matching Exercise

Match the appropriate term with its definition or description:

1. _____ Cultures, such as those that characterize North American and European countries, in which the need to achieve emphasizes personal, individual success rather than the success of the group.

2. _____ The degree to which a person is subjectively convinced of his or her ability to effectively meet the demands of a situation.

3. _____ The view that people are motivated to maintain an optimal level of arousal, which is neither too high nor too low.

4. _____ Motivated behavior directed toward demonstrating ability and exercising control in a situation.

5. _____ Cultures, such as those of many Asian countries, in which achievement motivation is more socially oriented than individually oriented.

6. _____ Being motivated to experience high levels of arousal associated with varied and novel activities.

7. _____ Motivated behavior directed toward excelling, succeeding, or outperforming others at some task.

8. _____ Test in which a person is asked to make up a story about each of a series of ambiguous pictures; the story is coded in terms of its achievement themes and imagery.

> Check your answers and review any areas of weakness before going on to the next section.

Emotion

Preview Questions

Consider the following questions as you study this section of the chapter.

- What functions do emotions serve in human behavior and relationships?
- What are the three components of emotion, and what are basic emotions?
- How do culture and individual differences influence emotional experience?
- What physical changes are associated with different emotions?
- What evidence supports the idea that the facial expressions associated with the basic emotions are innate?
- How are facial expressions affected by cultural display rules?

*Read the section "Emotion" and **write** your answers to the following:*

1. (a) We are motivated to seek out experiences that produce _____ emotions and to avoid experiences that produce _____ emotions.

   (b) _____ are intense but short-lived and are more likely to have a specific cause, to be directed toward some particular object, and to motivate a person to take some sort of action; in contrast, a _____ involves a milder emotional state that is more general and pervasive, such as gloominess or contentment, that lasts for a few hours or days.

   (c) Emotion can be formally defined as a psychological state involving three distinct components: _____ experience, _____ arousal, and a _____ or expressive response.

2. (a) Considerable _____ (agreement/disagreement) exists among psychologists regarding the definition and classification of emotions.

   (b) Some psychologists assert that there are a limited number of universal _____ emotions that are biologically determined products of evolution; these include anger, happiness, sadness, fear, disgust, surprise, anxiety, shame, and interest.

   (c) Some emotion theorists suggest that more complex emotions are produced by various combinations of _____ emotions; combining anger and disgust yields _____ , sadness plus surprise equals _____ , and _____ is the result of combining joy and acceptance.

   (d) Other theorists reject the idea of basic emotions and instead believe that a large number of _____ emotions exist.

   (e) People often experience a _____ of emotions rather than a "pure" form of any single given emotion. In more complex situations, people may experience _____ emotions, in which different emotions are experienced simultaneously or in rapid succession.

   (f) When emotions are compared, they tend to be arranged along two dimensions, how _____ or _____ the emotion is and how much arousal is present; joy and rage involve _____ (high/low) levels of arousal or intensity, whereas contentment and resentment involve relatively _____ (high/low) levels of arousal.

3. (a) People from different cultures experience emotions in _____ (different ways/much the same way) as Americans. Furthermore, there is general _____ (agreement/disagreement) among cultures regarding the subjective experience of different basic emotions such as joy, anger, fear, disgust, and sadness.

(b) Researchers have also found some key _____ (similarities/differences) in cultural descriptions of emotion; for example, the Japanese perceive an additional dimension to Americans' two basic dimensions of pleasantness and arousal, called interpersonal engagement.

(c) Some people are "more emotional" than others; that is, people vary greatly in the _____ of the emotions they experience.

(d) People who experience very intense positive emotions _____ (do/do not) tend to experience very intense negative emotions.

4. (a) When you experience an intense emotion such as anger or extreme fear, the _____ , or _____ , component of emotions is especially evident

(b) Physiological arousal involves the activation of the sympathetic division of the _____ nervous system, which gears you up for action, affecting heart rate, blood pressure, respiration, perspiration, and other bodily activities.

(c) In contrast to emotions such as anger or fear, emotions such as contentment are characterized by a _____ of bodily arousal.

(d) Research has shown that there _____ (are/are not) distinct differences in the pattern of physiological responses for different emotions.

(e) Surveys of many different cultures have suggested that distinct patterns of _____ changes may well be universal across cultures, at least for basic emotions such as joy, fear, anger, sadness, and disgust, but perhaps not for every emotion.

(f) The fact that changes in bodily functions accompany many emotions is the basis for the use of the _____ , commonly called a lie detector.

5. (a) In addition to their subjective and physiological components, emotions usually involve a(n) _____ or _____ component; we also show our emotions through our _____ , such as our gestures, changes in posture, and, most important, our facial expressions.

(b) Paul Ekman and his colleagues have coded different facial expressions by carefully analyzing which facial _____ are involved in producing each expression. They have been able to precisely classify the facial expressions that characterize happiness, disgust, surprise, sadness, anger, and fear.

(c) Facial expressions for basic emotions seem to be _____ , or _____ , rather than learned.

(d) Psychologist Carroll Izzard found that facial expressions of pain, interest, and disgust are present at birth; the social smile emerges by _____ or _____ weeks of age; sadness and anger are evident by _____ months; and fear is displayed by _____ or _____ months of age.

6. (a) Studies have shown that people from many different cultures accurately recognize the emotions expressed in photographs of facial expressions, even when the facial expressions display _____ of emotion.

(b) The social context, as well as culture, can influence the expression of emotion; cultural differences in the management of facial expressions are called

_____ ; these rules can vary greatly from culture to culture.

Graphic Organizer 2

Identify the emotion (relaxation, alarm, annoyance, boredom, astonishment) associated with each of the following descriptions and indicate where it should go on the matrix on the right.

1. Natasha receives an A+ in her third-year history course and can hardly believe it.

   _____

2. In the middle of the night, Harry, who lives alone, is startled out of a deep sleep by strange noises coming from the basement.

   _____

3. During his three o'clock calculus class Nathan finds the topic totally uninteresting and starts losing his concentration. _____

4. On Saturday Dawn sleeps in and spends most of the morning propped up on comfortable pillows reading a romantic novel.

   _____

5. Five minutes after the meter has expired Dhillon arrives at his car only to find he has been given a $20 ticket. _____

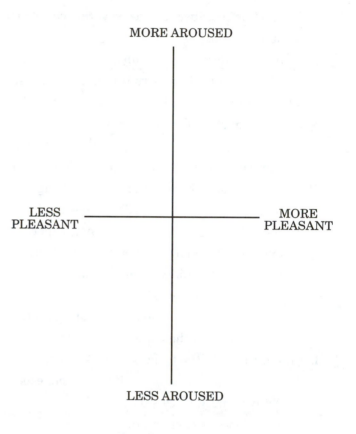

Explaining Emotions: Key Theories

Preview Questions

Consider the following questions as you study this section of the chapter.

- What are the James-Lange and Cannon-Bard theories of emotion, and how did Cannon refute the James-Lange theory?
- What are the main features of the facial feedback hypothesis?
- How does the two-factor theory account for emotions, and what aspects of the theory have been supported by research?
- What is the cognitive-mediational theory of emotion?

*Read the section "Explaining Emotions: Key Theories" and **write** your answers to the following:*

1. (a) Theories of emotion tend to differ in terms of which component of emotion—

   _____ responses, expressive

   _____ , or _____

   experience—receives the most emphasis.

   (b) The James-Lange theory proposes that emotions follow this sequence: we

   _____ a stimulus, physiological and behavioral changes occur, and we

   _____ these reactions as a particular emotion.

2. Walter Cannon challenged the James-Lange theory, criticizing it on a number of grounds:

    (a) Bodily reactions are similar for many emotions, yet our _____ experience of various emotions is very different.

    (b) Our emotional reaction to a stimulus is often faster than our _____ reaction, because it takes several seconds for activation of the _____ to take effect, but the subjective experience of emotion is often virtually instantaneous.

    (c) When physiological changes are artificially induced, as by drugs, people _____ (always/do not necessarily) report feeling a related emotion.

    (d) People cut off from feeling bodily changes (as a result of spinal cord injuries, for example) _____ (do/do not) experience true emotions; although physiological arousal can amplify emotional feelings, the perception of physical arousal _____ (does/does not) seem to be essential to the experience of emotion.

3. (a) According to the facial feedback hypothesis, _____ a specific emotion, especially facially, causes us to _____ experience that emotion.

    (b) Our bodily responses, including feedback from our muscles, can affect our _____ experience. _____ behavior helps to activate and regulate emotional experience, intensifying or lessening emotion.

4. (a) The Cannon-Bard theory suggests that when an emotion-arousing stimulus is perceived, information is relayed _____ to the sympathetic nervous system and to the cortex in the brain.

    (b) When the sympathetic nervous system is activated, it causes the _____ response; the activation of the cortex causes the _____ experience of emotion. These events occur _____, with neither causing the other.

5. (a) According to Schachter and Singer's two-factor theory (also called the cognitive arousal theory), emotion is a result of the _____ of physiological arousal and the cognitive label we attach to explain the stirred-up state; if one of these _____ is absent, emotion will not be experienced.

    (b) Research has suggested that there is little evidence for the two-factor theory's claim that arousal is a(n)_____ (necessary/unnecessary) condition for an emotional state, or the idea that emotional states can result from _____ unexplained arousal, but some aspects of the theory have been supported.

6. (a) Richard Lazarus's cognitive-mediational theory emphasizes that the most important aspect of emotional experience is our _____ interpretation, or appraisal, of the emotion-causing stimulus or event.

    (b) For Lazarus, _____ (only some/all) emotions are the result of _____ appraisals of the personal meaning of events and experiences.

    (c) Although it's clear that _____ appraisals can make a great deal of difference in emotional responses and experiences, emotion researchers differ in how much they emphasize the role of _____ .

    (d) Which process in emotion is most important is the subject of continuous debate, but an interactive approach, which conceptualizes emotion as a dynamic system, might acknowledge that _____ appraisals, _____ arousal, and _____ expression all contribute to subjective emotional experience.

7. Read the following and write the correct term in the space provided.

   (a) Since the end of the semester, Ellen had been feeling very contented and relaxed. When she received her transcript in the mail and discovered that she had received an A+ in statistics, she was overjoyed. Ellen's two different states (contentment and joy) illustrate the difference between _____ and _____ .

   (b) Walking to the parking lot late at night, Camellia suddenly hears footsteps behind her. Her heartbeat and blood pressure increase, her muscles tense, her mouth goes dry, and she begins to perspire. These physiological reactions were activated by her _____ nervous system.

   (c) Mr. Hashimoto is very careful to hide his true feelings and control his facial expressions when in the presence of his company's chief executive officers. This example illustrates the _____ of his culture.

   (d) Whenever she feels a bit gloomy, Danica sings the song "Pretend you're happy when you're blue"; if she follows the advice of the song, she actually experiences an elevation in her mood. This example is consistent with the _____ of emotion.

   (e) When Harbinder first rode on the High Peak ski lift, he looked down at the steep slopes beneath him and became aware of his high level of physiological arousal. Suddenly, he felt fearful. Harbinder's experience is best explained by the _____ theory of emotion.

Review of Terms, Concepts, and Names 4

Use the terms in this list to complete the Matching Test, then to help you answer the True/False items correctly.

emotion
mood
basic emotions
mixed emotions
interpersonal
   engagement
sympathetic nervous
   system
polygraph (lie detector)
nonverbal behavior
display rules
William James
James-Lange theory of
   emotion

Walter B. Cannon
Cannon-Bard theory of
   emotion
facial feedback
   hypothesis
two-factor theory of
   emotion
Richard Lazarus
cognitive-mediational
   theory of emotion
interactive approach to
   emotion

Matching Exercise

Match the appropriate term/name with its definition or description:

1. _____ View that expressing a specific emotion, especially facially, causes the subjective experience of that emotion.

2. _____ American psychologist who proposed the cognitive-mediational theory of emotion.

3. _____ Distinct psychological state that involves subjective experience, physical arousal, and a behavioral or expressive response.

4. _____ Schachter and Singer's theory that emotion is a result of the interaction of physiological arousal and the cognitive label that we apply to explain the arousal.

5. _____ Universal emotions that are biologically determined products of evolution; they include anger, happiness, sadness, fear, disgust, surprise, anxiety, shame, and interest.

6. _____ A third dimension, added by the Japanese to the two basic dimensions of emotion (pleasantness and arousal), that describes the degree to which each emotion involves relationships with others.

7. _____ Emotional expressions such as gestures, changes in posture, and facial expressions that don't rely on language or spoken communication.

8. _____ Approach to emotion that emphasizes the notion that cognitive appraisals, physiological arousal, and behavioral expression all contribute to subjective emotional expression.

9. _____ Social and cultural rules that regulate the expression of emotions, particularly facial expressions.

True/False Test

Indicate whether each item is true or false by placing T or F in the space next to each item.

1. ____ Walter B. Cannon was an American psychologist who developed an influential theory of emotion called the two-factor theory of emotion.

2. ____ The cognitive-mediational theory of emotion is Lazarus's theory that emotions result from the cognitive appraisal of the effect of a situation on personal well-being.

3. ____ The fact that changes in bodily functions accompany many emotions is the basis for the use of the polygraph, commonly called a lie detector.

4. ____ The James-Lange theory suggests that emotions arise from the perception and interpretation of bodily changes.

5. ____ Arousal of the sympathetic nervous system gears you up for action, affecting many bodily activities such as heartbeat, blood pressure, respiration, perspiration, and blood-sugar levels.

6. ____ The Cannon-Bard theory proposes that emotions arise from simultaneous activation of the nervous system, which causes arousal, and the cortex, which causes the subjective experience of that emotion.

7. ____ In more complex situations we may experience mixed emotions; these very different emotions are experienced simultaneously or in rapid succession.

8. ____ William James was an American psychologist who developed an influential theory of emotion called the facial feedback hypothesis.

9. ____ A mood is intense but rather short lived, is likely to have a specific cause, tends to be directed toward some particular object, and will motivate a person to take some sort of action.

Check your answers and review any areas of weakness before going on to the next section.

Something to Think About

1. Many Americans are obsessed with achieving, or at least getting closer to, the socially desirable goal of thinness. Approximately one-third of all American women and one-fifth of all American males are trying to lose weight, and the weight-loss industry is a $30 billion a year enterprise. Based on what you have read in your text, what advice would you give to a friend who is trying to lose weight?

2. Most people have heard about the polygraph, or lie detector, as it is commonly called. Many news articles have been written about the use of a polygraph to screen employees for drug use or theft. Also, scientists continue to debate its use in police interrogations and the admissibility of evidence based on polygraph results in courts of law. In addition, people who claim to have been abducted by aliens have taken polygraph tests to prove that they are not lying. What would you say to someone who is confused by all these reports?

Check your answers and review any areas of weakness before doing the progress tests.

Progress Test 1

Review the complete chapter (including Concept Reviews and the boxed inserts), review all your study notes, and then test yourself on the following progress test. Check your answers. If you make a mistake, review your notes, review the relevant section of the study guide, and, if necessary, go back and read the appropriate part of your textbook.

1. It is an innate characteristic of the European cuckoo to lay her eggs in other birds' nests. This behavior is an example of
   (a) an instinct.
   (b) a drive.
   (c) incentive motivation.
   (d) homeostasis.

2. Mrs. Kim talks proudly about her daughter Koko, who studies hard and earns good grades in college, and about how Koko intends to go to medical school and become a brain surgeon. Mrs. Kim is referring to Koko's

(a) motivation.
(b) extrinsic desires.
(c) instincts.
(d) drive.

3. About ten or fifteen minutes into his weightlifting routine Scott usually begins to perspire heavily. His body's tendency to maintain a steady temperature through the cooling action of sweating is a function of

(a) instinct.
(b) incentive motivation.
(c) homeostasis.
(d) self-actualization.

4. Tim buys a lottery ticket every Friday with the expectation that he is going to win some money. His behavior illustrates

(a) instinct.
(b) incentive motivation.
(c) drive.
(d) self-actualization.

5. Nicole feels that she has all the material possessions she needs in life and is now determined to devote all her energy to her art. According to Maslow's hierarchy of needs, Nicole is probably striving

(a) to fulfill her fundamental biological need to paint.
(b) to fulfill her basic safety needs.
(c) toward the realization of her personal potential.
(d) toward the realization of her social needs.

6. Dr. Dorfman destroys the lateral hypothalamus of a laboratory rat. This procedure is likely to

(a) permanently lower the rat's set point.
(b) decrease the rat's rate of metabolism.
(c) cause the rat to eat until it becomes obese.
(d) cause the rat to stop eating.

7. After her fourth piece of pizza, Mary feels quite full. Her satiation is due, at least in part, to increased levels of the hormone

(a) insulin.
(b) testosterone.
(c) cholecystokinin (CCK).
(d) estrogen.

8. Whenever he sees Amanda, Richard's heart beats faster and he gets a trembling feeling inside. Richard now thinks that he must be in love with Amanda. Which theory of emotion is represented in this example?

(a) James-Lange theory
(b) Cannon-Bard theory
(c) two-factor theory
(d) cognitive-mediational theory

9. Mr. Jackson is about thirty-five pounds overweight. Compared to people who are not overweight, Mr. Jackson is likely to have

(a) higher metabolism.
(b) lower metabolism.
(c) the same metabolism.
(d) all of the above; there is no relationship between weight and metabolism.

10. Erin has been diagnosed with bulimia nervosa. The main characteristic of her eating disorder is

(a) being 15 to 20 percent below the ideal body weight.
(b) a distorted self-perception about body shape and body weight.
(c) binge eating and purging by self-induced vomiting and occasionally by using laxatives or enemas.
(d) an obsession with food and a denial of being hungry.

11. Jill is independent, open-minded, and unconventional; loves the outdoors; and includes among her many interests skydiving, downhill skiing, white water kayaking, and hang-gliding. Jill is likely to be classified as

(a) a sensation seeker.
(b) shy and timid.
(c) an external.
(d) a nonexternal.

12. As part of his overall vocational assessment Bertram took the Thematic Apperception Test (TAT). His score on this test is most likely to reveal his level of

(a) competence motivation.
(b) achievement motivation.
(c) self-efficacy.
(d) emotionality.

13. When Willard's relationship ended, he felt pretty confused and experienced a combination of relief, sadness, nostalgia, anger, and jealousy. Willard's experience illustrates
    (a) basic emotions.
    (b) mixed emotions.
    (c) mood fluctuations.
    (d) interpersonal engagement.

14. Some people claim that subliminal self-help tapes will quickly and easily produce changes in our motivation, learning ability, attitudes, and other behaviors. According to Science Versus Pseudoscience 8.1,
    (a) all these claims have been supported by empirical evidence.
    (b) subliminal self-help tapes are effective but only for highly suggestible people.
    (c) because university and college bookstores sell subliminal self-help tapes, they probably work for improving study habits and passing exams.
    (d) there is no scientific support for the claims made by subliminal self-help tapes.

15. One of the most pervasive gender stereotypes is that women are more emotional than are men. Culture and Human Behavior 8.3 concludes that
    (a) women are more emotionally expressive compared to men.
    (b) males and females do not differ in their experience of emotion.
    (c) men mask their emotions more so than do women.
    (d) all of the above are true.

Progress Test 2

After you have checked your understanding of the material in Progress Test 1 and reviewed the chapter with special focus on any areas of weakness, you are ready to assess your knowledge of Progress Test 2. Check your answers. If you make a mistake, review your notes, the relevant section of the study guide, and, if necessary, the appropriate part of your textbook.

1. Mr. Lotz, like most men in his community, would be embarrassed to be caught crying in public. This examples illustrates
   (a) a cultural display rule.
   (b) machismo.
   (c) nonverbal behavior.
   (d) an interpersonal engagement rule.

2. Dr. Spearpoint believes that emotions arise from the perception and interpretation of bodily changes. His views are most consistent with the
   (a) James-Lange theory
   (b) Cannon-Bard theory
   (c) facial feedback hypothesis
   (d) two-factor theory

3. If he's feeling sad or unhappy, Milton "puts on a happy face." When he does this, his mood often improves. This result is best predicted by the
   (a) cognitive-mediational theory.
   (b) two-factor theory.
   (c) Cannon-Bard theory.
   (d) facial feedback hypothesis.

4. Both Javid and Jamal received a 10 percent pay raise to their base salary of $15 an hour. Javid is very happy, but Jamal is disappointed. Their different emotional reactions to the same pay raise reflect their different interpretations of the event. This example illustrates the _____ theory of emotion.
   (a) James-Lange
   (b) Cannon-Bard
   (c) two-factor
   (d) cognitive-mediational

5. After reviewing the major theories of motivation, Zomobia decided that a key problem with _____ theories was that they merely described and labeled behaviors rather than actually explaining them.
   (a) drive
   (b) instinct
   (c) incentive
   (d) humanistic

6. Jasbir has a term paper to write so she heads for the library to do the necessary research. Despite an initial failure to locate material related to her topic, Jasbir continues her catalogue search for many hours until she comes up with sufficient relevant information. She writes, rewrites, and edits her paper until she feels it is almost perfect. Jasbir is demonstrating which basic characteristic commonly associated with motivation?
   (a) activation
   (b) persistence
   (c) intensity
   (d) all of the above

7. Dr. Zascow thinks that emotion is best conceptualized as a dynamic system in which cognitive appraisals, physiological arousal, and behavioral expression all contribute to subjective emotional experience. Dr. Zascow's view is most consistent with the
   (a) integrative approach to emotion.
   (b) cognitive-mediational theory of emotion.
   (c) two-factor theory of emotion.
   (d) James-Lange theory of emotion.

8. While writing a term paper for her motivation course, Cara notes that the majority of people do not experience or achieve self-actualization, despite the claim that it is a goal common to all people. She decides that this is an important limitation of
   (a) instinct theories.
   (b) drive theories.
   (c) incentive theories.
   (d) humanistic theories.

9. Although Raymond has just eaten a very big meal, smelling his neighbor's barbecue makes him hungry again. Psychologists would most likely consider Raymond to be
   (a) an external.
   (b) an internal.
   (c) a nonexternal.
   (d) suffering from bulimia nervosa.

10. About six months ago, fifteen-year-old Kirsten went on a drastic weight-loss diet that caused her to drop from 115 to 85 pounds. Although she is dangerously underweight and undernourished, she continues to think she looks fat. Kirsten probably suffers from
   (a) obesity.
   (b) a very high metabolic rate.
   (c) bulimia nervosa.
   (d) anorexia nervosa.

11. Shortly after eating lunch, Marty is daydreaming in class. Imagining the taste and smell of his favorite pizza, he starts to feel hungry. In this instance, his feelings of hunger are probably caused by
   (a) increased levels of insulin.
   (b) decreased levels of insulin.
   (c) increased levels of cholecystokinin (CCK).
   (d) satiation.

12. Irfan's weight increased seven pounds above his normal set-point body weight. According to set-point theory, Irfan is likely to experience a(n) _____ in hunger and a(n) _____ in his metabolic rate.
   (a) increase; increase
   (b) decrease; decrease
   (c) increase; decrease
   (d) decrease; increase

13. Merv is in his early twenties. If he is typical of people his age, his basic metabolic rate (BMR) has _____ since he was a child.
   (a) decreased
   (b) increased
   (c) remained relatively the same
   (d) done any of the above (there is no relationship between age and BMR)

14. The Application contains a number of suggestions for increasing your level of happiness. Which of the following is *not* one of those suggestions?
   (a) Make happiness a goal.
   (b) Strengthen your closest relationships and be more social and outgoing.
   (c) Keep busy doing things that you enjoy and engage in activities that you find personally meaningful.
   (d) Stop worrying and develop positive, optimistic thinking patterns.
   (e) All of the above are suggestions for increasing happiness.

15. When Alfie applied for a job with a government security agency, he was told that he would have to take a polygraph test as part of his evaluation. According to In Focus 8.4, which of the following is true?
   (a) The polygraph test will reliably determine if he is lying.
   (b) The polygraph can easily determine if he is a regular drug user.
   (c) It is possible that he could be judged guilty of lying even when he is telling the truth.
   (d) Both his physiological arousal and psychological state will be accurately measured by the polygraph.

Progress Test 3

After you have checked your understanding of the material in Progress Tests 1 and 2, and have done a complete chapter review with special focus on any areas of weakness, you are ready to further assess your knowledge on Progress Test 3. Check your answers. If you make a mistake, review your notes, the appropriate parts of the study guide, and if necessary, the relevant sections of your textbook.

1. Pat experiences very intense positive emotions and is generally considered to be a very emotionally expressive person. It is likely that Pat
   (a) also tends to experience very intense negative emotions.
   (b) is very unpopular as compared with people who are emotionally inhibited.
   (c) almost never experiences negative emotions.
   (d) is very low in both achievement and competence motivation.

2. Five-year-old Nemanja was excited and very curious about the various animals he saw when he was taken to the zoo for the first time. His exploratory behavior was quickly inhibited, however, when he was suddenly startled and frightened by a loud roar from the lion's enclosure. His initial curiosity rapidly gave way to extreme fear and withdrawal. Nemanja's behavior is best explained by _____ theory.
   (a) drive
   (b) incentive
   (c) arousal
   (d) instinct

3. The desire to drink when thirsty is to _____ theory as the desire to avoid boredom is to _____ theory.
   (a) humanistic; drive
   (b) arousal; incentive
   (c) drive; arousal
   (d) self-actualization; homeostasis

4. During a discussion of motivational theories, Harland pointed out that people often engage in behaviors that serve to increase tension and physiological arousal. Harland's observation most strongly argues against which theory of motivation?
   (a) instinct theory
   (b) drive theory
   (c) arousal theory
   (d) humanistic theory

5. Cyril has a strong need for privacy and independence; he has an accurate perception of himself, other people, and external reality; and he appreciates the simple pleasures in life. According to Maslow, Cyril is probably
   (a) a sensation-seeker.
   (b) an external.
   (c) a nonexternal.
   (d) self-actualized.

6. Danny believes that if the food we eat equals the energy we expend, our weight will tend to remain fairly constant. Danny's statement best reflects the
   (a) arousal theory of motivation.
   (b) homeostatic theory of weight regulation.
   (c) incentive theory of motivation.
   (d) energy balance model of weight regulation.

7. Thirty-year-old Ali is very similar to his parents in physical appearance. Like both his mother and father, Ali is of short stature, heavy set, broad shouldered, and overweight. The fact that Ali's adult weight resembles that of his parents illustrates the influence of _____ on weight regulation and metabolism.
   (a) genetic factors
   (b) age
   (c) gender
   (d) environmental factors

8. Wilda is a diplomat and was trained in the customs, language, and religions of Slakia, where she is now posted. It is very unlikely that Wilda needed special training to correctly interpret her hosts' expressions of emotion as revealed by their
   (a) songs.
   (b) dancing.
   (c) facial expressions.
   (d) eating etiquette.

9. Tasleem is about 30 percent heavier than her optimal body weight. If she is like most obese people, she probably differs from nonobese people in the daily regulation of her eating behavior by
   (a) being highly responsive to external cues associated with food.
   (b) physiologically reacting to food-related stimuli with greater insulin production.
   (c) having a generally higher body level of insulin.
   (d) all of the above.

10. When Moira was preparing for her first solo landing in a single-engine plane, she experienced a number of physiological reactions such as a racing heart, sweaty palms, and tension in her muscles. These physiological reactions were activated by her _____ nervous system.
    (a) central
    (b) sympathetic
    (c) skeletal
    (d) parasympathetic

11. When Ulricke lost twelve pounds on a diet, her weight fell below her set-point weight. She is likely to experience a(n) _____ in hunger and a(n) _____ in her basal metabolic rate.
    (a) increase; increase   (c) increase; decrease
    (b) decrease; decrease   (d) decrease; increase

12. After working in the garden all afternoon on a hot day, Mrs. Ulman is very thirsty and drinks a big glass of iced tea. Her motivation to drink to reduce her feeling of thirst can best be explained by
    (a) instinct theory.
    (b) drive theory.
    (c) incentive motivation.
    (d) humanistic theory.

13. Dr. Gilbert destroyed the ventromedial hypothalamus of a laboratory rat. This procedure is most likely to
    (a) cause the animal to eat until it becomes obese.
    (b) cause the animal to stop eating.
    (c) lower the animal's set point for body weight.
    (d) raise the animal's set point for body weight.

14. According to In Focus 8.2, which of the following is true?
    (a) Level of self-efficacy is a function of innate or inborn mechanisms.
    (b) Self-efficacy is measured by the Thematic Apperception Test (TAT).
    (c) Claims that positive self-talk and positive mental imagery can help improve self-efficacy are pseudoscientific nonsense.
    (d) There are a number of useful techniques that can improve self-efficacy.

15. According to the Application, which two components underlie happiness?
    (a) having lots of money and having lots of material possessions
    (b) hardship caused by poverty and poor health
    (c) life satisfaction and the experience of positive emotions
    (d) being too thin and being too rich

Answers

Introduction: Motivation and Emotion
1. (a) initiate; direct
   (b) activation; persistence; intensity
2. (a) emotions
   (b) emotion

The Study of Motivation: From Then to Now
1. (a) instinct
   (b) instincts
   (c) described; labeled; explained
   (d) innate; genetically
2. (a) drive
   (b) drives; homeostasis
   (c) homeostasis
   (d) steady state; homeostasis
   (e) drive; need
   (f) drive; increasing
3. (a) incentive
   (b) learning
   (c) expectation
   (d) drive; incentive; incentive
4. (a) psychological; cognitive
   (b) inborn; environment
   (c) hierarchy of needs
   (d) self-actualization
   (e) biological; safety; social; growth-oriented
   (f) self-actualization
   (g) self-actualization
   (h) psychological; cognitive
5. (a) specific types of motivated behavior
   (b) biological, behavioral, cognitive
6. (a) motivation
   (b) homeostasis
   (c) unlikely
   (d) incentive
   (e) instinct
   (f) emotions

Matching Exercise 1

1. humanistic theories
2. motivation
3. persistence
4. Abraham Maslow
5. drive
6. instinct theories
7. hierarchy of needs

True/False Test 1

1. T	3. F	5. T	7. T
2. T	4. T	6. F	

The Motivation to Eat: What Causes Us to Start and Stop Eating? (Part 1)

1. (a) psychological, biological, social
   (b) emotional states
   (c) relationships

2. (a) do not; do
   (b) receptors; satiation
   (c) hormone; neurotransmitter
   (e) slowing; stretch receptors

3. (a) insulin; more; more
   (b) insulin; classically conditioned
   (c) externals; nonexternals
   (d) externals; nonexternals

4. (a) hypothalamus; ventromedial hypothalamus (VMH)
   (b) lateral hypothalamus (LH)
   (c) start eating; stop eating
   (d) appeal

5. (a) multiple
   (b) hypothalamus
   (c) psychological
   (d) interaction

The Motivation to Eat: The Regulation of Body Weight (Part 2)

1. (a) energy balance
   (b) food (energy); energy
   (c) glucose; fat
   (d) one-third; two-thirds
   (e) basal metabolic rate; BMR

2. (a) food intake
   (b) lower; higher; decreases
   (c) genetics

3. (a) BMR
   (b) homeostasis; basal metabolic rate
   (c) number; size
   (d) size; number

(e) set-point; number; size
(f) describes; explain

4. (a) 20; cannot
   (b) external
   (c) insulin
   (d) higher
   (e) insulin
   (f) metabolism; less
   (g) metabolic
   (h) exercise

5. (a) near self-starvation; refuses; weight; fat; body
   (b) females
   (c) appetites; diet
   (d) self-perception

6. (a) are; overweight
   (b) binge
   (c) do; high-caloric
   (d) genetic; are

7. (a) high
   (b) external
   (c) lateral; LH
   (d) basal metabolic rate; BMR
   (e) obese
   (f) anorexia nervosa

Matching Exercise 2

1. cholecystokinin (CCK)
2. oral signals
3. basal metabolic rate (BMR)
4. externals/nonexternals
5. ventromedial hypothalamus (VMH)
6. set-point weight
7. insulin
8. obese

True/False Test 2

1. T	4. T	6. F
2. F	5. T	7. T
3. T		

Arousal Motives: Curiosity and Sensation Seeking

1. (a) increase; reduce
   (b) curiosity, exploration; Incentive

2. (a) unpleasant
   (b) low; increase; high; reduce
   (c) optimal

3. (a) pace
   (b) gradually
   (c) pace; inhibited

4. (a) life experiences; increases
   (b) temperamental

5. (a) sensation seekers
   (b) Sensation seekers; flexible; tolerant

Competence and Achievement Motivation

1. (a) competence
   (b) achievement
   (c) need to achieve
   (d) Thematic Apperception Test; TAT
   (e) achievement; does

2. (a) individualistic; collectivistic

3. (a) self-efficacy
   (b) avoid

4. (a) achievement
   (b) pace
   (c) low
   (d) collectivistic
   (e) competence

Graphic Organizer 1

1. drive theory

2. humanistic theory

3. instinct theory

4. incentive theory

5. arousal theory

Matching Exercise 3

1. individualistic cultures

2. self-efficacy

3. arousal theory

4. competence motivation

5. collectivistic cultures

6. sensation seeking

7. achievement motivation

8. Thematic Apperception Test (TAT)

Emotion

1. (a) pleasurable; unpleasant
   (b) Emotions; mood
   (c) subjective; physical; behavioral

2. (a) disagreement
   (b) basic
   (c) basic; contempt; disappointment; love
   (d) qualitatively different
   (e) blend; mixed
   (f) pleasant; unpleasant; high; low

3. (a) much the same way; agreement
   (b) differences

(c) intensity
(d) do

4. (a) physiological; physical
   (b) autonomic
   (c) lowering
   (d) are
   (e) physiological
   (f) polygraph

5. (a) expressive; behavioral; nonverbal behavior
   (b) muscles
   (c) inborn; innate
   (d) three; four; two; six; seven

6. (a) blends
   (b) display rules

Graphic Organizer 2

1. astonish-ment
2. alarm
3. boredom
4. relaxation
5. annoyance

Explaining Emotions: Key Theories

1. (a) physical; behavior; subjective
   (b) perceive; interpret

2. (a) subjective
   (b) physiological; sympathetic nervous system
   (c) do not necessarily
   (d) do; does not

3. (a) expressing; subjectively
   (b) subjective; Expressive

4 (a) simultaneously
   (b) physical; subjective; at the same time

5. (a) interaction; factors
   (b) necessary; labeling

6. (a) cognitive
   (b) all; cognitive
   (c) cognitive; cognition
   (d) cognitive; physiological; behavioral

7. (a) mood; emotion
   (b) sympathetic
   (c) display rules
   (d) facial feedback hypothesis
   (e) James-Lange theory

Matching Exercise 4

1. facial feedback hypothesis
2. Richard Lazarus
3. emotion
4. two-factor theory of emotion
5. basic emotions
6. interpersonal engagement
7. nonverbal behavior
8. interactive approach to emotion
9. display rules

True/False Test 4

1. F	4. T	7. T
2. T	5. T	8. F
3. T	6. T	9. F

Something to Think About

1. Losing weight and keeping it off is a big problem for many people. You might begin your discussion by noting that our motivation to eat is influenced by psychological, biological, social, and cultural factors. For example, biologically, hunger and satiation are regulated by oral sensations, stomach signals, CCK, and insulin. Psychologically, some people are more strongly influenced by food-related external stimuli. Socially, women, in particular, are affected by society's ideal of thinness. Next, describe the energy balance model and the role of BMR in relation to weight regulation. In addition, set-point theory and the principle of homeostasis will help your friend to understand why some people keep a relatively constant weight and why some are obese.

Applying the above to losing weight, note that obese people do not necessarily eat more than nonobese people. Instead, they may be highly responsive to external cues associated with food; they also produce more insulin; and they operate with higher body levels of insulin. Moreover, obese people gain weight more easily than nonobese people, and dieting may sharply reduce their metabolic rate and keep it low for long periods of time.

The best advice for someone trying to lose weight is to modify his or her eating patterns and follow a regular exercise program. It's an uphill battle, and despite the gloomy statistics, many people have successfully kept weight off by following this advice.

2. The first thing to note about the polygraph is that it does not detect lies. It might be more accurate to refer to the polygraph as an "emotion detector" because it measures physiological arousal. Changes in heart rate, blood pressure, respiration, and perspiration, which are all associated with emotional arousal, can be detected by the polygraph. These changes may be associated with many different emotional states, such as anxiety, fear, irritation, and general nervousness. There is no specific pattern of responding associated with lying, and the polygraph can't specify which response is which. In addition, some people are able to lie without experiencing anxiety or arousal, whether they are guilty or not. Even if someone "passes" a polygraph test, as some alien abductees have, it does not necessarily mean that they are telling the truth; it may simply reflect the fact that they believe they are.

Research suggests that polygraph experts are prone to error in interpretation; about one-third of innocent people may be thought guilty and about one-fourth of guilty people may be declared innocent. Because of the high error rate, many states do not allow polygraph results to be used as evidence in court, and it is now illegal for nongovernmental agencies and companies to use a lie detector to routinely screen prospective employees for drug use or theft.

Progress Test 1

1. a	6. d	11. a
2. a	7. c	12. b
3. c	8. c	13. b
4. b	9. a	14. d
5. c	10. c	15. d

Progress Test 2

1. a	6. d	11. a
2. a	7. a	12. d
3. d	8. d	13. a
4. d	9. a	14. e
5. c	10. d	15. c

Progress Test 3

1. a	6. d	11. c
2. c	7. a	12. b
3. c	8. c	13. a
4. b	9. d	14. d
5. d	10. b	15. c

CHAPTER
9

Lifespan
Development

PREVIEW

Reading the section below first will give you a general sense of the chapter's contents and an initial introduction to some of the major concepts and terms. This will prime you for what you are about to read and help you to develop a "cognitive map" that will guide your study of the material in this chapter. Likewise, reading the **preview questions** at the beginning of each major section will improve your ability to understand, learn, and retain the information.

CHAPTER 9 . . . AT A GLANCE

Chapter 9 examines the scope of developmental psychology and major themes such as the stages of lifespan development, the nature of change, and the interaction between heredity and environment. The first two sections explain genetic contributions to development and describe the stages of prenatal development.

Development during infancy and childhood and the capacities and capabilities of the newborn are explored, including social and personality development, with special attention paid to the nature of temperament and the concept of attachment. This is followed by a description of the stages of language development. The section concludes with a detailed analysis of Piaget's theory of cognitive development and an examination of Vygotsky's information-processing model.

Adolescence is defined as a distinctive stage of development, with important changes in adolescent–parent relationships occurring during this period. Erikson's theory of psychosocial development and Kohlberg's theory of the development of moral reasoning are discussed next. Erikson maintains that identity versus identity diffusion is the main conflict associated with adolescence.

The final sections describe the three phases of adult development as well as the contributions of genetics, environment, and the individual's lifestyle. Love and work are the key themes that dominate adult development. Late adulthood does not necessarily involve a steep decline in physical and cognitive functioning. Erikson identified the task of ego integrity as the key psychosocial task of old age. In discussing dying and death, which can occur at any point in the lifespan, the text outlines Kübler-Ross's five-stage model of dying, noting that dying is an individual process much as any other during the lifespan.

Introduction: Your Life Story

Preview Questions

Consider the following questions as you study this section of the chapter.

- What do developmental psychologists study?
- What are the major themes in developmental psychology?

Read the section "Introduction: Your Life Story" and ***write*** *your answers to the following:*

1. (a) At every age and every stage of life, developmental psychologists investigate the influence of multiple factors on development, including _____ , _____ , _____ , _____ , and behavioral factors.

   (b) The impact of these factors on development is greatly influenced by our _____ , _____ , and _____ characteristics. Although we are influenced by the events we experience, we also shape the meaning and consequences of life events.

   (c) Along with studying common patterns of growth and change, developmental psychologists look at the ways that people _____ in their development and life stories.

2. (a) Developmental psychologists often conceptualize the lifespan in terms of basic _____ of development, usually defined by age and age-related changes; some aspects of development, such as language and prenatal development, are closely tied to _____ , which are periods during which the child is maximally sensitive to environmental influences; while some of life's transitions are rather abrupt, most of our physical, mental, and social changes occur _____ .

   (b) Another important theme in developmental psychology is the interaction between _____ and _____ ,

traditionally called the nature-nurture issue.

   (c) Although we are born with a specific _____ potential that we inherit from our biological parents, our _____ influences and shapes how that potential is expressed; in turn, our _____ inheritance influences the ways in which we experience and interact with the _____ .

Genetic Contributions to Your Life Story

Preview Questions

Consider the following questions as you study this section of the chapter.

- What are chromosomes, DNA, and genes, and what role do they play in determining each individual's unique genetic makeup?
- What role does the environment play in the relationship between genotype and phenotype?
- How do dominant and recessive genes differ, and what are sex-linked recessive characteristics?

Read the section "Genetic Contributions to Your Life Story" and ***write*** *your answers to the following:*

1. (a) Each chromosome is a long, threadlike structure composed of twisted parallel strands of _____ , or _____ , which is the chemical basis of all heredity; _____ contain the chemical genetic code that has directed the growth and development of many of your unique characteristics.

   (b) The DNA code carried on each chromosome is arranged in thousands of segments called _____ , each of which is a unit of DNA instructions pertaining to some characteristic, such as eye or hair color, height, or handedness.

   (c) At conception, _____ chromosomes from your biological mother's ovum were paired with

_____ chromosomes from

your biological father's sperm, resulting in

_____ *pairs* of chromo-

somes.

2. (a) The underlying genetic makeup of an indi-

vidual is called the _____ ; the

traits that are actually displayed constitute

what is referred to as the

_____ .

(b) When a genotype combines conflicting genet-

ic information (one gene for blue eyes and

one gene for brown eyes, for example), the

_____ gene will influ-

ence the trait you actually display.

(c) Traits such as freckles, dark eyes, dark hair,

and dimples are referred to as

_____ characteristics because

only one member of a gene pair must be

dominant in order for the trait to be

displayed.

(d) If both members of the gene pair happen to

be dominant, the genes will simply act in

harmony, and your _____ will

express the dominant characteristic.

(e) In order to get a nondominant characteristic

such as light hair or light eyes, each gene in

a gene pair must be a(n)

_____ gene, whose instruc-

tions are not expressed if combined with a

dominant gene; _____ genes

are expressed only if paired with an identi-

cal _____ gene.

(f) Traits whose expression requires two identi-

cal recessive genes, like light hair and being

dimple free, are called _____

characteristics.

(g) What we really inherit from our biological

parents is a genetic _____

that can be influenced by environmental

conditions; the phenotype *expression* of that

genetic programming may be influenced by

the environment.

3. (a) Some _____ characteristics,

such as color blindness and hemophilia, are

much more common in men than women,

and that has to do with the

_____ chromosome, the

23rd pair of chromosomes—the ones that

determine biological sex.

(b) There are two types of _____

chromosomes, the large X chromosome and

the smaller Y chromosome.

(c) In _____ (males/females), the

23rd pair of chromosomes is made up of two

large X chromosomes, and in

_____ (males/females), it is

made up of a large X chromosome and a

smaller Y chromosome.

(d) Following the normal pattern,

_____ (males/females) require

the presence of two recessive genes, one on

each X chromosome, in order for recessive

characteristics associated with the 23rd

chromosome pair to be displayed.

(e) For _____ (males/females), how-

ever, the smaller Y chromosome often does

not contain a corresponding gene segment to

match the one on their X chromosome; this

means that _____

(males/females) can display certain recessive

characteristics as a result of only one reces-

sive gene carried on the X chromosome of

their XY pair.

(f) Traits determined by recessive genes on the

X chromosomes are referred to as

_____ characteristics.

(g) Because _____ (males/females)

require only one recessive gene on their X

chromosome to display these traits, they are

more common in _____

(males/females) than in _____

(males/females); thus, there is a gender difference in the heritability of recessive characteristics that are communicated on the sex chromosome.

Graphic Organizer 1

There is a dominant gene (D) for "dimples" and a recessive gene (r) for "no dimples." The matrix below shows the four possible combinations. Decide which combinations (genotype) will result in "dimples" or "no dimples" (phenotype).

	Dominant (D)	Recessive (r)
Dominant (D)	Cell 1 DD	Cell 2 Dr
Recessive (r)	Cell 3 Dr	Cell 4 rr

Cell 1: The genotype DD results in the phenotype of

_____ .

Cell 2: The genotype Dr results in the phenotype of

_____ .

Cell 3: The genotype Dr results in the phenotype of

_____ .

Cell 4: The genotype rr results in the phenotype of

_____ .

Prenatal Development

Preview Questions

Consider the following questions as you study this section of the chapter.

- What happens to the single-cell zygote during prenatal development?
- What are the three stages of prenatal development?
- What are teratogens, and what general principles seem to govern their impact on the fetus?

*Read the section "Prenatal Development" and **write** your answers to the following:*

1. (a) During the germinal period, also called the _____ period, the fertilized egg undergoes rapid cell division before becoming implanted on the mother's uterine wall.

   (b) Some of the cells of the _____ will eventually form the structures that house and protect the developing fetus and provide nourishment from the mother; by the end of the two-week germinal period, the single cell has developed into a cluster of cells called the _____ .

2. (a) The embryonic period extends through week _____ ; during this time of rapid growth and intensive cell _____ , the organs and major systems of the body form.

   (b) Protectively housed in the fluid-filled _____ sac, the embryo is supplied with nutrients, oxygen, and water and gets rid of carbon dioxide and other wastes through its lifeline, the

   _____ .

   (c) The umbilical cord attaches the embryo to the _____ , a disk-shaped tissue on the mother's uterine wall; the _____ prevents the mother's blood from mingling with that of the developing embryo, acting as a filter to prevent harmful substances that might be present in the mother's blood from reaching the embryo.

   (d) Harmful agents or substances that can cause abnormal development or birth defects are called _____ ; these include exposure to radiation, toxic industrial chemicals, a number of diseases, and drugs such as alcohol, cocaine, and heroin.

3. (a) The third month marks the beginning of the _____ period, the final and longest stage of prenatal development; the main task of this period is for the body systems to grow and reach maturity in preparation for life outside the mother's body.

(b) By the end of the _____ month, the fetus can move its arms, legs, mouth, and head; it also becomes capable of _____ responses, such as fanning its toes and squinting its eyes.

(c) During the fourth month, the mother can feel the fetus moving; that is, she experiences _____ . By the fifth month, essentially all the _____ the person will ever have are present, though they will continue to develop long after birth.

(d) During the sixth month, the fetus's brain activity becomes similar to that of a newborn baby, and the fetus has distinct _____ cycles.

(e) The _____ month is considered the transitional month because fetuses can now survive outside the uterus with the help of intensive medical care and a protective environment.

(f) During the final two months, the fetus will double its weight, gaining an additional three to four pounds of _____ , which helps the newborn adjust to changing temperatures outside the womb.

4. Read the following and write the correct term in the space provided.

(a) Dr. Dalliwhal's research focuses on the relationship between various teratogens and birth defects. Dr. Dalliwhal is most likely a _____ psychologist.

(b) From the day Franco was born, people have always responded very positively to his good looks. Now that he is growing older, it is clear that he is developing a socially confident and outgoing personality. This best illustrates the interaction of _____ and _____ .

(c) Paul and Paula are brother and sister; in terms of chromosomes, Paul received a(n) _____ from his mother and a(n) _____ from his father, and Paula received a(n) _____ from her mother and a(n) _____ from her father.

(d) It is now six weeks since Jennifer conceived. The human organism she is carrying is called a(n) _____ ; after the eighth week, it will be called a(n) _____ .

Review of Terms and Concepts 1

Use the terms in this list to complete the Matching Test, then to help you answer the True/False items correctly.

developmental psychology
critical period
nature-nurture issue
chromosome
deoxyribonucleic acid (DNA)
gene
genotype
phenotype
dominant gene
dominant characteristics
recessive gene
recessive characteristics
sex chromosomes
sex-linked recessive characteristics
prenatal stage
zygote
germinal period (zygotic period)
embryo
embryonic period
teratogens
fetal period
fetus

Matching Exercise

Match the appropriate term with its definition or description.

1. _____ The stage of development before birth; divided into the germinal, embryonic, and fetal periods.

2. _____ The basic unit of heredity that directs the development of a particular characteristic; the individual unit of DNA instructions on a chromosome.

3. _____ The branch of psychology that studies how people change over the lifespan.

4. _____ Traits determined by recessive genes located on the X chromosome; in males, these characteristics require only one recessive gene to be expressed.

5. _____ Harmful agents or substances that can cause malformations or defects in an embryo or fetus.

6. _____ Long, threadlike structure composed of twisted parallel strands of DNA; found in the nucleus of the cell.

7. _____ In a pair of genes, the gene containing genetic instructions that will not be expressed unless paired with another recessive gene.

8. _____ The first two weeks of prenatal development.

9. _____ Cluster of cells that develop from the single-celled zygote by the end of the two-week germinal period.

10. _____ Traits whose expression requires two identical recessive genes, like those for light hair and being dimple free.

11. _____ Chromosomes designated as X or Y that determine biological sex; the 23rd pair of chromosomes in humans.

True/False Test

Indicate whether each statement is true or false by placing T or F in the blank space next to each item.

1. ____ The fetus is the name given to the growing organism at the beginning of the third month.

2. ____ A critical period during development is a time during which the child is maximally sensitive to environmental influences.

3. ____ Deoxyribonucleic acid (DNA) is the chemical basis of heredity; carries genetic instructions in the cell.

4. ____ The fetal period is the second period of prenatal development, extending from the third week through the eighth week.

5. ____ At conception, chromosomes from the biological mother and father combine to form a single cell called the fertilized egg, or zygote.

6. ____ In a pair of genes, the gene containing genetic instructions that will be expressed whether paired with another dominant gene or with a recessive gene is called the dominant gene.

7. ____ The embryonic period is the third and longest period of prenatal development, extending from the eighth week until birth.

8. ____ An important theme in developmental psychology is the interaction between heredity and environment; traditionally called the nature-nurture issue.

9. ____ The genotype refers to observable traits or characteristics of an organism determined by the interaction of genetic and environmental factors.

10. ____ Traits such as freckles, dark eyes, dark hair, and dimples are referred to as dominant characteristics because they require only one member of a gene pair to be present in order for the trait to be displayed.

11. ____ Phenotype refers to the underlying genetic makeup of a particular organism, including the genetic instructions for traits that are not actually displayed.

Check your answers and review any areas of weakness before going on to the next section.

Development During Infancy and Childhood: Physical Development

Preview Questions

Consider the following questions as you study this section of the chapter.

- What reflexes and sensory capabilities are physically helpless infants equipped with that enhance their chances for survival?

- How do the sensory capabilities of the newborn promote the development of relationships with caregivers?

- How does the brain develop after birth?

*Read the section "Development During Infancy and Childhood" and **write** your answers to the following:*

1. (a) The newly born infant enters the world with an impressive array of _____ and _____ capabilities, mostly reflexive in nature, that enhance the chances of survival.

   (b) When you touch a newborn's check, the infant turns toward the source of the touch and opens the mouth, which is the _____ reflex. Touching the newborn's lips triggers the _____ reflex, and putting a finger in the baby's palm triggers the _____ reflex.

2. (a) Vision is the _____ (most/least) developed sense at birth; the optimal viewing distance for the newborn is about _____ to _____ inches, the perfect distance for a nursing baby to easily focus on the mother's face and make eye contact.

    (b) When adults interact with very young infants, they almost always position themselves so that their face is relatively close to the baby's face; this, along with exaggerated head movements and facial expressions, makes it _____ (harder/easier) for the baby to see them.

    (c) At birth, infants are alert to the sound of human voices; they _____ (can/cannot) distinguish between their mother's voice and that of another woman.

    (d) Especially if breast-fed, the newborn quickly becomes sensitized to the _____ of his mother's body, and the mother becomes keenly attuned to her infant's characteristic appearance, _____ , and _____ texture.

3. (a) By the time infants begin crawling, at around _____ to _____ months of age, their view of the world, including distant objects, will be as clear as that of their parents.

    (b) At birth, the brain is an impressive _____ percent of its adult weight, whereas birth weight is only about 5 percent of eventual adult weight; during infancy, the brain will grow to about _____ percent of its adult weight, whereas body weight will reach only about 20 percent of adult weight.

    (c) The newborn enters the world with essentially _____ (half/all) the neurons the brain will ever have, an estimated 100 billion; after birth, however, the brain continues to develop rapidly.

    (d) The number of _____ (dendrites/neurons) increases dramatically during the first two years of life, and the axons of many neurons acquire _____ , the white, fatty covering that increases a neuron's communication speed.

    (e) The basic _____ of motor skill development is universal, but the _____ can vary greatly; each infant has his or her own genetically programmed timetable of physical maturation and developmental readiness to master different motor skills.

Development During Infancy and Childhood: Social and Personality Development

Preview Questions

Consider the following questions as you study this section of the chapter.

-   What is temperament, and what are the temperamental patterns that have been identified?
-   What is attachment, and how is it measured?
-   What is the basic premise of attachment theory?

*Read the section "Social and Personality Development" and **write** your answers to the following:*

1. (a) From birth, forming close social and emotional relationships with caregivers is essential to the infant's _____ and _____ well-being; the young infant _____ (does/does not) play a passive role in forming these relationships.

    (b) Infants come into the world with very distinct and consistent _____ styles; some babies are fussy, some are active and outgoing, and others seem shy. Psychologists refer to these styles as the baby's _____ .

2. (a) Research by Thomas and Chess has shown that about two-thirds of babies can be classified into one of three broad temperamental patterns: _____ .

(b) About one-third of infants can be characterized as _____ babies because they do not fit neatly into one of the three categories

(c) These broad patterns of temperamental qualities are remarkably_____ (stable/unstable) from infancy through childhood.

(d) Virtually all temperament researchers agree that individual differences in temperament have a _____ and _____ basis, but they also agree that _____ experiences can modify a child's basic temperament.

3. (a) During the first year of life, attachment usually takes place; this refers to the _____ that forms between the infant and caregivers, especially the mother; according to attachment theory, an infant's ability to thrive _____ and _____ depends in part on the quality of attachment.

(b) In homes where both parents are present, infants tend to form attachments to both parents at about the same time. An infant is also capable of forming attachments to other consistent caregivers, such as relatives or workers at a day-care center; thus, an infant is capable of forming _____ attachments.

(c) In general, when parents are consistently warm, responsive, and sensitive to their infant's needs, the infant develops a(n) _____ attachment; when parents are neglectful, inconsistent, or insensi-

tive to the infant's moods or behaviors, a(n) _____ attachment may develop.

4. (a) In order to measure attachment, Mary Ainsworth devised a procedure called the _____ , which is used with infants who are between one and two years old.

(b) In this technique, the baby and mother are brought into an unfamiliar room with a variety of toys; a few minutes later, a _____ enters the room; the mother departs after a few minutes, returns after a few more minutes, and then departs and returns again, and the infant's behavior is observed throughout the sequence.

(c) When the mother is present, the _____ attached infant will use her as a secure base from which to explore the new environment, periodically returning to her side; the infant will show distress when the mother leaves the room and will greet her warmly when she returns and is easily soothed.

(d) A(n) _____ attached infant is less likely to explore the environment even when his or her mother is present; the infant may appear either very anxious or completely indifferent and will tend to _____ or _____ the mother when she is present. In addition, these infants become extremely distressed when their mothers leave the room, and when reunited with their mothers, they are _____ (easy/hard) to soothe and comfort.

(e) Preschoolers with a history of being _____ attached tend to be more prosocial, empathetic, and socially competent than preschoolers with a history of _____ attachment; adolescents who were _____ attached in infancy have fewer problems, do better in school, and have more successful relationships with their peers than do adolescents who were _____ attached in infancy.

Development During Infancy and Childhood: Language Development

Preview Questions

Consider the following questions as you study this section of the chapter.

- How does a biological predisposition to learn language function in language development?
- How is language development encouraged by caregivers?
- What are the stages of language development?

*Read the section "Language Development" and **write** your answers to the following:*

1. (a) Children will have learned approximately 3,000 words and the complex rules of language by the time they are _____ years old.

   (b) According to linguist _____ , every child is born with a biological predisposition to learn language, any language; each child possesses a universal _____ , a basic understanding of the common principles of language organization.

   (c) At birth, infants _____ (can/cannot) distinguish among the speech sounds of all the world's languages; by 10 months of age, infants have _____ (gained/lost) this ability and can distinguish only among the speech sounds that are present in the language to which they have been exposed.

2. (a) Parents also seem to be biologically programmed to encourage language development by the way they speak to infants and toddlers; people in every culture, especially

parents, use a style of speech called _____ , or infant-directed speech, with babies.

   (b) The content of _____ tends to be restricted to topics that are familiar to the child, and _____ is often used.

   (c) The adult use of

   _____

   seems to be instinctive; as infants mature and become more sophisticated in language skills, the speech patterns of parents change to fit the child's developing language abilities.

3. The stages of language development appear to be universal, and in virtually every culture, infants follow the same sequence of language development at roughly similar ages:

   (a) At about three months of age, infants begin to _____ . At about five months of age, infants start to _____ , and at about nine months of age, they begin to _____ more in the sounds specific to their language.

   (b) Somewhere around their first birthday, infants produce their first real _____ , but before this, infants' _____ vocabulary (the words they understand) is much larger than their _____ vocabulary (the words they can say).

   (c) During the _____ stage, babies use a single word and vocal intonation to stand for an entire sentence.

   (d) Somewhere around their second birthday, infants begin putting words together to construct simple "sentences," such as "Mama go" and "No potty!" This is called the _____ stage.

   (e) The _____ stage reflects the first understanding of grammar.

(f) At around _____ years of age, children begin to rapidly increase the length and grammatical complexity of their sentences; there is a dramatic increase in the number of words that they can comprehend and produce, and by _____ age, a child may have a production capacity of over 10,000 words.

4. Read the following and write the correct term in the space provided.

(a) Dr. Snow is interested in the abilities of newborn children. While testing visual perception, she is likely to find that newborns will look longer at the image of a(n) _____ compared to other visual patterns.

(b) Kathy gave birth to a normal, healthy, eight-and-half-pound baby. In terms of brain development, the baby has _____ (50 percent/75 percent/100 percent) of the brain cells she will ever have.

(c) As Kathy's baby develops, it becomes apparent that she readily adapts to new experiences, displays positive moods and emotions, and has regular sleeping and eating patterns. She is likely to be classified as a temperamentally _____ baby.

(d) Kathy and her husband are consistently warm, responsive, and sensitive to their infant's needs, and the baby has developed the expectation that her needs will be met. It is very probable that the baby will form a(n) _____ attachment to her parents.

Review of Terms, Concepts, and Names 2

Use the terms in this list to complete the Matching Test, then to help you answer the True/False items correctly.

infancy
rooting reflex
sucking reflex
grasping reflex
temperament

easy temperament
difficult temperament
slow-to-warm-up
 temperament
attachment

secure attachment
insecure attachment
Strange Situation
Mary Ainsworth
Noam Chomsky
motherese (infant-
 directed speech)

cooing and babbling
 stage
one-word stage
comprehension
 vocabulary
production vocabulary
two-word stage

Matching Exercise

Match the appropriate term/name with its definition or description.

1. _____ The first two years of life.

2. _____ Measure of attachment devised by Mary Ainsworth, typically used with infants who are between one and two years old.

3. _____ Automatic response elicited by touching a newborn's lips.

4. _____ Temperamental category for babies who have a low activity level, who withdraw from new situations and people, and adapt to new experiences very gradually.

5. _____ Universal style of speech used with babies and characterized by very distinct pronunciation, a simplified vocabulary, short sentences, a high pitch, and exaggerated intonation and expression.

6. _____ Biologically programmed stage in language development that occurs between about three months of age and nine months of age.

7. _____ Emotional bond that forms between infants and their caretaker(s), especially parents.

8. _____ Words that are understood by an infant or child.

9. _____ Form of attachment that may develop when parents are neglectful, inconsistent, or insensitive to their infant's moods or behaviors and reflects an ambivalent or detached emotional relationship between infant and mother.

10. _____ Universal stage in language development, starting around two years of age, in which infants combine two words to construct simple "sentences" that reflect the first understanding of grammar.

True/False Test

Indicate whether each statement is true or false by placing T or F in the blank space next to each item.

1. ____ Noam Chomsky is the psychologist who devised the Strange Situation procedure to measure attachment; contributed to attachment theory.

2. ____ Production vocabulary refers to the words that an infant or child can speak.

3. ____ An infant's response to having his or her palms touched is called the rooting reflex.

4. ____ Babies with a difficult temperament tend to be intensely emotional, are irritable and fussy, cry a lot, and have irregular sleeping and eating patterns.

5. ____ During the one-word stage, babies use a single word and vocal intonation to stand for an entire sentence.

6. ____ Secure attachment is likely to develop when parents are consistently warm, responsive, and sensitive to their infant's needs.

7. ____ Mary Ainsworth is the American linguist who proposed that people have an innate understanding of the basic principles of language, which is called a universal grammar.

8. ____ Babies with an easy temperament readily adapt to new experiences, generally display positive moods and emotions, and have regular sleeping and eating patterns.

9. ____ Touching the newborn's cheek elicits the grasping reflex; the infant turns toward the source of the touch and opens the mouth.

10. ____ Temperament is the inborn predisposition to consistently behave and react in a certain way.

> Check your answers and review any areas of weakness before going on to the next section.

Development During Infancy and Childhood: Cognitive Development

Preview Questions

Consider the following questions as you study this section of the chapter.

- What are Piaget's four stages of cognitive development?
- What are the characteristics of each stage?
- What are the main criticisms of Piaget's theory?

Read the section "Cognitive Development" and **write** *your answers to the following:*

1. (a) The development of gender schemas is one reflection of the child's increasing sophistication in thinking, remembering, processing information, and other _____ processes.

   (b) The most influential theory of cognitive development is that of Swiss psychologist Jean Piaget, who believed that rather than passively soaking up information about the world children _____ try to make sense out of their environment.

   (c) According to Piaget, children progress through four distinct biologically programmed cognitive stages: the sensorimotor stage, from _____ to age _____ ; the preoperational stage, from age _____ to age _____ ; the concrete operational stage, from age _____ to age _____ ; and the formal operational stage, which begins during _____ and continues into _____ .

   (d) As a child advances to a new stage, the child's thinking is _____ different from that used in the previous stage; this progression is assumed to be a continuous, gradual process, common to all cultures, although there can be individual variation in the rate of progress.

   (e) Children develop a new understanding of the world in each progressive stage, building on the understanding acquired in the previous stage; as children _____ new information and experiences, they eventually change their way of thinking to _____ new knowledge.

2. (a) During the sensorimotor stage, infants acquire knowledge about the world through

motor _____ that allow them to directly experience and manipulate objects; they expand this practical knowledge by reaching, grasping, pushing, pulling, and pouring, in the process gaining a basic understanding of the effects that their own _____ can produce.

(b) At the beginning of the sensorimotor stage, an object exists only if the infant can directly sense it; by the end of this stage, the child acquires a new cognitive understanding that an object continues to exist even if it can't be seen; this is called

_____ .

(c) Infants gradually acquire an understanding of _____ as they gain experience with objects, as their memory abilities improve, and as they develop mental representations of the world, which Piaget called _____ .

3. (a) In Piaget's theory, _____ refer to logical, mental activities; thus, the preoperational stage is a prelogical stage.

(b) The hallmark of preoperational thought is the child's capacity to engage in _____ thought, which refers to the ability to use words, images, and symbols to represent the world.

(c) Indications for the expanding capacity for _____ thought are the child's impressive gains in language and the use of fantasy and imagination while playing.

(d) The preoperational child's thought is characterized by _____ , _____ , and _____ .

(e) The preoperational child is unable to understand that two equal physical quantities remain equal even if the appearance of one is changed and as long as nothing is added or subtracted, which is the principle of _____ .

4. (a) With the beginning of the concrete opera-

tional stage, children become capable of true logical thought, are much less _____ in their thinking, can _____ mental operations, and can focus simultaneously on two aspects of a problem; in short, they understand the principle of _____ .

(b) In this stage, children's thinking and use of logic tends to be limited to tangible objects and events; they are incapable of thinking logically about _____ situations or _____ ideas, unless they are related to their personal experiences or actual events.

5. (a) The formal operational stage is characterized by the gradual emergence of the ability to think logically even when dealing with _____ concepts or _____ situations; this ability continues to increase in sophistication throughout adolescence and adulthood.

(b) While an adolescent may deal effectively with _____ ideas in one domain of knowledge, his or her thinking may not reflect the same degree of sophistication in other areas; even among many _____ , formal operational thinking is often limited to areas in which they have developed expertise or a special interest.

6. (a) Although scientific research _____ (has/has not) supported Piaget's most fundamental idea that infants, young children, and older children use distinctly different cognitive abilities to construct their understanding of the world, his theory has been criticized in several areas.

(b) Piaget often _____ (overestimated/underestimated) the cognitive abilities of infants and children; many researchers believe that Piaget confused _____ limitations with _____ limitations.

(c) In several studies to assess an infant's understanding of object permanence, psychologist Renée Baillargeon used _____ tasks rather than _____ tasks. She concluded that infants have _____ (less/more) sophisticated cognitive abilities than Piaget believed.

7. (a) Piaget's notion that the stages unfold universally has been _____ (supported/challenged); studies have shown that many adults display _____ thought only in limited areas of knowledge, and some adults never display formal operational thought processes.

   (b) Piaget later suggested that formal operational thinking may not be a _____ phenomenon, but rather may be the product of an individual's expertise in a specific area.

   (c) Many developmental psychologists reject the Piagetian notion of distinct stages, emphasizing instead the

   _____

   model of cognitive development, which focuses on investigating the development of fundamental mental processes such as attention, memory, and problem solving. In this approach cognitive development is viewed as a process of _____ change over the lifespan.

8. (a) Another criticism is that Piaget underestimated the impact of the _____ and _____ environment on cognitive development.

   (b) Unlike Piaget, Russian psychologist _____ believed that cognitive development is strongly influenced by _____ and _____ factors such as the support and guidance that children receive from parents, other

adults, and older children; research has supported this position.

   (c) How these supportive social interactions are displayed varies from culture to culture; cross-cultural research has shown that cognitive development is strongly influenced by the _____ that are valued and encouraged in a particular environment.

   (d) Despite these criticisms, Piaget's documentation of the many _____ changes that occur during infancy and childhood ranks as one of the most outstanding contributions to developmental psychology.

9. Read the following and write the correct term in the space provided.

   (a) Four-year-old Tiborg is not completely egocentric, and five-year-old Natasha exhibits some understanding of conservation. Observations such as these suggest that Piaget may have _____ (overestimated/underestimated) the cognitive abilities of infants and children.

   (b) Eight-year-old Nadia has the ability to think logically about visible and tangible objects and situations. She is in the _____ stage of cognitive development.

   (c) Young Adrienne attempts to retrieve her toy bear after her father hides it under a blanket. This suggests that Adrienne has developed a sense of _____ .

   (d) When Mrs. Goodley cut Janet's hot dog into eight pieces and Simon's into six pieces, Simon started to cry and complained that he wasn't getting as much hot dog as Janet. Piaget would say that Simon doesn't understand the principle of _____ .

   (e) Three-year-old Rita calls all unfamiliar four-legged animals "doggies." She appears to be _____ these new experiences into her existing concept of a dog.

(f) Piaget would call Rita's mental representation or concept of dog a _____ .

(g) During a tutorial devoted to the pros and cons of genetic engineering, Vasilis raised some important issues about the ownership of fertilized eggs and whether destroying them constitutes taking a life. Piaget would say that Vasilis is in the _____ operational stage of cognitive development.

Review of Terms, Concepts, and Names 3

Use the terms in this list to complete the Matching Test, then to help you answer the True/False items correctly.

cognitive processes
Jean Piaget
qualitative difference in
  thinking
sensorimotor stage
object permanence
schemas
preoperational stage
operations
symbolic thought
egocentrism

irreversibility
centration
conservation
concrete operational
  stage
formal operational stage
Renée Baillargeon
information-processing
  model of cognitive
  development
Lev Vygotsky

Matching Exercise

Match the appropriate term/name with its definition or description.

1. _____ The ability to use words, images, and symbols to represent the world.

2. _____ The mental functions used in thinking, remembering, and processing information.

3. _____ The understanding that an object continues to exist even when it can no longer be seen.

4. _____ Piaget's fourth stage of cognitive development, which lasts from adolescence through adulthood and is characterized by the ability to think logically about abstract principles and hypothetical situations.

5. _____ Swiss child psychologist whose influential theory proposed that children progress through distinct stages of cognitive development.

6. _____ The model that views cognitive development as a continuous process over the lifespan and that studies the development of basic mental processes such as attention, memory, and problem solving.

7. _____ Piaget's term for the mental representations of the world that children acquire as their memories improve and as they gain an understanding of object permanence.

8. _____ Piaget's first stage of cognitive development, from birth to about age two; the period during which the infant explores the environment and acquires knowledge through sensing and manipulating objects.

9. _____ In Piaget's theory, the inability to take another person's perspective or point of view.

True/False Test

Indicate whether each statement is true or false by placing T or F in the blank space next to each item.

1. ____ In Piaget's theory, the word *operations* refers to logical, mental activities.

2. ____ Renée Baillargeon was the Russian psychologist who stressed the importance of social and cultural influences on cognitive development.

3. ____ In Piaget's theory, the concrete operational stage is the second stage of cognitive development, which lasts from about age two to age seven and is characterized by increasing use of symbols and prelogical thought processes.

4. ____ In Piaget's theory, irreversibility is the inability to reverse a sequence of events or logical operations mentally.

5. ____ In Piaget's theory, centration refers to the understanding that two equal quantities remain equal even though the form or appearance is rearranged, as long as nothing is added or subtracted.

6. ____ According to Piaget, as children advance to a new stage, their thinking is qualitatively different from that used in the previous stage; each new stage represents a fundamental shift in *how* children think and understand the world.

7. ____ In Piaget's theory, the tendency to focus on only one aspect of a situation and ignore other important aspects of the situation is called conservation.

8. ____ Lev Vygotsky is a Canadian-born American psychologist whose highly original studies of cognitive development in infancy, using visual rather than manual tasks, challenged Piaget's beliefs about the age at which object permanence first appears.

9. ____ In Piaget's theory, the preoperational stage is the third stage of cognitive development, which lasts from about age seven to adolescence and is characterized by the ability to think logically about concrete objects and situations.

Check your answers and review any areas of weakness before going on to the next section.

Adolescence

Preview Questions

Consider the following questions as you study this section of the chapter.

- How is adolescence defined, and what characteristics are evident during this stage of development?
- What characterizes relationships between parents and peers in adolescence?
- How do adolescents begin the process of identity formation?
- What is Erikson's psychosocial theory of life-span development?
- What are the stages and levels in Kohlberg's theory of moral development?
- How is moral reasoning influenced by gender and culture?

*Read the section "Adolescence" and **write** your answers to the following:*

1. (a) Adolescence begins around age _____ and lasts until the individual assumes _____ roles and responsibilities.

   (b) Parent-adolescent relationships are generally _____ ; most teenagers report that they admire their parents and turn to them for _____ . If the relationships have been good before adolescence, they continue to be relatively smooth during adolescence.

   (c) The influence of parents _____ (does/does not) continue throughout adolescence; however, relationships with _____ become increasingly important

   (d) Although peer influence can lead to undesirable behaviors in some instances, researchers have found that peer relationships _____ the traits and goals that parents fostered during childhood.

2. (a) Identity refers to the _____ , _____ , and ideals that guide an individual's behavior. Identity formation is a process that _____ (does/does not) continue throughout the lifespan.

   (b) For the first time in the lifespan, the adolescent possesses the _____ skills necessary to deal with identity issues in a meaningful way. Before adolescence, children tend to use _____ social and behavioral descriptions; adolescents use more _____ self-descriptions.

   (c) Some aspects of personal identity involve characteristics over which the adolescent has no control, such as gender, race, ethnic background, and socioeconomic level; these identity characteristics are _____ and already _____ by the time an individual reaches the adolescent years.

   (d) Adolescents begin to _____ themselves on several different dimensions; social acceptance by peers, academic and athletic abilities, work abilities, personal appearance, and romantic appeal are some aspects of _____ .

   (e) Another challenge facing adolescents is to

develop an _____ that is independent of their parents while retaining a sense of connection to the family; adolescents thus have several _____ that they must integrate into a coherent and unified whole to answer the question, "Who am I?"

3. (a) The adolescent's task of achieving an integrated identity is one important aspect of psychoanalyst Erik Erikson's influential theory of _____ development.

  (b) Erikson proposed that each of eight stages of life is associated with a particular _____ that can be resolved in either a positive or negative direction; relationships with others play an important role in determining the outcome of each conflict.

  (c) The key psychosocial conflict facing the adolescent is _____ . In the process of resolving this conflict, adolescents experiment with different roles, beliefs, and values, referred to as a _____ period.

  (d) Psychological research has generally _____ (supported/not supported) Erikson's description of the process of identity formation.

  (e) The process of identity formation only begins to take on serious meaning during _____ ; for most people, a stable and fully integrated identity probably does not occur until well into the _____ years.

4. (a) An important aspect of _____ development during adolescence is a change in moral reasoning, that is, in how an individual thinks about moral decisions.

  (b) The most influential theory of moral development was proposed by psychologist _____ , who used short stories to investigate moral reasoning. He concluded that there are distinct

_____ of moral development that unfold in an age-related, step-by-step fashion.

  (c) Kohlberg proposed three distinct _____ of moral reasoning, each of which is based on the degree to which a person conforms to the conventional standards of society; each _____ has two _____ that represent different degrees of sophistication in moral reasoning.

  (d) Reasoning based on self-interest is found at the _____ level, reasoning that emphasizes social rues and obligations is found at the _____ level, and moral reasoning guided by internalized legal and moral principles is found at the _____ level.

  (e) Research has shown that only a few exceptional individuals display the philosophical ideals associated with _____ moral reasoning; the normal course of changes in moral reasoning for most people seems to be captured by Kohlberg's first four _____ . By adulthood, the prominent form of moral reasoning is _____ moral reasoning.

5. (a) Kohlberg's theory is not without its critics; psychologist Carol Gilligan points out that Kohlberg's early research was conducted entirely with _____ subjects, yet it became the basis for a theory applied to both _____ and _____ .

  (b) Gilligan also notes that most of Kohlberg's stories involve a _____ as the main actor facing the moral dilemma to be resolved; when _____ are present in the stories, they often play a subordinate role.

  (c) To Gilligan, Kohlberg's model is based on an ethic of _____ rights and justice, which is a more common perspective for

_____ ; Gilligan's model is based on an ethic of care and responsibility.

(d) In her studies, Gilligan found that _____ tended to stress the importance of maintaining interpersonal relationships and responding to the needs of others, rather than focusing primarily on individual rights.

(e) Other researchers have found that whereas men and women may approach moral matters from slightly different perspectives, there _____ (does/does not) seem to be systematic gender differences in

moral reasoning when subjects are carefully matched on critical factors, such as level of education.

6. (a) Moral reasoning seems to be affected by _____ ; it has been argued that Kohlberg's stories and scoring system reflect a Western emphasis on individual rights, harm, and justice that is not shared in many _____ .

(b) For example, Kohlberg's moral stages do not reflect the sense of interdependence and the concern for the overall welfare of the _____ that is more common in _____ cultures.

Graphic Organizer 2

For each of the following, identify the appropriate stage of Piaget's theory and the stage and level of Kohlberg's theory.

Statement	Theory	Stage/Level
1. Jeremy refuses to pay taxes and risks going to jail because he does not believe in supporting a government that spends so many tax dollars on weapons of mass destruction. Jeremy enjoys discussing his position and is very articulate in developing logical arguments.	Piaget	
	Kohlberg	
2. Mary is convinced that her older sister Natalie has more soda than she does after her mother poured Natalie's can of soda into a long, thin glass and hers into a short, fat one. Despite being tempted to take a big drink out of Natalie's glass when she is in the washroom, Mary refrains because she thinks she might get punished.	Piaget	
	Kohlberg	
3. While playing a game of cards with his friends, Mark insists that everyone should have a chance to be dealer because that is the fair thing to do. Mark is also able to explain the rules to everyone by dealing a couple of practice hands; later, he has difficulty trying to explain the game to his Dad without using the cards.	Piaget	
	Kohlberg	
4. During a discussion with her therapist, Mrs. Bradshaw is asked to describe her husband. Among other things, she notes that he is very law abiding, always drives with extreme care, and frequently boasts that he has never received a ticket. He never completed high school because he couldn't handle all that abstract, hypothetical stuff and is fairly content working as a custodian in an office building.	Piaget	
	Kohlberg	

Adult Development

Preview Questions

Consider the following questions as you study this section of the chapter.

- What physical changes take place in adulthood?
- What general patterns of social development occur?
- How does the transition to parenthood affect adults?

Read the section "Adult Development" and **write** *your answers to the following:*

1. (a) Your unique _____ blueprint greatly influences the unfolding of certain physical changes during adulthood, such as when your hair begins to thin, lose its color, and turn gray.

   (b) These influences can vary significantly from one person to another; for example, the cessation of menstruation that signals the end of reproductive capacity in women, called _____ , may occur anywhere from the late thirties to the early fifties.

   (c) One key _____ factor that can influence the aging process is a person's lifestyle; staying mentally and physically active and eating a proper diet can both slow and minimize the degree of physical decline associated with aging.

   (d) Another factor is the passage of _____ .

2. (a) According to Erikson, the primary psychosocial task of _____ adulthood is to form a committed, mutually enhancing, intimate relationship with another person; during _____ adulthood, the primary psychosocial task becomes contributing to future generations through children, career, and other meaningful activities, referred to as _____ .

   (b) _____ (Male/Female) friends tend to confide in one another about their feelings, problems, and interpersonal relationships; _____ (male/female) friends typically minimize discussions about relationships or personal feelings or problems and instead tend to do things together, such as activities related to sports or hobbies.

   (c) Getting married and starting a family are the traditional tasks of _____ adulthood; in contrast to their parents, today's young adults are marrying at _____ (an earlier/a later) average age.

   (d) We tend to be attracted to and marry people who are _____ (different from/similar to) us on a variety of dimensions, including physical attractiveness, social and educational status, ethnic background, attitudes, values, and beliefs.

3. (a) Although it is commonly believed that children _____ (weaken/strengthen) the marital bond, marital satisfaction tends to _____ (decline/increase) after the birth of the first child.

   (b) With the birth or adoption of your first child, you take on a commitment to nurture the physical, emotional, social, and intellectual well-being of the next generation; this can fundamentally alter your _____ as an adult.

   (c) The hassles and headaches of child rearing can be minimized if the marital relationship is _____ and _____ and if both husband and wife share household and child-care responsibilities.

   (d) Although marital satisfaction often _____ (declines/increases) when people first become parents, it _____ (rises/drops) again after children leave home.

4. (a) There is much diversity in adult relationships; for example, the number of unmarried
couples living together has
_____ (decreased/increased)
dramatically in the last 20 years; currently,
better than _____ percent of all
children are being raised by a single parent.

(b) Reasons for the diversity in adult relationships include an increase in the number of
_____ , resulting in more single
parents and stepfamilies; an increasing
number of married couples opting for a
_____ life together, and
the number of gay and lesbian couples who
are committed to long-term,
_____ relationships.

(c) Such diversity in adult relationships reflects
the fact that adult _____ devel-
opment does not always follow a predictable
pattern; in the final analysis, any relationship that promotes the overall sense of happiness and well-being of the people involved
is a successful one.

5. (a) Most people explore different career options,
narrow down their options, and tentatively
commit to a particular job in a particular
field in _____ adulthood; close
to a _____ of people in their
late twenties and early thirties do not
change jobs in a particular field but completely switch occupational fields.

(b) Dual-career families have become increasingly common. If the couple has children,
the career tracks of men and women often
_____ (are the same/are different); married women with children are
much _____ (more/less) likely
than single women or childless women to
interrupt their careers, leave their jobs, or
switch to part-time work because of child-
rearing responsibilities.

(c) Generally, both men and women have a
greater potential for increased feelings of
self-esteem, happiness, and competence
when they perform _____ (a
single role/multiple roles). The critical factor
is the _____ of their experiences
on the job, in marriage, and as a parent.

Late Adulthood and Aging

Preview Questions

- What cognitive changes take place in late
adulthood?
- What factors can influence social development
during this period?

Read the section "Late Adulthood and Aging" and
write *your answers to the following:*

1. (a) The average life expectancy for men is about
_____ years; for women, it is
_____ years. The majority of
older adults _____ (do/do not)
live healthy, active, and self-sufficient lives.

(b) The stereotypical image that most of the
elderly live in nursing homes _____
(is/is not) true.

(c) Although they have _____
(more/fewer) chronic medical conditions, the
elderly tend to see themselves as relatively
healthy, partly because they have
_____ (more/fewer) acute illnesses, such as colds and the flu, than
younger people; even during the final years
of life, the majority of older adults enjoy relatively good health, mental alertness, and
self-sufficiency.

2. (a) In his longitudinal studies, K. Warner
Schaie has found that general intellectual
abilities gradually _____
(increase/decrease) until one's early forties
and then become relatively stable; after age
60, a small but steadily increasing percent-

age of older adults experience _____ (sharp/slight) declines on tests of general intellectual abilities, but most remain unaffected.

(b) When declines in _____ abilities occur during old age, the explanation is often simply a lack of practice or experience with the kinds of tasks on tests of these abilities; a few hours training _____ (can/cannot) improve test scores for most older adults.

(c) Schaie found the smallest declines in mental abilities in those who were better _____ and engaged in _____ and _____ activities throughout older adulthood.

3. (a) According to the _____ theory of aging, life satisfaction in late adulthood is highest when you maintain your previous level of activity, either by continuing old activities or finding new ones; the optimal level of activity varies from person to person.

(b) Along with satisfying social relationships, the prescription for psychological well-being in old age includes achieving what Erikson called _____ , the feeling that one's life has been meaningful.

(c) Older adults experience _____ when they look back on their lives and feel satisfied with their accomplishments, accepting whatever mistakes or missteps they may have made; those filled with regrets or bitterness about past mistakes, missed opportunities, or bad decisions experience _____ , a sense of disappointment in life.

(d) Often, these themes emerge as older adults engage in a _____ , thinking about or retelling their life story to others.

The Final Chapter: Dying and Death

Preview Questions
- How did Kübler-Ross describe the stages of dying and how valid is her theory?

Read the section "The Final Chapter: Dying and Death" and **write** *your answers to the following:*

1. (a) Attitudes toward death in old age _____ (show/do not show) the same diversity that is reflected in other aspects of adult development; _____ (all/not all) older adults are resigned to death, even when poor health has severely restricted their activities.

(b) In general, anxiety about death tends to peak in _____ adulthood and to decrease in _____ adulthood; at any age, people respond with a wide variety of emotions when faced with the prospect of imminent death, such as when they are diagnosed with a terminal illness.

(c) Elisabeth Kübler-Ross proposed that the dying go through five stages; first, they _____ that death is imminent; second, they feel and express _____ ; third, they _____ ; fourth, they become _____ ; and finally they _____ their fate.

(d) Although Kübler-Ross's research did much to sensitize the public and the medical community to the emotional experience of dying, it now seems clear that the dying individual in fact _____ (does/does not) progress through a predictable series of stages.

(e) Faced with impending death, some older adults react with passive _____ , others with _____ and

_____ ; some plunge into activity and focus their attention on _____ matters whereas others turn _____ , searching for the meaning of their life's story as the close of the final chapter draws near.

2. Read the following and write the correct term in the space provided.

(a) Delbert resists stealing cookies from the cookie jar because he is afraid his mother will punish him if he does. According to Kohlberg's theory, Delbert is demonstrating level _____ and stage _____ of moral reasoning.

(b) Compared with their grandparents, Mr. and Mrs. Belmont's children are likely to marry for the first time at _____ (an earlier/a later) age.

(c) David, a sixty-five-year-old retired civil servant, feels that his life has been unproductive and ultimately meaningless. According to Erikson, David has failed to achieve a sense of _____ .

(d) Andrew, a forty-five-year-old accountant, has just learned he has a terminal illness. According to Kübler-Ross, as soon as Andrew gets over his initial denial, he will experience _____ .

(e) Seventeen-year-old Brendan questions his parent's values but is not sure that his peer group's standards are totally correct either. His confusion about what is really important in life suggests that Brendan is struggling with the problem of _____ .

(f) Sarah is a twenty-five-year-old, white, middle class, well-educated, moderately religious person. If she is typical, she will marry someone very _____ (different from/similar to) herself.

(g) The last of the Sandwells' four children has just left home to pursue a career with NASA. If the Sandwells are like most parents whose children have left home, they are likely to experience a steady _____ (decline/increase) in marital satisfaction.

Graphic Organizer 3

Identify the theorist related to each of the following statements.

Statement	Theorist
1. I believe that social and cultural influences are the most important factors in cognitive development.	
2. I study attachment, and I have devised a measure of attachment called the Strange Situation.	
3. In my view people have an innate understanding of the basic principles of language, which I call a "universal grammar."	
4. As a result of my research on cognitive development in infants using visual rather than manual tasks, I have concluded that Piaget was wrong about the age at which object permanence first appears.	
5. I believe that development continues throughout the lifespan and that individuals pass through eight distinct stages during which they are faced with resolving important psychosocial conflicts.	
6. As a result of my longitudinal research on lifespan development, I believe that intellectual decline is not a natural and inevitable result of the biological aging process.	
7. My primary interest is in how children develop intellectually and cognitively, and my theory proposes that children progress through four distinct stages in succession, each stage characterized by a qualitatively different way of thinking from the previous stage.	
8. The primary goal of my research has been to map out the development of moral reasoning in humans; it is my view that there are three levels, each consisting of two stages, and that humans progress through these stages in sequence, until reaching the highest level.	

Review of Key Terms and Key Names 4

Use the terms in this list to complete the Matching Test, then to help you answer the True/False items correctly.

adolescence
identity
Erik Erikson
identity diffusion
moratorium period
integrated identity
moral reasoning
Lawrence Kohlberg
preconventional level
conventional level
postconventional level

ethic of individual rights
   and justice
ethic of care and
   responsibility
menopause
early adulthood
middle adulthood
late adulthood
generativity
activity theory of aging

authoritarian parenting
   style
permissive parenting
   style

authoritative parents
induction

Matching Exercise

Match the appropriate term/name with its definition or description.

1. _____ Discipline technique that combines parental control with explaining why a behavior is prohibited.

2. _____ The natural cessation of menstruation and the end of reproductive capacity in women.

3. _____ Carol Gilligan's categorization of women's moral development and reasoning, based on her research that showed women tended to stress the importance of maintaining interpersonal relationships and responding to the needs of others, rather than focusing primarily on individual rights.

4. _____ Baumrind's term for a parenting style in which parents are extremely tolerant and not demanding; permissive-indulgent parents are responsive to their children, whereas permissive-indifferent parents are not.

5. _____ In Erikson's theory, the period following identity diffusion during which the adolescent experiments with different roles, values, and beliefs.

6. _____ Transitional stage between late childhood and the beginning of adulthood, during which sexual maturity is reached.

7. _____ Kohlberg's level of moral reasoning that begins in late childhood and continues through adolescence and adulthood; characterized by moral reasoning that emphasizes social roles, rules, and obligations.

8. _____ Stage of adulthood, roughly from the forties to the mid-sixties, when physical strength and endurance gradually decline.

9. _____ A person's self-definition or description, including the values, beliefs, and ideals that guide the individual's behavior.

10. _____ Psychosocial theory that life satisfaction in late adulthood is highest when people maintain the level of activity they displayed earlier in life.

11. _____ In Erikson's theory, the primary psychosocial task of middle adulthood in which the person contributes to future generations through children, career, and other meaningful activity.

12. _____ American psychologist who proposed an influential theory of moral development.

True/False Test

Indicate whether each item is true or false by placing T or F in the space next to each item.

1. ____ Moral reasoning refers to the aspect of cognitive development related to the way an individual reasons about moral decisions.

2. ____ Erik Erikson was the German-born American psychoanalyst who proposed an influential theory of psychosocial development throughout the lifespan.

3. ____ Early adulthood refers to the stage of development during the twenties and thirties when physical strength typically peaks.

4. ____ Authoritarian parenting style is Baumrind's term for parents who set clear standards for their children's behavior but are also responsive to the children's needs and wishes.

5. ____ Late adulthood refers to the stage of development from the mid-sixties on, when physical stamina and reaction time tend to decline further and faster.

6. ____ In Erikson's theory, the adolescent's path to successfully achieving an identity begins with identity diffusion, which is characterized by little sense of commitment to the various issues he or she has to grapple with and the social demands made on him or her.

7. ____ The ethic of individual rights and justice is Carol Gilligan's term for the ethic that she believes is the basis for Kohlberg's theory and that she suggests is a more common perspective for males.

8. ____ Following the moratorium period, during which the adolescent experiments with different roles, values, and beliefs, he or she may then choose among alternatives and make commitments and gradually arrive at an integrated identity.

9. ____ Kohlberg and his colleagues found that responses of children under age ten reflect post-conventional moral reasoning based on self-interest and the tendency to avoid punishment and maximize personal gain.

10. ____ According to Baumrind, authoritative parents are demanding and unresponsive toward their children's needs or wishes.

11. ____ In Kohlberg's theory, the preconventional level is characterized by moral reasoning that reflects self-chosen ethical principles that are universally applied.

Check your answers and review any areas of weakness before going on to the next section.

Something to Think About

1. A popular and controversial topic in any discussion of raising children is the effect of day care on a child's development. Discussions like this can become quite heated, with people holding strong views on both sides of the debate. On the basis of what you have read in this chapter, what light could you shed on this controversial topic?

2. You may be planning to have a family one day if you haven't already done so. For most people this is quite a responsibility and a lot of work. Unlike many other areas in life, no formal training is available or required for the job of parent. You, however, are fortunate because you are taking an introductory psychology course and have learned a few things about child development. What advice would you give to people who are planning to have a family?

Check your answers and review any areas of weakness before doing the progress tests.

Progress Test 1

Review the complete chapter (including Concept Reviews and the boxed inserts), review all your study notes, and then test yourself on the following progress test. Check your answers. If you make a mistake, review your notes, review the relevant section of the study guide, and, if necessary, go back and read the appropriate part of your textbook.

1. When Thomas was conceived, he was a single fertilized egg called a(n)
   (a) zygote.   (c) fetus.
   (b) embryo.   (d) infant.

2. When Thomas was growing up, it became apparent that he was red-green color-blind. This disorder
   (a) is probably a sex-linked recessive characteristic.
   (b) is more common in males than females.
   (c) has to do with the 23rd pair of chromosomes.
   (d) is all of the above.

3. In her research, Dr. Joacim found that a pregnant mother's use of a certain chemical substance caused harm to the fetus. The chemical substance could be classified as
   (a) deoxyribonucleic acid.
   (b) a chromosome.
   (c) a phenotype.
   (d) a teratogen.

4. Kalbiar has dimples, which is a dominant characteristic determined by a single pair of genes. Kalbiar's genotype
   (a) could be a dimples/no dimples combination.
   (b) could be a no dimples/no dimples combination.
   (c) could be expressed phenotypically as no dimples, depending on the amount of sunlight she was exposed to.
   (d) could be all of the above.

5. When Mrs. Euland touched her newborn's lips, he produced an automatic response called the _____ reflex.
   (a) rooting   (c) grasping
   (b) sucking   (d) greedy

6. It has become apparent to Mr. and Mrs. Euland that their baby has a low activity level, tends to withdraw from new situations and people, and adapts to new experiences very gradually. The baby would be classified as a(n) _____ baby.
   (a) easy   (c) slow-to-warm-up
   (b) difficult   (d) securely attached

7. When two-year old Kerry was tested in the Strange Situation, she did not explore the environment even when her mother was present. She appeared very anxious, and she became extremely distressed when her mother left the room. Kerry is a(n)
   (a) insecurely attached infant.
   (b) securely attached infant.
   (c) conventional infant.
   (d) concrete operational infant.

8. When she was almost eleven months old, Jessica said "ba ba" when she pointed at her bottle and "ma ma" when she pointed at her Mom. Jessica is in the _____ stage of language development.
   (a) cooing   (c) one-word
   (b) babbling   (d) two-word

9. When Neil's mother hides his favorite toy under a blanket, Neil acts as though it no longer exists and makes no attempt to retrieve it. Neil is in Piaget's _____ stage.
   (a) sensorimotor
   (b) preoperational
   (c) concrete operational
   (d) formal operational

10. In the above example Neil's behavior suggests that he
   (a) has developed object permanence.
   (b) has not developed object permanence.
   (c) is capable of reversible thinking.
   (d) understands the principle of conservation.

11. Danielle has switched college majors four times and does not know what she wants to do after she gets her degree. Erikson would suggest that Danielle has not achieved
   (a) an integrated identity.
   (b) a sense of generativity.
   (c) the conventional level of moral reasoning.
   (d) the concrete operational stage of development.

12. Preconventional morality is to postconventional morality as _____ is to _____ .
   (a) social approval; ethical principle
   (b) self-interest; social approval
   (c) self-interest; ethical principle
   (d) social approval; self-interest

13. Gordon, a fifty-year-old lawyer, has just learned from his physician that he has only one year to live. According to Kübler-Ross, his first reaction to hearing the news is likely to be
   (a) "No, it's not possible, there's obviously been some mix-up, some terrible mistake."
   (b) "Life is not worth living any more."
   (c) "Why me? This is very unfair and makes me mad."
   (d) "Well, that's the way it goes, I guess."

14. According to the Application, a parenting style in which parents set clear standards for their children's behavior but are also responsive to the children's needs and wishes is called
   (a) authoritarian.
   (b) permissive-indulgent.
   (c) permissive-indifferent.
   (d) authoritative.

15. According to Culture and Human Behavior 9.1, infants typically sleep in their own bed and usually in a separate room from their parents in
   (a) all cultures.
   (b) all Western cultures.
   (c) the United States.
   (d) all Latin cultures.

Progress Test 2

After you have checked your understanding of the material in Progress Test 1 and have done a complete chapter review with special focus on any areas of weakness, you are ready to assess your knowledge of Progress Test 2. Check your answers. If you make a mistake, review your notes, the relevant section of the study guide, and, if necessary, the appropriate part of your textbook.

1. Dr. Strayer is conducting longitudinal research on factors that correlate with getting older. She is likely to find that
   (a) intellectual abilities decline sharply with age.
   (b) there is severe memory impairment as people reach late adulthood.
   (c) most people maintain their intellectual abilities as they age.
   (d) no matter how much older people practice their mental skills, they still do very poorly on intellectual tasks.

2. Mr. Danzig is a sixty-eight-year-old retired accountant. If he is typical of people his age, he is probably living
   (a) in his own home.
   (b) in a nursing home.
   (c) with his grown-up children.
   (d) in a mental health facility.

3. Darlene and Mike have been married for two years and have a nine-month-old infant. If they are like most young married couples, their level of marital satisfaction is probably
   (a) increasing dramatically.
   (b) increasing slightly.
   (c) declining.
   (d) the same as it was when they first got married.

4. Miguel is a twenty-five-year-old, college-educated middle-class engineer. Like his Mexican parents, he is a devout Catholic. If Miguel is like most people, he will probably marry someone who is
   (a) completely different from him in every way as long as she is Catholic.
   (b) very much like he is.
   (c) much older than he is.
   (d) much richer than he is.

5. Mrs. Grant is forty-nine years old and has recently ceased to menstruate. Mrs. Grant has experienced
   (a) moratorium.   (c) induction.
   (b) menopause.   (d) centration.

6. Late adulthood is to _____ as adolescence is to _____ .
   (a) ego integrity; generativity
   (b) generativity; intimacy
   (c) intimacy; ego integrity
   (d) ego integrity; integrated identity

7. Mr. Gates believes in law and order, obeys all rules and regulations, and has respect for authorities just because they are authorities. Mr. Gates is likely at Kohlberg's _____ level of moral reasoning.
   (a) conventional   (c) concrete operational
   (b) preconventional   (d) formal operational

8. Sixteen-year-old Jade is reading books about different religions and philosophies and is trying out different approaches to how one should live one's life. Jade is in Erikson's
   (a) moratorium period.
   (b) generativity stage.
   (c) ego integrity period.
   (d) formal operational stage.

9. The Atwells have two teenage children. If they are like most parents, their relationship with their kids
   (a) is very negative and getting worse.
   (b) is full of fights, arguments, anger, and hostility.
   (c) is just about as positive as it was when the children were younger.
   (d) was positive at first but has deteriorated as the children aged.

10. Marcel is researching a paper for his child developmental course and discovers the work of Lev Vygotsky. In summarizing Vygotsky's contribution to developmental psychology, Marcel is likely to note that the theorist emphasized
    (a) genetic factors.
    (b) clearly defined biological stages of cognitive development.
    (c) clearly defined biological stages of moral development.
    (d) social and cultural factors in cognitive development.

11. Kelly is five years old and has a good imagination. Recently, for example, she used a discarded box as a make-believe castle and made up a very interesting dialogue between the "king" and "queen" of her castle. This illustrates
    (a) centration.   (c) symbolic thought.
    (b) conservation.   (d) object permanence.

12. In the Strange Situation procedure, little Anthony used his mother as a safe base from which to explore the environment, showed distress when she left the room, and greeted her warmly when she returned. Anthony would be classified as
    (a) an difficult baby.
    (b) a securely attached baby.
    (c) an insecurely attached baby.
    (d) a slow-to-warm-up baby.

13. During a class debate on the issue of whether war is ever justified, Dominique argued that it is never justified because war involves killing people and killing people is against the law. Dominique is in the conventional stage of
    (a) Kohlberg's model of moral development.
    (b) Piaget's model of cognitive development.
    (c) Erikson's model of psychosocial development.
    (d) Chomsky's model of language development.

14. According to Critical Thinking 9.2, putting young children in a high-quality day-care facility
    (a) is detrimental to their physical health.
    (b) severely disrupts the attachment process.
    (c) has no detrimental effect on the children.
    (d) is detrimental to their psychological health.

15. According to the Application, psychologist Diana Baumrind has described a number of basic parenting styles. In her research, she found that children of _____ parents were likely to be moody, unhappy, fearful, withdrawn, unspontaneous, and irritable.

    (a) permissive-indulgent
    (b) permissive-indifferent
    (c) authoritative
    (d) authoritarian

Progress Test 3

After you have checked your understanding of the material in Progress Tests 1 and 2, and have done a complete chapter review with special focus on any areas of weakness, you are ready to further assess your knowledge on Progress Test 3. Check your answers. If you make a mistake, review your notes, the appropriate parts of the study guide, and if necessary, the relevant sections of your textbook.

1. Seventy-year-old Redner feels that his life has been full, interesting, and meaningful. According to Erikson, Redner has achieved a sense of

    (a) generativity.   (c) identity.
    (b) ego integrity.   (d) initiative.

2. Nine-year-old Adam has acquired the mental operations to comprehend such things as conservation and reversibility and can solve tangible problems in a logical manner. Adam is in Piaget's _____ stage of development.

    (a) sensorimotor   (c) concrete operational
    (b) preoperational   (d) formal operational

3. Piaget is to cognitive development as Erikson is to _____ development.

    (a) moral   (c) emotional
    (b) physical   (d) psychosocial

4. Despite the fact that he uses only one word utterances when he attempts to talk, one-year-old Vincent immediately does what he is told when his mother says, "Bring Mommy the teddy bear, Vincent." This suggests that

    (a) Vincent's comprehension vocabulary is much larger than his production vocabulary.
    (b) Vincent is in the embryonic stage of language development.
    (c) Vincent has a sex-linked recessive characteristic that has retarded his development.
    (d) Vincent's production vocabulary is much larger than his comprehension vocabulary.

5. When Kiran was born, his brain was about 25 percent of its adult weight; during infancy, it reached about 75 percent of its adult weight. This increase in weight is due to the fact that

    (a) millions of new neurons were formed daily during this period.
    (b) the number of dendrites increased dramatically and the axons of many neurons acquired myelin.
    (c) neurons grew bigger in size and the dendrites acquired a white fatty covering called myelin.
    (d) the number of new neurons increased dramatically and the original neurons increased in size and weight.

6. Nine months after conception, baby Tracy is born. The stages of her prenatal development, from first to last, were

    (a) embryonic, fetal, germinal.
    (b) fetal, embryonic, germinal.
    (c) germinal, embryonic, fetal.
    (d) germinal, fetal, embryonic.

7. Mrs. Hoff uses very distinct pronunciation, a simplified vocabulary, short sentences, a high pitch, and exaggerated intonation and expression whenever she interacts with her baby. This is an example of

    (a) motherese, or infant-directed speech.
    (b) a sex-linked recessive characteristic.
    (c) an insecurely attached mother.
    (d) cooing and babbling.

8. Michael has red-green color blindness, which is a sex-linked recessive characteristic, but his sister Eileen has normal color vision. It is likely that

    (a) Eileen has the recessive gene for red-green color blindness on each of her X chromosomes.
    (b) Michael has the recessive gene for red-green color blindness on each of his X chromosomes.
    (c) Eileen has the recessive gene for red-green color blindness on each of her Y chromosomes.
    (d) Michael has the recessive gene for red-green color blindness on the X chromosome of his XY chromosomes.

9. Which of the following utterances is two-year-old Quentin likely to have used during his recent birthday party?
   (a) "May I please have another cookie, Mama?
   (b) "ah-ah-ah, ba-ba-ba, ca-ca-ca!"
   (c) "Mama cookie."
   (d) "Quentin wants another cookie."

10. Gretchen is freckle free, which is a recessive characteristic determined by a single gene pair. She hopes that she will have a child who is also freckle free. In order for this to happen, her daughter will need to inherit the
    (a) genotype combination of no freckles/no freckles.
    (b) phenotype combination of freckles/no freckles.
    (c) genotype combination of freckles/no freckles.
    (d) genotype combination of freckles/freckles.

11. Young Allison doesn't understand that adding together one and three is the same as adding together three and one. Allison is demonstrating _____ and is in Piaget's _____ stage of development.
    (a) conservation; concrete operational
    (b) egocentrism; preoperational
    (c) centration; sensorimotor
    (d) irreversibility; preoperational

12. Fourteen-year-old Jason has the ability to reason abstractly and think logically even about hypothetical situations. Jason is in Piaget's _____ stage of cognitive development.
    (a) sensorimotor
    (b) preoperational
    (c) concrete operational
    (d) formal operational

13. Tasha is a newborn healthy infant. She has all
    (a) the neural connections she will ever have.
    (b) the dendrites she will ever have.
    (c) the myelin she will ever have.
    (d) the brain cells, or neurons, she will ever have.
    (e) of the above.

14. According to Culture and Human Behavior 9.3
    (a) the level of conflict between parents and adolescents tends to be higher in Chinese families compared with European-American families.

(b) although the level of conflict may vary, parent-adolescent conflict is a common dimension of family life in all cultures.
(c) regardless of which culture they belonged to, adolescents showed a high level of respect for parental authority, a strong sense of family obligation, and a keen desire for harmony within the family
(d) there is significantly less parent-adolescent conflict in individualistic cultures compared to collectivistic culture.

15. According to the Application, which of the following is *not* recommended for raising psychologically healthy children?
    (a) Work with your children's temperamental qualities.
    (b) Use induction to teach as you discipline.
    (c) Let your children know that you love them.
    (d) Strive to be an authoritarian parent.
    (e) Listen to your children.

Answers

Introduction: Your Life Story

1. (a) biological; environmental; social; cultural
   (b) attitudes, perceptions; personality
   (c) differ

2. (a) stages; critical periods; gradually
   (b) heredity; environment
   (c) genetic; environment; genetic; environment

Genetic Contributions to Your Life Story

1. (a) deoxyribonucleic acid; DNA; DNA
   (b) genes
   (c) 23; 23; 23

2. (a) genotype; phenotype
   (b) dominant
   (c) dominant
   (d) phenotype
   (e) recessive; recessive; recessive
   (f) recessive
   (g) potential

3. (a) recessive; sex
   (b) sex
   (c) females; males
   (d) females
   (e) males; males
   (f) sex-linked recessive
   (g) males; males; females

Graphic Organizer 1

Cell 1: dimples

Cell 2: dimples

Cell 3: dimples

Cell 4: no dimples

Prenatal Development

1. (a) zygotic
   (b) zygote; embryo

2. (a) eight; differentiation
   (b) amniotic; umbilical cord
   (c) placenta; placenta
   (d) teratogens

3. (a) fetal
   (b) third; reflexive
   (c) quickening; brain cells
   (d) sleep-wake
   (e) seventh
   (f) body fat

4. (a) developmental
   (b) nature (heredity); nurture (environment)
   (c) X; Y; X; X
   (d) embryo; fetus

Matching Exercise 1

1. prenatal stage
2. gene
3. developmental psychology
4. sex-linked recessive characteristics
5. teratogens
6. chromosome
7. recessive gene
8. germinal period (zygotic period)
9. embryo
10. recessive characteristics
11. sex chromosomes

True/False Test 1

1. T	5. T	9. F
2. T	6. T	10. T
3. T	7. F	11. F
4. F	8. T	

Development During Infancy and Childhood: Physical Ddevelopment

1. (a) physical; sensory
   (b) rooting; sucking; grasping

2. (a) least; 6; 12
   (b) easier
   (c) can
   (d) smell; smell; skin

3. (a) seven; eight
   (b) 25; 75
   (c) all
   (d) dendrites; myelin
   (e) sequence; average age

Development During Infancy and Childhood: Social and Personality Development

1. (a) physical; psychological; does not
   (b) behavioral; temperament

2. (a) easy, difficult, and slow to warm up
   (b) average
   (c) stable
   (d) genetic; biological; environmental

3. (a) emotional bond; physically; psychologically
   (b) multiple
   (c) secure; insecure

4. (a) Strange Situation
   (b) stranger
   (c) securely
   (d) insecurely; ignore; avoid; hard
   (e) securely; insecure; securely; insecurely

Development During Infancy and Childhood: Language Development

1. (a) three
   (b) Noam Chomsky; grammar
   (c) can; lost

2. (a) motherese
   (b) motherese, "baby talk"
   (c) infant-directed speech (motherese)

3. (a) coo; babble; babble
   (b) words; comprehension; production
   (c) one-word
   (d) two-word
   (e) two-word
   (f) two-and-a-half; school

4. (a) human face
   (b) 100 percent
   (c) easy
   (d) secure

Matching Exercise 2

1. infancy
2. Strange Situation
3. sucking reflex

4. slow-to-warm-up temperament
5. motherese (infant-directed speech)
6. cooing and babbling stage
7. attachment
8. comprehension vocabulary
9. insecure attachment
10. two-word stage

True/False Test 2

1. F	5. T	9. F
2. T	6. T	10. T
3. F	7. F	
4. T	8. T	

Development During Infancy and Childhood: Cognitive Development

1. (a) cognitive
   (b) actively
   (c) birth; two; two; seven; seven; eleven; adolescence; adulthood
   (d) qualitatively
   (e) assimilate; accommodate

2. (a) actions; actions
   (b) object permanence
   (c) object permanence; schemas

3. (a) operations
   (b) symbolic
   (c) symbolic
   (d) egocentrism, irreversibility; centration
   (e) conservation

4. (a) egocentric; reverse; conservation
   (b) hypothetical; abstract

5. (a) abstract; hypothetical
   (b) abstract; adults

6. (a) has
   (b) underestimated; motor-skill; cognitive
   (c) visual; manual; more

7. (a) challenged; abstract-hypothetical
   (b) universal
   (c) information-processing; continuous

8. (a) social; cultural
   (b) Lev Vygotsky; social; cultural
   (c) skills
   (d) cognitive

9. (a) underestimated
   (b) concrete operational
   (c) object permanence
   (d) conservation

(e) assimilating
(f) schema
(g) formal

Matching Exercise 3

1. symbolic thought
2. cognitive processes
3. object permanence
4. formal operational stage
5. Jean Piaget
6. information-processing model of cognitive development
7. schemas
8. sensorimotor stage
9. egocentrism

True/False Test 3

1. T	4. T	7. F
2. F	5. F	8. F
3. F	6. T	9. F

Adolescence

1. (a) 12; adult
   (b) positive; advice
   (c) does; friends and peers
   (d) reinforce

2. (a) values, beliefs; does
   (b) cognitive; concrete; abstract
   (c) fixed; internalized
   (d) evaluate; self-definition
   (e) identity; self-concepts

3. (a) psychosocial
   (b) psychosocial conflict
   (c) identity versus identity diffusioin; moratorium
   (d) supported
   (e) adolescence; adult

4. (a) cognitive
   (b) Lawrence Kohlberg; stages
   (c) levels; level; stages
   (d) preconventional; conventional; postconventional
   (e) postconventional; stages; conventional

5. (a) male; males; females
   (b) male; females
   (c) individual; males
   (d) women
   (e) does not

6. (a) culture; cultures
   (b) group; collectivistic

Graphic Organizer 2

1. Piaget: formal operational stage; Kohlberg: postconventional level, stage 6

2. Piaget: preoperational stage; Kohlberg: preconventional level, stage 1

3. Piaget: concrete operational stage; Kohlberg: preconventional level, stage 2

4. Piaget: concrete operational stage; Kohlberg: conventional level, stage 4

Adult Development

1. (a) genetic
   (b) menopause
   (c) environmental
   (d) time

2. (a) early; middle; generativity
   (b) Female; male
   (c) early; a later
   (d) similar to

3. (a) strengthen; decline
   (b) identity
   (c) warm; positive
   (d) declines; rises

4. (a) increased; 30
   (b) divorces; child-free; monogamous
   (c) social

5. (a) young (early); third
   (b) are different; more
   (c) multiple roles; quality

Late Adulthood and Aging

1. (a) 72; 79; do
   (b) is not
   (c) more; fewer

2. (a) increase; slight
   (b) mental; can
   (c) educated; physical; mental

3. (a) activity
   (b) ego integrity
   (c) ego integrity; despair
   (d) life review

The Final Chapter: Dying and Death

1. (a) show; not all
   (b) middle; late
   (c) deny; anger; bargain; depressed; accept
   (d) does not

(e) resignation; bitterness; anger; external; inward

2. (a) 1; 1
   (b) a later
   (c) ego integrity
   (d) anger
   (e) identity
   (f) similar to
   (g) increase

Graphic Organizer 3

1. Lev Vygotsky
2. Mary D. Salter Ainsworth
3. Noam Chomsky
4. Renée Baillargeon
5. Erik Erikson
6. K. Warner Schaie
7. Jean Piaget
8. Lawrence Kohlberg

Matching Exercise 4

1. induction
2. menopause
3. ethic of care and responsibility
4. permissive parenting style
5. moratorium period
6. adolescence
7. conventional level
8. middle adulthood
9. identity
10. activity theory of aging
11. generativity
12. Lawrence Kohlberg

True/False Test 4

1. T	5. T	9. F
2. T	6. T	10. F
3. T	7. T	11. F
4. F	8. T	

Something to Think About

1. Most psychologists today agree that the *quality* of the child-care arrangements is the key factor in promoting secure attachment in early child-

hood and preventing problems in later childhood. In fact, many studies have found that children who experience high-quality day care tend to be more sociable, better adjusted, and more academically competent than children who experience poor-quality day care. In addition, some researchers have found that grade school children enrolled in high-quality day care from infancy experience no negative effects of their day-care experience. Research in Sweden has supported these findings.

High-quality day care is characterized by a number of key factors: caregivers should be warm and responsive, developmentally appropriate activities and a variety of play materials should be available, caregivers should have some training and education in child development, low staff turnover is important, and the ratio of caregivers to children should be low.

2. A short discussion of the various stages of cognitive, psychosocial, and moral development would be appropriate. Raising psychologically healthy children is possible if parents adopt some of the strategies suggested by the experts. Psychologist Diana Baumrind has described three basic parenting styles: authoritarian, permissive, and authoritative. Research has shown that the authoritative style produces the best results. Can parents learn to be authoritative in their parenting style? The Application has a number of practical suggestions: let your children know that you love them, listen to your children, use induction to teach as you discipline, work with your children's temperamental qualities, and understand your child's age-related cognitive abilities and limitations.

Although all children inherit genetic predispositions from both parents, research has shown that environmental factors, such as the social and cultural influences, educational experiences, and parenting style have very powerful effects on a child's development.

Progress Test 1

1. a	6. c	11. a
2. d	7. a	12. c
3. d	8. c	13. a
4. a	9. a	14. d
5. b	10. b	15. c

Progress Test 2

1. c	6. d	11. c
2. a	7. a	12. b
3. c	8. a	13. a
4. b	9. c	14. c
5. b	10. d	15. d

Progress Test 3

1. b	6. c	11. d
2. c	7. a	12. d
3. d	8. d	13. d
4. a	9. c	14. b
5. b	10. a	15. d

CHAPTER

10

Gender and Sexuality

| PREVIEW | Reading the section below first will give you a general sense of the chapter's contents and an initial introduction to some of the major concepts and terms. This will prime you for what you are about to read and help you to develop a "cognitive map" that will guide your study of the material in this chapter. Likewise, reading the **preview questions** at the beginning of each major section will improve your ability to understand, learn, and retain the information. |

CHAPTER 10 . . . AT A GLANCE

To help you distinguish between sex and gender, the text first defines all the relevant terms *sex, gender, gender roles, gender identity, sexual orientation,* and *gender-role stereotype*. Similarities and differences in the cognitive abilities and sexual attitudes and behaviors of men and women are discussed. Gender-role development and the influence of social and cultural factors are examined. Two theories of gender-role development—social learning theory and gender schema theory—explain current thinking about how gender roles develop.

Human sexuality is discussed next. The four phases of the human sexual response cycle are presented, and sexual motivation in both humans and other animals is explored. Sexual orientation appears to develop at an early age, and genetics and brain structure may be involved. During early and middle childhood, children become increasingly aware of their own bodies and increasingly curious about sexual matters. At puberty, adolescents reach sexual maturity, when they must deal with many physical changes as well as romantic and sexual relationships. Details of human sexuality in early, middle, and late adulthood are presented, including the frequency and type of sexual behavior and people's fantasies about sexual activity.

The chapter ends with a discussion of various sexual disorders and problems, including the paraphilias and gender identity disorder. The most common types of sexual dysfunctions in men and women are described. Sexually transmitted diseases (STDs) and AIDS are discussed.

Introduction: Gender and Sexuality

Preview Questions

Consider the following questions as you study this section of the chapter.

- How is sex defined, and how does it differ from gender?
- How do the terms *gender role, gender identity,* and *sexual orientation* differ in meaning?

*Read the section "Introduction: Gender and Sexuality" and **write** your answers to the following:*

1. (a) Sex refers to _____ determined physical characteristics, such as differences in genetic composition and reproductive anatomy and function; gender refers to the _____ and _____ meanings that are associated with maleness and femaleness.

   (b) Gender roles consist of the _____ , _____ , and personality traits that a given culture designates as either masculine or feminine; gender identity refers to a given person's _____ sense of being either male or female; and sexual orientation refers to whether a person's _____ and _____ attraction is directed toward members of the opposite sex, the same sex, or both sexes.

   (c) Often, without our awareness, our behavior, attitudes, and aspirations have been strongly influenced by the gender-role expectations of our particular _____ . By the time most people reach adulthood, both _____ and _____ are well established, but it is important to note that these can be independent of each other.

Gender Stereotypes and Gender Roles

Preview Questions

Consider the following questions as you study this section of the chapter.

- What are gender-role stereotypes?
- How do men and women differ in terms of personality characteristics, cognitive abilities, and sexual attitudes and behaviors?

*Read the section "Gender Stereotypes and Gender Roles" and **write** your answers to the following:*

1. (a) The beliefs that people have about the typical characteristics and behaviors of each sex are referred to as gender-role _____ ; in our culture, these are very different for men and women.

   (b) Women are thought (expected) to be more _____ , _____ , and patient than men; men are thought (expected) to be more _____ , _____ , and mechanically minded than women.

   (c) Research has shown that there is a high degree of _____ (agreement/disagreement) on the characteristics associated with each sex across different cultures; in general, the characteristics associated with _____ (males/females) tended to be stronger and more active than the characteristics associated with _____ (males/females).

2. (a) In many aspects of behavior, including social, personality, and cognitive aspects, men and women are very _____ (different/similar); men and women _____ (do/do not) tend to perceive themselves as being diametrically opposite.

(b) Some significant _____ between the sexes do exist, but these are averages, and the causes can't be easily specified.

3. (a) On *most* personality characteristics, there _____ (are/are no) significant average differences between men and women.

(b) Women tend to be more _____ (assertive/nurturant) than men and men more _____ (assertive/nurturant) than women; in general, _____ (men/women) tend to manifest behaviors that can be described as socially sensitive, friendly, and concerned with others' welfare, whereas _____ (men/women) tend to manifest behaviors that can be described as dominant, controlling, and independent.

4. (a) On most cognitive abilities, there _____ (are/are no) significant differences between males and females.

(b) On tests of verbal fluency, reading comprehension, spelling, and, especially, basic writing skills, _____ consistently score much higher than _____ .

(c) On some, but not all, tests of spatial skills, _____ outscore _____ .

(d) Although the average difference is very small, _____ do slightly better than _____ on tests of mathematical ability; although this gender gap has been steadily narrowing over the last several decades, twice as many _____ as _____ score in the top 3 percent on math ability tests.

(e) Some researchers believe that _____ differences between the sexes, such as the female advantage on verbal skills and the male advantage on spatial skills, are due to sex differences in brain function or organization.

5. (a) A meta-analysis of over 170 previous studies comparing males and females on a wide variety of sexual attitudes and behaviors found that men and women were very _____ (similar/dissimilar) on many dimensions.

(b) The analysis also found that _____ had more permissive sexual attitudes and more sexual partners, experienced their first intercourse at an earlier average age, and masturbated more than _____ .

(c) Even though men and women are more _____ than _____ , there is a vast difference between growing up female and growing up male in most societies, including American society.

Gender-Role Development: Blue Bears and Pink Bunnies

Preview Questions

Consider the following questions as you study this section of the chapter.

- What role does gender play in our culture?
- How are boys and girls treated differently, and what gender differences develop during childhood?
- How do social learning theory and gender schema theory explain the development of gender roles?

*Read the section "Gender-Role Development: Blue Bears and Pink Bunnies" and **write** your answers to the following:*

1. (a) Even though male and female infants are _____ (totally different/virtually indistinguishable) in terms of size, appearance, or behavior, they are treated _____ (very differently/the same) from the moment of birth on.

(b) The fact that people don't dress their male and female children identically illustrates the persuasiveness and force of _____ and _____ expectations.

(c) When one-year-olds are dressed identically, adults cannot tell male and female infants apart, but it appears that

_____ can; even at that age they may already be sensitive to subtle gender differences in behavior and mannerisms, which suggests that gender awareness emerges at a very early age.

2. (a) Roughly between the ages of

_____ and _____ , children can identify themselves and other children as boys or girls without understanding that sex is determined by physical characteristics; they tend, instead, to identify the sexes in terms of attributes such as hair style, clothing, and activities.

(b) From about the age of 18 months to 2 years,

_____ in behavior begin to emerge, and they become more pronounced throughout early childhood.

(c) Roughly between the ages of _____ and _____ , preschoolers start acquiring gender-role stereotypes for toys, clothing, household objects, games, and work; from about the age of

_____ , there are consistent gender differences in preferred toys and play activities that continue throughout childhood.

(d) Throughout the remainder of childhood, boys and girls play primarily with members of _____ (their own/the opposite) sex; boys tend to play in _____ (larger/smaller) groups, whereas girls tend to establish and maintain _____ with one or two friends.

(e) In terms of belief in gender-role stereotypes; _____ (children/adults) are far more rigid than _____ (children/adults); as _____ (girls/

boys) grow older, they become even more flexible in their views of sex-appropriate activities and attributes, but _____ (girls/boys) become even less flexible.

3. (a) Based on the principles of learning, social learning theory contends that gender roles and gender-appropriate behavior are learned through _____ ,

_____ , and modeling by parents and caregivers.

(b) Research findings suggest that the effects of parental socialization in many areas of gender differences are relatively

_____ (large/small); for the most part, parents treat their male and female children rather _____ (differently/similarly).

(c) Children also learn gender differences when they observe and then imitate the sex-typed behavior of significant adults, older children, people on television, or characters in children's book; this is called _____ .

4. (a) Gender schema theory was developed by

_____ . Although it incorporates some aspects of social learning theory, it approaches gender-role development from a more strongly _____ perspective; children actively develop mental categories (or schemas) for masculinity and femininity.

(b) According to gender schema theory, children, like many adults, look at the world through "gender lenses"; gender schemas influence how people pay attention to,

_____ , _____ , and _____ gender-relevant behavior. Children readily _____ new information into their existing gender schemas.

(c) Gender schemas also include a broad range of more abstract or metaphorical qualities and attributes such as associating "gentle-

ness" with _____ and "tough-
ness" with _____ .

(d) Beyond the concrete associations children might have learned through _____ or _____ , even preschool-ers seem to be aware of the underlying meanings of gender stereotypes.

5. Read the following and write the correct term in the space provided:

(a) During a sex education talk, the teacher describes the differences in genetic composi-tion and reproductive anatomy that are bio-logically determined characteristics that define a person as being male or female. The teacher is describing _____ .

(b) Sheila contends that children actively devel-op cognitive categories for masculinity and femininity and that these mental represen-tations influence how children perceive, interpret, and remember relevant aspects of what is appropriate for boys and girls. Sheila's views are most consistent with _____ theory.

(c) Liam describes his girlfriend as gentle, car-ing, empathetic, and very feminine. Liam is referring to his girlfriend's

_____ .

(d) Pat and Les are fraternal twins. Pat consis-tently scores higher than Les on tests of ver-bal fluency, reading comprehension, and basic writing skills; Les outscores Pat on spatial skills and tests of mathematical abil-ity. It is very probable that Pat is _____ (male/female) and Les is _____ (male/female).

(e) As part of an experiment investigating gen-der-role development, Dr. Beach decides to dress a number of male and female one-year-olds in identical clothes. It is very like-ly that adults _____ (will/will not) be able to tell male and female infants apart but that other one-year-olds _____ (will/will not) be able to do so.

(f) Frank is very fit and works out in the gym almost every day. He is considered by many to be very masculine, especially by his boyfriend. Frank's sense of maleness is his _____ , and his attraction to members of the same sex is his

_____ .

Review of Terms, Concepts, and Names 1

Use the terms in this list to complete the Matching Test, then to help you answer the True/False items correctly.

sex	gender-role stereotypes
gender	social learning theory
gender roles	Sandra Bem
gender identity	gender schema theory
sexual orientation	schemas

Matching Exercise

Match the appropriate term/name with its definition or description.

1. _____ American psychologist who has conducted extensive research on sex roles and gender identity; proposed gender schema theory to explain gender-role development.

2. _____ The cultural, social, and psychological meanings that are associated with masculinity and femininity.

3. _____ The direction of a person's emotional and erotic attraction toward mem-bers of the opposite sex, the same sex, or both sexes.

4. _____ The beliefs and expectations that people hold about the typical characteris-tics, preferences, and behavior of men and women.

5. _____ In gender schema theory, the mental categories or representations of masculinity and femininity.

True/False Test

Indicate whether each statement is true or false by placing T or F in the blank space next to each item.

1. ____ Social learning theory contends that gen-der roles are acquired through the basic processes of learning, including reinforcement, punishment, and modeling.

2. ____ Sex refers to (1) the biological category of male or female as defined by physical differences in genetic composition and in reproductive anatomy and function and (2) the behavioral manifestations of the sexual urge; sexual intercourse.

3. ____ Gender identity refers to the behaviors, attitudes, and personality traits that are designated as either masculine or feminine in a given culture.

4. ____ Gender schema theory states that gender-role development is influenced by the formation of schemas, or mental representations, of masculinity and femininity.

5. ____ Gender roles refer to people's psychological sense of being male or female.

> Check your answers and review any areas of weakness before going on to the next section.

Human Sexuality

Preview Questions

Consider the following questions as you study this section of the chapter.

- What factors are involved in human sexuality?
- What are the four stages of the human sexual response?
- How does sexual motivation differ for lower and higher animals?
- What biological factors are involved in sexual motivation?

*Read the section "Human Sexuality" and **write** your answers to the following:*

1. (a) The human sexual response cycle was first mapped by sex researcher pioneers _____ and _____, who, in the name of science, observed hundreds of people engage in more than 10,000 episodes of sexual activity in their laboratory; their findings indicated that the human sexual response can be described as a cycle with four stages.

(b) The beginning of sexual arousal, which can occur in response to sexual fantasies or other sexually arousing stimuli, physical contact with another person, or masturbation, is called the _____ phase; this stage is accompanied by a variety of bodily changes in anticipation of sexual interaction.

(c) In the second phase, physical arousal builds as pulse and breathing rates continue to increase; this is called the _____ phase. During the first and second stages, the degree of arousal may fluctuate up and down.

(d) The third and shortest phase of the sexual response cycle, during which blood pressure and heart rate reach their peak, is called the _____ phase; both men (many of whom experience one intense orgasm) and women (many of whom are capable of multiple orgasms) describe the subjective experience of _____ in similar and very positive terms.

(e) Arousal slowly subsides and returns to normal levels during the _____ phase. At this point, males are incapable of having another erection or orgasm; this is called a _____ period, and it varies in length but tends to increase with age.

2. (a) In most animals, sexual behavior is biologically determined and triggered by _____ changes in the female; during the cyclical period known as _____, a female animal is fertile and receptive to male sexual advances.

(b) As you go up the evolutionary scale, moving from relatively simple to more sophisticated animals, sexual behavior becomes less _____ determined and more subject to learning and _____ influences.

(c) Sexual behavior also becomes less limited to the goal of _____ ; in some primate species, sexual interaction serves important _____ functions, defining and cementing relationships among members of the group.

3. (a) In humans, sexual behavior is not limited to the goal of _____ or to a female's fertile period. Although a woman's fertility is regulated by monthly hormonal cycles, these hormonal changes _____ (do/do not) seem to have an effect on a female's sexual motivation.

(b) Even when a woman's ovaries, which produce the female sex hormone _____ , are surgically removed or stop functioning during menopause, there is little or no drop in sexual interest.

(c) In many nonhuman female mammals, removal of the ovaries results in _____ (a complete/no) loss of interest in sexual activity.

(d) In male animals, removal of the testes (castration) typically _____ (has no effect on/causes a steep drop in) sexual activity and interest; castration causes a significant decrease in levels of _____ , the hormone responsible for male sexual development.

(e) When human males experience lowered levels of _____ due to illness or castration, a similar drop in sexual interest tends to occur, although the effects vary among individuals.

(f) The hormone _____ is also involved in female sexual motivation; when levels are abnormally low, sexual interest often wanes or diminishes.

Sexual Orientation

Preview Questions

Consider the following questions as you study this section of the chapter.

- What does sexual orientation refer to?
- Why is sexual orientation sometimes difficult to define?
- What factors have been associated with sexual orientation?

Read the section "Sexual Orientation" and **write** *your answers to the following:*

1. (a) Sexual orientation refers to whether a person is sexually aroused by members of the same sex, the opposite sex, or both sexes; a _____ is sexually attracted to individuals of the other sex, a _____ to individuals of the same sex, and a _____ to individuals of both sexes.

(b) Technically, the term *homosexual* can be applied to either males or females; however, females usually use the term _____ and males use the term _____ to describe their sexual orientation.

(c) There _____ (is/is not) always a perfect correspondence between a particular person's sexual identity, sexual desires, and sexual behaviors.

2. (a) Psychologists and other researchers cannot say with certainty why people are homosexual or bisexual; evidence from twin studies suggests that _____ plays a role in determining a homosexual orientation.

(b) While studying gay twins, researchers found that the closer the degree of _____ relationship, the more likely it was that both brothers would be homosexual; both brothers are more likely to be homosexual if they are _____ twins than if they are _____ twins.

(c) Because only about half the identical twins were both homosexual, it's clear that _____ alone cannot explain sexual orientation.

3. (a) Neurobiologist Simon LeVay discovered a small but significant difference between heterosexuals and homosexuals in a tiny cluster of neurons in the _____, which is known to be involved in sexual behavior; in male homosexuals and female heterosexuals, the cluster was only half the size as in heterosexual men.

(b) LeVay notes that there is no way of knowing if this difference in brain structure is the cause or the result of homosexual behavior in men. In general, the only conclusion we can draw from these studies is that some _____ and _____ factors are correlated with a homosexual orientation, but more definitive research is needed before causality can be determined.

4. Researchers investigating the effects of early life experience on sexual orientation concluded that:

(a) Homosexuality is _____ (due to/not due to) an unpleasant early heterosexual experience, such as being sexually abused during childhood by a member of the opposite sex.

(b) Homosexuality _____ (is/is not) the result of an abnormal relationship between the parents and the child, such as having a father who is an inadequate male role model or having an overly dominant mother.

(c) Research suggests that there _____ (are/are no) consistent differences between homosexual and heterosexual adults in their

patterns of early experiences; that is, in both, sexual orientation appears to be determined before adolescence and long before the beginning of sexual activity.

(d) Some researchers now believe that sexual orientation is established as early as age _____ and, once established, _____ (is/is not) highly resistant to change. Furthermore, evidence suggests that male and female homosexuals are _____ (more/less) likely to have followed the typical pattern of gender-specific behaviors.

5. (a) Psychological, biological, social, and cultural factors are undoubtedly involved in determining sexual orientation; however, researchers are _____ (able/still unable) to pinpoint exactly what those factors are and how they interact.

(b) Homosexuality in itself _____ (is still/is no longer) considered a sexual disorder by clinical psychologists and psychiatrists.

(c) Like heterosexuals, gays and lesbians can be found in every _____ and at every _____ level, and many are involved in long-term, committed, and caring relationships.

(d) Children who are raised by gay or lesbian parents _____ (are/are not) as well adjusted as children who are raised by heterosexual parents; also, they _____ (are/are not) more likely to be gay or lesbian in adulthood than are children who are raised by heterosexual parents.

Sexual Behavior over the Lifespan

Preview Questions

Consider the following questions as you study this section of the chapter.

- What elementary forms of sexuality appear during infancy and childhood?
- What is puberty, and what are primary and secondary sex characteristics?
- What factors influence the onset of menarche, and what are the effects of the timing of puberty?
- What characterizes the sexual relationships that develop in adolescence?
- What characterizes the sexual behavior patterns of adults, and what are some important aspects of sexual relationships in late adulthood?

Read the section "Sexual Behavior over the Lifespan" and **write** *your answers to the following:*

1. (a) Sexuality does not just magically appear with the onset of puberty during adolescence; the capacity of the human body to show reflexive sexual responses is present at _____ .

   (b) Infants as young as _____ or _____ months of age will smile or coo as they engage in genital play, fondling their own genitals in a very elementary form of masturbation; by the _____ birthday, genital play is a common occurrence, especially when the little one is being bathed.

   (c) Signs of sexual activation or genital play _____ (should/should not) cause alarm in the parent because such behaviors reflect _____ (abnormal/normal) developmental patterns.

   (d) During early childhood, roughly ages _____ to _____ , the child often becomes increasingly curious about his or her own body and its functions.

   (e) Young children also become keenly attuned to parental _____ , especially if they are negative, concerning nudity, genital touching, and genital exploration. Gradually, the young child begins to notice the anatomical differences between males and females.

   (f) With each advancing year from age _____ onward, children tend to show increased interest in exploring sexual topics; by about age _____ , most children are aware that certain behaviors produce erotic feelings, and sexual curiosity continues to rise during the late childhood years.

2. (a) Puberty is the physical process of attaining _____ maturation and _____ capacity that begins during the early adolescent years.

   (b) Internally, puberty involves the development of the _____ sex characteristics, which involve the sex organs that are directly involved in reproduction (the uterus in females and the testes in males).

   (c) Externally, development of the _____ sex characteristics, which are not directly involved in reproduction, signals increasing sexual maturity. These include changes in height, weight, and body shape, appearance of body hair, voice changes, and in girls, breast development.

   (d) The period of marked acceleration in weight and height gains, commonly called the _____ , along with sexual maturation, occurs about two years earlier in females than in males.

   (e) A female's first menstrual period, which is termed _____ , typically occurs around age 12 or 13 but may take place as early as age 9 or 10 or as late as age 16 or 17; for boys, the _____ typically begin enlarging around age eleven or twelve, but the process can begin before age nine or after age fourteen.

   (f) Genetics and environmental factors such as nutrition, health, body size, and degree of physical activity all can influence the timing of puberty; well-nourished and healthy children begin puberty _____ (earlier/later) than less healthy or poorly nourished children; heavy children begin puberty _____ (earlier/later) than lean children; and girls involved in physically demanding athletic activities can experience delays in _____ of up to two years beyond the average age.

3. (a) For _____ (boys/girls), early maturation is generally advantageous in terms of popularity, social maturity, academic achievement, and athletics; for _____ (boys/girls), early maturation is accompanied by negative feelings about their body image and pubertal changes, lack of factual information concerning development, and embarrassment due to unwanted attention from older males.

(b) During early and middle adolescence, the physical changes of puberty prime the adolescent's interest in sexuality, but _____ and _____ factors significantly influence when, why, and how sexual behavior is initiated.

(c) With increasing age, there is a corresponding increase in the number of adolescents who have engaged in such sexual activities as kissing or petting; between the ages of _____ and _____ , there is a sharp increase in the cumulative percentage of those who have had sexual intercourse, and by age _____ approximately 70 percent of females and 80 percent of males have lost their virginity.

(d) It is often assumed that a key role in the sexual socialization of adolescent children is played by _____ , but there is usually little direct communication regarding sexual matters; the adolescent's _____ gradually replaces his or her _____ as a source of sexual information.

4. (a) Most men and women develop an intimate relationship with another adult during their _____ ; they are part of a couple (either married or living with someone) by age _____ .

(b) Today's young adults have more sex partners than 30- to 50-year-olds because the latter group tended to have their first sexual experience when they _____ .

(c) Young adults today tend to become sexually active at a(n) _____ (earlier/later) age and are marrying at a(n) _____ (earlier/later) age.

(d) The vast majority of people (about 80 percent) had either one or no sexual partner in the previous year because they are _____ or _____ .

5. (a) The media image of frequent, frolicking sex as normal _____ (does/does not) reflect what is going on in American bedrooms.

(b) Married or cohabiting couples have the _____ (least/most) active sex lives.

(c) The vast majority of people reported that they _____ (are/are not) physically and emotionally satisfied with their sexual relationships.

6. (a) The most practiced, and nearly universal, sexual activity among heterosexual couples is _____ .

(b) With the exception of having sex with a(n) _____ , at least 90 percent of men _____ (agreed/disagreed) with women about the most unappealing sexual practices.

7. (a) Among older people, sexual interest and potency _____ (does/does not) disappear.

(b) Older men and women take longer to become sexually aroused and achieve

_____ . Despite physical changes (slower vaginal lubrication and less firm erections), _____ (some/most/all) sexually active senior adults report a high level of sexual enjoyment.

(c) For older women, the major obstacle to enjoying sexual relations is the

_____ .

(d) For older adults who have lost their spouse through death or divorce, _____ serves to fill the need for sexual and emotional intimacy as well as companionship; these are needs that continue throughout the lifespan.

8. Read the following and write the correct term in the space provided.

(a) Mary and her husband James have just shared a fulfilling sexual experience. Unlike Mary, James is not likely to be able to experience another orgasm for a period of time; this is called the _____ period.

(b) Mrs. Jacobson had her ovaries removed because of cancer and is now in perfect health. As a result of the operation, the level of the female sex hormone will _____ ; the level of her interest in sexual activity will _____ (increase/decrease/stay the same).

(c) Dr. Jamison surgically removed the testes of an experimental laboratory rat. It is very probable that the rat will experience a(n) _____ in sexual activity and interest.

(d) Hamish, a twenty-five-year-old medical student, is heterosexual; his brother Stuart, a twenty-one-year-old philosophy major, is homosexual. The two brothers differ in their

_____ .

(e) When she was almost thirteen, Manjit experienced her first menstrual period. She has reached _____ .

(f) Adam is fifteen and has gained both height and weight, some body hair, and a deeper voice during the past year. These changes are referred to as _____ sex characteristics.

(g) Mr. and Mrs. Dempster are in their seventies and enjoy good health and an active lifestyle. If they are like many adults in their age range, they are very _____ (unlikely/likely) to have an interest in sex.

(h) Twelve-year-old Sonia is taller than most of her classmates, has been wearing a bra for more than a year and a half, and had her first menstrual period when she was only ten. Compared with late-maturing girls, Sonia is likely to have had some _____ (positive/negative) experiences related to her early maturation.

Review of Terms, Concepts, and Names 2

Use the terms in this list to complete the Matching Test, then to help you answer the True/False items correctly.

William H. Masters	heterosexual
Virginia E. Johnson	homosexual
excitement phase	bisexual
plateau phase	puberty
orgasm	primary sex
resolution phase	characteristics
refractory period	secondary sex
estrus	characteristics
estrogen	adolescent growth spurt
testosterone	menarche
sexual orientation	

Matching Exercise

Match the appropriate term/name with its definition or description.

1. _____ American behavioral scientist who, along with William H. Masters, conducted pioneering research in the field of human sexuality and sex therapy.

2. _____ The second stage in the human sexual response cycle in which physical arousal builds as pulse and breathing rates con-

tinue to rise; the penis becomes fully erect, the testes enlarge, the clitoris withdraws but remains sensitive, the vaginal entrance tightens, and vaginal lubrication continues.

3. _____ The stage of adolescence in which an individual reaches sexual maturity and becomes physiologically capable of sexual reproduction.

4. _____ A female's first menstrual period, which occurs during puberty.

5. _____ A person who is sexually attracted to individuals of the other sex.

6. _____ Period of accelerated growth during puberty, involving rapid increases in height and weight.

7. _____ For a male, a period of time following orgasm during which he is incapable of having another erection or orgasm.

8. _____ A person who is attracted to individuals of the same sex.

9. _____ American physician who, along with Virginia E. Johnson, conducted pioneering research in the field of human sexuality and sex therapy.

10. _____ The first stage in the human sexual response cycle that marks the beginning of sexual arousal and can occur in response to sexual fantasies or other sexually arousing stimuli, physical contact with another person, or masturbation.

True/False Test

Indicate whether each statement is true or false by placing T or F in the blank space next to each item.

1. ____ Secondary sex characteristics are the sexual organs that are directly involved in reproduction, such as the uterus, ovaries, penis, and testicles.

2. ____ Estrus refers to the cyclical period during which a female nonhuman animal is fertile and receptive to male sexual advances.

3. ____ The fourth stage of the sexual response cycle, during which both sexes tend to experience a warm physical glow and sense of well-being and arousal returns to normal, is called the resolution phase.

4. ____ A bisexual is sexually attracted to individuals of both sexes.

5. ____ Testosterone, the female sex hormone produced by the ovaries, influences a woman's monthly reproductive cycle.

6. ____ Orgasm is the third and shortest phase of the sexual response cycle, during which blood pressure and heart rate reach their peak and muscles in the vaginal walls and uterus contract rhythmically, as do the muscles in and around the penis as the male ejaculates.

7. ____ Primary sex characteristics are sexual characteristics that develop during puberty and are not directly involved in reproduction but differentiate between the sexes, such as male facial hair and female breast development.

8. ____ Estrogen, the male sex hormone produced by the testes, is responsible for male sexual development.

9. ____ Sexual orientation refers to the cultural, social, and psychological meanings associated with masculinity or femininity.

Check your answers and review any areas of weakness before going on to the next section.

Sexual Disorders and Problems

Preview Questions

Consider the following questions as you study this section of the chapter.

- What are sexual dysfunctions, and what characterizes these disorders?
- What are the paraphilias, and how do they differ from dysfunctions?
- What is gender identity disorder?
- What are sexually transmitted diseases (STDs), and why do they pose serious health problems?
- What effects does the HIV virus have on the body, and who is most at risk for AIDS?

Read the section "Sexual Disorders and Problems" and write your answers to the following:

1. (a) Feeling tired, being grumpy with your partner, drinking too much alcohol, and being

anxious (including being anxious over your sexual performance) are all factors that can interfere with sexual

_____ ; such disruptions in sexual response _____ (are/are not) temporary.

(b) Sexual dysfunctions are consistent disturbances in sexual desire, arousal, or orgasm that cause _____ distress and interpersonal difficulties.

2. (a) A sexual dysfunction characterized by little or no sexual desire is called

_____ disorder. It is important to keep in mind that the frequency with which people want to have sex varies over the lifespan and according to personal preference.

(b) More extreme is a disorder in which a person actively avoids genital contact with a sexual partner because of extreme anxiety, fear, or disgust over sexual contact; this is called _____ disorder. Either men or women can chronically experience genital pain before, during, or after intercourse, a condition called _____ .

(c) When a male experiences a recurrent inability to achieve or maintain an erection, it is called male _____ ; at the opposite extreme, an erect male may experience recurring delays or a complete absence of the ability to achieve orgasm through intercourse, a condition called male

_____ .

(d) A male sexual dysfunction characterized by orgasm occurring before it is desired, often immediately or shortly after penetration, is referred to as _____ .

(e) When a female experiences distress over consistent delays in achieving orgasm or over her complete inability to achieve orgasm, it's called female

_____ ; another condition that can plague a woman is the persistent, involuntary contraction of the vaginal muscles, resulting in uncomfortable or painful intercourse, or if the muscle spasms are severe, the prevention of penetration; this is called _____

3. (a) Sexual dysfunctions may be the result of _____ or _____ conditions, such as diabetes or alcoholism; others are caused by

_____ factors, such as anxiety about sex or the association of pain with early sexual experiences.

(b) _____ (Many/Very few) sexual dysfunctions can be successfully treated by psychologists and physicians who have received specialized training in sex therapy.

(c) When a person's sexual gratification is highly or completely dependent on fantasies, urges, or behaviors that fall outside the socially accepted range of sexual behavior, the person is said to have a(n)

_____ . Such fantasies may involve nonhuman objects, suffering or humiliation, children, or another nonconsenting adult.

4. Identify the following sexual fantasies, urges, or behaviors.

(a) Sexual arousal achieved by exposing one's genitals to shocked strangers:

_____

(b) Sexual arousal from touching and rubbing against a nonconsenting person, usually in a crowded public situation, such as a crowded bus or subway car:

_____

(c) Sexual arousal in response to inanimate objects or body parts that are not primarily associated with sexual arousal:

_____

(d) For a heterosexual male, sexual arousal from cross-dressing in women's clothes:

_____

(e) Sexual fantasies, urges, or behavior involving sexual activity with a prepubescent child (generally age thirteen or younger):

_____

(f) Sexual arousal from observing an unsuspecting person who is disrobing, naked, or engaged in sexual activity:

_____

(g) Sexual arousal achieved through intentionally inflicting psychological or physical suffering on another person:

_____

(h) Sexual arousal in response to actually being humiliated, beaten, bound, or otherwise made to suffer:

_____

5. (a) The person with a sexual dysfunction _____ (is/is not) usually psychologically distressed by it; the person who has a paraphilia _____ (is/is not) usually psychologically distressed by it. Some paraphilias, such as _____ and _____ , are illegal.

(b) The exact causes of paraphilia remain obscure, although theories involving _____ and _____ causes exist.

6. (a) When a person expresses persistent discomfort about his or her assigned gender and repeatedly expresses a desire to be a member of the opposite sex, he or she is said to have _____ disorder (formerly called _____).

(b) When it occurs in children, _____ disorder is marked by an intense preoccupation with the play activities, games, and toys traditionally associated with the opposite sex. During the

teenage years, the individual may exhibit other kinds of cross-gender behaviors, such as a male shaving his legs.

(c) Adults with sexual identity disorder are extremely _____ (comfortable/ uncomfortable) about being regarded as a member of their assigned gender; in private, and sometimes in public, they may cross-dress and display mannerisms typical of the opposite sex.

(d) People with sexual identity disorder often resort to _____ treatments, _____ intervention, such as the surgical reduction of the Adam's apple in males, and _____ surgery.

7. (a) Sexually transmitted diseases (STDs) are almost always transmitted through sexual contact and include _____ , _____ , and parasitic infections.

(b) Gonorrhea, syphilis, and chlamydia are examples of _____ STDs; Pubic lice is an example of a(n) _____ STD; and _____ STDs include herpes and AIDS.

(c) Left untreated, many STDs can eventually cause significant health problems; a person _____ (may/may not) be aware that he or she is infected with an STD and thus unknowingly pass the STD on to sexual partners.

8. (a) AIDS, or acquired immune deficiency syndrome, is a disease caused when the human immunodeficiency virus (HIV) enters the bloodstream through exchange of infected body fluids, primarily _____ , _____ , and _____ products.

(b) Once a person is infected, HIV can exist in his or her body for a decade or longer without causing any apparent symptoms; however, the person is an HIV _____ and can infect others.

(c) As HIV weakens the immune system by attacking the _____ , the person becomes greatly susceptible to other diseases, including _____ , _____ , and encephalitis (inflammation of the brain and spinal cord).

(d) The groups most at risk of becoming infected by HIV are _____ men, _____ users, and people with _____ sex partners; however, no one is immune to HIV.

9. Read the following and write the correct term in the space provided.

(a) Marshall went to his doctor because his complete lack of sexual desire was causing interpersonal problems with his wife. He is most likely to be diagnosed as having a disorder called

_____ disorder.

(b) Recently, Herbert was arrested when he was caught peering through the window of a woman who was getting undressed. It turned out that Herbert had a long history of similar behavior. Herbert suffers from

_____ .

(c) Axel uses public transport during rush hour because he gets sexually aroused from touching and rubbing against strangers. Axel has a paraphilia called

_____ .

(d) When Julian was a child, he loved playing with dolls and joining in girls' games; as a teenager, he shaved his legs and under his arms. Now, he frequently dresses in women's clothes and hopes one day to undergo sex-reassignment surgery. Julian has

_____ disorder, formerly called _____ .

(e) Margorie, who is an intravenous drug user, became infected with the HIV virus after using a contaminated needle; she has now been diagnosed with _____ .

(f) Jennifer sought medical help for a problem she discovered she had after she started living with her boyfriend. After she described her symptoms of chronic genital pain during intercourse, her doctor diagnosed her condition as _____ .

Graphic Organizer 1

Read the following and decide whether the statement is more characteristic of a paraphilia (P) or a sexual dysfunction (SD):

Statement	P	SD
1. Consistent disturbances in sexual desire, arousal, or orgasm.		
2. Much more prevalent among men than women.		
3. Is not usually accompanied by psychological distress.		
4. Sexual gratification is almost always dependent on fantasies, urges, or behaviors that fall outside the socially accepted range of sexual behavior.		
5. Is usually accompanied by psychological distress and interpersonal difficulties.		
6. Typically come to the attention of mental health professionals when a person's behavior causes problems for his or her partner, family member, or coworker or has resulted in the person's arrest.		
7. Can be successfully treated by psychologists and physicians who have received specialized training in sex therapy.		
8. Some forms of the disturbance are illegal.		
9. Although biological and psychological theories have been proposed, the cause or causes remain obscure.		
10. While there is no reliable data on the prevalence of these problems, it is known that they affect both men and women about equally.		

Review of Terms and Concepts 3

Use the terms in this list to complete the Matching Test, then to help you answer the True/False items correctly.

sexual dysfunction
hypoactive sexual desire
  disorder
sexual aversion disorder
dyspareunia
male erectile disorder
male orgasmic disorder
premature ejaculation
female orgasmic
  disorder
vaginismus
paraphilia
exhibitionism
frotteurism

fetishism
transvestic fetishism
pedophilia
voyeurism
sexual sadism
sexual masochism
gender identity disorder
  (transsexualism)
sexually transmitted
  diseases (STDs)
AIDS (acquired immune
  deficiency syndrome)
human immunode-
  ficiency virus (HIV)

Matching Exercise

Match the appropriate term with its definition or description.

1. _____ Paraphilia characterized by sexual arousal in response to inanimate objects (for example, female undergarments, shoes, leather) or body parts that are not typically associated with sexual arousal (for example, feet, hair, legs).

2. _____ Infectious diseases that are transmitted primarily through sexual intercourse or other intimate sexual contact.

3. _____ In males, sexual dysfunction characterized by a recurring inability to achieve or maintain an erect penis.

4. _____ In females, sexual dysfunction characterized by consistent delays in achieving orgasm or the inability to achieve orgasm.

5. _____ Paraphilia in which a heterosexual male achieves sexual arousal from cross-dressing in women's clothes.

6. _____ Sexual dysfunction characterized by persistent, involuntary contractions or spasms of the vaginal muscles, which result in uncomfortable or painful intercourse.

7. _____ Nontraditional sexual behavior in which a person's sexual gratification depends on an unusual sexual experience, object, or fantasy.

8. _____ Virus that enters the bloodstream through the exchange of bodily fluids, primarily semen, blood, and blood products, and causes the disease called acquired immune deficiency syndrome, or AIDS.

9. _____ Consistent disturbance in sexual desire, arousal, or orgasm that causes psychological distress and interpersonal difficulties.

10. _____ In males, sexual dysfunction characterized by delayed orgasm during intercourse or the inability to achieve orgasm during intercourse.

11. _____ In males, sexual dysfunction characterized by orgasm occurring before it is desired, often immediately or shortly after penetration.

True/False Test

Indicate whether each item is true or false by placing T or F in the space next to each item.

1. ____ A paraphilia in which sexual arousal is achieved through intentionally inflicting psychological or physical suffering on another person is called sexual masochism.

2. ____ A paraphilia in which sexual fantasies, urges, or behavior involves sexual activity with a prepubescent child is called pedophilia.

3. ____ Dyspareunia is a sexual dysfunction characterized by active avoidance of genital sexual contact because of extreme anxiety, fear, or disgust.

4. ____ The disease caused by the exchange of body fluids (semen, blood, or blood products) containing the human immunodeficiency virus (HIV),

which attacks and weakens the immune system, is called AIDS (acquired immune deficiency syndrome).

5. ____ Voyeurism is a paraphilia in which sexual arousal is obtained from observing an unsuspecting person disrobing, naked, or engaging in sexual activity.

6. ____ Hypoactive sexual desire disorder is a sexual dysfunction characterized by abnormally high and persistent levels of sexual desire.

7. ____ A paraphilia in which sexual arousal is achieved by exposing one's genitals to shocked strangers is called exhibitionism.

8. ____ Sexual sadism is a form of paraphilia in which sexual arousal is achieved in response to actually being humiliated, beaten, bound, or otherwise made to suffer.

9. ____ Frotteurism is a paraphilia in which the person achieves sexual arousal from touching and rubbing against a nonconsenting person, usually in a crowded public situation, such as a crowded bus or subway car.

10. ____ Persons who express persistent discomfort about their assigned gender and repeatedly express a desire to be a member of the opposite sex are said to have gender identity disorder (formerly called transsexualism).

11. ____ A sexual dysfunction characterized by genital pain before, during, or after sexual intercourse is called sexual aversion disorder.

> Check your answers and review any areas of weakness before going on to the next section.

Something to Think About

1. Just about everyone experiences some kind of relationship problem at one time or another. Most frequently, problems tend to arise in intimate relationships between men and women. Imagine you are a therapist and a couple comes to you for help in resolving their ongoing interpersonal conflicts. Based on what you have discovered in this chapter, what advice would you give them?

2. The French saying "Vive la difference!" refers to the differences between men and women. When people use it, they may simply be celebrating the most obvious anatomical features and behaviors associated with masculinity and fem-

ininity. Male-female differences, however, continue to be a topic of debate. For instance, some popular books and the media have suggested that male and female brains are fundamentally different and that the two sexes are like creatures from two different planets (Mars and Venus, respectively). Now that you know quite a bit about gender and sexuality, what would you add to a discussion of the issue?

Check your answers and review any areas of weakness before doing the progress tests.

Progress Test 1

Review the complete chapter (including Concept Reviews and the boxed inserts), review all your study notes, and then test yourself on the following progress test. Check your answers. If you make a mistake, review your notes, review the relevant section of the study guide, and, if necessary, go back and read the appropriate part of your textbook.

1. In a recent tutorial discussion, Michael stated that women are more nurturing, patient, and emotional than men, and that men are more logical, rational, and aggressive than women. Michael's beliefs about male and female differences best illustrates
   (a) sexual orientation.
   (b) gender identity.
   (c) sex.
   (d) gender-role stereotypes.

2. Aldred believes that gender roles develop as a result of young children observing others modeling particular gender-appropriate behaviors and that children are rewarded when they behave accordingly and are punished when they don't. Aldred's view is most consistent with the _____ theory of gender-role development.
   (a) gender schema
   (b) Masters and Johnson's
   (c) social learning
   (d) evolutionary

3. When Kathy's baby was born, the doctor took one look at its genitals and said "It's a girl!" by definition, the doctor was referring to the newborn's
   (a) gender.   (c) sexual orientation.
   (b) sex.   (d) gender role.

4. Testosterone is to _____ as estrogen is to _____ .
   (a) female sexual development; male sexual development
   (b) premature ejaculation; vaginismus
   (c) male sexual development; female sexual development
   (d) female orgasmic disorder; male orgasmic disorder

5. Because of an illness, thirty-year-old Mandy had her ovaries surgically removed. As a result of this operation, Mandy is likely to experience
   (a) homosexual feelings and urges.
   (b) an increase in estrogen production.
   (c) a steep drop in sexual activity and interest.
   (d) a decrease in estrogen production.

6. Laureen is a lesbian. It is very probable that
   (a) her sexual orientation was determined before adolescence and before any sexual activity occurred.
   (b) she experienced some early childhood sexual abuse by a member of the opposite sex.
   (c) her father was overly domineering and her mother was ineffectual and provided her with a poor feminine role model.
   (d) her first sexual experience occurred in childhood with a member of the same sex.

7. Thomas and Shauna have just completed a number of tests of cognitive abilities. If they are typical, Thomas is likely to score _____ than Shauna on spatial skills and Shauna is likely to score _____ than Thomas on verbal, reading, and writing skills.
   (a) lower; higher   (c) higher; lower
   (b) lower; lower   (d) higher; higher

8. In preschool, four-year-old Michael is _____ likely to play with other boys than with other girls, and four-year-old Marie is _____ likely to play with other girls than with other boys.
   (a) more; more   (c) more; less
   (b) less; less   (d) less; more

9. After her husband died, sixty-eight-year-old Mrs. Jaspers started dating seventy-year-old Sidney. At their age
   (a) it is very unlikely that they will engage in sexual activity.
   (b) they will want to get married almost immediately.

(c) dating fills their needs for companionship and sexual intimacy.

(d) all of the above are true.

10. Frank and his wife Joanne have not managed to start a family yet because Frank is unable to achieve orgasm during intercourse but is able to do so through other means. Frank has a problem called

(a) premature ejaculation.

(b) male erectile disorder.

(c) dyspareunia.

(d) male orgasmic disorder.

11. Nancy and Bruce are newlyweds. They are going to a sex therapist because Nancy experiences persistent, involuntary contraction of the vaginal muscles, resulting in painful intercourse. Nancy suffers from

(a) female orgasmic disorder.

(b) vaginismus.

(c) hypoactive sexual desire disorder.

(d) frotteurism.

12. When Desmond and Mona met, they found that they shared certain sexual interests. Desmond achieves sexual arousal through intentionally inflicting psychological or physical suffering on another person, and Mona is sexually aroused by being humiliated, beaten, bound, or otherwise made to suffer. Desmond is a(n) _____ and Mona is a(n) _____ .

(a) exhibitionist; voyeur

(b) sexual sadist; sexual masochist

(c) pedophiliac; frotteurist

(d) sexual masochist; sexual sadist

13. Steve is uncomfortable with his own assigned gender, fantasizes about being a woman, and frequently dresses in female clothes and displays the mannerisms typical of a very feminine person. Steve suffers from

(a) exhibitionism.

(b) fetishism.

(c) hypoactive sexual desire disorder.

(d) gender identity disorder (transsexualism).

14. According to the Application, a key ingredient in successful intimate relationships is

(a) suppressing one's true emotions.

(b) resolving conflict.

(c) stonewalling.

(d) flooding.

15. According to Critical Thinking 10.1, which discusses brain differences in males and females, which of the following is true?

(a) Even the best-substantiated brain differences are small and inconsistent.

(b) The meaning and practical significance of any known brain differences are unclear and open to many different interpretations.

(c) Male and female brains are much more alike than they are dissimilar.

(d) All of the above are true.

Progress Test 2

After you have checked your understanding of the material in Progress Test 1 and have done a complete chapter review with special focus on any areas of weakness, you are ready to assess your knowledge of Progress Test 2. Check your answers. If you make a mistake, review your notes, the relevant section of the study guide, and, if necessary, the appropriate part of your textbook.

1. Julian is a heterosexual male who has a transvestic fetishism. Cross-dressing in women's clothes and wearing women's cosmetics sexually arouses him. Because his behavior falls outside the socially accepted range of sexual behaviors, he is likely to be classified as having

(a) dyspareunia.

(b) male orgasmic disorder.

(c) hypoactive sexual desire disorder.

(d) a paraphilia.

2. Elsie is thinking of going to a sex therapist. She is worried because she has never experienced an orgasm during sexual intercourse with her husband, despite having an otherwise very warm and loving relationship. Elsie probably has a sexual dysfunction called

(a) dyspareunia.

(b) sexual aversion disorder.

(c) female orgasmic disorder.

(d) vaginismus.

3. Mary and Martin are fraternal twins who will be celebrating their sixth birthday very soon. If they are typical of children at this age, Mary will ask for _____ and Martin will ask for _____ as birthday presents.

(a) dolls and a dollhouse; toy cars and trucks

(b) sports equipment; dolls and a dollhouse

(c) toy cars and trucks; sports equipment

(d) toy guns and soldiers; sports equipment

4. Psychologists at State University's Gerontology Center are conducting research on sexual behavior over the lifespan. They are most likely to discover that by the time people reach their seventies and eighties
   (a) they have no interest in sexual activity.
   (b) women outnumber men by a margin of almost two to one.
   (c) they are usually confined to old age homes.
   (d) men outnumber women by a margin of almost two to one.

5. Keith will be twenty-one years old next month. If he is like most young people his age, he
   (a) is still a virgin.
   (b) had sexual intercourse for the first time before he was fourteen.
   (c) has been married for about a year.
   (d) has already lost his virginity.

6. Hagar and Helga were both early-maturing children. Their respective experiences, as a result of early puberty, were likely to have been
   (a) very similar in all respects.
   (b) very negative for both.
   (c) very different in many respects.
   (d) very positive for both.

7. Between the age of fifteen and sixteen, Sean grew almost five inches. Sean experienced _____ during this year.
   (a) the development of primary sex characteristics
   (b) the adolescent growth spurt
   (c) the development of mammary glands
   (d) menarche

8. Whenever eight-month-old Tristan is being bathed, he fondles his own genitals and smiles and gurgles with apparent delight. Tristan is
   (a) engaging in genital play.
   (b) behaving normally.
   (c) not experiencing sexual arousal.
   (d) not expressing a desire for erotic contact
   (e) doing all of the above.

9. When he was thirteen, Kyle experienced several physical changes: his testicles started to enlarge, his height and weight increased, and his voice deepened. Kyle experienced
   (a) menarche.
   (b) puberty.
   (c) sexual dysfunction.
   (d) paraphilia.

10. In a term paper on child development, Sima made the case that children actively develop categories for masculinity and femininity and suggested that these mental representations influence how children perceive, interpret, and remember relevant aspects of what is appropriate for girls and boys. Sima's position is most consistent with the _____ theory of gender-role development.
    (a) gender schema
    (b) evolutionary
    (c) Masters and Johnson
    (d) social learning

11. Barney and Bailey are identical twins. Barney is gay. Therefore, there is
    (a) about a 50 percent chance that Bailey will also be homosexual.
    (b) almost 100 percent chance that Bailey will also be homosexual.
    (c) about a 20 percent chance that Bailey will also be homosexual.
    (d) no way to predict Bailey's sexual orientation because there is no correlation between genetic factors and sexual behavior.

12. In the human sexual response cycle, the first phase is _____ and the last phase is _____ .
    (a) plateau; resolution
    (b) excitement; orgasm
    (c) orgasm; plateau
    (d) excitement; resolution

13. Dr. MacKinnon is doing cross-cultural research on gender-role stereotypes. She is likely to discover that
    (a) across cultures, there is a high degree of agreement on the characteristics associated with each sex.
    (b) in every culture, the characteristics associated with the male stereotype are identical.
    (c) across cultures, there is a high degree of disagreement on the characteristics associated with each sex.
    (d) in every culture, the female stereotype is more widely believed than is the male stereotype.

14. According to In Focus 10.3, which of the following is true?
    (a) Sexual fantasies are psychologically unhealthy.

(b) Male and female sexual fantasies are almost identical in content and frequency.

(c) Sexual fantasies are a sign of sexual frustration and dissatisfaction with a relationship.

(d) All of the above are true.

(e) None of the above are true.

15. According to the Application, research has found that both _____ typically occur during emotional conflict.

(a) screaming and physical assault

(b) physical assault and homicide

(c) flooding and stonewalling

(d) cursing and swearing followed by a visit to a marriage counselor

Progress Test 3

After you have checked your understanding of the material in Progress Tests 1 and 2, and have done a complete chapter review with special focus on any areas of weakness, you are ready to further assess your knowledge on Progress Test 3. Check your answers. If you make a mistake, review your notes, the appropriate parts of the study guide, and if necessary, the relevant sections of your textbook.

1. When Oliver played with dolls and domestic toys, his mother would show her disapproval; when he played with toy vehicles and building blocks, his mother would respond in a positive manner. As Oliver grew older, he played less and less with dolls, dollhouses, and domestic toys and more and more with stereotypical "boys'" toys. This description of gender-role development illustrates

(a) gender identity theory.

(b) gender schema theory.

(c) social learning theory.

(d) evolutionary theory.

2. When Rex was a young pup, his owners took him to the vet to have him neutered. If Rex is like most animals, the removal of his testes will very likely result in a(n) _____ in the levels of the hormone testosterone, and a(n) _____ in sexual interest and sexual activity.

(a) increase; decrease

(b) decrease; decrease

(c) decrease; increase

(d) increase; increase

3. Dr. LaSage conducted twin studies on sexual orientation. If his findings are consistent with previous research on this topic, he is likely to conclude that

(a) sexual orientation is at least partly influenced by genetics.

(b) having an inadequate male role model or having an overly dominant mother is the primary cause of homosexuality.

(c) sexual orientation is almost completely influenced by environmental factors.

(d) homosexuality is the result of unpleasant early heterosexual experiences.

4. Barbara and Bob have decided to live together. She discovers that he can achieve sexual arousal only from contact with her stockings, shoes, or underwear. It appears that Bob has a disorder called

(a) voyeurism.   (c) exhibitionism.

(b) pedophilia.   (d) fetishism.

5. Heinz has a rather passive, weak father who provides a poor masculine role model. His mother, on the other hand, is a very strong, assertive, domineering woman. On the basis of research on early life experiences and sexual orientation, you would be justified in concluding that

(a) Heinz's experiences with his parents are not likely to cause him to become homosexual.

(b) by the time he is a young adult Heinz is almost certain to be a homosexual.

(c) Heinz will be a heterosexual during his teens, a bisexual in his early adult years, and eventually a homosexual in middle to late adulthood.

(d) by the time he reaches puberty, Heinz will suffer from gender identity disorder and one or more of the paraphilias.

6. Robert is very distressed and embarrassed because he frequently reaches sexual climax within minutes of becoming sexually aroused and before he has intercourse with his partner. Robert's problem is called

(a) hypoactive sexual desire disorder.

(b) premature ejaculation.

(c) male orgasmic disorder.

(d) male erectile disorder.

7. Doug was infected with HIV from contaminated blood during a blood transfusion many years ago. It is very likely that he will develop
   (a) chlamydia.
   (b) herpes.
   (c) syphilis.
   (d) acquired immune deficiency syndrome (AIDS).

8. Nathan is a homosexual. If the work of neurobiologist Simon LeVay is replicated and confirmed by other researchers, it is likely that Nathan may have a tiny cluster of neurons in his hypothalamus, which is known to be involved in sexual behavior, that is about
   (a) half the size of heterosexual men's.
   (b) half the size of heterosexual women's.
   (c) twice the size of heterosexual men's.
   (d) twice the size of heterosexual women's.

9. Larry is married, but he and his wife rarely have intercourse because the thought of any genital contact with his wife fills him with fear, anxiety, and disgust. Larry suffers from
   (a) hypoactive sexual desire disorder.
   (b) dyspareunia.
   (c) sexual aversion disorder.
   (d) male orgasmic disorder.

10. Noreen is almost thirteen and has just had her first menstrual period. Noreen has experienced
    (a) menopause.   (c) vaginismus.
    (b) menarche.   (d) a refractory period.

11. Sharina is writing a term paper on human sexuality. Her library research is likely to indicate that the normal order of the four stages in the human sexual response cycle is
    (a) excitement, resolution, plateau, and orgasm.
    (b) excitement, orgasm, plateau, and resolution.
    (c) plateau, excitement, resolution, and orgasm.
    (d) excitement, plateau, orgasm, and resolution.

12. Elizabeth has had to seek treatment because of persistent itching due to pubic lice. Elizabeth has contracted
    (a) a parasitic STD.
    (b) AIDS (acquired immune deficiency syndrome).
    (c) a bacterial STD.
    (d) chlamydia.

13. John is now serving a long jail sentence after his third conviction for engaging in sexual activities with prepubescent girls. John suffers from a paraphilia called
    (a) frotteurism.   (c) voyeurism.
    (b) fetishism.   (d) pedophilia.

14. In order to break the vicious circle of flooding-stonewalling-flooding, the Application suggests that couples should
    (a) become aware of the gender differences in handling emotion.
    (b) call a time-out whenever either one begins to feel overwhelmed or in danger of flooding.
    (c) spend the time-out period thinking about ways to resolve the conflict, not about ways to mount a more effective counterattack.
    (d) recognize that males need to try to stop avoiding conflict and females should try to raise issues in need of resolution in a calm manner and without personal attack.
    (e) do all of the above.

15. According to research by David Buss (Culture and Human Behavior 10.2)
    (a) mutual attraction and love are the most important factors in selecting a mate in all cultures studied.
    (b) men are more likely than women to value youth and physical attractiveness in a potential mate.
    (c) women value financial security, access to material resources, and high status and education in a potential mate.
    (d) all of the above are true.

Answers

Introduction: Gender and Sexuality

1. (a) biologically; cultural; social
   (b) behaviors, attitudes; psychological; emotional; erotic
   (c) culture; gender identity; sexual orientation

Gender Stereotypes and Gender Roles

1. (a) stereotypes
   (b) emotional, nurturing; aggressive, decisive
   (c) agreement; males; females

2. (a) similar; do not
   (b) differences

3. (a) are no
   (b) nurturant; assertive; women; men

4. (a) are no
   (b) females; males
   (c) males; females
   (d) males; females; males; females
   (e) cognitive

5. (a) similar
   (b) men; women
   (c) similar; dissimilar

Gender-Role Development: Blue Bears and Pink Bunnies

1. (a) virtually indistinguishable; very differently
   (b) cultural; social
   (c) other one-year-olds

2. (a) two; three
   (b) sex differences
   (c) two; three; three
   (d) their own; larger; close relationships
   (e) children; adults; girls; boys

3. (a) reinforcement, punishment
   (b) small; similarly
   (c) modeling

4. (a) Sandra Bem; cognitive
   (b) perceive, interpret; remember; assimilate
   (c) females; males
   (d) reinforcement; observation

5. (a) sex
   (b) gender schema
   (c) gender role
   (d) female; male
   (e) will not; will
   (f) gender identity; sexual orientation

Matching Exercise 1

1. Sandra Bem
2. gender
3. sexual orientation
4. gender-role stereotypes
5. schemas

True/False Test 1

1. T	3. F	5. F
2. T	4. T	

Human Sexuality

1. (a) William Masters; Virginia Johnson
   (b) excitement
   (c) plateau
   (d) orgasm; orgasm
   (e) resolution; refractory

2. (a) hormonal; estrus
   (b) biologically; environmental
   (c) reproduction; social

3. (a) reproduction; do not
   (b) estrogen
   (c) a complete
   (d) causes a steep drop in; testosterone
   (e) testosterone
   (f) testosterone

Sexual Orientation

1. (a) heterosexual; homosexual; bisexual
   (b) lesbian; gay
   (c) is not

2. (a) genetics
   (b) genetic; identical; fraternal
   (c) genetics

3. (a) hypothalamus
   (b) biological; genetic

4. (a) not due to
   (b) is not
   (c) are no
   (d) six; is; less

5. (a) still unable
   (b) is no longer
   (c) occupation; socioeconomic
   (d) are; are not

Sexual Behavior over the Lifespan

1. (a) birth
   (b) three; four; first
   (c) should not; normal
   (d) two; six
   (e) attitudes
   (f) five; eight

2. (a) sexual; reproductive
   (b) primary
   (c) secondary
   (d) adolescent growth spurt
   (e) menarche; testes
   (f) earlier; earlier; menarche

3. (a) boys; girls
   (b) social; cultural
   (c) 15; 18; 19
   (d) parents; peer group; parents

4. (a) twenties; thirty
   (b) married
   (c) earlier; later
   (d) married; cohabiting

5. (a) does not

(b) most

(c) are

6. (a) vaginal intercourse
   (b) stranger; agreed

7. (a) does not
   (b) orgasm; most
   (c) lack of a sexual partner
   (d) dating

8. (a) refractory
   (b) decrease; stay the same
   (c) decrease
   (d) sexual orientation
   (e) puberty
   (f) secondary
   (g) likely
   (h) negative

Matching Exercise 2

1. Virginia E. Johnson
2. plateau phase
3. puberty
4. menarche
5. heterosexual
6. adolescent growth spurt
7. refractory period
8. homosexual
9. William H. Masters
10. excitement phase

True/False Test 2

1. F	4. T	7. F
2. T	5. F	8. F
3. T	6. T	9. F

Sexual Disorders and Problems

1. (a) performance; are
   (b) psychological

2. (a) hypoactive sexual desire
   (b) sexual aversion; dyspareunia
   (c) erectile disorder; orgasmic disorder
   (d) premature ejaculation
   (e) orgasmic disorder; vaginismus

3. (a) physical; medical; psychological
   (b) Many
   (c) paraphilia

4. (a) exhibitionism
   (b) frotteurism
   (c) fetishism
   (d) transvestic fetishism

(e) pedophilia

(f) voyeurism

(g) sexual sadism

(h) sexual masochism

5. (a) is; is not; pedophilia; voyeurism
   (b) biological; psychological

6. (a) gender identity; transsexualism
   (b) gender identity
   (c) uncomfortable
   (d) hormone; surgical; sex-reassignment

7. (a) bacterial; viral
   (b) bacterial; parasitic; viral
   (c) may not

8. (a) blood; semen; blood
   (b) carrier
   (c) helper T cells; cancer; pneumonia
   (d) gay; intravenous drug; multiple

9. (a) hypoactive sexual desire
   (b) voyeurism
   (c) frotteurism
   (d) gender identity; transsexualism
   (e) AIDS
   (f) dyspareunia

Graphic Organizer 1

1. SD	5. SD	9. P
2. P	6. P	10. SD
3. P	7. SD	
4. P	8. P	

Matching Exercise 3

1. fetishism
2. sexually transmitted diseases (STDs)
3. male erectile disorder
4. female orgasmic disorder
5. transvestic fetishism
6. vaginismus
7. paraphilia
8. human immunodeficiency virus (HIV)
9. sexual dysfunction
10. male orgasmic disorder
11. premature ejaculation

True/False Test 3

1. F	5. T	9. T
2. T	6. F	10. T
3. F	7. T	11. F
4. T	8. F	

Something to Think About

1. Resolving conflicts is a key ingredient in successful intimate relationships. Men and women differ significantly in the way they communicate, especially when they are trying to deal with emotional issues and interpersonal conflicts; these fundamental differences can sabotage conflict resolution. There is hope, however. John Gottesman's research provides evidence of a number of constructive ways for overcoming these communication differences.

   First, conflict can play a key role in a healthy, happy relationship; a couple's relationship will grow if the couple successfully reconciles the inevitable differences that occur. Men and women react differently to conflict, particularly if it involves strong emotions. Typically, men have learned to suppress and contain their emotions, whereas women tend to be more comfortable with emotional expression. During emotional conflicts, people may experience flooding (the feeling of being overwhelmed emotionally); in reaction to this intense physiological arousal, they may engage in stonewalling (withdrawing to contain their uncomfortable emotions). Men tend to get more physiologically aroused during relationship conflicts than do women and are therefore more likely to engage in stonewalling. Women tend to experience stonewalling as disapproval and rejection and typically react by flooding. And that's how the vicious circle of flooding-stonewalling-flooding begins.

   A number of things can be done to break this vicious circle. First, both parties need to become aware of the gender differences in handling emotion. Men need to remember that women experience stonewalling as rejection, disapproval, and abandonment, and women need to accept men's need to temporarily withdraw from the situation. Second, calling for a 20- to 30-minute time-out period during a conflict is a good idea so long as both parties use the time to think about ways to resolve the conflict, rather than rehearsing or preparing vengeful comments and counterattack strategies. Third, men need to make a conscious effort to embrace, rather than avoid, the problem; sidestepping the issue won't make it go away. If the woman didn't care about the relationship, she wouldn't keep confronting her partner; generally, she wants both people to resolve the issue together. Fourth, women should try raising the issue in a more calm and less emotionally confrontational manner. Frame the problem in the context of maintaining a loving relationship and avoid personal attacks. Finally, tell the couple to buy, read, and discuss John Gottman's book—together!

2. The first point to make in any discussion of differences between men and women is that the sexes are much more alike than they are different. The similarities extend across many different and important aspects of behavior and ability, including brain structure. We tend to overlook these similarities when we focus on the differences that have been found between men and women. In addition, if the data on sex differences are examined, there is often a great deal of overlap between men and women.

   Second, note that any sex differences in behavior and cognitive functioning are not necessarily because male and female brains are structurally different. There is considerable *individual* variation in brain structure and function; thus, the average range of differences *within* each sex is larger than the average differences between the sexes. Indeed, some individual females are found to be more similar to the average male pattern than average female pattern, and vice versa. There are more similarities than differences between male and female brains.

   Third, even if we assume, for the sake of argument, that there are reliable sex differences in brain structure, no one knows the functional significance of those differences. The human brain is incredibly complex, and researchers have not yet managed to unravel all the interrelated organizational and functional aspects of this complicated organ. Clearly, we know a lot more than we used to, but we are still a long way from being able to specify the precise significance of any subtle sex difference that has been found or may be found in the future. It certainly can't be concluded that male and females "think differently" because of structural differences in their brains, as some headlines have claimed.

   If we accept that there may be some small and inconsistent differences in the structure of male and female brains, it does not necessarily follow that we are born with these differences. The brain's structure changes in response to experience, so it is entirely possible that any sex differences in the brain could be due to men's and women's different environmental and learning experiences.

Finally, and worth repeating, male and female brains are much more alike than they are dissimilar.

Progress Test 1

1. d	6. a	11. b
2. c	7. d	12. b
3. b	8. a	13. d
4. c	9. c	14. b
5. d	10. d	15. d

Progress Test 2

1. d	6. c	11. a
2. c	7. b	12. d
3. a	8. e	13. a
4. b	9. b	14. e
5. d	10. a	15. c

Progress Test 3

1. c	6. b	11. d
2. b	7. d	12. a
3. a	8. a	13. d
4. d	9. c	14. e
5. a	10. b	15. d

CHAPTER

11

Personality

PREVIEW

Reading the section below first will give you a general sense of the chapter's contents and an initial introduction to some of the major concepts and terms. This will prime you for what you are about to read and help you to develop a "cognitive map" that will guide your study of the material in this chapter. Likewise, reading the **preview questions** at the beginning of each major section will improve your ability to understand, learn, and retain the information.

CHAPTER 11 . . . AT A GLANCE

Chapter 11 focuses on the four major perspectives on personality. Freud's psychoanalysis stresses the unconscious, the importance of sex and aggression, and the influences of early childhood experiences. The major defense mechanisms, as well as the psychosexual stages of development and the various conflicts associated with each, are examined. The contributions of Freud's early followers, the neo-Freudians, are explored, and criticisms of Freud's theory are discussed.

Carl Rogers's humanistic theory and his optimistic view of human nature are examined, including his ideas about the self-concept, unconditional positive regard, the actualizing tendency, and the fully functioning person.

The social cognitive perspective stresses the role of conscious thought processes, goals, self-regulation, and reciprocal determinism. The influence of self-efficacy on behavior, performance, motivation, and persistence is explored. The notion that the interaction of multiple factors determines personality and behavior is examined.

The trait perspective focuses on measuring and describing individual differences. Cattell initially suggested sixteen basic personality factors, then Eysenck proposed three. The five-factor model is the current view of the number of source traits. The text concludes that traits are generally stable across time and across situations.

Behavioral genetics research uses twin and adoption studies to measure the relative influences of genetics and environment. The heritability estimate is explained, and personality factors that appear to have a genetic basis are identified.

The final section examines projective tests and self-report inventories, as well as their strengths and weaknesses.

Introduction: What Is Personality?

Preview Questions

Consider the following questions as you study this section of the chapter.

- How is personality defined, and what is a personality theory?
- What are the four major theoretical perspectives in personality?

*Read the section "Introduction: What Is Personality?" and **write** your answers to the following:*

1. (a) Personality is defined as an individual's unique and relatively consistent patterns of _____ , _____ , and _____ .

   (b) A personality theory is an attempt to describe and explain how people are _____ , how they are _____ , and why every individual is unique; in short, a personality theory ambitiously tries to explain the _____ person, but no single theory can explain all aspects of human personality.

2. There are many personality theories, but they can be roughly grouped under four basic perspectives.

   (a) The psychoanalytic perspective emphasizes the importance of _____ processes and the influence of _____ experience.

   (b) The humanistic perspective represents an optimistic look at human nature, emphasizing the _____ and the fulfillment of a person's _____ .

   (c) The social cognitive perspective emphasizes _____ and conscious _____ processes, including the importance of _____ about the self, goal setting, and self-regulation.

   (d) The trait perspective emphasizes the _____ and _____ of specific personality differences among individuals.

The Psychoanalytic Perspective on Personality

Preview Questions

Consider the following questions as you study this section of the chapter.

- Who was the founder of psychoanalysis, and what did he consider to be the main factors that influenced personality development?
- What were some of the key influences on Freud's thinking?

*Read the section "The Psychoanalytic Perspective on Personality" and **write** your answers to the following:*

1. (a) Freud was trained in _____ and _____ and was among the first to investigate the anesthetic and mood-altering properties of _____ ; his initial enthusiasm for its medical potential faded when he finally recognized that the drug is _____ .

   (b) Freud gave up physiological research for a private practice in _____ . His theory gradually evolved during his first 20 years of private practice based on observations of his patients as well as _____ .

   (c) Joseph Breuer, an early mentor of Freud, described a case in which the free expression of pent-up _____ associated with memories that only emerged under hypnosis resulted in the disappearance of psychological and physical symptoms. Breuer called this phenomenon _____ .

   (d) Because hypnosis did not work with many of his patients, Freud developed his own technique of _____ to help his patients uncover forgotten memories; patients would spontaneously report their uncensored _____ , _____ , and _____ as they came to mind.

2. (a) Freud and Breuer described several of their case studies in their landmark book *Studies in Hysteria*; its publication in 1895 marks the beginning of _____ .

   (b) For the next 30 years, Freud continued to refine his theory. Although he had previously asserted that the fundamental instinctual human motive was _____ , during this period he added _____ as a second powerful human motive.

   (c) In 1930, Freud published *Civilization and Its Discontents*, in which he applied his psychoanalytic perspective to _____ as a whole; he argued that _____ and _____ are in basic conflict, a conflict that cannot be resolved.

The Psychoanalytic Perspective on Personality: Freud's Dynamic Theory of Personality

Preview Questions

Consider the following questions as you study this section of the chapter.

- How do we access unconscious mental processes?
- What are the three basic structures of personality, and what are their functions?
- What are the main defense mechanisms, and what role do they play?

Read the section "The Psychoanalytic Perspective: Freud's Dynamic Theory of Personality" and ***write*** *your answers to the following:*

1. (a) Freud saw personality and behavior as the constant interplay of conflicting psychological forces that operate at three different levels of awareness: the _____ , _____ , and _____ levels.

   (b) Information of which you are not currently aware but is easily capable of entering your consciousness resides in the _____ .

   (c) The bulk of your thoughts, feeling, wishes, and drives are submerged in the _____ , which exerts an enormous influence on your _____ thoughts and behavior.

2. (a) Although it is not directly accessible, Freud believed that _____ material often seeps through to the _____ level in distorted, disguised, or symbolic forms.

   (b) Freud carefully analyzed his patients' reports of dreams and free associations for evidence of _____ wishes, fantasies, and conflicts.

   (c) Dream analysis was particularly important to Freud; beneath the surface images, or _____ content, of a dream lay its _____ content, or the true, hidden, unconscious meaning of the dream symbols.

   (d) Freud believed that the unconscious could also be revealed in _____ actions, such as accidents, mistakes, instances of forgetting, and inadvertent slips of the tongue, which are often referred to as "_____ slips."

3. (a) The three basic structures of personality evolved from the _____ that each person possesses.

   (b) The id, the most primitive part of the personality, is entirely _____ , is present at birth, and is completely immune to logic, values, morality, danger, and the demands of the _____ world.

(c) The id's reservoir of psychological energy is derived from two conflicting instinctual drives, the life instinct, called _____ , which consists of biological urges that perpetuate the existence of the individual and the species, and the death instinct, called _____ , which is a destructive energy reflected in aggressive, reckless, and life-threatening behaviors.

(d) The id is ruled by the _____ principle—the relentless drive toward immediate satisfaction of the instinctual urges, especially sexual urges; Freud used the word _____ to refer specifically to sexual energy or motivation.

(e) The id strives to increase _____ , reduce _____ , and avoid pain; even though it operates unconsciously, Freud saw the _____ principle as the most fundamental human motive.

4. (a) The ego is _____ (completely/partly) conscious and develops from part of the id's psychological energy; it represents the _____ , _____ , and planning dimensions of personality.

(b) As the mediator between the id's instinctual demands and the restrictions of the outer world, the ego operates on the _____ principle, which is the capacity to postpone _____ until the appropriate time or circumstances exist in the external world.

(c) The ego is the _____ part of the personality that learns various compromises to reduce the tension of the id's instinctual urges. If the ego can't identify an acceptable compromise to satisfy an instinctual urge, it can _____ the impulse, or remove it from conscious awareness.

(d) The ego must deal with _____ demands and limitations, such as the parents' values and morals (their ideas of right or wrong ways to think, act, and feel) and society's values as advocated by teachers and religious and legal authorities; gradually, these social values, which had been _____ imposed demands, become _____ rules and values.

5. (a) By about age five or six, the young child has developed a(n) _____ , parental voice that is partly conscious, called the superego.

(b) The superego is partly the _____ representation of parental and societal values, and it evaluates the acceptability of behavior; put simply, your superego represents your _____ and judges your own behavior as right or wrong, good or bad, acceptable or unacceptable.

(c) If you fail to live up to these moral ideals, the superego can be harshly punitive, imposing feelings of inferiority, _____ , _____ , _____ , and _____ .

6. (a) The ego must be strong, flexible, and resourceful to successfully mediate conflicts between the _____ demands of the id, the _____ authority of the superego, and _____ restrictions. According to Freud, everyone experiences an ongoing daily battle among these three warring personality processes.

(b) When the demands of the id or the superego threaten to overwhelm the ego, _____ results; if id impulses overpower the ego, a person may act _____ and perhaps _____ ; if superego demands overwhelm the ego, an individual may suffer from _____ ,

_____ , or even suicidal impulses for failing to live up to the superego's moral standards.

(c) If a realistic solution or compromise is not possible, the ego may temporarily reduce _____ by _____ thoughts or perceptions of reality through processes that Freud called ego defense mechanisms. These largely unconscious self-deceptions help maintain an integrated sense of self.

(d) The most fundamental ego defense mechanism, which in simple terms is unconscious forgetting, is called _____ ; to some degree, it occurs in every ego defense mechanism.

(e) Although anxiety-producing thoughts, feelings, or impulses may be pushed out of _____ awareness into the _____ , if you encounter a situation similar to the one you've _____ , bits and pieces of memories of the previous situation may begin to surface. In such cases, other defense mechanisms may be deployed to keep the urge partially conscious.

7. (a) When emotional impulses are redirected to a substitute object or person, _____ has occurred. The productive and creative contributions of people and even of whole societies are largely the result of a special form of this defense mechanism called

_____ .

(b) The main drawback to any defense mechanism, in Freud's view, is that maintaining self-deceptions requires _____ , which is needed to cope effectively with the demands of daily life.

(c) When ego defense mechanisms are used in limited areas on a short-term basis, _____ is not seriously depleted, but when they delay or interfere with our

use of more constructive coping strategies, they can be counterproductive.

The Psychoanalytic Perspective: Personality Development

Preview Questions

Consider the following questions as you study this section of the chapter.

- What are the five psychosexual stages of personality development?
- What are the core conflicts of the oral, anal, and phallic stages, and what are the consequences of fixation?
- What role does the Oedipus complex play in personality development?

Read the section "The Psychoanalytic Perspective: Personality Development" and **write** *your answers to the following:*

1. (a) According to Freud, people progress through five _____ stages of development; the foundations of adult personality development are established during the first five years of life, as the child progresses through the _____ , _____ , and _____ stages; the _____ stage occurs during late childhood; and the _____ stage begins in adolescence.

(b) Freud believed that the child expresses primitive _____ urges by seeking sensual pleasure from different areas of the body; thus, the psychosexual stages are _____ developmental periods.

(c) Over the first five years of life, the expression of primitive _____ urges progresses from one bodily zone to another in a distinct order. The first year of life is characterized by the _____ stage; during this time, the infant derives pleasure through the _____ activities of sucking, chewing, and biting; during the next two years, the _____ stage, pleasure is derived through elimination and acquiring control over elimination; in the _____ stage, the child's pleasure seeking is focused on his or her _____ .

2. (a) At each psychosexual stage, Freud believed that the infant or young child is faced with a developmental _____ that must be successfully resolved in order to move on to the next stage.

   (b) The heart of this _____ is the degree to which parents either _____ or _____ the child's expression of pleasurable feelings through activities pertaining to different bodily zones.

   (c) The result of an unresolved developmental conflict is _____ at a particular stage; the person continues to seek pleasure through behaviors that are similar to those associated with that stage.

3. (a) The most critical conflict that the child must successfully resolve for healthy personality and sexual development occurs during the _____ stage.

   (b) As the child becomes more aware of pleasure derived from the _____ area, Freud believed that the child develops a sexual attraction to the _____ parent and hostility toward the _____ parent; this is the famous Oedipus complex.

4. (a) For boys, the Oedipus complex unfolds as a confrontation with the _____ for the affections of the _____ ; when he realizes that his adversary is more physically powerful and may punish him by cutting off his genitals, the little boy experiences _____ anxiety.

   (b) To resolve the Oedipus complex and these anxieties, the little boy ultimately joins forces with his former enemy by resorting to

the defense mechanism of _____ ; that is, he imitates and internalizes his _____ values, attitudes, and mannerisms.

   (c) The problem with this is that only the father can enjoy the sexual affections of the mother; this limitation becomes internalized as a taboo against _____ urges in the boy's developing superego.

5. (a) A girl also ultimately resolves the Oedipus complex by _____ with the same-sex parent and developing a strong superego taboo against _____ urges.

   (b) The underlying sexual drama in a girl follows different themes. Because she feels deprived that she does not have a penis, she feels contempt and resentment toward her mother. In her attempt to take her mother's place with the father, she also _____ with her mother and _____ the attributes of the same-sex parent.

   (c) Freud's views on female sexuality, particularly the concept of _____ , are among his most severely criticized ideas.

6. (a) Freud felt that because of the intense anxiety associated with the Oedipus complex, the sexual urges of male and female children become _____ during the latency stage in late childhood.

   (b) Outwardly, children in the latency stage express a strong desire to associate with _____ peers, a preference that strengthens the child's sexual identity.

   (c) The final resolution of the Oedipus complex occurs in adolescence, during the _____ stage. As _____ urges start to resurface, they are prohibited by the moral ideals of the superego as well as by societal restrictions; instead, the person directs sexual urges toward socially acceptable substitutes, who often resemble the person's _____ parent.

(d) In Freud's theory, a healthy personality and sense of sexuality result when the _____ are successfully resolved at each _____ stage of development; this results not only in the person's capacity to _____ but also in expressions of productive living through one's life work, child rearing, and other accomplishments.

7. Read the following and write the correct term in the space provided.

(a) Wilma typically responds to stress and stressful situations in a very agitated, panic-stricken manner. Gloria, on the other hand, usually stays calm and handles things in a careful and thoughtful manner. The reactions of Wilma and Gloria indicate that each has a distinctive _____ .

(b) Colleen, who is suffering from some puzzling physical and psychological symptoms that don't appear to have any physiological cause, has decided to seek help from a Freudian psychoanalyst. The therapist is most likely to use _____ in an attempt to explore Colleen's unconscious.

(c) During a heated argument, David inadvertently called his wife Joanne by his mother's name. From the psychoanalytic perspective, this "Freudian slip" reveals something about David's _____ (conscious/preconscious/unconscious) motivation.

(d) Amelia had a very strange dream in which she was with a very handsome man on a train traveling through the Swiss Alps. The train kept going in and out of tunnels and going faster and faster as it made its way through the mountains. According to Freudian theory, the _____ (manifest/latent) content of the dream should give some clue as to what is going on in Amelia's unconscious.

(e) When two-year-old Tyler was told that he would get no dessert unless he finished eating all his vegetables, he turned the plate upside down and said he hated his Mom and Dad. Freud would have said that Tyler was responding to the demands of the

_____ .

(f) Kato found a wallet containing $200 in cash. For just a moment he was tempted to keep the money, but the thought of doing so made him feel guilty and anxious, and he immediately took the wallet to the lost-and-found office. According to Freud, Kato's good deed was motivated by his _____ .

(g) Leslie sometimes thinks that the real reason her husband became a psychotherapist was to provide himself with a socially acceptable way to indulge his excessive inquisitiveness about other people's private lives. Leslie is suggesting that her husband is using a special form of displacement called

_____ .

(h) Nine-year-old Danny looks up to his father and, when he grows up, wants to be an engineer just like him. Freud would suggest that Danny is exhibiting signs of the process of

_____ .

Graphic Organizer 1

Read the following and match each one with the appropriate stage of psychosexual development:

Description	Stage
1. Sixteen-year-old Graham has started going steady with Julie and is experiencing all the sensations of being in love.	
2. Five-year-old Annette has become very competitive with her mother for her father's affections and quite defiantly states that she is "Going to marry Daddy when I grow up!"	
3. Vivian is eight years old and does not like boys very much. In fact, she plays with her girlfriends almost exclusively.	
4. It seems that no matter what Marie gives her baby to play with, she immediately puts it in her mouth.	
5. Darcy is not quite two but seems to take great pleasure in refusing to obey his parents and by asserting his control and independence. His favorite word is "No!"	

Review of Terms, Concepts, and Names 1

Use the terms in this list to complete the Matching Test, then to help you answer the True/False items correctly.

personality
personality theory
Sigmund Freud
psychoanalysis
catharsis
free association
conscious
preconscious
unconscious
id
Eros
libido
Thanatos
pleasure principle
ego
reality principle

superego
ego defense mechanisms
repression
displacement
sublimation
psychosexual stages
oral stage
anal stage
phallic stage
fixation
Oedipus complex
castration anxiety
identification
penis envy
latency stage
genital stage

Matching Exercise

Match the appropriate term/name with its definition or description.

1. _____ In Freud's theory, the psychological and emotional energy associated with expressions of sexuality; the sex drive.

2. _____ An individual's unique and relatively consistent patterns of thinking, feeling, and behaving.

3. _____ In Freud's theory, the partly conscious self-evaluative, moralistic component of personality that is formed through the internalization of parental and societal rules.

4. _____ In Freud's theory, a child's unconscious sexual desire for the opposite-sex parent, usually accompanied by hostile feelings toward the same-sex parent.

5. _____ Latin for "I"; in Freud's theory, the partly conscious rational component of personality that regulates thoughts and behavior and is most in touch with the demands of the external world.

6. _____ Level of awareness that contains information that is not currently in conscious awareness but is easily accessible.

7. _____ The first psychosexual stage of development, during which the infant derives pleasure through the activities of sucking, chewing, and biting.

8. _____ In psychoanalytic theory, the ego defense mechanism that involves unconsciously shifting the target of an emotional urge to a substitute target that is less threatening or dangerous.

9. _____ Austrian neurologist who founded psychoanalysis, which is both a comprehensive theory of personality and a form of psychotherapy; emphasized the role of unconscious determinants of behavior and early childhood experiences in the development of personality and psychological problems; key ideas include id, ego, and superego, the psychosexual stages of development, and the ego defense mechanisms.

10. _____ The second psychosexual stage of development, during which the infant derives pleasure through elimination and acquiring control of elimination.

11. _____ Theory that attempts to describe and explain individual similarities and differences.

12. _____ Latin for "the it"; in Freud's theory, the completely unconscious, irrational component of personality that seeks immediate satisfaction of instinctual urges and drives; ruled by the pleasure principle.

13. _____ The fourth psychosexual stage of development, during which the sexual urges of male and female children become repressed; outwardly, children express a strong desire to associate with same-sex peers, a preference that strengthens the child's sexual identity.

14. _____ Sigmund Freud's theory of personality, which emphasizes unconscious determinants of behavior, sexual and aggressive instinctual drives, and the enduring effects of early childhood experiences on later personality development.

15. _____ In psychoanalytic theory, largely unconscious distortions of thought or perception that act to reduce anxiety.

16. _____ In Freud's theory, age-related developmental periods in which the child's sexual urges are expressed through different areas of the body and the activities associated with those areas.

True/False Test

Indicate whether each statement is true or false by placing T or F in the blank space next to each item.

1. ____ The final psychosexual stage of development, during which the person directs sexual urges toward socially acceptable substitutes and away from morally and societally prohibited ones, is called the phallic stage.

2. ____ As the Oedipus complex unfolds, the little boy feels affection for his mother and hostility and jealousy toward his father but realizes that his father is more physically powerful than he is; the boy experiences castration anxiety, or the fear that his father will punish him by castrating him.

3. ____ Fixation occurs if the child is frustrated or overindulged in his or her attempts to resolve the conflict associated with a stage, and the individual will continue to seek pleasure through behaviors that are similar to those associated with that psychosexual stage.

4. ____ In Freud's theory, the death instinct, reflected in aggressive, destructive, and self-destructive actions, is called Eros.

5. ____ In psychoanalytic theory, sublimation refers to the unconscious exclusion of anxiety-provoking thoughts, feelings, and memories from conscious awareness; the most fundamental ego defense mechanism.

6. ____ The term *unconscious* is used in Freud's theory to describe thoughts, feelings, wishes, and drives that are operating below the level of conscious awareness.

7. ____ Catharsis is a phenomenon that occurs when puzzling physical and psychological problems disappear after a person expresses pent-up emotions associated with traumatic events that may have been related to his or her problems.

8. ____ In psychoanalytic theory, an ego defense mechanism that involves redirecting sexual

urges toward productive, socially acceptable, nonsexual activities is called repression.

9. ___ As part of the resolution of her Oedipus complex, the little girl discovers that little boys have a penis and that she does not; she experiences a sense of loss, or deprivation, that Freud termed *penis envy*.

10. ___ The genital stage is the third psychosexual stage of development; during this stage, the child's pleasure seeking is focused on his or her genitals.

11. ___ In psychoanalytic theory, identification is an ego defense mechanism that involves reducing anxiety by modeling the behavior and characteristics of another person.

12. ___ The reality principle refers to the awareness of environmental demands and the capacity to accommodate them by postponing gratification until the appropriate time or circumstances exist.

13. ___ In Freud's theory, Thanatos refers to the self-preservation, or life, instinct, reflected in the expression of basic psychological urges that perpetuate the existence of the individual as well as the species.

14. ___ Free association is a psychoanalytic technique in which the patient spontaneously reports all thoughts, feelings, and mental images as they come to mind.

15. ___ All thoughts, feelings, and sensations that a person is aware of at any given moment represent the conscious level of awareness.

16. ___ The pleasure principle refers to the motive to obtain pleasure and avoid tension or discomfort; the most fundamental human motive and the guiding principle of the id.

> Check your answers and review any areas of weakness before going on to the next section.

The Psychoanalytic Perspective: The Neo-Freudians

Preview Questions

Consider the following questions as you study this section of the chapter.

- What are the similarities and differences in the approaches taken by Freud and the neo-Freudians?

- What are the key ideas of Jung, Horney, and Adler?

*Read the section "The Psychoanalytic Perspective: The Neo-Freudians" and **write** your answers to the following:*

1. In general, the neo-Freudians disagreed with Freud on three key points:
   (a) Freud's belief that the primary motivation behind behavior is _____ urges.
   (b) Freud's contention that personality is fundamentally determined by _____ experiences; the neo-Freudians believed that personality can also be influenced by experiences throughout the lifespan.
   (c) Freud's generally _____ (optimistic/pessimistic) view of human nature.

2. (a) Carl Jung rejected Freud's belief that human behavior is fueled by the instinctual drives of _____ and _____ ; instead, he believed that people are motivated by a more general psychological energy that pushes them to achieve psychological _____ , self-_____ , and psychic wholeness and harmony.
   (b) Jung believed that the deepest part of the individual psyche is the _____ unconscious, which is shared by all people and reflects humanity's _____ evolutionary history.
   (c) The mental images of universal human instincts, themes, and preoccupations, called _____ , are contained in the _____ unconscious.
   (d) Jung described two important archetypes: the _____ and the _____—the representations of feminine and masculine qualities. To achieve psychological harmony, men must recognize

and accept their _____ aspects and women must recognize and accept the _____ side of their nature.

(e) Jung's ideas make sense if you think of the _____ unconscious as reflecting shared human experiences and _____ as symbols that represent the common, universal themes of the human life cycle, such as birth, achieving a sense of self, parenthood, the spiritual search, and death.

(f) Jung was the first to describe two basic personality types: the _____ and the _____ ; Jung's emphasis on the drive toward psychological growth and self-realization anticipated some of the basic ideas of the _____ perspective on personality.

3. (a) In contrast to Freud, Karen Horney stressed the importance of _____ and _____ factors; specifically, she emphasized the importance of _____ relationships, especially the parent–child relationship, in the development of personality.

(b) Horney believed that disturbances in _____ relationships, not sexual conflicts, are the cause of psychological problems; such psychological problems arise from the attempt to deal with the feeling a child has of being isolated and helpless in a potentially hostile world; Horney called this apprehension and fear _____ .

(c) Horney described three patterns of behavior that the individual uses to defend against _____ : moving toward, against, or away from other people.

(d) Those who move toward other people have an excessive need for _____ and _____ ; those who move against others have an excessive need for _____ , and they are often

_____ , _____ , and domineering and need to feel superior to others; and those who move away from other people have an excessive need for _____ and self- _____ , which often makes them aloof and detached from others.

(e) Horney contended that people with a healthy personality are _____ in balancing these different needs; when one pattern becomes the predominant way of dealing with other people and the world, psychological conflict and problems can result.

(f) Horney disagreed with Freud's notion of _____ envy and instead proposed that men suffer from _____ envy; like Jung, she believed that people are not doomed to psychological conflict and problems and contended that the drive to grow psychologically and achieve one's potential are basic human motives.

4. (a) Alfred Adler believed that the most fundamental motive was the desire to improve oneself, master challenges, and move toward self-perfection and self-realization, which he called _____ . This arises from universal feelings of _____ that are experienced during infancy and childhood, when the child is helpless and dependent on others.

(b) These feelings motivate people to _____ for their real or imagined weaknesses by emphasizing their talents and abilities and by working hard to improve themselves. Adler saw the universal feelings of _____ as ultimately being constructive and valuable.

(c) When people are unable to compensate for specific weaknesses or when their feelings of are excessive, they can develop a(n) _____ complex.

(d) At the other extreme, people can

_____ for their feelings of inferiority, which may result in exaggerating
one's accomplishments and importance in an
effort to cover up weaknesses and denying
the reality of one's limitations; Adler called
this a _____ .

The Psychoanalytic Perspective: Evaluating Freud and the Psychoanalytic Perspective on Personality

Preview Questions

Consider the following questions as you study this section of the chapter.

- What influences has the psychoanalytic perspective had on Western culture and on psychology?
- What are the three criticisms of Freud's theory and, more generally, the psychoanalytic perspective?

Read the section "Evaluating Freud and the Psychoanalytic Perspective on Personality" and **write** *your answers to the following:*

1. Although Sigmund Freud's ideas have had a profound and lasting effect on psychology and on society, there are several valid criticisms of Freud's theory and psychoanalysis:

    (a) First, Freud's theory relies wholly on data derived from a relatively small sample of patients and from his self-analysis. He did not take notes during his private therapy sessions, and so we have only Freud's interpretations of the cases; this problem has to do with the ability to _____ evaluate the evidence.

    (b) Many psychoanalytic concepts, because they are so vague and ambiguous, are very difficult to scientifically _____ . In addition, because even seemingly contradictory information can be used to support

Freud's theory, psychoanalytic concepts are often impossible to _____ .
Psychoanalysis is also better at explaining past behavior than at predicting future behavior.

    (c) Several of Freud's ideas have been substantiated by empirical evidence, including the ideas that much of mental life is

    _____ ; that early _____ experiences have a critical influence on interpersonal relationships and psychological adjustment in adulthood; and that people differ significantly in the degree to which they are able to _____ their impulses, emotions, and thoughts toward adaptive and socially acceptable ends.

    (d) Many people feel that Freud's theories reflect a(n) _____ view of women; Freud's theory uses _____ psychology as a prototype, and women are essentially viewed as a deviation from the norm of masculinity.

2. Read the following and write the correct term in the space provided.

    (a) Wilfred suffered a lot of physical hardship and abuse as a child; as an adult, he lacks confidence, can't hold a job for long, and feels that nothing is really worth striving for. Adler would have said that Wilfred suffers from feelings of _____ .

    (b) In a class discussion, Louanne disputed Freud's assumption that women are inferior to men and that they suffer from penis envy; instead, she suggested that men suffer from womb envy and feel inadequate because they are incapable of bearing children. Louanne's views are most consistent with those of personality theorist

    _____ .

    (c) Adrian's therapist suggested that, to achieve psychological harmony, Adrian has to recognize and accept his feminine side, or anima. The therapist is referring to an important archetype in _____ theory of personality.

(d) Terry has an excessive need to exert power over people; he is very competitive, critical, and domineering and needs to feel superior to others. Horney would have suggested that Terry is defending against _____ by moving _____ other people.

(e) Frank is very sociable and outgoing and has a keen interest in sports and outdoor activities. Jung would probably describe Frank as a(n) _____ personality type.

Review of Terms, Concepts, and Names 2

Use the terms in this list to complete the Matching Test, then to help you answer the True/False items correctly.

neo-Freudians	Karen Horney
Carl Jung	basic anxiety
collective unconscious	womb envy
archetypes	Alfred Adler
anima	striving for superiority
animus	feelings of inferiority
introvert	inferiority complex
extravert	superiority complex

Matching Exercise

Match the appropriate term/name with its definition or description.

1. _____ German-born American psychoanalyst who emphasized the role of social relationships and culture in personality; sharply disagreed with Freud's characterization of female psychological development, especially his notion that women suffer from penis envy; key ideas included basic anxiety.

2. _____ In Jung's theory, the inherited mental images of universal human instincts, themes, and preoccupations that are the main components of the collective unconscious.

3. _____ In Adler's theory, the desire to improve oneself, master challenges, and move toward self-perfection and self-realization, considered to be the most fundamental human motive.

4. _____ Fundamental emotion that Horney described as the feeling a child has of being isolated and helpless in a potentially hostile world.

5. _____ Adler's term for the personality characteristic that people who are unable to compensate for specific weaknesses develop; a general sense of inadequacy, weakness, and helplessness.

6. _____ In Jung's theory, the basic personality type that focuses attention and energy toward the outside world.

7. _____ An important archetype that, according to Jung, represents the feminine side in every person.

8. _____ In Jung's theory, the hypothesized part of the unconscious mind that is inherited from previous generations and that contains universally shared ancestral experiences and ideas.

True/False Test

Indicate whether each statement is true or false by placing T or F in the blank space next to each item.

1. ____ The term *neo-Freudians* was given to the early followers of Freud who developed their own theories yet still recognized the importance of many of Freud's basic notions, such as the influence of unconscious processes and early childhood experiences.

2. ____ Carl Jung was an Austrian physician who broke with Freud and developed his own psychoanalytic theory of personality, which emphasized social factors and motivation toward self-improvement and self-realization; key ideas included the inferiority complex and the superiority complex.

3. ____ The animus is the archetype in Jung's theory that represents the masculine side of every female.

4. ____ According to Adler's theory, people can overcompensate for their feelings of inferiority and develop a superiority complex, which is characterized by exaggeration of one's accomplishments and importance in an effort to cover up weaknesses and limitations.

5. ____ Horney used the term *womb envy* to

describe the envy that men feel about women's capacity to bear children.

6. ___ In Jung's theory, the introvert is a basic personality type that focuses attention inward.

7. ___ Alfred Adler was the Swiss psychiatrist who broke with Freud to develop his own psychoanalytic theory of personality, which stressed striving toward psychological harmony; key ideas included the collective unconscious and archetypes.

8. ___ According to Adler's theory, striving for superiority arises from universal feelings of inferiority that are experienced during infancy and childhood, when the child is helpless and dependent on others.

Check your answers and review any areas of weakness before going on to the next section.

The Humanistic Perspective on Personality

Preview Questions

Consider the following questions as you study this section of the chapter.

- What is the focus of the humanistic perspective?
- What role do the self-concept, the actualizing tendency, and unconditional positive regard play in Rogers's personality theory?
- What are the key strengths and weaknesses of the humanistic perspective?

*Read the section "The Humanistic Perspective on Personality" and **write** your answers to the following:*

1. (a) In contrast to Freud's pessimistic view of people as being motivated by unconscious sexual and destructive instincts, humanistic psychologists saw people as being innately _____ . They also differ in their focus on the _____ personality.

    (b) In contrast to the behaviorist view that human and animal behavior is due largely to environmental reinforcement and punishment, the humanistic psychologists empha-

sized human _____ and such uniquely human characteristics as _____ and _____ . They contended that the most important factor in personality is the individual's _____ , _____ perception of his or her self.

    (c) The two most important contributors to the humanistic perspective were Carl Rogers and Abraham Maslow. Maslow is famous for his _____ of needs, and his research identified several qualities of _____ people.

2. (a) Like Freud, Rogers's personality theory developed out of his clinical experiences with his patients, whom he referred to as "clients" to emphasize their _____ and _____ participation in therapy. In contrast to Freud, Rogers was continually impressed by his clients' drive to _____ and _____ their potential.

    (b) Rogers's observations convinced him that the most basic human motive is the _____ .

3. (a) The cornerstone of Rogers's personality theory is the idea of the _____ .

    (b) People are motivated to act in accordance with their _____ and will deny or distort experiences that create contradictions.

    (c) Because they are motivated by the _____ tendency, infants and young children naturally gravitate toward self-enhancing experiences. As they become more self-aware, they experience an increasing need for _____ regard, which is the sense of being loved and valued by other people, especially one's parents.

4. (a) Rogers maintained that most parents pro-

vide their children with the sense that they are valued and loved only when they behave in a way that is acceptable to others; Rogers called this _____ and suggested that it may cause children to deny or distort genuine feelings.

(b) When people's self-concept conflicts with their actual experience, they are said to be in a state of _____ .

(c) As people continually defend against genuine feelings and experiences that are inconsistent with their _____ , they become progressively more out of touch with their true feelings and essential self, often experiencing psychological problems as a result.

(d) The child's sense of being unconditionally loved and valued, even if he or she doesn't conform to the standards and expectations of others, is called _____ . When parents use this approach, the child's _____ tendency is allowed its fullest expression.

(e) Rogers did not advocate _____ parenting; he thought that parents _____ (were/were not) responsible for controlling their children's behavior and for teaching them acceptable standards. Parents can discipline their child's specific behavior without undermining the child's sense of _____ .

5. (a) Rogers believed that one becomes a psychologically healthy, fully functioning person through consistent experiences of

   _____ .

(b) The fully functioning person has a flexible, constantly evolving _____ ; she is _____ , _____ to new experiences, capable of _____

in response to new experiences, and likely to be creative and spontaneous and to enjoy harmonious relationships with others.

(c) Rather than defending against or distorting her own thoughts or feelings, the person experiences _____ . Her sense of self is consistent with her emotions and experiences, and the _____ tendency is fully operational in her; and she makes conscious choices that move her in the direction of greater _____ and fulfillment of potential.

6. (a) Humanistic psychology has been influential in _____ and in such diverse areas as education, parenting, and even business management practices.

(b) The humanistic perspective has been criticized on two particular points. First, humanistic theories are hard to _____ or _____ scientifically; they tend to be based on philosophical assumptions or clinical observations rather than on _____ research. Some humanistic concepts are difficult to define or measure objectively.

(c) Second, many psychologists believe that humanistic psychology's view of human nature is too _____ (pessimistic/optimistic); for example, if self-actualization is a universal human motive, why are self-actualized people so hard to find?

(d) The influence of humanistic psychology has _____ (increased/decreased) since the 1960s and early 1970s. However, humanistic psychology promoted the scientific study of such topics as the healthy personality and creativity and focused attention on the importance of _____ experience and the _____ .

The Social Cognitive Perspective on Personality

Preview Questions

Consider the following questions as you study this section of the chapter.

- What is the focus of the social cognitive perspective?
- What is the principle of reciprocal determinism, and what is the role of self-efficacy beliefs in personality?
- What are the key strengths and weaknesses of the social cognitive perspective?

Read the section "The Social Cognitive Perspective on Personality" and **write** *your answers to the following:*

1. (a) One important characteristic of the social cognitive perspective is the idea that a person's _____ thought processes in different _____ strongly influences his or her actions.

   (b) People are seen as actively processing information from their _____ experiences; this information influences their _____ , _____ , _____ , and behavior as well as the specific environments they choose.

2. The social cognitive perspective differs from psychoanalytic and humanistic perspectives in several ways:

   (a) First, rather than basing their approach on _____ or insights derived from psychotherapy, social cognitive theorists rely heavily on _____ findings.

   (b) Second, the social cognitive perspective emphasizes _____ , self-regulated behavior rather than _____ mental influences and instinctual drives.

   (c) Third, social cognitive theory emphasizes that our sense of self can vary, depending on our _____ , _____ , and behaviors in a given situation.

3. (a) Although several contemporary personality theorists have embraced the social cognitive approach, probably the most influential is

   _____ .

   (b) This theorist's approach to personality reflects his ideas on observational learning and _____ .

   (c) Social cognitive theory emphasizes the social origins of thoughts and action, but also stresses the active _____ processes and the human capacity for

   _____ .

4. (a) Bandura's research has shown that we attend not only to the actions of others, but also to the _____ that follow the actions, to the rules and standards that apply to behavior in specific situations, and to the ways in which people _____ their own behavior.

   (b) The environment influences our thoughts and actions, our thoughts influence our actions and the environments we choose, and our actions influence our thoughts and the environments we choose; thus, Bandura's process of _____ operates in a circular fashion.

5. (a) Collectively, the emerging cognitive skills, abilities, attitudes, and especially beliefs of self-efficacy represent our _____ , which guides how we perceive, evaluate, and control our behavior in different situations.

   (b) The degree to which we are subjectively convinced of our own capabilities and effectiveness in meeting the demands of a particular situation is called _____ .

   (c) Our self-system is very _____ ; how we regard ourselves and our abilities varies depending on the situations or tasks we're facing; in turn, the tasks we are willing to try and how persistent we'll be in the face of obstacles is influenced by our

_____ about our self-efficacy.

(d) When we perform a task successfully, our sense of _____ becomes stronger; when we fail to deal effectively with a particular task or situation, our sense of _____ is undermined.

(e) From very early in life, children develop feelings of self-efficacy from _____ in dealing with different tasks and situations, such as athletics and social and academic activities; this is a lifelong process.

6. (a) A key strength of the social cognitive perspective on personality is its grounding in empirical, laboratory research; it is built on research in _____ , _____ psychology, and _____ psychology rather than on clinical impressions.

(b) Unlike the vague psychoanalytic and humanistic concepts, the concepts of social cognitive theory are scientifically _____ ; they can be operationally defined and measured.

(c) However, some psychologists believe that real-life, everyday situations are not adequately captured in the typical laboratory research situation because they are more _____ , with _____ factors converging to affect behavior and personality. They have argued, therefore, that _____ data may, in fact, be more reflective of the whole person.

(d) Other psychologists argue that the social cognitive perspective ignores _____ influences, emotions, and conflicts; it lacks the richness of psychoanalytic or humanistic theories, which strive to explain the whole person, including _____ , irrational, and emotional aspects of personality.

(e) The social cognitive perspective recognizes the complex combination of factors that influence our everyday behavior because it emphasizes the reciprocal interaction of _____ , _____ , and _____ factors.

(f) The social cognitive perspective also offers a developmental explanation of human functioning that persists throughout our lifetime because it emphasizes the important role of _____ , especially observational _____ .

(g) Finally, the social cognitive perspective places most of the responsibility for our behavior and the consequences that we experience squarely on our shoulders because it emphasizes the _____ of behavior.

The Trait Perspective on Personality

Preview Questions

Consider the following questions as you study this section of the chapter.

- What is the focus of trait theories, and what are three influential trait theories?
- How are traits defined, and what is the difference between surface traits and source traits?
- How is the expression of personality traits affected by situational demands?

*Read the section "The Trait Perspective on Personality" and **write** your answers to the following:*

1. (a) The psychoanalytic, humanistic, and social cognitive theories emphasize the _____ among people, whereas the trait approach to personality focuses primarily on describing individual _____ . Trait theorists view the person as being a unique combination of relatively stable, enduring personality _____ or _____ , called traits.

(b) People possess traits to different

_____ . Thus, traits are typically described in terms of a range from one extreme to its opposite, with most people falling in the middle of the range and fewer people falling at opposite poles.

2. (a) Surface traits, as the name implies, lie on the surface and can be easily inferred from observable _____ (for example, gloomy, cheerful, anxious, forgetful). To narrow down the number of traits to investigate, trait theorists systematically _____ related surface traits in order to identify broader source traits.

    (b) Source traits are thought to be more _____ than surface traits and can give rise to a vast number of them. One goal of trait theorists has been to identify the most basic set of universal source traits that can be used to describe all individual _____ .

3. (a) Pioneer trait theorist Raymond Cattell used a statistical technique called _____ to identify the traits that were most closely related to one another; he eventually reduced the number of source traits to _____ key personality factors.

    (b) To measure these traits, Cattell developed what has become one of the most widely used personality tests, the _____ Questionnaire (abbreviated _____).

4. Hans Eysenck's conception of personality includes just three dimensions.
    (a) The first dimension, the degree to which a person directs his or her energies outward toward the environment and other people versus inward toward inner and self-focused experiences, is called _____ .

    (b) The second major dimension is

_____ ; surface traits, such as anxiety, tension, depression, and guilt are associated with _____ ; at the opposite end, surface traits such as being calm, relaxed, and even-tempered are associated with _____ .

    (c) Eysenck believed that by combining these two dimensions people could be classified into four basic types:

_____ ,

_____ ,

_____ ,

and _____ ; each type is associated with a different combination of surface traits.

    (d) In later research, Eysenck identified a third personality dimension, called _____ ; a person high on _____ is antisocial, cold, hostile, and unconcerned about others, whereas a person low on this trait is warm and caring toward others.

5. (a) Eysenck believes that individual differences in personality are due to _____ differences among people and that an _____ (introvert's/extravert's) nervous system is more easily aroused than an _____ (introvert's/extravert's) nervous system. Research _____ (has/has not) provided some tentative support for this idea.

    (b) Assuming that people tend to seek out an optimal level of arousal, _____ would seek stimulation from their environment more than _____ would.

    (c) Research has shown that _____ preferred to study in a relatively noisy, open area with ample opportunities for socializing, whereas _____ preferred to study in a quiet section of the library.

6. (a) Today, the consensus among many trait

researchers is that the essential building blocks of personality can be described in terms of _____ basic personality dimensions, which are sometimes called the Big _____ ; these dimensions represent the structural organization of personality traits.

(b) The most commonly accepted factors according to the five-factor model of personality traits are _____ , _____ , _____ , _____ , and _____ to experience; these appear to be universal.

(c) Research has shown that traits are remarkably _____ (stable/unstable) across time. Today, most psychologists generally agree that personality traits are basically _____ (consistent/inconsistent) over time and in different situations.

(d) Human behavior, however, is the result of a complex _____ between traits and situations; the situations that people choose and the characteristic way they respond to similar situations are likely to be _____ (consistent/inconsistent) with their individual personality dispositions.

Personality Traits and Genetics: Just a Chip Off the Old Block?

Preview Questions

Consider the following questions as you study this section of the chapter.

- What is the focus of behavioral genetics?
- What is a heritability estimate, and how is it determined?
- To what degree are personality traits inherited, and what role do environmental influences play?
- What are the key strengths and weaknesses of the trait perspective?

*Read the section "Personality Traits and Genetics: Just a Chip Off the Old Block?" and **write** your answers to the following:*

1. (a) The field of behavioral genetics studies the effects of genes and heredity on behavior; research involves measuring _____ and _____ among members of a large group of people who are genetically related to different degrees.

(b) One strategy is to study _____ twins who were separated at birth or in early infancy and raised in different families; another method is to compare _____ individuals to adoptive siblings, their adoptive parents, or their biological parents.

(c) If a trait is genetically influenced, you would expect the degree of similarity between people to follow the degree of relatedness; thus, on a given trait, the most similar individuals would be _____ ; those who share approximately 50 percent of their genes, _____ and _____ , would be somewhat less similar; unrelated individuals, such as _____ children, would be even less similar; and the least similar individuals would be_____ _____ .

2. (a) When adoption studies and twins-reared-apart investigations are used with large groups of subjects, behavior geneticists can calculate a rough measurement of the degree to which differences within a given population are influenced by genetics; this is called a(n) _____ .

(b) If a particular trait was completely due to genetics, its heritability estimate would be

_____ ; if genetics played no role in the trait, the heritability estimate would be _____ .

(c) It's important to stress that a heritability estimate describes only the degree to which _____ within a specific group of people are due to genetics; it cannot be used to account for the characteristics of a particular individual.

(d) Heredity seems to play a significant role in two personality traits: _____ and _____ ; it plays a somewhat lesser role in the traits of _____ to experience and _____ . However, the influence of environmental factors is at least equal to the influence of genetics.

3. (a) Overall, sibling personality _____ (differences/similarities) are far greater than their _____ (differences/similarities). It has been suggested that nonshared experiences account for much of the personality _____ among siblings; siblings growing up in the same family _____ (do/do not) experience identical environmental influences.

(b) A child's genetically influenced traits _____ (may/may not) influence how he or she is treated by parents.

(c) Another significant effect on children's personalities is the interaction between _____ . In addition, other varied experiences, such as relationships with peers and teachers, accidents, illnesses, and events that affect the whole family, such as divorce, job loss, or a family move, may be experienced _____ (in the same way/quite differently) by each child in the family.

4. (a) Psychologists _____ (agree/disagree) on how many basic traits exist; psychologists _____ (agree/disagree)

that people can be described and compared in terms of basic personality traits.

(b) One criticism of trait theories is that they don't really _____ human personality; instead, they simply _____ general predispositions to behave in a certain way.

(c) A second criticism is that trait theorists don't attempt to _____ how or why individual differences develop.

(d) A third criticism is that trait approaches generally fail to address other important personality issues, such as the basic _____ that drive human personality, the role of _____ mental processes, how beliefs about the self influence personality, or how psychological _____ and _____ occur.

(e) Conspicuously absent are the grand conclusions about the essence of human nature that characterize the _____ and _____ theories.

5. Read the following and write the correct term in the space provided.

(a) Dunja is confident in her ability to service her own car but is less sure of her ability to bake cakes and cookies. According to Bandura, Dunja's different beliefs about her own abilities are her _____ beliefs.

(b) Eileen is consistently cheerful, optimistic, talkative, and impulsive. These traits, which are inferred from her observable behavior, are referred to as _____ traits.

(c) Navi is viewed by her family and friends as a flexible, creative, spontaneous, open, caring person who likes and is liked by most people. Carl Rogers would probably describe her as a(n) _____ person.

(d) Alfred believes that from an early age we

develop a set of perceptions and beliefs about ourselves, our nature, and our personal qualities and are motivated to act in accordance with these perceptions. Alfred's belief about personality development is most consistent with

_____

theory.

(e) Dr. Bhatt is concerned with describing, classifying, and measuring the numerous ways in which individuals may differ from one another. Her approach is most characteristic of the _____ perspective on personality.

(f) Whenever her son misbehaves, Rochelle's

disciplinary strategy is to make sure he clearly understands that his behavior is not acceptable while taking care to reassure him that he is loved and valued. Rachel is using Rogers's concept of

_____ .

(g) Dr. Lavalle studies the effects of heredity on behavior. In his research, he studies identical and fraternal twins who were separated at birth, identical and fraternal twins raised together, and the similarities and differences between adopted children and their adoptive and biological parents. Dr. Lavalle works in the field of

_____ .

Graphic Organizer 2

Read the following statements and match the personality theorist and theory/perspective associated with each:

Statement	Theorist	Theory/Perspective
1. I believe that people can be classified into four basic types: introverted-neurotic, introverted-stable, extraverted-neurotic, and extraverted-stable.		
2. It is my belief that people have an innate drive to maintain and enhance themselves. This actualizing tendency is the most basic human motive, and all other motives, whether biological or social, are secondary.		
3. I reduced Allport's 4,000 terms to 171, and then, by using factor analysis, I eventually came up with 16 personality factors that represent the essential source of human personality.		
4. My theory of personality stresses the influence of unconscious mental processes, the importance of sexual and aggressive instincts, and the enduring effects of early childhood experiences on personality.		
5. For me the most fundamental human motive is striving for superiority, which arises from universal feelings of inferiority. Depending on how people deal with these feelings, they may develop either an inferiority complex or a superiority complex.		
6. My research suggests that human functioning is caused by the interaction of behavioral, cognitive, and environmental factors, a process I call reciprocal determinism.		
7. For me the impact of social relationships and the nature of the parent-child interaction are the main determinants of personality. Different patterns of behavior develop as people try to deal with their basic anxiety. Males have an additional problem to deal with, womb envy.		
8. I am most well known for my theory of motivation and the notion of a hierarchy of needs. I also identified the qualities most associated with self-actualized people.		
9. It is apparent to me, from my observations of different cultures and my own patients, that the deepest part of the individual psyche is the collective unconscious, which contains universal archetypes. Personality can be described on two basic dimensions, introversion and extraversion.		

Review of Terms, Concepts, and Names 3

Use the terms in this list to complete the Matching Test, then to help you answer the True/False items correctly.

humanistic psychology
Abraham Maslow
Carl Rogers
actualizing tendency
self-concept
positive regard
conditional positive
  regard
incongruence
unconditional positive
  regard
fully functioning person
congruence
Albert Bandura
self-efficacy
social cognitive theory
reciprocal determinism

self-system
trait
trait theory
surface trait
source traits
Raymond Cattell
Hans Eysenck
introversion
extraversion
neuroticism
emotional stability
psychoticism
five-factor model of
  personality
behavioral genetics
heritability estimate

Matching Exercise

Match the appropriate term/name with its definition or description.

1. _____ A relatively stable, enduring predisposition to consistently behave in a certain way.

2. _____ People's beliefs about their ability to meet the demands of a specific situation; feelings of self-confidence or self-doubt.

3. _____ Contemporary American psychologist who is best known for his research on observational learning and his social cognitive theory of personality; key ideas include self-efficacy beliefs and reciprocal determinism.

4. _____ In Rogers's theory, the innate drive to maintain and enhance the human organism.

5. _____ Trait theory of personality that identifies five basic source traits (extraversion, neuroticism, agreeableness, conscientiousness, and openness to experience) as the fundamental building blocks of personality.

6. _____ American psychologist who was one of the founders of humanistic psychology and emphasized the study of healthy person-

ality development; developed a hierarchical theory of motivation based on the idea that people will strive for self-actualization, the highest motive, only after more basic needs have been met; key ideas included the hierarchy of needs and self-actualization.

7. _____ In Eysenck's theory, a third dimension of personality; a person high on this trait is antisocial, cold, hostile, and unconcerned about others, whereas a person low on this trait is warm and caring toward others.

8. _____ In Rogers's theory, the term for the sense of being loved and valued by other people, especially one's parents.

9. _____ A numerical estimate of the degree to which differences within a specific group of people are due to genetics.

10. _____ Bandura's theory of personality, which emphasizes the importance of observational learning, conscious cognitive processes, social experiences, self-efficacy beliefs, and reciprocal determinism.

11. _____ Theory of personality that focuses on identifying, describing, and measuring individual differences in attributes.

12. _____ In Eysenck's theory, the dimension of personality that describes people who direct their energies outward toward the environment and other people; a person high on this dimension would be outgoing and sociable, enjoying new experiences and stimulating environments.

13. _____ American psychologist who was one of the founders of humanistic psychology; developed a theory of personality and form of psychotherapy that emphasized the inherent worth of people, the innate tendency to strive toward one's potential, and the importance of the self-concept in personality development; key ideas included actualizing tendency and unconditional positive regard.

14. _____ Theoretical viewpoint on personality that generally emphasizes the inherent goodness of people, human potential, self-actualization, the self-concept, and healthy personality development.

15. _____ Albert Bandura's model that explains human functioning and personality as caused by the interaction of behavioral, cognitive, and environmental factors.

True/False Test

Indicate whether each statement is true or false by placing T or F in the blank space next to each item.

1. ____ Behavioral genetics is an interdisciplinary field that studies the effects of genes and heredity on behavior.

2. ____ In Rogers's theory, people are in a state of congruence when their feelings and experiences are denied and distorted because they contradict or conflict with their self-concept.

3. ____ Hans Eysenck was a British-born American psychologist who developed a trait theory that identifies 16 essential source traits or personality factors; also developed the widely used self-report personality test, the Sixteen Personality Factor Questionnaire (16PF).

4. ____ Personality characteristics or attributes that can easily be inferred from observable behavior are called source traits.

5. ____ In Rogers's theory, the sense that you will be valued and loved only if you behave in a way that is acceptable to others is called conditional positive regard.

6. ____ Self-concept is the set of perceptions and beliefs that you hold about yourself.

7. ____ In Eysenck's theory, neuroticism refers to a person's predisposition to become emotionally upset.

8. ____ In Rogers's theory, the fully functioning person has a flexible, constantly evolving self-concept and is realistic, open to new experiences, and capable of changing in response to new experiences.

9. ____ Unconditional positive regard, in Rogers's theory, is the sense that you will be valued and loved even if you don't conform to the standards and expectations of others.

10. ____ A surface trait is the most fundamental dimension of personality; these broad basic traits are hypothesized to be universal and relatively few in number.

11. ____ In Rogers's theory, people are in a state of incongruence when their sense of self (their self-concept) is consistent with their emotions and experiences.

12. ____ Raymond Cattell was a German-born British psychologist who developed a trait theory of personality that identifies the three basic dimensions of personality as neuroticism, extraversion, and psychoticism.

13. ____ In Eysenck's theory, emotional stability reflects a person's predisposition to be emotionally even.

14. ____ Cognitive skills, abilities, and attitudes that emerge through developmental experiences involving the interaction of behavioral, cognitive, and environmental factors represent the person's self-system.

15. ____ In Eysenck's theory, introversion is a personality dimension in which the person directs his or her energies inward, toward inner, self-focused experiences; a person high on this dimension might be quiet, solitary, and reserved, avoiding new experiences.

Check your answers and review any areas of weakness before going on to the next section.

Assessing Personality: Psychological Tests

Preview Questions

Consider the following questions as you study this section of the chapter.

- How are self-report inventories and projective tests used to measure personality, and how are they administered and scored?

- What are the key strengths and weaknesses of self-report inventories and projective tests?

*Read the section "Assessing Personality: Psychological Tests" and **write** your answers to the following:*

1. (a) There are literally hundreds of psychological tests that can be used to assess abilities, aptitudes, interest, and personality; they are useful insofar as they accurately and consistently reflect a person's _____ on some dimension and can predict a person's future _____ functioning or _____ .

   (b) Tests developed out of the psychoanalytic approaches to personality are called _____ . A person's response to a vague image, such as an inkblot or an ambiguous scene, is thought to be a(n) _____ of his or her unconscious conflicts, motives, psychological defenses, and personality traits.

(c) The first projective test, which consists of ten cards, five that show black and white inkblots and five that depict colored inkblots, is the _____ . As the person describes what he sees in each inkblot, his responses are recorded verbatim and his behavior, gestures, and reactions are observed.

(d) Numerous scoring systems exist for the Rorschach. Interpretation is based on such criteria as whether the person reports seeing _____ or _____ objects, _____ or _____ figures, and movement, and whether the person deals with the whole blot or just part of it.

2. (a) In a more structured test, the person is asked to look at a series of cards, each depicting an ambiguous scene, and create a story about the scene, including what the characters are feeling and how the story turns out. This is the

_____ ,

abbreviated as _____ .

(b) The stories are scored for the

_____ , _____ ,

_____ , and conflicts of the main character and how conflicts are resolved. As with the Rorschach, interpreting the TAT involves the subjective judgment of the examiner.

3. (a) Projective tests are used mainly to help assess emotionally disturbed individuals. Their primary strength is that they provide a wealth of _____ information about an individual's psychological functioning that can be explored further in psychotherapy.

(b) There are several drawbacks to projective tests: a person's responses can be influenced

by the _____ situation or the examiner's _____ . The scoring of these tests is highly _____ (objective/subjective), with low interrater reliability; because the same person may obtain different results on separate occasions, the tests often fail to produce _____ results. Finally, the tests are poor at predicting future behavior.

(c) Despite their widespread use, especially among clinical psychologists, hundreds of studies of projective tests seriously question their _____ (that the tests measure what they purport to measure) and their _____ (the consistency of test results).

4. (a) Tests that typically use a paper-and-pencil format and take a direct, structured approach to assessing personality are called _____ . The person answers specific questions or rates herself on various dimensions of behavior and psychological functioning.

(b) Often called objective personality tests, _____ inventories contain items that have been shown by previous research to differentiate between people on a particular personality characteristic; they are _____ (objectively/subjectively) scored against standardized norms.

(c) The most widely used self-report inventory is the Minnesota Multiphasic Personality Inventory (MMPI), which consists of 500 statements that the subject responds to with "True," "False," or "Cannot say." Topics include social, political, religious, and _____ attitudes, physical and _____ health, interpersonal relationships, and _____ thoughts and behaviors.

(d) The MMPI is widely used by _____ psychologists and _____ to assess patients; it is also used to evaluate the _____ health of candidates for such occupations as police officers, doctors, nurses, and professional pilots.

(e) Like many other self-report inventories, the MMPI has special scales to detect whether a person is answering honestly and _____ .

5. (a) In contrast to the MMPI, the California Personality Inventory (CPI) and the Sixteen Personality Factor Questionnaire (16PF) are personality inventories that are designed to assess _____ populations.

(b) The CPI provides measures on such characteristics as _____ effectiveness, self-_____ , independence, and empathy; profiles generated are used to predict such things as high school and college grades, delinquency, and _____ performance.

(c) The 16PF was originally developed by

_____

and is based on his trait theory. It uses a _____ format in which the person must respond to each item by choosing one of three alternatives.

(d) The results generate a profile on Cattell's 16 personality factors; each factor represents a range, with a person's score falling somewhere along the continuum between two extremes. The 16PF is widely used for _____ counseling, _____ counseling, and evaluating employees and executives.

6. (a) The two most important strengths of self-report inventories are their _____ on a comparable population and the use of established _____ ; the results of self-report inventories are _____ (subjectively/objectively) scored (by hand or by com-

puter) and compared to _____ established by previous research.

(b) The reliability and validity of self-report inventories are _____ (far less/far greater) than those of projective tests; research has demonstrated that the MMPI, the CPI, and the 16PF provide accurate, consistent results that can be used to generally _____ behavior.

(c) Weaknesses of self-report inventories include the fact that people can successfully fake responses and answer in _____ desirable ways; some people are prone to responding in a set way, such as answering "True" to all items; finally, people are not always accurate _____ of their own behavior, attitudes, attributes, and true feelings.

(d) Personality tests are generally useful strategies that can provide insights about the _____ makeup of people but are unlikely to provide a definitive description of a given individual; people can and often do change over time, so projective tests and self-report inventories provide a barometer of _____ and _____ functioning only at the time of the test.

7. Read the following and write the correct term in the space provided.

(a) Michelle was given a psychological test in which she was asked to look at a series of cards with ambiguous scenes and make up stories for each one. She was told to give as much detail as possible about what the characters are feeling and how the story ends. Michelle was given a(n) _____ test called the

_____ .

(b) When Roger was assessed for his suitability to be a police officer, he was given a 500-item test that was used to evaluate his mental health. The test he was given was most likely the _____ .

(c) Mr. and Mrs. Sheldrake want to get some idea of how their son is going to do in high school. The test that is best at predicting their son's high school grades is the

_____ .

(d) In his psychoanalytic practice Dr. Coles tries to understand his client's unconscious conflicts, motives, psychological defenses, and personality traits. It is very probable that Dr. Coles uses a(n) _____ test called the _____ .

(e) Dr. Cera sees a lot of married couples in his counseling practice. In an effort to help them resolve their conflicts, he frequently administers a test to each partner, which generates a profile of their personality characteristics. Dr. Cera most likely uses the

_____ .

Review of Terms and Concepts 4

Use the terms in this list to complete the Matching Test, then to help you answer the True/False items correctly.

psychological test
projective test
Rorschach Inkblot Test
Thematic Apperception Test (TAT)
self-report inventory
Minnesota Multiphasic Personality Inventory (MMPI)
California Personality Inventory (CPI)
Sixteen Personality Factor Questionnaire (16PF)
possible selves
graphology

Matching Exercise

Match the appropriate term with its definition or description.

1. _____ Type of psychological test in which a person's responses to standardized questions are compared with established norms.

2. _____ Projective test that uses inkblots, developed by Swiss psychiatrist Hermann Rorschach in 1921.

3. _____ Self-report inventory that assesses personality characteristics in normal populations.

4. _____ Test that assesses a person's abilities, aptitudes, interests, or personality, based on a systematically obtained sample of behavior.

5. _____ Self-report inventory developed by Raymond Cattell that generates a personality profile with ratings on 16 trait dimensions.

True/False Test

Indicate whether each statement is true or false by placing T or F in the blank space next to each item.

1. ___ A projective test is a type of personality test that involves a person's interpreting an ambiguous image and is used to assess unconscious motives, conflicts, psychological defenses, and personality traits.

2. ___ Possible selves refers to an aspect of the self-concept that includes images of the selves that you hope, fear, or expect to become in the future.

3. ___ The Minnesota Multiphasic Personality Inventory (MMPI) is a projective personality test that involves creating stories about each of a series of ambiguous scenes.

4. ___ The Thematic Apperception Test (TAT) is a self-report inventory that assesses personality characteristics and psychological disorders; used to assess both normal and disturbed populations.

5. ___ Graphology is a pseudoscience that claims to assess personality as well as social and occupational attributes based on a person's distinctive handwriting, doodles, and drawing style.

Check your answers and review any areas of weakness before going on to the next section.

Something to Think About

1. The use of psychological tests has been and will continue to be an interesting topic of discussion for most people. Almost everyone has heard of the famous inkblot test, but not everyone knows its purpose or its limitations. Considering what you have learned about psychological tests in this chapter, what would you tell someone about the inkblot test and psychological tests in general?

2. The history of astrology can be traced back over 4,000 years. Astrology's basic premise is that the positions of the planets and stars at the time and place of your birth determine your personality and destiny. Today, belief in astrological predictions remains widespread. Indeed,

you probably know a number of people who, even if they are not true believers, at least read their daily horoscope in the paper. How might you enlighten these people about scientific research on astrology?

> Check your answers and review any areas of weakness before doing the progress tests.

Progress Test 1

Review the complete chapter (including Concept Reviews and the boxed inserts), review all your study notes, and then test yourself on the following progress test. Check your answers. If you make a mistake, review your notes, review the relevant section of the study guide, and, if necessary, go back and read the appropriate part of your textbook.

1. Marvin is angry and upset after an argument with his boss. At home that evening he is harshly and unreasonably critical of his son for not getting all his homework assignments completed. According to Freud, Marvin is using an ego defense mechanism called

   (a) identification.   (c) rationalization.
   (b) repression.   (d) displacement.

2. Seven-year old Salvatore prefers to play with his male friends and does not like playing with girls very much. Salvatore is probably in the _____ stage of psychosexual development.

   (a) anal   (c) latency
   (b) phallic   (d) genital

3. Although Tim has many fond memories of his college days, he only vaguely remembers the girl he was engaged to but who left him suddenly for another man. Tim's unconscious forgetting is an ego defense mechanism called

   (a) identification.   (c) displacement.
   (b) sublimation.   (d) repression.

4. Every time two-year-old Kate is given a bath, she plays with her genital area. If her parents chastise or punish her, she is likely to experience frustration, which could lead to an unresolved developmental conflict called

   (a) fixation.   (c) displacement.
   (b) sublimation.   (d) denial.

5. Zachary considers himself to be an outgoing, fun-loving type of person, and he goes to a lot of parties. Sondra, on the other hand, thinks of herself as fairly quiet and shy, and enjoys being by herself, reading a book and listening to classical music. In Jung's theory, Zachary's and Sondra's different behaviors reflect

   (a) the two basic personality type, the extravert and the introvert.
   (b) the two important archetypes, the anima and the animus.
   (c) a superiority complex and an inferiority complex.
   (d) penis envy and womb envy.

6. Read the example in question 5 again. According to social cognitive theory, the different personalities of Zachary and Sondra reflect the interaction of behavioral, cognitive, and environmental factors, a process Bandura called

   (a) identification.
   (b) moving toward others and moving away from others.
   (c) the actualizing tendency.
   (d) reciprocal determinism.

7. As part of a research project, Jasbinder was given the same psychological test three times at two-month intervals by three different therapists. Her results on the tests were all very different. It is most probable that she was given the

   (a) MMPI.   (c) CPI.
   (b) 16PF.   (d) TAT.

8. When Jasmine was researching a term paper for her history of psychology course, she was intrigued by the ideas of the neo-Freudian Karen Horney. She was particularly intrigued by Horney's description of basic patterns of behavior that develop to defend against basic anxiety. These are

   (a) the introvert and the extravert.
   (b) the anal, the oral, and the phallic type.
   (c) striving for superiority and striving for inferiority.
   (d) moving toward others, against others, and away from others.

9. When asked to describe her husband, Mrs. Roech said that he is prone to exaggerating his accomplishments and importance, seems unaware of the reality of his limitations, and tends to overcompensate for his feelings of inferiority and weakness. Adler would probably have said that Mr. Roech has

(a) an inferiority complex.
(b) an extraverted personality.
(c) a superiority complex.
(d) an anal fixation.

10. Katrina thinks of herself as fairly laid back, easygoing, and relatively calm. She believes that she is above average academically and intellectually and sees herself as very conscientious at work and caring and loving with her family. Carl Rogers's term for Katrina's perceptions and beliefs about herself would be
(a) self-efficacy.   (c) self-system.
(b) self-concept.   (d) possible selves.

11. Miguel is giving a lecture on the five-factor model of personality. Which of the following personality dimensions is *not* likely to be included in his talk?
(a) anal retentiveness
(b) extraversion
(c) neuroticism
(d) agreeableness
(e) openness to experience

12. Dr. Markowitz studies the effects of heredity on behavior. One of his areas of research focuses on similarities and differences in identical twins who were separated at birth or early infancy and raised by different families. Dr. Markowitz is most probably a(n)
(a) psychoanalyst.
(b) humanistic psychologist.
(c) social cognitive psychologist.
(d) behavioral geneticist.

13. Zintyre was very impressed when told by an astrologer that, "You are gregarious, outgoing, and fond of travel. You tend to react negatively to authority figures and you have had a number of confrontations as a result. You enjoy good food and good wine and you don't suffer fools gladly." According to Science and Pseudoscience 11.4, which of the following is true?
(a) The astrologer probably has an extraordinary gift for accurately assessing personality.
(b) The astrologer is probably operating at chance level in assessing personality.
(c) The astrologer is using a proven scientific method in his personality assessment of Zintyre.
(d) Zintyre is probably extremely accurate in assessing the accuracy of the astrologer's personality description.

14. According to the Application, the term *possible selves* refers to
(a) the unconscious part of the mind that motivates our behavior.
(b) the major symptom of a fixated personality.
(c) the aspect of the self-concept that includes images of the selves that you hope, fear, or expect to become in the future.
(d) delusional thought processes.

15. According to the Critical Thinking 11.1, which of the following is true?
(a) Freud's view of human nature was deeply pessimistic.
(b) Rogers's view of human nature was deeply pessimistic.
(c) Freud believed that humans are positive, forward-moving, constructive, realistic, and trustworthy.
(d) Rogers believed that the essence of human nature is destructive but that societal, religious, and cultural restraints make people behave in good and moral ways.

Progress Test 2

After you have checked your understanding of the material in Progress Test 1 and have done a complete chapter review with special focus on any areas of weakness, you are ready to assess your knowledge of Progress Test 2. Check your answers. If you make a mistake, review your notes, the relevant section of the study guide, and, if necessary, the appropriate part of your textbook.

1. Nathan chews the end of his pen, bites his nails, overeats, smokes cigarettes, and talks incessantly. According to Freud, Nathan has probably fixated at the _____ stage of psychosexual development due to some unresolved conflict.
(a) oral   (c) phallic
(b) anal   (d) genital

2. Marsha, Matthew, and Maxwell are siblings. They share about 50 percent of their genes and were brought up in the same household by the same parents. It would be safe to predict that their personalities
(a) are more different than they are similar.
(b) are very unlikely to be influenced by genetic variables.
(c) are more similar than they are different.
(d) are very unlikely to be influenced by environmental variables.

3. Shelly was often rejected by her parents; as a result, she mistrusts other people and treats them with hostility, which leads to their rejection of her. This cycle of rejection, mistrust, hostility, and further rejection illustrates what Bandura called

   (a) self-efficacy.
   (b) identification.
   (c) displacement.
   (d) reciprocal determinism.

4. During a class discussion of various perspectives on personality, Sasha points to all the evidence that human beings are destructive and aggressive. He points to the millions who died in two world wars and the ongoing killings and massacres that continue in many parts of the world today. Sasha's observation about basic human nature supports the _____ perspective and is a criticism of the _____ perspective.

   (a) humanistic; psychoanalytic
   (b) trait; social cognitive
   (c) social cognitive; trait
   (d) psychoanalytic; humanistic

5. Dr. Sheenan is a clinical psychologist who wants to assess the extent to which a client is suffering from depression, delusions, and other mental health problems. Dr. Sheenan is most likely to use the

   (a) 16PF.   (c) MMPI.
   (b) CPI.   (d) TAT.

6. When Cindy was given the Rorschach Inkblot Test, she reported seeing a number of inanimate objects and some animal figures and tended to concentrate on very small details in each inkblot. Her therapist observed her behavior, gestures, and reactions as she responded to each card. It is most probable that her therapist is

   (a) interested in her unconscious conflicts, motives, and psychological defenses.
   (b) assessing her suitability for a particular occupation, such as police officer or pilot.
   (c) trying to generate a personality profile based on a number of personality traits.
   (d) trying to predict how she will perform academically when she goes to college.

7. In analyzing data from large numbers of subjects in adoption and twins-reared-apart studies, Dr. Producesk has arrived at a rough measure of the degree to which differences within a specific group are due to genetics. Dr. Producesk has calculated

   (a) the actualizing tendency of people.
   (b) the reciprocal determinism factor.
   (c) the factor analysis coefficient.
   (d) a heritability estimate.

8. Five-year-old Dunstan has recently become very possessive of his mother and appears to be jealous of his father. He is sometimes openly hostile, telling his father, "Don't kiss my Mommy!" According to Freud, Dunstan is in the _____ stage of psychosexual development and showing manifestations of _____ .

   (a) oral; fixation
   (b) anal; fixation
   (c) phallic; the Oedipus complex
   (d) latency; the Oedipus complex

9. Wendy believes that the most fundamental human motive is striving for superiority. She thinks that this drive arises from global feelings of inferiority and that human personality and behavior reflect our attempts to compensate for or overcome our perceived weaknesses. Which personality theorist is most likely to agree with Wendy's views?

   (a) Freud   (c) Horney
   (b) Jung   (d) Adler

10. David is very quiet, pessimistic, anxious, and moody and becomes emotionally upset very easily. In terms of Eysenck's four basic personality types, he would be classified as

    (a) introverted-neurotic.
    (b) introverted-stable.
    (c) extraverted-neurotic.
    (d) extraverted-stable.

11. In a term paper on Carl Jung's theory of personality, Justin quoted Jung as saying that the _____ contains "the whole spiritual heritage of mankind's evolution, born anew in the brain structure of every individual."

    (a) personal preconscious
    (b) collective conscious
    (c) personal unconscious
    (d) collective unconscious

12. Ursula's therapist instructs her to relax, close her eyes, and state aloud whatever thoughts come to mind no matter how trivial, silly, or absurd they seem. The therapist is using a technique called
    (a) free association.   (c) sublimation.
    (b) displacement.   (d) repression.

13. Leanne studies very hard, but she always feels that she hasn't studied enough. If she takes a break to socialize with her friends, she starts feeling guilty and anxious. Freud would say that Leanne has a
    (a) strong superego.   (c) weak superego.
    (b) strong id.   (d) weak id.

14. According to Culture and Human Behavior 11.3, which of the following is true?
    (a) Any two randomly chosen people of the same age, sex, and culture will likely have absolutely no similarities.
    (b) Some similarities between separated identical twins may be genetically influenced.
    (c) Personality is almost completely determined by genes.
    (d) Personality is almost completely determined by environmental factors.

15. According to Science Versus Pseudoscience 11.5, graphologists' claims that handwriting reveals temperament, personality traits, intelligence, and reasoning ability
    (a) have been empirically tested and supported by numerous scientific studies.
    (b) have not been supported by scientific reseach.
    (c) should be believed because thousands of U.S. companies have used graphologists to assist in hiring new employees.
    (d) have much greater validity and reliability than similar claims made by astrologers.

Progress Test 3

After you have checked your understanding of the material in Progress Tests 1 and 2, and have done a complete chapter review with special focus on any areas of weakness, you are ready to further assess your knowledge on Progress Test 3. Check your answers. If you make a mistake, review your notes, the appropriate parts of the study guide, and if necessary, the relevant sections of your textbook.

1. During a class reunion Adeil reminisced with some of his high school friends about their last year at school and had no problem recalling many of the fun times they had together. In terms of Freud's theory of personality, Adeil's ability to recall these events would suggest that they are stored at the _____ level of awareness.
    (a) unconscious   (c) latency
    (b) conscious   (d) preconscious

2. Researchers conducting a study involving identical twins who were separated at birth are likely to conclude that differences in the twins' personality traits are due to _____ , whereas similarities in personality traits are due to _____ .
    (a) environmental influences; genetic influences
    (b) unconditional positive regard; conditional positive regard
    (c) genetic influences; environmental influences
    (d) displacement; sublimation

3. Juan is a very experienced car mechanic who believes he can fix just about any problem in any make of car or truck. According to Bandura, Juan's confidence in his ability to handle mechanical problems is his
    (a) self-concept.
    (b) superiority complex.
    (c) self-efficacy.
    (d) actualizing tendency.

4. When Romwaldo was given the results of his psychological test, he was told that he scored high on the extraverted-stable dimension and that he has a tendency to be sociable, outgoing, talkative, and responsive. This description of Romwaldo's source and surface traits is most consistent with
    (a) Hans Eysenck's view of personality.
    (b) Rorschach's theory of personality.
    (c) Alfred Adler's model of personality.
    (d) Carl Rogers's humanistic approach to personality.

5. The pleasure principle is to _____ as the reality principle is to _____ .
    (a) the oral stage; the anal stage
    (b) Thanatos; Eros
    (c) the id; the ego
    (d) the ego; the superego

6. Ellen has an excessive need for approval and affection. According to Karen Horney, Ellen's pattern of behavior is typical of those who move _____ other people.
    (a) toward
    (b) against
    (c) away from
    (d) neither toward nor against

7. Dr. Selnick believes in the importance of unconscious psychological conflicts, sexual and aggressive drives, and the formative influence of early childhood experiences. Dr. Selnick's views are most consistent with the _____ perspective.
    (a) psychoanalytic
    (b) humanistic
    (c) social cognitive
    (d) trait

8. Raffi is shown a series of cards with ambiguous scenes and is told to make up a story about each one, describing the characters' feelings and their motives. Raffi has been given the
    (a) Thematic Apperception Test (TAT).
    (b) Rorschach Inkblot Test.
    (c) California Personality Inventory (CPI).
    (d) Minnesota Multiphasic Personality Inventory (MMPI).

9. Sheldon has frequently been rebellious, inconsiderate, and self-centered. His parents are consistent in disciplining him for his inappropriate behaviors while communicating to him that they value and love him. The person most likely to agree with their parenting approach and use of unconditional positive regard is
    (a) Sigmund Freud.
    (c) Joseph Breuer.
    (b) Carl Rogers.
    (d) Carl Jung.

10. Dr. Welch is a clinical psychologist who uses the MMPI and the 16PF. If asked to identify the key strength of these tests, he is most likely to note that
    (a) they provide a wealth of qualitative information about the individual.
    (b) scoring relies on the examiner's subjective judgment and clinical experience and expertise.
    (c) they accurately measure the individual's unconscious motives and conflicts.
    (d) they are standardized and objectively scored.

11. When Professor Mainprize was going through a very painful divorce, he tended to mark student papers very harshly and to make the exams difficult. A psychoanalyst would be most likely to view the professor's treatment of his students as an example of
    (a) identification.
    (c) displacement.
    (b) repression.
    (d) sublimation.

12. Dr. Sharma stresses the importance of identifying, measuring, and describing individual differences in terms of various personality characteristics. His views are most representative of the _____ perspective on personality.
    (a) psychoanalytic
    (c) social cognitive
    (b) humanistic
    (d) trait

13. According to the Application section, which of the following is false?
    (a) A person's self-concept is a multifaceted system of related images and ideas.
    (b) Possible selves influence our behavior in important ways.
    (c) We're often unaware of how possible selves we've mentally constructed influence our beliefs, actions, and self-evaluations.
    (d) A person's self-concept is a singular mental self-image.

14. According to Critical Thinking 11.2, which of the following is true?
    (a) Freud viewed aggression as a universal, unconscious, human instinct.
    (b) Bandura believed that the essence of human nature is aggressive but that societal, religious, and cultural restraints make people behave in nonaggressive ways.
    (c) Freud believed human aggression, like other human behavior, is driven by conscious, rational goals and motives.
    (d) Bandura viewed aggression as a universal, unconscious, human instinct.

15. Science versus Pseudoscience 11.4, which discusses astrology and personality, concluded that
    (a) the position of the planets and stars at the time and place of your birth determines your personality and destiny.
    (b) today, virtually nobody believes in astrological interpretations and predictions.
    (c) science has not been able to refute the claims, predictions, and interpretations of astrology.
    (d) neither popular nor serious astrology has any reliable basis in scientific fact.

Answers

Introduction: What Is Personality?

1. (a) thinking; feeling; behaving
   (b) different; similar; whole

2. (a) unconscious; early childhood
   (b) self; unique potential
   (c) learning; cognitive; beliefs
   (d) description; measurement

The Psychoanalytic Perspective on Personality

1. (a) medicine; physiology; cocaine; addictive
   (b) neurology; self-analysis
   (c) emotions; catharsis
   (d) free association; thoughts, mental images; feelings

2. (a) psychoanalysis
   (b) sexuality; aggression
   (c) civilization; human nature; civilization

The Psychoanalytic Perspective: Freud's Dynamic Theory of Personality

1. (a) conscious, preconscious; unconscious
   (b) preconscious
   (c) unconscious; conscious

2. (a) unconscious; conscious
   (b) unconscious
   (c) manifest; latent
   (d) unintentional; Freudian

3. (a) psychological energy
   (b) unconscious; external
   (c) Eros; Thanatos
   (d) pleasure; *libido*
   (e) pleasure; tension; pleasure

4. (a) partly; organized, rational
   (b) reality; gratification
   (c) pragmatic; repress
   (d) external; externally; internalized

5. (a) internal
   (b) conscious; conscience
   (c) guilt, shame, self-doubt; anxiety

6. (a) instinctual; moral; external
   (b) anxiety; impulsively; destructively; guilt, self-reproach
   (c) anxiety; distorting
   (d) repression
   (e) conscious; unconscious; repressed

7. (a) displacement; sublimation
   (b) psychological energy
   (c) psychological energy

The Psychoanalytic Perspective: Personality Development

1. (a) psychosexual; oral, anal; phallic; latency; genital
   (b) sexual; age-related
   (c) sexual; oral; oral; anal; phallic; genitals

2. (a) conflict
   (b) conflict; frustrate; overindulge
   (c) fixation

3. (a) phallic
   (b) genital; opposite-sex; same-sex

4. (a) father; mother; castration
   (b) identification; father's
   (c) incestual

5. (a) identifying; incestual
   (b) identifies; internalizes
   (c) penis envy

6. (a) repressed
   (b) same-sex
   (c) genital; incestual; opposite-sex
   (d) conflicts; psychosexual; love

7. (a) personality
   (b) free association
   (c) unconscious
   (d) latent
   (e) id
   (f) superego
   (g) sublimation
   (h) identification

Graphic Organizer 1

1. genital
2. phallic
3. latency
4. oral
5. anal

Matching Exercise 1

1. libido
2. personality
3. superego
4. Oedipus complex
5. ego
6. preconscious
7. oral stage
8. displacement

9. Sigmund Freud

10. anal stage

11. personality theory

12. id

13. latency stage

14. psychoanalysis

15. ego defense mechanisms

16. psychosexual stages

True/False Test 1

1. F	7. T	13. F
2. T	8. F	14. T
3. T	9. T	15. T
4. F	10. F	16. T
5. F	11. T	
6. T	12. T	

The Psychoanalytic Perspective: The Neo-Freudians

1. (a) sexual
   (b) early childhood
   (c) pessimistic

2. (a) sex; aggression; growth; realization
   (b) collective; collective
   (c) archetypes; collective
   (d) anima and animus; feminine; masculine
   (e) archetypes
   (f) introvert; extravert; humanistic

3. (a) social; cultural; social
   (b) human; basic anxiety
   (c) basic anxiety
   (d) approval; affection; power; competitive, critical; independence; sufficiency
   (e) flexible
   (f) penis; womb

4. (a) striving for superiority; inferiority
   (b) compensate; inferiority
   (c) inferiority
   (d) overcompensate; superiority complex

The Psychoanalytic Perspective: Evaluating Freud and the Psychoanalytic Perspective on Personality

1. (a) objectively
   (b) measure or confirm; disprove
   (c) unconscious; childhood; regulate
   (d) sexist; male

2. (a) inferiority
   (b) Karen Horney
   (c) Jung's

(d) basic anxiety; against
(e) extravert

Matching Exercise 2

1. Karen Horney

2. archetypes

3. striving for superiority

4. basic anxiety

5. inferiority complex

6. extravert

7. anima

8. collective unconscious

True/False Test 2

1. T	4. T	7. F
2. F	5. T	8. T
3. T	6. T	

The Humanistic Perspective on Personality

1. (a) good; healthy
   (b) growth; self-awareness; free will; conscious, subjective
   (c) hierarchy; self-actualized

2. (a) active; voluntary; grow; develop
   (b) actualizing tendency

3. (a) self-concept
   (b) self-concept
   (c) actualizing; positive

4. (a) conditional positive regard
   (b) incongruence
   (c) self-concept
   (d) unconditional positive regard; actualizing
   (e) permissive; were; self-worth

5. (a) unconditional positive regard
   (b) self-concept; realistic, open; changing
   (c) congruence; actualizing; growth

6. (a) psychotherapy
   (b) validate; test; empirical
   (c) optimistic
   (d) decreased; subjective; self-concept

The Social Cognitive Perspective on Personality

1. (a) conscious; situations
   (b) social; goals, expectations, beliefs

2. (a) self-analysis; experimental
   (b) conscious; unconscious
   (c) thoughts, feelings

3. (a) Albert Bandura
   (b) self-efficacy
   (c) cognitive; self-regulation

4. (a) consequences; regulate
   (b) reciprocal determinism

5. (a) self-system
   (b) self-efficacy
   (c) flexible; beliefs
   (d) self-efficacy; self-efficacy
   (e) experiences

6. (a) learning, cognitive; social
   (b) testable
   (c) complex; multiple; clinical
   (d) unconscious; unconscious
   (e) mental; behavioral; situational
   (f) learning; learning
   (g) self-regulation

The Trait Perspective on Personality

1. (a) similarities; differences; characteristics; attributes
   (b) degrees

2. (a) behavior; group
   (b) basic; differences

3. (a) factor analysis; 16
   (b) Sixteen Personality Factor; 16PF

4. (a) introversion–extraversion
   (b) neuroticism–emotional stability; neuroticism; stability
   (c) introverted-neurotic, introverted-stable, extraverted-neurotic; extraverted-stable
   (d) psychoticism; psychoticism

5. (a) biological; introvert's; extravert's; has
   (b) extraverts; introverts
   (c) extraverts; introverts

6. (a) five; Five
   (b) extraversion, neuroticism; agreeableness; conscientiousness; openness
   (c) stable; consistent
   (d) interaction; consistent

Personality Traits and Genetics: Just a Chip Off the Old Block?

1. (a) similarities; differences
   (b) identical; adopted
   (c) identical twins; fraternal twins; siblings; adopted; genetically unrelated individuals who grew up in different homes

2. (a) heritability estimate
   (b) 100 percent; 0 percent
   (c) differences

3. (d) extraversion, neuroticism, openness; conscientiousness

3. (a) differences; similarities; differences; do not
   (b) may
   (c) siblings; quite differently

4. (a) disagree; agree
   (b) explain; label
   (c) explain
   (d) motives; unconscious; change; growth
   (e) psychoanalytic; humanistic

5. (a) self-efficacy
   (b) surface
   (c) fully functioning
   (d) social cognitive
   (e) trait
   (f) unconditional positive regard
   (g) behavioral genetics

Graphic Organizer 2

1. Hans Eysenck; trait
2. Carl Rogers; humanistic
3. Raymond Cattell; trait
4. Sigmund Freud; psychoanalytic
5. Alfred Adler; psychoanalytic (neo-Freudian)
6. Albert Bandura; social cognitive
7. Karen Horney; psychoanalytic (neo-Freudian)
8. Abraham Maslow; humanistic
9. Carl Jung; psychoanalytic (neo-Freudian)

Matching Excercise 3

1. trait
2. self-efficacy
3. Albert Bandura
4. actualizing tendency
5. five-factor model of personality
6. Abraham Maslow
7. psychoticism
8. positive regard
9. heritability estimate
10. social cognitive theory
11. trait theory
12. extraversion
13. Carl Rogers
14. humanistic psychology
15. reciprocal determinism

True/False Test 3

1. T	6. T	11. F
2. F	7. T	12. F
3. F	8. T	13. T
4. F	9. T	14. T
5. T	10. F	15. T

Assessing Personality: Psychological Tests

1. (a) characteristics; psychological; behavior
   (b) projective; projection
   (c) Rorschach
   (d) animate; inanimate; human; animal

2. (a) Thematic Apperception Test; TAT
   (b) motives, needs, anxieties

3. (a) qualitative
   (b) testing; behavior; subjective; consistent
   (c) validity; reliability

4. (a) self-report inventories
   (b) self-report; objectively
   (c) sexual; psychological; abnormal
   (d) clinical; psychiatrists; mental
   (e) consistently

5. (a) normal
   (b) interpersonal; control; job
   (c) Raymond Cattell; forced-choice
   (d) career; marital

6. (a) standardization; norms; objectively; norms
   (b) far greater; predict
   (c) socially; judges
   (d) psychological; personality; psychological

7. (a) projective; Thematic Apperception Test (TAT)
   (b) MMPI
   (c) CPI
   (d) projective; Rorschach Inkblot Test
   (e) 16PF

Matching Exercise 4

1. self-report inventory

2. Rorschach Inkblot Test

3. California Personality Inventory (CPI)

4. psychological test

5. Sixteen Personality Factor Questionnaire (16PF)

True/False Test 4

1. T	3. F	5. T
2. T	4. F	

Something to Think About

1. In any discussion of psychological testing it is always a good idea to point out the important characteristics of a good test, namely, reliability and validity. In terms of personality testing, you should first describe the two categories of tests, projective tests and self-report inventories.

   The famous Rorschach Inkblot Test is, of course, a projective test. In other words, it is assumed that people will project their unconscious feelings, motives, drives, thoughts, and so on in their responses to the series of inkblots. Similarly, the Thematic Apperception Test (TAT) gives subjects an opportunity to project unconscious information into the stories they make up about ambiguous scenes. Both tests developed out of the psychoanalytic approaches to personality, and scoring involves the subjective interpretations of the examiner. A brief discussion of Freud's theory as it relates to personality would probably be in order. A review of the most damaging criticisms of psychoanalysis may shed light on the topic, and the issue of the validity and reliability of projective tests should not be overlooked. Despite the criticisms, projective tests are widely used and can provide a wealth of qualitative data about an individual.

   Self-report inventories are used by clinical psychologists to evaluate both normal and abnormal populations in a variety of settings and for a variety of purposes. The most common are the MMPI, the CPI, and the 16PF. These are often called objective personality tests because they are standardized and objectively scored and measured against established norms. Self-report inventories are far more reliable and valid than are projective tests. These tests do have some drawbacks, including a person's ability to fake responses and answer in a socially desirable manner, some people's tendency to answer in a set way to all questions, and the fact that people are not always the best judges of their own behavior.

   Personality tests are generally useful strategies that can provide insights about the psychological makeup of a person. However, no personality test, by itself, is likely to provide a definitive description of a given individual. In addition, because people can and often do change over time, any personality test provides a profile of the person only at the time of the test.

2. Many people believe in astrology, and a large number consult professional astrologers to find out what they should do and what lies ahead of them in the future. Belief in astrology is not restricted to any class or group of individuals. People from all walks of life, from senior managers to assembly line workers, from government leaders to junior clerks, consult their horoscopes on a regular basis. As is the case with many strongly held beliefs, it is often difficult to get true believers in astrology to listen to any information that might contradict what they feel is a valid point of view. It is always important to be aware of this and to respect their right to believe whatever they wish. However, if the opportunity does arise to have an open-minded discussion, presenting the results of Shawn Carlson's (1985) carefully designed study could be useful. Remember, a panel of astrological advisers were involved in helping Carlson design the study, and thirty of the top American and European astrologers were involved. All the participating astrologers agreed beforehand that Carlson's study was a fair test of astrological claims. Although the astrologers who approved the design predicted that 50 percent was the minimum effect they would expect to see, the results showed that astrologers performed at a chance level. In other words, anybody simply guessing would have done as well as the astrologers. Carlson's results are consistent with those of many other researchers. A careful review of the scientific research on astrology came to the conclusion that astrology has absolutely no reliable basis in scientific fact and cannot stand up to any valid statistical test. Of course, if the astrologers had any real insight from their reading of the planets, they could easily have foreseen the outcome of Carlson's study!

Progress Test 1

1. d	6. d	11. a
2. c	7. d	12. d
3. d	8. d	13. b
4. a	9. c	14. c
5. a	10. b	15. a

Progress Test 2

1. a	6. a	11. d
2. a	7. d	12. a
3. d	8. c	13. a
4. d	9. d	14. b
5. c	10. a	15. b

Progress Test 3

1. d	6. a	11. c
2. a	7. a	12. d
3. c	8. a	13. d
4. a	9. b	14. a
5. c	10. d	15. d

Social
Psychology

PREVIEW   Reading the section below first will give you a general sense of the chapter's contents and an initial introduction to some of the major concepts and terms. This will prime you for what you are about to read and help you to develop a "cognitive map" that will guide your study of the material in this chapter. Likewise, reading the **preview questions** at the beginning of each major section will improve your ability to understand, learn, and retain the information.

CHAPTER 12 . . . AT A GLANCE

Chapter 12 discusses social psychology—the scientific study of the way individuals think, feel, and behave in social situations—as broadly divided into two major research areas: social cognition and social influence. The chapter first explores person perception, including the factors that influence our perceptions of others. This is followed by a discussion of the process of attribution, including three important attributional biases and the influence of culture on attributional processes.

Once we form impressions of people, we tend to interpret their behavior in terms of our attitudes about them. The conditions under which attitudes determine behavior are identified. The role of cognitive dissonance in behavior and cognition is explored. In discussing prejudice, the text describes such cognitive influences as stereotypes, ingroups, out-groups, the out-group homogeneity effect, in-group bias, and ethnocentrism. The emotional roots of prejudice and techniques for reducing prejudice are also considered.

Conformity occurs when people change their behavior, attitudes, or beliefs in response to real or imagined group pressure. The original experimental design and the results of Stanley Milgram's research on a type of conformity called obedience are presented in detail. Conditions that influence people to obey and to resist obeying authority figures are identified.

Latané and Darley's research on helping behavior, bystander intervention, and diffusion of responsibility is discussed, and their model, which identifies the factors that increase and decrease the likelihood of bystander intervention, is presented. Individual behavior can be strongly influenced by the presence of others; the phenomena of social loafing, social striving, social facilitation, and deindividuation are examined.

Introduction: Social Psychology

Preview Questions

Consider the following questions as you study this section of the chapter:

- What is social psychology?
- What is meant by social cognition and social influence?

*Read the section "Introduction: Social Psychology" and **write** your answers to the following:*

1. (a) Social psychology is the scientific study of how individuals _____ ,
   _____ , and _____
   in social situations.
   (b) Social cognition refers to how we form _____ of other people, how we _____ the meaning of other people's behavior, and how our behavior is affected by our _____ .
   (c) Social influence focuses on how our behavior is affected by _____ factors and other people. It includes such questions as why we _____ to group norms, what compels us to _____ an authority figure, and the conditions under which people will _____ a stranger.

Person Perception: Forming Impressions of Other People

Preview Questions

Consider the following questions as you study this section of the chapter:

- What is person perception?
- What four principles does the mental process of forming judgments of others follow?
- How do social categories, implicit personality theories, and physical attractiveness influence person perception?

*Read the section "Person Perception: Forming Impressions of Other People" and **write** your answers to the following:*

1. (a) Person perception refers to the _____ processes we use to form _____ and draw _____ about the characteristics of others; it is an active and subjective process that always occurs in some interpersonal context.
   (b) Every interpersonal context has three key components: the _____ of the individual you are attempting to size up, your own _____ as the perceiver, and the specific _____ in which the process occurs; each component influences the conclusions you reach about other people.

2. Person perception follows four basic principles:
   (a) Your reactions to others are determined by your _____ of them, not by who or what they really are.
   (b) The amount and kind of information you collect about others is determined by your _____ in a particular situation.
   (c) In every situation, how you expect people to act in that situation partly determines how you _____ them; you make reference to the _____ for the appropriate behavior in a particular social situation.
   (d) How you perceive others and how you act on your perceptions is also influenced by your _____ .
   (e) In combination, these four basic principles underscore that person perception is not a one-way process in which we objectively survey other people, then logically evaluate their characteristic. Instead, the _____ , our _____ , and the perception we have of others all interact.

3. (a) Social categorization is the _____ process of classifying people into _____ on the basis of common characteristics; this is mostly automatic and

spontaneous and occurs outside of conscious awareness.

(b) With limited time to form impressions, we rely on very broad _____ , such as gender, race, and age.

(c) Using social categories has both disadvantages and advantages; relegating someone to a social category on the basis of _____ information ignores that person's _____ qualities. On the other hand, relying on social categories is a natural, adaptive _____ process that is efficient and effective for mentally organizing information about others.

(d) When it is important to your goals to perceive another person as accurately as possible, you're less likely to rely on automatic categorization; instead, you _____ and _____ exert mental effort to understand the other person better and to form a more accurate impression.

4. (a) An implicit personality theory is a network of assumptions or beliefs about the relationships among various types of _____ , _____ , and _____ . Through our previous social experiences, each of us has formed cognitive _____ about the traits and behaviors associated with different "types" of people and expect them to behave accordingly.

(b) Like social categories, implicit personality theories _____ (are/are not) useful as mental shortcuts in perceiving other people; however, they are not always _____ and in some instances can be dangerously misleading.

(c) Although implicit personality theories can lead to inaccurate conclusions, they represent another important _____

cognition strategy in our efforts to make sense of other people; they provide a mental framework that helps us organize our _____ , _____ , and beliefs about people.

5. (a) As a result of cultural conditioning, most people associate physical _____ with a wide range of desirable characteristics; physically _____ people are perceived as being more intelligent, happier, socially competent, sexier, and better adjusted than other people. They are also perceived as being more vain and less modest than _____ people.

(b) Physical attractiveness _____ (is/is not) correlated with being popular, less lonely, and less anxious in social situations; it _____ (is/is not) correlated with intelligence, mental health, or self-esteem.

Attribution: Explaining Behavior

Preview Questions

Consider the following questions as you study this section of the chapter.

- How is attribution defined?
- What are the fundamental error, the actor-observer discrepancy, and the self-serving bias, and how do these biases shape the attributions we make?

*Read the section "Attribution: Explaining Behavior" and **write** your answers to the following:*

1. (a) The process of inferring the cause, or the why, behind someone's behavior, including your own, is called _____ . Psychologists also use the word to refer to the _____ you make for a particular behavior. These inferences have a strong influence on your thoughts and feelings about others.

(b) The fundamental attribution error is the tendency to spontaneously attribute the behavior of others to _____ , _____ characteristics while downplaying or underestimating the effects of _____ , _____ factors.

(c) The fundamental attribution error plays a role in a common explanatory pattern called _____ ; the victim of a crime, disaster, or serious illness is blamed for having somehow _____ the problem or for not having taken steps to avoid or prevent it.

(d) A second bias contributes to unfairly blaming the victim, which is based on our need to believe that the world is fair. This is called the _____ .

2. (a) When we explain our own behavior, however, we don't make the fundamental attribution error; instead, we're more likely to use a(n) _____ , _____ attribution than a(n) _____ , _____ attribution.

(b) This common attributional bias is called the _____ discrepancy because there is a discrepancy between the attributions you make when you are the _____ in a given situation and those you make when you are the _____ of other people's behavior.

(c) One explanation for this bias is that we have more _____ about the potential causes of our own behavior than we do about the causes of other people's behavior; when we're more aware of the possible situational influences on the behavior, such as with people we know well, we are less susceptible to the _____ discrepancy and are better at seeing situations from their point of view.

3. (a) The self-serving bias is the tendency to attribute _____ (successful/unsuccessful) outcomes of our own behavior to internal causes and _____ (successful/unsuccessful) outcomes to external, situational causes.

(b) In a wide range of situations, people tend to credit themselves for their _____ and to blame their _____ on external circumstances. Psychologists explain the self-serving bias as being partly due to an attempt to save face and to protect self-esteem in the face of _____ .

4. Read the following and write the correct term in the space provided.

(a) Adam got an A in his philosophy class and concluded that he had quite a talent for writing coherently and thinking logically. When he got a C in his sociology class, he expressed dissatisfaction with the course content, the teaching ability of the professor, and the quality and clarity of the exams. This best illustrates the _____ .

(b) Rachel has just learned that her neighbor's teenage son, Brad, was involved in an automobile accident at a nearby intersection. She said to her husband, "Well, Brad's recklessness has finally got him into trouble!" Rachel's comment suggests that she has made the _____ .

(c) When Allen observed Mark miss what looked to him like an easy point, Allen concluded that Mark was not a skilled basketball player. Later, in an identical position, Allen also failed to score. However, this time he concluded that it was the strong opposing team that prevented him from scoring. It would appear that Allen is committing the _____ .

(d) When Cheryl first met Charles, who is an archivist in the university library, she concluded that he was probably very quiet, introverted, and introspective. She was later surprised to learn that he was the lead singer in a heavy metal band. Cheryl's surprise is probably the result of using a(n)

_____

to make judgments about the traits and characteristics associated with certain types of people.

(e) After learning about some interesting social psychology phenomena in his introductory class, Patrick decided he would like to test one of the concepts by facing the back instead of the front while riding the eleva-tor. Much to his surprise, he found that he could not carry out his plan. After a second or two, he was overcome with embarrass-ment and ended up facing the front like everyone else. Patrick's behavior was governed by the

_____ of the situation.

(f) Grover does not support any charities because he believes that people who are poor, hungry, or homeless did something to deserve their situation. Grover's explanatory style is called

_____ ; it probably reflects his strong need to believe the world is fair, an assumption called the

_____ .

Graphic Organizer 1

The following statements represent attributional processes. Decide which is (A) the fundamental attribution error, (B) the actor–observer discrepancy, or (C) the self-serving bias, and decide whether the attribution is to the self or to others or to both and whether it is internal (INT) or external (EXT).

Statement	Process	Attribution
1. I got an A in biology because I'm smart; I got a C in chemistry because the professor was disorganized, couldn't teach, and gave exams that were grossly unfair.		
2. My sister had a fender-bender because she is a typical female driver; when I had a fender-bender, it was because the other driver was an idiot.		
3. I don't care what he said about his car breaking down; he was fifteen minutes late for the first class so he must be one of those inconsiderate professors who is more concerned with his research than with his students.		

Review of Terms and Concepts 1

Use the terms in this list to complete the Matching Test, then to help you answer the True/False items correctly.

social psychology
social cognition
social influence
person perception
social norms
social categorization
implicit personality
  theory
attribution

fundamental attribution
  error
actor–observer
  discrepancy
self-serving bias
blaming the victim
just-world hypothesis
self-effacing bias
  (modesty bias)

Matching Exercise

Match the appropriate term with its definition or description.

1. _____ The "rules," or expectations, for appropriate behavior in a particular social situation.

2. _____ Mental process of inferring the causes of people's behavior, including one's own. Also used to refer to the explanation made for a particular behavior.

3. _____ Tendency to attribute successful outcomes of one's own behavior to internal causes and unsuccessful outcomes to external, situational causes.

4. _____ Branch of psychology that studies how people think, feel, and behave in social situations.

5. _____ Network of assumptions or beliefs about the relationships among various types of people, traits, and behaviors.

6. _____ Tendency to attribute one's own behavior to external, situational causes while attributing the behavior of others to internal, personal causes; especially likely to occur with regard to behaviors that lead to negative outcomes.

7. _____ Tendency to blame an innocent victim of misfortune for having somehow caused the problem or for not having taken steps to avoid or prevent it.

True/False Test

Indicate whether each statement is true or false by placing T or F in the blank space next to each item.

1. ___ The effect that situational factors and other people have on an individual's behavior is called social cognition.

2. ___ The fundamental attribution error refers to the tendency to attribute the behavior of others to internal, personal characteristics while ignoring or underestimating the effects of external, situational factors; an attributional bias that is common in individualistic cultures.

3. ___ The mental processes we use to form judgments and draw conclusions about the characteristics and motives of others are called person perception.

4. ___ Social categorization refers to the mental process of classifying people into groups (or categories) on the basis of their shared characteristics.

5. ___ Social influence is the study of the mental processes people use to make sense of their social environment; it includes the study of person perception, attribution, attitudes, and prejudice.

6. ___ The self-effacing bias (modesty bias) involves blaming failure on internal, personal factors while attributing success to external, situational factors; more common in collectivistic cultures than individualistic cultures.

7. ___ People have a tendency to blame the victim because they have a strong need to believe that the world is fair and that we get what we deserve and deserve what we get; this is called the just-world hypothesis.

Check your answers and review any areas of weakness before going on to the next section.

The Social Psychology of Attitudes

Preview Questions

Consider the following questions as you study this section of the chapter.

- How is the term *attitude* defined, and what are its three components?

- Under what conditions are attitudes most likely to determine behavior?

- What is cognitive dissonance, and how does it affect behavior?

Read the section "The Social Psychology of Attitudes" and **write** *your answers to the following:*

1. (a) Psychologists formally define an attitude as a _____ tendency to evaluate

some _____ , _____ , or _____ in a particular way; attitudes are typically positive or negative, but they can also be _____ , as when you have mixed feelings about an issue or a person.

(b) Attitudes can be made up of several related components: (1) an attitude may have a(n) _____ component (your thoughts and conclusions about a given topic or object); (2) an attitude may have a(n) emotional, or _____ , component; and (3) an attitude can have a(n) _____ component, in which your attitude is reflected in your actions.

2. (a) Psychologists have found that people _____ (always/don't always) act in accordance with their attitudes.

(b) You are most likely to behave in accordance with your attitudes when (1) your attitudes are _____ or are _____ expressed; (2) your attitudes have been formed through direct _____ ; (3) you are very _____ about the subject; (4) you have a vested _____ in the subject; and (4) you anticipate a _____ outcome or response from others.

3. (a) Cognitive dissonance is an unpleasant state of _____ tension (dissonance) that occurs when there is _____ (consistency/an inconsistency) between two thoughts or perceptions. The state of disso-

nance is so unpleasant that we are strongly motivated to reduce it.

(b) Cognitive dissonance commonly occurs in situations in which you become uncomfortably aware that your behavior and your attitudes _____ with each other. Thus, you are simultaneously holding two _____ cognitions, your original attitude and the way you have behaved.

(c) If you can easily _____ your behavior to make it _____ with your attitude, then any dissonance can be quickly and easily resolved. When your behavior cannot be easily _____ , you will tend to change your attitude to make it _____ with your behavior. Attitude change due to cognitive dissonance is quite _____ (uncommon/common) in everyday life.

(d) Cognitive dissonance can also change the _____ of an attitude so that it is _____ with some behavior you've already performed.

(e) Cognitive dissonance also operates when choosing between two basically equal alternatives; each choice has _____ and _____ features, creating dissonance. Once you make a choice, however, you immediately bring your attitudes more closely into line with that commitment, reducing the dissonance; you emphasize the _____ features of the choice you rejected and the _____ features of the choice you made.

Graphic Organizer 2

The following statements reflect attitudes about certain topics. Decide which component—cognitive, affective, or behavioral— is represented by each statement.

Statement	Component
1. I believe that the automobile is the single most destructive element on this planet.	
2. I consistently recycle paper, plastic, soda cans, glass, and other waste.	
3. I vote for antigun control advocates and give them my full support.	
4. I get really angry when I see people carelessly throwing their litter on the ground.	
5. I don't want to contribute to the pollution of our city, so I ride my bicycle or take public transportation.	
6. I am very happy when I see women doing well in what used to be male-dominated occupations.	
7. In my opinion, a woman's place is in the home, raising the kids and doing housework.	
8. I get really upset when motorists are rude and inconsiderate.	
9. I believe that the automobile is the greatest invention ever, and we need to elect politicians who will promise to build more roads and freeways.	

Understanding Prejudice

Preview Questions

Consider the following questions as you study this section of the chapter.

- How is prejudice defined?
- What are stereotypes, what are their functions, and what problems are associated with their use?
- What are in-groups, out-groups, and ethnocentrism, and what effect does in-group/out-group thinking have on our social judgments?
- How can prejudice be overcome, and what conditions are essential for reducing tensions between groups?

Read the section "Understanding Prejudice" and ***write*** *your answers to the following:*

1. (a) Prejudice is a(n) _____ toward people who belong to a specific social group.

   (b) Much of the psychological research on prejudice has focused on relations between white and African-Americans; increasingly, however, prejudice has become an inter-group affair, as mutual distrust and dislike have taken hold among many different _____ and _____ groups.

(c) Prejudice is ultimately based on the exaggerated notion that members of "other" social groups are different from members of our own social group; however, racial and ethnic groups are far more _____ (similar/different) than they are _____ (similar/different). Any differences that may exist between members of racial and ethnic groups are _____ (smaller/larger) than differences among various members of the same group.

2. (a) A specific kind of social category is a stereotype, which is defined as a cluster of _____ that are attributed to members of a specific social group or category; in other words, stereotypes are based on the assumption that people have certain _____ because of their membership in a particular group.

(b) Like other social categories, stereotypes simplify social information so that we can sort out, process, and _____ information about other people more easily; use of stereotypes seems to be a natural _____ process and an inescapable fact of social _____ but can have some very negative consequences.

3. (a) Stereotypes not only determine what people see but also what they _____ . Attributing a stereotypic cause for an outcome or event can _____ us to the true cause of events.

(b) Once formed, stereotypes are _____ (easy/hard) to shake. Stereotypic beliefs can

be very misleading, or even damaging, when they become _____ that are applied to all members of a given group; the result may be prejudice.

(c) When confronted by evidence that contradicts a stereotype, people will tend to _____ that information in a variety of ways; for example, they may see it as a(n) _____ to the stereotype, or if they find several instances of contradictory evidence, they may create a mental subgroup that includes the _____ and still maintain their more general stereotype.

4. (a) People have a very strong tendency to perceive others in terms of two very basic social categories: the _____ ("us") refers to the group or groups to which we belong, whereas _____ ("them") refer to groups of which we are not a member; we're more likely to resort to _____ biased stereotypes to describe members of other groups than fellow members of our own group.

(b) _____ and _____ aren't necessarily limited to racial, ethnic, or religious boundaries but can include virtually any characteristic that can create a distinction.

(c) We typically describe members of our own group as being quite _____ (similar/different), whereas we tend to see members of the out-group as much more _____ (similar/different) to one another; this tendency is called the _____ effect.

(d) The tendency to make more favorable, positive attributions for behaviors by members of our own group and unfavorable, negative attributions for behaviors by members of the out-group is called the _____ .

(e) One form of in-group bias is the belief that one's culture or ethnic group is superior to others, called _____ . This type of thinking contributes to the formation of _____ about cultures whose customs differ from our own.

5. (a) Stereotypes and in-group to out-group bias form the _____ basis for prejudicial attitudes; but prejudice also has a strong _____ component that is characterized by being intensely negative.

(b) Behaviorally, prejudice can be displayed in the form of _____ , and it can occur against men, women, and children just because they are members of a particular out-group.

(c) One theory holds that _____ and intergroup _____ increase when two groups are competing for scarce resources (jobs, land, oil, water, political power); they also increase during times of social change.

(d) Because prejudice often exists in the absence of these factors, social psychologists are examining the _____ basis of prejudice. One researcher has found that prejudice occurs when out-groups are perceived as threatening important in-group _____ and values.

6. (a) Contact theory holds that bringing members of different groups into contact with one another would inevitably _____ prejudice among groups; however, under some circumstances, contact between different groups can _____ prejudice by confirming negative stereotypes or failing to meet positive expectations.

(b) Muzafer Sherif's research helped clarify the conditions that produce intergroup _____ and _____ ;

and that intergroup conflict can be decreased when groups engage in a(n) _____ effort to achieve a common goal.

(c) Using the jigsaw classroom technique, other researchers showed that _____ learning can reduce prejudice in the classroom. This technique requires each student in a small, ethnically diverse group to become an expert in one aspect of their project and to teach it to the other members of the group; _____ and _____ replaced competition.

(d) As compared with children in traditional classrooms, children in jigsaw classrooms had _____ (lower/higher) self-esteem, a _____ liking for children in other ethnic groups, a decreased use of negative stereotypes and prejudice, and a reduction of intergroup hostility,

7. Some social psychologists argue that prejudice reduction at the individual level is a three-step process.

(a) First, individuals must _____ that prejudiced responses are wrong and _____ reject prejudice and stereotyped thinking.

(b) Second, they must _____ their nonprejudiced beliefs so that they become an integral part of their self-concept.

(c) Third, individuals must learn to _____ automatic prejudicial reactions and deliberately replace them with nonprejudiced responses that are based on their personal standards.

8. Read the following and write the correct term in the space provided.

(a) In Zeegland, where Majib grew up, women manage all the household finances, make all the major decisions regarding the family, and earn most of the family income. The men, on the other hand, tend to spend their time "hanging out" and trying to impress each other with the way they dress. Majib's belief that all women are naturally more assertive and domineering than men reflects her _____ about gender.

(b) In a discussion about gun control laws, Jerrilee said, "In my opinion, easy access to guns is the major contributing factor to the high homicide rate in the United States." This statement reflects the _____ component of Jerrilee's attitude about gun control.

(c) At lunch one day, a group of fine arts majors happened to sit next to a group of engineering students. During a discussion after lunch, one of the fine arts students remarked, "Boy, those engineering students are all alike. They are so loud, pushy, and aggressive, and, unlike us, they haven't got a scrap of creativity among them!" This statement reflects the

_____

effect.

(d) During a sociology class, the instructor mentioned that the Heckawe tribe considers chopped-up earthworms, sheep's eyeballs, water buffalo testicles, and live caterpillars to be delicacies. Later, while having a hamburger and fries for lunch, a student remarked that the Heckawe diet was disgusting and repulsive. Another suggested that the tribe would someday become civilized and maybe even start eating good food "just like us." These remarks illustrate a form of in-group bias called

_____

(e) Sylvester was having a tough time deciding which computer to buy: the model Z5000

Spartan or its equivalent, the LX5000 MBI. With a toss of a coin, he chose the Z5000 Spartan. Initially, he was worried about his choice; however, after talking with many enthusiastic Z5000 Spartan owners, he is now very pleased that he chose the better of the two options. It is very likely that Sylvester experienced _____ when he purchased his PC, and his subsequent behavior was an attempt to _____ this unpleasant state of psychological tension.

Review of Terms, Concepts, and Names 2

Use the terms in this list to complete the Matching Test, then to help you answer the True/False items correctly.

attitude	in-group bias
cognitive dissonance	ethnocentrism
prejudice	discrimination
stereotype	contact theory
in-group	Muzafer Sherif
out-group	jigsaw classroom
out-group homogeneity	technique
effect	

Matching Exercise

Match the appropriate term/name with its definition or description.

1. _____ American social psychologist who is best known for his "Robbers Cave" experiments to study prejudice, conflict resolution, and group processes.

2. _____ The belief that one's own culture or ethnic group is superior to all others and the related tendency to use one's own culture as a standard by which to judge other cultures.

3. _____ Learned tendency to evaluate some object, person, or issue in a particular way; such evaluations may be positive, negative, or ambivalent.

4. _____ A social group to which one belongs.

5. _____ Unpleasant state of psychological tension or arousal (dissonance) that occurs when two thoughts or perceptions (cognitions) are inconsistent; typically results from awareness that attitudes and behavior are in conflict.

6. _____ A social group to which one does not belong.

7. _____ A negative attitude toward people who belong to a specific social group.

True/False Test

Indicate whether each statement is true or false by placing T or F in the blank space next to each item.

1. ____ Contact theory proposed that bringing members of different groups into contact would inevitably reduce prejudice among the groups; the theory has not been supported.

2. ____ When prejudice is displayed behaviorally, it is called discrimination.

3. ____ The out-group homogeneity effect refers to the tendency to judge the behavior of in-group members favorably and out-group members unfavorably.

4. ____ A stereotype is a cluster of characteristics that are associated with all members of a specific social group, often including qualities that are unrelated to the objective criteria that define the group.

5. ____ The jigsaw classroom technique is a teaching technique that stresses cooperative, rather than competitive, learning situations.

6. ____ The in-group bias refers to the tendency to see members of out-groups as very similar to one another.

> Check your answers and review any areas of weakness before going on to the next section.

Conformity: Following the Crowd

Preview Questions

Consider the following questions as you study this section of the chapter.

- What is social influence, and how is it related to conformity?
- Why do people conform, and what factors influence the degree to which people conform?
- How does culture affect conformity?

*Read the section "Conformity: Following the Crowd" and **write** your answers to the following:*

1. (a) The psychological study of how our behavior is influenced by the social environment and other people is called _____ .
   (b) Conformity occurs when we change our _____ , _____ , or _____ in response to real or imagined group pressure.
   (c) The fact that we act or present ourselves in the same way as other people _____ (does/does not) necessarily mean that we're conforming to group standards; conformity is acting _____ from the way we would act alone.
   (d) If you think one thing in _____ and behave the same way as the group in _____ , that's conformity. If you alter both your _____ beliefs and outward behavior as a result of group pressure, that's conformity, too.

2. (a) The psychologist who studied the degree to which people would conform to the group even when the group opinion was clearly wrong was _____ ; he found that _____ (very few/the vast majority) conformed with the group judgment on at least one of the critical trials.
   (b) We conform to the larger group for two basic reasons: (1) we want to be liked and accepted by the group, which is referred to as _____ social influence; and (2) we want to be right. When we're uncertain or doubt our own judgment, we may look to the group as a source of accurate information, which is called _____ social influence.
   (c) In experiments on conformity, subjects are more likely to go _____ (along with/against) the majority if one other participant dissents; any dissent _____ (increases/decreases) resistance to the

majority opinion, even if the other person's dissenting opinion is wrong; conformity _____ (increases/lessens) even if the other dissenter's competence is questionable.

3. (a) One explanation for the steady decline in levels of conformity since _____ conducted his studies is that the cultural climate of American society was fundamentally different in the 1950s.

   (b) In a wide-ranging meta-analysis, British psychologists found that conformity is generally higher in _____ cultures than in _____ cultures.

   (c) Because independence, self-expression, and standing out from the crowd is emphasized in _____ cultures, the whole notion of conformity tends to carry a negative connotation. In _____ cultures, publicly conforming while privately disagreeing tends to be regarded as socially appropriate tact or sensitivity, whereas publicly challenging the judgments of others is considered rude, tactless, and insensitive.

Obedience: Just Following Orders

Preview Questions

Consider the following questions as you study this section of the chapter.

- How is obedience defined, and what was the basic design of Milgram's obedience experiments?
- What aspects of the experimental situation increased the likelihood of obedience?
- What factors did Milgram later discover that decreased the level of obedience?

Read the section "Obedience: Just Following Orders" and **write** your answers to the following:

1. (a) Stanley Milgram is best known for his studies of obedience, which is defined as the _____ of an action in response to the _____ of an authority or person of higher status, such as a teacher or a supervisor.

   (b) Milgram wanted to find out if a person could be _____ by others into committing a(n) _____ act, some action that violated his or her own conscience, such as hurting a stranger.

   (c) To find out, Milgram embarked on one of the most systematic and controversial investigations in the history of psychology: how and why people _____ the destructive _____ of an authority figure.

2. (a) Milgram's subjects were fairly _____ of the population in terms of educational background and occupation, and the experiment was rigged so that the subjects were always in the role of the _____ in the experiment; the other subject, who was an accomplice, was always the _____ .

   (b) The role of the _____ was to shock the _____ , who was strapped to a chair in a separate room, every time he made a mistake on the memorization task; a realistic but nonfunctioning shock generator with increments of 15 to 450 volts was used to deliver the "punishment."

   (c) Each time the _____ made an error, the _____ was told to progress to the next level on the shock generator and announce the voltage before delivering the shock; the _____ followed a set scripted series of responses as the voltage increased until he eventually stopped responding altogether.

   (d) If the teacher protested that he wished to stop or that he was worried about the learner's safety, the experimenter _____ (would/would not) insist that the teacher continue.

(e) According to the script, the experiment would be halted when the teacher _____ the experimenter's orders to continue or when the voltage reached the maximum level of 450 volts.

3. (a) The results showed that all estimates of the level of shock that people would give in this experimental situation were wrong; _____ of Milgram's subjects went to the full 450-volt level, and of those who defied the experimenter, _____ (none/most/all) stopped before the 300-volt level.

(b) Milgram's obedience study has been _____ many times in the United States and other countries, and by Milgram himself on numerous occasions using variations of his basic experimental design, including one with all female subjects.

(c) Although Milgram's subjects appeared genuinely upset about hurting another person, _____ (a few/many/the majority) of them continued to administer stronger and stronger shocks, obediently following the experimenter's commands.

4. Milgram and other researchers identified several aspects of the experimental situation that had a strong impact on the subjects' willingness to continue obeying the experimenter's orders.

(a) A previously well-established _____ framework to obey. When they arrived in the lab, they had the _____ that they would obediently follow the directions of the person in charge—the experimenter.

(b) They believed the experiment would advance scientific knowledge and may have

felt that defying the experimenter's orders would make them appear arrogant, rude, disrespectful, or uncooperative. Thus, the _____ , or _____ , in which the obedience occurred influenced them.

(c) The gradual, repetitive _____ of the task. At the beginning of the experiment, the subject administered a very low level of shock (15 volts), and like the learner's protests, the shocks _____ very gradually, 15 volts at a time.

(d) The experimenter's _____ and _____ . The experimenter took responsibility for the learner's well-being; thus, the subjects could believe that they were not responsible for the _____ of their actions.

(e) The teacher was _____ and _____ separated from the learner. First, the learner was not _____ ; only his voice could be heard. Second, punishment was _____ ; the subject simply pushed a switch on the shock generator. Finally, the learner never appealed directly to the teacher to stop the shocks.

5. (a) By varying his experiments, Milgram identified several conditions that _____ (increase/decrease) the likelihood of destructive obedience.

(b) Willingness to obey _____ (diminishes/increases) sharply when the buffers that separate the teacher from the learner are lessened or removed, as when both of them are in the same room.

(c) If the experimenter left the room and spoke to the subject over the phone instead of face to face, complete obedience dropped to 23 percent. Thus, the _____ of the experimenter was another critical element.

6. (a) When subjects (teachers) were allowed to act as their own authority and freely choose the shock level, 95 percent of them _____ (did/did not) go beyond 150 volts; clearly, they _____ (were/were not) responding to their own aggressive, sadistic impulses.

(b) Milgram found that people are _____ (more/less) likely to muster up the courage to defy an authority when they see others do so; when they observed what they thought were two other subjects disobeying the experimenter, the real subject _____ (failed to follow/followed) their lead 90 percent of the time.

7. The scientific study of conformity and obedience has produced some important insights:

(a) It is psychologically uncomfortable to be at odds with the majority or the authority, enough so that our judgment and perceptions can be distorted and we may act in ways that violate our conscience. Thus, _____ factors are very important.

(b) Each of us _____ (does/does not) have the capacity to resist group or authority pressures; some subjects _____ (did/did not) refuse to conform or obey despite considerable social and situational pressure.

(c) No specific personality trait consistently _____ conformity or obedience in experimental situations such as the ones created by Asch and Milgram.

(d) Conformity and obedience are not completely bad in and of themselves; they are necessary for an orderly society. The critical issue is whether the norms we conform to or the orders we obey reflect values that respect the _____ , _____ , and _____ of others.

8. Read the following and write the correct term in the space provided.

(a) Trent hates to wear ties but wears one to his sister's wedding to avoid the disapproval of his family. Trent's behavior illustrates the importance of _____ social influence.

(b) Harold is a subject in a replication of Milgram's obedience experiment. If he is like most of the subjects in the experiment, he _____ (will/will not) administer high levels of shock to the learner.

(c) If Harold was allowed to act as his own authority and freely choose the shock level, it is very _____ (likely/unlikely) that he will use a shock over 150 volts, the first point at which the learner is likely to protest.

(d) At the end of a music concert featuring his favorite group, Jamal joined everyone else in giving them a standing ovation. Jamal's behavior _____ (is/is not) an example of conformity.

Review of Terms, Concepts, and Names 3

Use the terms in this list to complete the Matching Test, then to help you answer the True/False items correctly.

conformity
Solomon Asch
normative social
 influence

informational social
 influence
Stanley Milgram
obedience

Matching Exercise

Match the appropriate term/name with its definition or description.

1. _____ American social psychologist who is best known for his controversial investigation of destructive obedience to an authority.

2. _____ The tendency to adjust one's behavior, attitudes, or beliefs to group norms in response to real or imagined group pressure.

3. _____ Source of behavior that is motivated by the desire to gain social acceptance and approval.

4. _____ Performance of an action in response to the direct orders of an authority or person of higher status.

5. _____ American social psychologist who is best known for his pioneering studies of conformity.

6. _____ Source of behavior that is motivated by the desire to be correct.

> Check your answers and review any areas of weakness before going on to the next section.

Helping Behavior: Coming to the Aid of Strangers

Preview Questions

Consider the following questions as you study this section of the chapter.

- What is prosocial behavior, and how does it differ from altruism?
- What are the components of Latané and Darley's model of helping behavior?
- What factors increase or decrease the likelihood that people will help others?

Read the section "Helping Behavior: Coming to the Aid of Strangers" and **write** *your answers to the following:*

1. (a) When we help another person with no expectation of a personal reward or benefit, we're displaying _____ ; an individual is motivated purely by the desire to help someone in need.

   (b) Altruistic actions fall under the broader heading of _____ behavior, which describes any behavior that helps another person, whatever the underlying motive.

   (c) Sometimes we help others in order to gain something, such as recognition, reward, increased self-esteem, reduced guilt, or having the favor returned; thus, _____ behaviors are not necessarily _____ .

2. (a) Beginning in the 1960s, Bibb Latané and John Darley pioneered the study of when and why people decide to help others, or _____ , by conducting ingenious experiments in which people appeared to need help.

   (b) On the basis of their research findings, they developed a model of the process people follow when they decide whether or not to help another person. People are most likely to help if (1) they _____ the event or incident, (2) they _____ it is a situation in which help is needed, (3) they feel some sense of _____ to help, and (4) they know _____ with the situation.

3. Beyond the general model, Latané, Darley, and other researchers identified specific factors that influence the decision to help. Which factors increase the likelihood of helping behavior?

   (a) The "feel _____ , do _____ " effect. People who feel _____ , successful, happy, or fortunate are more likely to help others.

   (b) We tend to be more helpful when we're feeling _____ , such as after telling a lie or inadvertently causing an accident.

   (c) Seeing others who are _____ to help. People's behavior is often influenced by observing other people, and the same holds true for helping behavior.

   (d) Perceiving the other person as _____ help. We're more likely to help people who are in need through no fault of their own.

   (e) Knowing _____ to help. People who help tend to have more medical, police, and first aid training; simply knowing what to do contributes to the decision to help someone else.

   (f) Any sort of _____ relationship, even the most minimal social interaction, such as making eye contact or engaging in small talk, increases the likelihood that one person will help another.

4. Which factors *decrease* the likelihood of helping behavior?

   (a) The _____ of other people. People are much more likely to help when they are _____ (alone/with others); if other people are present, helping behavior _____ (increase/declines), a phenomenon called the bystander effect.

   (b) There appear to be two reasons for the bystander effect: (1) the presence of other people creates a _____ ; the responsibility to intervene is shared (or diffused) among the other onlookers, and because no one person feels all the pressure to respond, each bystander becomes _____ (more/less) likely to help; (2) each of us is motivated to some extent by the desire to behave in a socially acceptable way (_____ social influence) and to appear correct (_____ social influence); we often rely on the reactions of others to help us define the situation and guide our responses.

   (c) Being in a big city or a very small town. People are _____ (more/less) likely to help a stranger in very big cities (300,000 people or more) or in very small towns (5,000 people or less); people are _____ (more/less) likely to help a stranger in towns with populations in between these two extremes.

   (d) When situations are _____ or _____ , and people are not certain that help is needed, such as in domestic disputes or a lovers' quarrel, they're less likely to help.

   (e) As a general rule, we tend to weigh the _____ as well as the

_____ of helping in deciding whether to act, and when the _____ for helping outweigh the _____ , we tend not to help.

   (f) On a small yet universal scale, the murder of Kitty Genovese dramatically underscores the power of _____ and _____ influences on our behavior.

The Influence of Groups on Individual Behavior

Preview Questions

Consider the following questions as you study this section of the chapter.

- How does the presence of other people influence individual behavior?
- What are social loafing and social striving, and how does culture affect performance in a group?
- What are social facilitation and deindividuation, and under what conditions do these phenomena occur?

*Read the section "The Influence of Groups on Individual Behavior" and **write** your answers to the following:*

1. (a) Whether it is cheering, clapping, or rope pulling, people tend to expend less effort on _____ tasks than when they perform the same task _____ , a phenomenon called social loafing.

   (b) Social loafing is more pronounced when it is difficult or impossible to assess each individual's contribution to the _____ effort; as a general rule, the _____ (fewer/greater) the number of people involved in a collective effort, the lower each individual's output.

   (c) Research has shown that social loafing is reduced or eliminated when (1) the group is composed of people we _____ (know/don't know), (2) we are members of a(n) _____ group, or

(3) the task is _____ or

_____ .

(d) Women are generally _____
(more/less) likely to engage in social loafing
than men. And when the group size increases, the degree of social loafing
_____ for men, but not for
women.

2. (a) The diffusion of responsibility that occurs
among bystanders in a helping situation
also seems to occur among group members
working on a(n) _____ task.
The responsibility or effort for attaining the
group goal is spread across all the group
members, resulting in _____
(increased/reduced) effort by each individual
group member.

(b) Social loafing can also occur because people
_____ (do/do not) expect other
group members to slack off. To keep the situation even-handed or equitable, people
_____ (increase/reduce) their
efforts to match the level of effort they
expect other group members to display.

3. (a) Social loafing is a common phenomenon in
_____ cultures and is not only
absent but reversed in many _____
cultures, where individuals work _____
(less/harder) when they are in groups than
when they are alone, a pattern referred to
as social striving.

(b) Group success tends to be more highly valued than individual success in
_____ cultures, and the contributions made by individuals to group success are more highly valued than they are in
_____ cultures.

(c) The social norms in _____ cultures encourage a sense of social responsibility and hard work within the group.

4. (a) When a task is relatively simple or well

rehearsed, the _____ (absence/
presence) of other people tends to enhance
individual performance, a pattern called
social _____ . If the task is complex or poorly learned, the _____
of other people is likely to hinder performance.

(b) Our level of arousal and motivation tends to
_____ (decrease/increase) in the
presence of other people. When the task is
simple or well learned, this _____
(interferes with/enhances) performance;
when the task is complex or poorly learned,
arousal coupled with apprehension about
being negatively evaluated tends to
_____ (diminish/enhance) our
performance.

5. (a) In combination, increased arousal and a(n)
_____ sense of responsibility
can lead to deindividuation, which refers to
the reduction of self-awareness and inhibitions that can occur when a person is part of
a group whose members feel

_____ .

(b) Because of deindividuation, people may do
things that they wouldn't do if they were
_____ or _____ ,
which can lead to irresponsible or antisocial
behavior.

(c) Deindividuation, heightened _____ ,
and the sense of _____ that
large crowds and social chaos engender can
lead to mobs of rioting people who smash
windows, steal, and injure innocent
bystanders.

(d) An important element of deindividuation is
the _____ (increased/reduced)
sense of self-awareness; thus, one way to
counteract deindividuation is to
_____ (increase/reduce) self-
awareness.

6. Read the following and write the correct term in the space provided.

(a) Keith and his friends, who are normally law-abiding teenagers, put on masks and costumes on Halloween and smashed a number of pumpkins in the neighborhood. Social psychologists suggest that acts of vandalism such as this may be the result of

_____ .

(b) While practicing for the bike race, Roberto's best time on the course was 47 minutes and 12 seconds. During the actual race, however, his time improved by almost 3 minutes. Roberto's improvement when other people were watching may be the result of

_____ .

(c) Carmichael was elated when he won $1,000 in the lottery. Later that day, he gladly volunteered to spend a few hours on the weekend to help collect food for the local food bank. This illustrates the

" _____ "

effect.

(d) Two evenings a week Dr. Valdez volunteers his time at an AIDS clinic purely because he wants to help people. His behavior is an example of _____ .

(e) While about twenty subjects were filling out a questionnaire in a classroom, an odorless vapor started seeping into the room from one of the heating vents. The room slowly began to fill with the vapor, yet nobody stopped what they were doing and nobody went to report the incident. This bystander effect occurred because the presence of other people creates a(n)

_____ .

(f) In a social psychology experiment, college students pulled less hard on a rope if they believed others were also pulling on the same rope than if they thought they were pulling alone. This exemplifies the phenomenon of _____ .

Graphic Organizer 3

Describe the main research findings of the following social psychologists. (For example, Zimbardo's grasshopper study showed how behavior can change attitude through the process of cognitive dissonance.)

Researcher	Main Research Findings
1. Asch	
2. Sherif	
3. Milgram	
4. Latané and Darley	

Review of Terms, Concepts, and Names 4

Use the terms in this list to complete the Matching Test, then to help you answer the True/False items correctly.

altruism
prosocial behavior
Bibb Latané
John M. Darley
"feel good, do good" effect
bystander effect
diffusion of responsibility

social loafing
social striving
social facilitation
deindividuation
persuasion

Matching Exercise

Match the appropriate term/name with its definition or description.

1. _____ Contemporary American social psychologist who, along with co-researcher Bibb Latané, is best known for his pioneering studies of bystander intervention in emergency situations.

2. _____ Deliberate attempt to influence the attitudes or behavior of another person in a situation in which that person has some freedom of choice.

3. _____ Phenomenon in which the greater the number of people present, the less likely each individual is to help someone in distress.

4. _____ The reduction of self-awareness and inhibitions that can occur when a person is part of a group whose members feel anonymous.

5. _____ Helping another person with no expectation of personal reward or benefit.

6. _____ Contemporary American social psychologist who, along with co-researcher John M. Darley, is best known for his pioneering studies of bystander intervention in emergency situations.

True/False Test

Indicate whether each item is true or false by placing T or F in the space next to each item.

1. ___ Prosocial behavior refers to any behavior that helps another, whether the underlying motive is self-serving or selfless.

2. ___ Social facilitation is the tendency for the presence of other people to enhance individual performance.

3. ___ The phenomenon in which the presence of other people makes it less likely that any individual will help someone in distress because the obligation to intervene is shared among all the onlookers is called diffusion of responsibility.

4. ___ Social loafing refers to a situation in which individuals work harder when they are in groups than when they are alone.

5. ___ The "feel good, do good" effect refers to the fact that when people feel good, successful, happy, or fortunate, they are more likely to help others.

6. ___ The tendency to expend less effort on collective tasks than on the same task performed alone is called social striving.

Check your answers and review any areas of weakness before going on to the next section.

Something to Think About

1. People often ask, "Why are so many people reluctant to help others who are in distress and need help?" The most usual responses are that people suffer from apathy and that big cities alienate and depersonalize people. What would you say if someone asked you that question?

2. We are subjected to a wide variety of situations and stimuli that are designed to influence our attitudes or behavior. The most obvious of these are media advertisements, but we regularly encounter many other more subtle sources of attempted influence. These attempts to influence us all use techniques of persuasion. Imagine that you are hired by a company, and management wants you to write a brief summary of the factors that are most powerful in changing people's attitudes or behaviors. What would you put in your report?

Check your answers and review any areas of weakness before doing the progress tests.

Progress Test 1

Review the complete chapter (including Concept Reviews and the boxed inserts), review all your study notes, and then test yourself on the following progress test. Check your answers. If you make a mistake, review your notes, review the relevant section of the study guide, and, if necessary, go back and read the appropriate part of your textbook.

1. Dr. Lopez is a social psychologist who studies the mental processes people use to make sense of their social environment, including such topics as person perception, attribution, attitudes, and prejudice. His specific area of research is called
   (a) social cognition.
   (b) abnormal psychology.
   (c) social influence.
   (d) personality.

2. About a dozen students were sitting in a small research laboratory room filling out a questionnaire when they head a crash followed by groaning from the room next door. While many of them appeared to notice, nobody went to inform the researcher, who said he would be in his office just down the hall. This example illustrates
   (a) deindividuation.
   (b) diffusion of responsibility.
   (c) obedience.
   (d) informational social influence.

3. Michael, who is an accountant, often wonders why people are surprised when they find out that he is also a skydiving instructor on the weekends. The most obvious explanation is that people form cognitive schemas for different types of people and occupations. The use of these types of assumptions is called
   (a) ethnocentrism.
   (b) altruism.
   (c) implicit personality theory.
   (d) the self-serving bias.

4. If Marcello is typical of most people who are considered to be physically attractive, he is very likely to be
   (a) of above-average in intelligence.
   (b) better adjusted than most people.
   (c) more assertive than unattractive people.
   (d) less lonely, more popular, and less anxious in social situations than unattractive people.

5. Sally did very poorly on her last math test. If her fifth-grade teacher concludes that Sally did poorly because she is not motivated to do well in school, the teacher may be committing the
   (a) fundamental attribution error.
   (b) actor–observer discrepancy.
   (c) self-serving bias.
   (d) social categorization error.

6. When Allison landed a big contract for her firm, she accepted the credit for her hard work and smart "wheeling and dealing." When she failed to get the contract in another situation, she blamed the sneaky and dishonest tactics of the competition. This illustrates
   (a) social loafing.
   (b) the self-serving bias.
   (c) social striving.
   (d) the actor–observer discrepancy.

7. During a discussion on fast food and fast-food outlets, Reginald stated, "Fast food is great. I just love southern fried chicken, fries, coleslaw, and milkshakes." This statement represents the _____ component of Reginald's positive attitude toward fast-food restaurants.
   (a) cognitive   (c) behavioral
   (b) affective   (d) ambivalent

8. Faced with the equally attractive choice of either a baconburger or a cheeseburger, Jill finally decided on the cheeseburger. Shortly after she made her choice, she decided that the cheeseburger was a healthier choice and probably had fewer calories than the baconburger. Her tendency to emphasize the positive aspects of her choice and the negative aspects of the choice she rejected is an example of
   (a) social facilitation.
   (b) altruism.
   (c) prejudice.
   (d) cognitive dissonance.

9. One of Manfred's college classmates was from Turkey, and he loved turkey sandwiches, turkey pizza, turkey burgers, and turkey sausages. Manfred now believes that the main diet of all people from Turkey is centered around meals made from turkey meat, and he has little doubt why the country is called Turkey. Manfred's beliefs about the culture of Turkey reflect
   (a) ethnic stereotyping.   (c) deindividuation.
   (b) ethnocentrism.   (d) in-group bias.

10. Jackson joined the Alpine cross-country ski club because he couldn't afford the cost of downhill skiing. Many members of his club think that downhill skiing is destroying the natural environment, and they often make derogatory remarks about downhillers. Since joining the club, Jackson has changed his attitude about downhill skiing; he now promotes the benefits of cross-country skiing and joins his new buddies in categorizing all downhill skiers as self-centered, uncaring destroyers of the environment. This example illustrates
    (a) the out-group homogeneity effect.
    (b) in-group bias.
    (c) stereotyping.
    (d) all of the above.

11. Greg, who is a new faculty member, is on a college committee concerned with student evaluation. Greg disagrees with the proposal to institute a collegewide percentage system for grading. The other five members have already stated that they are in favor of the proposal. Which of the following is likely to persuade Greg in his decision about how to vote?
    (a) normative social influence
    (b) informational social influence
    (c) neither (a) nor (b); Greg may stick with his own view and vote against the proposal
    (d) all of the above

12. Henny is working on a project with four other students. If he is typical of most people involved in a collective task, he is likely to
    (a) work harder than if he were working on the same task alone.
    (b) expend less effort than if he were working on the same task alone.
    (c) credit external, situational factors if the project is a success and blame himself if the project is unsuccessful.
    (d) suffer from deindividuation.

13. Just moments after dozens of people get off a crowded bus, a badly dressed man stumbles and falls on the sidewalk near the bus stop. Research on bystander intervention would suggest that
    (a) he will get immediate help from many people.
    (b) the presence of others will decrease the diffusion of responsibility.
    (c) if one person stops to help him, other people are likely to help as well.
    (d) no one in the crowd will perceive that he may need help.

14. According to Critical Thinking 12.2, which of the following is true?
    (a) Two-thirds of the subjects completely obeyed the experimenter's destructive demands and progressed to the full 450-volt level.
    (b) Milgram was criticized because he failed to debrief the subjects after the experiment was over.
    (c) Less than 1 percent of the subjects obeyed the experimenter's destructive demands and progressed to the full 450-volt level.
    (d) The vast majority of Milgram's subjects experienced long-term traumatic reactions, such as depression, decreased self-esteem, and psychotic episodes.

15. According to the Application, which of the following is correct?
    (a) Persuasion refers to the deliberate attempt to influence the attitudes or behaviors of another person in a situation in which the person has some freedom of choice.
    (b) Persuasion techniques are not effective in manipulating people in any way.
    (c) Professional persuaders can easily manipulate and change the attitudes and behaviors of the vast majority of people.
    (d) Because of the flexible nature of social norms, the vast majority of people can resist conforming to any societal standards.

Progress Test 2

After you have checked your understanding of the material in Progress Test 1 and have done a complete chapter review with special focus on any areas of weakness, you are ready to assess your knowledge of Progress Test 2. Check your answers. If you make a mistake, review your notes, the relevant section of the study guide, and, if necessary, the appropriate part of your textbook.

1. Jake lost his job two months ago when his company downsized its operations; despite his efforts, he has not yet found another job. One of his neighbors stated that Jake is just like most unemployed people—irresponsible, unmotivated, and basically lazy. The neighbor has committed the
    (a) self-serving bias.
    (b) actor–observer discrepancy.
    (c) social categorization error.
    (d) fundamental attribution error.

2. When their town was threatened by a flood, two families who had been enemies for years ended up working together to try to save the town from the overflowing river. Generalizing from Sherif's findings, you might conclude that this act of cooperative behavior may lead to

   (a) increased antagonism once the danger has passed.
   (b) an increase in social loafing.
   (c) reduced conflict and increased harmony between the two families.
   (d) diffusion of responsibility.

3. As part of a social psychology experiment, one group of male college students are asked to wear masks and clothes that hide their identities. Compared with a similar group wearing name tags and whose faces are not covered, the anonymous group demonstrated significantly more aggression. The reason for the increased aggression in the anonymous condition is

   (a) social facilitation.   (c) social loafing.
   (b) deindividuation.   (d) altruism.

4. When Rachel found out that she had straight As in all her courses, she was elated. Later that day, when she was asked if she could donate some money to the restore-the-church fund, she readily made a donation, even though she is not religious and does not go to church. This illustrates

   (a) cognitive dissonance.
   (b) the "feel good, do good" effect.
   (c) conformity.
   (d) informational social influence.

5. Wolfgang's best typing speed was 50 words a minute during practice. However, in a typing competition with 10 other people, he improved his speed to 55 words a minute. His improved performance in the presence of others reflects

   (a) informational social influence.
   (b) normative social influence.
   (c) social facilitation.
   (d) social striving.

6. When Inge was first elected to the student finance committee, she was asked to make a decision on some important financial matter with which she was not familiar. All the other members of the committee stated that they were going to vote against the proposal. Inge voted with the group because she assumed that they must have the correct information. This example illustrates

   (a) social facilitation.
   (b) normative social influence.
   (c) informational social influence.
   (d) deindividuation.

7. Martha is a subject in a replication of Milgram's original obedience experiment that involves female subjects only. Compared with a similar study involving only male subjects,

   (a) at least 60 percent of the females will refuse to continue with the experiment at the 300-volt level.
   (b) a much higher percentage of the females will obey the experimenter and progress to the 450-volt level.
   (c) only about 10 percent of the female subjects will obey the experimenter and progress to the 450-volt level.
   (d) the results of the all-female replication will be the same as the all-male condition.

8. In the study described in question 7, if the experimenter leaves the room and gives the directions over the phone, it is very likely that

   (a) the level of compliance will be the same as if the experimenter was in the room.
   (b) the level of compliance will be greater than if the experimenter was in the room.
   (c) the level of compliance will be significantly lower than if the experimenter was in the room.
   (d) none of the subjects will follow the experimenter's instructions and progress to the 450-volt level.

9. Quincy has reviewed the literature on conformity and obedience for a term paper. He is most likely to conclude that

   (a) virtually nobody is capable of resisting group or authority pressure.
   (b) all people are innately predisposed to be cruel and aggressive.
   (c) conformity and obedience are not necessarily bad in and of themselves and are important for an orderly society.
   (d) all of the above are true.

10. Jorge thought that either horse, Con Brio or White Lightening, had an equal chance of winning the next race and was debating which one to bet on. After he placed his money on Con Brio, however, he felt very confident that he had backed the winner. This example illustrates the effect of

   (a) cognitive dissonance.
   (b) the self-serving bias.
   (c) conformity.
   (d) social influence.

11. Jenny got 90 percent on her biology midterm exam, Jean got 60 percent, and Jackie got 75 percent. On the basis of their scores on the exam, Jackie thinks to herself that Jenny must be really intelligent and that Jean must be a little slow. Which of the following is true?

   (a) Jackie has made an attribution.
   (b) Jackie's assessment of her classmates' intelligence is accurate.
   (c) Jackie's evaluation reflects the in-group bias.
   (d) Jackie's assessment of her classmates' intelligence reflects her prejudice.

12. During a discussion about gun control laws, Marylou said, "I believe it is every American's fundamental right to own a gun and that the government has no right to pass laws banning the ownership of guns under any circumstances." This statement reflects the _____ component of Marylou's attitude about guns and gun-control laws.

   (a) cognitive   (c) behavioral
   (b) affective   (d) dissonant

13. Yoko was late for work because the traffic was particularly heavy. When she arrived at the office, she apologized to her boss, insisting that it was her fault for being late; if she were less lazy, it wouldn't have happened. This example of blaming an accidental occurrence on an internal, personal disposition rather than on situational factors is called the

   (a) self-serving bias.
   (b) fundamental attribution error.
   (c) actor–observer discrepancy.
   (d) self-effacing bias (modesty bias).

14. According to Culture and Human Behavior 12.1, collectivistic and individualistic cultures differ in their attributional biases. In general, compared with members of individualistic cultures, how likely are members of collectivistic cultures to commit the fundamental attribution error?

   (a) more likely
   (b) less likely
   (c) just as likely
   (d) All of the above are equally likely.

15. A number of persuasion techniques are used by professional marketers. According to the Application, which of the following is *not* one of those techniques?

   (a) the door-in-the-face technique
   (b) the that's-not-all technique
   (c) the foot-in-the-mouth technique
   (d) the low-ball technique
   (e) the foot-in-the-door technique

Progress Test 3

After you have checked your understanding of the material in Progress Tests 1 and 2, and have done a complete chapter review with special focus on any areas of weakness, you are ready to further assess your knowledge on Progress Test 3. Check your answers. If you make a mistake, review your notes, the appropriate parts of the study guide, and if necessary, the relevant sections of your textbook.

1. Dr. Saroya is a social psychologist whose research interests focus on how our behavior is affected by situational factors and other people, and in particular why we conform to group norms and why we help or don't help strangers. The basic area of social psychology that Dr. Saroya studies is called

   (a) social cognition.   (c) social influence.
   (b) social facilitation.   (d) social loafing.

2. When Ruby got on the subway, she quickly looked around and decided it would be safer to sit next to the middle aged, well-dressed woman than the man with bright orange hair and earrings. Ruby has engaged in the process of

   (a) deindividuation.   (c) ethnocentrism.
   (b) person perception.   (d) cognitive dissonance.

3. When Mr. Denbridge was asked to donate to a fund to help people infected with hepatitis B and the HIV virus, he responded that he would not help these people because they caused their own misfortunes. It appears that Mr. Denbridge is
   (a) blaming the victim.
   (b) demonstrating the out-group homogeneity effect.
   (c) being altruistic.
   (d) reducing his cognitive dissonance.

4. During a tour of a Latin America country, Susanne was surprised to find that almost everyone took a long three-hour break in the middle of the day. She concluded that, compared with the United States, this country was not doing well economically because everyone was lazy, lacked motivation, and spent too much time sleeping. Susanne's conclusion reflects a form of in-group bias called
   (a) ethnocentrism.
   (b) deindividuation.
   (c) social loafing.
   (d) the actor-observer discrepancy.

5. During the annual spring clean-up at her school, Heidi noticed that students who were part of a group did much less work per person than students who were given tasks that required them to work alone. Heidi's observation is most consistent with the phenomenon of
   (a) social facilitation.
   (b) social loafing.
   (c) prosocial behavior.
   (d) altruistic behavior.

6. Vince suggests that his sister's aggressive behavior results from her insecurity. Vince's explanation for his sister's behavior is an example of
   (a) deindividuation.
   (b) the bystander effect.
   (c) an attribution.
   (d) cognitive dissonance.

7. Kyle is in sixth grade and, like most children in his school, he believes that his school is better than all the other schools in town. This best illustrates
   (a) in-group bias.
   (b) ethnic stereotyping.
   (c) cognitive dissonance.
   (d) the fundamental attribution error.

8. Seeing a skier wipe out on a steep section of the run, Jenny comments, "A klutz like that shouldn't be allowed on the slopes!" Later, when Jenny wipes out in the same place, she blames the icy conditions. This is an example of
   (a) the self-serving bias.
   (b) the actor–observer discrepancy.
   (c) deindividuation.
   (d) social loafing.

9. Pietro notices that when there are empty seats on the bus, nobody ever sits beside a stranger, but when the bus is crowded, people sit beside strangers all the time. He noticed that the same thing happens in movie theaters, the cafeteria, and even the classroom. Pietro's observation suggests that people's behavior in these situations is governed by
   (a) prejudice.   (c) stereotypes.
   (b) social categorization. (d) social norms.

10. Fraser loves wearing sandals or thongs and hates wearing shoes. However, when he went to dinner with his girlfriend's family, he wore shoes because he did not want to evoke their disapproval. Fraser's behavior best illustrates the importance of
    (a) informational social influence.
    (b) normative social influence.
    (c) social facilitation.
    (d) obedience.

11. While Lyle was alone in a classroom filling out a questionnaire, an odorless vapor started seeping slowly into the room from one of the heating vents. In this situation it is very likely that Lyle will leave the room and report the strange odor to someone. If Lyle was in the room with a large group of other people who were also filling out questionnaires, it is much less likely that he would report the vapor. The difference in Lyle's behavior is best explained by
    (a) the bystander effect.
    (b) social facilitation.
    (c) altruism.
    (d) cognitive dissonance.

12. When Maryjane steps into the elevator, she quickly looks at the other passengers and decides that the gray-haired man with the beard must be a professor at the college. Maryjane has engaged in the process of
    (a) prejudicial thinking.
    (b) discrimination.
    (c) social categorization.
    (d) deindividuation.

13. Rita volunteers three or four evenings a week at a local shelter for the homeless because she believes in helping those less fortunate than herself. Richard also volunteers at the shelter because he believes the work experience will increase his chances of getting accepted into the Masters of Social Work program. In this situation, Rita's motivation is an example of _____ , and Richard's motivation reflects _____ .
    (a) altruism; prosocial behavior
    (b) social facilitation; social striving
    (c) prosocial behavior; altruism
    (d) normative social influence; informational social influence

14. According to Critical Thinking 12.2, which of the following is true of Milgram's research?
    (a) It created a controversy that led to the establishment of ethical safeguards by the American Psychological Association and the federal government regarding experiments involving human subjects.
    (b) It was criticized for causing his subjects emotional stress, tension, and loss of dignity.
    (c) It demonstrated, much to everyone's surprise, that the majority of subjects would obey an authority figure even if it apparently meant hurting another person.
    (d) All of the above are true.

15. According to Culture and Human Behavior 12.1, which of the following is true of the self-effacing bias (modesty bias)?
    (a) It refers to the tendency to expend less effort on collective tasks than on the same task performed alone.
    (b) It involves blaming failure on internal, personal factors while attributing success to external, situational factors.
    (c) It refers to the tendency to work harder on collective tasks than on the same task performed alone.
    (d) It involves attributing successful outcomes of one's own behavior to internal causes and unsuccessful outcomes to external, situational causes. ·

Answers

Introduction: Social Psychology
1. (a) think, feel; behave
   (b) impressions; interpret; attitudes
   (c) situational; conform; obey; help

Person Perception: Forming Impressions of Other People
1. (a) mental; judgments; conclusions
   (b) characteristics; characteristics; situation
2. (a) perceptions
   (b) goals
   (c) evaluate; social norms
   (d) self-perception
   (e) context; self-perceptions
3. (a) mental; groups
   (b) social categories
   (c) superficial; unique; cognitive
   (d) consciously; deliberately
4. (a) people, traits; behaviors; schemas
   (b) are; accurate
   (c) social; observations, memories
5. (a) attractiveness; attractive; unattractive
   (b) is; is not

Attribution: Explaining Behavior
1. (a) attribution; explanation
   (b) internal, personal; external, situational
   (c) blaming the victim; caused
   (d) just-world hypothesis
2. (a) external, situational; internal, personal
   (b) actor–observer; actor; observer
   (c) information; actor–observer
3. (a) successful; unsuccessful
   (b) successes; failures; failure
4. (a) self-serving bias
   (b) fundamental attribution error
   (c) actor–observer discrepancy
   (d) implicit personality theory
   (e) social norms
   (f) blaming the victim; just-world hypothesis

Graphic Organizer 1
1. C; INT for own success; EXT for own failure
2. B; EXT for self; INT for other
3. A; INT for other

Matching Exercise 1
1. social norms
2. attribution
3. self-serving bias
4. social psychology
5. implicit personality theory
6. actor–observer discrepancy
7. blaming the victim

True/False Test 1

1. F	4. T	6. T
2. T	5. F	7. T
3. T		

The Social Psychology of Attitudes

1. (a) learned; object, person; issue; ambivalent
   (b) cognitive; affective; behavioral

2. (a) don't always
   (b) extreme; frequently; experience; knowledge-able; interest; favorable

3. (a) psychological; an inconsistency
   (b) conflict; conflicting
   (c) rationalize; consistent; justified (rationalized); consistent; common
   (d) strength; consistent
   (e) desirable (positive); undesirable (negative); negative; positive

Graphic Organizer 2

1. cognitive
2. behavioral
3. behavioral
4. affective
5. behavioral
6. affective
7. cognitive
8. affective
9. cognitive

Understanding Prejudice

1. (a) negative attitude
   (b) majority; minority
   (c) similar; different; smaller

2. (a) characteristics; characteristics
   (b) remember; cognitive; cognition

3. (a) do not see; blind
   (b) hard; expectations
   (c) discount; exception; exceptions

4. (a) in-group; out-groups; negatively
   (b) in-groups; out-groups
   (c) different; similar; out-group homogeneity
   (d) in-group bias
   (e) ethnocentrism; negative stereotypes

5. (a) cognitive; emotional
   (b) discrimination
   (c) prejudice; hostility
   (d) emotional; norms

6. (a) reduce; increase
   (b) conflict; harmony; cooperative
   (c) cooperative; interdependence; cooperation
   (d) higher; greater

7. (a) decide; consciously
   (b) internalize
   (c) inhibit

8. (a) stereotype
   (b) cognitive
   (c) out-group homogeneity
   (d) ethnocentrism
   (e) cognitive dissonance; reduce

Matching Exercise 2

1. Muzafer Sherif
2. ethnocentrism
3. attitude
4. in-group
5. cognitive dissonance
6. out-group
7. prejudice

True/False Test 2

1. T	3. F	5. T
2. T	4. T	6. F

Conformity: Following the Crowd

1. (a) social influence
   (b) behavior, attitudes; beliefs
   (c) does not; differently
   (d) private; public; private

2. (a) Solomon Asch; the vast majority
   (b) normative; informational
   (c) against; increases; lessens

3. (a) Asch
   (b) collectivistic; individualistic
   (c) individualistic; collectivistic

Obedience: Just Following Orders

1. (a) performance; direct orders
   (b) pressured; immoral
   (c) obey; orders

2. (a) representative; teacher; learner
   (b) teacher; learner
   (c) learner; teacher; learner
   (d) would
   (e) refused to obey

3. (a) two-thirds; none

(b) repeated (replicated)

(c) the majority

4. (a) mental; expectation

(b) situation, context

(c) escalation; escalated

(d) behavior; reassurances; consequences

(e) physically; psychologically; visible; depersonalized

5. (a) decrease

(b) diminishes

(c) proximity

6. (a) did not; were not

(b) more; followed

7. (a) situational

(b) does; did

(c) predicts

(d) rights, well-being; human dignity

8. (a) normative

(b) will

(c) unlikely

(d) is not

Matching Exercise 3

1. Stanley Milgram

2. conformity

3. normative social influence

4. obedience

5. Solomon Asch

6. informational social influence

Helping Behavior: Coming to the Aid of Strangers

1. (a) altruism

(b) prosocial

(c) prosocial; altruistic

2. (a) bystander intervention

(b) notice; believe; responsibility; how to deal

3. (a) good; good; good

(b) guilty

(c) willing

(d) deserving

(e) how

(f) personal

4. (a) presence; alone; declines

(b) diffusion of responsibility; less; normative; informational

(c) less; more

(d) vague; ambiguous

(e) costs; benefits; costs; benefits

(f) situational; social

The Influence of Groups on Individual Behavior

1. (a) collective; alone

(b) collective; greater

(c) know; highly valued; meaningful; unique

(d) less; increases

2. (a) collective; reduced

(b) do; reduce

3. (a) individualistic; collectivistic; harder

(b) collectivistic; individualistic

(c) collectivistic

4. (a) presence; facilitation; presence

(b) increase; enhances; diminish

5. (a) diminished; anonymous

(b) alone; identifiable

(c) arousal; anonymity

(d) reduced; increase

6. (a) deindividuation

(b) social facilitation

(c) feel good, do good

(d) altruism

(e) diffusion of responsibility

(f) social loafing

Graphic Organizer 3

1. Naive subjects yielded to group pressure in the line-judging task even though the group opinion was wrong.

2. The Robbers Cave study helped clarify the conditions that produce intergroup conflict and harmony and led to the use of the jigsaw classroom technique to promote cooperative behavior.

3. Dramatic illustration of the pressure to obey an authority figure's request to shock another person in a mock learning experiment.

4. Showed the conditions under which people are more likely to help a stranger in distress as well as the factors that decrease helping behavior.

Matching Exercise 4

1. John M. Darley

2. persuasion

3. bystander effect

4. deindividuation

5. altruism

6. Bibb Latané

True/False Test 4

1. T   4. F
2. T   5. T
3. T   6. F

Something to Think About

1. The first thing to note is the distinction between altruism and prosocial behavior and that people do perform many acts of kindness and help each other on a daily basis. Many times these behaviors are altruistic; the individual helps someone with no expectation of a personal reward or benefit. Other times, helping behaviors have some pay-off, such as reduced guilt, increased self-esteem, rewards, recognition, or the expectation that the favor will be returned.

   In some instances, such as in the Kitty Genovese case, people could easily help someone by simply making a phone call but they don't. Latané and Darley have developed a model that addresses the question of why people don't intervene. For intervention to occur, people have to notice the event or incident, believe it is a situation in which help is needed, feel some sense of responsibility to help, and, finally, know how to deal with the situation.

   The final model identifies six specific factors that increase the likelihood that bystanders will help: (1) the "feel good, do good" effect, (2) feeling guilty, (3) seeing others who are willing to help, (4) perceiving others as deserving help, (5) knowing how to help, and (6) a personal relationship with the person who needs help.

   A number of factors decrease the likelihood of bystanders helping: (1) the presence of others, called the bystander effect, and the resulting diffusion of responsibility; (2) being in a big city or a very small town; (3) a vague or ambiguous situations; and (4) when the personal costs for helping outweigh the benefits. In a discussion of this issue it is important to be able to explain and give examples of each factor.

2. The summary in the Application "The Persuasion Game" provides the information you need to answer this question. First, define persuasion, then paraphrase the main strategies that professional persuaders use to manipulate people's attitudes and behaviors. These include the role of reciprocity, the door-in-the-face technique, the that's-not-all technique, the rule of commitment, the foot-in-the-door technique, and the low-ball technique. You might also want to integrate material from the chapter, such as the finding that we often form more positive impressions of beautiful people than of those who are physically unattractive, the role of cognitive dissonance in changing cognitions and behavior, and aspects of conformity and obedience research. Finally, you should discuss the ways in which people can defend themselves against professional persuasion techniques—for example, sleeping on it, playing the devil's advocate, and paying attention to gut feelings.

Progress Test 1

1. a   6. b   11. d
2. b   7. b   12. b
3. c   8. d   13. c
4. d   9. a   14. a
5. a   10. d   15. a

Progress Test 2

1. d   6. c   11. a
2. c   7. d   12. a
3. b   8. c   13. d
4. b   9. c   14. b
5. c   10. a   15. c

Progress Test 3

1. c   6. c   11. a
2. b   7. a   12. c
3. a   8. b   13. a
4. a   9. d   14. d
5. b   10. b   15. b

Stress, Health, and Coping

PREVIEW

Reading the section below first will give you a general sense of the chapter's contents and an initial introduction to some of the major concepts and terms. This will prime you for what you are about to read and help you to develop a "cognitive map" that will guide your study of the material in this chapter. Likewise, reading the **preview questions** at the beginning of each major section will improve your ability to understand, learn, and retain the information.

CHAPTER 13 . . . AT A GLANCE

Chapter 13 deals with the effects of stress on health and the ways in which people cope with stress. Health psychologists study stress and other psychological factors that influence health, illness, and treatment and are guided by the biopsychosocial model. The life events approach to stress first developed in the 1960s is critically examined. More recently, researchers have focused on the importance of daily hassles, conflict, and social and cultural factors as sources of stress.

The physical effects of stress are discussed. Walter Cannon's fight-or-flight response and Hans Selye's three-stage general adaptation syndrome are described. Ader and Cohen's research on conditioning the immune system and its influence on the foundation of psychoneuroimmunology are presented along with research findings on the effects of stress on the immune system.

Psychological factors can also influence our response to stress. People's sense of personal control and their explanatory style—optimistic or pessimistic—are important in determining how a person responds to stress. The text notes that chronic negative emotions are related to the development of some chronic diseases and that Type A behavior patterns can predict the development of heart disease, with the most critical component being hostility. The role of social support in how people deal with stressful situations is explored.

The final section covers coping strategies. Depending on the situation, people use problem-focused or emotion-focused coping. Culture affects the choice of coping strategies; individualistic and collectivistic coping strategies are compared and contrasted.

Introduction: What Is Stress?

Preview Questions

Consider the following questions as you study this section of the chapter.

- How is stress defined, and what is the main focus of health psychology?
- What is the biopsychosocial model, and how are health psychologists guided by it?

*Read the section "Introduction: What Is Stress?" and **write** your answers to the following:*

1. (a) Stress is widely defined as a negative _____ state occurring in response to events that are perceived as taxing or _____ a person's resources or ability to cope.

   (b) Whether or not we experience stress largely depends on our _____ of an event and the _____ we have to deal with the event.

2. (a) Health psychology is one of the most rapidly growing specialty areas in psychology. Along with the study of _____ , it focuses on how psychological factors influence _____ , _____ , _____ , and health-related behaviors.

   (b) Health psychologists are guided by the biopsychosocial model, according to which health and illness are determined by the complex interaction of _____ , _____ , and _____ factors.

What Is Stress?: Sources of Stress

Preview Questions

Consider the following questions as you study this section of the chapter.

- What are stressors, and what are some of the most important sources of stress?
- What is the life events approach, and what problems are associated with this approach?

- How do daily hassles and conflict contribute to stress?
- How can social and cultural factors become sources of stress?

*Read the section "What Is Stress?: Sources of Stress" and **write** your answers to the following:*

1. (a) Stressors are _____ or _____ that are perceived as harmful, threatening, or challenging.

   (b) Early stress researchers Holmes and Rahe believed that any _____ that required you to adjust your _____ and _____ would cause stress. They developed the Social Readjustment Rating Scale in an attempt to measure the amount of stress people experienced.

   (c) The scale includes 43 life events (both positive and negative), each of which is assigned a numerical rating that estimates its relative impact in terms of _____ , which range from 11 for the least stress-producing to 100 for the most stress-producing.

   (d) According to this approach, any change, whether positive or negative, is inherently stress-producing; researchers found that people who had more than _____ life change units within a year had an increased rate of physical or psychological illness.

2. Several problems with the life events approach have been pointed out:

   (a) The link between scores on the Social Readjustment Rating Scale and the development of physical and psychological problems is relatively _____ (weak/strong); most people _____ (do/don't) develop physical or mental problems as a result of major life events.

   (b) The Social Readjustment Rating Scale does

not take into account a person's subjective _____ of an event, response to that event, or ability to cope with the event. It assumes that a given life event will have _____ (the same/a different) impact on virtually everyone.

(c) The life events approach assumes _____ in itself, whether good or bad, produces stress. Research has shown that health is most adversely affected by _____ life events, especially when they are unexpected or uncontrollable, whereas _____ events are much less likely to affect health adversely.

(d) Researchers generally agree that _____ events are significant sources of stress, but that _____ in itself is not necessarily stressful.

3. (a) A scale to measure daily hassles—everyday occurrences that annoy and upset people—was developed by stress researcher _____ and his colleagues. They believed that these might be an important source of stress.

(b) The frequency of daily hassles _____ (is/is not) linked to psychological distress and physical symptoms; in fact, the number of daily hassles people experience is a _____ (worse/better) predictor of physical illness and symptoms than the number of major life events experienced.

(c) One explanation is that minor stressors are _____ ; each hassle may be relatively unimportant in itself, but after a day filled with minor hassles, the effects add up.

(d) Daily hassles also contribute to the stress produced by

_____ ; whether positive or negative, any _____ can

create a ripple effect, generating a host of new daily hassles.

4. (a) Another common source of stress results from the feeling of being pulled between two opposing desires, motives, or goals, which is called _____ . An individual is motivated to _____ desirable or pleasant outcomes and to _____ undesirable or unpleasant outcomes.

(b) Being faced with a choice between two equally appealing outcomes is a win-win situation; this is called an

_____ conflict. As a rule, these conflicts are usually easy to resolve and don't produce much stress.

(c) More stressful is having to choose between two unappealing or undesirable outcomes; this is referred to as an

_____ conflict. A natural response to this conflict is to delay making a decision or to bail out of the situation altogether.

(d) Most stressful of all is when a single goal has both desirable and undesirable aspects; this called a(n) _____ conflict. People often vacillate, unable to make a decision; the result is a significant increase in feelings of stress and anxiety.

5. (a) Crowding, crime, unemployment, poverty, racism, inadequate health care, and substandard housing are all _____ conditions that can be important sources of stress. When people live in an environment that is inherently stressful, they often experience ongoing, or _____ , stress.

(b) People in the _____ (highest/lowest) socioeconomic levels of society tend to have the highest levels of psychological distress, illness, and death; in _____ neighborhoods, people are likely to be exposed to more negative life events, including daily hassles, and to have fewer resources available to cope with those events.

(c) Stress can also result when _____ clash; for refugees, immigrants, and their children, adapting to a new _____ can be extremely stress-producing.

6. Read the following and write the correct term in the space provided.

(a) Dr. Woodworth studies stress, how psychological factors influence health, illness, treatment, and health-related behaviors. Dr. Woodworth is a _____ psychologist.

(b) If Dr. Woodworth is like most psychologists in his specialty area, he adheres to the theory that health and illness are determined by the complex interaction of biological, psychological, and social factors. In other words, he is guided by the _____ model.

(c) In the past year, Frank has been divorced, moved twice, and started a new relation-

ship. In addition, he has received a promotion and a big raise at work but now has many more responsibilities. His score on the Social Readjustment Rating scale is likely to be _____ (high/low), and according to its developers, Homes and Rahe, Frank has a(n) _____ (increased/decreased) likelihood of developing serious physical or psychological problems.

(d) According to Richard Lazarus, Frank's major life events may create a ripple effect and generate a host of _____ that may accumulate to cause even greater stress.

(e) Janet can only take one course this semester because of work commitments. She is torn between two courses she really wants to take, each of which fits her work schedule. Janet is probably experiencing an

_____ conflict.

Graphic Organizer 1

Read the following descriptions and decide which type of stress-producing conflict is involved: approach-approach, avoidance-avoidance, or approach-avoidance. In addition, label each one as producing either a high, medium, or low level of stress.

Description	Type of Conflict/ Level of Stress (low/medium/high)
1. Lyndle wants to maintain a high grade-point average and needs to study hard before his exam tomorrow, but he has been asked by his girlfriend to go with her to a party this evening.	
2. A rat in the start box of a Y-shaped maze with two separate goal boxes at the end of each prong will receive an equally desirable food pellet in each one.	
3. Annalee is very happy to be doing well on her diet but now has to decide whether to go for lunch with her friends at her favorite Greek taverna or stay in the lunchroom and eat her low-calorie snack.	
4. In order to be able to borrow the family car for the evening, Jason has to decide between doing two equally unappealing chores, the family laundry or washing and waxing the bathroom and kitchen floors.	
5. Virginia entered her name in a contest and was overwhelmed when she won a seven-day Caribbean cruise. She has to decide between a seven-day eastern Caribbean cruise or a seven-day western Caribbean cruise.	
6. Melvin is overweight and out of shape and is given a choice of two daily exercise regimens by his doctor, one involving 40 minutes of running, riding an exercise bike, and weightlifting and the other involving 40 minutes of rowing machine, step-up machine, and weightlifting.	

Review of Terms, Concepts, and Names 1

Use the terms in this list to complete the Matching Test, then to help you answer the True/False items correctly.

stressors
stress
health psychology
biopsychosocial model
Social Readjustment
  Rating Scale
Richard Lazarus
daily hassles

conflict
approach-approach
  conflict
avoidance-avoidance
  conflict
approach-avoidance
  conflict
acculturative stress

Matching Exercise

Match the appropriate term/name with its definition or description.

1. _____ American psychologist who helped promote the cognitive perspective in the study of emotion and stress; developed the cognitive appraisal model of stress and coping with coresearcher Susan Folkman.

2. _____ Basic type of conflict in which you're faced with a choice between two equally appealing outcomes. As a rule, these conflicts are usually easy to resolve and don't produce much stress.

3. _____ Situation in which a person feels pulled between two or more opposing desires, motives, or goals.

4. _____ Everyday minor events that annoy and upset people.

5. _____ The branch of psychology that studies how psychological factors influence health, illness, medical treatment as well as health-related behaviors.

6. _____ Model that guides the work of health psychologists. According to this model, health and illness are determined by the complex interaction of biological, psychological, and social factors.

True/False Test

Indicate whether each statement is true or false by placing T or F in the blank space next to each item.

1. ____ Stress refers to events or situations that are perceived as harmful, threatening, or challenging.

2. ____ The Social Readjustment Rating Scale was developed by Thomas Holmes and Richard

Rahe in an attempt to measure the amount of stress people experienced as a function of life events that are likely to require some level of adaptation.

3. ____ An approach-avoidance conflict has a single goal with both desirable and undesirable aspects. When faced with this conflict, people often vacillate, or repeatedly go back and forth in their minds, unable to decide to approach or avoid the goal.

4. ____ Stressors refer to negative emotional states that occur in response to events that are perceived as taxing or exceeding a person's resources or ability to cope.

5. ____ An avoidance-avoidance conflict involves choosing between two unappealing or undesirable outcomes. People often delay making a decision when faced with this conflict, or they may bail out altogether.

6. ____ The stress that results from the pressure of adapting to a new culture is called acculturative stress.

Check your answers and review any areas of weakness before going on to the next section.

Physical Effects of Stress: The Mind–Body Connection

Preview Questions

Consider the following questions as you study this section of the chapter.

- How can stress contribute to health problems both directly and indirectly?

- How did the work of Cannon and Selye contribute to the early understanding of stress?

- What endocrine pathways are involved in the flight-or-fight response and the general adaptation syndrome?

*Read the section "Physical Effects of Stress: The Mind–Body Connection" and **write** your answers to the following:*

1. (a) People under chronic stress are more likely to use alcohol, coffee, and cigarettes than people under less stress. Thus, stress can

indirectly affect a person's health by

_____ that jeopardizes physical

well-being.

(b) High levels of stress can also interfere with

_____ abilities, such as atten-

tion, concentration, and memory; in turn,

such disruptions can increase the likelihood

of accidents and injuries.

(c) Stress can directly affect physical health by

altering _____ , leading to

symptoms, illness, or disease; for example,

stress can cause neck and head muscles to

contract and tighten, resulting in stress-

induced headaches.

2. (a) To explain the connection between stress

and health, researchers have focused on how

the _____ system, including the

_____ , interacts with two other

important body systems, the _____

and _____ systems.

(b) A rapidly occurring chain of internal physi-

cal reactions prepares people either to

_____ or to take

_____ from an immediate

threat.

(c) This fight-or-flight response was first

described by American physiologist

_____ , one of the earliest

contributors to stress research. He discov-

ered that the fight-or-flight response

involved both the

_____ nervous system and

the _____ system.

(d) With the perception of a threat, the hypo-

thalamus and lower brain structures acti-

vate the _____

system to stimulate the adrenal medulla to

secrete hormones called catecholamines,

including _____ and

_____ .

(e) Circulating through the blood, cate-

cholamines _____ (inhibit/

trigger) the rapid and intense bodily

changes associated with the fight-or-flight

response. Once the threat is removed, the

high level of bodily arousal tends to

_____ , and within twenty to

sixty minutes, a _____ is

usually reestablished.

(f) As a short-term reaction, the fight-or-flight

response helps ensure _____ by

swiftly mobilizing internal physical

resources to defensively attack or flee an

immediate threat. However, when exposure

to an unavoidable threat is _____ ,

the intense arousal of the fight-or-flight

response can also become _____

and can prove harmful to physical health.

3. (a) Hans Selye was the Canadian endocrinolo-

gist whose pioneering scientific investiga-

tions confirmed Cannon's suggestion that

_____ stress can be physically

harmful.

(b) Regardless of the condition that Selye used

to produce prolonged stress, he found the

same pattern of physical changes in experi-

mental rats; first, the _____

glands became enlarged; second,

_____ ulcers and loss of weight

occurred; and third, there was shrinkage of

the _____ gland and

_____ glands, two key compo-

nents of the immune system.

(c) Selye believed that these distinct

_____ changes represented the

essential effects of stress—the body's

response to any demands placed on it. If

stress continues, the effects became evident

in three progressive stages, which Selye

called the _____ syndrome.

4. (a) During the initial stage, intense arousal

occurs as the body mobilizes internal physical resources to meet the demands of the stress-producing event; Selye called this the _____ stage and found that the rapidly occurring changes are the result of the release of catecholamines by the _____ .

(b) In the second stage, the body actively tries to resist or adjust to the continuing stressful situation; this is called the _____ stage, and while the intense arousal of the _____ stage diminishes, physiological arousal remains above normal and _____ to new stressors is impaired.

(c) If the stress-producing event persists, the _____ stage may occur; the symptoms of the _____ stage reappear, only this time irreversibly. As the body's energy reserves become depleted, adaptation begins to break down, leading to _____ , physical disorders, and, potentially, death.

5. (a) Selye found that prolonged stress activates a second _____ pathway that involves the _____ , the _____ gland, and the _____ cortex, which is the outer portion of the adrenal gland.

(b) In response to a stressor, the _____ signals the _____ gland to secrete a hormone called adrenocorticotropic hormone (ACTH), which in turn stimulates the _____ cortex to release stress-related hormones called corticosteroids, the most important being cortisol.

(c) In the short run, the corticosteroids provide several benefits, helping to protect the body against the harm caused by stressors; they _____ (increase/reduce) inflammation of body tissues and _____ (lessen/enhance) muscle tone in the heart and blood vessels. However, continued high levels of corticosteroids can weaken important body systems, lowering immunity and increasing susceptibility to physical symptoms and illness.

Physical Effects of Stress: Stress and the Immune System

Preview Questions

Consider the following questions as you study this section of the chapter.

- How can stress undermine health and impair the immune system?
- How did the work of Ader and Cohen challenge the existing view of the immune system?
- What is psychoneuroimmunology, and how does the immune system interact with the nervous system?
- What kinds of stressors affect immune system functioning?

*Read the section "Physical Effects of Stress: Stress and the Immune System" and **write** your answers to the following:*

1. (a) The immune system is your body's _____ system; it detects and battles foreign invaders, such as bacteria, viruses, and tumor cells, and its effectiveness can be diminished by stress.

(b) The most important elements of the immune system are the specialized white blood cells that fight bacteria, viruses, and other foreign invaders, called _____ ; these cells are initially manufactured in the _____ and then migrate to other immune system organs, such as the thymus and spleen, where they develop more fully and are stored until needed.

2. (a) In the mid-1970s, psychologist Robert Ader teamed up with immunologist Nicholas

Cohen and demonstrated that the immune system response in rats could be _____ conditioned.

(b) Ader and Cohen's landmark study challenged the prevailing scientific view that the immune system operates _____ of the brain and psychological processes. It also triggered interest in other possible influences on the immune system, including the effects of _____ and _____ states.

(c) Ader and Cohen's study helped establish a new interdisciplinary field called

_____ , which is the scientific study of the interconnections among psychological processes (_____), the nervous system (_____) and the endocrine system (_____), and the immune system (_____).

(d) Psychoneuroimmunology researchers discovered that (1) the central nervous system and the immune system are directly linked; _____ nervous system fibers go into virtually every organ of the immune system, directly influencing the production and functioning of lymphocytes; (2) the surfaces of lymphocytes contain receptor sites for _____ and _____ , including catecholamines and cortisol; and (3) lymphocytes themselves produce _____ and _____ , which in turn influence the nervous and endocrine systems.

(e) Thus, there is ongoing interaction and communication among the _____ system, the _____ system, and the _____ system; each system influences and is influenced by the other systems.

3. (a) Extremely stressful events _____ (enhance/reduce) immune system functioning. Furthermore, more common negative life events, such as the end or disruption of important interpersonal relationships and chronic stressors that continue for years, can _____ (enhance/diminish) immune system functioning.

(b) Psychologist Janice Kiecolt-Glaser and her husband, immunologist Ronald Glaser, found that even the rather commonplace stress of exams _____ affects the immune system. Brief exposure to a psychological stressor, such as performing a frustrating task for 30 minutes or less, _____ (can/cannot) temporarily alter immune system responses.

(c) While stress-related immune system decreases may _____ (lower/heighten) our susceptibility to health problems, exposure to stressors _____ (does not translate/translates) automatically into poorer health.

(d) Your physical health is affected by the interaction of many factors, such as your unique _____ makeup, _____ , _____ , personal habits, and access to medical care. Also required, of course, is exposure to _____ , _____ , and other disease-causing agents.

(e) It's important to keep in mind that the stress-induced decreases in immune functioning that have been demonstrated experimentally are often _____ (large/ small); as psychoneuroimmunology researchers are careful to point out, these decreases in immune function _____ (may/may not) translate into an added health risk for most people.

4. Read the following and write the correct term in the space provided.

(a) When Hans was hiking on a trail in the wilderness, he unexpectedly encountered a large brown bear and her two cubs. Hans froze in his tracks, and his heartbeat, blood pressure, and pulse increased dramatically. Fortunately, the bear and the cubs took off into the bush. The rapidly occurring chain of internal physical reactions that Hans experienced was described by Walter Cannon as the _____ response.

(b) The physiological changes that Hans experienced when he was startled resulted from his sympathetic nervous system stimulating the adrenal medulla to secrete hormones called _____ .

(c) After overcoming the initial shock of finding her new car badly damaged by a hit-and-run driver, Wilma phones the police and becomes actively involved in seeking witnesses to the incident. At this point it is most likely that Wilma is in the _____ stage of the general adaptation syndrome.

(d) Dr. Laslo believes that there is an interaction among psychological processes, the nervous and endocrine systems, and the immune system and that each system influences and is influenced by the other systems. It is very likely that Dr. Laslo works in the new interdisciplinary field called

_____ .

(e) When Georgia was under a lot of stress, she became ill due to a viral infection. In response to this infection, the most important elements in her immune system, called _____ , will try to defend against the foreign invader.

Review of Terms, Concepts, and Names 2

Use the terms in this list to complete the Matching Test, then to help you answer the True/False items correctly.

fight-or-flight response
Walter Cannon
catecholamines
Hans Selye
general adaptation
  syndrome
alarm stage
resistance stage

exhaustion stage
corticosteroids
immune system
lymphocytes
Robert Ader
psychoneuroimmunology
Janice Kiecolt-Glaser

Matching Exercise

Match the appropriate term/name with its definition or description.

1. _____ American psychologist who made several important contributions to psychology, especially in the study of emotions; he described the fight-or-flight response, which involves the sympathetic nervous system and the endocrine system.

2. _____ Specialized white blood cells that are responsible for immune defenses.

3. _____ Hormones, including adrenaline and noradrenaline, secreted by the adrenal medulla that cause rapid physiological arousal.

4. _____ Canadian endocrinologist who was a pioneer in stress research; defined stress as "the nonspecific response of the body to any demand placed on it" and described a three-stage response to prolonged stress that he called the general adaptation syndrome.

5. _____ Hormones released by the adrenal cortex that play a key role in the body's response to long-term stressors.

6. _____ The first stage of the general adaptation syndrome, during which intense arousal occurs as the body mobilizes internal physical resources to meet the demands of the stress-producing event.

7. _____ Body system that produces specialized white blood cells that protect the body from viruses, bacteria, and tumor cells.

True/False Test

Indicate whether each statement is true or false by placing T or F in the blank space next to each item.

1. ____ Robert Ader is the American psychologist who, with immunologist Nicholas Cohen, first demonstrated that immune system responses could be classically conditioned; helped establish the new interdisciplinary field of psychoneuroimmunology.

2. ____ The rapidly occurring chain of internal physical reactions that prepare people to either fight or take flight from an immediate threat is called the general adaptation syndrome.

3. ____ In the resistance stage of the general adaptation syndrome, the body actively tries to resist or adjust to the continuing stressful situation.

4. ____ Janice Kiecolt-Glaser is the American psychologist who, with immunologist Ronald Glaser, conducted extensive research on the effect of stress on the immune system.

5. ____ The fight-or-flight response is Hans Selye's term for the three-stage progression of physical changes that occur when an organism is exposed to intense and prolonged stress.

6. ____ Psychoneuroimmunology is an interdisciplinary field that studies the interconnections among psychological processes, nervous and endocrine system functions, and the immune system.

7. ____ In the exhaustion stage of the general adaptation syndrome, the symptoms of the alarm stage reappear, only this time irreversibly; as the body's energy reserves become depleted, adaptation begins to break down, leading to exhaustion, physical disorders, and, potentially, death.

> Check your answers and review any areas of weakness before going on to the next section.

Individual Factors That Influence the Response to Stress

Preview Questions

Consider the following questions as you study this section of the chapter.

- What are the psychological factors that can affect our response to stress?

- How do feelings of control, explanatory style, and negative emotions influence stress and health?

- What is Type A behavior, and what role does hostility play in its relationship to health?

Read the section "Individual Factors That Influence the Response to Stress" (up to "Social Factors") and ***write*** *your answers to the following:*

1. (a) Individual differences in reacting to stressors are due to how people _____ an event and their _____ for coping.

   (b) Psychological research has consistently shown that having a sense of _____ over a stressful situation _____ (increases/reduces) the impact of stressors and _____ (increases/decreases) feelings of anxiety and depression.

   (c) Those who can _____ a stress-producing situation often show _____ (no more/more) psychological distress or physical arousal than people not exposed to the stressor.

   (d) Researchers Rodin and Langer found that having _____ over even minor aspects of their environment had powerful effects on the health of nursing home residents.

2. (a) If you feel that you can control a stressor by taking steps to minimize or avoid it, you will experience _____ (more/less) stress, both subjectively and physiologically.

   (b) Having a sense of personal control also works by _____ (decreasing/enhancing) positive emotions, such as feelings of self-confidence, self-efficacy, autonomy, and self-reliance.

   (c) In contrast, feeling a lack of control over events produces all the landmarks of the stress response: levels of catecholamines and corticosteroids _____ (increase/decrease) and the effectiveness of immune

system functioning _____
(increases/decreases).

(d) It is important to note that the perceptions
of personal control in a stressful situation
must be _____ to be adaptive;
_____ perceptions of personal
control contribute to stress and poor adjust-
ment.

3. (a) According to psychologist Martin Seligman,
how people characteristically explain their
failures and defeats makes the difference;
people who have an optimistic explanatory
style tend to use _____ ,
_____ , and _____
explanations for negative events; people who
have a pessimistic explanatory style use
_____ , _____ , and
_____ explanations for negative
events.

(b) Pessimists are also inclined to believe that
_____ (a large amount/no
amount) of personal effort will improve their
situation; pessimists tend to experience
_____ (more/less) stress than
optimists.

(c) Most people fall _____
(at one extreme/somewhere along) the opti-
mism-pessimism spectrum. Although a person's characteristic explanatory style, particularly for negative events, is relatively
_____ across the lifespan, it
may vary somewhat in different situations.

(d) Like personal control, explanatory style is
related to health consequences; explanatory
style in early adulthood _____
physical health status decades later; those
with _____ explanatory styles
had significantly better health than those
with _____ explanatory styles.

4. (a) Research has shown that people who are
habitually _____ ,

_____ , _____ , and
hostile are more likely to develop a chronic
disease such as arthritis or heart disease.

(b) People who are tense, angry, and unhappy
experience _____ (less/more)
stress than happier people; they also report
_____ (less/more) frequent and
intense daily hassles and react much
_____ (less/more) intensely to
the stressful events they encounter.

(c) Transient negative moods may also be associated with health risks; a series of studies
showed that immune system functioning
_____ (increased/decreased) on
days when participants experienced negative events and bad moods and _____
(got worse/improved) on days when they
experienced positive events and good moods.

5. (a) The original formulation of the Type A
behavior pattern included a cluster of three
characteristics: (1) an exaggerated sense of
_____ urgency, with the person
often trying to do more and more in less and
less time; (2) a general sense of
_____ , with the person fre-
quently displaying anger and irritation; and
(3) intense _____ and
_____ . In contrast, people who
were classified as displaying the Type B
behavior pattern were more
_____ and _____ .

(b) Initial research showed that Type A men
were _____ (half/twice) as likely
to develop heart disease as Type B men.
Later research suggested that some components of the Type A behavior pattern, time
urgency and achievement striving,
_____ (were/were not) associat-
ed with the development of heart disease.

(c) The critical component that emerged as the
strongest predictor of cardiac disease was

_____ , which refers to the tendency to feel anger, annoyance, and contempt and to hold negative beliefs about human nature in general.

(d) Hostile men and women are also prone to believing that the disagreeable behavior of others is _____ directed against them; thus, they tend to be suspicious, mistrustful, cynical, and pessimistic. They are much _____ (less/more) likely than other people to develop heart disease.

(e) High levels of hostility _____ (decreases/increases) the likelihood of dying from all natural causes, including cancer.

(f) Hostile Type A people experience _____ (smaller/larger) increases in blood pressure, heart rate, and the production of stress-related hormones, experience stress _____ (more/ less) frequently, and have _____ (fewer/more) severe negative life events and daily hassles than other people do.

Individual Factors That Influence the Response to Stress: Social Factors

Preview Questions

Consider the following questions as you study this section of the chapter.

- What is meant by social support, and how does it benefit health?
- How can social supports sometimes increase stress?
- What gender differences have been found in social support?

*Read the section "Individual Factors That Influence the Reaction to Stress: Social Factors" and **write** your answers to the following:*

1. (a) Psychologists have become increasingly aware of the importance that close relationships play in our ability to deal with stressors and, ultimately, in our physical health.

Research has shown that socially isolated people have _____ (better/poorer) health and _____ (higher/lower) death rates than people who have many social contacts or relationships.

(b) To investigate the role played by personal relationships in stress and health, psychologists measure the level of _____ support, which refers to the resources provided by other people in times of need.

2. (a) Social support of friends and relatives can modify our _____ of a stressor's significance, including the degree to which we perceive it as threatening or harmful. Simply knowing that support and assistance are readily available may make the situation seem _____ (less/more) threatening.

(b) The presence of supportive others seems to _____ (increase/decrease) the intensity of physical reactions to a stressor.

(c) Social support can influence our health by making us _____ (more/less) likely to experience negative emotions. In contrast, loneliness and depression are unpleasant emotional states that _____ levels of stress hormones and _____ affect immune system functioning.

3. (a) Conversely, relationships with others can also be a significant _____ of stress; negative interactions with other people are _____ (less/more) effective in creating psychological distress than positive interactions are in improving well-being.

(b) When people are perceived as being judgmental, their presence may _____ (decrease/increase) the individual's physical reaction to a stressor. In one study, the presence of a favorite dog was more effective than the presence of a friend in _____ (increasing/lowering) reactivity to a stressor.

4. (a) Women are _____ (less/more) likely than men to serve as providers of support, which can be a very stressful role. Women may be more likely to suffer from the _____ effect, becoming upset about negative life events that happen to other people whom they care about.

(b) In contrast, men are _____ (less/more) likely to be distressed only by negative events that happen to their immediate family—their wives and children.

(c) In general, men tend to rely heavily on a close relationship with their spouse, placing _____ (more/less) importance on relationships with other people; women, in contrast, are _____ (more/less) likely to list close friends along with their spouse as confidants.

(d) Having a strong network of social support _____ (is/is not) generally advantageous in your ability to cope with stressors and maintain health.

Coping: How People Deal with Stress

Preview Questions

Consider the following questions as you study this section of the chapter.

- How is *coping* defined?
- What are the two basic forms of coping, and when is each typically used?
- What are some of the most common coping strategies, and how does culture affect coping style?

Read the section "Coping: How People Deal with Stress" and **write** *your answers to the following:*

1. (a) The strategies that you use to deal with distressing events are examples of

_____ , which refers to the ways in which we try to change circumstances, or our interpretations of circumstances, to make them more favorable and less threatening.

(b) Coping tends to be a(n) _____ , ongoing process.

(c) When coping is effective, we _____ to the situation, and stress is reduced. When it is not—when it is _____ —coping can involve thoughts and behaviors that intensify or prolong distress or that produce self-defeating outcomes.

(d) Adaptive coping serves many functions: (1) it involves realistically _____ the situation and determining what can be done to minimize the impact of the stressor; (2) it often includes developing _____ tolerance for negative life events, maintaining self-esteem, and keeping emotions in balance; and (3) it is directed toward _____ important relationships during stressful experiences.

2. (a) Coping aimed at managing or changing a threatening or harmful stressor is called _____ coping.

(b) If we think nothing can be done to change the situation, we direct our efforts toward relieving or regulating the emotional impact of a stressful situation by using _____ coping. Although this strategy doesn't change the problem, it can help you feel better about the situation.

3. (a) When people rely on aggressive or risky efforts to change the situation, they are engaging in _____ coping. Ideally, this type of coping is direct and assertive; when this coping style is _____ or _____ , it

may generate negative emotions in the people being confronted, damaging future relations with them.

(b) In contrast, efforts to rationally analyze the situation, identify potential solutions, and then implement them is referred to as
_____ .

(c) When you shift your attention away from the stressor and toward other activities, you're engaging in the _____-focused coping strategy called
_____ . The basic goal is to escape or avoid the stressor and neutralize distressing emotions.

(d) Examples of this strategy might include escaping into _____ (also called wishful thinking), _____ , or immersing yourself in work, studies, or hobbies; maladaptive forms include drug use or excessive sleeping.

(e) When the stressor is severe or long lasting, strategies such as wishful thinking may be
_____ .

4. (a) Seeking social support is the coping strategy that involves turning to friends, relatives, or other people for _____ ,
_____ , or _____ support.

(b) When you acknowledge the stressor but attempt to minimize or eliminate its emotional impact, you're engaging in the coping strategy called _____ ; in certain high-stress occupations, this strategy can help people cope with painful human problems.

(c) The refusal to acknowledge that the problem even exists is called _____ ; this strategy can compound problems in situations that require immediate attention.

(d) Perhaps the most constructive emotion-focused coping strategy is the one in which

the person not only tries to minimize the _____ emotional aspects of the situation but also tries to create positive meaning by focusing on
_____ ; this is called _____ .

(e) Most people use multiple coping strategies in stressful situations, often combining _____ and _____ forms of coping; different coping strategies may be used at different stages of dealing with a stressful encounter.

5. (a) Culture _____ (does/ does not) seem to play a role in our choice of coping strategy.

(b) Members of individualistic cultures tend to emphasize personal _____ and personal _____ in dealing with problems; thus they are _____ (more/less) likely to seek social support in stressful situations than are members of collectivistic cultures. Members of collectivistic cultures tend to be _____ (more/less) oriented toward their social group, family, or community and to seek help with their problems.

(c) Individualists tend to favor problem-focused strategies, such as _____ coping and _____ , which involve directly changing the situation to achieve a better fit with their wishes or goals.

(d) In collectivistic cultures, a _____ (lesser/greater) emphasis is placed on controlling your personal reactions to a stressful situation rather than trying to control the situation itself; this _____-focused coping style emphasizes gaining control over inner feelings by accepting and accommodating yourself to existing realities.

6. Read the following and write the correct term in the space provided:

(a) When Marie turned down Massimo's offer to go out for dinner on Friday night, he was very disappointed. Upon reflection, however, he decided that Marie was really not his type anyway, and he'd be better off going out with someone else. Massimo's rationalization of the situation reflects a(n) _____ explanatory style.

(b) When asked by her therapist to describe her husband, Cheryl said that he was very competitive and ambitious, he was always very busy, and any demands made on his time angered and irritated him. Cheryl's description suggests that her husband may have a(n) _____ behavior pattern.

(c) Irene constantly complains about her health, her job, and in general everything about her life. She tends to dislike most of the people she meets and always seems to be in a grouchy mood. It appears that Irene suffers from _____ emotions.

(d) Masayuki is a member of a group of engineers in a large industrial plant in Tokyo. When things get stressful, Masayuki tries to control the outward expression of his emotions and endeavors to accept the situation with maturity, serenity, and flexibility. Masayuki is using a _____ coping strategy, which is more characteristic of collectivistic cultures than of individualistic cultures.

(e) Shortly after he lost his job and his relationship with his girlfriend ended, Jim went to visit his family. Unfortunately, being with his family made him feel worse. The only time he felt better was when he was with the family dog. It is possible that Jim perceived his family as being _____ and the dog as being _____ and unconditionally supportive.

(f) Although Lambert was very disappointed when he didn't even come close to winning his first mountain bike race, he concluded that all his training and the knowledge he gained from the experience were beneficial. Lambert is using a very constructive emotion-focused strategy called _____ .

Graphic Organizer 2

*Read the following statements and decide which researcher(s)
is (are) most likely to have expressed these views:*

Statement	Researcher(s)
1. I believe that when we are faced with danger or any threatening or stress-producing situation we have an immediate physical reaction that involves the sympathetic nervous system and the endocrine system and the release of catecholamines. I call these internal physical changes the fight-or-flight response.	
2. When we published the results of our research, we realized that we were challenging the prevailing scientific view that the immune system operates independently of the brain and psychological processes. However, our results, which demonstrated that the immune response in rats could be classically conditioned, have been replicated by many other researchers.	
3. We were two of the earliest researchers to study stress. In an attempt to measure the amount of stress people experienced, we developed the Social Readjustment Rating Scale. Our view at the time was that any changes, either positive or negative, would cause stress and that high levels of stress, as measured by life change units, would lead to the development of serious physical and psychological problems.	
4. My research on stress, which I define as the nonspecific response of the body to any demand, led me to postulate a three-stage model to prolonged stress, called the general adaptation syndrome. I believe that the stress response involves the hypothalamus, pituitary gland, adrenal cortex, and release of hormones such as ACTH and corticosteroids.	
5. My view is that what causes us problems in the long run is not so much the major life events, which do cause stress, but the cumulative effect of daily hassles that annoy, irritate, and upset people. I have developed a scale to measure these hassles. The number of daily hassles is a better predictor of physical illness and symptoms than the number of major life events experienced.	
6. In my view, it is the way people characteristically explain their failures and defeats that determines who will persist and who will not. I think there are two basic types of explanatory style, an optimistic explanatory style and a pessimistic explanatory style. Those who use a pessimistic explanatory style experience more stress than those who use an optimistic explanatory style.	
7. We are a husband-and-wife team who collected immunological and psychological data from medical students, who face three-day exam periods several times each academic year. We have consistently found that even the rather commonplace stress of exams adversely affects the immune system.	

Review of Terms, Concepts, and Names 3

Use the terms in this list to complete the Matching Test, then to help you answer the True/False items correctly.

Martin Seligman
optimistic explanatory style
pessimistic explanatory style
Type A behavior pattern
Type B behavior pattern
social support
stress contagion effect
coping
problem-focused coping

emotion-focused coping
confrontive coping
planful problem solving
escape-avoidance
seeking social support
distancing
denial
positive reappraisal
emotional support
tangible support
informational support

Matching Exercise

Match the appropriate term/name with its definition or description.

1. _____ Behavioral and cognitive responses used to contend with stressors; involves efforts to change circumstances, or one's interpretations of circumstances, to make them more favorable and less threatening.

2. _____ Problem-focused coping strategy in which the person relies on aggressive or risky efforts to change the situation.

3. _____ American psychologist who conducted research on explanatory style and the role it plays in stress, health, and illness; also developed the learned helplessness model.

4. _____ Emotion-focused coping strategy in which the person shifts his or her attention away from the stressor and toward other activities.

5. _____ Behavioral and emotional style characterized by a sense of time urgency, hostility, and competitiveness.

6. _____ Category of social support that includes the expression of concern, empathy, and positive regard.

7. _____ Gender difference in the effects of social support that results from women becoming upset about negative life events that happen to other people.

8. _____ Resources provided by other people in times of need, including emotional support, tangible support, and informational support.

9. _____ Emotion-focused coping strategy that involves turning to friends, relatives, or other people for emotional, tangible, or informational support.

10. _____ Emotion-focused coping strategy that involves the refusal to acknowledge that the problem exists.

True/False Test

Indicate whether each item is true or false by placing T or F in the space next to each item.

1. ___ An optimistic explanatory style involves accounting for negative events or situations with internal, stable, and global explanations.

2. ___ The Type B behavior pattern is a behavioral and emotional style characterized by a relatively relaxed and laid-back approach to situations and problems.

3. ___ Informational social support involves direct assistance, such as providing transportation, lending money, or helping with meals, child care, or household tasks.

4. ___ Emotion-focused coping efforts are aimed primarily at relieving or regulating the emotional impact of a stressful situation.

5. ___ The most constructive emotion-focused coping strategy is positive reappraisal, which involves not only minimizing the negative emotional aspects of the situation but also trying to create positive meaning by focusing on personal growth.

6. ___ A pessimistic explanatory style involves accounting for negative events or situations with external, unstable, and specific explanations.

7. ___ An emotion-focused coping strategy in which the individual acknowledges the stressor but attempts to minimize or eliminate its emotional impact is called distancing.

8. ___ Problem-focused coping efforts are aimed primarily at directly changing or managing a threatening or harmful stressor.

9. ___ A problem-focused coping strategy that involves efforts to rationally analyze the situation, identify potential solutions, and then implement them is called planful problem solving.

10. ___ Tangible social support involves offering helpful suggestions and advice to a person in distress.

> Check your answers and review any areas of weakness before going on to the next section.

Something to Think About

It sometimes seems that everyone you meet is stressed out. There are things to be done, deadlines to be met, social and family obligations, financial pressures, work-related problems, and so on. How can people cope with all this stress? Is there anything that can be done? Fortunately, there are several strategies for coping with stress. What advice would you give someone who is experiencing stress?

> Check your answers and review any areas of weakness before doing the progress tests.

Progress Test 1

Review the complete chapter (including Concept Reviews and the boxed inserts), review all your study notes, and then test yourself on the following progress test. Check your answers. If you make a mistake, review your notes, review the relevant section of the study guide, and, if necessary, go back and read the appropriate part of your textbook.

1. Natasha experienced a great deal of anxiety when she had three exams on the same day. In this situation the exams are _____ and her response is called _____ .
   (a) stress; stressor
   (b) the biological component; the cognitive component
   (c) stressors; stress
   (d) the social component; the biological component

2. Dr. Turnbull uses the biopsychosocial model to guide his research into how psychological factors influence health, illness, and treatment. Dr. Turnbull is most likely a
   (a) developmental psychologist.
   (b) health psychologist.
   (c) psychoneuroimmunologist.
   (d) psychiatrist.

3. Donald scored 300 points on the Social Readjustment Rating Scale. What does that mean?
   (a) It is absolutely certain that Donald will develop physical and psychological problems.
   (b) It is impossible to accurately predict whether Donald will develop physical and psychological problems.
   (c) Donald has probably experienced very few daily hassles during the past year.
   (d) Donald's subjective appraisal of the events in his life during the previous year will have no bearing on his health and well-being.

4. Del got up late and nicked himself three times while shaving. When he poured his coffee, he found that there was no cream in the fridge; then, as he was tying his shoe laces, one of them broke. Richard Lazarus would call these incidents
   (a) major life events.   (c) minor life events.
   (b) daily hassles.   (d) life change units.

5. To earn money so that he can buy a ticket to a rock concert, Ken has to either wash and wax the two family cars or wash and wax the kitchen and bathroom floors. In trying to decide between these two equally unappealing choices, Ken is likely to experience an _____ conflict.
   (a) approach-avoidance
   (b) approach-approach
   (c) avoidance-avoidance
   (d) escape-avoidance

6. Yui is leaving Japan to work and live in the United States and is very excited about the move. When Yui arrives and starts work in the United States, she is likely to
   (a) be much more relaxed and laid back than she was in Japan.
   (b) experience increased levels of stress due to the acculturation process.
   (c) become physically and psychologically ill within weeks.
   (d) adapt to the new environment without experiencing any stress whatsoever.

7. When Nibras was chased and attacked by a dog during his regular morning run, he experienced the classic symptoms of the fight-or-flight response. According to Walter Cannon, it is likely that his sympathetic nervous system stimulated his adrenal medulla to secrete hormones called

    (a) catecholamines.   (c) corticosteroids.
    (b) ACTH.   (d) lymphocytes.

8. After overcoming the initial shock of having his house broken into and many of his personal possessions stolen, Vincent calls the police for help and starts thinking of ways to help catch the burglar and retrieve his belongings. At this point, Vincent is most likely in the _____ stage of the general adaptation syndrome.

    (a) alarm   (c) exhaustion
    (b) resistance   (d) denial

9. When Claudia became ill because of a viral infection, her immune system kicked into high gear to defend her by producing

    (a) lymphocytes.   (c) catecholamines.
    (b) corticosteroids.   (d) noradrenaline.

10. Dr. Blackman studies the interconnections among psychological processes, the nervous and endocrine systems, and the immune system. Like other specialists in the field of psychoneuroimmunology, Dr. Blackman is aware that researchers have discovered that

    (a) the central nervous system and the immune system are directly linked.
    (b) the surfaces of lymphocytes contain receptor sites for neurotransmitters and hormones, including catecholamines and cortisol.
    (c) lymphocytes themselves produce neurotransmitters and hormones.
    (d) all of the above are true.

11. When Darcy was taking his statistics exam, he was very anxious and nervous. According to researchers such as Janice Kiecolt-Glaser, the stress of exams

    (a) adversely affects the immune system.
    (b) has no effect on the immune system.
    (c) has a beneficial effect on the immune system.
    (d) does none of the above

12. Whenever anything goes wrong in his life, Dean typically feels that it must be something about him that causes the problem; he also believes that no amount of personal effort will improve his situation. Martin Seligman would say that Dean has

    (a) a Type A behavior pattern.
    (b) an optimistic explanatory style.
    (c) a Type B behavior pattern.
    (d) a pessimistic explanatory style.

13. After his third month of low sales, Allen is called into the sales manager's office and told that he had better start meeting his quota or he will be laid off. The manager appears to be coping with the problem of low sales by using a(n) _____ strategy called _____ .

    (a) problem-focused; confrontive coping
    (b) emotion-focused; escape-avoidance
    (c) problem-focused; planful problem solving
    (d) emotion-focused; distancing

14. According to Culture and Human Behavior 13.1, which of the following is not a pattern of acculturation?

    (a) integration   (d) marginalization
    (b) assimilation   (e) disembarkation
    (c) separation

15. Critical Thinking 13.3, which discusses personality and disease, points out that psychologists and other scientists are cautious in reaching conclusions about the connection between personality and health for which of the following reasons?

    (a) Many studies investigating the role of psychological factors in disease are correlational.
    (b) Personality factors might indirectly lead to disease via poor health habits.
    (c) It may be that the disease influences a person's emotions, rather than the other way around.
    (d) All of the above factors are true.

Progress Test 2

After you have checked your understanding of the material in Progress Test 1 and have done a complete chapter review with special focus on any areas of weakness, you are ready to assess your knowledge of Progress Test 2. Check your answers. If you make a mistake, review your notes, the relevant section of the study guide, and, if necessary, the appropriate part of your textbook.

1. When Janeen was caught in a large traffic jam, she experienced a severe headache. In this case, the traffic jam is to _____ as her headache is to _____ .
   (a) fight; flight
   (b) stressor; stress
   (c) flight; fight
   (d) stress; stressor

2. For his birthday Liam has to decide between a pair of skis and a mountain bike. In trying to decide between these two equally attractive alternatives, Liam is likely to experience an _____ conflict.
   (a) approach-avoidance
   (b) approach-approach
   (c) avoidance-avoidance
   (d) escape-avoidance

3. Fifty-five-year-old Maxwell is a very impatient and competitive defense lawyer who feels that he must be the best in his field. In addition, he has a reputation for being hostile toward judges and prosecuting attorneys. Maxwell is likely to be classified as having a(n)
   (a) Type A behavior pattern.
   (b) pessimistic explanatory style.
   (c) Type B behavior pattern.
   (d) optimistic explanatory style.

4. In the above example it is very likely that Maxwell is at high risk for developing heart disease. The component of his behavior that is most likely to contribute to health problems is his
   (a) impatience.
   (b) competitiveness
   (c) achievement orientation.
   (d) hostility.

5. Heloise is an emergency room nurse. Whenever she has a particularly hectic and stressful shift, she and some of the other nurses find themselves making fun of the patients and the doctors. Heloise is using an emotion-focused coping strategy called
   (a) confrontive coping.
   (b) denial.
   (c) distancing.
   (d) positive reappraisal.

6. Madge wants advice on how to cope with the stress of returning to college after being out of school for a number of years. She would be best advised to approach her classes
   (a) with a sense of personal control and optimism.
   (b) with a realistic but pessimistic attitude.
   (c) using an emotion-focused coping strategy called distancing.
   (d) using an emotion-focused coping strategy called denial.

7. Whenever Beth experiences problems in her relationship with her fiancee, she typically talks to her family about her troubles. Beth is using a(n) _____ strategy called _____ .
   (a) problem-focused; confrontive coping
   (b) emotion-focused; distancing
   (c) problem-focused; planful problem solving
   (d) emotion-focused; seeking social support

8. While researching a paper for her psychology class, Joyce came across the research of Ader and Cohen on conditioning and immune system functioning. She is likely to conclude that their work was important for which of the following reasons?
   (a) It challenged the prevailing scientific view that the immune system operates independently of the brain and psychological processes.
   (b) It demonstrated that humans could be conditioned to salivate just like Pavlov's dogs.
   (c) Before their research was published, everyone believed that there was a strong interconnectedness among psychological processes, nervous and endocrine system functions, and the immune system.
   (d) It proved conclusively that the immune system could not be classically conditioned.

9. After a bank was robbed, the bank tellers and the customers got up off the floor, where they had been held at gunpoint. Because it was such a frightening experience, they are likely to have experienced a rapidly occurring chain of internal physical reactions called
   (a) daily hassles.
   (b) the fight-or-flight response.
   (c) the general adaptation syndrome.
   (d) the stress contagion effect.

10. Following the bank robbery, the people who were very frightened probably experienced increased activation of the sympathetic nervous system, stimulation of the adrenal medulla, and release of hormones called
    (a) lymphocytes.   (c) testosterone.
    (b) catecholamines.   (d) estrogen.

11. During her final year of medical training, Lissette was under constant pressure; she never seemed to get enough sleep, was anxious and nervous most of the time, and experienced many physical symptoms and disorders. As a result of this prolonged stress, it is likely that her hypothalamus, pituitary gland, and adrenal cortex will work together to release stress-related hormones called
    (a) lymphocytes.   (c) corticosteroids.
    (b) catecholamines.   (d) acetylcholine.

12. Gregory was very disappointed when he wasn't accepted to the graduate program at State University. Upon reflection, however, he decided that the preparations he made in putting his application together and the knowledge he gained from the interview were very beneficial experiences. Gregory is using a(n) _____ strategy called _____ .
    (a) problem-focused; confrontive coping
    (b) emotion-focused; positive reappraisal
    (c) problem-focused; planful problem solving
    (d) emotion-focused; escape-avoidance

13. According to the Application, which of the following is *not* recommended for helping someone in distress?
    (a) Express affection for the person, whether by a warm hug or simply a pat on the arm.
    (b) Be a good listener and show concern and interest.
    (c) Ask questions that encourage the person under stress to express his or her feelings and emotions.
    (d) Give advice that the person has not asked for.
    (e) Be willing to invest time and attention in helping.

14. In Focus 13.2, which discusses the relationship between stress and the common cold, concludes that
    (a) stress reduces the effectiveness of the immune system and its ability to fight off viruses, bacteria, and other foreign invaders.
    (b) factors such as health-compromising behaviors provide the underlying stress-illness connection.
    (c) highly stressed people get sick more often because they interact with more people than do people with little stress.
    (d) all of the above are true.

15. According to Culture and Human Behavior 13.1, the term *acculturative stress* refers to the
    (a) coping strategies used by immigrants.
    (b) stress that results from the pressure of adapting to a new culture.
    (c) stress-producing events and situations that occur when people leave home and move to a different city.
    (d) final stage of the general adaptation syndrome.

Progress Test 3

After you have checked your understanding of the material in Progress Tests 1 and 2, and have done a complete chapter review with special focus on any areas of weakness, you are ready to further assess your knowledge on Progress Test 3. Check your answers. If you make a mistake, review your notes, the appropriate parts of the study guide, and if necessary, the relevant sections of your textbook.

1. Richard Lazarus is to _____ as Hans Selye is to _____ .
    (a) daily hassles; the general adaptation syndrome
    (b) the fight-or-flight response; the cognitive appraisal model
    (c) classically conditioning the immune system; the general adaptation syndrome
    (d) daily hassles; life event units

2. When Argento encountered a wild cougar on the hiking trail, he experienced acute stress. Which of the following would Walter Cannon consider the correct sequence involved in Argento's fight-or-flight response?
   (a) pituitary; hypothalamus; ACTH release, sympathetic nervous system.
   (b) secretion of corticosteroids, ACTH release, perspiration, cognitive appraisal.
   (c) hypothalamus, sympathetic nervous system, adrenal medulla, secretion of catecholamines
   (d) perspiration, ACTH release, respiration, parasympathetic nervous system, secretion of catecholamines

3. If Dr. Penman is like most researchers in the field of psychoneuroimmunology he is likely to hold the view that
   (a) it is impossible to classically condition the immune system.
   (b) the immune system works independently of other body systems.
   (c) there are interconnections between the endocrine system and the immune system functions, but psychological processes operate independently.
   (d) there are interconnections among psychological processes, nervous and endocrine system functions, and the immune system.

4. Rita and Richard both have a large network of social relationships, including close friends and family members. Compared with Richard, Rita may be potentially vulnerable to some of the problematic aspects of social support because
   (a) women are less likely that men to serve as providers of support.
   (b) women, in general, are more likely than men to suffer from the stress contagion effect.
   (c) women tend to rely on a close personal relationship with their spouse and place less importance on relationships with other people.
   (d) women are less likely than men to become upset about what happens to their friends and relatives.

5. Reena has a very successful accounting practice and frequently works sixty hours or more a week. She has to manage her time efficiently in order to keep up with the demands of her career and family life. Despite all the pressure, Reena loves her job, is always kind and considerate to her employees, and has a very cheerful personality. Which of the following is most likely to be true of Reena?
   (a) Because of her very stressful lifestyle, she is likely to have very high levels of corticosteroids.
   (b) She is at a very high risk for coronary disease and other health problems.
   (c) She is very likely to develop coronary disease because of her Type A behavior pattern.
   (d) Because she is low in hostility, her risk of developing coronary disease is no higher than that of anyone else.

6. Forty-year-old Lannie is a widow, lives alone, has very few friends, and rarely interacts with other people except at work. Research suggests that compared with people who have many social contacts and relationships, social isolation such as Lannie's is correlated with
   (a) higher-than-normal levels of catecholamines.
   (b) poor health and higher death rates.
   (c) lower-than-normal levels of corticosteroids.
   (d) good health and lower death rates.

7. In replicating Ader and Cohen's original research, Dr. Andrews and his colleagues also found that the suppression of the immune system was influenced by
   (a) Type A behavior.
   (b) the general adaptation syndrome.
   (c) classical conditioning.
   (d) aerobic exercise.

8. Kari is a very laid-back, easygoing mail carrier. She loves her job because it allows her to meet people and get daily exercise. Kari is likely to be classified as having a
   (a) Type A behavior pattern.
   (b) high risk of heart disease.
   (c) Type B behavior pattern.
   (d) stress contagion syndrome.

9. Jacob was one of the unsuccessful candidates for a job, and naturally he was disappointed. However, in his habitual manner, he thought that he would have better luck next time, especially if he took some additional training to make him more qualified for the position. Martin Seligman would say that Jacob has a(n)

   (a) Type A behavior pattern.
   (b) optimistic explanatory style.
   (c) problem-focused coping style.
   (d) pessimistic explanatory style.

10. Helga, a college student, was offered a new job. On the plus side the higher salary and increased benefits are appealing, but on the down side she will have to work longer hours, take on extra responsibilities, and have a longer commute to work. She needs the extra money but she also needs to keep her high GPA at college. Helga is likely experiencing a type of conflict called _____ conflict.

    (a) approach-approach
    (b) avoidance-avoidance
    (c) escape-avoidance
    (d) approach-avoidance

11. Anders, a fifty-two-year-old insurance salesman, is unexpectedly called into the sales manager's office and told that he is going to be laid off because the company is downsizing. Which stage of the general adaptation syndrome is Anders likely experiencing?

    (a) alarm stage   (c) exhaustion stage
    (b) resistance stage   (d) denial stage

12. Dr. Chambers has a very busy clinical practice. To clear his mind of all the problems he faces each day and to cope with the high level of stress, he goes to the gym for a workout four or five times a week. Dr. Chambers is using a(n) _____ coping strategy called _____ .

    (a) emotion-focused; escape-avoidance
    (b) problem-focused; denial
    (c) emotion-focused; wishful thinking
    (d) problem-focused; confrontive coping

13. When Lester was having personal and academic problems in college, he went to see one of the counselors, who provided some helpful suggestions to improve his study habits and advised him to enroll in a remedial course to improve his writing skills. According to the Application, the type of social support that Lester received is called _____ support.

    (a) emotional   (c) informational
    (b) tangible   (d) confrontive

14. According to In Focus 13.4, which of the following strategies is recommended for minimizing stress?

    (a) Exercise regularly.
    (b) Avoid or minimize stimulants.
    (c) Regularly practice a relaxation technique.
    (d) All of the above are recommended.

15. Having moved to the United States from China two years ago, Mi-Ling feels equally comfortable with her new American friends and with her Chinese relatives. According to Culture and Human Behavior 13.1, Mi-Ling has adopted the acculturation pattern of

    (a) assimilation.   (c) marginalization.
    (b) separation.   (d) integration.

Answers

Introduction: What Is Stress?

1. (a) emotional; exceeding
   (b) cognitive appraisal; resources

2. (a) stress; health, illness, treatment
   (b) biological, psychological; social

What Is Stress?: Sources of Stress

1. (a) events; situations
   (b) change; behavior; lifestyle
   (c) life change units
   (d) 150

2. (a) weak; don't
   (b) appraisal; the same
   (c) change; negative; positive or desirable
   (d) negative; change

3. (a) Richard Lazarus
   (b) is; better
   (c) cumulative
   (d) major life events; major life event

4. (a) conflict; approach; avoid
   (b) approach-approach
   (c) avoidance-avoidance
   (d) approach-avoidance

5. (a) social; chronic
   (b) lowest; poverty-stricken
   (c) cultures; culture

6. (a) health
   (b) biopsychosocial
   (c) high; increased
   (d) daily hassles
   (e) approach-approach

Graphic Organizer 1

1. approach-avoidance; high
2. approach-approach; low
3. approach-avoidance; high
4. avoidance-avoidance; medium
5. approach-approach; low
6. avoidance-avoidance; medium

Matching Exercise 1

1. Richard Lazarus
2. approach-approach conflict
3. conflict
4. daily hassles

5. health psychology
6. biopsychosocial mode

True/False Test 1

1. F   3. T   5. T
2. T   4. F   6. T

Physical Effects of Stress: The Mind–Body Connection

1. (a) prompting behavior
   (b) cognitive
   (c) body functions

2. (a) nervous; brain; endocrine; immune
   (b) fight; flight
   (c) Walter Cannon; sympathetic; endocrine
   (d) sympathetic nervous; adrenaline; noradrenaline
   (e) trigger; gradually subside; normal level
   (f) survival; prolonged; prolonged

3. (a) prolonged
   (b) adrenal; stomach; thymus; lymph
   (c) physical; general adaptation

4. (a) alarm; adrenal medulla
   (b) resistance; alarm; resistance
   (c) exhaustion; alarm; exhaustion

5. (a) endocrine; hypothalamus; pituitary; adrenal
   (b) hypothalamus; pituitary; adrenal
   (c) reduce; enhance

Physical Effects of Stress: Stress and the Immune System

1. (a) surveillance
   (b) lymphocytes; bone marrow

2. (a) classically
   (b) independently; stress; emotional
   (c) psychoneuroimmunology; psycho- ; -neuro- ; -immunology
   (d) sympathetic; neurotransmitters; hormones; neurotransmitters; hormones
   (e) nervous; endocrine; immune

3. (a) reduce; diminish
   (b) adversely; can
   (c) heighten; does not translate
   (d) genetic; nutrition, exercise; bacteria, viruses
   (e) small; may not

4. (a) fight-or-flight
   (b) catecholamines
   (c) resistance
   (d) psychoneuroimmunology
   (e) lymphocytes

Matching Exercise 2

1. Walter Cannon
2. lymphocytes
3. catecholamines
4. Hans Selye
5. corticosteroids
6. alarm stage
7. immune system

True/False Test 2

1. T   5. F
2. F   6. T
3. T   7. T
4. T

Individual Factors That Influence the Response to Stress

1. (a) appraise; resources
   (b) control; reduces; decreases
   (c) control; no more
   (d) control

2. (a) less
   (b) enhancing
   (c) increase; decreases
   (d) realistic; unrealistic

3. (a) external, unstable; specific; internal, stable; global
   (b) no amount; more
   (c) somewhere along; stable
   (d) predicts; optimistic; pessimistic

4. (a) anxious, depressed; angry
   (b) more; more; more
   (c) decreased; improved

5. (a) time; hostility; ambition; competitiveness; relaxed; laid back
   (b) twice; were not
   (c) hostility
   (d) intentionally; more
   (e) increases
   (f) larger; more; more

Individual Factors That Influence the Response to Stress: Social Factors

1. (a) poorer; higher
   (b) social

2. (a) appraisal; less
   (b) decrease
   (c) less; increase; adversely

3. (a) source; more
   (b) increase; lowering

4. (a) more; stress contagion
   (b) more
   (c) less; more
   (d) is

Coping: How People Deal with Stress

1. (a) coping
   (b) dynamic
   (c) adapt; maladaptive
   (d) evaluating; emotional; preserving

2. (a) problem-focused
   (b) emotion-focused

3. (a) confrontive; hostile; aggressive
   (b) planful problem solving
   (c) emotion; escape-avoidance
   (d) fantasy; exercising
   (e) counterproductive

4. (a) emotional, tangible; informational
   (b) distancing
   (c) denial
   (d) negative; personal growth; positive reappraisal
   (e) problem-focused; emotion-focused

5. (a) does
   (b) autonomy; responsibility; less; more
   (c) confrontive; planful problem solving
   (d) greater; emotion

6. (a) optimistic
   (b) Type A
   (c) chronic negative
   (d) emotion-focused
   (e) judgmental; nonjudgmental
   (f) positive reappraisal

Graphic Organizer 2

1. Walter Cannon
2. Robert Ader and Nicholas Cohen
3. Thomas Holmes and Richard Rahe
4. Hans Selye
5. Richard Lazarus
6. Martin Seligman
7. Janice Kiecolt-Glaser and Ronald Glaser

Matching Exercise 3

1. coping
2. confrontive coping

3. Martin Seligman

4. escape-avoidance

5. Type A behavior pattern

6. emotional support

7. stress contagion effect

8. social support

9. seeking social support

10. denial

True/False Test 3

1. F	5. T	9. T
2. T	6. F	10. F
3. F	7. T	
4. T	8. T	

Something to Think About

A good place to start in giving advice to someone is to explain what stressors are and what the stress reaction is. Identifying potential sources of stress, from major life events to daily hassles, is useful, and noting how our subjective cognitive appraisal of stressors influences our reactions is also important. It is also helpful to know about physical reactions and psychological and social factors that influence our response to stress.

People vary a great deal in the way they respond to distressing events. Psychologists have identified several different factors that influence an individual's response to stressful events. Having a sense of control reduces the impact of stressors and decreases feelings of anxiety and depression. The type of explanatory style we use—optimistic, pessimistic, or, as in most cases, somewhere in between—can also have an effect on our health. People with a pessimistic explanatory style tend to have poorer physical health, whereas people with an optimistic, confident, and generally positive outlook have better immune system responses and better physical health. Furthermore, chronically grouchy people experience more stress, have more frequent and intense daily hassles, and generally react with far greater distress to stressful events.

Many different strategies can be used to deal with stress, some of which are more adaptive than others. Having good social support is beneficial, but so too are the types of strategies that we adopt to cope with distressing events. Problem-focused and emotion-focused coping strategies are two that the text discusses in detail. In addition, we can minimize the impact of stressors by exercising regularly, avoiding or minimizing stimulants such as coffee, tea, or cigarettes, and by regularly practicing a relaxation technique such as meditation or progressive muscle relaxation. Stress is an unavoidable part of life and can influence both our physical and psychological well-being. How we choose to cope with stress can reduce and minimize its destructive effects.

Progress Test 1

1. c	6. b	11. a
2. b	7. a	12. d
3. b	8. b	13. a
4. b	9. a	14. e
5. c	10. d	15. d

Progress Test 2

1. b	6. a	11. c
2. b	7. d	12. b
3. a	8. a	13. d
4. d	9. b	14. a
5. c	10. b	15. b

Progress Test 3

1. a	6. b	11. a
2. c	7. c	12. a
3. d	8. c	13. c
4. b	9. b	14. d
5. d	10. d	15. d

CHAPTER 14

Psychological Disorders

PREVIEW

Reading the section below first will give you a general sense of the chapter's contents and an initial introduction to some of the major concepts and terms. This will prime you for what you are about to read and help you to develop a "cognitive map" that will guide your study of the material in this chapter. Likewise, reading the **preview questions** at the beginning of each major section will improve your ability to understand, learn, and retain the information.

CHAPTER 14 . . . AT A GLANCE

Chapter 14 begins by addressing the distinction between normal and abnormal behavior and the criteria for diagnosing psychological disorders, according to DSM-IV.

Anxiety is a common experience for all people, but only when it becomes maladaptive is it considered a disorder. The prevalence, course, and possible causes of anxiety disorders, including generalized anxiety disorder, panic disorder, phobias, posttraumatic stress disorder, and obsessive-compulsive disorder, are discussed.

Mood disorders involve serious, persistent disturbances in emotions that cause psychological discomfort and/or impair the ability to function. The symptoms of major depression and bipolar disorder are identified, and the course and potential causes of these mood disorders are discussed.

Personality disorders are characterized by inflexibility and maladaptive personality traits. Paranoid personality disorder, along with antisocial personality disorder, and borderline personality disorder are discussed in terms of symptoms, causation, and treatment.

Dissociative experiences involve a disruption in awareness, memory, and personal identity. The symptoms and possible causes of dissociative amnesia, dissociative fugue, and dissociative identity disorder (DID) are examined.

The main symptoms of schizophrenia are identified. Positive symptoms represent excesses in normal functioning, and negative symptoms reflect deficits or decreases in normal functioning. Three subtypes of schizophrenia are discussed, and the course and prevalence of the disorder are presented. Various theories of the causes of schizophrenia are explored, and the conclusion is reached that no single factor has emerged as causing this psychological disorder.

Introduction: Understanding Psychological Disorders

Preview Questions

Consider the following questions as you study this section of the chapter.

- What is psychopathology, and what characterizes abnormal behavior?
- What is DSM-IV, and how was it developed?
- How prevalent are psychological disorders?

Read the section "Introduction: Understanding Psychological Disorders" and **write** *your answers to the following:*

1. (a) The line that divides normal and abnormal behavior _____ (is/is not) sharply defined; in many instances, the difference between normal and abnormal behavior is a matter of _____ and is often determined by the social or cultural context in which a particular behavior occurs.

    (b) Psychopathology is defined as the scientific study of the _____ , _____ , and development of psychological disorders.

    (c) Most of us respond differently to _____ and _____ disorders. When we are troubled with _____ symptoms, we typically seek help and are not reluctant to talk about the problem; with _____ disorders, people are often reluctant to seek professional help and try to hide the fact that they have problems.

2. (a) Although the terms are interchangeable, _____ (psychologists/psychiatrists) generally prefer the term *psychological disorder*, whereas _____ (psychologists/psychiatrists) tend to prefer the term *mental disorder*.

    (b) A psychological, or mental, disorder can be defined as a pattern of _____ or

_____ symptoms that cause significant personal _____ , impair the ability to _____ in one or more important areas of life, or both. These symptoms must represent a serious departure from prevailing social and cultural norms.

(c) DSM-IV stands for the _____ and _____ *Manual of Mental Disorders*, fourth edition. Published by the American Psychiatric Association in 1994, it represents the consensus of a wide range of mental health professionals and organizations.

(d) DSM-IV describes approximately 250 specific psychological disorders, including their _____ , the exact _____ that must be met to make a _____ , and the typical course of a particular mental disorder.

(e) DSM-IV provides mental health professionals with (1) a common _____ to label mental disorders and (2) comprehensive _____ to diagnose mental disorders.

3. (a) In surveying a representative sample of Americans aged 15 to 54, the National Comorbidity Survey (NCS) found that almost one in two adults (48 percent) had experienced the symptoms of a psychological disorder at some point during _____ ; 30 percent of the people had experienced the symptoms of a psychological disorder during _____ .

    (b) About 80 percent of those who had suffered from the symptoms of a mental disorder during the previous year _____ (had/had not) sought any type of treatment or help for their symptoms.

(c) Clearly, many people who could potentially benefit from mental health treatment _____ (do/do not) seek it. This may reflect lack of awareness about psychological disorders or the fact that a _____ still exists when it comes to seeking treatment for psychological symptoms, or lack of services or resources.

(d) Even though the incidence of mental disorders is much higher than previously believed, _____ (very few/most) people weather the symptoms without becoming completely debilitated and without professional intervention. Really serious conditions that demanded immediate treatment affected 3 to 5 percent of the people surveyed.

(e) The NCS also found that the prevalence of certain mental disorders was _____ (the same/different) for men and women; women had a _____ (higher/lower) prevalence of anxiety and depression, whereas men had a _____ (higher/lower) prevalence of substance abuse disorders.

(f) DSM-IV has five categories of mental disorders that are some of the most common ones that mental health professionals encounter; these are _____ disorders, _____ disorders, _____ disorders, _____ disorders, and _____ .

Anxiety Disorders

Preview Questions

Consider the following questions as you study this section of the chapter.

- What are the main symptoms of anxiety disorder, and how does pathological anxiety differ from normal anxiety?

- What characterizes generalized anxiety disorder and panic disorder?

- What are the phobias, and how have they been explained?

*Read the section "Anxiety Disorders" (up to "Posttraumatic Stress Disorder") and **write** your answers to the following:*

1. (a) Anxiety is defined as an unpleasant emotional state characterized by _____ arousal and feelings of _____ , _____ , and worry that often hit during personal crises and everyday conflicts. When it alerts you to a realistic threat, anxiety is _____ and _____ .

   (b) As your internal alarm system, anxiety puts you on _____ alert, preparing you to defensively fight or flee potential dangers; it also puts you on _____ alert, making you focus your attention squarely on the threatening situation and become extremely vigilant.

   (c) In the anxiety disorders, however, the anxiety is _____ , disrupting everyday activities, moods, and thought processes.

   (d) Three features distinguish normal anxiety from pathological anxiety: First, pathological anxiety is _____ ; it is provoked by perceived threats that are _____ or _____ , and the anxiety response is out of proportion to the actual importance of the situation. Second, pathological anxiety is _____ ; the person can't shut off the alarm reaction, even when he or she knows it's unrealistic. Third, pathological anxiety is _____ ; it _____ with relationships, job or academic performance, or everyday activity.

2. (a) As a symptom, anxiety occurs in many different mental disorders. In anxiety disorder, however, anxiety is the _____ symptom and is manifested differently in each of the anxiety disorders.

    (b) Intense anxiety, which often does not seem to be triggered by anything specific, is the main symptom of both _____ anxiety disorder and _____ disorder.

    (c) When severe anxiety occurs in response to a specific object or situation, the disorder is called a _____ .

    (d) When anxiety is triggered by memories of a traumatic experience, the person is suffering from _____ disorder.

    (e) When pathological anxiety occurs in response to uncontrollable thoughts or urges to perform certain actions, the person is suffering from _____ disorder.

3. (a) The main feature of generalized anxiety disorder is _____ , _____ , _____ , and excessive apprehension. People with this disorder are constantly tense and anxious, and their anxiety is pervasive.

    (b) In generalized anxiety disorder, when one source of worry is removed, another quickly moves in to take its place; because of this, generalized anxiety disorder is sometimes referred to as _____ anxiety.

4. (a) A panic attack is a(n) _____ episode of _____ anxiety that rapidly escalates in intensity. The most common symptoms are a(n) _____ heart, _____ breathing, breathlessness, and a choking sensation, often accompanied by sweating, trembling, lightheadedness, chills, or hot flashes.

    (b) Along with these symptoms are feelings of _____ and the belief that one is about to die, go crazy, or completely lose control; a panic attack typically peaks within _____ minutes of onset and then gradually subsides.

    (c) When panic attacks occur _____ and _____ , the person is said to be suffering from panic disorder. The _____ of panic attacks is highly variable and quite unpredictable; understandably, people with panic disorder are quite apprehensive about when and where the next panic attack will hit.

5. (a) Both _____ and _____ causes seem to be implicated in panic disorder; on the _____ side, family and twin studies have found that panic disorder tends to run in families, but genetics alone does not provide a complete explanation.

    (b) Psychologically, people with panic disorder are unusually sensitive to the signs of physical arousal, and they may be _____ . For example, when normal subjects and panic disorder patients are given a substance, such as caffeine, that triggers _____ arousal, only the panic disorder patients react with a full-blown panic attack.

    (c) People with panic disorder tend to misinterpret the physical signs of arousal as catastrophic and dangerous, according to the _____ theory of panic disorder. After a frightening initial attack, the person becomes extremely _____ about suffering another attack; in turn, he or she becomes sensitized to physical changes that might signal the onset of another frightening episode.

    (d) After a series of panic attacks, the person becomes behaviorally _____ to respond with fear to the physical symptoms of arousal; once established, such a _____ response, combined with catastrophic thoughts, can act as a spring-board for repeated panic attacks, leading to panic disorder.

(e) Syndromes resembling panic disorder have been reported in many _____ ; other symptoms of panic, such as becoming hysterical, screaming, swearing, striking out at others, and breaking things, along with the circumstances that trigger panic attacks, are influenced by _____ .

6. (a) A phobia is a(n) _____ , _____ fear that is triggered by a specific object or situation; encountering the feared situation or object can provoke a full-fledged _____ in some people.

(b) People with a specific phobia are terrified of a particular object or situation and go to great lengths to _____ that object or situation, even though they know the fear is _____ .

(c) In the general population, mild phobias, such as fear of dogs or snakes, are extremely _____ (common/uncommon). In comparison, severe phobias are character-ized by incapacitating _____ and _____ that significantly interfere with daily life.

(d) About 10 percent of the population will experience a _____ phobia at some point in their lives; women are _____ (half/twice) as likely as men to suffer from a _____ phobia.

7. The objects or situations that produce specific phobias tend to fall into four broad categories:

(a) Fear of particular _____ , such as flying, driving, or being in tunnels, bridges, elevators, or enclosed places.

(b) Fear of _____ of the natural _____ , such as heights, water, thunderstorms, or lightning.

(c) Fear of _____ or _____ , including fear of injec-tions, needles, and medical or dental procedures.

(d) Fear of _____ and _____ , such as snakes, spiders, dogs, cats, slugs, or bats.

8. (a) People with agoraphobia fear having a _____ in a public place from which it might be difficult to escape or get help; consequently, they tend to avoid situa-tions that they think might provoke a _____ and situations from which they would be unable to escape or get help.

(b) Many agoraphobics become prisoners in their own homes, unable to go beyond their front doors; not surprisingly, then, agoraph-obia is the phobia for which people _____ (least/most) often seek professional help.

(c) The difference between those with a _____ phobia and those with agoraphobia is that the former will avoid the object or situation because of the irrational fear evoked, whereas the latter are not so much worried about the danger or threat but rather fear that they might have a _____ and be trapped or unable to escape or get help.

9. (a) A person with _____ phobia is paralyzed by fear of _____ situ-ations, especially if the situation involves performing even routine behaviors in front of others. The core of this phobia seems to be an irrational fear of being embarrassed, judged, or critically evaluated by others.

(b) People with social phobia recognize that their fear is excessive and unreasonable, but they still approach _____ situa-tions with tremendous anxiety. In severe cases, they may even suffer a(n) _____ in social situations.

(c) People with social phobia often have very low _____ , poor _____ skills, and few friends; they may also suffer from occupational or academic underachievement, have intense test anxiety, and have a fear of asking questions or making comments.

(d) When the fear of being embarrassed or failing in public significantly interferes with daily life, it qualifies as a(n) _____ phobia.

10. (a) Classical conditioning may well be involved in the development of a specific phobia that can be traced back to some sort of traumatic event; the feared object is the _____ stimulus and the learned fear is the _____ , which can generalize to other similar stimuli.

(b) Operant conditioning can also be involved in the avoidance behavior that characterizes phobias; the _____ of avoiding the feared object is _____ (positively/negatively) reinforced by the relief from anxiety and fear that the behavior brings about.

(c) Observational learning can also be involved in the development of phobias; people can learn to be phobic of certain objects or situations by _____ the fearful reactions of someone else who acts as a _____ in the situation or through seeing media accounts of disasters and catastrophes.

(d) Although learning principles can explain the genesis of some phobias, they cannot account for all cases of phobia; many individuals _____ (can/cannot) remember any traumatic or upsetting event

associated with the feared object or situation, and even though many people directly experience traumatic events, _____ (only a few/most) of those people do not develop phobias associated with the frightening situation or object.

11. (a) Humans seem to be _____ prepared to acquire fears of certain animals and situations that were important survival threats in human evolutionary history. People also seem predisposed to develop phobias toward creatures that arouse _____ , such as slugs, maggots, rats, or cockroaches, which are relatively harmless.

(b) Instinctively, it seems, many people find these creatures repulsive, possibly because they are associated with _____ , infection, or _____ ; the predisposition to develop phobias for such creatures may reflect a fear of contamination or _____ that is also based on human evolutionary history.

(c) In combination, _____ principles and _____ predispositions provide several useful insights into the development of phobias, but they have a number of shortcomings.

Anxiety Disorders: Posttraumatic Stress Disorder and Obsessive-Compulsive Disorder

Preview Questions

Consider the following questions as you study these sections of the chapter.

- How is posttraumatic stress disorder (PTSD) defined?
- What are the main characteristics of PTSD, and what causes the disorder?
- What is obsessive-compulsive disorder, and what are the most common types of obsessions and compulsions?

Read the sections "Anxiety Disorders: Posttraumatic Stress Disorder" and "Obsessive-Compulsive Disorders" and **write** *your answers to the following:*

1. (a) Posttraumatic stress disorder (PTSD) is a long-lasting anxiety disorder that develops in response to an extreme _____ or _____ trauma; extreme traumas are events that produce intense feelings of horror and _____ , such as a serious physical injury or threat of injury to yourself or to loved ones.

   (b) Originally, PTSD was primarily associated with direct experiences of _____ ; it's now known that PTSD can also develop in survivors (as well as witnesses) of other sorts of extreme traumas, such as natural _____ , physical or sexual _____ , and random shooting sprees and can be experienced by children as well as adults.

   (c) Three core symptoms characterize PTSD: (1) the person _____ recalls the event, replaying it in his or her mind; it is often unwanted or intrusive, which means that it interferes with normal thought processes; (2) the person avoids _____ or _____ that tend to trigger memories of the experience and undergoes a general numbing of emotional responsiveness; and (3) the person experiences the increased physical _____ associated with anxiety; he or she may be easily _____ , experience _____ disturbances, have problems concentrating and remembering, and be prone to irritability or angry outbursts.

   (d) Not surprisingly, PTSD seriously interferes with the ability to function in daily life.

   Along with their PTSD symptoms, people experience _____ and feelings of _____ over surviving the trauma when close friends or relatives did not. In order to ease their emotional distress, they commonly engage in _____ abuse. Many individuals also display other psychological disorders, such as _____ , _____ , or generalized anxiety disorder.

   (e) Several factors influence the likelihood of developing posttraumatic stress disorder: (1) people with a personal or family history of psychological disorders are _____ (more/less) likely to develop PTSD when exposed to extreme trauma; (2) the magnitude of the trauma plays _____ (a small/an important) role—_____ (less/more) extreme stressors are more likely to produce PTSD; and (3) when people undergo _____ , the incidence of PTSD can be quite high.

2. (a) Obsessive-compulsive disorder is an anxiety disorder in which a person's life is dominated by _____ thoughts (_____) and behaviors (_____).

   (b) Obsessions are _____ , _____ , _____ thoughts or mental images that cause the person great anxiety and distress; they have little basis in reality and are often extremely far-fetched.

   (c) A compulsion is a(n) _____ behavior that the person feels driven to perform; typically, compulsions are _____ behaviors that must be carried out in a certain pattern or sequence.

   (d) Compulsions may be _____

(overt/covert) physical behaviors, such as repeatedly washing the hands, or they may be _____ (overt/covert) mental behaviors, such as counting or reciting certain phrases to yourself; when the person tries to resist performing the behavior, unbearable _____ , _____ , and distress result.

(e) True obsessive-compulsives do not find any _____ in their obsessions and compulsions; instead, the obsessions and compulsions they experience are very _____ and _____ .

3. (a) Generally, people with this disorder experience _____ (just obsessions/just compulsions/both obsessions and compulsions). Obsessions and compulsions are often linked in some way, even if the behaviors bear little logical relationship to the feared consequences. In all cases, obsessive-compulsives feel that something terrible will happen if the compulsive action is left undone.

(b) Obsessions and compulsions take a _____ (different/similar) shape in different countries; the _____ of the obsessions and compulsions tends to mirror the particular culture's concerns and beliefs.

(c) Although researchers are far from fully understanding the causes of obsessive-compulsive disorder, _____ factors seem to be involved; a deficiency in the neurotransmitter _____ has been implicated in the disorder.

(d) In addition, obsessive-compulsive disorder has been linked with dysfunction in specific brain areas, such as the _____ lobes, which play a key role in our ability to think and plan ahead, and the caudate nucleus, which is involved in regulating _____ .

4. Read the following and write the correct term in the space provided.

(a) Dr. Janz is a psychiatrist who assesses and treats patients in a mental institution. Dr. Sloane is a clinical psychologist who works with a similar population of patients in a mental health clinic. Dr. Janz is likely to describe his patients as suffering from _____ disorders, whereas Dr. Sloane is more likely to use the term _____ disorder when referring to his patients' problems.

(b) Seventeen-year-old Brad has a shaven head, and he has rings in his nose, ears, and navel. Shortly after purchasing a new pair of jeans, he cut and tore horizontal slits across the thigh and knee areas of each leg. In our present culture, Brad would be classified as _____ .

(c) Mr. and Mrs. Jefferson want to hire a new housekeeper. Mr. Jefferson suggests that the best person would be someone who has an excessive dislike and fear of dirt, germs, and insects and who deals with anxiety about contamination by using a very thorough cleaning, washing, and disinfecting routine. Mrs. Jefferson thinks that any person fitting that description might have a problem called _____ disorder.

(d) Mr. Alviro suffers from intense anxiety most of the time. He is nervous and worried and is overly concerned about a wide range of life circumstances with little or no justification. Mr. Alviro probably suffers from _____ disorder.

(e) Maurice is very quiet and introverted. He is painfully shy in the presence of other people and has dropped many courses at college simply because they involved oral presentations. He can't get a job because he is intensely afraid and anxious about being interviewed. Maurice would probably be classified as having

_____ .

(f) Mr. Ng frequently recalls the horrors he and his family experienced in his native Cambodia. He suffers from sleep disturbances and is often awakened by terrifying nightmares. Mr. Ng is experiencing _____ disorder.

(g) Ever since the sudden death of her husband,

Mrs. Baxter has experienced a number of terrifying and unexpected episodes in which her heart suddenly starts to pound hard for no apparent reason; she typically feels a choking sensation, has trouble breathing, and starts to sweat and tremble. Mrs. Baxter is probably experiencing

_____ .

Graphic Organizer 1

List the main symptoms of each of the following anxiety disorders:

Generalized Anxiety Disorder	Panic Disorder	Phobias

Posttraumatic Stress Disorder	Obsessive-Compulsive Disorder

Review of Terms and Concepts 1

Use the terms in this list to complete the Matching Test, then to help you answer the True/False items correctly.

psychopathology
psychological disorder
  (mental disorder)
DSM-IV
anxiety
anxiety disorders
generalized anxiety
  disorder
panic attack
panic disorder

phobia
specific phobia
agoraphobia
social phobia
posttraumatic stress
  disorder (PTSD)
obsessive-compulsive
  disorder
obsessions
compulsions

Matching Exercise

Match the appropriate term with its definition or description.

1. _____ The scientific study of the origins, symptoms, and development of psychological disorders.

2. _____ Abbreviation for the *Diagnostic and Statistical Manual of Mental Disorders*, fourth edition; the book published by the American Psychiatric Association that describes the specific symptoms and diagnostic guidelines for different psychological disorders.

3. _____ Anxiety disorder in which the symptoms of anxiety are triggered by intrusive, repetitive thoughts and urges to perform certain actions.

4. _____ Unpleasant emotional state characterized by physical arousal and feelings of tension, apprehension, and worry.

5. _____ Irrational fear triggered by a specific object or situation.

6. _____ Anxiety disorder in which chronic and persistent symptoms of anxiety develop in response to an extreme physical or psychological trauma.

7. _____ Anxiety disorder involving the extreme and irrational fear of experiencing a panic attack in a public situation and being unable to escape or get help.

8. _____ Anxiety disorder characterized by an extreme or irrational fear of a specific object or situation that interferes with the ability to function in daily life.

True/False Test

Indicate whether each statement is true or false by placing T or F in the blank space next to each item.

1. ____ Compulsions refer to repeated, intrusive, and uncontrollable irrational thoughts or mental images that cause extreme anxiety and distress.

2. ____ A psychological (or mental) disorder is a pattern of behavioral and psychological symptoms that cause significant personal distress, impair the ability to function in one or more important areas of daily life, or both.

3. ____ Generalized anxiety disorder is characterized by excessive, global, and persistent symptoms of anxiety; also called free-floating anxiety.

4. ____ Panic disorder is an anxiety disorder in which the person experiences frequent and unexpected panic attacks.

5. ____ Obsessions refer to repetitive behaviors or mental acts that are performed to prevent or reduce anxiety.

6. ____ Social phobia is an anxiety disorder involving the extreme and irrational fear of being embarrassed, judged, or scrutinized by others in social situations.

7. ____ Anxiety disorders are a category of psychological disorders in which extreme anxiety is the main diagnostic feature and causes significant disruptions in the person's cognitive, behavioral, and interpersonal functioning.

8. ____ A panic attack is a sudden episode of extreme anxiety that rapidly escalates in intensity.

Check your answers and review any areas of weakness before going on to the next section.

Mood Disorders: Emotions Gone Awry

Preview Questions

Consider the following questions as you study this section of the chapter.

- What are mood disorders, and how do disturbed emotions cause psychological distress and impair daily functioning?

- What are the symptoms of major depression, and what is dysthymic disorder?
- What is the course of depression, and how prevalent is it?

Read the section "Mood Disorders: Emotions Gone Awry" and **write** *your answers to the following:*

1. (a) In mood disorders, emotions violate the _____ of normal moods in quality, intensity, and duration; mood changes persist much longer than the normal fluctuations in moods that we all experience.

   (b) DSM-IV formally defines a mood disorder as a(n) _____ , _____ disturbance in a person's emotions that causes _____ discomfort, impairs the ability to _____ , or both.

2. (a) Major depression is characterized by extreme and persistent feelings of despondency, worthlessness, and hopelessness, causing impaired _____ , _____ , _____ , and _____ functioning.

   (b) Emotionally, the person feels overwhelming sadness, often accompanied by feelings of _____ , worthlessness, inadequacy, emptiness, and hopelessness. Even if surrounded by close friends and loving family members, the person feels _____ and _____ from others.

   (c) Behaviorally, the depressed person's feelings are reflected in dejected and spiritless facial expressions; _____ , _____ , and gestures seem awkward and slower than usual; _____ spells may occur for no apparent reason. Depressed people make less eye contact with others and may withdraw from activities that they once enjoyed.

(d) Cognitively, memory is often impaired; thought processes feel dull and sluggish, and the person may have problems _____ . Routine tasks such as making simple decisions, studying, making dinner, or balancing a checkbook become increasingly difficult. Self-esteem plummets as the person's _____ become globally pessimistic and negative about their self, the world, and the future; and _____ is always a potential risk in major depression.

(e) Physically, major depression is characterized by a general loss of _____ and _____ energy, along with vague physical aches and pains. Some depressed people experience a sense of _____ restlessness and anxiety, demonstrated by fidgeting or aimless pacing; in fact, the physical symptoms of anxiety often accompany depression.

3. (a) Along with a general loss of energy, _____ and _____ diminish; appetite and eating patterns are _____ ; and sexual interest _____ . Depressed people often lose weight because they lose all interest in food, and less commonly, people may eat excessively and gain weight.

   (b) Abnormal sleep patterns are another hallmark of major depression; the amount of time spent in _____ , deeply relaxed sleep is greatly _____ , and the person experiences sporadic _____ periods of varying lengths. Episodes of sleeplessness are common; less commonly, some depressed people sleep excessively, sometimes as much as eighteen hours a day.

   (c) To be diagnosed with major depression, a person must display most of these symptoms for _____ weeks or longer; in many cases, there doesn't seem to be any _____ reason for the persistent feeling of depression; in other cases, a person's downward emotional spiral has been triggered by some _____ event or _____ situation.

(d) If a family member or close friend dies, it is completely _____ to feel despondent and sad for several months as part of the mourning or bereavement process. As a general rule, if a person's ability to function after the death of a loved one is still seriously impaired after _____ months, major depression is suspected.

4. (a) In contrast to major depression, which significantly impairs a person's ability to function, some people experience a less severe form of depression called _____ disorder; this mood disorder is a _____ , low-grade depression that is characterized by many of the symptoms of depression, but the symptoms are less intense.

(b) Usually, this disorder develops in response to some _____ event or trauma; although the person functions adequately, the negative mood can persist indefinitely, creating a chronic case of the blues.

(c) Some people with _____ disorder experience _____ depression; that is, they experience one or more episodes of major depression on top of their ongoing _____ disorder; as they recover from the episode of major depression, they return to the less intense depressed symptoms of dysthymic disorder.

5. (a) Depression is the _____

(least/most) common of all the psychological disorders.

(b) Women are about _____ (half/twice) as likely as men to be diagnosed with major depression.

(c) People in the 15–24 and 35–44 age bracket are _____ (least/most) at risk. People with little education or income, homemakers, or those who are are divorced, widowed, or separated are also at _____ (lesser/ greater) risk.

(d) Most people who experience major depression try to cope with the symptoms _____ (by themselves/ by seeking professional help). When depression _____ (is/is not) treated, it may become a recurring mental disorder that progressively becomes more severe.

(e) Better than _____ of all people who have been through one episode of major depression can expect a relapse, usually within two years. With each recurrence, the symptoms _____ (decrease/ increase) in severity, and the time between major depression episodes _____ (decreases/increases).

(f) For millions of people with seasonal affective disorder (SAD), repeated episodes of depression are as predictable as the changing _____ , especially the onset of _____ and _____ . In the most common form of SAD episodes of depression recur in the _____ and _____ months, when there is the least amount of sunlight; it is more common among _____ and those who live in the northern latitudes.

Mood Disorders: Bipolar Disorder

Preview Questions

Consider the following questions as you study this section of the chapter.

- How is bipolar order defined?
- What characterizes a manic episode, and what is cyclothymic disorder?
- How prevalent is bipolar disorder, and what factors contribute to mood disorders?

Read the section "Mood Disorders: Bipolar Disorder" and **write** *your answers to the following:*

1. (a) In contrast to major depression, bipolar disorder (previously called

    _____) almost always involves abnormal moods at

    _____ end(s) of the emotional spectrum.

   (b) Episodes of incapacitating _____ alternate with shorter periods of extreme euphoria called _____ episodes. For most people with the disorder, a

    _____ episode immediately precedes or follows a bout with major

    _____ , with a small percentage of people experiencing only _____ episodes.

2. (a) Manic episodes typically begin

    _____ , and symptoms

    _____ ; people sleep little, have boundless energy, and are uncharacteristically euphoric, expansive, and excited for several days or longer.

   (b) Typically, the person in the midst of a manic episode does not recognize what is happening to him and resists the efforts of others to help; his _____ is wildly inflated, and he exudes supreme

    _____ that is reflected in grandiose (but often delusional) plans for obtaining wealth, power, and fame.

   (c) Frenzied goal-directed behavior abounds during a manic episode; to an outside observer, the behavior seems disorganized and bizarre, but the _____ person believes that he is simply seizing golden opportunities.

   (d) Words are spoken at a rapid rate and are often slurred as the manic person tries to keep up with his own thought processes; attention is easily distracted by virtually anything, triggering a(n)

    _____ , in which thoughts rapidly and loosely shift from topic to topic.

   (e) The ability to function during a manic episode is severely impaired;

    _____ is usually required, partly to protect people from the potential consequences of their own poor judgment and inappropriate behavior.

   (f) During manic episodes, people can run up a mountain of bills, disappear for weeks at a time, become sexually promiscuous, or commit illegal acts; very commonly, the person becomes _____ or

    _____ abusive when others question his grandiose plans.

3. (a) Some people experience a milder but chronic form of bipolar disorder called

    _____ disorder.

   (b) In this disorder, people experience moderate but frequent mood swings for two years or longer. These mood swings are not severe enough to qualify as either _____ disorder or major _____ .

   (c) Often, people with _____ disorder are perceived as being extremely moody, unpredictable, and inconsistent.

4. (a) The onset of bipolar disorder typically occurs in the person's _____ . The mood swings tend to start and stop much more abruptly than the mood changes of major depression, and the _____

and _____ episodes tend to be much shorter, lasting from a few days to a couple of months.

(b) Unlike major depression, bipolar disorder _____ (does/does not) show any sex differences in the rate at which it occurs.

(c) In the vast majority of cases, bipolar disorder is a(n) _____ mental disorder; a small percentage of the cases display _____ , experiencing four or five _____ or _____ episodes every year. More commonly, bipolar disorder tends to recur every couple of years, especially when individuals stop taking _____ , a medication that helps control the disorder.

5. (a) There is ample indirect evidence from family, twin, and adoption studies that some people inherit a(n)

_____ , or a greater vulnerability, to develop a mood disorder.

(b) Researchers have consistently found that both major depression and bipolar disorder tend to run in families; if a person has a mood disorder, that person's immediate relatives are up to _____ times more likely than the general population to have a mood disorder.

(c) Twin studies have shown that if one identical twin suffers from major depression or bipolar disorder, the other twin has about a _____ percent chance of also developing the disorder. This shared risk rate _____ (has/has not) been found in studies of identical twins who were adopted and raised apart.

6. (a) There is a great deal of indirect evidence that implicates at least two important neurotransmitters, _____ and _____ , in major depression. Antidepressants seem to lift the symptoms of depression by increasing the availability of _____ and _____ in the brain. In general, antidepressants are highly _____ (ineffective/effective).

(b) Since the 1960s, in most cases, bipolar disorder has been treated, and its recurrence prevented, by use of the drug _____ . Apparently, this drug seems to regulate the availability of a neurotransmitter called _____ , which acts as an excitatory neurotransmitter in many areas of the brain.

7. (a) Major depression is often triggered by _____ and _____ events; exposure to these events are the best predictors of major depression episodes. This is especially true for people who have experienced _____ episodes of depression and who have a family history of mood disorders.

(b) Even in people with no family or personal history of mood disorders, _____ alone can produce major depression. There is also some evidence that _____ life events play a role in the course of bipolar disorder.

Graphic Organizer 2

List the main symptoms of the mood disorders:

Major Depression	Bipolar Disorder
1.	1.
2.	2.
3.	3.
4.	
5.	
6.	
Dysthymic Disorder	**Cyclothymic Disorder**
1.	1.

Personality Disorders: Maladaptive Traits

Preview Questions

Consider the following questions as you study this section of the chapter.

- What are the main characteristics of personality disorder?
- What are the ten personality disorders that are included in DSM-IV?
- What characterizes the behavior of someone with a paranoid, antisocial, or borderline personality disorder?

*Read the section "Personality Disorders: Maladaptive Traits" and **write** your answers to the following:*

1. (a) Someone with a personality disorder has personality traits that are _____ and _____ across a broad range of personal and social situations; these people deviate markedly from social and cultural norms. Personality disorders become evident during adolescence or early adulthood and tend to be very _____ (stable/unstable) over time.

(b) DSM-IV identifies ten personality disorders, which are grouped in three basic clusters: (1) the odd, eccentric cluster includes _____ , _____ , and _____ personality disorders; (2) the dramatic, emotional, or erratic cluster consists of _____ , _____ , _____ , and _____ personality disorders; and (3) the anxious, fearful cluster includes people who display _____ , _____ , or _____ personality disorders.

(c) Personality disorders are evident in up to 15 percent of the general population. It _____ (is/ is not) possible for a person to display the characteristics of more than one personality disorder at a time.

2. (a) The defining features of the paranoid personality disorder are _____ and _____ of the motives of others. About 3 percent of the general population display this disorder, which occurs most frequently in _____ (men/women).

(b) People with paranoid personality disorder are very _____ (likely/reluctant) to form close attachments or confide in others; they have _____ (little or no/a strong) tendency to blame others for their own shortcomings; they are _____ (seldom/often) critical of what they perceive as the shortcomings of others. In addition, pathological jealousy _____ (commonly/rarely) characterizes the intimate relationships of the person with paranoid personality disorder.

(c) Although there is not a great deal known about what causes paranoid personality disorder, it does tend to co-occur with _____ and _____ personality disorders.

3. (a) The individual with antisocial personality disorder, (also called a _____ or _____), has the ability to _____ , _____ , _____ , and otherwise manipulate and harm other people. The person shows _____ (a great deal of/little or no) remorse for having caused pain, damage, or loss to others.

(b) The central feature of antisocial personality disorder is a pattern of blatantly

_____ .

In the general population, approximately 6 percent of _____ (men/women) and 1 percent of _____ (men/women) display this pattern.

(c) The pattern of behavior associated with antisocial personality disorder is _____ (rarely seen/often seen) in childhood or the early adolescent years. By middle to late adulthood, the antisocial behaviors of deceiving and manipulating others for their own personal gain, disregarding and violating the rights of others,

and so on, tend to _____ (increase/diminish).

(d) A number of factors have been identified as contributing to antisocial personality disorder: (1) _____ stress, (2) _____ during childhood and adolescence, (3) disrupted _____ , (4) poor _____ or a pathological _____ environment, (5) _____ personality traits, and (6) _____ factors.

(e) The person with antisocial personality disorder often feels _____ (little/ a great deal of) anxiety about his behaviors and the consequences he experiences. Attempts to treat this disorder _____ (are usually successful/often fail).

4. (a) Borderline personality disorder is primarily characterized by chronic instability in _____ , _____ , and relationships; moods are _____ , _____ , and fluctuate quickly.

(b) This chaotic disorder is the _____ (least/most) commonly diagnosed of the personality disorders. Of the estimated 10 million Americans with borderline personality disorder, about 75 percent are _____ (men/women).

(c) The person with borderline personality disorder often has a pervasive feeling of _____ and is desperately afraid of _____ . Interpersonal relationships are _____ (unstable/stable) and the person sees herself and others in absolute terms (perfect or worthless, ecstatic or miserable).

(d) Borderline personality disorder is also characterized by _____ behaviors, such as self-mutilation, suicide threats and attempted suicide, and lack of impulse control. People with this disorder may _____ , drive recklessly; _____ drugs, be _____ promiscuous, and suffer from eating disorders and depression.

(e) Some researchers believe that a disruption in _____ in early childhood are important causal factors; other researchers have suggested that _____ , _____ , or _____ abuse and neglect during childhood may contribute to the development of borderline personality disorder.

The Dissociative Disorders: Fragmentation of the Self

Preview Questions

Consider the following questions as you study this section of the chapter.

- How is a dissociative experience defined?
- What are dissociative amnesia and dissociative fugue?
- What is dissociative identity disorder (DID), and what is thought to cause it?
- Why are some psychologists skeptical about DID?

*Read the section "The Dissociative Disorders: Fragmentation of the Self" and **write** your answers to the following:*

1. (a) A normal personality is one in which awareness, memory, and personal identity are _____ and _____ ; in contrast, a dissociative experience is one in which a person's awareness, memory, and personal identity become _____ or _____ .

   (b) Dissociative experiences _____ (are/are not) inherently pathological; in fact, they are quite _____ and completely _____ .

(c) In some cultures, dramatic disruptions in an individual's sense of personal identity are perceived as _____ and even highly valued; for example, _____ is common in many cultures, typically within a religious context.

(d) Another phenomenon that occurs in some cultures is one in which the person loses her sense of personal identity or is unaware of her surroundings, referred to as a _____ .

(e) Speaking in tongues, or _____ , is common in some North American Christian churches and is another example of a dissociative possession state; the person is temporarily possessed by the Holy Spirit, who supposedly speaks through the individual.

(f) As DSM-IV points out, dissociative possession or trance states _____ (are/are not) considered pathological if (1) they occur within the context of accepted cultural or religious practice; (2) they occur voluntarily; and (3) they don't cause distress or impair functioning.

2. (a) Dissociative experiences are not necessarily _____ . But when a dissociative disorder occurs, the dissociative experiences are far more _____ and _____ , are more _____ , and severely disrupt everyday functioning.

   (b) Awareness or recognition of familiar surroundings may be completely obstructed; _____ of pertinent personal information may be unavailable to consciousness; and _____ may be lost, confused, or fragmented.

3. (a) The partial or total inability to recall important information that is not due to a medical

condition, such as an illness or injury, or a drug, is referred or as

_____ .

(b) Usually, the person develops _____ for personal events and information rather than for general knowledge or skills; in most cases, dissociative _____ is a response to stress, trauma, or an extremely painful situation, such as combat, marital problems, or physical abuse.

(c) A closely related disorder in which the person outwardly appears normal but has extensive _____ and is confused about his identity is called dissociative _____ . The person may suddenly and inexplicably travel away from his home, wander to other cities or countries, and in some cases adopt a completely new identity.

4. (a) Dissociative identity disorder (DID), formerly known as _____ disorder, involves extensive memory disruptions for personal information along with the presence of two or more distinct _____ , or "_____," within a single person.

(b) Typically, each _____ has its own name, and each will be experienced as if it has its own personal history and self-image; these alternative _____ , often called alters, may be of widely varying ages and of different genders.

(c) The number of alternative personalities can range from 2 to over a 100, but having _____ to _____ alters is most common.

5. (a) Alters are not really separate _____ but rather constitute a "system of mind." That is, alters seem to embody different aspects of the individual's

_____ that, for some reason, cannot be integrated into the primary personality; each holds memories, emotions, and motives that are not admissible to the individual's conscious mind.

(b) At different times, different alters take control of the person's experience, thoughts, and behavior. Typically, the primary _____ is _____ (aware/unaware) of the existence of the alternate personalities; however, the alters _____ (may/may not) have knowledge of each other's existence and share memories; sometimes, the experiences of one alter are accessible to another alter but not vice versa.

(c) Differences between the different personalities in visual functioning, allergies, _____ , and handedness have been reported, but many of these physiological differences have yet to be convincingly demonstrated under controlled conditions.

(d) Virtually all people with DID show symptoms of _____ and _____ problems for recent and childhood experiences. Commonly, they _____ (are/are not) able to remember their behavior or whereabouts during specific time periods.

(e) People with DID typically have numerous _____ and _____ problems as well as a chaotic personal history.

(f) Symptoms of major _____ , _____ , posttraumatic stress disorder, substance abuse, _____ disorders, and self-destructive behavior are also common; often, the DID patient has been diagnosed with a variety of other _____ disorders before the DID diagnosis is made.

6. (a) According to one explanation, DID represents an extreme form of dissociative _____ . A very _____ (low/high) percentage of DID cases report having suffered extreme physical or sexual abuse in childhood.

   (b) In order to cope with the trauma, the child "_____" himself or herself from it, creating alternate _____ . Over time, alters are created to deal with the memories and emotions associated with intolerably painful experiences.

   (c) Feelings of _____ , _____ , _____ , and guilt that are too powerful for the child to consciously integrate can be dissociated into these alternate personalities. In effect, dissociation becomes a pathological _____ that the person uses to cope with overwhelming experiences.

   (d) The dissociative _____ theory is difficult to test empirically, but some researchers have provided independent evidence and correlational data confirming the link between childhood trauma and frequency of dissociative experiences in adulthood.

7. Read the following and write the correct term in the space provided.

   (a) Ursula is generally happy about her move to northern Canada six years ago, but at regular intervals since then she has suffered episodes of depression during the fall and winter months. Ursula is probably suffering from _____ disorder.

   (b) Laura suffers from a mood disorder. Her therapist has taken a family history and found that Laura's mother and two sisters also suffer from the same problem. Although her therapist is aware that multiple factors may be involved in her problem, he is most likely to conclude that Laura may have a(n) _____ predisposition for the disorder.

   (c) Dr. Markoff has prescribed lithium for Sandro's mood disorder. It is most likely that Sandro suffers from _____ disorder.

   (d) Nedzad has a chronic disorder involving moderate but frequent mood swings that are not severe enough to qualify as bipolar disorder or major depression. He is perceived as being very moody, unpredictable, and inconsistent; taken together, these symptoms may indicate _____ disorder.

   (e) Tony has a rigid preoccupation with orderliness, personal control, and rules; he is also a perfectionist. His friend Parnell has a grandiose sense of self-importance, constantly exaggerates his abilities and accomplishments, and has an excessive need for admiration. It is most likely that Tony has _____ personality disorder, and Parnell has _____ personality disorder.

   (f) Marion Einer, a fifth-grade schoolteacher in Jersey City, disappeared a few days after her husband left her. One year later, she was discovered working as a waitress in a cocktail lounge in San Diego. Calling herself Faye Bartell, she claimed to have no recollection of her past life and insisted she had never been married. This example illustrates _____ .

   (g) When Vanessa goes to a movie, she tends to become totally absorbed in the plot and loses all track of time and place; she is also often momentarily disoriented when she leaves the theater. These episodes represent _____ .

(h) Karlson recently survived an airline crash. Although he escaped from the burning plane with very few injuries, three of his friends were killed in the crash. Karlson is unable to recall any details from the time of the accident until a week later. Karlson has experienced _____ .

(i) Dr. Rendell studies people who typically disregard and violate the rights of others and who appear to have no remorse or conscience about their destructive behaviors. Her colleague Dr. Gideon studies people who have a pervasive distrust and suspiciousness of the motives of others without any good reason. Dr. Rendell studies

_____ personality disorder, and Dr. Gideon studies _____ personality disorder.

Review of Terms and Concepts 2

Use the terms in this list to complete the Matching Test, then to help you answer the True/False items correctly.

mood disorders
major depression
dysthymic disorder
seasonal affective
    disorder (SAD)
bipolar disorder
manic episode
cyclothymic disorder
personality disorder
paranoid personality
    disorder
antisocial personality
    disorder (psychopath
    or sociopath)

borderline personality
    disorder
dissociative experience
spirit possession
trance state
glossolalia
dissociative disorders
dissociative amnesia
dissociative fugue
dissociative identity
    disorder (DID)

Matching Exercise

Match the appropriate term with its definition or description.

1. _____ Personality disorder characterized by a pervasive pattern of disregarding and violating the rights of others; such individuals are also referred to as psychopaths or sociopaths.

2. _____ Often called manic depression, this mood disorder involves periods of incapacitating depression alternating with periods of extreme euphoria and excitement.

3. _____ Mood disorder in which episodes of depression typically recur during fall and winter and disappear during spring and summer.

4. _____ Nonpathological dissociative experience, usually within a religious context, in which the occupant of the person's body is supposedly displaced by a "spirit" that takes control of the body, and the person often has no memory of the experience.

5. _____ Mood disorder characterized by extreme and persistent feelings of despondency, worthlessness, and hopelessness, causing impaired emotional, cognitive, behavioral, and physical functioning.

6. _____ Sudden, rapidly escalating emotional state characterized by extreme euphoria, excitement, physical energy, and rapid thoughts and speech.

7. _____ Break or disruption in consciousness during which awareness, memory, and personal identity become separated or divided.

8. _____ Inflexible, maladaptive patterns of thoughts, emotions, behavior, and interpersonal functioning that are stable over time and across situations; they deviate from the expectations of the individual's culture.

9. _____ Formerly called *multiple personality disorder*; dissociative disorder involving extensive disruptions along with the presence of two or more distinct identities or "personalities."

10. _____ A category of mental disorders in which significant and chronic disruption in mood is the predominant symptom, causing impaired cognitive, behavioral, and physical functioning.

True/False Test

Indicate whether each statement is true or false by placing T or F in the blank space next to each item.

1. ____ A personality disorder characterized by a pervasive distrust and suspiciousness of the motives of others without sufficient basis is called paranoid personality disorder.

2. ___ In some cultures, a person may enter a trance state in which he loses his sense of personal identity or is unaware of his surroundings.

3. ___ Dissociative fugue involves the inability to recall information but does not involve sudden, unexpected travel from home.

4. ___ Glossolalia, or speaking in tongues, is common in some North American Christian churches; it is a dissociative state in which the person is temporarily possessed by the Holy Spirit, who speaks through the individual in an unknown language.

5. ___ Dissociative amnesia involves sudden and unexpected travel away from home, extensive amnesia, and identity confusion.

6. ___ Cyclothymic disorder involves chronic, low-grade feelings of depression that produce subjective discomfort but do not seriously impair the ability to function.

7. ___ Dissociative disorders are a category of psychological disorders in which extreme and frequent disruptions of awareness, memory, and personal identity impair the ability to function.

8. ___ Borderline personality disorder is characterized by instability of interpersonal relationships, self-image, and emotions, as well as by marked impulsivity.

9. ___ Dysthymic disorder is a milder but chronic form of bipolar disorder in which the person experiences moderate but frequent mood swings.

> Check your answers and review any areas of weakness before going on to the next section.

Schizophrenia: A Different Reality

Preview Questions

Consider the following questions as you study this section of the chapter.

- How is schizophrenia characterized?
- How do positive and negative symptoms differ, and what are the core symptoms of schizophrenia?
- What are the main subtypes of schizophrenia?
- What factors have been implicated in the development of schizophrenia?

- What evidence points to the involvement of genetic factors and brain abnormalities in the development of schizophrenia?
- How do environmental factors affect the development of schizophrenia?

*Read the section "Schizophrenia: A Different Reality" and **write** your answers to the following:*

1. (a) Schizophrenia is a psychological disorder that involves severely distorted _____ , _____ , and _____ processes. During a schizophrenic episode, people lose their grip on reality and experience an entirely different inner world that is often characterized by mental _____ , _____ , and frustration.

   (b) Positive symptoms reflect an excess or distortion of normal functioning and include (1) _____ , or false beliefs; (2) _____ , or false perceptions; and (3) severely disorganized _____ processes, _____ , and behavior.

   (c) Negative symptoms reflect a restriction or reduction of normal functioning, such as greatly reduced _____ , _____ expressiveness, or production of _____ .

   (d) According to DSM-IV, schizophrenia is diagnosed when two or more of these characteristic symptoms are actively present for a _____ or longer. Usually, schizophrenia also involves a longer personal history, typically _____ months or more, of odd behavior, beliefs, perceptual experiences, and other less severe signs of mental disturbance.

   (e) There is enormous individual variation in the _____ , _____ , and duration of schizophrenic symptoms.

2. (a) A delusion is a(n) _____ held _____ that persists in spite of contradictory evidence or appeals to reason. Schizophrenic delusions are usually bizarre and far-fetched and typically cause great _____ distress and interfere with _____ or _____ functioning.

(b) Although the content of delusions is wide-ranging, delusions are almost always centered on the _____ who is _____ them.

(c) Certain themes also tend to surface consistently. If the delusional person believes that other people are constantly talking about her and that everything that happens is somehow related to her, it is a delusion of _____ .

(d) The belief that one is extremely important, powerful, or wealthy is the basic theme of delusions of _____ .

(e) If the person believes that others are plotting against or trying to harm him or someone close to him, it is a delusion of _____ .

(f) Because people with schizophrenia find their delusions so convincing, the delusions can sometimes provoke _____ or _____ behavior. In some instances, delusional thinking can lead to dangerous behaviors, such as the person who responds to his delusional ideas by hurting himself or attacking others.

3. (a) Hallucinations are _____ or _____ perceptions that seem vividly real. The hallucinations of schizophrenia are often _____ and _____ , such as hallucinated voices that constantly tell a person what to do.

(b) The most common hallucinations experienced in schizophrenia are _____ , followed by _____ hallucinations. The most frequent form of _____ hallucination is hearing a voice or voices.

(c) The content of hallucinations is often tied to the person's _____ beliefs. If a person harbors _____ of _____ , hallucinated voices may reinforce her grandiose ideas by communicating instructions from God or angels; if the person harbors _____ of _____ , hallucinated voices or images may be extremely frightening, threatening, or accusing.

(d) When a schizophrenic episode is severe, hallucinations _____ (are easily distinguished/can be virtually impossible to distinguish) from objective reality; but when the symptoms are less severe, the person _____ (may/may not) recognize that the hallucination is a product of his own mind. In some cases of schizophrenia, the auditory hallucinations can last for _____ or even _____ .

4. (a) People often report that during a schizophrenic episode, sights, sounds, and other sensations feel _____ . Along with these disturbances, the person may experience severely disorganized _____ ; it can be very difficult to _____ , _____ , and integrate important information while ignoring irrelevant information, and the person's mind drifts from topic to topic in an unpredictable, illogical manner.

(b) Such disorganized _____ is also often reflected in the person's _____ ; ideas, words, and images are sometimes strung together in

ways that seem completely nonsensical to
the listener.

5. (a) Excesses or distortions in normal function-
        ing, such as _____ ,
        _____ , and disrupted
        _____ , reflect positive symp-
        toms; in contrast, negative symptoms reflect
        marked deficits or decreases in
        _____ or _____
        functioning.

    (b) In one commonly seen negative symptom,
        there is a greatly reduced or complete lack
        of emotional responsiveness or facial expres-
        sion; this is referred to as
        _____ or
        _____ ;
        regardless of the situation, the person
        responds in an emotionally _____
        way. In addition, few expressive
        _____ are made, and the per-
        son's _____ is slow and monoto-
        nous, lacking normal vocal inflections.

    (c) A closely related negative symptom involv-
        ing a greatly reduced production of speech is
        called _____ . Because verbal
        responses are limited to brief, empty com-
        ments, this symptom is also referred to as
        poverty of _____ .

    (d) The inability to initiate or persist in even
        simple forms of goal-directed behavior, such
        as dressing, bathing, or engaging in social
        activities, is called _____ ; the
        person seems to be completely
        _____ , sometimes sitting for
        hours at a time.

6. (a) The most common type of schizophrenia is
        characterized by the presence of delusions,
        hallucinations, or both; this is the
        _____ type. However, the per-
        son shows no _____ impair-
        ment, disorganized _____ , or

negative symptoms; instead, well-organized
delusions of persecution or grandeur are
operating.

    (b) A very rare type of schizophrenia is marked
        by highly disturbed movement or actions
        and is referred to as the _____
        type. Symptoms may include bizarre
        _____ or grimaces, extremely
        agitated behavior, complete
        _____ , echoing words just spo-
        ken by another person, or imitating the
        _____ of others.

    (c) In this type of schizophrenia, the person will
        resist direction from others and may also
        assume rigid _____
        to resist being moved; _____
        schizophrenia is often characterized by
        another unusual symptom, called waxy flexi-
        bility; like a wax figure, the person can be
        molded into any position and will hold that
        position indefinitely.

    (d) Extremely disorganized behavior, disorga-
        nized speech, and flat affect are the promi-
        nent features of the
        _____ type of
        schizophrenia.

    (e) A person with _____ type
        of schizophrenia sometimes experiences
        delusions and hallucinations but they are
        not well organized and integrated. Instead,
        they contain fragmented, shifting themes.
        Silliness, laughing, and giggling may occur
        for no apparent reason, and the person's
        behavior is very peculiar; this type of schizo-
        phrenia was formerly called
        _____ schizophrenia, and
        that term is still sometimes used.

    (f) When an individual displays a combination
        of positive and negative symptoms that do
        not clearly fit the criteria for the
        _____ , _____ , or

_____ types of schizophrenia, the label _____ type is used..

7. (a) The onset of schizophrenia typically occurs during _____ .

(b) Worldwide, no society or culture is immune to this mental disorder; most cultures _____ (do/do not) correspond very closely to the very low rate of schizophrenia seen in the United States.

(c) The course of schizophrenia _____ (is/is not) marked by enormous individual variability, but a few global generalizations are possible. About one-quarter of those who experience an episode of schizophrenia _____ (do/do not) recover completely and never experience another episode; another one-quarter experience _____ episodes of schizophrenia, but often with only minimal impairment in the ability to function.

(d) For the rest of those who have suffered an episode of schizophrenia, schizophrenia becomes a _____ mental illness, and the ability to function normally in society may be severely impaired. The people in this category face the prospect of repeated _____ and extended treatment, which places a heavy emotional, financial, and psychological burden on people with the disorder, their families, and society.

8. (a) Studies of families, twins, and adopted individuals have firmly established that _____ factors play a significant role in many cases of schizophrenia.

(b) First, studies have consistently shown that schizophrenia tends to cluster in certain _____ ; second, family and twin studies have consistently shown that the _____ a person is to someone who has schizophrenia, the greater the risk that she will be diagnosed with the disorder at some point in her lifetime; third, adoption studies have consistently shown that if either _____ parent of an adopted individual had schizophrenia, the adopted individual is at greater risk to develop schizophrenia.

(c) The strongest evidence that points to genetic involvement in schizophrenia—the _____ percent risk rate for a person whose identical twin has schizophrenia—is the same evidence that underscores the importance of environmental factors.

9. (a) According to the dopamine hypothesis, schizophrenia is related to _____ (excessive/reduced) dopamine activity in the brain.

(b) The idea that schizophrenia is the result of abnormal brain chemistry is supported largely by two pieces of _____ (direct/indirect) evidence: first, antipsychotic drugs that reduce schizophrenic symptoms in many people _____ or _____ dopamine activity in the brain; second, drugs such as amphetamines or cocaine _____ dopamine activity in the brain; use of these drugs can produce schizophrenia-like symptoms in normal adults or increase symptoms in people who already suffer from schizophrenia.

(c) Although the dopamine hypothesis is compelling, there are inconsistencies. Not all individuals who have schizophrenia experience a reduction of symptoms in response to antipsychotic drugs that _____ dopamine activity in the brain. And for many patients, these drugs reduce some, but not all, schizophrenic symptoms.

10. (a) Researchers have found that about half of the people with schizophrenia show some type of _____ structure abnormality.

(b) The most consistent finding has been the enlargement of the fluid-filled cavities called _____ located deep within the brain, but researchers are not sure how this might be related to schizophrenia.

(c) Differences in brain activity between schizophrenic and normal individuals have been revealed by _____ scans.

(d) These findings _____ (prove/do not prove) that schizophrenia is definitely caused by brain abnormalities; first, about _____ percent of the people suffering from schizophrenia do not show brain structure abnormalities; second, the evidence is _____ , and researchers are still investigating whether differences in brain structures and activity are the _____ or the _____ of schizophrenia; third, the kinds of brain abnormalities seen in schizophrenia are also seen in other mental disorders, and rather than specifically causing schizophrenia, it's possible that the brain abnormalities might contribute to mental disorders in general.

11. (a) One provocative theory is that schizophrenia might be caused by exposure to an influenza _____ or other _____ infection during prenatal development or shortly after birth. Such exposure is assumed to affect the developing brain, producing changes that make individuals more vulnerable to schizophrenia later in life.

(b) There is _____ (little/some) evidence to support the _____ infection theory. First, children whose mothers were exposed to a flu virus during the second trimester of pregnancy _____ (do/do not) show an increased rate of schizophrenia; second, schizophrenia occurs _____

(more/less) often in people who were born in the winter and spring months, when upper respiratory infections are most common.

12. (a) Researchers have investigated such psychological factors as dysfunctional _____ , disturbed _____ communication styles, and critical or guilt-inducing _____ styles as possible contributors to schizophrenia; however, no single psychological factor seems to emerge consistently as causing schizophrenia; rather, it seems that those who are _____ predisposed to develop schizophrenia may be more vulnerable to the effects of disturbed family environments.

(b) Researchers have found that adopted children with schizophrenic biological mothers have a much _____ (higher/lower) rate of schizophrenia and schizophrenia-related disorders than the children in a control group whose biological mothers were not schizophrenic.

(c) This finding was true only when the children were raised in a psychologically disturbed adoptive home; when children with a _____ background of schizophrenia were raised in a psychologically healthy adoptive family, they were _____ (more/no more) likely to develop schizophrenia than control-group children.

(d) Although adopted children with no genetic history of schizophrenia were _____ (more/less) vulnerable to the psychological stresses of a disturbed family environment, 33 percent of the control-group adoptees _____ (did/did not) develop symptoms of a serious mental disorder if they were raised in a disturbed family environment.

(e) A healthy psychological environment may

_____ a person's _____ vulnerability for schizophrenia; a psychologically unhealthy environment can act as a catalyst for the onset of schizophrenia, especially for those with a(n) _____ history of the disease.

(f) Thus far, no single _____ , _____ , or _____ factor has emerged as the causal agent in schizophrenia. Nevertheless, in the last few years, new antipsychotic drugs have been developed that are much more effective in treating both the _____ and _____ symptoms of schizophrenia.

13. Read the following and write the correct term in the space provided.

(a) Franko and Alberto are identical twins. Franko has developed schizophrenia. The probability that Alberto will also develop schizophrenia is about _____ percent.

(b) Dr. Hansen is conducting research on the viral infection theory. He is likely to find that people born in the winter and spring months, when upper respiratory infections are most common, are _____ (more/less) likely to suffer from schizophrenia than those born at other times of the year.

(c) Derrick hears voices that tell him to be careful because he is being watched by aliens. Kirk believes that he is a famous rock star. Derrick suffers from _____ , and Kirk suffers from _____ .

(d) Quincy falsely believes that others are plotting against him and are trying to kill him. He believes that these agents are putting poison in the hospital's coffee supply and will attack him if he ever tries to leave the ward. This example illustrates a positive symptom of schizophrenia called _____ .

(e) Regardless of the situation she is in, Parminder responds in an emotionally flat way, and she consistently shows a greatly reduced or complete lack of emotional responsiveness. She shows little in the way of expressive gestures or facial expressions, and her speech is slow and monotonous, without normal vocal inflections. These schizophrenic symptoms indicate that Parminder suffers from _____ , or _____ .

(f) Mrs. Perez usually sits passively in a motionless stupor, but if the nurse moves her arms to a new position, she will stay in that position for a very long time. This symptom of catatonic schizophrenia is called _____ .

(g) When Darcy was examined by his psychologist, she noted that he displayed some combination of positive and negative symptoms that did not clearly fit the criteria for _____ , _____ , or _____ types of schizophrenia, so she diagnosed him as having an undifferentiated type of schizophrenia.

Graphic Organizer 3

Write the main positive and negative symptoms of schizophrenia in the spaces provided.

Positive Symptoms	Negative Symptoms
1.	1.
2.	2.
3.	3.

Review of Terms and Concepts 3

Use the terms in this list to complete the Matching Test, then to help you answer the True/False items correctly.

schizophrenia
positive symptoms
negative symptoms
delusion
delusions of reference
delusions of grandeur
delusions of persecution
hallucination
flat affect
alogia (poverty of speech)
avolition

paranoid type of schizophrenia
catatonic type of schizophrenia
waxy flexibility
disorganized type of schizophrenia (hebephrenic schizophrenia)
undifferentiated type of schizophrenia
dopamine hypothesis

Matching Exercise

Match the appropriate term with its definition or description.

1. _____ View that schizophrenia is related to, and may be caused by, excess activity of the neurotransmitter dopamine in the brain.

2. _____ Mental disorder in which the ability to function is impaired by severely distorted beliefs, perceptions, and thought processes.

3. _____ Subtype of schizophrenia that is characterized by the presence of delusions, hallucinations, or both; the person shows virtually no cognitive impairment, disorganized behavior, or negative symptoms, but instead, well-organized delusions of persecution or grandeur are operating, and auditory hallucinations are often evident.

4. _____ Unusual symptom of catatonic schizophrenia in which the person can be molded into any position and will hold that position indefinitely.

5. _____ Commonly seen negative symptom of schizophrenia in which an individual consistently shows a dramatic reduction in emotional responsiveness and a lack of normal facial expression; few expressive gestures are made, and the person's speech is slow and monotonous, lacking normal vocal inflections.

6. _____ Falsely held belief that persists in spite of contradictory evidence.

7. _____ Delusion in which the person believes that other people are constantly talking about her or that everything that happens is somehow related to her.

8. _____ False or distorted perception that seems vividly real to the person experiencing it.

9. _____ Label for a subtype of schizophrenia that is used when an individual displays some combination of positive and negative symptoms that does not clearly fit the criteria for the paranoid, catatonic, or disorganized type.

True/False Test

Indicate whether each item is true or false by placing T or F in the space next to each item.

1. ___ In schizophrenia, positive symptoms reflect defects or deficits in normal functioning and include flat affect, alogia, and avolition.

2. ___ Avolition refers to the inability to initiate or persist in even simple forms of goal-directed behaviors, such as dressing, bathing, or engaging in social activities.

3. ___ The catatonic type of schizophrenia is marked by highly disturbed movements or actions and may include bizarre postures or grimaces, waxy flexibility, extremely agitated behavior, complete immobility, echoing words spoken by others, and assuming rigid postures that resist being moved.

4. ___ Alogia, which is also referred to as poverty of speech, is used to describe the symptom in which speech production is greatly reduced.

5. ___ The basic theme of delusions of grandeur is that the person is extremely important, powerful, or wealthy.

6. ___ In schizophrenia, negative symptoms reflect excesses or distortions of normal functioning and include delusions, hallucinations, and disorganized thoughts and behaviors.

7. ___ In delusions of persecution, the person believes that others are plotting against or trying to harm him or someone close to him.

8. ___ The prominent features of the disorganized type of schizophrenia are extremely disorganized behavior, disorganized speech, and flat affect; this subtype is sometimes called hebephrenic schizophrenia.

Check your answers and review any areas of weakness before going on to the next section.

Something to Think About

1. One of the most common misconceptions about mental, or psychological, disorders is that schizophrenia and multiple personality are the same thing. This myth is fostered by inaccurate portrayals and misinformation in the media. What are the important distinctions between these two disorders, and what would you say to someone who thought they were the same thing?

2. Most people are curious about mental, or psychological, disorders. Students frequently recog-

nize aspects of themselves in the descriptions they read and wonder if they could end up suffering from some form of psychological disorder. What is normal, and what is abnormal? What are the chances of developing symptoms of psychopathology, and what causes such disorders? How would you answer these questions?

Check your answers and review any areas of weakness before doing the progress tests.

Progress Test 1

Review the complete chapter (including Concept Reviews and the boxed inserts), review all your study notes, and then test yourself on the following progress test. Check your answers. If you make a mistake, review your notes, review the relevant section of the study guide, and, if necessary, go back and read the appropriate part of your textbook.

1. Phoebe believes that she is the president of the United States and thinks that her indecipherable scribblings are actually top secret memos. Phoebe is most clearly suffering from a(n)
   (a) delusion.   (c) hallucination.
   (b) panic attack.   (d) obsession.

2. Shayna has very erratic, unstable relationships, emotions, and self-image. She is extremely impulsive and goes to great lengths to avoid real or imagined abandonment. It is most probable that Shayna has a disorder called _____ personality disorder.
   (a) paranoid   (c) antisocial
   (b) borderline   (d) avoidant

3. Dr. Koopman deals with people who suffer from a variety of problems that cause significant personal distress and impair their ability to function in one or more important areas of their lives. Like most people in his profession, Dr. Koopman uses the term *mental disorder* to describe these symptoms. Dr. Koopman is most likely a
   (a) clinical psychologist.
   (b) psychiatrist.
   (c) social psychologist.
   (d) developmental psychologist.

4. Kaila often appears nervous and agitated. She frequently talks in a loud voice and giggles at almost everything she hears. Her behavior is most likely to be diagnosed as a psychological disorder if it
   (a) is not caused by some biological dysfunction.
   (b) is the result of a genetic predisposition.
   (c) represents a significant departure from the prevailing social and cultural norms.
   (d) is caused by drugs or medication.

5. Sidney, a college student, complains that he feels nervous and fearful most of the time but doesn't know why. He worries constantly about everything in his life, and if he manages to deal with one problem, he starts worrying about a dozen more things. Sidney most likely suffers from _____ disorder.
   (a) generalized anxiety
   (c) dissociative
   (b) bipolar
   (d) cyclothymic

6. Imogene, a third-grade teacher, sometimes experiences a pounding heart, rapid breathing, breathlessness, and a choking sensation. She breaks out in a sweat, starts to tremble, and experiences light-headedness and chills. These symptoms last for about ten minutes and are characteristic of
   (a) posttraumatic stress disorder (PTSD).
   (b) dysthymic disorder.
   (c) cyclothymic disorder.
   (d) panic attack.

7. Paula has been diagnosed with agoraphobia. Her symptoms include which of the following?
   (a) an extreme and irrational fear of experiencing a panic attack in a public place and being unable to escape or get help
   (b) a sudden, rapidly escalating emotional state characterized by extreme euphoria, excitement, physical energy, and rapid thoughts and speech
   (c) partial or total inability to recall important personal information
   (d) all of the above

8. Dr. Weinberg believes that phobias develop because humans are biologically prepared to acquire fears of certain animals and situations. Dr. Weinberg's position is most consistent with the _____ theory of phobias.
   (a) cognitive
   (c) evolutionary
   (b) learning
   (d) psychoanalytic

9. Jaime brushes her teeth 12 times every day. Each time, she uses exactly 35 strokes up and 35 strokes down and three different brands of toothpaste. Jaime suffers from a(n) _____ disorder.
   (a) obsessive-compulsive
   (b) panic
   (c) cyclothymic
   (d) bipolar

10. Kevin was working in a building when an explosion occurred; although he escaped with relatively minor injuries, he can't stop thinking about all the dead and seriously injured people he saw. He has frequent nightmares about the event and feels guilty that he survived when many of his coworkers did not. Kevin's symptoms are indicative of
    (a) dissociative fugue.
    (b) dysthymic disorder.
    (c) cyclothymic disorder.
    (d) posttraumatic stress disorder (PTSD).

11. Mrs. Landon has been diagnosed as suffering from major depression. Which of the following symptoms is she most likely to be experiencing?
    (a) feelings of guilt, worthlessness, inadequacy, emptiness, and hopelessness
    (b) awkward and slower than usual speech, movement, and gestures and frequent crying spells for no apparent reason
    (c) dull and sluggish thought processes and problems concentrating
    (d) loss of physical energy and vague aches and pains
    (e) all of the above

12. Karla suffers from a chronic, low-grade depression characterized by many of the symptoms of major depression but less intense; these problems started many years ago when both her parents were killed in a car accident. Karla is likely to be diagnosed as suffering from
    (a) dysthymic disorder.
    (b) agoraphobia.
    (c) cyclothymic disorder.
    (d) dissociative amnesia.

13. After living in Anchorage for a number of years, Juanitta was diagnosed with seasonal affective disorder (SAD). Episodes of depression are most likely to occur
    (a) when she travels south to visit her family in Florida.
    (b) during the fall and winter months.
    (c) during the day but not at night.
    (d) during the spring and summer months.

14. According to the Application, the best way to help prevent someone from committing suicide is to
    (a) use some well-known platitudes like "every cloud has a silver lining."
    (b) not let the person talk too much about what is bothering him because it will only make him more depressed.
    (c) suggest that seeking professional help would be a total waste of time and money in the present situation.
    (d) ask the person to delay his decision and encourage him to seek professional help.

15. According to Critical Thinking 14.1, which of the following is true?
    (a) People with mental disorders are generally portrayed with great accuracy in the media.
    (b) The statistical risk of violent behavior associated with mental illness is far higher than the risks associated with being young, male, or poorly educated.
    (c) The incidence of violent behavior among current or former mental patients is grossly exaggerated in media portrayals.
    (d) The statistical risk of violent behavior is greater among people with catatonic schizophrenia than among those with any other mental disorder.

Progress Test 2

After you have checked your understanding of the material in Progress Test 1 and have done a complete chapter review with special focus on any areas of weakness, you are ready to assess your knowledge of Progress Test 2. Check your answers. If you make a mistake, review your notes, the relevant section of the study guide, and, if necessary, the appropriate part of your textbook.

1. Dr. Moretti believes that schizophrenia is the result of abnormal brain chemistry. Her views are consistent with the
    (a) viral infection theory.
    (b) dopamine hypothesis.
    (c) genetic predisposition theory.
    (d) cognitive-behavioral theory.

2. When dealing with patients, psychiatrists, psychologists, and other mental health professionals are likely to refer to _____ to determine the criteria for a particular diagnosis.
    (a) pop psychology books
    (b) standard medical textbooks
    (c) DSM-IV
    (d) astrology charts

3. Dr. Crewe believes that people with panic disorder tend to misinterpret the physical signs of arousal as catastrophic and dangerous, and this misinterpretation only adds to the problem by causing even more physiological arousal. Eventually, they become conditioned to respond with fear to the physical symptoms of arousal, and repeated panic attacks lead to panic disorder. Dr. Crewe's explanation is most consistent with the _____ of panic disorder.
    (a) social-cultural explanation
    (b) biological theory
    (c) cognitive-behavioral theory
    (d) genetic predisposition explanation

4. Nima suffers from a type of schizophrenia that is characterized by hallucinations and delusions of grandeur, but she shows virtually no cognitive impairment, disorganized behavior, or negative symptoms. Nima suffers from _____ -type schizophrenia.
    (a) paranoid   (c) disorganized
    (b) catatonic   (d) undifferentiated

5. Tara, a young married women, has wandered from her home to a distant city where she has completely forgotten her family and her identity. This example illustrates
    (a) undifferentiated-type schizophrenia.
    (b) dissociative fugue.
    (c) disorganized-type schizophrenia.
    (d) dissociative amnesia.

6. Maury repeatedly checks to see if the stove is turned off and frequently turns around on his way to work to go back home to double check. This is an example of a(n)
    (a) delusion.   (c) hallucination.
    (b) obsession.   (d) compulsion.

7. Otis turned down a very highly paid job because it meant he would have to fly to the head office in Tokyo two or three times a year. He doesn't know why, but the thought of flying absolutely terrifies him. Otis may have
(a) undifferentiated-type schizophrenia.
(b) a phobia.
(c) bipolar disorder.
(d) posttraumatic stress disorder (PTSD).

8. Every semester just before midterm exams, Lilly gets very anxious and worries about how she is going to do. To reduce her apprehension, she studies very hard. Lilly suffers from
(a) anxiety disorder.
(b) free-floating disorder.
(c) panic disorder.
(d) obsessive-compulsive disorder.
(e) none of the above; her symptoms are quite normal.

9. Jessica rarely leaves her home. She doesn't go shopping because she is frightened of having a panic attack and getting lost or trapped in a crowd. Jessica has symptoms that indicate she may have
(a) agoraphobia.
(b) cyclothymic disorder.
(c) posttraumatic stress disorder (PTSD).
(d) seasonal affective disorder (SAD).

10. Yvette usually stands motionless and will echo words just spoken to her. She resists directions from others and sometimes assumes a rigid posture to prevent people from moving her. These symptoms suggest that Yvette has a type of _____ called _____ type.
(a) schizophrenia; catatonic
(b) mood disorder; cyclothymic
(c) schizophrenia; disorganized
(d) mood disorder; systemic

11. Brandy's doctor prescribed lithium for her symptoms, and as long as she keeps taking the medication, she feels fine. It is very likely that Brandy suffers from
(a) schizophrenia.
(b) generalized anxiety disorder.
(c) bipolar disorder.
(d) dissociative identity disorder (DID).

12. Regardless of the situation he is in, Phillip responds in an emotionally flat manner and consistently shows greatly reduced lack of emotional responsiveness or facial expression. His speech is slow and monotonous, and he is unable to initiate even simple forms of goal-directed behavior, such as dressing, bathing, or engaging in social activities. Phillip is suffering from _____ and his symptoms are _____ .
(a) schizophrenia; positive
(b) anxiety disorder; positive
(c) schizophrenia; negative
(d) anxiety disorder; negative

13. Perry has dropped out of college because of the extreme distress that being in social situations causes him. He is unemployed because he is unable to bring himself to partake in an interview. Perry has
(a) disorganized-type schizophrenia.
(b) a dissociative disorder.
(c) a generalized anxiety disorder.
(d) social phobia.

14. Within the last two years John has been fired from four different jobs for stealing money and goods from his employers. He feels no remorse and thinks his bosses were stupid for making it so easy to steal from them. John has a long history of problems with the law, which started in his early teens when he was diagnosed as having a conduct disorder. It is most likely that John has a(n) _____ personality disorder.
(a) antisocial   (c) borderline
(b) obsessive-compulsive (d) paranoid

15. According to Culture and Human Behavior 14.3, which of the following is true?
(a) The content of schizophrenic hallucinations and delusions is virtually identical across cultures.
(b) People with a mental disorder who are not actively suffering from the symptoms of the disorder are twice as dangerous and violent as normal people.
(c) The content of schizophrenic hallucinations and delusions can vary tremendously from one culture to another.
(d) Schizophrenia is much more prevalent in North America than in any other part of the world.

Progress Test 3

After you have checked your understanding of the material in Progress Tests 1 and 2, and have done a complete chapter review with special focus on any areas of weakness, you are ready to further assess your knowledge on Progress Test 3. Check your answers. If you make a mistake, review your notes, the appropriate parts of the study guide, and if necessary, the relevant sections of your textbook.

1. Wendell repeatedly steals small items that he doesn't need and could easily pay for if he wanted to. Harman frequently sets fire to property for no obvious reason other than the pleasure he derives from seeing buildings on fire. According to Table 14.1: Some Key Diagnostic Categories in DSM IV, Wendell suffers from _____ and Harman has a disorder called _____ .
   - (a) kleptomania; pyromania
   - (b) Tourette's disorder; hypochondriasis
   - (c) autistic disorder; fetishism
   - (d) agoraphobia; pyrophobia

2. Fear of having a panic attack in a public situation is to _____ as an extreme and irrational of being embarrassed, judged, or scrutinized by others in social situations is to _____ .
   - (a) claustrophobia; pyrophobia
   - (b) monophobia; xenophobia
   - (c) agoraphobia; social phobia
   - (d) cynophobia; claustrophobia

3. Shayne suffers from posttraumatic stress disorder (PTSD). If he is similar to most people who have this disorder, he is likely to exhibit which of the following symptoms?
   - (a) frequent, intrusive recollections of a traumatic event, numbing of emotional responsiveness, and avoidance of particular situations
   - (b) recurrent episodes of unintended sleep in inappropriate situations, such as during a meeting or while driving a car
   - (c) repetitive behaviors or mental acts that are performed to prevent or reduce anxiety
   - (d) the urge to set fires for pleasure, gratification, or relief of tension

4. Mandy is a forty-five-year-old administrative assistant. Based on the National Comorbidity Survey (NCS), the chance that Mandy may have experienced the symptoms of a psychological disorder at some point in her life is about _____ percent.
   - (a) 10
   - (b) 50
   - (c) 80
   - (d) 100

5. Dr. Burstein explains the development of phobias in terms of basic learning principles. Which of the following are likely to be included in his explanation?
   - (a) classical conditioning
   - (b) operant condition
   - (c) observational learning
   - (d) All of the above may be involved in his explanation.

6. After several weeks of feeling very apathetic and dissatisfied with his life, Elmiro has suddenly become extremely euphoric and full of energy. He talks so rapidly that he is hard to understand, sleeps very little, and has gone on a number of very expensive shopping sprees. He gets very irritated when anyone tells him to take it easy and slow down. Elmiro is exhibiting all the signs of
   - (a) obsessive-compulsive disorder.
   - (b) catatonic schizophrenia.
   - (c) dissociative identity disorder (DID).
   - (d) bipolar disorder.

7. Lucille suffers from dissociative identity disorder (DID). If she is like most people diagnosed with this disorder, she is likely to have experienced
   - (a) extreme physical or sexual abuse in childhood.
   - (b) episodes when she believed she was the reincarnation of some famous and powerful person.
   - (c) exposure to a viral infection during prenatal development or early infancy.
   - (d) excess dopamine in her brain during childhood.

8. During a religious ceremony in his local Christian church, Billy Joe suddenly starts speaking very rapidly in what appears to be a number of different languages and appears to be in a trancelike state. This form of dissociative experience is called _____ and is classified in DSM-IV as _____ .
   - (a) fugue state; pathological
   - (b) glossolalia; normal
   - (c) fugue state; normal
   - (d) glossolalia; pathological

9. Dr. Krane is involved in the scientific study of the origins, symptoms, and development of psychological disorders. Dr. Krane's specialty area is
   - (a) psychopathology.
   - (b) personality.
   - (c) perception.
   - (d) psychosocioimmunology.

10. Vera has been diagnosed with cyclothymic disorder. Her symptoms are likely to include
    - (a) moderate but frequent mood swings for two years or longer.
    - (b) chronic low-grade feelings of depression that produce subjective discomfort but do not seriously impair her ability to function.
    - (c) partial or total inability to recall important personal information.
    - (d) irrational fears of a specific object or situation.
    - (e) all of the above.

11. Nester's sense of self-esteem is wildly inflated, and he exudes supreme self-confidence. He has delusional, grandiose plans for obtaining wealth, power, and fame and is engaged in a frenzy of goal-directed activities that could cost thousands of dollars. This is an example of a(n)
    - (a) manic episode.
    - (b) obsession.
    - (c) social phobia.
    - (d) hallucination.

12. Deidre suffers from frequent and unexpected panic attacks. Despite her apprehension about these episodes, Deidre functions fairly well in her job and has a relatively normal social life. Deidre is likely to be diagnosed with
    - (a) panic disorder.
    - (b) social phobia.
    - (c) bipolar disorder.
    - (d) dissociative fugue.

13. Scott repeatedly thinks that he might get a gun and kill all his colleagues at work. These thoughts are very disturbing, intrusive, and uncontrollable and cause Scott great distress and anxiety. Scott is experiencing a(n)
    - (a) delusion.
    - (b) obsession.
    - (c) hallucination.
    - (d) compulsion.

14. Regarding the classification of personality disorders, the odd, eccentric cluster is to _____ personality disorder as the dramatic, emotional, erratic cluster is to _____ personality disorder.
    - (a) obsessive-compulsive; narcissistic
    - (b) histrionic; avoidant
    - (c) borderline; antisocial
    - (d) paranoid; antisocial

15. According to Critical Thinking 14.2, which of the following statements about DID is (are) true?
    - (a) Much of the skepticism about DID is related to the fact that the number of reported cases has decreased dramatically in the last two decades.
    - (b) Some psychologists suggest that DID patients are consciously or unconsciously faking the symptoms, responding to the therapists suggestions, or mimicking the symptoms of sensational DID cases portrayed in the media.
    - (c) Cross-cultural research has shown that the incidence of DID outside the United States is almost zero.
    - (d) Most psychologists believe that DID and schizophrenia are identical disorders.
    - (e) All of the above are true.

Answers

Introduction: Understanding Psychological Disorders

1. (a) is not; degree
   (b) origins, symptoms
   (c) mental; physical; physical; psychological

2. (a) psychologists; psychiatrists
   (b) behavioral; psychological; distress; function
   (c) *Diagnostic; Statistical*
   (d) symptoms; criteria; diagnosis
   (e) language; guidelines

3. (a) their lifetimes; the past 12 months
   (b) had not
   (c) do not; stigma
   (d) most

(e) different; higher; higher

(f) anxiety; mood; dissociative; personality; schizophrenia

Anxiety Disorders

1. (a) physical; tension, apprehension; adaptive; normal
   (b) physical; mental
   (c) maladaptive
   (d) irrational; exaggerated; nonexistent; uncontrollable; disruptive; interferes

2. (a) main
   (b) generalized; panic
   (c) phobia
   (d) posttraumatic stress
   (e) obsessive-compulsive

3. (a) global, persistent, chronic
   (b) free-floating

4. (a) sudden; extreme; pounding; rapid
   (b) terror; 10
   (c) frequently; unexpectedly; frequency

5. (a) biological; psychological; biological
   (b) panic prone; physiological
   (c) cognitive-behavioral; apprehensive
   (d) conditioned; conditioned
   (e) cultures; culture

6. (a) intense, irrational; panic attack
   (b) avoid; irrational
   (c) common; terror; anxiety
   (d) specific; twice; specific

7. (a) situations
   (b) features; environment
   (c) injury, blood
   (d) animals; insects

8. (a) panic attack; panic attack
   (b) most
   (c) specific; panic attack

9. (a) social; social
   (b) social; panic attack
   (c) self-esteem; social
   (d) social

10. (a) conditioned; conditioned response
    (b) conditioned response; negatively
    (c) observing; model
    (d) cannot; most

11. (a) biologically; disgust
    (b) disease; filth; infection
    (c) learning; biological

Anxiety Disorders: Posttraumatic Stress Disorder and Obsessive-Compulsive Disorder

1. (a) physical; psychological; helplessness
   (b) military combat (war); disasters; assault
   (c) frequently; stimuli; situations; arousal; startled; sleep
   (d) depression; guilt; substance; depression, panic disorder
   (e) more; an important; more; multiple traumas

2. (a) repetitive; obsessions; compulsions
   (b) repeated, intrusive, uncontrollable
   (c) repetitive; ritualistic
   (d) overt; covert; tension, anxiety
   (e) satisfaction; distressing; anxiety-provoking

3. (a) both obsessions and compulsions
   (b) similar; content
   (c) biological; serotonin
   (d) frontal; movements

4. (a) mental; psychological
   (b) normal
   (c) obsessive-compulsive
   (d) generalized anxiety
   (e) social phobia
   (f) posttraumatic stress
   (g) panic attacks

Graphic Organizer 1

Generalized Anxiety Disorder
Persistent, chronic, unreasonable worry and anxiety, characterized by general symptoms of anxiety, including persistent physical arousal.

Panic Disorder
Frequent and unexpected panic attacks, with no specific or identifiable trigger.

Phobias
Intense anxiety or panic attack triggered by a specific object or situation leads to persistent avoidance of feared object or situation.

Posttraumatic Stress Disorder
Anxiety triggered by memories of an extreme physical or psychological traumatic experience.

Obsessive-Compulsive Disorder
Anxiety caused by uncontrollable, persistent, recurring, and intrusive thoughts (obsessions) and/or urges to perform certain actions (compulsions).

Matching Exercise 1

1. psychopathology
2. DSM-IV
3. obsessive-compulsive disorder
4. anxiety
5. phobia
6. posttraumatic stress disorder (PTSD)
7. agoraphobia
8. specific phobia

True/False Test 1

1. F   4. T   7. T
2. T   5. F   8. T
3. T   6. T

Mood Disorders: Emotions Gone Awry

1. (a) criteria
   (b) serious, persistent; psychological; function
2. (a) emotional, behavioral, cognitive; physical
   (b) guilt; alone; disconnected
   (c) speech, movement; crying
   (d) concentrating; thoughts; suicide
   (e) mental; physical; physical
3. (a) motivation; drive; disturbed; diminishes
   (b) nondreaming; reduced; REM
   (c) two; external; negative; stressful
   (d) normal; two
4. (a) dysthymic; chronic
   (b) stressful
   (c) dysthymic; double; dysthymic
5. (a) most
   (b) twice
   (c) most; greater
   (d) by themselves; is not
   (e) half; increase; decreases
   (f) seasons; autumn (fall); winter; fall; winter; women

Mood Disorders: Bipolar Disorder

1. (a) manic depression; both
   (b) depression; manic; manic; depression; manic
2. (a) suddenly; escalate rapidly
   (b) self-esteem; self-confidence
   (c) manic
   (d) flight of ideas
   (e) hospitalization
   (f) obnoxious; verbally
3. (a) cyclothymic

(b) bipolar; depression
(c) cyclothymic

4. (a) early twenties; manic; depressive
   (b) does not
   (c) recurring; rapid cycling; manic; depressive; lithium
5. (a) genetic predisposition
   (b) three
   (c) 70; has
6. (a) serotonin; norepinephrine; norepinephrine; serotonin; effective
   (b) lithium; glutamate
7. (a) traumatic; stressful; previous
   (b) chronic stress; stressful

Graphic Organizer 2

Major Depression

1. Loss of interest or pleasure in almost all activities
2. Despondent mood, feelings of emptiness or worthlessness, or excessive guilt
3. Preoccupation with death or suicidal thoughts
4. Difficulty sleeping or excessive sleeping
5. Diminished ability to think, concentrate, or make decisions
6. Diminished appetite and significant weight loss or excessive eating and weight gain

Bipolar Disorder

1. One or more manic episodes characterized by euphoria, high energy, grandiose ideas, flight of ideas, inappropriate self-confidence, and decreased need for sleep
2. Usually also has one or more episodes of major depression
3. May alternate rapidly between symptoms of mania and major depression

Dysthymic Disorder

1. Chronic, low-grade depressed feelings that are not severe enough to qualify as major depression

Cyclothymic Disorder

1. Moderate, recurring, up-and-down mood swings that are not severe enough to qualify as major depression or bipolar disorder

Personality Disorders: Maladaptive Traits

1. (a) inflexible; maladaptive; stable
   (b) paranoid, schizoid; schizotypal; antisocial; borderline; histrionic; narcissistic; avoidant, dependent; obsessive-compulsive
   (c) is

2. (a) pervasive mistrust; suspiciousness; men
   (b) reluctant; a strong; often; commonly
   (c) schizotypal; avoidant

3. (a) psychopath; sociopath; lie, cheat, steal; little or no
   (b) disregarding and violating the rights of others; men; women
   (c) often seen; diminish
   (d) childhood; substance abuse; brain chemistry; parenting; family; parental; genetic
   (e) little; often fail

4. (a) emotions, self-image; uncontrollable, intense
   (b) most; women
   (c) emptiness; abandonment; unstable
   (d) self-destructive; gamble; abuse; sexually
   (e) attachment relationships; physical, sexual; emotional

The Dissociative Disorders: Fragmentation of the Self

1. (a) associated; well integrated; separated; divided
   (b) are not; common; normal
   (c) normal; spirit possession
   (d) trance state
   (e) glossolalia
   (f) are not

2. (a) abnormal; extreme; frequent; persistent
   (b) memories; identity

3. (a) dissociative amnesia
   (b) amnesia; amnesia
   (c) amnesia; fugue

4. (a) multiple personality; identities; personalities
   (b) personality; personalities
   (c) 10; 15

5. (a) people; personality
   (b) personality; unaware; may
   (c) brain function
   (d) amnesia; memory; are not
   (e) psychiatric; physical
   (f) depression, anxiety; sleep; psychological

6. (a) coping; high
   (b) dissociates; personalities
   (c) anger, rage, fear; defense mechanism
   (d) coping

7. (a) seasonal affective
   (b) genetic
   (c) bipolar
   (d) cyclothymic
   (e) obsessive compulsive; narcissistic
   (f) dissociative fugue
   (g) dissociative experience

(h) dissociative amnesia
(i) antisocial; paranoid

Matching Exercise 2

1. antisocial personality disorder
2. bipolar disorder
3. seasonal affective disorder (SAD)
4. spirit possession
5. major depression
6. manic episode
7. dissociative experience
8. personality disorders
9. dissociative identity disorder (DID)
10. mood disorders

True/False Test 2

1. T	4. T	7. T
2. T	5. F	8. T
3. F	6. F	9. F

Schizophrenia: A Different Reality

1. (a) beliefs; perceptions; thought; chaos, disorientation
   (b) delusions; hallucinations; thought; speech
   (c) motivation, emotional; speech
   (d) month; six
   (e) onset; intensity

2. (a) falsely; belief; psychological; social; occupational
   (b) person; experiencing
   (c) reference
   (d) grandeur
   (e) persecution
   (f) inappropriate; bizarre

3. (a) false; distorted; ongoing; persistent
   (b) auditory; visual; auditory
   (c) delusional; delusions; grandeur; delusions; persecution
   (d) can be virtually impossible to distinguish; may; months; years

4. (a) distorted; thinking; concentrate, remember
   (b) thinking; speech

5. (a) delusions, hallucinations; sensations; behavior; emotional
   (b) flat affect; affective flattening; "flat"; gestures; speech
   (c) alogia; speech
   (d) avolition; apathetic

6. (a) paranoid; cognitive; behavior
   (b) catatonic; postures; immobility; movements
   (c) postures; catatonic
   (d) disorganized
   (e) disorganized; hebephrenic
   (f) paranoid, catatonic; disorganized; undifferentiated

7. (a) young adulthood
   (b) do
   (c) is; do; recurrent
   (d) chronic; hospitalizations

8. (a) genetic
   (b) families; more closely related; biological
   (c) 50

9. (a) excessive
   (b) indirect; reduce; block; enhance
   (c) reduce

10. (a) brain
    (b) ventricles
    (c) PET
    (d) do not prove; 50; correlational; cause; consequence

11. (a) virus; viral
    (b) some; viral; do; more

12. (a) parenting; family; parenting; genetically
    (b) higher
    (c) genetic; no more
    (d) less; did
    (e) counteract; inherited; genetic
    (f) biological, psychological; social; positive; negative

13. (a) 50
    (b) more
    (c) hallucinations; delusions
    (d) delusions of persecution
    (e) flat affect; affective flattening
    (f) waxy flexibility
    (g) paranoid, catatonic; disorganized

Graphic Organizer 3

Positive Symptoms
1. delusions
2. hallucinations
3. disorganized thoughts and behavior

Negative Symptoms
1. flat effect
2. alogia (poverty of speech)
3. avolition

Matching Exercise 3

1. dopamine hypothesis
2. schizophrenia
3. paranoid type of schizophrenia
4. waxy flexibility
5. flat affect
6. delusion
7. delusions of reference
8. hallucination
9. undifferentiated type of schizophrenia

True/False Test 3

1. F	4. T	7. T
2. T	5. T	8. T
3. T	6. F	

Something to Think About

1. Multiple personality disorder, now called dissociative identity disorder (DID), involves extensive memory disruptions for personal information along with the presence of two or more distinct identities or personalities. Typically, each personality has its own name and each will be experienced as if it has its own personal history and self-image. These alternate personalities, or alters, may be of widely varying ages and of different genders. Typically, the primary personality is unaware of the existence of the alternate personalities. However, the alters may have knowledge of each other's existence and share memories. Sometimes the experiences of one alter are accessible to another alter but not vice versa. From this description of the disorder, it is clear that symptoms of amnesia and memory problems are a central part of DID. In addition, people with DID have numerous psychiatric and physical symptoms as well as a chaotic personal history.

   Contrast DID with a description of schizophrenia, and the differences between the two disorders become apparent. Schizophrenia is a psychological disorder that involves severely distorted beliefs, perceptions, and thought processes. During a schizophrenic episode, people lose their grip on reality. The positive symptoms of schizophrenia reflect an excess or distortion of normal functioning and include hallucinations, delusions, and severely disorganized thought processes, speech, and behavior. The negative symptoms reflect a restriction or reduction of normal functions and include flat affect, alogia (poverty of speech), and avolition, or the inability to initiate or persist in even simple forms of goal-directed behavior. There are four different subtypes of schizophrenia: paranoid type, catatonic type, disorganized type, and undifferentiated type. In addition, as noted in the text, the prevalence, course, and cause of schizophrenia are markedly different from those of DID.

2. The first thing to note is that the line that divides normal and abnormal behavior is not clearly defined. In addition, it is affected by the social and cultural context in which the behavior occurs. Psychopathology is the scientific study of the origins, symptoms, and development of psychological disorders, and as you learned in this chapter, DSM-IV is the book that describes about 250 specific disorders, including their symptoms, the exact criteria that must be met to make a diagnosis, and the typical course of each psychological disorder. The main categories of psychological disorders are the anxiety disorders, mood disorders, personality disorders, dissociative disorders, and schizophrenia.

According to your text, the chance that someone will experience symptoms of psychological disorder some time in his or her lifetime is fifty-fifty. About one in three people will have experienced the symptoms of psychological disorder during the last year. However, about 80 percent of those people will not have sought professional help. The good news is that most people seem to weather the symptoms without becoming completely debilitated and without professional intervention. It is estimated that 3 to 5 percent of people have really serious symptoms that demand immediate treatment, and these people usually have developed several mental disorders over time, not just one disorder that suddenly appears. Women tend to have a higher prevalence of anxiety and depression, whereas men tend to have a higher prevalence of substance abuse disorders.

Nobody knows for sure what causes psychological disorders. There is no shortage of theories, however. Biological and genetic factors have been implicated, as have abnormalities in brain structure and chemical imbalances. Various environmental and social explanations have also been suggested. Research continues, and someday we may be closer to finding the cause or causes of these abnormalities.

Progress Test 1

1. a	6. d	11. e
2. b	7. a	12. a
3. b	8. c	13. b
4. c	9. a	14. d
5. a	10. d	15. c

Progress Test 2

1. b	6. d	11. c
2. c	7. b	12. c
3. c	8. e	13. d
4. a	9. a	14. a
5. b	10. a	15. c

Progress Test 3

1. a	6. d	11. a
2. c	7. a	12. a
3. a	8. b	13. b
4. b	9. a	14. b
5. d	10. a	15. b

CHAPTER 15

Therapies

CHAPTER 15 . . . AT A GLANCE

Chapter 15 discusses the use of psychotherapies and biomedical therapies to treat psychological disorders. Psychoanalysis, which is based on Freud's theory of personality, is described, including its basic assumptions and the techniques used in the psychoanalytic process. Client-centered therapy is discussed as the prime example of the humanistic approach to psychotherapy, and the basic assumptions of this form of insight therapy are explored. Behavior therapy is based on learning principles and assumes that maladaptive behaviors are learned. The techniques used to facilitate change are examined. The cognitive therapies, which assume that psychological problems are caused by maladaptive patterns of thinking, are explored next.

Group and family therapies are contrasted with individual therapy, and the advantages and benefits of each are examined. The relationship between culture and psychotherapy is discussed, and cross-cultural differences in assumptions, expectations, and techniques are noted. The effectiveness of psychotherapy is explored, and it is concluded that, in general, psychotherapy is better than no treatment at all and that no particular form of psychotherapy is superior to any other.

In introducing the biomedical therapies, the text notes that the most common biomedical therapy is psychoactive medication. The discussion includes the nature of these drugs, their effects on the brain, their side effects, and the disorder for which they are prescribed. The main categories of drugs are antipsychotic, antianxiety, and antidepressant medications. Lithium is prescribed for bipolar disorder. Electroconvulsive therapy (ECT), a different type of biomedical therapy, is used for treating severe depression.

Introduction: Psychotherapy and Biomedical Therapy

Preview Questions

Consider the following questions as you study this section of the chapter.

- How is psychotherapy defined, and what types of problems are treated using psychotherapy?
- What is the basic assumption common to all forms of psychotherapy?
- What is biomedical therapy, and how does it differ from psychotherapy?

*Read the section "Introduction: Psychotherapy and Biomedical Therapy" and **write** your answers to the following:*

1. (a) Many people seek help from mental health professionals because they are suffering from some form of _____ ; in addition, many people seek help in dealing with _____ relationships, such as an unhappy marriage, or in dealing with life's _____ , such as coping with the death of a loved one or adjusting to retirement.

    (b) Psychotherapy refers to the use of _____ techniques to treat _____ , _____ , and _____ problems; although there are hundreds of forms of psychotherapy, they all share the assumption that _____ factors play a significant role in a person's troubled feelings, behaviors, or relationships.

    (c) Biomedical therapies involve the use of _____ or other _____ procedures to treat the symptoms associated with psychological disorders; these treatments are based on the assumption that the symptoms of many _____ disorders involve _____ factors, such as abnormal brain chemistry.

    (d) There has been a steadily growing trend to combine biomedical therapy and psychotherapy in treating _____ disorders. Traditionally, only licensed physicians, such as _____ , have been allowed to prescribe the different forms of biomedical therapy, but in recent years, some clinical psychologists with additional training have been allowed to prescribe medications to treat these disorders.

    (e) The most influential approaches in psychotherapy are _____ , _____ , _____ , and _____ .

Psychoanalytic Therapy

Preview Questions

Consider the following questions as you study this section of the chapter.

- What is psychoanalysis, and who developed this form of therapy?
- What techniques are used in psychoanalysis, and what is their purpose?
- What role does insight play, and what are short-term dynamic therapies?

*Read the section "Psychoanalytic Therapy" and **write** your answers to the following:*

1. (a) Psychoanalysis is a form of psychotherapy originally developed by Sigmund Freud in the early 1900s and is based on his theory of _____ ; its assumptions and techniques _____ (are no longer/continue to be) influential today.

    (b) Freud stressed that _____ experiences lay the foundation for later personality development. When these experiences result in _____ conflicts and _____ urges, these emotionally charged memories are _____ , or pushed out of conscious awareness, but continue to influence a person's thoughts and behavior, including the dynamics of relationships with others.

(c) According to Freud, these conflicts festering in the unconscious are at the core of _____ behavior and _____ disorders. To achieve psychological health, Freud believed it is essential to move these conflicts from the _____ to _____ awareness.

(d) Psychoanalysis is designed to help unearth past conflicts so that the patient attains _____ as to the real source of her problems. Central to this process is the intense _____ that gradually forms between the psychoanalyst and the patient in order for the patient to reexperience and resolve the conflicts.

(e) Freud believed that unconscious material can be glimpsed in disguised form in _____ , _____ lapses, inadvertent _____ , and even apparent accidents.

2. (a) Freud also developed several techniques to coax a patient's _____ conflicts to _____ awareness. In the famous technique called _____ , the patient lies on a couch and spontaneously reports all _____ , _____ , and _____ as they come to mind; along with the general themes that keep resurfacing, the psychoanalyst notes occasional _____ comments and these are explored for their possible meaning.

(b) Even more significant are blocks in _____ , an abrupt change in topic, or sudden silences; these may be signs of _____ , which is the patient's unconscious attempts to block the process of revealing _____ memories and conflicts.

(c) Another technique that Freud made famous is _____ interpretation; because psychological defenses are reduced during _____ , he believed that frustrated desires, impulses, and motives are expressed symbolically in _____ .

(d) According to Freud, we consciously remember the _____ content, or actual dream images, but beneath these surface images is the _____ content, which is the true, hidden, and unconscious meaning of the dream that is disguised in dream symbols.

(e) In addition to asking _____ , confronting patterns of _____ , and encouraging the patient to _____ on thoughts, the analyst makes carefully timed _____ ; these involve explaining the possible meaning of _____ , _____ , instances of _____ , or the patient's reactions to the psychoanalyst.

(f) One of the most important processes that occurs in the relationship between the patient and the psychoanalyst is called _____ ; this occurs when the patient unconsciously responds to the therapist as though the therapist were a significant person in the patient's life, often a parent. This process is encouraged by the therapist's neutrality.

(g) All these psychoanalytic techniques are designed to help the patient see how _____ conflicts influence his current _____ and _____ ; once these kinds of _____ are achieved, the psychoanalyst helps the patient work through and resolve longstanding conflicts.

(h) On average, traditional psychoanalysis is a _____ , expensive process.

3. (a) Today, _____ (few/many) psychotherapists practice traditional psychoanalysis lasting for years; people are usually looking for help with _____ problems that require only weeks or months to resolve. Regardless of which type of therapy is used, the average duration of therapeutic contact is only about _____ sessions.

(b) Today, there are many different forms of short-term dynamic therapies that are based on traditional psychoanalytic notions and have many features in common: (1) contact lasts for no more than _____ ; (2) the patient's problems are _____ assessed at the beginning of therapy; (3) the therapist and patient agree on _____ , _____ , and attainable goals; and (4) in the actual sessions, most psychodynamic therapists are more _____ than traditional psychoanalysts, actively engaging the patient in a dialogue.

(c) As in traditional psychoanalysis, the therapist uses _____ to help the patient recognize hidden _____ and _____ that may be occurring in important relationships in her life; therapy also focuses on helping the patient identify _____ resources she can use to cope with the current difficulty as well as future problems.

(d) Traditional, lengthy psychoanalysis is _____ (frequently/seldom) practiced today, but Freud's basic assumptions and techniques _____ (are no longer/continue to be) influential.

4. Read the following and write the correct term in the space provided.

(a) Felicity had a very bizarre dream in which she was playing pool with a very big cue and she didn't miss a single shot. According to Freud, this account represents the _____ content of her dream.

(b) Her psychoanalyst interpreted the big cue, the pool balls, and the pockets in Felicity's dream as symbols of sexual organs. The therapist is focusing on the _____ content of her dream.

(c) When she was asked to elaborate on the dream and talk about her feelings, Felicity said that the dream was simply about playing pool, nothing more. This response is likely to be interpreted as a sign of _____ .

(d) Although her therapist has remained neutral and nonjudgmental throughout their sessions, Felicity is beginning to express feelings of hostility and anger toward him. This part of the psychoanalytic process is called _____ .

Review of Terms, Concepts, and Names 1

Use the terms in this list to complete the Matching Test, then to help you answer the True/False items correctly.

psychotherapy
biomedical therapies
psychoanalysis
Sigmund Freud
insight
free association
resistance
dream interpretation
manifest content
latent content
interpretation
transference
short-term dynamic therapies

Matching Exercise

Match the appropriate term/name with its definition or description.

1. _____ Founder of psychoanalysis who theorized that psychological symptoms are the result of unconscious and unresolved conflicts stemming from early childhood.

2. _____ The treatment of emotional, behavioral, and interpersonal problems through the use of psychological techniques designed to encourage understanding of problems and modify troubling feelings, behaviors, or relationships.

3. _____ Psychoanalytic technique in which the psychoanalyst offers a carefully timed explanation of the patient's dreams, free associations, or behavior to facilitate the recognition of unconscious conflicts or motivations.

4. _____ Type of psychotherapy originated by Sigmund Freud in which free association, dream interpretation, and analysis of resistance and transference are used to explore repressed or unconscious impulses, anxieties, and internal conflicts.

5. _____ The use of medications, electroconvulsive therapy, or other medical treatment to treat the symptoms associated with psychological disorders.

6. _____ Psychotherapies that are based on traditional psychoanalytic notions in which therapeutic contact typically lasts for no more than a few months rather than years.

7. _____ In psychoanalysis, the process by which emotions and desires originally associated with a significant person in the patient's life, such as a parent, are unconsciously transferred to the psychoanalyst.

True/False Test

Indicate whether each statement is true or false by placing T or F in the blank space next to each item.

1. ____ Psychoanalysts believe that it is essential to move conflicts from the patient's unconscious to his or her conscious awareness. The process of recognizing and ultimately resolving these longstanding repressed conflicts is called insight.

2. ____ Freud called the remembered story or the actual dream images the latent content of the dream.

3. ____ In psychoanalysis, the patient's unconscious attempts to block the revelation of repressed memories and conflicts is called resistance.

4. ____ Dream interpretation is a technique used in psychoanalysis in which the content of dreams is analyzed for disguised or symbolic wishes, meanings, and motivations.

5. ____ Free association is a technique used in psychoanalysis in which the patient spontaneously reports all thoughts, feelings, and mental images as they come to mind as a way of revealing unconscious thoughts and emotions.

6. ____ Freud called the true, hidden, and unconscious meaning of the dream that is disguised in dream symbols the manifest content.

> Check your answers and review any areas of weakness before going on to the next section.

Humanistic Therapy

Preview Questions

Consider the following questions as you study this section of the chapter.

- What is the main humanistic therapy, and who developed it?
- What therapeutic conditions and techniques are important in client-centered therapy?
- How do client-centered therapy and psychoanalysis differ as insight therapies?

*Read the section "Humanistic Therapy" and **write** your answers to the following:*

1. (a) The humanistic perspective in psychology emphasizes human _____ , self-_____ , and freedom of _____ . The most important factor in personality is the individual's _____ , _____ perception of him- or herself.

   (b) Humanistic psychologists see people as being innately _____ and motivated by the need to grow _____ . If people are raised in a genuinely accepting atmosphere and given freedom to make _____ , they will develop healthy self-concepts and strive to fulfill their unique _____ as human beings.

2. (a) Probably the most influential of the humanistic psychotherapies is

_____ therapy, also called _____ therapy, developed by Carl Rogers.

(b) Rogers believed that the medical term _patient_ implies that people in therapy are "_____" and are seeking treatment from an all-knowing authority figure who can "_____" them; instead of stressing the therapist's expertise or perceptions of the patient, _____ therapy emphasizes the client's _____ perception of himself and his environment.

(c) Like Freud, Rogers saw the therapeutic relationship as the catalyst that leads to _____ and lasting personality change. Unlike Freud, Rogers believed that the therapist should not exert power by offering carefully timed _____ , but instead should be _____ .

(d) The therapist must not _____ , make _____ , offer _____ , or pass judgment on the client's thoughts or feelings. Change must be chosen and directed by the _____ , and the therapist's role is to create the conditions that allow the client to direct the focus of therapy.

3. Rogers believed that three qualities of the therapist are critical in creating the therapeutic conditions that promote self-awareness, psychological growth, and self-directed change:

(a) Genuineness means that the therapist _____ and _____ shares her thoughts and feelings with the client; the therapist is modeling _____ and, by thoughtfully expressing her feelings without defensiveness or pretense, encourages the client to exercise more fully this capability in himself.

(b) The therapist must value, accept, and care for the client, whatever his problem or behavior; Rogers called this quality _____ ; Rogers believed that a person develops psychological problems largely because he has consistently experienced only _____ , which results in his cutting off or denying unacceptable aspects of himself and his experience, distorting his _____ and thinking and behaving in unhealthy, unproductive ways.

(c) The therapist must communicate _____ by _____ listening and reflecting the content and personal meaning of feelings being experienced by the client. In effect, the therapist creates a psychological mirror, reflecting the client's _____ and _____ as they exist in the client's private inner world, allowing him to explore and clarify them and to see himself and his problems more clearly.

(d) Rogers believed that when the therapeutic atmosphere contains _____ , _____ , and _____ , change is more likely to occur; such conditions foster feelings of being psychologically safe, accepted, and valued and allow the client to move in the direction of _____ , which is the realization of his unique potentials and talents.

(e) Research has generally _____ (supported/not supported) Rogers's ideas of the therapeutic qualities needed for change; along with being influential in individual psychotherapy, the client-centered approach

has been applied to _____ counseling, _____ , education,
_____ , and even community
and international relations.

Behavior Therapy

Preview Questions

*Consider the following questions as you study this
section of the chapter.*

- What is the basic premise of behavior therapy?
- How are classical and operant conditioning
  principles used to treat and modify problem
  behaviors?

*Read the section "Behavior Therapy" and **write** your
answers to the following:*

1. (a) In sharp contrast to the therapies of Rogers
       and Freud, which assume that gaining
       insight into the source of the problem is suf-
       ficient to bring about desirable changes in
       behavior and emotions, the goal of behavior
       therapy is to _____ specific
       problem behaviors, not to change the entire
       _____ ; rather than focusing on
       the _____ , behavior therapists
       focus on _____ behavior.

   (b) Behavior therapists assume that maladap-
       tive behaviors are _____ , just
       as adaptive behaviors are. Thus, the basic
       strategy in behavior therapy involves
       _____ maladaptive behaviors
       and _____ more adaptive
       behaviors in their place.

   (c) Behavior therapists employ techniques that
       are based on the learning principles of
       _____ conditioning,
       _____ conditioning, and
       _____ learning.

2. (a) John Watson _____ conditioned
       an infant called Little Albert to fear a tame
       laboratory rat by repeatedly pairing the rat
       with a loud clanging sound, and over time,

Albert's conditioned fear _____
to other furry objects, including a fur coat,
cotton, and a Santa Claus mask.

   (b) Watson's research inspired one of his stu-
       dents, Mary Cover Jones, to explore ways of
       _____ conditioned fears; she
       used a procedure that has become known as
       _____ , which refers to
       the learning of a new conditioned response
       that is incompatible with a previously
       learned response.

   (c) Jones's procedure involved gradually intro-
       ducing the _____ stimulus and
       at the same time pairing it with a(n)
       _____ stimulus, such as food,
       which elicits a positive response that is
       incompatible with the original conditioned
       response. This procedure also
       _____ (increased/eliminated)
       fear of objects that were similar to the origi-
       nal feared stimulus.

   (d) Along with counterconditioning, Jones used
       social imitation, or _____
       _____ techniques; she
       demonstrated that seeing others acting in a
       fearless manner encourages the fearful indi-
       vidual to _____ the behavior.

3. (a) Based on the same premise as
       counterconditioning, systematic desensitiza-
       tion involves learning a new conditioned
       response (relaxation) that is
       _____ with or
       _____ the old conditioned
       response (fear and anxiety).

   (b) First, the behavior therapist teaches you
       _____ ,
       which involves successively
       _____ one muscle group after
       another until a deep state of
       _____ is achieved.

   (c) Second, the therapist helps you construct a
       list of specific anxiety-provoking images

associated with the feared stimulus or situation, arranged in a(n) _____ from least to most anxiety provoking; the therapist would also have you create a very _____ , unrelated _____ scene, such as imagining yourself walking on the beach on a warm sunny day.

(d) During desensitization, when you are deeply relaxed, with your eyes closed, you vividly imagine the least threatening scene at the bottom of the _____ . After you can do this three or four times while maintaining complete _____ , you move up to the next scene in your _____ .

(e) If you start to feel twinges of anxiety or tension, the therapist will guide you back to imagining a previous scene or the _____ scene and, if necessary, will use the _____ technique.

(f) Over several sessions, you gradually work your way up the anxiety _____ , imagining each scene while maintaining complete _____ . Very systematically, desensitization to the feared situation occurs as each imagined scene becomes paired with a conditioned response of _____ rather than anxiety, until eventually the person can encounter the actual feared situation.

(g) In practice, systematic desensitization is often combined with other techniques, such as _____ learning; patients may visit the actual feared setting or watch videotapes of other people being calm and relaxed in the anxiety-provoking situation. These behavioral techniques are _____ (highly/not very) effective.

4. (a) Children who are chronic bedwetters spend _____ (less/more) time in the very relaxed, deep stages of nondreaming sleep than other children. Behavior therapists assume that bedwetting occurs because the child has not learned to _____ in response to the physical sensation of a full bladder.

(b) The goal of the bell and pad treatment is to _____ condition arousal so that a child awakens when his bladder is full. When the child starts to wet the bed, a loud _____ goes off and awakens the child, who then shuts off the alarm, uses the bathroom, changes the sheet, and resets the alarm.

(c) Over the course of a few weeks, the child's body becomes conditioned so that the sensations of a full bladder (the conditioned _____) triggers waking arousal (the desired conditioned _____).

(d) Behavior therapists are not inclined to dwell on the _____ meaning of bedwetting; instead, the behavior therapist attempts to _____ the problem behavior.

(e) In contrast, Freud explained bedwetting as a form of _____ gratification and _____ behavior caused by extreme anxiety. According to psychoanalysts, conditioning methods will lead to symptom substitution, such as _____ problems later in life. There is no scientific support for this position.

(f) The bell and pad treatment is significantly _____ (less/more) effective in dealing with bedwetting than are the insight-oriented therapies. School-age children who achieve success with this technique experience a _____ (lesser/greater) sense of self-control, self-esteem, and happiness at being able to remain dry.

5. (a) Aversive conditioning attempts to create a(n) _____ conditioned response to a harmful stimulus such as cigarette smoking or alcohol consumption; the goal is to replace the former _____ conditioned response with one that produces distaste or nausea.

   (b) Aversive conditioning techniques have been used to treat alcohol addiction, sexual deviance, compulsive gambling, and overeating. For example, if a person who is taking the medication Antabuse consumes any alcohol, extreme _____ is induced.

   (c) In general, aversive conditioning is _____ (very/not very) effective. The problem seems to be that the aversive conditioning procedures do not _____ very well to situations beyond the specific therapy setting.

6. (a) B. F. Skinner's operant conditioning model of learning is based on the simple principle that behavior is _____ and maintained by its _____ . When a behavior increases as a result of a desirable consequence, _____ has occurred; when a behavior decreases because it no longer leads to reinforcement, _____ has occurred; and when behavior decreases in response to an unpleasant consequence, _____ has occurred.

   (b) Behavior therapists use a variety of techniques based on operant conditioning, including _____ reinforcement for desired behaviors and nonreinforcement, or _____ , of undesired behaviors.

   (c) The token economy is an example of the use of operant conditioning techniques to modify the behavior of _____ . A token economy is a very structured environment, a system for _____ desired behaviors through _____ reinforcement.

   (d) Basically, tokens or points are awarded as _____ reinforcers for desirable behaviors and withheld or taken away for undesirable behaviors. The tokens can be exchanged for other _____ , such as special privileges or desirable items or activities.

   (e) Token economies have been used in _____ , _____ , juvenile correction institutes, and _____ hospitals and have been effective even with severely disturbed patients who have been hospitalized for many years; the use of token economies has declined because of problems of implementation, time and training involved, and legal challenges related to withholding of privileges.

7. Read the following and write the correct term in the space provided.

   (a) Dr. Soos does not analyze or interpret his clients' motives or problems. Instead, he believes that the client is in the best position to discover his or her own ways of effectively dealing with problems and that the role of the therapist is to provide the right conditions that foster self-awareness, psychological growth, and self-directed change. Dr. Soos is obviously a(n) _____ psychologist who uses _____ therapy.

   (b) In an attempt to help her husband overcome his deep fear of traveling by sea, Mrs. Bowman brings home travel brochures showing exotic destinations reached by cruise ships; she asks her husband to imagine both of them sitting in their deck chairs enjoying the warm sunshine and cool beverages, and at the same time she reassures him that these big ships are totally safe and comfortable and that he has nothing to worry about. Mrs. Bowman's efforts to reduce her husband's fear most closely resembles techniques used in

_____ .

(c) To help Trevor overcome his addiction to nicotine, Dr. Clarke asks him to smoke some cigarettes and at the same time administers electric shock to his arm. Dr. Clarke is using a technique called _____ conditioning.

(d) Retarded children in a group home are given plastic chips for making their beds, brushing their teeth, washing their hands, and being on time for meals. They are allowed to exchange these chips for candy, cookies, or additional TV time. The group home is using a behavioral technique called the

_____ .

(e) Eight-year-old Darryl has problems with bedwetting. His mother takes him to a behavior therapist who recommends a procedure that fixes the problem in a matter of weeks. The therapist most likely is using the

_____ .

(f) Desiree told her therapist, "I feel so inadequate and useless, and I can't seem to cope with even the smallest things in my life. What should I do?" Her therapist answered, "You are feeling very helpless about things in your life, and sometimes you feel unable to cope. Can you think where these feelings come from?" The therapist is using

_____ therapy and appears to be communicating with

_____ .

Review of Terms, Concepts, and Names 2

Use the terms in this list to complete the Matching Test, then to help you answer the True/False items correctly.

humanistic perspective
client-centered therapy
Carl Rogers
genuineness
unconditional positive regard
conditional acceptance
empathic understanding
behavior therapy
Mary Cover Jones
counterconditioning
systematic desensitization
progressive relaxation
control scene
bell and pad treatment
aversive conditioning
reinforcement
extinction
punishment
token economy

Matching Exercise

Match the appropriate term/name with its definition or description.

1. _____ American psychologist who conducted the first clinical demonstrations of behavior therapy.

2. _____ Psychological perspective that emphasizes human potential, self-awareness, and freedom of choice.

3. _____ Form of behavior therapy in which the therapeutic environment is structured to reward desired behaviors with tokens or points that may eventually be exchanged for tangible rewards.

4. _____ In client-centered therapy, the critical quality of the therapist that involves honestly and openly sharing his or her thoughts and feelings with the client.

5. _____ Type of psychotherapy that focuses on directly changing maladaptive behavior patterns by using basic learning principles and techniques; also called behavior modification.

6. _____ American psychologist who helped found humanistic psychology and developed client-centered therapy.

7. _____ The first step in systematic desensitization, which involves successively relaxing one muscle group after another until a deep state of relaxation is achieved.

8. _____ Behavior therapy technique used to treat nighttime bedwetting by conditioning arousal from sleep in response to body signals of a full bladder.

9. _____ Type of psychotherapy developed by humanist Carl Rogers in which the therapist is nondirective and reflective, and the client directs the focus of each therapy session; also called person-centered therapy.

10. _____ In behavior therapy, the process of increasing a behavior as the result of a desirable consequence.

True/False Test

Indicate whether each statement is true or false by placing T or F in the blank space next to each item.

1. ____ Aversive conditioning is a behavior therapy technique based on classical conditioning that involves modifying behavior by conditioning a new response that is incompatible with a previously learned response.

2. ____ In client-centered therapy, empathic understanding involves active listening and reflecting the content and personal meaning of feelings being experienced by the client.

3. ____ Systematic desensitization is a type of behavior therapy in which phobic responses are reduced by pairing relaxation with a series of mental images or real-life situations that the person finds progressively more fear provoking; it is based on the principle of counterconditioning.

4. ____ In behavior therapy, when a behavior decreases because it no longer leads to a reinforcer, extinction has occurred.

5. ____ In systematic desensitization, the therapist may have the client create a very relaxing scene, unrelated to the hierarchy of anxiety-provoking images, called a control scene.

6. ____ In client-centered therapy, unconditional positive regard is created when the therapist values, accepts, and cares for the client, whatever her problems or behaviors.

7. ____ In behavior therapy, punishment causes a decrease in a behavior because the behavior no longer leads to a reinforcer.

8. ____ When a person has received acceptance by significant others only if she conforms to their expectations, she is said to have experienced conditional acceptance.

9. ____ Counterconditioning is a relatively ineffective type of behavior therapy that involves repeatedly pairing an aversive stimulus with occurrence of undesirable behaviors or thoughts.

Check your answers and review any areas of weakness before going on to the next section.

Cognitive Therapies

Preview Questions

Consider the following questions as you study this section of the chapter.

- On what assumption is cognitive therapies based?
- What is rational-emotive therapy (RET), and who developed it?
- What is Beck's cognitive therapy (CT), and how does it differ from rational-emotive therapy?

*Read the section "Cognitive Therapies" and **write** your answers to the following:*

1. (a) Cognitive therapies assume that most people blame unhappiness and problems on _____ events and situations, but the real cause of unhappiness is the way the person _____ about the events, not the events themselves.

   (b) Thus, the goal of cognitive therapy is to focus on the faulty patterns of _____ and then to _____ them to more adaptive, healthy patterns.

2. (a) Rational-emotive therapy (RET) was developed by _____ because he believed that people's difficulties are caused by their faulty _____ and _____ beliefs. RET focuses on changing the patterns of _____ thinking that are believed to be the primary cause of the client's emotional distress and psychological problems.

(b) In RET, psychological problems are explained by the ABC model; when a(n) _____ event (A) occurs, it is the person's _____ (B) about the event that cause emotional _____ (C). This differs from the common-sense view that (A) causes (C).

(c) Identifying the core _____ beliefs that underlie personal distress is the first step in RET. The second step is for the therapist to vigorously _____ and _____ the irrational beliefs.

(d) The consequences of irrational beliefs are _____ , such as extreme anger, despair, resentment, and feelings of worthlessness, which interfere with constructive attempts to change disturbing situations. According to RET, the result is _____ behaviors, _____ disorders, _____ , and other psychological problems.

(e) From the client's perspective, RET requires admitting her irrational beliefs and accepting the fact that those beliefs are _____ and _____ . In addition, the client must radically change her way of _____ and _____ to stressful events.

(f) According to RET, appropriate emotions are the consequence of _____ beliefs; such _____ mental and emotional responses encourage people to work toward constructively changing or coping with difficult situations.

(g) RET has been shown to be generally _____ (effective/ineffective) in the treatment of _____ , _____ , and certain _____ disorders and in helping people overcome self-defeating behaviors.

3. (a) Aaron Beck's development of cognitive therapy (CT) grew out of his research on _____ . He discovered that _____ people have an extremely negative view of the past, present, and future.

(b) Rather than realistically evaluating their situation, _____ patients have developed a negative _____ bias, consistently _____ their expectations in a negative way; these negative _____ are shaped by deepseated, self-deprecating thoughts, and CT essentially focuses on correcting the _____ biases that underlie _____ and other psychological disorders.

(c) Like Ellis, Beck believes that what people _____ creates their moods and emotions; like RET, CT involves helping clients to identify faulty _____ and to replace unhealthy patterns of thinking with healthier ones.

(d) In contrast with RET's emphasis on _____ thinking, Beck believes that _____ and other psychological problems are caused by _____ thinking and _____ beliefs. The cognitive therapist encourages the client to _____ test the accuracy of his or her assumptions and beliefs.

4. (a) The first step in CT is to help the client learn to recognize and monitor _____ that occur without conscious effort or control. Whether negative or positive, _____ can control your emotional and behavioral reactions to events.

(b) In the second step of CT, the therapist helps the client learn how to _____ test the reality of the

_____

that are so upsetting. The cognitive therapist may also assign behavior tasks to _____ the accuracy of the negative automatic thoughts.

(c) Initially, the cognitive therapist acts as a(n) _____ , showing the client how to evaluate the accuracy of

_____ ; in this way, he hopes to eventually teach the client to do the same on her own. Unlike the confrontational tactics used in RET, the CT therapist strives to create a therapy climate of _____ that encourages the client to contribute to the evaluation of the logic and accuracy of her thinking.

(d) Beck's CT has been shown to be very _____ (ineffective/effective) in treating _____ and other psychological disorders, including _____ disorders, _____ disorders, PTSD, and relationship problems. It also has been adapted to treat psychotic symptoms associated with schizophrenia.

Group and Family Therapy

Preview Questions

Consider the following questions as you study this section of the chapter.

- How does group therapy work, and what are some of the advantages of this approach?
- What is family therapy, and how does it differ from individual therapy?

Read the section "Group and Family Therapy" and **write** *your answers to the following:*

1. (a) In contrast to psychotherapy, which is focused on a single client's problems,

thoughts, and emotions, group therapy involves one or more therapists working with several people _____ ; the group may be as small as three or four people or as large as ten or more people.

(b) Virtually any approach (psychodynamic, humanistic, behavior, or cognitive) can be used in _____ , and just about any problem that can be handled individually can be dealt with in group therapy.

(c) Regardless of whether the therapy group is made up of clients who share the same problem or is more diverse, the goals are the same as those for _____ therapy: resolving psychological problems and promoting more adaptive behaviors. The therapeutic success of group therapy often hinges on the group's collective sense of _____ , or togetherness.

(d) Group therapy has a number of advantages over individual psychotherapies: (1) group therapy is very _____ ; a single therapist can work simultaneously with several people; (2) rather than relying on the client's _____ about how he relates to other people, the therapist can observe his actual interactions with others; (3) the support and encouragement provided by the other group members may help a person feel less alone and understand that his problems are not _____ ; (4) group members may provide each other with helpful, practical _____ for solving common problems and can act as _____ for successfully overcoming difficulties; and (5) working within a group gives people an opportunity to try out new _____ in a safe, supportive environment.

(e) Group therapy is typically conducted by a mental health professional, whereas _____ groups and _____ groups are typically conducted by nonprofessionals.

2. (a) Family therapy operates on the premise that the problem is not solely within the individual but instead involves the _____ . The major goal of family therapy is to alter and improve the ongoing _____ among all family members, including important members of the extended family, such as grandparents or in-laws.

(b) Family therapy is based on the assumption that the family is a _____ , an interdependent unit, not just a collection of separate individuals; the family is seen as a _____ structure in which each member plays a unique role.

(c) Every family has certain unspoken "_____" of interaction and communication that often revolve around issues such as which family members exercise _____ and how, who makes _____ , who keeps the _____ , and what kinds of alliances members have formed among themselves. As such issues are explored, unhealthy _____ of family interaction can be identified and replaced with new ones that promote the psychological health of the family as a unit.

(d) Family therapy is often used to _____ the effectiveness of individual psychotherapy, especially in cases when the client's problems reflect conflict and disturbances in the entire family _____ . This therapy is also indicated when there is conflict among family members.

(e) Many family therapists also provide _____ or _____ therapy with the goal of improving communication and problem-solving skills and increasing intimacy between the pair.

(f) A current trend in _____ therapy is the focus on the _____ and _____ context within which the relationship functions; therapists are taking greater care not to impose their own expectations of what constitutes a healthy relationship, especially when the couple's _____ background differs from the therapist's in terms of values and expectations about gender roles and about the marital relationship.

Culture and Psychotherapy: Bridging the Culture Gap

Preview Questions

Consider the following questions as you study this section of the chapter.

- What happens when psychotherapists and clients hold different cultural values?
- What cultural values are inherent in Western psychotherapy, and how do these values clash with the values of other cultures?

*Read the section "Culture and Psychotherapy: Bridging the Culture Gap" and **write** your answers to the following:*

1. (a) Individualistic cultures emphasize the _____ , _____ self, behaving in accordance with _____ attributes and motives. Thus, Western psychotherapies focus on the individual, and problems are presumed to have _____ causes and are expected to be solved by the individual.

(b) Commonly, the client is encouraged to become more _____ , more self-sufficient, and less _____ on others in making decisions and conducting his or her life. The client may even be encouraged to disregard the demands of family members in the process of developing his or her own _____ .

(c) In many collectivistic cultures, however, the basic psychological unit is not the individual, but the _____ , the _____ , or the _____ . The needs of the individual are much more strongly identified with the needs of the _____ to which he or she belongs, and problems and successes reflect on the group as well as the individual.

(d) One type of traditional Native American therapy is conducted in the person's home and can involve as many as 40 to 70 members of the individual's community or tribe; it is called _____ therapy.

(e) Latino cultures also stress _____ over independence, with a strong emphasis on the family, including members of the extended family; it is recommended that members of the client's extended family be actively involved in _____ treatment.

(f) Many persons in Asian cultures define their identities in terms of the _____ and _____ to which they belong. According to the Japanese psychotherapy, Naikan therapy, being _____ is the surest path to psychological suffering.

(g) The goal of Naikan therapy is to replace the focus on the _____ with a sense of gratitude and obligation toward significant others; the client focuses on how much _____ and others have done for him and how he has failed to meet their needs.

2. (a) In many cultures, people are far more likely to turn to _____ or _____ than they are to mental health professionals; in many Native American cultures, for example, personal problems are considered to be _____ rather than psychological in nature, and so people are more likely to seek help from _____ leaders rather than psychologists or psychiatrists.

(b) Another barrier to seeking professional help is felt by _____ and _____ who have experienced government oppression in their native lands.

(c) Psychodynamic, humanistic, and cognitive therapies all stress the importance of a client's _____ into thoughts and feelings; many other cultures, however, do not emphasize the importance of soul searching in resolving psychological problems, but instead may encourage the depressed or anxious person to _____ focusing on upsetting thoughts and negative thinking.

(d) Many Western psychotherapies are based on the assumption that the client will _____ her deepest feelings and most private thoughts, but in many other cultures, intimate details of one's personal life are discussed only with a _____ and never with a _____ .

(e) In Asian cultures, people tend to avoid the _____ expression of emotions, often expressing thoughts and feelings _____ or _____ ; in a similar way, Native American cultures tend to value _____ of emotions rather than _____ expression of emotions.

(f) It's not surprising, then, that ethnic minorities are _____ (more/less) likely than European-Americans to consult mental health professionals; they're also _____ (less/more) likely to drop out after a single session when they do.

Evaluating the Effectiveness of Psychotherapy

Preview Questions

Consider the following questions as you study this section of the chapter.

- What is meta-analysis, and what has it demonstrated about the general effectiveness of psychotherapy?
- Is one form of psychotherapy superior to another?
- What common factors contribute to effective psychotherapy, and what is eclecticism?

*Read the section "Evaluating the Effectiveness of Psychotherapy" and **write** your answers to the following:*

1. (a) To help deal with the diversity among psychotherapy studies and arrive at general conclusions, researchers often combine the results of similar studies using _____ . This statistical technique involves _____ the results of several studies into a(n) _____ analysis, essentially creating one large study that can reveal overall trends.

    (b) Most people with psychological problems _____ (seek/do not seek) help from mental health professionals; they cope with the help and support of _____ and _____ or by using _____ strategies. Some people improve simply with the passage of time, a phenomenon called _____ .

    (c) The basic strategy to investigate whether psychotherapy offers significant benefits is to compare people who enter psychotherapy with a matched _____ group of people who do not receive psychotherapy.

    (d) When meta-analysis is used to summarize these studies, the researchers consistently arrive at the same conclusion: psychotherapy is significantly _____ (less/more) effective than no treatment.

    (e) The benefits of psychotherapy _____ (are/are not) usually apparent in a relatively short period of time.

2. (a) Looking at individual studies, it appears that people who are experiencing panic disorder, obsessive-compulsive disorder, and phobias are helped the most by _____ and _____ therapies as opposed to _____ therapies. When meta-analysis techniques are used, a consistent finding is that, in general, there is _____ difference in the effectiveness of different psychotherapies.

    (b) Researchers have identified a number of factors that are related to a positive therapy outcome: (1) the most important factors are those associated with the _____ relationship, such as mutual respect, trust, hope, and the experience of catharsis. Other factors include: (2) certain characteristics of the _____ , such as warmth, sensitivity, responsiveness, being perceived as sincere and genuine, and actively helping people to understand and face their problems; (3) the therapists' sensitivity to the _____ differences that may exist between themselves and their clients; (4) _____ characteristics, such as level of motivation, commitment to therapy, active involvement in the process, along with openness, a willingness to change, expressiveness, and social maturity; (5) _____

circumstances, such as having the support, understanding, and encouragement of family members or a spouse and having a stable living situation in which other people are psychologically well adjusted.

(c) None of these factors is _____ to any particular brand of psychotherapy; nevertheless, the _____ among psychotherapy techniques can be important; for therapy to be optimally effective, the individual should feel comfortable with both the therapist and the therapeutic techniques used by the therapist.

3. (a) Increasingly, a personalized approach to therapy is being facilitated by the movement of mental health toward the pragmatic and integrated use of diverse psychotherapeutic techniques, or _____ .

(b) Eclectic psychotherapists carefully tailor the therapy approach to the _____ and _____ of the person seeking help.

4. Read the following and write the correct term in the space provided.

(a) Dr. McGilvery wants to determine whether psychotherapy is effective for particular psychological disorders. In attempting to analyze the results of numerous published studies on the issue, he should use a technique called _____ .

(b) Mike, a mental health professional, tries to tailor his therapeutic approach to the prob-

lems and characteristics of the person seeking help. Mike's pragmatic and integrated use of diverse psychotherapeutic techniques would classify him as a(n) _____ therapist.

(c) Dr. Samson believes that a key aspect of resolving some psychological problems is getting individuals to realize that others have problems similar to their own. To achieve this goal, _____ therapy would be useful.

(d) Jay's therapist attacks and openly criticizes Jay's irrational and self-defeating ways of thinking. Jay's therapist is most likely a(n) _____ therapist.

(e) Dr. Beaven tries to help her clients learn to recognize and monitor the automatic thoughts that occur without conscious effort or control; she then encourages them to empirically test the reality of these thoughts. Dr. Beaven's approach is most consistent with _____ therapy.

(f) Dr. Sidhu believes that in order to understand psychological problems, it is important to investigate interactions among family members within the context of the dynamic family system in which each member plays a unique role. Dr. Sidhu is most likely a(n) _____ therapist.

Graphic Organizer 1

Fill in each of the following with the correct information.

Type of Therapy	Founder	Source of Problems	Treatment Techniques	Goals of Therapy
Psychoanalysis				
Client-Centered Therapy				
Behavior Therapy				
Rational-Emotive Therapy				
Cognitive Therapy				

Review of Key Terms and Key Names 3

Use the terms in this list to complete the Matching Test, then to help you answer the True/False items correctly.

cognitive therapies
Albert Ellis
rational-emotive therapy
Aaron T. Beck
cognitive therapy
group therapy
self-help groups and
    support groups

family therapy
network therapy
Naikan therapy
eclecticism
spontaneous remission

Matching Exercise

Match the appropriate term/name with its definition or description.

1. _____ Form of psychotherapy that is based on the assumption that the family is a system and that treats the family as a unit.

2. _____ Group of psychotherapies that are based on the assumption that psychological problems are due to maladaptive patterns of thinking; treatment techniques focus on recognizing and altering these unhealthy thinking patterns.

3. _____ Type of therapy, developed by psychiatrist Aaron Beck, that focuses on changing the client's unrealistic beliefs.

4. _____ Form of psychotherapy that involves one or more therapists working simultaneously with a small group of clients.

5. _____ Type of cognitive therapy, developed by psychologist Albert Ellis, that focuses on changing the client's irrational beliefs.

6. _____ Phenomenon in which people eventually improve or recover from psychological symptoms simply with the passage of time.

True/False Test

Indicate whether each item is true or false by placing T or F in the space next to each item.

1. ___ Albert Ellis founded cognitive therapy (CT), a psychotherapy based on the assumption that depression and other psychological problems are caused by biased perceptions, distorted thinking, and inaccurate beliefs.

2. ___ Eclecticism is the pragmatic and integrated use of techniques from different psychotherapies.

3. ___ Network therapy is a Native American therapy that is conducted in the person's home and can involve as many as 40 to 70 members of the individual's community or tribe.

4. ___ Self-help groups and support groups deal with a wide array of psychological, medical, and behavioral problems through group processes and interactions that are typically organized and led by nonprofessionals.

5. ___ Aaron T. Beck founded the cognitive psychotherapy called rational-emotive therapy (RET), which emphasizes recognizing and changing irrational beliefs.

6. ___ Naikan therapy is a Japanese psychotherapy that encourages the client to meditate on what he has received from significant others, what he has done in return, and the problems that he has caused for these significant people.

Check your answers and review any areas of weakness before going on to the next section.

Biomedical Therapies

Preview Questions

Consider the following questions as you study this section of the chapter.

- What is biomedical therapy?

- What are the most important antipsychotic, antianxiety, and antidepressant medications, how do they achieve their effects, and what are their advantages?

- What are lithium and ECT, and how are they used?

Read the section "Biomedical Therapies" and **write** *your answers to the following:*

1. (a) Today, the most common biomedical therapy is the use of

_____ ,

prescription drugs that alter mental functions and alleviate psychological symptoms.

(b) Because they are medical treatments, the biomedical therapies must be administered by a(n) _____ or other licensed physician; _____ physicians write many of the prescriptions for medications that affect psychological symptoms.

2. (a) The synthetic version of an herb that has been used in India and Japan to treat diverse medical conditions, including psychotic symptoms associated with schizophrenia, is called _____ .

   (b) In the 1950s, French scientists demonstrated that the the psychotic symptoms commonly seen in schizophrenia are diminished by the drug _____ ; this drug is better known today by its trade name _____ and is still widely used to treat psychotic symptoms.

   (c) Because _____ and _____ diminish the symptoms commonly seen in schizophrenia, they are called _____ medications.

   (d) Both drugs work by reducing levels of the neurotransmitter _____ ; since the development of these early drugs, more than thirty other _____ medications, which also act on _____ receptors in the brain, have been developed.

   (e) The first antipsychotics effectively reduced the so-called positive symptoms of schizophrenia, such as _____ , _____ , and disordered thinking and contributed to the dramatic decrease in the number of patients in mental hospitals.

3. The early antipsychotic drugs had a number of drawbacks:

   (a) They didn't actually _____ schizophrenia; psychotic symptoms often returned if a person stopped taking the medication.

   (b) They were less effective in eliminating the so-called negative symptoms of schizophrenia, such as _____ withdrawal, _____ , _____ emotions, or lack of emotional expressiveness; in some cases, the drugs even made the negative symptoms worse.

   (c) They often produced unwanted _____ , such as dry mouth, weight gain, constipation, sleepiness, and poor concentration.

   (d) These drugs also *globally* altered brain levels of _____ , which altered normal motor movements and created a number of motor-related _____ , such as muscle tremors, rigid movement, a shuffling gait, and a masklike facial expression.

   (e) The long-term use of these drugs causes a small percentage of people to develop a potentially irreversible motor disorder called _____ , which is characterized by severe, uncontrollable facial tics and grimaces, chewing movements, and other involuntary lip movements.

   (f) A further problem is the "_____" pattern of hospitalization, discharge, and rehospitalization. Once the symptoms of schizophrenia were stabilized by the drugs, the patients were discharged, but because of the unpleasant side effects, inadequate medical follow-up, or both, the patients eventually stopped taking the medication; when the symptoms returned, they were rehospitalized.

4. (a) A new generation of antipsychotic drugs, called _____ antipsychotics, act differently on the brain than the older drugs did; clozapine and risperidone affect levels of the neurotransmitter _____ as well as _____ in the brain.

   (b) The atypical antipsychotics have three

advantages over the traditional antipsychotic drugs: (1) clozapine and risperidone are much less likely to cause

_____

side effects because they act on

_____ receptors only in brain areas associated with psychotic symptoms, not globally; (2) they are much more effective than the older drugs in treating the

_____ symptoms of schizophrenia; and (3) a _____ (significant/very small) proportion of patients who have not responded to any of the traditional antipsychotic drugs improve after taking clozapine or risperidone, sometimes dramatically.

(c) While clozapine and risperidone bring the potential of new _____ ,
a new drug, _____ , that is structurally similar does not produce the same side effects. Two other new drugs, sertindole and quetrapine, produce greater _____ and fewer
_____ for people suffering from the most severe forms of mental disorders.

5. (a) The best-known antianxiety drugs are
_____ , which include the trade name drugs Valium and Xanax; they take effect rapidly and calm jittery feelings, relax muscles, and promote sleep by increasing the level of
_____ , a neurotransmitter that inhibits the transmission of nerve impulses in the brain and slows brain activity.

(b) The benzodiazepines have several potentially dangerous side effects: (1) they can reduce
_____ , _____ ,
and _____ time; (2) their effects can be _____ when they are combined with alcohol and many other

drugs, including over-the-counter antihistamines; and (3) benzodiazepines are physically _____ if taken in large quantities over a long period of time; if physical _____ occurs, the person must withdraw from the drug gradually, as abrupt withdrawal can produce life-threatening symptoms.

(c) A newer antianxiety drug with the trade name Buspar has fewer

_____

and lower risk of _____ and physical _____ ; its major drawback is that it must be taken for two to three weeks before it takes effect.

(d) The benzodiazepines are still regarded as the most effective medications currently available for immediate, short-term relief from _____ ; for the long-term treatment of chronic _____ ,
such as in _____ disorder or generalized _____ disorder, Buspar may be the most appropriate medication.

6. (a) The medication used to treat bipolar disorder is _____ , a naturally occurring substance; it counteracts both
_____ and _____
symptoms in patients with the disorder.

(b) Lithium stops acute manic episodes over the course of a week or two. Once these episodes are under control, the long-term use of lithium can help prevent relapses into either
_____ or _____ ; it is an effective treatment for most patients.

(c) Lithium has a very narrow range between the _____ dosage level and the _____ dosage level; if the level is too low, _____ symptoms persist, and if the level is too high, symptoms of lithium _____ may occur.

(d) How lithium works was a complete mystery

until recently; apparently, it stabilizes the availability of the excitatory neurotransmitter _____ , preventing both abnormal highs and abnormal lows.

(e) Recently, bipolar disorder has been treated with an anticonvulsant medicine, called _____ , which seems especially helpful in treating those who rapidly cycle through bouts of bipolar disorder several times a year.

7. (a) The antidepressant medications counteract the classic symptoms of depression, such as _____ , _____ , _____ , suicidal thoughts, difficulty _____ , and disruptions in _____ , energy, _____ , and sexuality.

(b) The first generation of antidepressants consists of two classes of drugs, called _____ and _____ inhibitors, both of which affect multiple neurotransmitter pathways in the brain. Evidence suggests that these drugs alleviate depression by increasing the availability of two key brain neurotransmitters, _____ and _____ .

(c) In about 75 percent of depressed patients, these drugs effectively eliminate depressive symptoms, but they can also produce numerous _____ , such as weight gain, dizziness, and dry mouth and eyes; in combination with other chemicals found in many foods, they can produce dangerously high blood pressure levels.

(d) The second generation of antidepressants include trazadone and bupropion, and although chemically different from the first generation, they were generally _____ (more/no more) effective and had _____ (many/none) of the same side effects.

(e) The third generation of antidepressants are the selective _____ reuptake _____ (SSRIs). Rather than acting on multiple neurotransmitter pathways, the SSRIs affect the availability of a single neurotransmitter, _____ .

(f) The first SSRI to be released was fluoxetine, with the trade name _____ , and it was quickly followed by its chemical cousins, Zoloft and Paxil; these drugs tend to have _____ and _____ side effects but can cause headaches, nervousness, sleeping problems, loss of appetite, and sexual dysfunction.

8. (a) About 40,000 patients a year receive electroconvulsive therapy (ECT) as a medical treatment for severe _____ , and it is sometimes used to treat mania, catatonia, and other severe mental disorders. The procedure involves _____ to induce a seizure in the brain, much like an epileptic seizure, but it is not known why inducing a convulsion relieves the symptoms of depression.

(b) Today, ECT is a relatively simple and quick medical procedure, usually performed in a hospital. The seizure lasts about a minute; when the anesthesia wears off and the patient wakes up, _____ and _____ may be present for a few hours.

(c) Not uncommonly, the patient experiences a temporary or permanent loss of _____ for the events leading up to the treatment; to treat major _____ , a series of 6 to 10 ECT treatments are usually spaced over a few weeks.

(d) ECT _____ (is/is not) a very effective treatment for severe depression

with a slightly _____
(lower/higher) overall effectiveness rate than
the antidepressant drugs.

(e) ECT has potential dangers; serious
_____ impairments can occur,
such as extensive amnesia (memory loss)
and disturbances in _____ and
_____ abilities. ECT is also the
most controversial medical treatment for
psychological disorders, and not everyone
agrees that it is either safe or effective.

9. Read the following and write the correct term
in the space provided.

(a) For no apparent reason, Mrs. Bell has constant and persistent feelings of anxiety, nervousness, and apprehension that interfere
with her ability to eat, sleep, and function.
Her psychiatrist is most likely to prescribe a
type of psychoactive medication called an
_____ medication.

(b) Mr. Millis still experiences intense feelings
of despondency, hopelessness, dejection, and
suicidal thoughts, despite extensive psychotherapy and months of psychoactive medication. Because of this lack of responsiveness, his doctor is likely to consider using
_____ therapy.

(c) After being on antipsychotic medications for
many years, Florence has developed a number of serious symptoms, such as severe,
uncontrollable facial tics and grimaces,
chewing movements, and other involuntary
movements of the lips, jaw, and tongue.
Florence suffers from

_____ .

(d) Dwayne has been diagnosed with bipolar
disorder. His doctor is most likely to prescribe _____ .

(e) To treat her symptoms, which included hallucinations, delusions, and disordered
thought processes, Debra's psychiatrist pre-

scribed one of the atypical antipsychotic
medications that affect the levels of the neurotransmitters serotonin and dopamine in
the brain. He is likely to have prescribed
either _____ or
_____ .

Review of Terms and Concepts 4

Use the terms in this list to complete the Matching Test.

psychoactive medications	lithium
antipsychotic medications	antidepressant medications
tardive dyskinesia	electroconvulsive therapy (ECT)
antianxiety medications	catharsis

Matching Exercise

Match the appropriate term with its definition or description.

1. _____ A naturally occurring substance that is used in the treatment of bipolar
disorder.

2. _____ Prescription drugs that alter
mental functions and alleviate psychological
symptoms.

3. _____ Biomedical therapy used primarily in the treatment of depression that
involves electrically inducing a brief brain
seizure; also called *shock therapy* and *electric
shock therapy*.

4. _____ Prescription drugs that are
used to alleviate the symptoms of anxiety.

5. _____ Prescription drugs that are
used to reduce the symptoms associated with
depression.

6. _____ Potentially irreversible
motor disorder that results from the long-term
use of antipsychotic medications and is characterized by severe, uncontrollable facial tics and
grimaces, chewing movements, and other involuntary movements of the lips, jaw, and tongue.

7. _____ Prescription drugs that are
used to reduce psychotic symptoms; frequently
used in the treatment of schizophrenia.

8. _____ The reduction of emotional

and physical tension that occurs simply as a result of talking about one's psychological problems.

> Check your answers and review any areas of weakness before going on to the next section.

Something to Think About

1. Many people suffer from fear and anxiety about such things as going to the dentist or doctor or to job interviews and taking exams. These kinds of fears are normal, and most people manage to cope with such anxiety-provoking situations. Other fears are more serious and may cause the person intense distress and somehow interfere with his or her normal functioning. Imagine a situation in which a friend or family member comes to you seeking help about how to overcome her fear of flying. Based on what you know about the behavior therapy technique of systematic desensitization, what might you say to this person?

2. Many people with psychological problems do not seek help from mental health professionals. There are many reasons for this. One reason may have to do with a lack of understanding about what to expect in psychotherapy. What are some of the important things a person should know about psychotherapy?

> Check your answers and review any areas of weakness before doing the progress tests.

Progress Test 1

Review the complete chapter (including Concept Reviews and the boxed inserts), review all your study notes, and then test yourself on the following progress test. Check your answers. If you make a mistake, review your notes, review the relevant section of the study guide, and, if necessary, go back and read the appropriate part of your textbook.

1. Jacqueline's therapist uses dream interpretation and free association to help her to become more aware of unresolved conflicts in her childhood. The therapist's techniques and goals best reflect the primary aim of
(a) psychoanalysis.
(b) client-centered therapy.
(c) behavior therapy.
(d) cognitive therapy.

2. Mrs. Alverz gives her third-grade students a silver sticker every time they get a perfect score on their weekly spelling test. At the end of the term, students can exchange their stickers for prizes. Mrs. Alverz is using a strategy based on _____ conditioning called the _____ .
(a) classical; bell and pad method
(b) classical; token economy
(c) operant; bell and pad method
(d) operant; token economy

3. Kayla dream that she arrived for her final exam just when everyone else was finishing; her professor, who had an uncanny resemblance to her father in the dream, started screaming and shouting at her in front of everyone. She suddenly awoke, feeling quite relieved that it was only a bad dream. When Kayla told her friend Lenny about her frightening dream, he suggested that the dream contained enough symbolism to indicate that Kayla had some unresolved childhood conflicts. Lenny appears to be basing his interpretation on the _____ content of the dream.
(a) token   (c) overt
(b) manifest   (d) latent

4. Lenny's interpretation of Kayla's dream is most consistent with the _____ approach.
(a) psychoanalytic   (c) behavioral
(b) humanistic   (d) cognitive

5. Twenty-five-year-old Melissa told her therapist that she felt worthless and unattractive because she didn't have a boyfriend; she was sure she was going to end up single and unloved. Her therapist said, "Your way of thinking is not only irrational but also totally stupid and absurd! You are worthless only if you *think* you are!" This statement would most likely be made by
   (a) a behavioral therapist.
   (b) a client-centered therapist.
   (c) a rational-emotive therapist.
   (d) a psychoanalyst.
   (e) none of the above; no therapist would talk like that to a client.

6. Once a week, Gardner attends a local health clinic, where he attempts to deal with some of his psychological problems by discussing them with five or six other people and two psychologists. Gardner is involved in
   (a) individual therapy.
   (b) group therapy.
   (c) a biomedical treatment program.
   (d) a self-help group.

7. Mr. Lansdon's intense feelings of despondency and helplessness are periodically interrupted by episodes in which he experiences excessive feelings of personal power and a grandiose optimism that he can change the world to fit his strange ideological beliefs. A biomedical therapist would most likely prescribe
   (a) electroconvulsive therapy.
   (b) lithium.
   (c) antipsychotic medications.
   (d) antidepressant medications.

8. Gabrielle's feelings of unhappiness, despondency, dejection, and hopelessness have become so extreme that she has attempted suicide. Which of the following treatments is likely to provide her with the quickest relief from her misery?
   (a) systematic desensitization
   (b) the bell and pad treatment
   (c) psychoanalysis
   (d) electroconvulsive therapy (ECT)

9. Because of his persistent psychological problems, Werner has been prescribed a benzodiazepine drug called Valium. It is most likely that Werner suffers from
   (a) bipolar disorder.   (c) anxiety.
   (b) schizophrenia.   (d) depression.

10. After a session with her therapist, in which she finally expressed all the anger and hostility she felt toward her parents and described the terrible guilt she felt about it, Charlene felt an enormous reduction in and relief from her emotional and physical tension. Charlene has probably experienced
    (a) resistance.
    (b) catharsis.
    (c) ECT.
    (d) counterconditioning.

11. Kathleen is on a committee at a community health-care facility that has the task of determining which of the major forms of psychotherapy is most effective. After she reviews studies that used meta-analysis to assess the results of treatment outcomes, she is most likely to conclude that
    (a) behavior therapy is the single most effective therapy available.
    (b) client-centered therapy has been consistently more effective than all the other forms of therapy.
    (c) in general, there is little or no difference in the effectiveness of the different forms of psychotherapy.
    (d) psychoanalysis works best for schizophrenia, and cognitive therapy works best for phobias.

12. Tyler has been diagnosed with schizophrenia. His doctor is most likely to prescribe
    (a) electroconvulsive therapy.
    (b) lithium.
    (c) antipsychotic medication.
    (d) antianxiety medication.

13. According to the Application, which of the following is true?
    (a) Therapy is a collaborative effort.
    (b) Expect therapy to challenge how you think and act.
    (c) Your therapist will not become a substitute friend.
    (d) Your therapist will not make decisions for you.
    (e) All of the above are true.

14. According to In Focus 15.2, phobias
    (a) are now being treated experimentally with virtual reality (VR) technology.
    (b) can be easily cured with Prozac.
    (c) are best treated using psychoanalytic techniques.
    (d) are eliminated using aversive therapy.

15. According to In Focus 15.1, which of the following is true of Mary Cover Jones?
    (a) She was a psychoanalyst.
    (b) She was the first behavior therapist.
    (c) She was one of the founders of the humanistic movement.
    (d) Along with Albert Ellis, she developed rational-emotive therapy.

Progress Test 2

After you have checked your understanding of the material in Progress Test 1 and have done a complete chapter review with special focus on any areas of weakness, you are ready to assess your knowledge of Progress Test 2. Check your answers. If you make a mistake, review your notes, the relevant section of the study guide, and, if necessary, the appropriate part of your textbook.

1. Dr. Rassmunsen uses medication and other medical procedures, including electroconvulsive therapy, to treat the symptoms of psychological disorders. Dr. Rassmunsen's approach would most likely be classified as
    (a) cognitive therapy.
    (b) behavioral therapy.
    (c) humanistic therapy.
    (d) biomedical therapy.

2. Mr. Damson suffers from auditory hallucinations and falsely believes his coworkers are not only trying to steal his "secret inventions" but are also plotting to kill him. A biomedical therapist would most likely prescribe
    (a) electroconvulsive therapy.
    (b) lithium.
    (c) antipsychotic medications.
    (d) antidepressant medications.

3. Mervyn's therapist prescribed a medication that is classified as a selective serotonin reuptake inhibitor (SSRI) for his psychological symptoms. It is most likely that Mervyn suffers from
    (a) schizophrenia.   (c) anxiety disorder.
    (b) bipolar disorder.   (d) depression.

4. When Freda told her therapist that she wanted to get his advice on what she should do about her relationship problems, he replied, "It sounds to me like you are experiencing some difficulties with you relationship. Is that right?" The therapist's response reflects the technique of
    (a) transference.
    (b) free association.
    (c) empathic understanding.
    (d) counterconditioning.

5. It is very probable that Freda's therapist is a _____ therapist.
    (a) cognitive   (c) behavior
    (b) psychoanalytic   (d) humanistic

6. When Greta's psychoanalyst asked her to elaborate on certain aspects of her dream, she couldn't think of anything to say. Her lack of responsiveness is likely to be interpreted as
    (a) resistance.
    (b) catharsis.
    (c) transference.
    (d) spontaneous remission.

7. Dr. Whelan believes that people can overcome their problems if they learn to recognize and monitor their automatic thoughts and then try to empirically test the reality of those thoughts. Her approach is most consistent with
    (a) behavior therapy.
    (b) biomedical therapy.
    (c) cognitive therapy.
    (d) psychoanalysis.

8. A behavior therapist trains a child who is a frequent bedwetter to awaken and use the bathroom by arranging for an alarm to sound every time the child wets the bed. This technique is called _____ and illustrates the use of _____ conditioning principles.
    (a) aversive therapy; operant
    (b) the bell and pad treatment; classical
    (c) aversive therapy; classical
    (d) the bell and pad treatment; operant

9. For which of the following is Dr. Kelly most likely to prescribe a benzodiazepine drug called Valium?

   (a) Celia, who smokes three packs of cigarettes a day
   (b) Rachel, who suffers from nervous apprehension, intense anxiety, and an inability to relax
   (c) Garth, who irrationally believes that aliens are trying to steal his thoughts
   (d) Manuel, who fluctuates between extreme moods of euphoria and depression

10. Quentin has an irrational fear of flying. His therapist first teaches him to relax completely, then he asks him to come up with a list of anxiety-provoking images associated with flying. Finally, the therapist asks Quentin to close his eyes and imagine very clearly the least fearful scene on the list. Quentin's therapist is a _____ therapist using _____ .

    (a) behavior; systematic desensitization
    (b) cognitive; rational-emotive techniques
    (c) humanistic; emphatic understanding
    (d) psychoanalytic; free association

11. Jeneen is taking a prescription drug that contains a naturally occurring substance called lithium. It is most probable that she is suffering from

    (a) schizophrenia.   (c) chronic depression.
    (b) bipolar disorder.   (d) anxiety disorder.

12. Ursula, who lives in a home for the mentally retarded, is able to earn points for getting dressed, maintaining personal hygiene, and engaging in appropriate social interactions. These points can be exchanged for access to desirable items or special privileges. This example illustrates the use of

    (a) aversive conditioning.
    (b) counterconditioning.
    (c) systematic desensitization.
    (d) a token economy.

13. Seven-year-old Niall chews the ends of all his pens and pencils, so his mother paints them with a foul-tasting, but harmless, substance. After a few days of this treatment, Niall stops chewing his pens and pencils. Niall's mother has used a form of

    (a) transference.
    (b) counterconditioning.
    (c) aversive therapy.
    (d) electroconvulsive therapy.

14. According to In Focus 15.1, which of the following is true of Mary Cover Jones?

    (a) She identified herself as a behaviorist and used behavioral principles throughout her research career.
    (b) She conducted longitudinal research that documented changes in the subjects' somatic, environmental, family, attitudinal, and behavioral growth and change over a 55-year period.
    (c) She pioneered the use of virtual reality (VR) technology in the treatment of phobias.
    (d) She promoted the use of the drug Prozac for the treatment of severe depression.

15. According to the Application, which of the following is true of catharsis?

    (a) It produces long-term relief from most psychological disorders.
    (b) It is the cornerstone of the relationship between the therapist and the person seeking help.
    (c) It refers to the emotional relief that people experience from the simple act of talking about their problems.
    (d) It refers to the repression of anxiety-provoking emotions into the unconscious mind.

Progress Test 3

After you have checked your understanding of the material in Progress Tests 1 and 2, and have done a complete chapter review with special focus on any areas of weakness, you are ready to further assess your knowledge on Progress Test 3. Check your answers. If you make a mistake, review your notes, the appropriate parts of the study guide, and if necessary, the relevant sections of your textbook.

1. Mr. Keiko, a middle-aged Japanese American, has been referred to a psychologist because he is displaying the classic symptoms of anxiety and depression. A problem that may occur with a Western-style therapist is that Mr. Keiko may
   (a) be reluctant to discuss personal, intimate details of his life with a stranger.
   (b) prefer to deal with a female rather than a male therapist.
   (c) believe that insight and awareness of all painful thoughts and feelings are necessary for mental health.
   (d) do all of the above.

2. Aaron Beck is to _____ as Carl Rogers is to _____ .
   (a) cognitive therapy; rational emotive therapy
   (b) behavior therapy; client-centered therapy
   (c) biomedical therapy; psychoanalysis
   (d) cognitive therapy; client-centered therapy

3. Because of Rhian's persistent feelings of hopelessness, dejection, and guilt, and her suicidal thoughts, her doctor is likely to prescribe an antidepressant drug called
   (a) Prozac.   (c) Valium.
   (b) chlorpromazine. (d) lithium.

4. Masahara goes to a therapist who specializes in a Japanese psychotherapy called Naikan therapy. It is very probable that he will be advised
   (a) that being self-absorbed is the surest path to psychological suffering.
   (b) to focus on developing a sense of gratitude and obligation towards significant others.
   (c) to meditate on how much his parents and others have done for him and how he may have failed to meet their needs.
   (d) to reflect on the trouble and problems he may have caused significant others.
   (e) to do all of the above.

5. Mrs. Blonska has been diagnosed with generalized anxiety disorder. Because her doctor is concerned with the long-term treatment of her global and persistent feelings of anxiety, he is likely to prescribe
   (a) Buspar.   (c) Depakote.
   (b) Prozac.   (d) Clozapine.

6. Mr. MacKaskill has a serious drinking problem. In order to reduce his intake of alcohol, a behavior therapist might give Mr. MacKaskill a medication called Antabuse, which induces nausea whenever it is taken with alcohol. This behavioral technique is called
   (a) counterconditioning.
   (b) systematic desensitization.
   (c) aversive therapy.
   (d) the token economy.

7. For no obvious reason, Mr. Henderson has recently begun to express feelings of annoyance, irritability, and anger toward his therapist, who has been consistently patient, concerned, and supportive. Freud would most likely consider Mr. Henderson's hostility toward his therapist to be an example of
   (a) insight.   (c) aversion.
   (b) counterconditioning. (d) transference.

8. Dr. Elson uses a therapeutic technique that involves modifying behavior by conditioning a new response that is incompatible with a previously learned undesired response. Dr. Elson is most likely a _____ therapist who is using _____ .
   (a) behavior; counterconditioning
   (b) cognitive; rational-emotive techniques
   (c) psychoanalytic; free association
   (d) biomedical; ECT

9. Nelson's therapist believes that a therapist should be nondirective, providing unconditional positive regard in an open, honest way. Nelson's therapist is most likely a _____ therapist.
   (a) psychoanalytic   (c) cognitive
   (b) behavioral   (d) humanistic

10. During a lecture to students interested in graduate work in clinical psychology, Dr. Barton is asked what factors contribute most to effective psychotherapy. He is most likely to respond that
   (a) mutual respect, trust, and hope in the therapeutic situation are important factors.
   (b) therapists who have warmth, sensitivity, sincerity, and genuineness are usually effective.
   (c) clients who are motivated, expressive, and actively committed to therapy enhance the success of therapy.
   (d) all of the above contribute to effective psychotherapy.

11. Brian's therapist attempts to tailor her approach to his particular problems and characteristics and, in doing so, makes use of techniques from different psychotherapies. Brian's therapist would most likely be classified as a(n) _____ therapist.
    (a) humanistic
    (b) eclectic
    (c) behavior
    (d) cognitive

12. Which of the following individuals is most likely to benefit from a psychoactive drug that affects the level of the neurotransmitter dopamine in the brain?
    (a) Herman, who hears imaginary voices telling him that he is going to be abducted by aliens
    (b) Marcel, who is very nervous and anxious all the time
    (c) Carla, who feels sad, despondent, dejected, and worthless most of the time
    (d) Faith, who drinks at least a six-pack of beer every day

13. Harriet has asked her psychology professor whether psychotherapy is more effective than no therapy at all. If her professor is familiar with the meta-analytic studies on the topic, he is most likely to answer that
    (a) psychotherapy is no more effective than talking to a friend.
    (b) it is not possible to measure the effectiveness of psychotherapy.
    (c) psychotherapy harms more people than it helps.
    (d) psychotherapy is significantly more effective than no treatment.

14. Self-help groups are discussed in In Focus 15.3. Which of the following points is made?
    (a) Compared with therapy provided by mental health professionals, self-help groups are generally ineffective for the vast majority of psychological problems.
    (b) All self-help groups are organized and led by nonprofessionals.
    (c) Compared with professional mental health services, self-help groups are much more likely to cause harm to the people involved.
    (d) Self-help groups are most useful for people with mood disorders.

15. According to Critical Thinking 15.4, which of the following is true?
    (a) Prozac helps seriously depressed people regain a normal level of functioning.
    (b) There is solid scientific evidence that Prozac can fundamentally alter and enhance functioning in every aspect of a normal person's life.
    (c) Prozac is an antipsychotic medication that alleviates the symptoms of schizophrenia.
    (d) Cosmetic pharmacology is now an accepted therapeutic approach used by most biomedical practitioners.

Answers

Introduction: Psychotherapy and Biomedical Therapy

1. (a) psychological disorder; troubled; transitions
   (b) psychological; emotional, behavioral; interpersonal; psychological
   (c) medication; medical; psychological; biological
   (d) psychological; psychiatrists
   (e) psychoanalytic, humanistic, behavioral; cognitive

Psychoanalytic Therapy

1. (a) personality; continue to be
   (b) early childhood; unresolved; frustrated; repressed
   (c) maladjusted; psychological; unconscious; conscious
   (d) insight; relationship
   (e) dreams, memory; slips of the tongue

2. (a) unconscious; conscious; free association; thoughts, mental images; feelings; inadvertent
   (b) free association; resistance; repressed
   (c) dream; sleep; dreams
   (d) manifest; latent
   (e) questions; resistance; elaborate; interpretations; dreams, free associations; resistance
   (f) transference
   (g) past; behavior; relationships; insights
   (h) slow

3. (a) few; specific; eight
   (b) a few months; quickly; specific, concrete; directive
   (c) interpretations; feelings; transferences; psychological
   (d) seldom; continue to be

4. (a) manifest
   (b) latent
   (c) resistance
   (d) transference

Matching Exercise 1

1. Sigmund Freud

2. psychotherapy

3. interpretation

4. psychoanalysis

5. biomedical therapy

6. short-term dynamic therapies

7. transference

True/False Test 1

1. T   3. T   5. T
2. F   4. T   6. F

Humanistic Therapy

1. (a) potential; awareness; choice; conscious, subjective
   (b) good; psychologically; choices; potential

2. (a) client-centered; person-centered
   (b) sick; heal (cure); client-centered; subjective
   (c) insight; interpretations; nondirective
   (d) direct; decisions; solutions; client

3. (a) honestly; openly; genuineness
   (b) unconditional positive regard; conditional acceptance; self-concept
   (c) empathic understanding; actively; thoughts; feelings
   (d) genuineness, unconditional positive regard; empathic understanding; self-actualization
   (e) supported; marital; parenting; business

Behavior Therapy

1. (a) modify; personality; past; current
   (b) learned; unlearning; learning
   (c) classical; operant; observational

2. (a) classically; generalized
   (b) reversing; counterconditioning
   (c) feared; pleasant; eliminated
   (d) observational learning; imitate

3. (a) incompatible; inhibits
   (b) progressive relaxation; relaxing; relaxation
   (c) hierarchy; relaxing; control
   (d) hierarchy; relaxation; hierarchy
   (e) control; progressive relaxation
   (f) hierarchy; relaxation; relaxation
   (g) observational; highly

4. (a) more; wake up
   (b) classically; bell
   (c) stimulus; response
   (d) psychological; modify
   (e) sexual; regressive; sexual
   (f) more; greater

5. (a) unpleasant; positive
   (b) nausea
   (c) not very; generalize

6. (a) shaped; consequences; reinforcement; extinction; punishment
   (b) positive; extinction
   (c) groups of people; strengthening; positive
   (d) positive; reinforcers
   (e) prisons, classrooms; psychiatric

7. (a) humanistic; client-centered
   (b) behavior therapy (systematic desensitization)
   (c) aversive
   (d) token economy
   (e) bell and pad treatment
   (f) client-centered; empathic understanding

Matching Exercise 2

1. Mary Cover Jones

2. humanistic perspective

3. token economy

4. genuineness

5. behavior therapy

6. Carl Rogers

7. progressive relaxation

8. bell and pad treatment

9. client-centered therapy

10. reinforcement

True/False 2

1. F   4. T   7. F
2. T   5. T   8. T
3. T   6. T   9. F

Cognitive Therapies

1. (a) external; thinks
   (b) thinking; change

2. (a) Albert Ellis; expectations; irrational; irrational
   (b) activating; beliefs; consequences
   (c) irrational; dispute; challenge
   (d) unhealthy negative emotions; self-defeating; anxiety; depression

(e) irrational; unhealthy; interpreting; responding

(f) rational; healthy

(g) effective; depression, social phobia; anxiety

3. (a) depression; depressed

(b) depressed; cognitive; distorting; perceptions; cognitive; depression

(c) think; thinking

(d) irrational; depression; distorted; unrealistic; empirically

4. (a) automatic thoughts; automatic thoughts

(b) empirically; automatic thoughts; test

(c) model; automatic thoughts; collaboration

(d) effective; depression; anxiety; eating

Group and Family Therapy

1. (a) simultaneously

(b) group therapy

(c) individual; cohesion

(d) cost-effective; self-perceptions; unique; advice; models; behaviors

(e) self-help; support

2. (a) whole family; interaction

(b) system; dynamic

(c) rules; power; decisions; peace; patterns

(d) enhance; system

(e) marital; couple

(f) couple; social; cultural; cultural

Culture and Psychotherapy: Bridging the Culture Gap

1. (a) independent, autonomous; internal; internal

(b) assertive; dependent; potential

(c) family; group; community; group

(d) network

(e) interdependence; psychological

(f) group; family; self-absorbed

(g) self; parents

2. (a) family members; friends; spiritual; spiritual

(b) refugees; immigrants

(c) insight; avoid

(d) disclose; friend; stranger

(e) public; indirectly; nonverbally; restraint; open

(f) less; more

Evaluating the Effectiveness of Psychotherapy

1. (a) meta-analysis; pooling; single

(b) do not seek; friends; family; self-help; spontaneous remission

(c) control

(d) more

(e) are

2. (a) cognitive; behavioral; insight-oriented; little or no difference

(b) therapeutic; therapist; cultural; client; external

(c) specific; differences

3. (a) eclecticism

(b) problems; characteristics

4. (a) meta-analysis

(b) eclectic

(c) group

(d) rational-emotive

(e) cognitive

(f) family

Graphic Organizer 1

Psychoanalysis:

Founder: Sigmund Freud

Source of Problems: Repressed, unconscious conflicts stemming from early childhood experiences

Treatment Techniques: Free association, analysis of dream content, interpretation, and transference

Goals of Therapy: To recognize, work through, and resolve longstanding conflicts

Client-Centered Therapy:

Founder: Carl Rogers

Source of Problems: Conditional acceptance and dependence that causes a person to develop a distorted self-concept and worldview

Treatment Techniques: Nondirective therapy, with therapist displaying unconditional positive regard, genuineness, and empathic understanding

Goals of Therapy: To develop self-awareness, self-acceptance, and self-determination

Behavior Therapy:

Founder: Various; derived from the fundamental principles of learning

Source of Problems: Learned maladaptive behavior patterns

Treatment Techniques: Systematic desensitization, bell and pad treatment, aversive conditioning, reinforcement and extinction, token economy, observational learning

Goals of Therapy: To unlearn maladaptive behaviors and learn adaptive behaviors in their place

Rational-Emotive Therapy

Founder: Albert Ellis

Source of Problems: Irrational beliefs

Treatment Techniques: Very directive therapy: identifying, logically disputing, and challenging irrational beliefs

Goals of Therapy: To surrender irrational beliefs and absolutist demands

Cognitive Therapy:
Founder: Aaron T. Beck
Source of Problems: Unrealistic, distorted perceptions and interpretations of events due to cognitive biases
Treatment Techniques: Directive collaboration: teaching client to monitor automatic thoughts; testing accuracy of conclusions; correcting distorted thinking and perception
Goals of Therapy: To accurately and realistically perceive self, others, and external events

Matching Exercise 3

1. catharsis
2. family therapy
3. cognitive therapies
4. cognitive therapy
5. group therapy
6. rational-emotive therapy
7. spontaneous remission

True/False Test 3

1. F   3. T   5. F
2. T   4. T   6. T

Biomedical Therapies

1. (a) psychoactive medications
   (b) psychiatrist; family
2. (a) reserpine
   (b) chlorpromazine; Thorazine
   (c) reserpine; chlorpromazine (Thorazine); antipsychotic
   (d) dopamine; antipsychotic; dopamine
   (e) hallucinations, delusions
3. (a) cure
   (b) social; apathy, flat
   (c) side effects
   (d) dopamine; side effects
   (e) tardive dyskinesia
   (f) revolving door
4. (a) atypical; serotonin; dopamine
   (b) movement-related; dopamine; negative; significant
   (c) side effects; olanzapine; benefits; side effects
5. (a) benzodiazepines; GABA
   (b) coordination, alertness; reaction; intensified; addictive; dependency
   (c) side effects; dependency; addiction
   (d) anxiety; anxiety; panic; anxiety

6. (a) lithium; manic; depressive
   (b) mania; depression
   (c) therapeutic; toxic; manic; poisoning
   (d) glutamate
   (e) Depakote
7. (a) hopelessness, guilt, dejection; concentrating; sleep; appetite
   (b) tricyclics; MAO; norepinephrine; serotonin
   (c) side effects
   (d) no more; many
   (e) serotonin; inhibitors; serotonin
   (f) Prozac; fewer; milder
8. (a) depression; a brief burst of electrical current
   (b) confusion; disorientation
   (c) memory; depression
   (d) is; higher
   (e) cognitive; language; verbal
9. (a) antianxiety
   (b) electroconvulsive
   (c) tardive dyskinesia
   (d) lithium
   (e) clozapine; risperidone

Matching Exercise 4

1. lithium
2. psychoactive medications
3. electroconvulsive therapy (ECT)
4. antianxiety medications
5. antidepressant medications
6. tardive dyskinesia
7. antipsychotic medications
8. catharsis

Something to Think About

1. The first thing to tell someone with a phobia is that there are many different therapeutic approaches in psychology, such as psychoanalysis, client-centered therapy, cognitive therapy, and behavior therapy. It would be appropriate to briefly explain the differences between each of these approaches and to advise the person to seek professional help if she feels that her problem is severe. Having said that, you can then go on to describe an approach that has been relatively effective in dealing with phobias—systematic desensitization.

   The first step in systematic desensitization is for the person to learn how to relax completely. This is because a state of complete relaxation is incompatible with being tense and anxious. The second step is to have the person generate a hierarchy of feared situations associated with flying. For example, the most feared situation the person can imagine might be sitting on the plane during take off and the least fearful might be hearing someone talking about flying. Once the person is totally relaxed, she can start imagining the least fearful situation in the hierarchy. When she can do that for a number of times without tensing up, she can move to the next situation in the hierarchy, and so on. It is also helpful for the person to create an unrelated, relaxing control scene, such as lying on the beach watching the waves roll in, which can be used to help her relax. Over a number of sessions, the person works her way up the hierarchy while relaxing completely, until eventually she can approach the real situation.

In practice, systematic desensitization is often combined with other techniques, such as counterconditioning (pairing pleasant associations, such as being able to travel to exotic islands, with the feared situation) and observational learning (using the real situation or a video), which involves watching other people being calm and relaxed in the anxiety-provoking situation. As noted in the In Focus Box 15.2, computer simulations using virtual reality technology are now being used with some success to treat certain phobias.

2. First, people seek help from mental health professionals not only for psychological problems but also for dealing with troubled relationships, coping with transitions in life, and other troubling situations. Second, there should be no stigma attached to getting help when it is needed. The prevalence of psychological disorders and similar types of problems is much higher than most people realize, so we all probably know someone who is or has been in therapy or perhaps needs to be. So, what should we expect from psychotherapy? The Application gives some important guidelines about the therapist-client relationship and the psychotherapy process.

The cornerstone of psychotherapy is the relationship between the therapist and the person seeking help. This relationship is a collaborative endeavor in which the client is actively involved in the therapeutic process. Therapy requires work not only during the therapy sessions but also outside them. So people should expect to be involved and active. In addition, people should not expect the therapist to make

decisions for them. Virtually all forms of therapy are designed to increase a person's sense of responsibility, confidence, and mastery in dealing with life's problems. The therapist is there to help.

A therapist is not a substitute friend. Rather, he or she is more of a consultant, responding objectively and honestly to issues and problems. In addition, ethically and legally, everything that goes on in therapy is totally confidential. And, under no circumstances does therapeutic intimacy include sexual intimacy.

A person should also expect therapy to challenge how he or she thinks and acts, which sometimes can be a painful process. But becoming aware that changes are needed is a necessary step toward developing healthier forms of thinking and behavior. It is important, however, not to confuse insight with change. Just because people gain an understanding of the sources and nature of their psychological problems does not mean that they will automatically resolve these problems. Likewise, the catharsis that often results from therapy is not synonymous with change. With some effort and the help of the therapeutic process, people can move toward changing how they think, behave, and react to other people, but this will not happen overnight.

Progress Test 1

1. a	6. b	11. c
2. d	7. b	12. c
3. d	8. d	13. e
4. a	9. c	14. a
5. c	10. b	15. b

Progress Test 2

1. d	6. a	11. b
2. c	7. c	12. d
3. d	8. b	13. c
4. c	9. b	14. b
5. d	10. a	15. c

Progress Test 3

1. a	6. c	11. b
2. d	7. d	12. a
3. a	8. a	13. d
4. e	9. d	14. b
5. a	10. d	15. a

Statistics: Understanding Data

PREVIEW

Reading the section below first will give you a general sense of the chapter's contents and an initial introduction to some of the major concepts and terms. This will prime you for what you are about to read and help you to develop a "cognitive map" that will guide your study of the material in this chapter. Likewise, reading the **preview questions** at the beginning of each major section will improve your ability to understand, learn, and retain the information.

APPENDIX A . . . AT A GLANCE

Appendix A explains how and when various statistical techniques are used. Descriptive statistics are used to organize and summarize data in a meaningful way. Examples discussed include frequency distributions, which can be presented as a table, histogram, or frequency polygon; measures of central tendency (mode, median, and mean); and measures of variability (range and standard deviation). z scores are explained, and the concept of the normal distribution is presented.

Correlation, which is introduced in Chapter 1, is described, and how the correlation coefficient is calculated is explained. The point is made that correlational research is restricted to prediction and cannot be used to identify cause-and-effect relationships. The scatter diagram can be used to depict graphically the relationship between two variables.

Inferential statistics are used to determine whether outcomes of a study can be generalized to a larger population, and they provide information about the probability of a particular result if only random factors are operating. The text notes that if the probability of the outcome resulting from chance factors is small, the findings are said to be statistically significant.

Descriptive Statistics

Preview Questions

Consider the following questions as you study this section of the chapter.

- What are descriptive statistics, and what are they used for?
- How do frequency distributions, histograms, and frequency polygons differ from each other?
- What are the three measures of central tendency, and how do they differ in the results they obtain?
- What are the two measures of variability, and how are *z* scores derived?

*Read the section "Descriptive Statistics" and **write** your answers to the following:*

1. (a) Descriptive statistics are used to
    _____ and _____
    data in a meaningful way.

    (b) A frequency distribution is a(n)
    _____ of how often various
    scores occur; _____ are set up,
    and occurrences of each _____
    are tallied to give the frequency of each.

    (c) A histogram is a way of _____
    representing a frequency distribution. It is
    like a bar chart with two special features:
    the bars are always _____ and
    they always _____ .

    (d) A frequency polygon is another way of
    _____ representing a frequency
    distribution. In contrast to a histogram, on a
    frequency polygon, a mark is made above
    each _____ at the point
    representing its frequency and these marks
    are then connected by

    _____ .

2. (a) An asymmetrical distribution with more
    scores piled up on one side of the distribu-
    tion than on the other is called a
    _____ distribution.

    (b) If most people have low scores, the distribu-
    tion is _____ .
    If most people have high scores, the distrib-
    ution is _____ .

    (c) A distribution in which scores fall equally on
    both halves of the graph is a(n)
    _____ distribution. An example
    of a(n) _____ distribution is the
    normal curve.

3. (a) A measure of central tendency is a single
    _____ that presents some infor-
    mation about the center of a
    _____ distribution.

    (b) The mode is the score or category that
    occurs most _____ in a set of
    raw scores or in a _____
    distribution.

    (c) The median is the score that falls in the
    _____ of a _____
    distribution; if the scores are arranged from
    lowest to highest, the median will have a(n)
    _____ number of scores on each
    side of it.

    (d) A problem with the _____ and
    the _____ is that both measures
    reflect only one score in the distribution.
    The mean is the _____ of a set
    of scores in a distribution _____
    by the number of scores; it is usually the
    most representative measure of central
    tendency.

    (e) Because each score in a distribution enters
    into its computation, the mean is particular-
    ly susceptible to _____ scores;
    any unusually _____ or
    _____ score will pull the mean
    in its direction.

4. (a) In addition to identifying the central tenden-
    cy in a distribution, researchers may want

to know how much scores in a distribution _____ from one another; a measure of _____ is a single number that presents information about the _____ of scores in a frequency distribution.

(b) A simple way to measure _____ is with the range, which is computed by subtracting the _____ score in a distribution from the _____ score; the range provides a limited amount of information because it depends on only the two most _____ scores in a distribution.

(c) The standard deviation is a measure of _____ that is expressed as the square root of the sum of the squared deviations around the mean divided by the number of scores in the distribution. The _____ the standard deviation, the more spread out are the scores in a distribution.

5. (a) Researchers can also describe the relative position of any individual score in a distribution by locating its distance from the mean in terms of

_____

units; a statistic called a _____ gives that information.

(b) If you subtract the mean from the score of interest (that is, calculate its deviation from the mean) and divide this quantity by the standard deviation, you have computed the _____ .

(c) A positive z score indicates that the score is _____ the mean; a negative z score shows that the score is _____ the mean.

(d) Some variables, such as height, weight, or IQ, if graphed for large numbers of people, fall into a characteristic pattern called the

_____

or the _____ .

This distribution is symmetrical, and the _____ , _____ , and _____ fall exactly in the middle.

6. Read the following and write the correct term in the space provided.

(a) Professor Wilson calculated the mode, median, and mean of the scores from the midterm exam. These are descriptive statistics referred to as

_____ .

(b) Professor Wilson noticed that the most frequently occurring score was 73; this score is called the _____ .

(c) In order to determine the spread of the scores, Professor Wilson subtracted the lowest score in the distribution from the highest. In this instance, he has calculated a measure of _____ called the _____ .

(d) Next, he subtracted the mean from each score in the distribution, squared each of these deviations, added them up, divided by the number of scores in the distribution, and finally took the square root of the number just calculated. Professor Wilson has calculated a measure of _____ called the _____ .

(e) Finally, Professor Wilson graphically represented the frequency distribution by placing a mark above each score at the point representing its frequency and then connecting these points with straight lines. This type of graph is called a(n)

_____ .

Review of Terms and Concepts 1

Use the terms in this list to complete the Matching Test, then to help you answer the True/False items correctly.

descriptive statistics
frequency distribution
histogram
frequency polygon
skewed distribution
positively skewed
  distribution
negatively skewed
  distribution
symmetrical distribution
measure of central
  tendency

mode
median
mean
measure of variability
range
standard deviation
z score
standard normal curve
  (standard normal
  distribution)

Matching Exercise

Match the appropriate term with its definition or description.

1. _____ A number, expressed in standard deviation units, that shows a score's deviation from the mean.

2. _____ Statistics used to organize and summarize data in a meaningful way.

3. _____ A symmetrical distribution forming a bell-shaped curve in which the mean, median, and mode are all equal and fall in the exact middle.

4. _____ A summary of how often various scores occur in a sample of scores. Score values are arranged in order of magnitude and the number of times each score occurs is recorded.

5. _____ Measure of variability; expressed as the square root of the sum of the squared deviations around the mean divided by the number of scores in the distribution.

6. _____ An asymmetrical distribution; more scores pile up on one side of the distribution than on the other.

7. _____ A single number that presents information about the spread of scores in a frequency distribution.

8. _____ Distribution in which the scores fall equally on both sides of the graph. The normal curve is an example.

9. _____ Measure of variability; the highest score in a distribution minus the lowest score.

True/False Test

Indicate whether each statement is true or false by placing T or F in the blank space next to each item.

1. ____ In a positively skewed distribution, most people have high scores.

2. ____ The mode is the most frequently occurring score in a distribution.

3. ____ A measure of central tendency is a single number that presents some information about the "center" of a frequency distribution.

4. ____ In a negatively skewed distribution, most people have low scores.

5. ____ A histogram is a way of graphically representing a frequency distribution where frequency is marked above each score category on the graph's horizontal axis and the marks are connected by straight lines.

6. ____ The mean is the sum of a set of scores in a distribution divided by the number of scores and is usually the most representative measure of central tendency.

7. ____ A frequency polygon is a way of graphically representing a frequency distribution and is a type of bar chart using vertical bars that touch.

8. ____ The median is the score that divides a frequency distribution exactly in half, so that the same number of scores lies on each side of it.

Check your answers and review any areas of weakness before going on to the next section.

Correlation and Inferential Statistics

Preview Questions

Consider the following questions as you study these sections of the chapter.

- How is correlation defined, and what is the difference between a negative and positive correlation?

- What is the correlation coefficient, and how is it depicted graphically?

- How are inferential statistics used, and what is meant by statistical significance?

- What is meant by the terms *population* and *sample*, and why is sampling used?

*Read the sections "Correlation" and "Inferential Statistics" and **write** your answers to the following:*

1. (a) Correlation is the _____ between two variables and is assessed by a statistic called the correlation coefficient; this is a measure of the _____ and _____ of the relationship between two variables.

   (b) To compute a correlation coefficient, the data from both variables of interest can be converted to _____ . This is done so that data in different forms can be put into a standard scale.

   (c) A correlation coefficient can range anywhere from _____ to _____ . The exact number tells us about the _____ of the relationship being measured and its _____ .

   (d) A number close to _____ indicates a strong relationship, whereas a number close to _____ indicates a weak relationship. The sign (+ or –) of the correlation tells us about the relationship's _____ .

   (e) A positive correlation coefficient means that as one variable _____ , the second variable tends to _____ ; a negative correlation coefficient indicates that as one variable _____ , the other tends to _____ .

2. (a) Plotting two variables together creates a _____ , or _____ .

   (b) A straight diagonal line starting in the lower lefthand corner of the graph and progressing to the upper right represents a perfect _____ correlation; a straight diagonal line starting in the upper lefthand corner of the graph and ending at the lower righthand corner represents a perfect _____ correlation. When data points fall randomly with no general direction to them, a _____ correlation is depicted.

   (c) In addition to describing the relationship between two variables, correlation coefficients are useful for another purpose: _____ ; knowing a person's score on one of two related variables helps _____ what the person's score will be on the other variable.

   (d) The one thing a correlation does not tell us is _____ ; the fact that two variables are highly correlated does not mean that one variable directly _____ the other. The only way to determine _____ and _____ is to conduct an experiment.

3. (a) Inferential statistics allow researchers to determine whether the outcome in a study is likely to be more than just a _____ event and whether it can be legitimately _____ to a larger population.

   (b) If the results of a study are more extreme than would be expected by _____ alone, we reject the idea that no _____ effect has occurred and conclude that the manipulation of the independent variable is the reason for the obtained results; when this happens, the results are _____ .

   (c) Generally, if the probability of obtaining a particular result if random factors alone are operating is less than _____ (5 chances out of 100), the results are considered _____ .

   Researchers who want to be even more sure set their probability value at _____ (1 chance out of a 100).

4. (a) A complete set of something—people, nonhuman animals, objects, or events is called a
_____ . Because the entire
_____ of interest usually cannot
be studied, researchers select a subset of the
population, called a _____ .

5. Read the following and write the correct term
in the space provided.

(a) Dr. Jabul discovers that the more education
people have, the more money they tend to
earn. Dr. Jabul has discovered a
_____ correlation.

(b) Based on his research, Dr. Jabul can use one
variable to _____ the other but
he cannot say that one variable
_____ the other.

(c) When Professor Alphonse plotted his data
on a scatter plot, he noticed that they clustered in a pattern that extends from the
upper lefthand hand corner of the graph to
the lower righthand corner. This pattern
suggests that the two variables are
_____ related.

(d) When Kayla analyzed the correlational data
for her psychology project, the correlation
coefficient was +.07. Kayla can conclude that
the two variables _____ (are/are
not) correlated.

(e) When researchers analyzed the data from
their experiment, they found large differences between the control group and the
experimental group that were not due to
chance. They can conclude that the results
are _____ .

(f) In order to discover how people feel about
the level of service provided, the ABC company asks a randomly selected subset of
their customers to fill in a brief questionnaire. ABC's customers represent the
_____ , and the subset surveyed
is a(n) _____ .

Review of Terms and Concepts 2

*Use the terms in this list to complete the Matching
Test, then to help you answer the True/False items
correctly.*

correlation	scatter diagram (scatter
correlation coefficient	plot)
positive correlation	inferential statistics
coefficient	statistically significant
negative correlation	population
coefficient	sample

Matching Exercise

*Match the appropriate term with its definition or
description.*

1. _____ Graph that represents the
relationship between two variables.

2. _____ Measure of the magnitude
and direction of the relationship (the correlation) between two variables; the closer the
number is to +1 or −1, the stronger the relationship.

3. _____ Statistical techniques that
allow researchers to determine whether the
outcomes in a study are likely to be more than
just chance events and whether they can be
legitimately generalized to a larger population.

4. _____ A complete set of something—people, nonhuman animals, objects, or
events.

5. _____ The relationship between
two variables.

True/False Test

*Indicate whether each statement is true or false by
placing T or F in the blank space next to each item.*

1. ____ Results can be considered statistically significant when the probability of obtaining them,
if chance factors alone are operating, is less
than .05 (5 chances out of 100).

2. ____ A positive correlation coefficient indicates
that as one variable increases, the other tends
to decrease.

3. ____ A sample is a subset of a population.

4. ____ A negative correlation coefficient indicates
that as one variable increases, the other tends
to increase.

Check your answers and review any areas of
weakness before doing the progress tests.

Progress Test 1

Review the complete chapter, review all your study notes, and then test yourself on the following progress test. Check your answers. If you make a mistake, review your notes, review the relevant section of the study guide, and, if necessary, go back and read the appropriate part of your textbook.

1. Professor Admunson used a scatter diagram to depict the relationship between her students' high school GPA and their first-year GPA in college. She noticed that the data points clustered in a pattern that extend from the lower left-hand corner of the graph to the upper right-hand corner. This pattern suggests that the two variables
   (a) are negatively correlated.
   (b) have no relationship.
   (c) are positively correlated.
   (d) have a cause-and-effect relationship.

2. A measure of variability is to _____ as a measure of central tendency is to _____ .
   (a) mode; median
   (b) correlation; scatter plot
   (c) standard deviation; mean
   (d) histogram; frequency polygon

3. One student in the class got an extremely low score of 10 out of 100 on a test. Which measure of central tendency is most affected by this low score?
   (a) mode   (c) median
   (b) mean   (d) range

4. Following the final exam, Professor Farrar calculated a number of statistics and noticed that the standard deviation was extremely small. This indicates that
   (a) the scores on the exam were clustered around the mean and not spread out.
   (b) the distribution was skewed.
   (c) the scores had a great deal of variability and were not clustered around the mean.
   (d) there were very few students in her class.

5. Mrs. Kodiak has seven children aged 3, 5, 8, 9, 12, 15, and 15. The median age of her children is
   (a) 9.   (c) 12.
   (b) 15.   (d) 67.

6. When the results of an experiment were examined and the appropriate statistics calculated, the researchers concluded that the probability of obtaining these results, if random factors alone were operating, was less than .01. The results are
   (a) probably due to chance.
   (b) statistically insignificant.
   (c) skewed.
   (d) statistically significant.

7. For his class presentation, Liam prepared a graph that depicted a frequency distribution with vertical bars that touched each other. Liam has constructed a
   (a) scatter diagram.
   (b) frequency polygon.
   (c) histogram.
   (d) standard deviation.

8. Liam's graph is a symmetrical distribution with an equal number of scores on each side of the graph. It is very likely that the
   (a) mean is larger than the median.
   (b) mode is larger than the mean.
   (c) mean, mode, and median have the same value.
   (d) median is larger than the mode.

9. When researchers calculated the correlation coefficients for two different sets of data, they discovered that set A had a negative correlation of −.85 and set B had a positive correlation of +.62. They can conclude that
   (a) set A has a stronger correlation than set B.
   (b) set A has a weaker correlation than set B.
   (c) set B has a stronger correlation than set A.
   (d) both (b) and (c).

10. When Gary calculated the mean, median, and mode of the data in his frequency distribution, he was using
    (a) inferential statistics.
    (b) descriptive statistics.
    (c) correlational statistics.
    (d) measures of variability.

Progress Test 2

After you have checked your understanding of the material in Progress Test 1 and have done a complete chapter review with special focus on any areas of weakness, you are ready to assess your knowledge of Progress Test 2. Check your answers. If you make a mistake, review your notes, the relevant section of the study guide, and, if necessary, the appropriate part of your textbook.

1. In addition to calculating the range, Matthew also calculated the standard deviation for his frequency distribution of scores. Matthew is using
   (a) measures of variability.
   (b) inferential statistics.
   (c) measures of central tendency.
   (d) correlational statistics.

2. When Professor Kitahara finished marking the final exams, he plotted the results on a graph by marking the frequency above each score category on the horizontal axis and then connected the marks using straight lines. Professor Kitahara has constructed a
   (a) frequency distribution.
   (b) histogram.
   (c) frequency polygon.
   (d) scatter diagram.

3. Professor Kitahara observed that the graph was a symmetrical distribution that resembled a bell-shaped curve and that the mean, median, and mode were all equal. A student who scored better than 84 percent of the other students in this distribution would have a z score of
   (a) +1.   (c) +.84.
   (b) −1.   (d) −.84.

4. Hanna has a grade point average of 3.5. What measure of central tendency was used to calculate this statistic?
   (a) median
   (b) standard deviation
   (c) mode
   (d) mean

5. In her research, Dr. Simiak found that the more credit cards people have, the less money they have in their savings accounts. Dr. Simiak has found a _____ correlation between the number of credit cards owned and savings.
   (a) positive   (c) negative
   (b) zero   (d) skewed

6. Range is to mode as _____ is to _____ .
   (a) correlation; scatter diagram
   (b) median; mode
   (c) correlation coefficient; z score
   (d) variability; central tendency

7. Fydor compared two frequency distributions and noticed that in the first distribution most people had low scores and in the second distribution most people had high scores. The first distribution is _____ , and the second distribution is _____ .
   (a) positively skewed; negatively skewed
   (b) symmetrical; normal
   (c) negatively skewed; positively skewed
   (d) a polygon; a histogram

8. When Tyborg calculated the mean and standard deviation for a set of scores, he found that the mean was 55 out of a 100 and the standard deviation was 15. If the scores are normally distributed, Tyborg can conclude that approximately 68 percent of the scores are between.
   (a) 40 and 70.   (c) 55 and 70.
   (b) 25 and 85.   (d) 40 and 55.

9. In the above example, a student with a z score of −1 would have a score of
   (a) 55.   (c) 70.
   (b) 40.   (d) 25.

10. During the past month Karianne read 8 books, Kyle read 2 books, Phylis read 4 books, and Phillip read 6 books. The mean number of books read by this group is
   (a) 5.   (c) 8.
   (b) 20.   (d) 6.

Progress Test 3

After you have checked your understanding of the material in Progress Tests 1 and 2, and have done a complete chapter review with special focus on any areas of weakness, you are ready to further assess your knowledge on Progress Test 3. Check your answers. If you make a mistake, review your notes, the appropriate parts of the study guide, and if necessary, the relevant sections of your textbook.

1. A complete set of something (people, objects, events, etc.) is to a _____ as a representative subset is to a _____ .
   (a) descriptive statistics; inferential statistics
   (b) sample; population

(c) inferential statistics; descriptive statistics
(d) population; sample

2. Dr. Soryun carried out the appropriate calculations on her data and noticed that results were more extreme than would be expected by chance. She concluded that the probability of obtaining these results if random factors alone were operating was less than 1 chance out of a 100. Dr. Soryun has used _____ statistics, and the results can be called

_____ .

(a) descriptive statistics; statistically significant
(b) inferential statistics; positively skewed
(c) descriptive statistics; positively skewed
(d) inferential statistics; statistically significant

3. Organizing and summarizing data is to _____ as making inferences and drawing conclusions is to _____ .
(a) descriptive statistics; inferential statistics
(b) correlational research; experimental research
(c) inferential statistics; descriptive statistics
(d) experimental research; correlational research

4. Researchers at State University are interested in determining to what extent personality variables such as impatience, aggressiveness, and hostility could be used to predict the risk of cardiovascular disease. These researchers are most likely to use _____ in their research.
(a) a measure of variability
(b) the correlation coefficient
(c) the standard normal distribution
(d) the standard deviation

5. After analyzing his data, Jamie decided to depict his results in a graph. He noticed that the data points clustered in a pattern that extended from the upper lefthand corner to the lower righthand corner on his graph. Jamie has constructed a _____ that shows a

_____ .

(a) polygon; skewed distribution
(b) scatter diagram; positive correlation
(c) histogram; symmetrical distribution
(d) scatter diagram; negative correlation

6. In his survey research, Dr. Khrod discovered that the more education people have, the less television they watch. Dr. Khrod has discovered a(n) _____ between television watching and level of education.
(a) negative correlation
(b) illusory correlation
(c) positive correlation
(d) cause-and-effect relationship

7. When Harpinder plotted his data, his graph closely resembled the normal curve and had a mean of 50 and a standard deviation of 5. Harpinder can be confident that approximately 68 percent of the scores are between
(a) +1 and –1 SDs.
(b) +2 and –2 SDs.
(c) +3 and –3 SDs.
(d) correlation coefficients of +1 and –1.

8. Raphael's z-score on the midterm was +1. If the class scores are normally distributed, Raphael has
(a) scored better than 34.13 percent of the class.
(b) scored worse than 34.13 percent of the class.
(c) scored better than 84 percent of the class.
(d) scored worse than 84 percent of the class.

9. When Professor Exman compared the statistics from her two introductory biology classes, she noticed that the standard deviation was 8.24 in class A and 3.76 in class B. She can conclude that
(a) the students in class A studied much harder than those in class B.
(b) the scores in class A had much more variability than those in class B.
(c) the range for both classes is likely to be identical.
(d) one very extreme score probably distorted the standard deviation for class A.

10. As a first step in analyzing her data, Tracianne calculated the mean, the mode, and the median. Tracianne has
(a) used inferential statistics.
(b) determined the statistical significance of her results.
(c) used descriptive statistics.
(d) calculated measures of variability.

462   Appendix A Statistics: Understanding Data

Answers

Descriptive Statistics

1. (a) organize; summarize
   (b) summary; categories; category
   (c) graphically; vertical; touch
   (d) graphically; category; straight lines

2. (a) skewed
   (b) positively skewed; negatively skewed
   (c) symmetrical; symmetrical

3. (a) number; frequency
   (b) frequently; frequency
   (c) middle; frequency; equal
   (d) mode; median; sum; divided
   (e) extreme; high; low

4. (a) differ; variability; spread
   (b) variability; lowest; highest; extreme
   (c) variability; larger

5. (a) standard deviation; z score
   (b) z score
   (c) above; below
   (d) standard normal curve; standard normal distribution; mean, median; mode

6. (a) measures of central tendency
   (b) mode
   (c) variability; range
   (d) variability; standard deviation
   (e) frequency polygon

Matching Exercise 1

1. z score
2. descriptive statistics
3. standard normal curve (standard normal distribution)
4. frequency distribution
5. standard deviation
6. skewed distribution
7. measure of variability
8. symmetrical distribution
9. range

True/False Test 1

1. F	4. F	7. F
2. T	5. F	8. T
3. T	6. T	

Correlation and Inferential Statistics

1. (a) relationship; magnitude; direction
   (b) z scores

(c) −1; +1; magnitude; direction
(d) 1; 0; direction
(e) increases; increase; increases; decrease

2. (a) scatter diagram; scatter plot
   (b) positive; negative; zero
   (c) prediction; predict
   (d) causation; causes; cause; effect

3. (a) chance; generalized
   (b) chance; real; statistically significant
   (c) .05; statistically significant; .01

4. (a) population; population; sample

5. (a) positive
   (b) predict; causes
   (c) negatively
   (d) are not
   (e) statistically significant
   (f) population; sample

Matching Exercise 2

1. scatter diagram (scatter plot)
2. correlation coefficient
3. inferential statistics
4. population
5. correlation

True/False Test 2

1. T	3. T
2. F	4. F

Progress Test 1

1. c	5. a	9. a
2. c	6. d	10. b
3. b	7. c	
4. a	8. c	

Progress Test 2

1. a	5. c	9. b
2. c	6. d	10. a
3. a	7. a	
4. d	8. a	

Progress Test 3

1. d	5. d	9. b
2. d	6. a	10. c
3. a	7. a	
4. b	8. c	

Industrial/Organizational Psychology

APPENDIX B . . . AT A GLANCE

Appendix B identifies and describes five major subfields of industrial/organization (I/O) psychology. Work settings, type of training, and employment outlook in the area of I/O psychology are examined.

Of the five subfields, personnel psychology and organizational behavior are explored in depth. Job analysis, personnel selection, effective job training programs, and accurate evaluation of job performance are all part of the work carried out in personnel psychology. These psychologists use many devices to help with the goal of selecting the best applicants for jobs and are concerned with the validity of these selection devices.

The discussion of organizational behavior begins with the topic of job satisfaction, noting the various hypotheses used to explain different levels of job satisfaction. Leadership and leadership effectiveness are also discussed. Three approaches to explaining leadership effectiveness are explored, and the text concludes that situational theories seem to do the best job. How leaders emerge in a group and how the glass ceiling prevents women and others from attaining positions of leadership in organizations are also examined.

Finally, trends for the future and their implications for I/O psychology are presented.

What Is Industrial/Organizational Psychology?

Preview Questions

Consider the following questions as you study this section of the chapter.

- What is industrial/organizational psychology?
- What are the five major subareas of industrial/organizational psychology?

*Read the section "What Is Industrial/Organizational Psychology?" and **write** your answers to the following:*

1. (a) Industrial/organizational psychology is the branch of psychology that focuses on the study of _____ at work; the field consists of five major _____ .

   (b) Personnel psychology focuses on the measurement of human characteristics, such as _____ , _____ , _____ , and personality dimensions. The major goals are to match people's characteristics with the characteristics required in a particular job and to accurately measure _____ performance and assess employee _____ needs.

   (c) Organizational behavior (OB) focuses on how the organization and the social environment in which people work affect their _____ and _____ ; these include job satisfaction, motivation, and organizational commitment.

   (d) The human factors subfield focuses on the _____ of equipment and the _____ of work procedures in light of human capabilities and limitations. The science of applying knowledge of physical characteristics to the _____ of equipment in order to minimize fatigue and discomfort and maximize productivity is

called _____ .

   (e) Vocational and career counseling is a combination of _____ psychology and _____ psychology and focuses on helping people choose occupations that best match their preferences, needs, and values. Psychologists in this specialty area also often help people, as they gain job knowledge and experience, to plan for _____ or _____ moves.

   (f) The goal of _____ (OD) is to bring about positive change in an organization, such as greater profitability or improvement in the quality of products. Changing the cultural beliefs and attitudes of an organization so that its members better appreciate the differences among human beings is called _____ .

Work Settings, Type of Training, and Employment Outlook

Preview Questions

Consider the following questions as you study this section of the chapter.

- What are the requirements for working in the field of I/O psychology, and what are the principal employment settings of I/O psychologists?
- What is the employment outlook for I/O psychologists?
- What jobs and careers are open to people with bachelor's degrees?

*Read the section "Work Settings, Type of Training, and Employment Outlook" and **write** your answers to the following:*

1. (a) Many I/O psychologists belong to a division of the American Psychological Association (APA) called the Society for Industrial and Organizational Psychologists (SIOP); of SIOP members, 89.8 percent have

_____ , 9.7 percent have
_____ degrees, and 0.4 percent
have _____ degrees.

(b) To work in the field of I/O psychology, a
_____ or a _____
degree is generally required. However, some
areas that are closely related to I/O are open
to those with _____ degrees.

(c) Over 39 percent of I/O psychologists work in
a university or college, 32.7 percent percent
work as _____ to organizations,
and the rest work in _____ or
_____ organizations.

(d) The employment outlook for those with
Ph.D.s and master's degrees appears
_____ (favorable/unfavorable).

2. (a) Although it is very difficult for people with
bachelor's degrees to find employment in the
field of I/O psychology, some related areas,
such as _____ ,
_____ , and
_____ and
managers, are open to them; the purpose of
these jobs is to help management make
effective use of employees'
_____ , _____ , and
abilities and to help employees find job
satisfaction.

(b) Another I/O-related career in which those
with bachelor's degrees may sometimes find
employment is that of
_____ .
These people deal with a variety of organizational problems, from helping organizations
relocate to helping them restructure; they
_____ , _____ , and
_____ information, make recommendations, and help to implement those
recommendations.

(c) A third I/O-related field open to those with
bachelor's degrees is

_____ .
These people typically work for
_____ supply firms, matching
employers with job applicants and job applicants with employers. Sales ability, self-
confidence as well as strong oral communication and interpersonal skills are needed.

Personnel Psychology

Preview Questions

_Consider the following questions as you study this
section of the chapter._

- What are the three major goals of personnel
psychology?
- What is the definition of job analysis, and how
is selection device validity used?
- What are the most common types of psychological tests and personnel selection devices used in
personnel psychology?

Read the section "Personnel Psychology" and **write**
your answers to the following:

1. (a) The three major goals of personnel psychologists are (1) _____ the best
applicant for the job; (2) _____
employees so that they perform their jobs
effectively; and (3) accurately
_____ employee performance.

(b) Job analysis is a technique in which the
major _____ of a job, along with
the human _____ needed to fill
it, are determined. Information about the
job is usually collected from employees who
currently hold the job or from their supervi-
sors; this may be done through a(n)
_____ , _____ , or
_____ .

(c) Selection devices such as tests and interviews are used to determine which applicants have the _____ ,
_____ , and _____
specified in a job analysis.

(d) Training program developers begin by comparing the current work _____ , _____ , and _____ of employees with the information obtained from the job analysis. They then design training programs to eliminate gaps between what currently exists and what is optimal.

(e) Job analysis is also the first step in the design of performance _____ systems; it defines and clarifies what effective performance is so that performance _____ instruments may be developed.

2. (a) Personnel psychologists are concerned with the degree to which selection devices are _____ ; selection device _____ refers to the extent to which a selection device is successful in distinguishing between those applicants who will become high performers and those who will not.

(b) Tests that are classified on the basis of what they measure and that are often used by employers are _____ tests.

(c) Tests that measure general intelligence or specific _____ skills, such as mathematical or verbal ability, are called _____ ability tests. _____ ability tests measure mechanical reasoning and may be used to predict job performance for engineering, carpentry, and assembly work. Tests that include measures of fine dexterity in fingers and hands, accuracy and speed of arm and hand movement, and eye-hand coordination are called _____ ability tests. _____ ability tests include measures of visual acuity, color vision, and hearing.

(d) Personality tests may be designed to measure either _____ or _____ personality characteris-

tics. An assessment of _____ personality characteristics might be appropriate for selecting people for sensitive jobs, such as nuclear plant operator, police officer, and airline pilot.

(e) Recently, tests designed to measure _____ personality traits, such as conscientiousness, extraversion, and agreeableness, have become more popular for the selection of employees.

(f) Tests that attempt to assess an applicant's attitudes about theft and the punishment of it, and perceptions about the prevalence of theft are called _____ tests. Because of the issues of faking and _____ , the Committee on Psychological Tests and Assessments of the APA has expressed concerns about the use of these tests in personnel selection.

3. (a) Work samples are typically used for jobs involving the manipulation of objects, whereas _____ exercises are usually used for jobs involving managerial or professional skills. In both, applicants are given a _____ of the job to perform; it is assumed that if they do well on this, they are likely to do well on the actual job.

(b) Although the general interview is one of the most commonly used selection devices, it typically possesses _____ ; that is, assessments of applicants in general interviews _____ (are/are not) strongly related to their subsequent job performance.

(c) The reason for the _____ of interviews is that they are often _____ ; questions may be vague and unrelated to job performance, and different questions are sometimes asked of different applicants.

(d) If developed and conducted properly,

_____ (structured/unstructured) interviews are adequate predictors of job performance; they should (1) be based on _____ ; (2) involve questions that elicit _____ information about the applicant; (3) involve questions that are asked of all applicants in the same _____ ; and (4) be _____ by a panel of interviewers who record and rate the applicant's responses.

Organizational Behavior and Trends for the Future

Preview Questions

Consider the following questions as you study these sections of the chapter.

- How is job satisfaction researched, and what are the main assumptions of the discrepancy hypothesis, the social influence hypothesis, and the dispositional factors approach?

- What is leadership, and how do trait, behavioral, and the situational (or contingency) theories explain leadership effectiveness?

- What is the glass ceiling, and how do gender and ethnicity affect leadership opportunities and career success?

- What are the main trends affecting the future of I/O psychology?

Read the sections "Organizational Behavior" and "Trends for the Future" and **write** _your answers to the following:_

1. (a) One approach used to explain differences in job satisfaction is based on the _____ hypothesis; its basic assumptions are (1) that people _____ in what they want from a job; (2) that people _____ in how they evaluate what they experience at work; and (3) that level of satisfaction is based on the differences between what is _____ and what is _____ .

    (b) A significant amount of research _____ (supports/does not support) the _____ hypothesis; negative _____ (getting less than desired) have been related to dissatisfaction, and positive _____ (getting more than desired) have also been related to dissatisfaction in some cases.

2. (a) The social influence hypothesis is based on the idea that people _____ their situations, in part, according to the reactions of others. When _____ their own job satisfaction, people may be influenced by the attitudes of their coworkers regarding the degree to which the job is satisfying.

    (b) Research has shown that people who heard others evaluate a task positively were _____ (likely/not likely) to evaluate the task positively when they performed it later. Similarly, people who heard others evaluate a task negatively were later _____ (likely/not likely) to evaluate the task negatively.

3. (a) Recently, _____ factors have been used to explain differences in job satisfaction. Some researchers believe that some people may be prone to negative _____ and _____ (such as suspicion, fear, worry, and dissatisfaction), whereas others may be prone to positive ones (such as trust, enthusiasm, and satisfaction).

    (b) In one study, researchers who examined identical twins raised apart found support for the idea that a tendency toward _____ or _____ outlooks may be _____ based; they concluded that job satisfaction may be explained, in part, by _____ factors.

(c) Theories based on _____ between desires and experiences, _____ influences, and _____ dispositions have each been successful in explaining some of the differences in job satisfaction among people. However, none of these approaches by itself can completely explain differences in job satisfaction.

(d) Job satisfaction has been found to be related to overall _____ satisfaction. This is one reason that high job satisfaction should be the goal of all organizations; in addition to reducing _____ and _____ , it contributes to employees' overall level of happiness.

4. (a) The approach to leader effectiveness that is based on the idea that leaders are born not made is called the _____ approach. According to this view, some people possess certain qualities or characteristics that make them _____ leaders.

(b) A large number of _____ , such as height, physical attractiveness, dominance, flexibility, and intelligence, have been examined to see if they determine how effective a leader will be. Research has demonstrated that personal _____ and leader effectiveness are _____ (closely/not closely) related.

5. (a) The theory of leader effectiveness that focuses on the differences in the behaviors of effective and ineffective leaders is the _____ theory.

(b) Researchers have identified two major types of leadership behavior: leaders who are deeply concerned about their followers and who spend time building trust, respect, and warmth between themselves and their fol-

lowers are examples of the _____ type of leadership; leaders who are task oriented, who structure tasks for their followers, and who push for things to get done are examples of the _____ type of leadership.

(c) Initiating structure _____ (has/has not) been related to high productivity but also to low job satisfaction and high personnel turnover; consideration _____ (has/has not) been related to high job satisfaction but also to low productivity in some situations.

6. (a) Theories of leadership that focus on how a particular situation influences a leader's effectiveness are called _____ (contingency) theories; these theories tend to be complicated but _____ (are/are no) better at explaining leader effectiveness than either trait or behavioral theories.

(b) The trait of charisma has received a lot of attention. Typically, charismatic leaders have a high need for _____ , are extremely _____ , and believe strongly in a particular cause; they are able to change the _____ and _____ of their followers and may even be able to evoke strong compliance from them.

(c) Research that examines who in a group is likely to become a group leader is studying the _____ of leaders; this topic differs from that of leader _____ , because not everyone who emerges as a leader is a good leader.

(d) A technique in which a group is given a problem to solve or a topic to discuss is called _____ group discussion. Researchers study the group to see who emerges as the leader. Personal qualities that have been related to leader emergence are _____ , _____ , _____ , and _____ .

7. (a) About 40 percent of all managerial jobs in the United States are held by women; however, only _____ to _____ percent of upper-level management positions are filled by women.

(b) The difficulty that women are having in advancing to high levels in most organizations may be due to subtle, unofficial _____ that creates an invisible but strong barrier to women's promotion to the top; this barrier is called the _____ and is reinforced by differences in socialization, educational and training opportunities, and family and child-care responsibilities of males and females.

(c) Another powerful reinforcer of the _____ is unfair performance evaluation; researchers have found that males and females are often evaluated differently for managerial jobs.

(d) Researchers have found _____ (differences/no differences) in the leadership effectiveness of men and women working in organizations and _____ (differences/practically no differences) in male and female leadership behavior; some research has found that _____ tend to be more autocratic, whereas _____ tend to be more democratic, with the effectiveness of each style depending on the situation.

(e) Leaders of different races hold _____ (similar/different) values. Cultivating a diverse work force is likely to be advantageous to organizations because heterogeneous groups, compared with homogenous ones, are more likely to be _____ and _____ .

(f) Some researchers have hypothesized that a familiarity with, understanding of, and sympathy toward the norms of two different cultures, called _____ , enables people to be more _____ when leading heterogeneous groups, because it provides them with a greater diversity of skills. One study found that Mexican-Americans high in _____ exhibited more leadership behavior than those low in this trait.

8. (a) Demographers predict that the work force will become _____ (less/more) diverse as we move into the twenty-first century. The workplace is also expected to become ever more _____ , with employees required to operate and maintain complicated machinery and equipment; organizations are likely to find themselves competing not only _____ but also _____ .

(b) Increased diversity in the work force will result in a greater demand for research on the ways in which _____ groups communicate, interact, and make decisions. As _____ participate in the work force in record numbers and as our population ages, the need for child care and elder care will continue to grow.

(c) Advances in communication (computers, modems, faxes, e-mail, and voice mail) have made it possible for greater numbers of employees to work from their homes; the _____ and _____ of home workers will need to be compared with those working on company premises.

(d) Human factors will become more important as technological advances continue; the _____ of equipment with human capabilities and limitations in mind will be vital to the _____ and _____ of employees as companies come to depend on more sophisticated techniques and equipment.

(e) It will be increasingly important to have systems for selecting managers who are able to function effectively in various _____ . In addition, managers must be trained in the _____ and _____ of different cultures; programs to help managers and their families adjust to living in foreign countries will also be needed.

(f) In the future, _____ will continue to have a significant impact on the workplace and will continue to adjust the focus of their research and its applications to meet the changing needs of people at work.

Review of Terms and Concepts

Use the terms in this list to complete the Matching Test, then to help you answer the True/False items correctly.

industrial/organizational (I/O) psychology	social influence hypothesis
personnel psychology	dispositional factors hypothesis
organizational behavior	trait approach to leader effectiveness
human factors	
ergonomics	behavioral theories of leader effectiveness
vocational and career counseling	situational (or contingency) theories of leader effectiveness
organizational development (OD)	
job analysis	glass ceiling
selection device validity	
discrepancy hypothesis	

Matching Exercise

Match the appropriate term with its definition or description.

1. _____ Assessment of the major responsibilities of a particular job and the human characteristics needed to fill it.

2. _____ Subarea of I/O psychology that focuses on bringing about positive change in an organization, such as increased profitability or improved products.

3. _____ Invisible but strong barrier of subtle, unofficial discrimination that prevents women or minorities from being promoted

to the highest levels of leadership in an organization.

4. _____ Branch of psychology that focuses on the study of human behavior at work.

5. _____ Theories that focus on how a particular situation influences a leader's effectiveness.

6. _____ Approach to explaining job satisfaction that focuses on the discrepancy, if any, between what a person wants from a job and how that person evaluates what is experienced at work.

7. _____ Subfield of I/O psychology that combines with counseling psychology to help people choose occupations that match their preferences and needs.

8. _____ View that a person's level of job satisfaction is influenced by the job satisfaction levels of other people.

True/False Test

Indicate whether each statement is true or false by placing T or F in the blank space next to each item.

1. ____ The dispositional factors hypothesis is the view that a person's level of job satisfaction may be due in part to a genetically based disposition toward a positive or negative outlook.

2. ____ Personnel psychology is a subarea of I/O psychology that focuses on how the organization and the social environment in which people work affect their attitudes and behaviors.

3. ____ Behavioral theories of leader effectiveness focus on differences in the behaviors of effective and ineffective leaders.

4. ____ Ergonomics is a subarea of I/O psychology that focuses on the design of equipment and the development of work procedures in light of human capabilities and limitations.

5. ____ Selection device validity is the extent to which a personnel selection device is successful in distinguishing between those who will become high performers at a certain job and those who will not.

6. ____ Human factors is the science of applying knowledge about human physical characteristics to the design of equipment that minimizes fatigue and discomfort and maximizes productivity.

7. ___ The trait approach to leader effectiveness focuses on the personal characteristics displayed by successful leaders.

8. ___ Organizational behavior is a subarea of I/O psychology that focuses on matching people's characteristics to job requirement, accurately measuring job performance, and assessing employee training needs.

> Check your answers and review any areas of weakness before doing the progress tests.

Progress Test 1

Review the complete chapter, review all your study notes, and then test yourself on the following progress test. Check your answers. If you make a mistake, review your notes, review the relevant section of the study guide, and, if necessary, go back and read the appropriate part of your textbook.

1. Mrs. Garcia is as talented and qualified as the male candidates who applied for a number of high-level management positions over the years, but she has never been selected. I/O psychologists are likely to attribute this to
   (a) ergonomic factors.
   (b) the glass ceiling.
   (c) the validity of the selection devices.
   (d) the results of accurate job analyses.

2. Dr. Foggerty focuses on the design of equipment and the development of work procedures in light of human capabilities and limitations. Dr. Foggerty's area of interest is called
   (a) human factors.
   (b) personnel psychology.
   (c) vocational and career counseling.
   (d) organizational behavior.

3. When Kamal goes to graduate school, she plans to specialize in a subarea of I/O psychology that focuses on matching people's characteristics to job requirements, accurately measuring job performance, and assessing employee training needs. Kamal is interested in
   (a) personnel psychology.
   (b) organizational psychology.
   (c) organizational development.
   (d) ergonomics.

4. Helmut has a bachelor's degree and is interested in working in the field of I/O psychology. Which of the following statements about Helmut's prospects is true?
   (a) It will be difficult for him to find employment in the field of I/O.
   (b) Some areas related to I/O, such as personnel, training, and labor relations specialists and managers, are open to him.
   (c) He may find a job as an employment interviewer.
   (d) All of the above are true.

5. Olivia's research focuses on how the organization and the social environment in which people work affect their attitudes and behaviors. Olivia works in a subarea of I/O psychology called
   (a) personnel psychology.
   (b) human factors.
   (c) ergonomics.
   (d) organizational behavior.

6. Gulbinder is the chief personnel officer for a large corporation. She is very concerned that the methods and techniques used in personnel selection are successful in distinguishing between applicants who will become high performers and those who will not. Gulbinder's concerns are related to
   (a) human factors.
   (b) ergonomics.
   (c) selection device validity.
   (d) organizational development (OD).

7. Bradford believes that leaders are born, not made, and he cites many examples of people who possess certain qualities or characteristics that make them natural leaders. Bradford's views are most consistent with the
   (a) situational (or contingency) theories of leader effectiveness.
   (b) behavioral theories of leader effectiveness.
   (c) dispositional factors hypothesis.
   (d) trait approach to leader effectiveness.

8. Although most Americans report that they are satisfied with their jobs, they appear less satisfied with some aspects than with others. In order to explain differences in job satisfaction, which of the following approaches is likely to be used?
   (a) discrepancy hypothesis
   (b) social influence hypothesis
   (c) dispositional factors hypothesis
   (d) All of the above are equally likely.

9. Mrs. Afyia uses a technique in which the major responsibilities of the job, along with the human characteristics needed to fill it, are determined. Her goal is to select appropriate people for the position. Mrs Afyia is using a technique called
   (a) ergonomics.
   (b) job analysis.
   (c) selection device validity.
   (d) human factors.

10. According to In Focus B.1, the valuing-differences culture of Digital Equipment Corporation was enhanced through a number of techniques. Which of the following is *not* one of those techniques?
    (a) creation of an awareness and skills training program
    (b) celebrating differences events sponsored by various employee groups
    (c) creation of leadership groups and support groups designed to provide emotional and career support for employees with similar backgrounds
    (d) segregation of employees on the basis of gender, ethnicity, or race, to minimize conflicts and confrontations between these various groups
    (e) establishment of core groups, or small groups of workers who meet on a regular basis to discuss key issues

Progress Test 2

After you have checked your understanding of the material in Progress Test 1 and have done a complete chapter review with special focus on any areas of weakness, you are ready to assess your knowledge of Progress Test 2. Check your answers. If you make a mistake, review your notes, the relevant section of the study guide, and, if necessary, the appropriate part of your textbook.

1. Dr. Kent uses her background in counseling psychology to help people choose occupations that match their preferences and needs. Dr. Kent is involved in
   (a) organizational development.
   (b) human factors.
   (c) vocational and career counseling.
   (d) personnel psychology.

2. Shortly after moving into a new office building, many employees complained about the layout of the offices, the lack of proper ventilation, and the uncomfortable chairs and desks. The employees' fatigue and discomfort decreased productivity and increased illness and absenteeism. There appears to be a problem with
   (a) organizational behavior.
   (b) ergonomics.
   (c) organizational development.
   (d) selection device validity.

3. In his research on leader effectiveness, Dr. Grether focuses on differences in the behavior of effective and ineffective leaders. Dr. Grether's work is most consistent with the _____ theories of leader effectiveness.
   (a) trait   (c) situational
   (b) behavioral   (d) dispositional

4. Lance wants to become an I/O psychologist but he is not sure what the future hold for this profession. Research on this topic is likely to reveal that
   (a) I/O psychologists will continue to have a significant impact on the workplace.
   (b) most I/O psychologists will become redundant in the near future due to technological advances.
   (c) increased diversity of the work force, technological advances, and a global economy will mean a gradual decline in the need for I/O psychologists as we move into the twenty-first century.
   (d) it will be very easy for people with bachelor's degrees to find employment in the field of I/O psychology.

5. Mr. Wentworth wants to bring about positive change in his organization, increase profitability, and improve the products he manufactures. The subarea of I/O psychology most concerned with these issues is
   (a) personnel psychology.
   (b) ergonomics.
   (c) organizational development (OD).
   (d) vocational and career counseling.

6. Gladys believes that job satisfaction results from the difference between what a person wants from a job and how that person evaluates what is experienced. Wilma disagrees and suggests that people's level of job satisfaction is probably due to their innate tendency to be positive or negative about life and work. Gladys's view supports the _____ hypothesis, and Wilma's position supports the _____ hypothesis.
   (a) discrepancy; social influence
   (b) dispositional; discrepancy
   (c) discrepancy; dispositional
   (d) social influence; dispositional

7. At a party recently, Justina was asked what she does for a living. She replied that her work focuses on the study of human behavior at work. Justina is most likely a(n)
   (a) counseling psychologist.
   (b) social psychologist.
   (c) industrial/organizational psychologist.
   (d) clinical psychologist.

8. When asked to elaborate on the type of work she does Justina said that her main interest lies in the design of equipment and in the development of work procedures in light of human capabilities and limitations. Justina works in a subarea of I/O psychology called
   (a) human factors.
   (b) personnel psychology.
   (c) organizational development.
   (d) ergonomics.

9. International Production Corporation is concerned with developing an organizational culture that would value the many differences among its employees. Their I/O consultant implements a program to help change the cultural beliefs and attitudes of the organization so that its members better appreciate the dif-

ferences among human beings. This type of program is called
   (a) diversity training.
   (b) situational exercises.
   (c) discrepancy training.
   (d) dispositional training.

10. In her work, Dr. Tahler uses a variety of psychological tests that measure cognitive ability, mechanical aptitude, motor and sensory ability, and normal and abnormal personality traits. It is most likely that Dr. Tahler is a(n)
   (a) human factors psychologist.
   (b) personnel psychologist.
   (c) organizational psychologist.
   (d) ergonomics psychologist.

Progress Test 3

After you have checked your understanding of the material in Progress Tests 1 and 2, and have done a complete chapter review with special focus on any areas of weakness, you are ready to further assess your knowledge on Progress Test 3. Check your answers. If you make a mistake, review your notes, the appropriate parts of the study guide, and if necessary, the relevant sections of your textbook.

1. When Brock finishes college he plans to go on to graduate school and focus on the study of human behavior at work. Brock wants to be a(n)
   (a) counseling psychologist.
   (b) statistician.
   (c) clinical psychologist.
   (d) industrial/organizational psychologist.

2. Dr. Addersly conducted research on gender and leadership, and male and female leadership behavior. If his research is consistent with previous research in this area, Dr. Addersly is likely to discover
   (a) men will tend to use a style of leadership called consideration and women will prefer initiating structure.
   (b) virtually no gender differences.
   (c) that men will encounter the glass ceiling more often than women.
   (d) vast gender differences.

3. Gregory believes that a leader's effectiveness is most likely a result of a particular combination of personality characteristics, rather than situational factors. Gregory's views are most consistent with _____ theories of leader effectiveness.
   (a) behavioral
   (b) contingency
   (c) dispositional
   (d) trait

4. Professor Kress focuses on the design of equipment and the development of work procedures in light of human capabilities and limitations. Professor Fergus focuses on applying knowledge about human physical characteristics to the design of equipment that minimizes fatigue and discomfort and maximizes productivity. Professor Krebs works in an area of I/O called _____ , and Professor Fergus works in _____ .
   (a) human factors; ergonomics
   (b) organizational development; organizational behavior
   (c) ergonomics; human factors
   (d) organizational behavior; organizational development

5. Breen has a high need for power, believes strongly in the feminist cause, is extremely self-confident, and has highly developed interpersonal skills. Breen fits the profile of a(n) _____ leader.
   (a) considerate
   (b) ergonomic
   (c) charismatic
   (d) initiating

6. The Zander Corporation is concerned about selecting the appropriate person for the job of production manager. Mrs. Juarez, the personnel manager, assesses and records the position's responsibilities and the personal characteristics required by the job. Mrs. Juarez is using a technique called
   (a) human factors analysis.
   (b) job analysis.
   (c) ergonomic analysis.
   (d) discrepancy analysis.

7. In a report for the personnel department of the Utopia Corporation, Dr. Raimundo makes recommendations regarding the validity and reliability of the company's various selection devices. Which of the following is Dr. Raimundo likely to suggest has the lowest validity?
   (a) work samples
   (b) general unstructured interviews
   (c) psychological testing
   (d) situational exercises

8. Stephanie and Steven both work as resource specialists for the same company. Stephanie is very satisfied with most aspects of her job, but Steven dislikes just about everything about his job. According to research by the Gallup Corporation
   (a) Stephanie is influenced by dispositional traits, and Steven is affected by discrepancy factors.
   (b) Steven is more typical of American workers than Stephanie is.
   (c) Stephanie's attitude is a function of the glass ceiling, and Steven's attitude is influenced by situational or contingency factors.
   (d) Stephanie is more typical of American workers than Steven is.

9. Hannalee wants to bring about positive changes in her business organization. She is concerned with improving the line of products, streamlining production, and increasing profitability. Hannalee should probably consult an I/O psychologist who specializes in a subarea called
   (a) personnel psychology.
   (b) ergonomics.
   (c) diversity training.
   (d) organizational development.

10. According to In Focus B.1, if a company is interested in developing an organizational culture that values the many differences among its employees it should
    (a) use diversity training, develop awareness and skills training programs, and create leadership and support groups.
    (b) separate employees of different genders, races, and ethnic backgrounds in order to minimize conflict and confrontation between various groups.
    (c) provide workshops that focus on enhancing group cohesion and conformity to the collectivistic corporate identity.
    (d) use transcendental meditation training, ergonomic workshops, and mandatory participation in employee group activities during lunch and coffee breaks

Answers

What Is Industrial/Organizational Psychology?

1. (a) human behavior; subareas
   (b) knowledge, skills, abilities; job; training
   (c) attitudes; behaviors
   (d) design; development; design; ergonomics
   (e) I/O; counseling; promotions; career
   (f) organizational development; diversity training

Work Settings, Type of Training, and Employment Outlook

1. (a) doctorates; master's; bachelor's
   (b) doctorate; master's; bachelor's
   (c) consultants; private; public
   (d) favorable
2. (a) personnel; training; labor relations specialists; knowledge, skills
   (b) management analysts and consultants; collect, review; analyze
   (c) employment interviewer; personnel

Personnel Psychology

1. (a) selecting; training; evaluating
   (b) responsibilities; characteristics; interview, observation; survey
   (c) knowledge, skills; abilities
   (d) procedures, knowledge; skills
   (e) appraisal; appraisal
2. (a) valid; validity
   (b) psychological
   (c) cognitive; cognitive; Mechanical; motor; Sensory

(d) abnormal; normal; abnormal
(e) normal
(f) honesty; false positives

3. (a) situational; mini-version
   (b) low validity; are not
   (c) low validity; unstructured
   (d) structured; job analysis; job-related; order; evaluated

Organizational Behavior and Trends for the Future

1. (a) discrepancy; differ; differ; desired; experienced
   (b) supports; discrepancy; discrepancies; discrepancies
2. (a) interpret; evaluating
   (b) likely; likely
3. (a) dispositional; perceptions; feelings
   (b) positive; negative; biologically; genetic
   (c) discrepancy; social; inherited
   (d) life; absenteeism; turnover
4. (a) trait; natural
   (b) traits; traits; not closely
5. (a) behavioral
   (b) consideration; initiating structure
   (c) has; has
6. (a) situational; are
   (b) power; self-confident; attitudes; beliefs
   (c) emergence; effectiveness
   (d) leaderless; intelligence, aggressiveness, decisiveness; dominance
7. (a) 2; 4
   (b) discrimination; glass ceiling
   (c) glass ceiling
   (d) no differences; practically no differences; men; women
   (e) similar; flexible; creative
   (f) biculturalism; flexible; biculturalism
8. (a) more; technical; nationally; globally
   (b) heterogeneous; women
   (c) job satisfaction; productivity
   (d) design; productivity; satisfaction
   (e) cultures; customs; languages
   (f) I/O psychologists

Matching Exercise

1. job analysis
2. organizational development (OD)
3. glass ceiling
4. industrial/organizational (I/O) psychology

5. situational (or contingency) theories of leader effectiveness
6. discrepancy hypothesis
7. vocational and career counseling
8. social influence hypothesis

True/False Test

1. T	4. F	7. T
2. F	5. T	8. F
3. T	6. T	

Progress Test 1

1. b	5. d	9. b
2. a	6. c	10. d
3. a	7. d	
4. d	8. d	

Progress Test 2

1. c	5. c	9. a
2. b	6. c	10. b
3. b	7. c	
4. a	8. a	

Progress Test 3

1. d	5. c	9. d
2. b	6. b	10. a
3. d	7. b	
4. a	8. d	